31/3/1993

Marilyn Monroe:
The Biography

The Art of Alfred Hitchcock

Stanley Kramer Film Maker

Camerado: Hollywood and the American Man

The Dark Side of Genius: The Life of Alfred Hitchcock

The Kindness of Strangers: The Life of Tennessee Williams

Falling in Love Again: Marlene Dietrich (A Photo-Essay)

Lenya: A Life

Madcap: The Life of Preston Sturges

Laurence Olivier: A Biography

Dietrich: A Biography

Marilyn Monroe:
The Biography

Donald Spoto

Chatto & Windus
LONDON

First published 1993

1 3 5 7 9 10 8 6 4 2

© Donald Spoto 1993

Donald Spoto has asserted his right under
the Copyright, Designs and Patents Act, 1988
to be identified as the author of this work

First published in the United Kingdom in 1993 by
Chatto & Windus Ltd
Random House, 20 Vauxhall Bridge Road, London SW1V 2SA

Random House Australia (Pty) Limited
20 Alfred Street, Milsons Point, Sydney,
New South Wales 2061, Australia

Random House New Zealand Limited
18 Poland Road, Glenfield
Auckland 10, New Zealand

Random House South Africa (Pty) Limited
PO Box 337, Bergvlei, South Africa

Random House UK Limited Reg. No. 954009

A CIP catalogue record for this book
is available from the British Library

ISBN 0 7011 4025 9

Filmset by SX Composing Ltd, Rayleigh, Essex
Printed and bound in Great Britain by
Mackays of Chatham PLC, Chatham, Kent

for Elaine Markson
with gratitude and devotion

She brings him good every day of his life,
and when she speaks it is always wisely.
Praise her for all she has accomplished.

The Book of Proverbs

It *is* glory – to have been tested, to have had our little quality and cast our little spell . . . to have made somebody care.

Henry James, *The Middle Years*

*

If one tells the truth, one is sure, sooner or later, to be found out.

Oscar Wilde, *Phrases and Philosophies for the Use of the Young*

Contents

Acknowledgements

The kindness and generosity of many people made this book a reality.

Lisa Callamaro, in the offices of my agent Elaine Markson, introduced me to Gordon Freedman, a film and television producer of admirable integrity and intelligence. He first suggested this book and introduced me to the family of Milton H. Greene and the representative's of Greene's Estate. As Marilyn Monroe's friend, photographer and business partner, Greene had kept massive and detailed archives covering much of Marilyn's life – materials that include her production and legal files as well as various personal documents, tapes and letters. I owe Gordon Freedman enormous gratitude for providing access to those who made this historic cache available to me.

Equally so, Joshua Greene and Anthony Greene were more than helpful, providing tangible assistance and amiable encouragement at every stage, as well as access to their father's photographs of Marilyn – especially that which graces the jacket. Amy Greene, their mother, opened her home and extended her family to include Marilyn for several years; candidly and generously, Amy shared unique and unprecedented memories, impressions and anecdotes with me. Knowing her and her sons (and, through them, more about Milton Greene himself), it is easy to understand how Marilyn matured so much in their company.

The writer Elaine Dundy, always a helpful colleague, put me in touch with the archivist and genealogist Roy Turner, who arranged for me to have exclusive access to documents gathered by him and Marilyn Gemme over almost two decades. Much nonsense has been written about my subject's early history and family background, but Roy Turner and Marilyn Gemme first pursued the facts with an honourable passion for truth. My research was immeasurably enriched by theirs.

Through my colleague James Spada, I met one of the most helpful people for this book: from the very beginning, I was assisted (almost daily) by Greg Schreiner, a gifted musician and composer who is also the co-founder and president of Marilyn Remembered. This association – more than a fan club – is made up of talented people, some of whom knew and worked with Monroe, all of whom are devoted to celebrating her talents. Greg provided me with crucial introductions to many people I might otherwise have overlooked; he pointed me to important bibliographies; and he was ever ready to answer questions and provide concrete help.

Likewise, I owe very much to Roman Hryniszak and Michelle Justice, who direct a similar group called All About Marilyn and who regularly publish a magazine that helps set the record straight on many matters pertinent to our subject. They could not have been more generous with their time and efforts in helping me reach people for major interviews.

Patrick Miller, whose encyclopedic knowledge of Hollywood history in general and of Marilyn Monroe's life and career in particular are remarkable, has for years hoped that a true and full account of her life would one day be published. This book would have suffered enormously without Patrick's extraordinary help and advice.

Marilyn Monroe's three husbands survive. James Dougherty cheerfully clarified much and provided more than a glimpse into his married life with Marilyn when she was Norma Jeane. On the matter of his brief marriage to Marilyn, their divorce and moving reunion, Joe DiMaggio's determined silence is well known and can only be respected. Arthur Miller pointed me to his own extended memoirs on his years with Marilyn and confirmed several important points I put to him in writing.

Acknowledgements

Eleanor Goddard – known as Bebe to her friends – is the stepdaughter of Norma Jeane's foster mother, Grace Goddard. Bebe spent part of her adolescence with Norma Jeane and has a clear understanding of how she became Marilyn. In tracing this dynamic, Bebe was unstintingly forthcoming in replying to my many questions.

Similarly, a special kind of relationship with Marilyn Monroe was enjoyed by her stand-in and good friend Evelyn Moriarty, who from 1960 to 1962 was very close to her indeed. Evelyn's detailed recounting of behind-the-scenes drama, her understanding of Marilyn, her important contributions during many interviews with me and her constant and warm encouragement were precious assets during the writing of this book.

Patricia Newcomb, Marilyn's last publicist and loyal ally, offered me unprecedented confidence and detailed many of the fine points of Marilyn's last two years. Rightly respected for her discretion, loyalty and veracity, Pat spoke at length and with admirable frankness: her signal contributions to this book are everywhere evident.

The late Rupert Allan was Marilyn's first publicist and her constant confidant. Loved and esteemed during his almost fifty years in Hollywood, Rupert encouraged me from the start, providing important introductions and offering me several lengthy, richly detailed interviews even when he was in failing health.

Jane Wilkie, a reporter, writer and editor who covered Hollywood for years, kept drafts of lengthy, revealing and unpublished conversations with James Dougherty and with Natasha Lytess – interviews she conducted during the 1950s. Jane welcomed me to her home and transferred to me the exclusive rights to these rich, hitherto unseen manuscripts.

John Miner was deputy district attorney of Los Angeles County and chief of its Medical Legal Section when Marilyn died, and in this capacity he was present during the autopsy. He pointed out details that enabled me to resolve at last one of the most disturbing and mysterious cases in modern history. Likewise, Arnold Abrams MD, director of the department of pathology at St John's Hospital, Santa Monica, guided me through the thickets of medical and chemical terminology and clarified important points of the coroner's report.

David Zeidberg and the staff of the Department of Special Collections at the University of California, Los Angeles, helped me to pore through cartons of the Ralph Greenson Papers.

Susan D'Entremont, at the John F. Kennedy Memorial Library in Dorchester, Massachusetts, provided direction in locating the Robert F. Kennedy Papers during his term as Attorney General.

In the Archives of Performing Arts at the University of Southern California, Ned Comstock was as usual a cheerful and thoughtful guide, pointing out several significant items in the Warner Bros, Jerry Wald and Constance McCormick collections.

Bob Dauner, Archivist in Special Collections at the Albuquerque Public Library, provided data relative to the life of John Murray.

The papers of Ben Hecht, who anonymously wrote major portions of Marilyn's early autobiography, are kept in Special Collections at the Newberry Library in Chicago. There, I was ably assisted by Margaret Kulis, Meg Bolger and Elizabeth Freebairn.

Just so, Pamela Dunn, in Special Collections at Stanford University, helped me make my way through the letters and papers of Spyros Skouras, president of Twentieth Century-Fox.

Myra T. Grenier at Seek Information Service, helped cull files in the *Los Angeles Times*.

Mona Newcomer, in the Office of Alumni Affairs at Urbana University, Urbana, Ohio, provided important documents regarding the family background of Eunice Joerndt (later Murray).

Doug McKinney, Director of Archives at CBS News, provided critical access to documents and to a tape of the historic interview Mike Wallace conducted with Norman Mailer on *60*

Minutes in 1973. Doug also provided special technical machinery with which I was able to hear antique dictabelt recordings from the Greene archives.

Diana L. Summerhayes, Deputy District Attorney in the Appellate Division of the District Attorney's Office, County of Los Angeles, cleared the way for examination of materials assembled by that office relative to the 1982 Investigator's Report on the death of Marilyn Monroe.

At the Discovery Unit of the Los Angeles Police Department, Larry Wulterin enabled me to obtain the official police report and ancillary documents on the death of Marilyn Monroe.

In the Louis B. Mayer Library at the American Film Institute in Los Angeles, Alan Braun and Gladys Irvis dashed from floor to floor locating boxes that disclosed the rich matter relevant to Marilyn's years as a client of agent and producer Charles K. Feldman. Similarly, the staff at the Billy Rose Theatre Collection at the Lincoln Center Library for the Performing Arts in New York was swift and efficient in locating clippings and secondary source materials.

Interviews with those who knew Marilyn Monroe were of course key elements in preparing this biography. In addition to those named above, the following people enlightened me on various unique aspects of her life and work, and I am grateful to them all: Bill Alexander, William Asher, George Axelrod, Milton Berle, Walter Bernstein, Mervin Block, David Brown, Jack Cardiff, Lucille Ryman Carroll, Ted Cieszynski, Mart Crowley, Alex D'Arcy, Ken DuMain, Milton Ebbins, George Erengis, Michael Gurdin MD, Edwin Guthman, Joe Hyams, Natalie Trundy Jacobs, Joseph Jasgur, Adele Jergens, Jay Kanter, Douglas Kirkland, Ernest Lehman, Peter Levathes, Jean Louis, Esther Maltz, Joseph L. Mankiewicz, George Masters, Albert Maysles, Robert Mitchum, John Moore, Dolores Naar, Joseph Naar, Sherle North, Ron Nyman, Lydia Bodrero Reed, Vanessa Reis, Ralph Roberts, Milton Rudin, Jane Russell, Hal Schaefer, Michael Selsman, Sam Shaw, Max Showalter, Arnold

Shulman, Allan and Marjorie Snyder, Mickey Song, Steffi Sidney Splaver, John Springer, Maureen Stapleton, Bert Stern, Susan Strasberg, Jule Styne, Henry Weinstein, Billy Wilder, Gladys Phillips Wilson, William Woodfield and Paul Wurtzel.

Others, although they did not know Marilyn personally, also provided interviews or practical assistance that clarified important points relative to her life and death: Sheldon Abend, Martin Baum, Gordon W. Blackmer, John Bates, John Bates Jr, Nancy Bates, Rick Carl, Ronald H. Carroll, Kay Eicher, George and Diane Fain, Will Fowler, Richard Goodwin, Milton Gould, Betsy Duncan Hammes, Margaret Hohenberg MD, Hilary Knight, Michael Korda, Phillip LaClair, Ted Landreth, Robert Litman MD, Don Marshall (Los Angeles Police Department, Ret.), John Milklian, Dan Moldea, Benson Schaeffer PhD, Henry Schipper, Roland Snyder, Richard Stanley and Edith Turner.

Those who shared with me their private collections of photographs have a special claim on my gratitude, too: Chris Basinger, Ted Cieszynski, T. R. Fogli, Eleanor Goddard, Sabin Grey, Evelyn Moriarty, Vanessa Reis, Greg Schreiner, Allan Snyder, Mickey Song and Gary Wares.

At HarperCollins in New York, there is a veritable litany of good souls for me to honour.

I am fortunate indeed to enjoy the friendship and unswerving loyalty of my editor, Gladys Justin Carr, Vice-President and Associate Publisher. With passionate dedication, sharp insights and constant good humour, Gladys guided this book at every stage, from contract to first copy; I am thus ever in her debt. Her assistant, Tracy Devine and Ari Hoogenboom, despatched numerous daily tasks with trusty good cheer, making many rough ways smooth.

William Shinker, Group Vice-President, was from the start an enthusiastic supporter of the book, demonstrating an especially amiable, personal interest and introducing me to those in house whose friendliness and commitment to the project enriched the process – James Fox, Brenda Marsh, Susan Moldow, Joseph Montebello, Brenda Segel, Steven Sorrentino and Martin Weaver.

For the sixth time, Michael Mattil brought to my manuscript his considerable gifts as copy editor: his keen eye and sharp pencil work wonders, and I marvel at his speed and accuracy.

At Chatto & Windus in London, Carmen Callil and Jonathan Burnham could not have been more gracious and sensitive editors, offering friendship in the bargain. Of more than a dozen of my foreign language publishers, I have had the pleasure of meeting only two: Hans-Peter Ubleis of Wilhelm Heyne Verlag, Munich; and Renaud Bombard at Presses de la Cité, Paris. Like their colleagues in England and America, they have accepted me and my work in amity and have offered very welcome suggestions. I cannot imagine a more fortunate writer than myself.

My attorney Kirtley Thiesmeyer was, as always, a perceptive advocate, bringing to my professional life talents that constantly amaze me, and my good friend John Darretta helped me proofread the American and British galleys.

During the early part of the research, Douglas Alexander was my tirelessly efficient and savvy assistant. He then accepted an opportunity to work on his own first book, an assignment that augurs well for the world of letters.

Subsequently there came to the project Charles Rappleye, an editor and writer with noteworthy credits, and I gratefully salute his collegial service. He tracked down obscure facts and remote people, conducted investigations requiring the delicate but dogged persistence of a private eye and cut clean paths through a tangle of civil, legal and police records – thus successfully bringing to light significant matters relative to the final year of Marilyn Monroe's life.

At the Elaine Markson Literary Agency in New York – my professional headquarters for fifteen years – things are in the hands of vigilant friends: Geri Thoma, Sally Cotton Wofford,

Lisa Callamaro, Caomh Kavanagh, Stephanie Hawkins, Sara DeNobrega and Tasha Blaine.

With very great love and gratitude, *Marilyn Monroe* is dedicated to my agent, Elaine Markson – the second time I make this gesture, and I pray not the last.

In a way, assembling the many thousand words of a biography is easier than finding the few to express adequately the depth of my admiration for Elaine, who more than anyone has guided my career to its present felicitous stage. If I mention only her wisdom and humour, her warmth and honour, I merely list those qualities long familiar to her many friends, to other clients and to countless people in publishing. Elaine is ever the most patient and solicitous counsellor, my prudent and devoted friend. Marilyn would have adored her.

D. S.
Los Angeles and New York
Christmas 1992

Chapter One

ANTECEDENTS – TO JUNE 1926

Marilyn Monroe's maternal great-grandfather was Tilford Marion Hogan, born in 1851 in Illinois to farmer George Hogan and his wife Sarah Owens not long after their emigration from Kentucky. By the age of twelve, Tilford was six feet tall and reed-thin, but strong enough for rough farm labour. In 1870, at nineteen, he was living in Barry County, Missouri, where he married Jennie Nance. To support her and, by 1878, their three children, Tilford worked long hours for miserable wages as a day labourer; notwithstanding his efforts, the Hogan family income was always inadequate. For over a decade, they seemed constantly on the move in Missouri, living variously in farmhouses, log cabins, shared servants' quarters and sometimes barns.

Despite the hardships and very little education, Tilford apparently had an inquiring and sensitive mind: he taught himself to read and took a fancy to poetry and the classics – genteel pursuits to which he could devote little time. Earnest, practical Jennie, citing the family's constant deprivations, offered him no encouragement in his literary interests. The marriage lasted twenty years and then, for reasons that remain unclear, they were divorced. Jennie took the children and returned to her mother's home in Chariton County, and Tilford went to live with his sister in Linn County.

Whatever the marriage problems, Hogan was much liked and respected by friends and neighbours, for he was a generous man who shared spontaneously from his own meagre supplies of

I

food and fuel. His empathetic nature was perhaps all the more remarkable since his entire adult life was blighted by severe rheumatoid arthritis and chronic respiratory infections, conditions exacerbated by hard work, poor diet and a ceaseless rhythm of poverty. In addition, he was virtually ostracized after his divorce, which was no commonplace among the zealous Christian citizenry of late nineteenth-century Missouri. After 1891 (when he turned forty), he worked harder than ever and seemed prematurely old and frail; he also suffered a terrible loneliness without his children, who visited but rarely.

The liveliest of these was Della May (who later sometimes signed herself Della Mae), the second of Tilford and Jennie's three children. She was born on 1 July 1876, while her parents were living briefly in Brunswick, Missouri. Not especially pretty but gay and mischievous, she was a precocious and energetic child who had no interest in her father's educational aspirations; quite the contrary, she was a habitual truant. Parents and teachers were outraged when, at the age of ten, she led classmates to a local pond for fishing and swimming. There was even graver concern over the matter of Della's conduct with those who often crept away into a family's barn in late afternoons for a game of 'Kiss-Me-Quick'. By fifteen she was long out of school, shuttling back and forth between her parents, enjoying the attentions of boys alert to her persuasive, unreserved charm.

Frisky young Della avoided marriage until she was twenty-two, an advanced age for espousals at the time. In 1898 she met a house painter recently arrived in Missouri from Indiana named Otis Elmer Monroe, ten years her senior. Like Della's father, Otis nurtured goals loftier than mere manual labour. He insisted that one day he would study art in Europe, and he spiced their conversations with talk of French painters and of *belle époque* Paris, of which he had seen gravures in magazines.

After a proper courtship, on which the groom-to-be insisted, Della May Hogan and Otis Elmer Monroe were married in late 1899. Photographs of her at the time show a woman of medium height with a strong, round face, dark eyes, an almost severe jaw and extraordinary poise: there is nothing demure in her stance. No portraits of Otis have survived, but Della later described him as fair-skinned, with reddish hair and hazel eyes. He was, she later said, 'neat as a pin, always turned out like a gentleman – or at least a gentleman's gentleman'. After a bad fall, he had a permanent scar on his left cheek, and this gave him a somewhat dashing, romantic look. Della seemed to think of him as a roué, a robust man of the world who had known danger.

Not long after the wedding, Otis told Della to pack their clothes. Because he was guaranteed better wages than for occasional house painting, he had accepted an offer to work for the Mexican National Railway. They settled just across the border from Eagle Pass, Texas, in a town later known as Piedras Negras (then called Porfirio Diaz in honour of Mexico's incumbent president). Della, at first unhappy to have left America, often stood on her front porch, gazing at the bridge across the Rio Grande into Texas. But she was an adaptable soul and soon relaxed into her self-appointed role as a kind of unofficial teacher to the Indian and Mexican women, for whom she was also occasional midwife. By autumn 1901, Della was herself pregnant, and on the morning of 27 May 1902 she delivered a child she named Gladys Pearl; a Mexican civil judge certified the birth five days later.

The following year Otis and Della learned that there were better jobs to be had in Los Angeles, where trams, trolleys and railway cars were proliferating to connect the various sections of that swiftly growing city. The Monroes moved to California in the spring, leasing a small, one-bedroom bungalow on West Thirty-seventh Street, in the south-central sector of the city, whence Otis went out to work for the Pacific Electric Railway. With a wife and daughter to support, his dreams of painting watercolours aboard a Seine houseboat faded into oblivion.

In 1905, Della gave birth to a boy named Marion Otis Elmer, and the family required larger quarters. Family notebooks record that theirs was a peripatetic life over the next several years, and that they lived in at least eleven rented and furnished houses or apartments between 1903 and 1909. With such instability and few possessions to call their own, Gladys and Marion, although not obviously deprived of necessities, had uprooted and insecure early lives; constantly on the move, as young Della herself had once been, there were also few opportunities to form sustained friendships. In addition, Otis often failed to return from work at night; just as often, when Della confronted him, he insisted he could not recall where he had been. Because he occasionally drank heavily, Della was not surprised at these memory lapses. The Monroe marriage was thus sorely tested throughout 1907.

Early the following year, at the age of forty-one, Otis Monroe's behaviour and health deteriorated with alarming rapidity. His memory was erratic, his responses often inappropriate, he suffered severe headaches and became uncharacteristically slovenly. Fits of rage, frightening to Della and the children, alternated with fits of weeping, and the poor man soon developed violent tremors in his hands and feet, sometimes followed by seizures that, at least once, sent six-year-old Gladys in a panic to stay with neighbours for two days.

Then, during the summer of 1908, Otis became semi-paralysed. Admitted in November to the Southern California State Hospital at Patton in San Bernardino County, he was diagnosed as suffering from general paresis, the final stage of neurosyphilis, or syphilis of the brain. The disease had been known and diagnosed in Western civilization for at least two centuries; the first successful drug treatment, by the German bacteriologist Paul Ehrlich, was being developed that very same year, too late to benefit Otis.

Della could endure visits to the hospital for only the first several months, after which her husband was completely demented and virtually beyond recognition; in addition, she found domestic day work to support her children. Nine months later, on 22 July 1909, without having left his hospital bed, Otis died at the age of forty-three.

His harrowingly swift mental deterioration had terrified Della, and she told her children that he had gone mad and died a lunatic – perhaps from drink, perhaps from bad conduct. But the medical file released to her after his death and preserved for decades in family records clearly reveals that Otis Elmer Monroe died of an organogenic (not a psychogenic) illness. The dementia, in other words, was the result of a systemic disease, not a genetic predisposition. More important, at least one physician believed the form of syphilis was of the so-called endemic type – that is, the deadly spirochete had been contracted not through sexual activity but through the dangerously unsanitary, viral-infested conditions in which he had worked in Mexico. (The incidence of syphilis in Mexico during the period 1880–1910 – although not always clearly demarcated in its types – was virtually epidemic.) Della, Gladys and Marion Monroe wrongly believed their husband and father had died of insanity, when in fact he was killed by an infection that destroyed his brain tissue.

How acutely this information affected Gladys and Marion at the ages of seven and four is difficult to know, but they must have taken their cue from Della. At first she affected a stoic, matronly melancholy, working earnestly and taking the children to one or another nearby Protestant church 'to pray for the health of their own spirit'. Despite this transient fit of piety, Della still had the restlessness and exuberance that had characterized her youth – she was, after all, only thirty-three years old. By 1910 she was entertaining eligible bachelors and widowers in her home at 2440 Boulder Street. Gladys, by all accounts an extroverted, active girl, thought she would soon have a new father: 'Mama liked men,' she said later, 'and we all wanted a papa.'

For that they waited two years, during which Della was engaged (or acted so) several times before she finally settled on a new husband. On 7 March 1912, at the age of thirty-five, she married Lyle Arthur Graves, a shy, earnest man of twenty-nine who had come from Green Bay, Wisconsin, worked with Otis at Pacific Electric and was that year a railway switchman supervisor. The new family moved to Graves's house at 324½ South

Hill Street, later part of the central Los Angeles business district.

Not much time passed before Della realized she had made a mistake, for Lyle, too, was inclined to excessive drinking – or so she claimed when she took the children after only eight months and moved to a residential hotel. A month later, at Christmas 1912, she went back to Graves, apparently because she needed the support. But the reconciliation did not last long, despite Lyle's generous gifts for the children during the holidays, and his ceding to Della the management of his salary. Five months later, on Gladys's eleventh birthday, Della left Graves; on 17 January 1914 she was divorced, charging him with 'failure to provide, dissipation and habitual intemperance'.

Della herself had known a rootless and restless childhood (her parents having separated when she was thirteen), and so although she may have expected more from adulthood, she knew not how to find or nurture the proper components for herself or her children: there was quite literally no place like home. Their father had died mysteriously after a terrible sickness; men were welcomed and then dismissed by their mother; gentlemen callers arrived and departed; Graves was a new father for only a few months, then he was not, then he was again, then he was not. For Gladys, on the edge of young womanhood, men were impermanent, unreliable transients; at the same time, her mother's conduct implied that men were also in some way necessary to a woman's life. Della continued to enjoy – indeed required – male companionship. Her daughter was, then, receiving mixed signals about marriage, family and parenthood.

By the end of 1916, Della and her children were living in one room of a boarding house at 26 Westminster Avenue, just a short walk from the Pacific Ocean in an area south of Santa Monica known as Venice, on the shore of Santa Monica Bay, twelve miles from downtown Los Angeles. Planned by a man named Abbot Kinney (who made his fortune in the manufacture of Sweet Caporal cigarettes), Venice, California, was planned to resemble its Italian namesake.

Kinney envisioned romantic canals connecting the streets, and beaches and shops linking homes on flower-banked shores via charming arched bridges across the canals. Construction of lagoons and cottages was begun in 1904, and in 1905 the canals were filled with water. Kinney persuaded merchants, hoteliers and restaurant owners to build in the architectural style of the Venetian Renaissance, and to complete the effect he imported two dozen gondoliers from Italy, who arrived with an appropriate repertoire of their native airs and lyrics. Throughout the first two decades of the century, Venice was the so-called Playland of the Pacific, and in 1925 it was incorporated into the City of Los Angeles. Della had visited the place once before; now she chose it as home for herself and her children.

When they arrived, Gladys was fourteen years old. Bright and flirtatious, she made her presence known in every school and social gathering. Her light brown hair sparkled with red highlights, she had a high, vivacious voice and was quick to laugh, and like Della she craved attention, especially from older men – not surprisingly, since she had so little from her own father. Her eleven-year-old brother Marion was soon despatched to live with cousins in San Diego, for Della believed a boy should be raised in a household headed by a man. Already tall and strong like his grandfather Hogan, Marion became a champion high-school swimmer and at nineteen he falsified his age and married a younger classmate named Olive Brunings. Marion Monroe was neither the first nor the last of his family to contract a teenage marriage.

On New Year's Eve of 1917, dancing at a waterfront parlour, Della slipped on an overwaxed patch of floor. Before falling, she was literally swept off her feet by a handsome, six-foot widower named Charles Grainger. Within days, he was visiting her almost every evening at Westminster Avenue.

To Della, Grainger's life was more impressively exotic than anything ever planned by Otis Monroe. Grainger had first worked as a rigger in the Los Angeles oil boom of the 1890s.

7

Then, in 1915, he shipped out to India, and from there he went on to South East Asia, where he was a drilling supervisor for the Burma Oil Company. After his return to Southern California, Grainger had been employed only sporadically by the Shell Company. He lived not far from Della, at 410 Carroll Canal Court, Venice, a modest two-room bungalow along one of the many channels of inland Venice. That address was more appealing than 26 Westminster, and when she saw it Della was charmed.

At that time cohabitation was no more socially acceptable than abortion or divorce, but Charles and Della discussed living together at Carroll Canal Court without marrying; she simply began to call herself Mrs Grainger and no one was the wiser. This decision was probably his, for Grainger's job prospects were frequently uncertain while he hoped for a new overseas assignment. Della's relationships with Otis and Lyle had been deeply troubled, and now she and Charles Grainger often lived apart for days or weeks at a time. In addition, he was helping to support two teenage sons in northern California and could not have rejoiced at the prospect of being legally required to provide for Della and her daughter. Wary of adjusting to yet another father and displeased that her mother was again living in an irregular situation providing her with no sure emotional support, Gladys was unhappy and let Grainger know it by surly moods or silence. As a result, Della found her daughter something of a nuisance, for Charles's offer for them to live with him was not forthcoming.

An expedient development then occurred. A twenty-six-year-old Kentucky businessman named John Newton Baker, visiting Los Angeles, was smitten with the fourteen-year-old Gladys, and she with him – not least because attachment to a man meant independence from Grainger. On 17 May 1917, swearing that her daughter was eighteen and had just moved from Oregon, Della cheerfully witnessed the marriage, turned over the room at 26 Westminster to the newlyweds, and promptly moved in to her lover's bungalow. By 1918, Grainger had found a job very different from oil-drilling, but at least he had regular wages as a supervisor at the Pickering Pleasure Pier in Santa Monica. All of them might, for the time being, have prided themselves on their various ingenuities.

At first, Gladys Baker was a happy young bride, and scarcely seven months later she bore a son they named Jack. The following year, in July 1919, their daughter Berniece Inez Gladys was born.

Given her father's death and her mother's subsequent emotional inconstancy, Gladys had no precedent for domestic stability, nor, apparently, did she herself desire a conventional home life. Quickly wearying of motherhood and its demands, Gladys preferred to leave Berniece with neighbours (just as she had given up Jack) while she went to dance halls and beach parties with friends or strangers; her husband, meanwhile, worked long hours as a general merchandising agent.

On 20 June 1921, Gladys filed for divorce, accusing Baker of 'extreme cruelty by abusing [her] and calling her vile names and using profane language at and in her presence, by striking [her] and kicking [her]', all this despite the fact that she had been 'a good and loyal wife'. Her virtue was not unchallenged by Baker, however, who counterclaimed Gladys's lewd and lascivious conduct. The court forbade her to take her children away from Los Angeles.

While this legal melodrama proceeded, so did the precarious affair between Della and Charles. By March 1922, Della had returned to him and again departed, moving with Gladys to a four-bedroom rented bungalow at 46 Rose Avenue, Venice – another street only as wide as an alley, and a few steps from the shore. Signing a lease as 'Della Monroe', she agreed to rent out two of the bedrooms, earn a wage as housekeeper there, and pay one hundred dollars a month to the absentee owners, Adele Weinhoff and Susie Noel. But as late as June not even the first rent cheque had been posted. This caused a furious dispute between Della and Gladys, each accusing the other of squandering or stealing cash. Neither of them held jobs, most of their funds came from Grainger (with only the remnant of a small final sum from Baker), and these amounts the two women spent on good times, for Della and her daughter had gentlemen admirers. Their brief span as roommates ended in July when a formal eviction notice arrived. With Grainger's permission, Della moved away from the beach, into an empty bungalow he owned in Hawthorne.

The Bakers' final divorce decree took effect in May 1923. That same month he took Berniece and Jack and went back to his native Kentucky. Gladys travelled there once, about a year later, but the children were strangers to her and she left them in the permanent custody of their father. Perhaps from guilt and remorse for her negligence, Gladys made only infrequent attempts to contact them over the years. Jack never saw his mother again (he was reported to have died in his twenties), and it would be several decades before Berniece was reunited with her. Gladys, who had not much experience of emotional stability with Della, could not provide it for her own children.

Free of every family encumbrance and obligation, Gladys then moved east to the section known as Hollywood, where she took a job on the fringe of the movie business – as a splicer (or cutter) of negative film stock at Consolidated Film Industries, located at the corner of Seward and Romaine Streets.

No matter how mechanical the work may have seemed to Gladys, she saw at her bench each day many of the images that were produced to entertain America. In 1923, 43 million people (40 per cent of the country's population) paid an average of ten cents each to see a total of 576 silent, black-and-white films released that year. This was the era of stars like glamorous, sophisticated Gloria Swanson and demurely heroic Lillian Gish; audacious Douglas Fairbanks and sensual Rudolph Valentino; exotic Pola Negri and comic Marion Davies. Among the biggest hits of the year were Lois Wilson and Ernest Torrence in *The Covered Wagon*; Lon Chaney in *The Hunchback of Notre Dame*; Mary Pickford in Ernst Lubitsch's *Rosita*; Edna Purviance in Charles Chaplin's *A Woman of Paris*; Cecil B.

DeMille's first version of *The Ten Commandments*; and Harold Lloyd in *Safety Last*. Gladys was one of a vast working population flooding into Hollywood: four years earlier 35,000 people worked in some capacity for the movie industry; by 1923 the count was 130,000.

Consolidated was one of several labs developing and printing the dailies or rushes, the first rough reel of scenes for viewing by producers, directors and executives the morning after filming. Working six days a week in a crowded room, Gladys, wearing white gloves to protect the negative film stock, cut the pieces of film marked by studio editors and passed them along to those who patched together the sections ordered for the final release negative.

Not long after she began work, Gladys was befriended by a supervisor named Grace McKee, who was soon to become the most important influence on Gladys after her mother. Even more significantly, Grace deeply affected the life of Gladys's next child, Norma Jeane. By the end of summer 1923, Grace and Gladys were sharing an apartment at 1211 Hyperion Avenue, east of Hollywood, in the section later known as Silver Lake.

Grace McKee had been born in Montana on New Year's Day 1895 and christened Clara Grace Atchinson. By 1915, divorced and living in Los Angeles, she was married to a twenty-one-year-old garage mechanic named Reginald Evans. She longed for a career as a movie actress but this never seemed a possibility despite a winsome smile and irrepressible ambition. Standing only five feet one inch tall, Grace was a spirited peroxide blonde who settled for her role as (in the idiom of the day) 'a good time girl', which meant that she was sometimes considered a bad one. Claiming that Evans had gone off to the Great War and died in 1918 (a fact that cannot be substantiated), Grace sliced three years off her age and in 1920, conveniently forgetting about her first husband from Montana as well as Reginald Evans, she wed a draughtsman two years younger than herself named John

Wallace McKee. They did not remain together long, although it would be years before they divorced.

Grace, a woman without inhibitions, felt free to dart from one relationship to another. 'She was a birdlike creature' – her volatile emotions, small stature and perky manner were aptly described years later by Olin G. Stanley, who worked with Grace at Consolidated.

> She was freewheeling, hard-working and fast-living. Ambitious to succeed. A busybody. Whoever and whatever she wanted, she went and got. Partying and booze seemed the most important things in her life, and work was just means to that end.

As friends, Stanley added, Grace and Gladys were ever on the lookout for dates. 'They did, as you'd say, lots of fast living, lots of dates with fellows at the lab or from the studios.' The women and their beaux hauled cartons of bootlegged liquor, widely available in the movie capital, for week-end jaunts to log cabins in the mountains, or to beach parties. When they cavorted an extra day and missed work or drifted off from the lab for an afternoon of fun, co-workers assumed Grace and Gladys's responsibilities in exchange for a dollar or a drink. Gladys Baker and Grace McKee were typical 'flappers' of the Roaring Twenties who chose to extend the recent women's suffrage amendment to include the various social and sexual autonomies long claimed by men.

In their way, they were simply imitating the more exotic and controversial movie stars whose startling images passed before them daily at their workbenches. On Grace's advice, Gladys lightened her brown hair to an almost defiant cherry red in 1924. 'Until Grace took her in hand,' according to Olin Stanley, 'Gladys was really nondescript – a plain Jane. I wouldn't have given her a second glance in a crowd of three before that.'

One who gave more than a second glance was a meterman for

the Southern California Gas Company named Martin Edward Mortensen, who met Gladys during the summer of 1924. Born in California in 1897, son of a Norwegian immigrant, he too had ended a first marriage several years earlier and now, at twenty-seven, was ready to settle down and start a family. He was instantly attracted to Gladys's pert, fey humour and her good nature. In addition, Mortensen, raised a devout Lutheran, was impressed by Gladys's interest in religion, although he perhaps did not know how novel and transitory a concern this was for her. That year, Grace had attended several Christian Science services with a boyfriend who visited their apartment on Hyperion Avenue and spoke of his creed. As usual, Grace's curiosities were at once shared by Gladys – although in neither case did the women consider joining the faith.

To Mortensen, then, Gladys seemed the ideal mate. For her part, she found him handsome, generous, stable and flatteringly jealous; he also looked more than five years older and bore a slight facial scar (and so she saw something of her father). In any case, she saw no good reason to reject his proposal of marriage and security.

But their marriage on 11 October 1924 was ill-considered, for, perhaps predictably, Gladys could not long match her husband in the area of marital fidelity. As she told Grace, Gladys found life with Martin respectable, secure and unendurably dull. Four months later, as if taking a cue from her mother's relationships Gladys simply left her husband and moved back with Grace. On 26 May 1925, Mortensen reluctantly filed a divorce petition in California Superior Court, claiming that Gladys 'wilfully and without cause deserted [him] and ever since has and now continues to . . . desert and abandon [him]'.

Gladys was slow to respond, and her husband several times tried to win her back. According to Olin Stanley, Mortensen often defended Gladys against detractors. Once, as Stanley arrived for work, he observed a colleague leering at Gladys and overheard him say to another man, 'I sure would like to have some of that.'

Some other guy then replied, 'I hear all you have to do is ask,' and with that a man sprang to his feet and grabbed this guy by the throat, shouting, 'Don't ever let me hear you say anything like that about her again!' You know who that was? Why, it was Mortensen. He was still crazy about that gal.

Mortensen waited and hoped, but when Gladys never replied to his repeated overtures for reconciliation, he at last requested a final decree of divorce, which was handed down uncontested on 15 August 1928. In 1929, Gladys learned from friends in Ohio that a man named Martin Edward Mortensen had been killed in a motorcycle accident. And that, she thought, was the end of it.

But in late 1925, almost ten months after she had left Mortensen, Gladys learned she was pregnant. No longer living with Grace, separated from her husband and cited in a divorce petition, she turned to her mother for help. While every man in Gladys's life was keeping his distance (several of them were married), no one could have been less responsive to Gladys's abandoned condition than Della. With righteous indignation – all the more ironic since she claimed to be Mrs Grainger – she ignored her daughter's pleas and plight and simply went ahead with her scheduled grand tour of South East Asia with her lover, travelling on business at the expense of Shell Oil.

For years it was asserted by biographers that Gladys's pregnancy was the result of her affair with Charles Stanley Gifford, foreman of the day shift at Consolidated Film. He had been separated from his wife, Lillian Priester, in October 1923 and a final divorce was granted to her in May 1925. Handsome and arrogant, he was known at home and at work as a wild philanderer, a designation of which he was frankly proud: his wife's uncontested divorce petition noted that he 'shamelessly boasted of his conquests with other women'. Among them was Gladys Baker.

But Gladys never claimed privately or publicly that Gifford was the child's father, nor did she ever seek from him relief or support for herself or the child. The simple truth is that the father could have been any of her boyfriends in 1925 – Harold Rooney, a co-worker who was besotted with her; or the adoring Clayton MacNamara; or, perhaps most likely of all, Raymond Guthrie, a film developer who ardently courted her for months that year.

As for the child, she never met Gifford and was never certain he was her father. To be sure, she tried to contact one or two men she said *might have been* her father (and Gifford *may* have been among them), but the accounts of her attempts at a meeting are notoriously contradictory. Evidence that Charles Stanley Gifford was the father of Gladys's child is, in fact, utterly lacking. When asked if Gladys and Gifford even had an affair, Olin Stanley, who knew them both well in 1925 and 1926, was unsure. 'Gladys was always shacking up with somebody . . . But Gifford as the father? Only God knows.'

The baby was born on 1 June 1926 at 9.30 AM in the Los Angeles General Hospital, and the birth certificate identifies her as the daughter of Gladys Monroe of 5454 Wilshire Boulevard. So easy was it, then as now, to omit, invent and alter one's record, that Gladys simply claimed that her two earlier children had died. She added creatively that the residence of her husband, a baker she designated as 'Edward Mortenson', was unknown. The child's birth registration in the California Board of Health's Bureau of Vital Statistics stated her name as Norma Jeane Mortenson. In her youth, she was sometimes known as Norma Jeane Baker. From the age of twenty, she was Marilyn Monroe, but she declined to make that her legal name until seven years before her death.

Chapter Two

In 1917, beautiful, doe-eyed Norma Talmadge, then twenty, married the thirty-eight-year-old independent producer Joseph M. Schenck, who founded a corporation named in honour of his wife and moulded her career with astonishing success. By 1926, when the couple separated, Norma Talmadge had appeared in more than sixty films, most of them somewhat damp melodramas with titles like *Smilin' Through* and *Secrets*, over which the star's luminous, expressive beauty somehow triumphed. For a film lab worker like Gladys, who coveted glamour and routinely saw images of Talmadge everywhere, the name was more than an imitation: 'Norma' expressed a kind of totemic longing, a benediction on her daughter's future. Double names for girls were popular at the time (Mary Lee, Carol Anne, and so on), and Gladys found 'Jeane' a suitable addition.*

Within two weeks of the child's birth, Gladys gave Norma Jeane over to a foster family sixteen miles away. The reasons for this are not difficult to fathom.

In the Roaring Twenties, moral and aesthetic standards were challenged in deed as well as discourse – not only in America, but round the world. After the horror of the Great War, there were extraordinary explosions of creativity as well as bolder (and sometimes dangerous) amusements everywhere. Along with New York, Berlin and Paris seemed simultaneously to inaugurate the 'Jazz Age', and life for a time seemed a cycle of

---

* Contrary to popular belief, Gladys could hardly have bestowed the second name in honour of Jean Harlow, for Harlean Carpenter did not change her name until 1928.

uninhibited fun, excitement and experimentation. Europeans eagerly imported the works of Americans like Hemingway, Dreiser, Gershwin and Jelly Roll Morton – but not the dark, imprecatory religious sentiments so deeply rooted in the American tradition.

The United States, however, was caught in the conflict between the new moral turmoil and the old puritan repressions. In the 1920s, higher hemlines were seen and coarser language heard in public than ever before; there was widespread use of drugs as recreational gear (especially cocaine and heroin); and plays and movies routinely dealt with the dark underside of life. In contrast, by that peculiarity known as Prohibition, alcohol was then illegal. As the voices of moral vigilance became more strident, the country's penchant for the bogus remedy of extreme moralism (as distinct from authentic morality) led to the emergence of thumpingly righteous fundamentalist religions – in California as in the South.

There were other factors encouraging Gladys to place the baby with a decent family: she could not give up her job, there was no one to care for Norma Jeane while she worked, and her restless, nomadic life (like her mother's, as she may have apprehended) was unsuitable for mothering.

And there were less tangible, more elusive, perhaps subconscious (but none the less potent) reasons to deliver Norma Jeane to the care of others. Gladys had seen her father's deterioration and death, which (she had been wrongly told) was due to madness – a condition then believed to be invariably inherited. Disappointed, like Della, in marriage, Gladys had also found herself incapable of effective mothering. Hostile to her mother on account of the past and Della's recent abandonment of her during the latter part of her pregnancy, Gladys may have been, in a way, a classic type of parent who resents an offspring of the same sex.* In addition, she was plainly terrified by the physical

---

* An important national study conducted during the 1920s suggested many parents who gave up their children 'were themselves children emotionally . . . and manifested this in their disinterest in and hostility toward their own offspring as children who needed to be reared' (see A. J. Simon, *The Nervous Child*, vol. 3,

responsibilities of caring for an infant. Further seasoned by sharing her friend Grace McKee's dedication to an unfettered life of gaiety (as if it were a vocation), Gladys had developed the habit of an essentially selfish life.

She was, then, ill prepared to be a diligent, effective and constant mother, and she knew it. Of this Gladys's own mother Della was similarly convinced, for as soon as she returned from her exotic South Seas adventure – when her granddaughter was a week old – she urged Gladys to place Norma Jeane in the care of a sober, devout couple named Bolender; they also lived on Rhode Island Street, the address of Della's bungalow at Hawthorne. (The street-name was changed several times as Hawthorne and adjacent El Segundo became business extensions of the Los Angeles International Airport.) 'I was probably a mistake,' Norma Jeane told a friend years later. 'My mother didn't want me. I probably got in her way, and I must have been a disgrace to her.'

Like many families of that time, the Bolenders supplemented their income by caring for foster children, a responsibility for which they were paid twenty or twenty-five dollars a month either by the natural parents or by the State of California.

And so on 13 June 1926, Norma Jeane Mortensen (her name variously noted on official forms as Mortensen, Mortenson or Baker) was delivered to Albert and Ida Bolender. He was a postman, and she devoted herself to mothering (she had one son), foster-parenting, housekeeping and local, Protestant parish life of the Low Church type. Among the many dramatic presentations of Norma Jeane's life was the account of her being shuttled to more than a dozen foster homes before she was ten. Like so many other tales of her childhood, this bit of manufactured autobiography conveniently fed the legend of a miserable, Dickensian childhood – a theme beloved of Hollywood publicists and sentimentally cherished by many people. But Norma

p. 119 [1944]; W. H. Newell in *The American Journal of Orthopsychiatry*, vol. 4, p. 387 [1934] and vol. 6, p. 576 [1936].)

Jeane's earliest years were geographically rather stable: she lived for seven years in the Bolenders' modest, four-room bungalow.

One unhappy event occurred during Norma Jeane's early years – something she could have hardly recalled from the age of one, but about which she learned from the Bolenders, Gladys and Grace.

In early 1927, Della suddenly fell ill with a weak heart and became susceptible to frequent respiratory infections. She now depended on Gladys, who moved in with her mother despite the long daily trolley-car ride to work. By late spring, Della was in wretched health. Her breathing became severely impaired by degenerative heart disease, and this caused her to suffer acute depressions. Medication provided only occasional relief and, as with many cardiopulmonary patients, the intervals were often characterized by pleasant fantasies, reveries and even periods of frank euphoria. Della could be withdrawn and tearful when Gladys departed for work, but then in the evening she might find her mother cheerfully preparing dinner. It would have been natural, in such circumstances, for Gladys to recall the unpredictable behaviour of her father years earlier. There is some evidence in the family files that Della suffered a stroke in the late spring of 1927 – an event which could also have caused unpredictable shifts of mood and temper.

At the end of July, Della was convinced death was near, and an array of guilty memories alternated with hallucinations: her parents, Tilford and Jennie Hogan, were reconciled, she told Gladys, and they were coming to rescue her, to take her home. Next morning she claimed that Charles Grainger (long since out of her life) had crept into her bed the night before and had made violent love to her. Not long after, she struggled from her home, walked over to the Bolenders to see her granddaughter and banged on the door. Angered when she saw that no one came to admit her, Della broke the door's glass with her elbow – 'for no reason I know of,' Ida said, adding, 'we called the police.'

On 4 August 1927, Della was carted away to the Norwalk State Hospital suffering from acute myocarditis, a general term for inflammation of the heart and surrounding tissues. After nineteen days of agonizing distress, she died on 23 August at the age of fifty-one. The death certificate gives the cause as simply myocarditis, adding a 'contributory manic depressive psychosis'. This latter term was imprecise, especially in those days, and was subjoined only because Gladys stressed to the physicians at Norwalk that her mother's moods and tempers had alternated unpredictably in recent weeks.

The fact is that little was done for Della's grave heart condition. She had seen doctors only three or four times and often forgot the hours and doses of her medication. When the ward supervisor signed papers a day after her death, Gladys's report on her mother's mental state made the addition of 'psychosis' understandable but really baseless; but among the documents of Della's case during confinement, there is no psychological profile, nor is there a record of an attending neurologist. Della Monroe (thus her name appeared in hospital records) died of heart disease which caused impaired mentation due to insufficient oxygenation of the brain. As in the case of her husband Otis Monroe, there is no evidence that she was also a psychiatric case. But for Gladys the myth of family madness deepened: after Della's death she was distressed and for several weeks failed to report for work. Shutting herself in her mother's bungalow, she pored over Della's few possessions; finally, she emerged and decided to sell the place. Bracing herself for a return to work, Gladys then moved back to Hollywood, obtaining jobs at two movie studios, weekdays and Saturdays.

Although there were quite different reasons to pity much in her life, the truth is that (contrary to later publicity reports), Norma Jeane's years with the Bolenders were essentially secure, she lacked no material necessities, and there is no evidence that she was abused or mistreated. But she was the only child to remain so long: more than a dozen other children arrived, grew and departed, or returned to their families.

'Despite all the inventions of later years,' according to Norma Jeane's first husband, 'she never had known grinding poverty, never had gone shoeless, never, to the best of my knowledge, had to skip a meal.' He felt that as her career improved she 'desperately wanted some colorful family tale of want and scarcity ... [while] the truth is that she was raised in a small but comfortable bungalow with every modern convenience, if not splendid luxury.' The Bolenders even owned a scarred old upright piano, used mostly for hymn-singing by Ida's church cronies. There were also toys and books, and a small room to accommodate a child's parent for an overnight visit.

Yet she was clearly scarred by the psychological and emotional stress of her uncertain identity and by not knowing when her mother might suddenly appear and just as suddenly vanish. When she did visit Norma Jeane, Gladys took her for outings or picnics. Mother and daughter rode the Pacific Electric trolley cars to Sunset Beach; alternatively, they made several changes and travelled south to tour the glass factories in Torrance; or, all the year round, they would simply ride and ride from one shoreline resort to another, stopping at Redondo, Manhattan and Hermosa for lunch or ice cream. Among Norma Jeane's earliest memories was Venice's own St Mark's Plaza, on the corner of Windward and Ocean Front Walk, where (then as decades years later) residents and tourists shopped and gaily-dressed crowds crossed to and from the beach. Gladys once bought a striped parasol her daughter kept for years, and Norma Jeane loved to watch the mimes, jugglers and fire-eaters at the Plaza. Frequently, mother and daughter rode the Venice Miniature Railway down Windward and then walked along the inland lagoons, where Gladys pointed out the weekend rendez-vous of Douglas Fairbanks and Mary Pickford, of Harold Lloyd, of William S. Hart. But such happy Saturdays grew increasingly rare, for Gladys visited less and less often. 'Her mother paid her board all the time,' Ida recalled, adding that Norma Jeane 'was never neglected and always nicely dressed'. But Gladys became for the most part an irregular, shadowy visitor at the edge of her daughter's life.

'One morning I called [Ida] "Mother", and she said, "Don't

call me that – I'm not your mother. Call me "Aunt Ida". Then I pointed to her husband, and I said, "But he's my Daddy!" and she just said, "No".' Later, 'she discussed her father more than anyone in her past,' according to a close friend. 'She remembered her mother, although without much feeling. But she missed a father terribly, although she was smart enough to be wary of anyone she took for a surrogate father.'

Ida Bolender was correct to speak truthfully about the situation; her manner and tone, however, seems to have lacked the kind of comforting explanation that would have protected the child, from bewilderment and the conviction that she was in some way markedly different from other children. At two and three, Norma Jeane could not have understood the sporadic arrivals and departures of the woman she was told to call mother. 'She didn't come very much,' she said later. 'She was just the woman with the red hair.' Gladys, whose visits meant good times, made guest appearances, but the major players of Norma Jeane's early life were the Bolenders, and in matters of conduct, religion and morality they yielded centre stage to none.

'To go to a movie was a sin,' Norma Jeane remembered of one Bolender doctrine. 'If the world came to an end with you sitting in the movies,' Ida warned, 'do you know what would happen? You'd burn along with all the bad people. We are churchgoers, not moviegoers.' The sharp disjunction between Gladys's attitudes and those of the Bolenders must have caused Norma Jeane considerable confusion about proper conduct and standards of right and wrong.

Confusion or no, photographs from these first several years show Norma Jeane a winsome child with ash-blond hair, an engaging smile and bright, clear eyes. But she always recalled that in the Bolender household 'no one ever called me pretty.' The plainspoken, decent, humourless Ida did not believe in flattery; prettiness might even be dangerous. She and her family lived within bustling, modern Los Angeles County, but Ida and Albert could have been the models for Grant Wood's *American*

Gothic. Norma Jeane's closest playmate was a stray dog she brought home. The Bolenders allowed her to keep the puppy so long as she cared for it, and Norma Jeane was usually seen followed two paces behind by the worshipping Tippy.

The family had in fact no inclination for mere worldly amusements; they placed primary emphasis on morality and religious responsibilities. The church they all attended (literally shaken to its foundations by the 1933 earthquake) was the focus of Bolender life – and therefore, by extension, the lives of the children committed to their care. 'We took her to Sunday school with us,' Ida said. 'I had not only Norma Jeane and my own son, but other children, too, with me.' This pious little platoon marched off to the pews not only on Sunday but also for prayer and instruction one afternoon and one evening during each week, as Marilyn later recalled. 'Every night I was told to pray that I would not wake up in hell. I had to say: "I promise, God helping me, not to buy, drink, sell or give alcohol while I live. From all tobacco I'll abstain and never take God's name in vain".' '. . . I always felt insecure.'

That the Bolenders were not prodigal with entertainments or compliments is entirely consistent with the austere and highly charged religious character of their lives. Perhaps the primary advantage of faith, they believed, was the certainty of their moral posture, and it was morality which assured salvation. They were members of a branch of the United Pentecostal Church much influenced by the famous Los Angeles Apostolic Faith Gospel Mission, a revival community founded on Azusa Street in 1906. Like many people with good intentions but a restrictive and potentially dangerous literal-mindedness, adherents of this kind of faith often equate true religion with unquestioning obedience to a certain code of right conduct; a sense of mystery (much less a mystical sense) is not even mentioned. For children especially, everything was to be made clear and immutable, and people of any age who questioned or complained were pitied, ignored or held in quiet contempt. This is not to imply, however, that there is any evidence that the Bolenders were other than attentive, caring foster parents. 'They were terribly strict,' Norma Jeane said years later. 'They didn't mean any harm – it was their religion. They brought me up harshly.'

For over a century, Roman Catholic, mainstream Protestant and then Jewish communities flourished in Los Angeles. But in the 1920s and 1930s, flamboyant evangelical sects proliferated along with the aromatic eucalyptus and acrid auto fumes. Unconventional, sometimes hysterical attempts at faith healing; bizarre costumes; midnight-to-dawn meetings where sinners were asked to 'testify'; services that resembled movie-set extravaganzas – all these were typical of local religious life. This is not remarkable in a place where the entertainment industry depended on the mechanisms of fanfare and promotion; the fringe churches, too, engaged advertising and public relations consultants.

The best example of this colourful spirit during Norma Jeane's childhood was the notorious Aimee Semple McPherson, greatly admired by the Bolenders, who took Norma Jeane and their other young charges to hear the famous evangelist. A Pentecostal minister born in 1890, Sister Aimee began her preaching career with itinerant evangelism, radio sermons and healing services at seventeen; eventually she found her greatest welcome in Los Angeles. There, after terminating two marriages but attracting many followers, she established her International Church of the Foursquare Gospel, whose Angelus Temple was built by her devotees in 1927 at the staggering cost of $1.5 million. Her congregations nationwide, augmented and united by radio broadcasting, numbered in the tens of thousands.

McPherson was quite a character. Usually present was her mother, sunnily addressed as 'Ma Kennedy', who led the applause for her daughter's highly theatrical revival services – rites ideally suited to Hollywood. To preach a sermon on God's law, she wore a police uniform; to address the topic of decency, her outfit was a Victorian overall; lights, music and mirrors were routinely used for the right effects. The saxophone, for example, was played by a young man named Anthony Quinn, later a movie star. Dynamic and attractive, McPherson was much loved by her faithful even after the collapse of her third marriage, the filing of at least fifty lawsuits against her, and widespread scandals involving (separately) sex and money. (She had an affair with Charles Chaplin.) For all that, the impression made by the exuberant blond Sister Aimee, who used the tools of the acting trade to arouse her congregants, was unforgettable for those who saw her.*

At home the Bolenders continued the ideals set before everyone at church. Dancing, smoking and card-playing were considered works of the demon, and neatness, order and discipline were marks of virtue; children's carelessness, impertinence or poor manners were sinful. Routines for mealtimes, chores and playtime were meticulously followed; household regulations were dutifully observed and deviation from them was to be avoided at all cost. Ida's face often bore an expression of exasperated disappointment over some minor childish foible: 'It was hard to please them. Somehow I was always falling short, although I can't remember being especially bad.' Standards were high for winning approval from Norma Jeane's first mother figure, while Albert Bolender remained mostly a quiet backer of his wife's domestic management, his silence severer than any open threat of punishment.

As a natural part of maturing, of establishing independence, of testing and claiming one's own personality, every child finds a way of rebellion. For Norma Jeane, rigorous discipline at home firmly forestalled mischief, tantrums and rank disobedience. She could, she always insisted, only withdraw to an inner world for her escape. In this regard, there was so much emphasis on propriety that a peculiar type of recurring childhood dream was perhaps inevitable:

I dreamed that I was standing up in church without any clothes on, and all the people there were lying at my feet on

* McPherson died of a barbiturate overdose in 1944 at the age of fifty-three.

the floor of the church, and I walked naked, with a sense of freedom, over their prostrate forms, being careful not to step on anyone.

The surreal scene was described and appropriately embellished in adulthood, and whether or not it actually haunted the pre-adolescent Norma Jeane is perhaps unimportant. More to the point, the dream represents what she later wanted the public to think of her childhood fantasies: that she had a kind of prophetic sense of who she would be and what effect she would have on others. She would be a woman to surprise and shock with a natural, guilt-free display of her body; she would also take care not to offend, and in some way this would be con-nected to her being (as she desired) accepted – even adored – with people lying at her feet. Dream or no, this became the reality.

The Bolenders would have been horrified to hear such a dream: the bathtub was the only licit place for nakedness. And because cleanliness was not only next to godliness but virtually a sign of it, the Bolenders' sole extravagance was the hot water lavishly poured for the children's baths. In a household obsessed with the taint of sin, Norma Jeane was encouraged to soak and scrub. But she never felt that she emerged quite clean enough to please her foster parents. 'You could have done better,' Ida or Albert said quietly as they brushed her hair and set out a clean dress. The religious injunctions of church echoed at home: *perfection* was the ideal to be ever kept before the growing child. Anything less – and of course everything is – deserves implicit belittling; and nothing is more dangerous than praise, which could lead to complacency, idleness or spiritual torpor. She recalled that in her childhood she never felt quite ready, quite clean enough, acceptable, presentable for the Bolenders. 'You can always do better.' It was a short route from a soiled blouse to eternal damnation.

She certainly could have done better than to be bored and dis-tracted at a religious pageant into which she was corralled at

Easter 1932. With fifty other black-robed youngsters arranged in the form of a living cross, she made her first public theatrical appearance at a sunrise service at the Hollywood Bowl:

> We all had on white tunics under the black robes and at a given signal we were supposed to throw off the robes, changing the cross from black to white. But I got so interested in looking at the people, the orchestra, the hills and the stars in the sky that I forgot to watch the conductor for the signal. And there I was – the only black mark on a white cross. The family I was living with never forgave me.

'I've got to get rid of that quiet little girl,' Norma Jeane overheard Ida Bolender say to her husband that night. 'She makes me nervous.'

In 1932 the domestic atmosphere of discipline and achievement was reinforced in the new demands of school life. 'Go down two blocks, turn left and keep going till you see the school,' Ida Bolender said one morning in early September, and with two older neighbouring children to accompany her, Norma Jeane set off for first-grade class at the Washington Street School in Hawthorne, then located at the corner of El Segundo Boulevard and Washington Street (just south of the area that included Los Angeles International Airport). Classroom discipline was simply a variant on home for Norma Jeane, but in the schoolyard, she remembered: 'I loved playing games, and everything seemed like it was pretending. Like all kids, we used to act out little dramas, exaggerate stories. But I loved to make things up – more than the others, I think – maybe because life with my foster parents was always so predictable.' On most days, Tippy followed her to school and waited outside for the return journey.

Another 'pretend game' that year seems to have been inspired by a recurring motif on a radio detective serial the Bolenders allowed. A few times that year, Norma Jeane slipped off to school with Albert's flashlight, prowling the route and (in broad daylight) shining the torch on the licence plate of every car and carefully jotting it down. Thus did she practise writing her numbers in early 1933.

And then, with the suddenness of the earthquake that rocked Southern California that March, life changed for Norma Jeane just after her seventh birthday. An angry neighbour, annoyed at Tippy's barking, grabbed a shotgun and killed the dog, causing the child a spasm of grief. The Bolenders summoned Gladys, who arrived in late June, transported by her friend Grace McKee, by this time more than ever Gladys's closest confidante, sometimes her emotional support, often her counsellor, always the arbiter of difficult decisions and the adjudicator of Gladys's personal and financial dilemmas. Then almost forty, single and childless after several marriages, generous, bohemian with an almost manic pertness, Grace was to become the most important influence in Norma Jeane's life. For the present, however, Gladys was at the centre of things.

Her mother helped Norma Jeane bury her pet. She then paid the Bolenders their last month's fee, packed her daughter's clothes and swept her off to a small apartment she had leased for the summer at 6012 Afton Place, Hollywood, near the studios where she and Grace worked as freelance cutters. Norma Jeane's time in the sleepy village suburb of Hawthorne had firmly ended, and with it the vigilant moralism to which the child had been subjected. At the same time, Gladys's decision to reverse the pattern of her life and to take on the care of her daughter seemed almost a desperate act, one of foreign or imposed conscience.

On 13 June, as part of President Roosevelt's assault on the Great Depression, the Home Owner Loan Corporation had been instituted. Low-cost mortgages were now available to hundreds of thousands of Americans, and Gladys, as a single parent, easily qualified. At once she negotiated the purchase of a house into which she and her daughter moved that autumn. Life was changing very rapidly indeed, as Norma Jeane found when, during that summer, Gladys and Grace acted as her tour guides for Hollywood and downtown Los Angeles.

A decade earlier, the city had had half a million people; now there were almost three times that number. This increase created an enormous suburban sprawl, with the emergence of various communities linked by the Pacific Electric streetcars; these travelled as far north-east as Pasadena and south-west to Long Beach for only twenty cents; out to the village of Lankershim (later North Hollywood) for fifteen cents; and out to Zelzah (Canoga Park) for a dime. Trolleys clanged along Hollywood and Santa Monica Boulevards – two of the major east–west arteries – while along Sunset Boulevard passengers rode in elegant double-decker buses.

The various sections of Los Angeles were characterized by the development of different industries and technology. Aircraft factories were busy near the shore, opening up Los Angeles to a world from which it had been much isolated with deserts on the eastern and the ocean on the western limits. Wells were operating round the clock in the hills south of Hollywood, and the port of Los Angeles was the country's largest oil terminal.

Ten miles inland was the epicentre of the motion picture industry, flourishing as never before with talkies, attracting technicians as well as hopeful actors from all over the world. Film companies owned more than two million dollars worth of real estate, studio space and equipment, while two hundred miles of new streets were being blocked out and paved with routes toward the studios. Los Angeles and Hollywood were, in the collective mind of the world, synonymous.

For all its business enterprises and efficient movie story-telling, there was little high culture – a fact at least partly due to the influx of migrant labourers to Los Angeles. From Iowa, Missouri, the Dakotas, Nebraska and Kansas there came, in the words of one historian, 'a people well stereotyped in American folklore – mainly derived from Low Church Protestant stock, puritan and materialistic to start with.' And from Central America came another kind of migrant worker: Hispanic Catholic, often with strong Indian roots – in other words, not European-American and therefore, so far as the sturdy Mid-westerner judged, not American at all. With Depression breadlines and Beverly Hills mansions, immigrant poor and movie-star rich, Los Angeles was evolving into an odd confusion of realms, a hedonistic hick town where the traditional American frontier values of hard work and land cultivation clashed with the allure of the fast buck, fame and a good life under perpetual sunshine.

Late in August, Gladys and Norma Jeane moved into their house at 6812 Arbol Drive, a furnished six-room, three-bedroom house not far from the Hollywood Bowl. The item that settled Gladys's mind on this particular residence was a Franklin baby grand piano, painted white. It could have come straight from a scene that had passed through her fingers at the lab – *Flying Down to Rio* with Fred Astaire (on which she had worked at RKO that year) – or from Busby Berkeley's *Gold Diggers of 1933*. For Gladys as for moviegoers, a white piano was virtually an omen of better times.

The house purchase was negotiated and a $5000 loan obtained from the Mortgage Guarantee Company of California – issued, interestingly, to 'Gladys Baker, a married woman'. To facilitate the payments, Gladys at once leased out the entire house to a married couple; she then rented back a bedroom for herself and her daughter, sharing the living-room, bathroom and kitchen with the other family. In Gladys and Norma Jeane's bedroom hung one small framed photograph – of Charles Gifford. From this fact sprang a subsequent false certainty, among several writers, concerning Norma Jeane's father, but all the child knew (or her mother admitted) was Gladys's residual affection for an old beau.

Gladys continued to work as a cutter, and her housemates were English film actors with great spirit but uneven fortunes: George Atkinson had small roles in a few George Arliss films, his wife was an extra in crowd scenes, and his daughter was a sometime stand-in for Madeleine Carroll. It was not surprising, therefore, that the talk at home was usually about movies: writing them, acting in them, editing them, going to see them. Suppers of hash, chipped beef or melted cheese on toast –

usually prepared by Grace, the constant visitor – were spiced by industry news, movie star gossip and studio schedules. That year Prohibition was repealed state by state, and on long, hot summer nights Gladys, Grace and their friends lingered on the porch after the evening meal, smoking cigarettes and sipping from tall beakers of lager. Norma Jeane often collected the empty beer bottles and filled them with flowers from the tiny backyard garden; into one bottle she poured some of her mother's lavender water for herself. Movies, cigarettes, beer, sweet lotions: nothing could have been more different from the years with the Bolenders, as she later recalled.

> Life became pretty casual and tumultuous, quite a change from the first family. They worked hard when they worked, and they enjoyed life the rest of the time. They liked to dance and sing, they drank and played cards, and they had a lot of friends. Because of that religious upbringing I'd had, I was kind of shocked – I thought they were all going to hell. I spent hours praying for them.

For a disciplined, quiet seven-year-old girl, this new adult conduct must have seemed precarious and perhaps more disorienting than refreshing. Most awkwardly, she had to adjust to a second mother. 'Aunt Ida was not my mother,' she kept saying to herself. 'The lady with the red hair is really my mother' – the woman who without hesitation dealt out a card game for her friends, poured beer, rolled back the carpet and danced. Here was a new woman to please, one completely different from Ida Bolender, and someone she really did not know.

Among the most remarkable differences was the acceptability – even the *necessity* – of the movies. When they guided Norma Jeane on weekend tours of Hollywood, Gladys and Grace naturally emphasized the great Hollywood movie palaces, those cathedrals of diversion that variously rivalled the Parthenon, Versailles, Far Eastern temples, Gothic churches and European opera houses. These theatres, the women said, were the places that showed 'our movies'. Sparing no expense, designers filled vast interior spaces with paintings and antiques, sculpture and splashing fountains. 'No kings or emperors have even wandered through more luxurious surroundings,' boasted the theatre decorator Harold Rambach.

Imaginations soared along with the construction fees. East of Vine Street on Hollywood Boulevard was the fabulous Pantages Theater, built in 1930 to accommodate 2288, where uniformed ushers with flashlights conducted patrons past Art Deco columns and vaults, sunbursts and statuary, to a gilt-edged auditorium. Sid Grauman, inspired by the excavations of King Tutankhamum's tomb in 1922, built the Egyptian Theater on Hollywood Boulevard that year. Eleven years later, the place was still in pristine condition: patrons walked down a long, dramatically decorated courtyard with stucco walls featuring mock tombs and vast effigies of ancient Egyptian gods, pharoahs and mummy cases, sphinxes, vultures and fancy grillework. Grauman's most famous achievement was the Chinese Theater, a little further west on Hollywood Boulevard, with the exterior of a Buddhist temple, the interior of a Chinese palace, elaborate chinoiserie throughout, and a great gong to herald the start of the feature movie.* Here Grauman assured his immortality along with that of movie stars by inviting them to imprint their hand and footprints into wet cement with appropriate greetings to him.

All that year and the next, the little girl who had once been told she belonged to a family of 'churchgoers, not moviegoers' was taken at weekends to these temples of the imagination, where she saw not dour preachers or the eccentric Sister Aimee, but self-reliant Katharine Hepburn as Jo in *Little Women*; Mae West sparkling with sexual self-confidence in *She Done Him Wrong*; Claudette Colbert bathing nude in *Cleopatra*; and Raquel Torres vamping Groucho Marx in *Duck Soup*. Most of

---

* Other notably fantastic creations – some of them downtown, on Broadway – included the Warner Brothers, the El Capitan, the Vine Street, the Palace, the Los Angeles Theater, the United Artists Theater and the Mayan.

all, she remembered how Gladys and Grace adored an incandescent blonde named Jean Harlow, a brazenly sexy social climber in *Dinner at Eight*. 'There's a movie star!' Grace whispered to Norma Jeane, pointing at Harlow and echoing the sentiments of millions of Americans – and from that moment, as Norma Jeane later said, 'Jean Harlow was my favorite actress.'

Weekdays that summer, while Gladys and Grace worked at film labs, their very livelihoods dependent on the gods and goddesses they saw, Norma Jeane was given money to stay cool and safe at the movies. 'There I'd sit, all day and sometimes way into the night – up in front, there with the screen so big, a little kid all alone, and I loved it. I didn't miss anything that happened – and there was no [money for] popcorn, either.'

In September, when Norma Jeane entered second grade at the Selma Avenue elementary school, she was registered as Norma *Jean*; this was a clerical error, but one which recurred with such frequency that it is easy to imagine Gladys and Grace comparing their girl to both Norma Talmadge and Jean Harlow.

That autumn, Gladys received news from Missouri. Her grandfather Tilford Hogan, the sympathetic and self-educated farmer whose divorce had caused a great emptiness in his life, had been dealt a great blow by the news of Della's death. The following year, when he was seventy-seven, two things happened: his health, never robust, suddenly began to fail, and he married a shy, generous, hard-working widow named Emma Wyett. She, too, soon became ill with heart disease.

After the stock market crash of 1929, hunger and hardship had become pandemic in the United States, and to its worst effects Tilford Hogan was not immune. Hundreds of suicides were reported daily across the country as families lost great fortunes or modest savings; in 1933, no less than fifteen million men were jobless – one of every four heads of households. Scores of banks closed, factories failed every week, countless rural folk became migrant workers and complacent middle- and upper-class families in large cities were living in tarpaper shacks, sifting through garbage dumps for food scraps. In February the nation seemed on the brink of a collective nervous breakdown when President-elect Franklin D. Roosevelt, visiting Miami, narrowly escaped an assassin's bullet. He was inaugurated in March and, although he and his new government announced radical steps to cure the country's dreadful health, everyone knew this was not the task of a week. In this time of widespread heartache and panic, Tilford Hogan was simply worn down after years of misfortune. By May 1933, his lungs and kidneys failing as quickly as the farm he tenanted, he was unable to provide for himself and Emma. That month came the final stroke of ill fortune: he was to be evicted from his farm.

Early in the afternoon of 29 May 1933, he waved from the window of the small house in Laclede as Emma cranked their ancient jalopy and went on a shopping errand to a nearby village. When she returned two hours later, she called to her husband but there was no reply in or near the house. Emma then walked over to the crumbling barn. As she entered the cavernous darkness, she saw him swinging by the neck, suspended from a rope thrown over a high beam. An inquest ordered by the Missouri State Board of Health had no difficulty confirming the doctor's report: Tilford Marion Hogan, bereft of pride and hope, was simply another suicide statistic in Linn County during the worst year of the Great Depression.

Although she had never known Tilford, Gladys (learning of his death in October in a letter from a cousin) took the news as a terrible shock and fell into a stupefied depression. Her father, she had been incorrectly told, had died of lunacy; her mother's death had been erroneously reported as caused by manic-depressive psychosis; now, her grandfather's death by his own hand convinced her that there was virtually a blight of mental illness on the family tree. From this belief Gladys could not be dissuaded. In the evenings she stalked the rooms of the house, muttering prayers and reading aloud from a family Bible. Inconsolable, she refused food and sleep, despite Grace's

ministrations. Frightened by her mother's unusual and protracted grief, Norma Jeane brought tea and held Gladys's hand,
begging her to rest, imploring her to stop weeping.

After several weeks of Gladys's depression, Grace took matters into her own hands and called in a neurologist. According
to Eleanor Goddard (later Norma Jeane's foster-sister), 'This
doctor prescribed some pills for Gladys. But she had a violent
reaction to them.' Psychopharmacology had not, it must be
emphasized, a sophisticated history in 1934 – much less was it
then (nor has it ever been) a precise science. The effects of certain psychotropic drugs simply cannot be foreseen, and without
careful monitoring and the swift administration of antidotes,
medications that are harmless to most patients may cause
dangerous, permanent and in some cases lethal side-effects.

By February 1934, Gladys was still withdrawn and depressed,
although once again there were no sure signs of outright psychosis: her inability to cope seems to have derived more from
her background (perhaps, too, from guilt and remorse over
neglect of her children) than from real psychiatric illness. She
had also taken on the burden of a house, even as she continued
to work six days a week, and she was trying to know her youngest child, hitherto a stranger. Her hopes for the future, in other
words, seemed suddenly to collide with the past and even with a
large dose of remorse for her lifestyle and her early neglect of
Norma Jeane. She also seems to have drunk excessively on at
least two occasions (as did many people when bottles and kegs
were broken open to celebrate the end of Prohibition), and
liquor would interact perilously with any mood-altering medication.

Gladys obviously required more sophisticated medical care
than she was receiving, and psychological counselling was
scarcely available at all in Los Angeles at that time. The assertion of insanity, established soon after under curious
circumstances, became the unquestioned truth only much later;
by then, it was the patched invention of the movie star's ace
publicists, a brilliant reporter and a legendary writer – all of

them committed to the creation of a Hollywood tale in Hollywood terms. The simpler, more poignant facts of Gladys's mismanaged care was the first casualty of the legend.

'The doctor who prescribed the drugs couldn't have known what effect they'd have on Gladys, and her condition was thought to be irreversible by 1935,' recalled Eleanor Goddard. 'Her attempt to care for herself and Norma Jeane was out of the question. Up to that point she did a really remarkable job.'

And so Gladys Pearl Monroe Baker Mortensen, not yet thirty-two years old, was taken to a rest home in Santa Monica in early 1934. There she remained, sedated and forlorn, for several months before being transferred to Los Angeles General Hospital, from which she was sometimes released for weekends to determine her ability to cope with 'reality' (according to one of the few remaining medical reports from that year). Never offered anything like competent psychiatric care, a field still in its infancy in the 1930s (and especially uncommon in California), Gladys gradually crept into the dark refuge of a lonely, solitary world from which she seldom emerged. At the same time, the care of her daughter was readily assumed by the childless, concerned, formidable Grace McKee – Norma Jean's third mother-figure in eight years.

For most of 1934, Norma Jeane remained at Arbol Drive, cared for by the Atkinsons but supervised by Grace, who visited almost daily. Again there were major changes and fresh expectations to bewilder her, and, inevitably, new patterns of behaviour to which she had to conform. Ida Bolender had regarded movie stars and their world as sinful: when she reported to Ida that her mother had taken her to a movie, Norma Jeane had been told this was a dangerous pastime. After that, Gladys had given her daughter the idea that movies were innocent entertainment – and thank God for them, for they brought a decent wage.

But Grace went further. One neither condemned nor merely watched Clara Bow or Jean Harlow: they were to be emulated. For a child not yet eight, this was an astonishing contradiction of creeds to absorb and, successively, to heed. Much of her childhood was defined, then, by a sequence of contradictions that could only cause guilt. The proper young lady formed by Ida tried to avoid wickedness and remain pure. The child visited by Gladys wanted to make herself agreeable, to comfort and to please; the girl taken in hand by Grace was encouraged to put all that aside and to become someone entirely new – an invention written, designed, produced and directed by Grace McKee herself. Until 1934, Grace's maternal instincts (and much of her money) had been lavished on two nieces. Then these children moved away from Los Angeles. But from the sadness of Gladys's departure came the sudden fortune of Grace McKee – she now had a child to raise, to form and shape.

'Grace loved and adored Norma Jeane,' recalled McKee's fellow-worker Leila Fields.

If it weren't for Grace, there would be no Marilyn Monroe ... Grace raved about Norma Jeane like she was her own. Grace said Norma Jeane was going to be a movie star. She had this feeling. A conviction. 'Don't worry, Norma Jeane. You're going to be a beautiful girl when you get big – an important woman, a movie star.'

And to advance the cause, Grace dressed Norma Jeane in a hand-made gingham dress, curling her hair and urging her to smile and pout like Mary Pickford. Eleanor Goddard, who knew Norma Jeane before she was Marilyn Monroe, agreed:

Grace was very perceptive. From this very early time she had the idea that Norma Jeane was going to be a movie star. And she did everything in her power to bring it about. Grace could have no children of her own, and so she lavished her affection on Norma Jeane, whom she considered to be as much or more hers than Gladys's.

'More hers than Gladys's' – precisely because Gladys was now regarded as incompetent and ineffectual. One must presume, given the financial sacrifices Grace made on Norma Jeane's behalf for so long, that the conscious motives animating Grace were benevolent; to be sure, she allowed the child more freedom than had the Bolenders, and provided more luxuries. But the freedom, pleasure and advantages Grace provided were not without benefit to Grace herself. 'Grace Goddard was nice enough – if she could benefit,' said Norma Jeane's first husband, tempering his otherwise high praise for her generosity and sacrifice.

The woman Norma Jeane now had to please, to whom she owed her safety, her bed and board, did not merely enjoy working in a sector of the so-called 'dream factory' – she supervised one of its most important departments. In Hollywood social life and in the celluloid stories she helped assemble for the public, Grace saw people in real life and characters in stories renamed and reinvented – just as she did for herself in her own capricious youth and whimsical bohemianism, in her airy unconcern for adding or subtracting a name here or losing a husband there.

If ever a girl was primed for Hollywood, it was Norma Jeane, watching Grace's own hair colour and hemlines alter. Grace knew how a woman's appearance could be changed by makeup, lights, filters and shadows; how, with a quick snip of the scissors, an unflattering image could be eliminated. She knew by profession what the studios successfully marketed, what 'worked', what the public wanted. The infinite varieties of cosmetic surgery, later one of Los Angeles' most heavily advertised and lucrative professions, became perhaps the logical extension of the movie world's craving for an impossible ideal. It was, in other words, Grace McKee's job to help perfect illusions. And with greater frequency and intensity during the next several years, Norma Jeane became the heiress of Grace's experience. In taking on the child's care and education, she had at last an opportunity to create the daughter nature had denied her.

In 1934, Olin G. Stanley was working as a temporary cutter with Grace in the Columbia Studios editing lab. As he recalled, cutters worked four hours on Saturdays, and for months Grace asked a friend to bring Norma Jeane to the lab an hour before noontime closing. 'We workers were introduced to her, and every introduction was the same, over and over. Grace said, "Baby, I want you to meet Olin – Olin, isn't she pretty?"'

Thus far, this was ordinary pride. But Grace went further: '"Norma Jeane, turn around and show the nice man the big bow on the back of your dress. Now walk down that way and turn around. Good, now walk back here again ... Oh, here comes Ella, Norma Jeane! You met Ella last month. Tell Ella again – she's probably forgotten, but *you* haven't forgotten! Tell Ella what you're going to be when you're all grown up. Say: 'a movie star,' baby! Tell her you're going to be a movie star!" This brainwashing continued every week for months and months.' Another worker confirmed Stanley's recollections: 'It was just a plain fact with Grace,' recalled Charlotte Engleburg. 'Norma Jeane was going to be a movie star, and that was that.'

For this goal there could be only one model. 'Grace was captivated by Jean Harlow,' said Norma Jeane, 'and so Jean Harlow was my idol.'

Chapter Three

The girl named Harlean Carpenter, born to a genteel Kansas family in 1911, came to Hollywood with her divorced mother, a woman who had ambitions of movie stardom for herself. But the daughter fared better, took her mother's name as her own, and as Jean Harlow worked as an unbilled extra in silent films and then more remarkably in comedy shorts with Laurel and Hardy. Her first major appearance was in *Hell's Angels* in 1930. The bond between mother and daughter continued to be so strong that even during her three marriages 'The Baby', as everyone affectionately called Jean, frequently spent nights at her mother's home.

In nine films released during the next two years (most notably *The Public Enemy*, *Platinum Blonde* and *Red Headed Woman*), Jean Harlow's overt sexuality, her shockingly dyed and cinematically lighted platinum-coloured hair and her shimmering screen image made her endlessly fascinating. The critical consensus, however, maintained that she was merely a cheap, sassy twenty-year-old playing a succession of cheap, erotic roles. Longing for better parts in more serious films, in 1932 she signed a contract with MGM, where producer Louis B. Mayer carefully guided her star image and where she developed a natural flair for comedy. She was also, contrary to what the public was led to believe, a rather sweet young woman with a genuine longing to supplement her brief formal education and greatly – perhaps neurotically – attached to her mother. Expressing the common sentiment of those who knew Jean

Harlow, the actress Maureen O'Sullivan remarked that 'there wasn't anyone at MGM who didn't love her, who wasn't amused by her or didn't think her an absolute darling.'

Playing opposite such stars as Clark Gable and Spencer Tracy, Jean Harlow at twenty-two was, despite promises of more serious roles, still asked to show more cleavage and disport herself with more blatant sultriness than any star of her day. When Grace McKee took Norma Jeane to see Harlow in *Dinner at Eight*, *Bombshell* and *The Girl from Missouri* (all released between the summers of 1933 and 1934) the critical tide was turning in Harlow's favour.

MGM, however, continued to keep her in skin-tight white gowns emphasizing her startling blond-white hair. This presentation of frank eroticism corresponded with something in her own character; she rarely wore underclothes, and in restaurants and at press conferences was often seen (apparently absent-mindedly) caressing and fondling herself. Like many stars of both sexes, she had no greater admirer than herself. Offscreen, Harlow's life lacked anything like sustained happiness. Married three times by the age of twenty-four, she spent her short life in a constant search for her missing father, from whom she was always separated. But audiences adored her, and even the mysterious circumstances surrounding the apparent suicide of her second husband (twenty-two years her senior) could not diminish public approval.

It is no exaggeration to say that during the Great Depression, Jean Harlow was America's great apotheosis of daring but often comically exaggerated carnality. There were stars who sometimes tried to imitate her hair colour or were given a similar studio build-up, but publicists and reporters insisted there would never be another like Harlow.*

This Grace McKee stoutly denied: 'There's no reason you can't grow up to be just like her, Norma Jeane. With the right

* Harlow's image was attempted by or forced on stars as various as Marion Davies, Joan Crawford, Carole Lombard, Betty Grable, Constance Bennett, Lyda Roberti, Alice Faye and Joan Blondell.

hair colour and a better nose . . .' For the child, then eight (and for those who overheard this oft-repeated refrain), Grace must have sounded a little ridiculous, not to say intimidating. But she was the importunate and prophetic screen mother. As if incarnating a hoary cliché, both she and Mama Jean transmuted their own dashed hopes of stardom into energies on behalf of others, through whom they lived and who, they hoped, would succeed where they themselves had failed. In September 1934, Grace added a lavender rinse to her own peroxide blond hair and applied touches of makeup to Norma Jeane's lips and cheeks. The race to stardom, insofar as it involved the child's unofficial guardian, was beginning with an Olympic sprint.

That year passed for Norma Jeane with the routines of grade school, regular movie-going with Grace, and irregular visits from Gladys, who went with them at least three times to Sunday lunch at the Ambassador Hotel, a rare and glamorous treat. Quiet, sad and remote, Gladys picked at her food while Grace chattered gaily, proudly showing off a dress she had bought for Norma Jeane and the pink ribbons she had tied into the child's curled hair. Such occasions must have been awkward for the mother, who could only have felt more incompetent than ever; and for the daughter, estranged again from a woman she had never really known.

On such visits, Gladys was inevitably disconnected from the 'real world' of family life to which her doctors wished her exposed. Nor could Gladys have felt more attuned to actuality when she met her daughter at the house on Arbol Drive. There the Atkinsons, still immured in their endless, unrealized fantasies of success, were packing for England and, they said, the certainty of stardom. Frightened of responsibility for Norma Jeane and doubtless guilty for failing her doctors, her daughter and her friend Grace, Gladys returned to the relative calm of the hospital. There, at least, was the comfort of a routine where she had no real chores and where maternal duties were nonexistent – and so Gladys could avoid any lingering guilt. The only reality was what she saw and heard; for her, Norma Jeane was a vague presence, lingering perhaps only like a phantom pain. 'My mother,' she said later, 'never really made any effort to be with me. I don't think I existed for her.'

The house on Arbol Drive was put up for sale that autumn; this portion of the street soon vanished, and the land became part of the Hollywood Bowl complex. Grace, however, did not take the child to live with her, and the reason for this was quite clear. She had decided to become Norma Jeane's legal guardian, but the State of California required proof that the living natural parent or parents were incompetent and likely to remain so. In addition, the prospective adoptee was required to spend at least six months in a county orphanage while the guardianship was approved.

The first requirement was readily met after Grace obtained a formal statement from doctors that Gladys was insane. Grace then arranged her transfer from Los Angeles General to Norwalk State Hospital, where Della Monroe had died. Gladys's condition had stabilized and Los Angeles General's staff said they could no longer accommodate her. 'Her illnesses,' proclaimed the chief medical officer's report, 'have been characterized by (1) preoccupation with religion at times, and (2) at other times deep depression and agitation. This appears to be a chronic state.' Such an assertion perfectly demonstrates the impoverished state of both diagnosis and treatment of emotional illness in 1935. One might reasonably ask whether a longing for spiritual health, often the result of depression and agitation, was not in fact an appropriate response to much of what Gladys had known in her life.

Since the house on Arbol Drive was no longer the family home, there was no alternative but further institutionalization for Gladys. In addition, Norwalk had (at least by comparison with General) a better reputation in managing chronic cases of various mental illnesses. Quite apart from Gladys's general apathy and loss of affect, county physicians at General were persuaded of the patient's incompetence by Grace's statement of Norma Jeane's illegitimacy as well as her presentation of the family 'history' – the now accepted account of mental illness afflicting Tilford, Otis and Della.

Thus in January 1935, Gladys was taken to Norwalk, where she remained one year before another transfer. 'I was sorry she was sick,' Norma Jeane said later, 'but we never had any kind of relationship. I didn't see her very often. To me, she was just the woman with the red hair.' Nor did Grace encounter difficulty in fulfilling the second legal mandate. She learned there was a place available for Norma Jeane the following September at the Los Angeles Orphans Home, and until then she arranged for a family in West Los Angeles named Giffen to take her in. Before doing so, however, Grace cannily determined that the Giffens were already a houseful, with their own and several other foster children: no, they could not keep Norma Jeane very long.

Because she was demonstrating such care for Norma Jeane and filing weekly reports with the appropriate authorities, Grace then re-petitioned the court, asking that the orphanage requirement be waived so that Norma Jeane might live with her after a time with the Giffens. 'You can imagine how happy I was when Grace told me I wouldn't be sent away to live at some kind of school with children I didn't know, and no family.'

And so, after two months with the Giffens, while the court investigated Grace McKee's fitness as legal guardian, Norma Jeane was allowed to live temporarily with Grace's mother, Emma Willette Atchinson. She had an apartment on Lodi Place, Hollywood, in a pleasant white stucco building with a Spanish tiled roof, a flowering courtyard and a gently splashing fountain. Norma Jeane moved there in early spring 1935.

That same month, Grace swung into action – not only expediting the cause of her guardianship, but also asking the court to award her sole control over the affairs of Gladys P. Baker. Grace rightly saw that Gladys's financial affairs must be kept regular to avoid seizure by the surprise appearance of someone claiming to be Norma Jeane's father, or by the tax authorities. She also knew that proper investments and sales of any cash or real property needed a careful eye, and that she could, on

Norma Jeane's behalf, draw on these monies for the girl's support. Accordingly, on 25 March, Grace swore an affidavit that Gladys needed a court-appointed guardian and that, despite the interim orphanage requirement, she was the proper candidate.

In April, the assets of Gladys's 'estate' were assessed: Gladys Baker, as she was then known, had $60 cash in the bank account, $90 in unendorsed insurance cheques (for loss of work due to illness); one table radio valued at $25, with a store balance due of $15; a debt of $250 on a 1933 Plymouth sedan she had scarcely used; and $200 owed on the white piano.

On 1 June, Norma Jeane's ninth birthday, Grace McKee received full possession of everything owned by Gladys Baker along with responsibility for its disposition. Within days she drove the Plymouth back to its original owner (who cancelled the debt); she sold the piano for $235 (duly returning the profit to the estate); and the house was repossessed by the mortgagee without penalty.

At the same time, Grace submitted items for reimbursement – sums to which she was entitled during her earlier care of Gladys and Norma Jeane: $24 for a fee to a nurse named Julia Bennett, for example; $25 to Emma Atchinson for custody of Norma Jeane; $49.30 in fees owed to the Santa Monica Rest Home; and a $43.16 bill for clothing purchased for Norma Jeane. Able to negotiate her way through the thicket of many legal and social matters, Grace McKee was a formidable conjunction of fantasist and pragmatist.

But some things cannot be anticipated or readily adjudicated – a surprise romance among them. For the first time in several years, as far as can be determined, love overturned Grace's life in the person of a man who for ever altered her plans and Norma Jeane's destiny.

Precisely how Grace McKee met Ervin Silliman Goddard that spring of 1935 is unknown; that there was a great mutual rush of passion is beyond dispute. Ten years younger than Grace, Goddard stood six feet five inches tall, was sometimes mistaken for film actor Randolph Scott and was engaged as Joel McCrea's stand-in on several movies. (One of his daughters later spotted him as one of the soldiers alongside Laurel and Hardy in *Babes in Toyland*.) A divorced Texan with three children he did not see for long periods, Goddard was, as his daughter Eleanor later described him, 'the ultimate Hail Fellow Well Met.' Charming and intelligent, he was an inveterate tinkerer and the son of a former surgeon, and so on both counts bore the nickname 'Doc'. But his handsome geniality and his dream of movie stardom often led to periods of indolence, and indolence to prolonged appointments with cronies at local saloons. Not unexpectedly, he found Grace's energy infectious, her passionate nature gratifying, her adoration and encouragement irresistible.

For her part, she was besotted by the flattery and ardent attention of a strong, young and comely man she described to everyone as a movie star. Side by side, Doc Goddard and Grace McKee were almost comical: she was a full foot shorter, thin and trim, and he was the proverbial brawny cowboy. Their own joviality forestalled laughter at them or sniggering at her seniority, and friends enjoyed their sheer luxuriant enjoyment of one another's company that spring and summer of 1935. They were married in August, after a wild weekend frolic in Las Vegas, where Grace's aunt was witness and hostess.

Returning to Los Angeles, the newlyweds gathered one of Goddard's daughters, Nona, who had come with him to California (she later became the actress Jody Lawrance), and the foursome took a small bungalow on Odessa Avenue in Van Nuys, in the San Fernando Valley just over the Hollywood hills. 'Norma Jeane was a shy, introverted little girl,' Jody Lawrance said years later, adding that they were both 'neurotic children [who] clammed up and were very sensitive toward our surroundings.' Lawrance remembered that the two girls assembled a makeshift tree house in a pepper tree, 'and we crawled up there when we thought we'd get in trouble. That tree house was our escape.'*

---

* Jody Lawrance assumed minor roles in six films between 1951 and 1962. She took her life soon after finishing the last.

Modest would be too grand a word to describe the bungalow itself, which was essentially a shack. Both Doc and Grace were at this time employed only intermittently, and neither had savings. Goddard insisted that Norma Jeane's was the unnecessary extra mouth to feed, and he prevailed on Grace to give the child up to the orphanage – for a short time, he promised, until his proverbial ship came in.

Given her clear dedication to Norma Jeane's welfare and the grand scheme for adopting her and guiding her toward stardom, it could not have been easy for Grace to tell the child that she would have to move into the orphanage that September. For Norma Jeane, here was another relationship suddenly ruptured, another promise broken; she was once again an unwanted commodity. As she had been told by Ida Bolender, her own mother had 'dropped her off', and Norma Jeane learned for herself that she could be turned away when she was an inconvenience. In adulthood, her lack of close female friends owed much to these early experiences: she had had no primary experience on which to base any trust of a woman, no experience (after the remote, obsessive Ida Bolender) of womanly constancy. Once again, any semblance of a normal pattern of early socialization was subverted.

On 13 September 1935, Grace packed Norma Jeane's clothes and delivered her to the Los Angeles Orphans Home, at 815 North El Centro, Hollywood, where she was registered as the 3463rd child in its twenty-five-year history. The place was nothing like a workhouse; on the contrary, it was an attractive and spacious red-brick colonial mansion. Nevertheless, it was an institution for orphans.

The Home could accommodate fifty or sixty children, not all of whom were actually without parents: in the 1920s, fully a third of the residents were runaways or street urchins forsaken by the poor or immigrant workers unable (or unwilling) to provide for unwanted offspring. In the 1930s many poverty-stricken parents could apply for a child's short-term lodging. These, like Norma Jeane, were classified as 'temporary guests or students'. She stayed there until 26 June 1937 (just after her eleventh birthday), by which time Doc Goddard's ship was still unberthed. 'Doc had a lot of trouble during the Depression,' as Norma Jeane's first husband later recalled. 'This was unfortunate, because he really had a great mind and seemed to me able to do just about anything.'

At the Home, boys and girls were housed in separate wings, four, five or six in each neat, tidy room. From 1952, Marilyn Monroe's statements to the press about the orphanage became more and more fantastic. In 1960 she said (among other embroideries) that she 'slept in a room with twenty-seven beds', and she added distressing tales of orphanage trauma: dreary accommodation, cold baths, rigid discipline and endless menial tasks such as toilet-scrubbing and washing hundreds of plates after meals. In fact, there was a team of adult employees to cook and clean at the Home, but, to encourage a sense of responsibility, the children were paid five or ten cents a week for less arduous minor chores suited to the age and strength of each.

According to Eleanor Goddard, Norma Jeane was inspired by the accounts of the really dreadful and abused situations Eleanor herself had known in Texas, when after her parents divorced and she was pitchforked miserably from stranger to stranger and house to house. But Norma Jeane's time on El Centro was quite decent, and because the Home was nonsectarian, the supervisors, while encouraging children to attend church on Sundays, imposed no religious obligations.

Norma Jeane's file noted that she was in 1935 'a normal, healthy girl who eats and sleeps well, seems content and uncomplaining and also says she likes her classes.' Formal education was not offered at the Home, but at the Vine Street Elementary School, a five-minute stroll away. Of her two years at Vine Street, in grades four and five, no records remain.

On Saturdays during these two years, Grace frequently appeared and took Norma Jeane for a day's outing, which usually meant lunch and a movie – especially if there was an early evening premiere, when they both applauded the stars and joined the throngs in the cries of adoration typical of the time. Among the pictures Norma Jeane especially remembered was *Mutiny on the Bounty*, with Clark Gable; he reminded her of the dark-haired, moustached man whose photograph had hung at Arbol Drive. Gable, she said repeatedly, was 'the man I thought of as my father'. Grace often said that she was still trying to 'fix things up so you can come back with me where you belong', by which, no doubt, she meant the Goddards' legal guardianship.

On such days, Norma Jeane was often taken to Grauman's Chinese, where she remembered 'trying to fit my feet into the footprints – but my school shoes were too big for the stars' slim, high-heeled ones. Then I measured my hands with theirs, but mine seemed too small – it was all very discouraging!'

But with Grace as tutor, Norma Jeane's dejection could not last long. The girl was routinely taken to a beauty parlour, Grace standing by anxiously as curlers, irons and brushes attempted the proleptic glamorization of Norma Jeane. She was sometimes hauled into the ladies' lavatory at a tea-room or movie theatre and shown the proper application techniques of face powder and lipstick; eye-liner and a delicate cologne completed a spectacle passers-by could only have regarded as the slightly bizarre, premature display of a pre-adolescent. 'Grace was something of a wizard with cosmetics,' according to Eleanor Goddard, 'and she loved to sweep down on us with all kinds of advice about makeup.'

In 1935, two Harlow films opened in Hollywood – *China Seas* and *Libeled Lady* – and Grace reiterated her conviction that Norma was going to follow Jean Harlow, a vision in sparkling black and white pictures: platinum hair, a shimmering white wardrobe whenever possible, white decor and props. After seeing several Harlow pictures in 1935 and 1936, Grace dyed her own hair blond, went into a period when she was seen only in white, bought only white clothes for Norma Jeane and briefly considered dying the girl's hair platinum but wisely drew back: the Home would not have admired such a change in a ten-year-old. As the *New York Times* reported, it was due to Harlow that platinum blondes 'made their appearance everywhere, among actresses, dancers, show girls and blues singers ... in the subways, in the streets and in the audiences at theatres.'

'Time after time, Grace touched a spot on my nose,' Norma Jeane said years later. '"You're perfect except for this little bump, sweetheart" she'd say. "But one day you'll be perfect – like Jean Harlow." But I knew that no matter what, I would never be perfect – as anyone else, let alone myself.' Looking at the girl, Grace imagined a young Harlow and said so to Norma Jeane (who later told this to friends so often it became an obsession). Both had blue-grey eyes and a slightly receding chin (that 'could also stand fixing,' Grace said); the hair colour would be altered in due course. Such early preparation and exhortation to become an imitation of a major movie star would naturally appeal to a child with a confused identity, a lack of normal home life and a pattern of needing to please so many mother-figures. She was, in other words, primed to be the ultimate, manufactured facsimile of a culture's fantasies.

There was also something of a stir in the gossip columns on 1 June 1936 (Norma Jeane's tenth birthday) when the blonde star announced that after almost a decade of acting under her mother's maiden name, she was at last formally changing her own to Jean Harlow. She would thenceforth no longer, after three marriages, be legally Harlean Carpenter McGrew Bern Rosson. About the same time, it was widely touted that Harlow was one of the celebrity volunteers campaigning vigorously for the re-election of President Franklin Roosevelt – a political involvement that much impressed Grace.

Saturdays with Grace were welcome breaks from school and communal living. But in a way it would have been surprising if Norma Jeane did not perceive her 'Aunt Grace' as a variation of Gladys – a fantastic creature who arrived at her own convenience, one to whom she might gradually become unimportant, even negligible.

In addition, Grace was not entirely reliable or predictable in her visits, although her account books (carefully preserved) reveal her regular payments to the Home and her purchase of clothes for the girl. (In 1936, for example, Grace paid the full fee to the Home, fifteen dollars monthly, and she spent almost the same amount on clothes, makeup and 'expenses for minor'.) Norma Jeane must have feared that, like Gladys, Grace might be taken away without warning, and so it seemed to be, when Grace failed to come to the Home for five consecutive Saturdays in late 1936. At that period the girl broke into sobs of despair at the slightest provocation. If she was 'almost perfect', she may have reasoned, why was she abandoned? One of the administrators, a good-natured soul named Mrs Dewey, reminded her that most of the children never had any visitors, but that was very cold comfort indeed. Years later, her third husband felt that 'she was able to walk into a crowded room and spot anyone there who had lost parents . . . or had spent time in orphanages.'

By early 1937, Norma Jeane's mood had darkened. 'I was never used to being happy during those years,' she told a reporter later. Indeed, a supervisor that year noted that she occasionally seemed 'anxious and withdrawn . . . and at such times she stutters slightly. Norma Jeane [*sic*] is also susceptible to a lot of coughs and colds . . . If she is not treated with much reassurance and patience at such times, she appears frightened. I recommend her to be put with a good family.'

Typically, Norma Jeane's yearning for solace evoked a vivid fantasy life. 'I sometimes told the other orphans I had real wonderful parents who were away on a long trip and would come for me any time, and once I wrote a postcard to myself and signed it from Mother and Daddy. Of course nobody believed it. But I didn't care. I wanted to think it was true. And maybe if I thought it was true it would come true.'

Inventing idealized fantasy-parents may sometimes have briefly eased the loneliness; later (even when she admitted the truth) she found relations with women difficult to negotiate.

Just as she found contradictory the injunctions set by Ida and Grace, just as they gently reminded her that she could always 'do better' and 'be perfect', so no one could match the expectations aroused by her lost parents. In addition to a pitiable cycle of search and inevitable disappointment, she sometimes chose unsuitable partners for friendship, romance or marriage – perhaps in the unacknowledged belief that by repeating the unhappiness of the past she might at last reverse its effects.

There was another outlet for her longing and her fantasy. To her first husband and to many friends, she later said that she often

> went up to the roof [of the Home] to look at the water tower at the RKO Studios a few blocks away, where my mother had once worked. Sometimes that made me cry, because I felt so lonely. But it also became my dream and my fantasy – to work where movies were made. When I told this to Grace, she almost danced for joy.

The child's bleakness and daydreams are easy to understand. The Home cared diligently for its young charges, but in the custodial manner of institutions and enforced communities. There was necessarily an atmosphere of impersonal affection that strictly discouraged particular friendships between children and mentors, to avoid unhealthy dependence as well as the erotic attachments inevitable in close quarters when adults are placed *in loco parentis*. As a result, there is often found in institutionalized children a paradoxical indifference to the welfare of others. Each child is, after all, merely one among dozens, and because the staff strive to act without favouritism, there is a kind of emotional insipidity. However dedicated the supervisors, orphanages are not usually happy places. Everyone tacitly understands the artificiality of the milieu, and children know very quickly that there has been something woefully incomplete about their lives.

There was, however, one notable exception to the general impersonality. Mrs Dewey saw Norma Jeane returning from a Saturday outing with Grace. Primped and fluffed, with new ribbons in her curled hair and makeup freshly applied, the girl approached the building. Later she remembered:

I suddenly stopped. I knew we weren't allowed to wear makeup [at the orphanage], and I forgot until that minute that I was wearing the makeup Grace had put on my face that day. I didn't know whether to go in or just run away. Another girl had been given some kind of punishment or de-merit . . . for wearing lipstick, which the teachers thought was pretty trashy.

But Mrs Dewey surprised Norma Jeane. 'You have very lovely skin,' she said, 'and you don't want to have a shiny face, but sometimes you hide it with a little too much rouge.' And with that she toned down Grace's handiwork without embarrassing the child.

Grace kept her promise to bring Norma Jeane home. Her final papers for guardianship were filed on 26 February 1936 and (with the slowness typical of bureaucracies) the petition was finally granted in the spring of 1937. She left the Los Angeles Orphans Home and arrived at the Goddard bungalow in Van Nuys on 7 June 1937 – a week after her eleventh birthday. Just as she was climbing into Grace's car that evening, radio bulletins announced the death of Jean Harlow, who died suddenly of uremic poisoning at twenty-six. Louis B. Mayer, Harlow's boss at MGM, summarized the consensus of those who knew her and those who simply admired her: 'This girl, whom so many millions adored, was one of the loveliest, sweetest persons I have known in thirty years of the theatrical business.' As one reporter wrote, 'She added little that was new to comedy, but she intensified in her person several comical ideas of her day: the gold-digger type, the under-educated, utilitarian, quick-

tongued, slightly unaware females then in vogue among car-
toonists, magazine writers, jokesters.' Grace was torn,
according to Marilyn years later, between grief at the death of
this beautiful young woman and her conviction that this made
Norma Jeane's future all the more certain.

Norma Jeane's residence with the Goddards was brief
because of a singularly unpleasant and even traumatic event.
According to her first husband, James Dougherty, Doc Goddard, very drunk one night, grabbed the girl and, fumbling and
fondling her crudely, tried to force himself on her. She managed
to disengage herself from his embrace and dashed off, shaking
and crying. Especially for so vulnerable and fatherless a girl, this
incident was alarming and repellent. Norma Jeane's initial experience of physical contact with a man dissociated sex from the
context of affection: what may have at first seemed like a gesture
of tenderness turned ugly and abusive.

At once, Norma Jeane complained to her 'Aunt Grace', who
must have thought her husband's drunken advance portended
more serious trouble. 'I can't trust anything or anyone,' Grace
muttered. And so in November 1937, Grace shipped the girl
away again, this time to board with relatives. 'At first I was
waking up in the mornings at the Goddards' and thinking I was
still at the orphanage,' she told friends eighteen years later.
'Then, before I could get used to them, I was with another aunt
and uncle, waking up and thinking I was still at the Goddards.'
She concluded the reminiscence poignantly: 'It was all very confusing.'

Chapter Four

From November 1937 to August 1938, Norma Jeane lived with cousins and a great-aunt in Compton, about twenty-five miles south-east of the San Fernando Valley but still in Los Angeles County. But instead of a pleasant new home, more challenges and trauma awaited. There was a general atmosphere of suspicion in the house, constant whispers of something sinister and tragic about the family's history. It was a milieu that could have sprung straight from the pages of a story by Edgar Allan Poe or Henry James – it could have been described as Gothic but for the prevailing Southern California sunshine. And the aroma of dread that hung in the rooms had nothing to do with Gladys or her daughter.

The woman to whom Grace made irregular payments for Norma Jeane's care was a divorcée named Ida Martin, who received sometimes five dollars a month, at other times ten or fifteen, often nothing. She was the mother of Olive Brunings, who had married Gladys's younger brother Marion in 1924. Olive and Marion Monroe, so far as the family knew, lived for five years in the Central California town of Salinas, where he worked as a mechanic, and there they had three children: Jack, born in 1925; Ida Mae, in 1927; and Olive, in 1929. When the youngest was nine months old, on the afternoon of 20 November 1929, Marion Monroe left the house, telling his wife he was going to buy a newspaper and would return before dinner. He was never seen or heard from again.

The Bureau of Missing Persons failed to locate him, and local police could not trace his itinerary that afternoon. The California Department of Motor Vehicles was no help, nor were police in four neighbouring states. Marion had not contacted anyone in his family, including Gladys to whom the news was relayed the next day. His most recent employer, Joe Zerboni (owner of the Union Storage and Transfer Company), was equally surprised and had no idea of Monroe's whereabouts, destination or fate. Ida Martin, Marion's mother-in-law, engaged the prestigious Shayer Detective Service of Los Angeles; after three years they had not a single clue.

In 1934, Olive ('destitute and in need of State aid', as her petition read) began legal proceedings to have her husband declared legally dead, so that her three children could be registered as half-orphans and thus eligible for public welfare funds. (Laws providing aid for single parents later changed, but this was Olive's only recourse for financial aid at that time.) But the State required ten years of a spouse's absence before a declaration of presumed death could be issued, and with it the concomitant financial benefits for the surviving family. Olive and her three children had no relief from a situation of grinding poverty until 1939.

When Norma Jeane arrived in Compton at the end of 1937, she met her three cousins for the first time, since Ida Martin was also caring for her three grandchildren while Olive worked with migrant farmers. The children were close in age: little Olive was then eight, Ida Mae ten, Jack twelve and Norma Jeane eleven. Years later, Ida Mae recalled one statement that Norma Jeane repeated: 'I remember she said over and over again that she was never going to marry. She said she was going to be a school teacher and have lots of dogs.'

Here again was a parentless household, with children trying to structure life after a father's mysterious disappearance, familial instability, abandoned and displaced children. Just as in the lives of Della, Gladys and Grace, there was the impression that men are both necessary and capricious – untrustworthy, volatile, unknowable, unpredictable and still achingly missed. Life was imperfect with and without them.

And here was yet another surrogate mother for Norma Jeane to know and to please. Ida Martin seems to have been an attentive provider, but she had no answer for Norma Jeane when she asked about her Uncle Marion's absence and the distance of Aunt Olive from the family. 'Once we decided to run away from home,' Ida Mae added. 'We had the idea we'd go to San Francisco to look for my dad, because someone had once said they had seen him there. But we didn't leave the house.' She remembered, too, that there was an odd and frightening lady who lived across the street – a demented woman named Dorothy Enright who sat on her porch, endlessly rocking in an old rattan chair. 'Her family kept her occupied with piles of movie magazines to pore over, and we got the hand-me-downs.'

Later, Norma Jeane's feelings about this period were complicated:

> The world around me then was kind of grim. I had to learn to pretend in order to – I don't know – block the grimness. The whole world seemed sort of closed to me . . . [I felt] on the outside of everything, and all I could do was to dream up any kind of pretend-game.

One of her more imaginative games was based on a movie magazine story that showed a picture of wine-making, 'and so she had the idea we would make wine,' Ida Mae recalled. 'We had a big old, discarded bathtub in the back yard, and we gathered grapes and piled them into the tub, then stomped on them with our bare feet. This went on for three or four days, but we ended up only with a rotten smell in the backyard, and no wine!'

In the spring of 1938, Olive Monroe visited Ida Martin and together they told the children that thenceforth they had to consider their father dead, not just absent – only in this way could they have enough money to remain a family. This idea was at once picked up by Norma Jeane, for she told her schoolteacher that she was living with relatives because her parents had been killed in an accident (as indeed, for her, they might as well have been). The teacher, a benign woman named Parker, was moved to tears and for the remainder of the sixth grade Norma Jeane was the subject of special attention and concern. Her student's quietly dramatized account was remarkably effective.

Some of Norma Jeane's other inspirations were more psychologically complex. In 1937, Grace had taken her twice to see Errol Flynn and the Mauch twins in the movie *The Prince and the Pauper*, and in early summer 1938 she saw it again with her cousins. The jaunty Flynn was a dashing leading man, but the identical boys were for ever after fascinating to Norma Jeane:

> Later, I thought it [the identical twins] was a little eerie, actually, but then I was very excited by seeing the two look-alikes, one a prince pretending to be a beggar-boy and the other an urchin pretending to be a prince.*

Besides the moustached Flynn, who reminded Norma Jeane of Clark Gable ('I told Jack and Ida Mae that Gable was my real father, but they just laughed'), the movie perhaps made its deepest impression on her precisely because of the exchange-of-roles fantasy. A waif only pretends to be so: he is actually a prince, and after considerable effort he is recognized as heir to the throne of Henry VIII.

Norma Jeane had already been routinely transformed from a kind of weekday orphanage Cinderella into a Saturday afternoon princess by the determined Grace McKee Goddard. Grace had primed her for stardom and said she would one day inherit the mantle of movie queen Jean Harlow. Norma Jeane then discovered that inventions about her family and her background both sweetened her own memories and occasionally made her lovable to others. No wonder the doubles of *The Prince and the Pauper*, with the neat replacement of a fantasy by a real royalty,

---

* The story is somewhat more complicated, but this later statement represents her girlhood résumé, and her *impression* is more significant than her inaccurate re-telling of the plot.

long haunted her. She had only to meet the heroic father-figure (à la Clark Gable or Errol Flynn) to set the matter right: the waif would be raised to the legitimate regal position.

Two events that year may well have fed the need for escape into fantasy. First, Grace visited in March and quietly told Norma Jeane that, after Gladys had tried to escape from the hospital at Norwalk, she had been transferred to a more secure environment – the state asylum at Agnew, near San Francisco.

The attempted breakout had a concrete and tragically ironic cause. Gladys had been terribly upset and disoriented after receiving telephone calls from her last husband, Martin Edward Mortensen, who she believed had died in a motorcycle accident in Ohio eight years earlier. In fact, Mortensen was alive and well in California; it had been a Midwesterner with the same name and a similar background whose death had been mistakenly reported to her by relatives as that of her husband.

Still solicitous for Gladys's welfare and willing to provide for some of her needs, Mortensen had tracked her to the hospital at Norwalk and put through several calls. Alternately confused and almost hysterical with relief that someone had remembered and was reaching out to her, Gladys tried to leave the Norwalk grounds to find her ex-husband. But the staff had been told Mortensen had died in 1929, and so Gladys's report of the telephone calls and her subsequent escape attempt were regarded as grave schizophrenic delusions requiring the more sophisticated treatment at Agnew. This was forthwith decreed, and Gladys had no further contact with Martin.*

Norma Jeane seemed to receive this news of her mother's condition as virtually an announcement of Gladys's death. Grace tried to soften the occasion with gifts (the details and cost of which were preserved by Grace's family): a sun-suit for the beach, a new hat, and three pairs of shoes. By that summer, to the consternation of Ida Martin and her grandchildren, Norma

---

* Mortensen died on 10 Feb. 1981, in Mira Loma, Riverside County, California.

Jeane, poorest of the cousins, had no less than ten pairs, all of them supplied by Grace (and charged to Gladys's dwindling account).

The second episode involved a violation that was even more traumatic than Doc Goddard's crude and abusive advance. Not long before Norma Jeane's twelfth birthday in June 1938 (according to her close friends Norman Rosten and Eleanor Goddard, among others), a cousin forced her into some kind of violent sexual contact. She was 'sexually assaulted' (although not raped, for her first husband claimed she was a virgin at the time of their wedding). The importunate cousin was thirteen-year-old Jack, of whose later life nothing is known; by his twenties he seems to have imitated his father's disappearing act. This incident reinforced her sense that she was desired as an object, but she was left feeling abused. She was, after all, only eleven years old, and the scene could only have been painful and upsetting both physically and psychologically. As Ida Mae recalled, Norma Jeane bathed obsessively for days after.

As if on cue in her role as fairy godmother, Grace returned to celebrate Norma Jeane's twelfth birthday. After spending $11.74 for Norma Jeane's new dress and the then outrageous sum of six dollars for a hair treatment, Grace meticulously prepared the girl's makeup and whisked her off for a professional photographic session. This was, she explained, the first step towards fame – towards growing up to become the new Jean Harlow. She also gave Norma Jeane a scrapbook in which to paste the photograph.

Grace's constant fussing over Norma Jeane's appearance, her obsession with the girl's future and even the gifts were more endured than enthusiastically received by Norma Jeane – who had (especially after her experiences with Doc and Jack) good reason to regard herself as a mere object for someone's pleasure. But she was legally subject to Grace's decisions about where she would live, and she was as well dependent on Grace's subsidies.

Another decision by Grace was soon announced. At summer's end, she decided Norma Jeane should quit the Martin household and return to Los Angeles – not only to have her ward closer and thus keep an alert eye on her adolescent development and forthcoming career, but also to enrol her in a junior high school of which she approved. Norma Jeane would not, however, be returning to the Goddard household: she was to board with Grace's aunt.

Edith Ana Atchinson Lower, always called Ana, was sister to Grace's father. Born on 17 January 1880, she was fifty-eight years old when Norma Jeane came to live with her. During the 1920s she and her husband, Edmund H. ('Will') Lower, had acquired a number of modest bungalows and cottages in various parts of Los Angeles County. They were divorced in about 1933 and, while Ana was by no means a rich divorcée, her settlement provided some rental income. (Will Lower died in 1935.) But Ana's circumstances were imperilled during the Depression, when a number of her tenants simply abandoned their residences.

By 1938 the Goddards were living virtually rent-free in one of Ana's houses on Odessa Street in Van Nuys, while Ana lived in a two-family duplex she owned at 11348 Nebraska Avenue, West Los Angeles, renting out the ground floor. She would have the income of thirty dollars a month from the State of California for boarding Norma Jeane Baker. (After the unhappy business of the Mortensen telephone calls, Grace everywhere registered Norma Jeane under Gladys's first married name, which Gladys herself had used most frequently.)

'Aunt Ana', as Norma Jeane called her, was a plump, white-haired, grandmotherly soul. She was also a very devout Christian Scientist, having advanced to the level of healing practitioner.

'She was very religious,' recalled Eleanor Goddard,

but not at all a fanatic. In fact she was very sensible, compassionate and accepting of others. She looked severe and stern and had an imposing carriage, but she was putty inside, not the dominating matron she was often made out to be.

Generous and outgoing, Ana's good works and devotion to her religion took her to the Lincoln Heights jail once weekly, where she spent time reading the Bible to inmates.

Alone in the life of Norma Jeane, Ana Lower warranted undiluted loving praise.

> She changed my whole life. She was the first person in the world I ever really loved and she loved me. She was a wonderful human being. I once wrote a poem about her [long since lost] and I showed it to somebody and they cried . . . It was called 'I Love Her'. She was the only one who loved and understood me . . . She never hurt me, not once. She couldn't. She was all kindness and all love.

Yet Ana Lower was, however kindly, the latest in an ongoing variety of mother figures. She could enfold Norma Jeane in a blanket of loving commitment and take her for the daughter she never had. But there was no way to alter the fact that she was also another woman whose attitude toward men and marriage was undeniably tainted (like that of Gladys, Grace and Ida Martin) by her own divorce. 'Talk about marriage and sex was certainly never on the agenda,' Marilyn Monroe said frankly years later.

There were, then, oddly ambivalent circumstances at this time, for Ana's broken marriage, her appearance of refined widowhood and the fact that she was the oldest of Norma Jeane's custodians denied the girl an effective female confidante. And this set of particulars was doubtless made more complex by Ana's earnest Christian Science faith and its impact on Norma Jeane – a sincere example, to be sure, but one set before the girl with considerable zeal. That August of 1938, Norma Jeane found herself at local Christian Science services, twice on Sunday and once during the week.

Ana Lower gently but somewhat simplistically guided Norma Jeane to see that only what was in the mind was real, and the mind could be uplifted. But the girl had already long sought refuge from insecurity in unreal movie images, a programme of transformation into Jean Harlow enjoined by Grace, and cultivation of her own fantasy life. Ana's brand of religion, in other words, complemented by a Victorian-Puritan sensibility and her seniority (with its implicit image, to youngsters, of sexlessness), was not altogether appropriate given Norma Jeane's past experience and her present adolescent needs.

In 1938 there were in America about 270,000 members in about two thousand congregations of Christian Science.* Founded in 1879 in Boston by Mary Baker Eddy, the religion is a system of therapeutic metaphysics. The vast majority of its adherents have always been middle-aged and elderly American women from the middle and upper classes, although the denomination is found in all countries with large Protestant populations. Central to its doctrine is a variation of subjective idealism: matter is unreal, there is only God (or Mind). The goal of Mrs Eddy's teachings (codified in *Science and Health with Key to the Scriptures*, 1891) is to bring the unreal material body into a condition of perfect harmony with our real spiritual condition: made in the Divine likeness, we are geared for spiritual perfection.

In a kind of intense Gnosticism linked to traditional American transcendentalism (which originated and flourished in Mrs Eddy's home territory, New England), there is an optimistic attitude towards the perceived world, which may ever be brought closer to its fulfilment by effort as well as by spiritual healing. (It should be stressed, however, that Christian Scientists have never been encouraged to withdraw from the world:

* As one scholar of the religion has noted: 'The controversy about the origins of Christian Science, the obscurity of periods of Mrs Eddy's life, and the inaccessibility of the archival materials of the Mother Church are together responsible for the absence of completely reliable standard works on the movement.' See B. R. Wilson, 'Christian Science', in the *Encyclopaedia Britannica*, 15th edn, 1983: vol. 4, p.564; and the same author's monograph, 'The Origins of Christian Science: A Survey', *Hibbert Journal*, vol. 57 (1959), 161–70.

responsibility in public and social life was exemplified by its foundation and long maintenance of one of America's great journals, *The Christian Science Monitor*, a newspaper commanding worldwide respect.)

The godly human being, for this denomination, constantly strives for a spiritual condition in which the counterfeit flesh and the mortal, fallible mind can be overcome. Taken in its purest form, Christian Science denies the reality of the senses, although allowance is made for a human level at which improvement is sought and achieved by right thinking. We do not sin, suffer or die: we are victims of unhealthy delusions. Linked to this doctrine is that of 'malicious animal magnetism', evil thought that *appears* real and powerful only because people wrongly assert its actuality. Advanced Scientists, especially the accredited, elite cadre of teachers known as practitioners, who are trained to read, pray and invoke therapeutic healing, learn how to counter the impact of this 'animal magnetism'.

Furthermore, the disharmony of sin, sickness and death may be overcome by right prayerful thinking and a dutiful attentiveness to Mrs Eddy's commentaries on the scriptures. Instead of drugs and medicines, spiritual truth must be affirmed, error denied, and the distinction made between absolute being and the frail mortal life. The symbol of Christian Science is thus immediately compelling: a cross (without the figure of the dead or dying Christ) surrounded by a crown. Glory overwhelms suffering, which has no real relation to humanity.

Because by a complicated and intriguing paradox Christian Science does not share American fundamentalism's contempt for the world and the flesh, recreation and entertainment are not forbidden, nor is the religion hostile to education, medical studies excepted. Because she chose not to seek any other employment, Ana Lower was eligible to be one of the Church's official practitioners, and in this capacity she was permitted to take fee-paying clients.

But when Norma Jeane began seventh grade at Emerson Junior High School on Selby Avenue, between Wilshire and

Santa Monica Boulevards in West Los Angeles, Aunt Ana's creed was at once challenged. That very September, the girl began to menstruate, and every monthly period for much of her life was a gruelling time during which she rarely found relief from severe cramps. In 1938 there were no readily obtainable medicines to counter the effects of what was for Norma Jeane very real agony (and it is unlikely that Ana would have made them available in any case). Friends from this and later times of Norma Jeane's life recall that each month she writhed on the floor, sobbing in pain. So began a lifelong history of gynaecological problems, including chronic endometriosis. She had, then, another conflict, but neither the spiritual nor intellectual sophistication with which to cope: if there was no real body and if God was All Goodness and Mind, why this torture? Why was her own body playing her false? Aunt Ana comforted her, prayed with her, embraced her, 'but nothing did any good. I just had to wait it out'.

At Emerson, there were 500 students in the seventh grade, and like those in the eighth and ninth they came from all parts of the western sector of Los Angeles. Some were chauffeured down from the gated mansions in the enclave known as Bel-Air, above Sunset Boulevard. Others were from the middle-class flatlands of West Los Angeles. And some – Norma Jeane among them – were within walking distance, from a poorer district known as Sawtelle.

A section of the so-called Western Front of the city, Sawtelle was bounded by four Boulevards: Sepulveda on the east, Bundy on the west, Wilshire on the north and Pico on the south. The area was a jumble of populations – Japanese immigrants; long-time California pioneers from the East and Midwest; recently arrived Dust Bowl 'Okies' who had sought work and refuge in sunny California during the Depression; Hispanics and Mexican-Indians; and older Los Angeles residents like Ana Lower.

'Los Angeles was a very divided, class-conscious society,' according to Norma Jeane's classmate Gladys Phillips (later

Wilson), 'and this was unfortunately true of school life, too. All the students were immediately, unofficially classified according to where they lived. And Sawtelle was simply not the place to be from.' Indeed Angelenos smiled and thought of beer halls when Sawtelle was mentioned, for there were many such gathering places for the working classes; the neighbourhood seemed synonymous with illiterate or semi-literate poor. Ana Lower was neither illiterate, out of work, nor on the dole, yet from her first day at school Norma Jeane Baker was marked by most of her classmates as (went on Gladys Phillips) 'from the wrong side of the tracks'.

Norma Jeane's courses, those designed for seventh grade girls not enrolled in the college prep track, were not overwhelmingly impressive from an academic standpoint, and her achievements were neither remarkably good nor bad:

Autumn 1938
Social Living (history, civics, geography): C
Physical education (gym class): B
Science: C
Office practice: A
Journalism: B
Spring 1939
Life Sciences (elementary biology): C
English: B
Bookkeeping: B
Physical education: C

'She was very much an average student,' recalled Mabel Ella Campbell, who taught the Life Sciences class. 'But she looked as though she wasn't well cared for. Her clothes separated her a little bit from the rest of the girls. In 1938 she wasn't well developed. Norma Jeane was a nice child, but not at all outgoing, not vibrant.'

Marilyn elaborated twenty years later:

I was very quiet, and some of the other kids used to call me The Mouse. The first year at Emerson, all I had was the two light blue dress-suits from the orphanage. Aunt Ana let them out because I'd grown a little, but they didn't fit right. I wore tennis shoes a lot, because you could get them for ninety-eight cents – and Mexican sandals. They were even cheaper. I sure didn't make any best-dressed list. You could say I wasn't very popular.

Reserved in her new environment, embarrassed about wearing the same uniform every day, and with no experience of socialization outside the confines of the orphanage, Norma Jeane found friendships difficult. 'She was neat but plain, as I remember,' recalled Ron Underwood, another classmate. 'She was also somewhat shy and withdrawn, and apparently had few friends.' Marian Losman (later Zaich) remembered that 'she always seemed to be alone,' and Gladys Phillips agreed: 'She really wasn't close to anyone at all.' Norma Jeane's isolation was intensified by the fact that Ana Lower had no telephone.

Close attachments to women were made even more problematic after her thirteenth birthday (1 June 1939), when Grace took Norma Jeane by train to San Francisco, where Gladys was living (as she would for several years) in a clinic-supervised boarding house. Her mother was not violent or unkind; she did not seem irrational or sedated; she was clean and evidently well looked after. But she spoke not a word, neither during the initial meeting nor during lunch – nothing until Norma Jeane and Grace prepared to depart. Gladys then looked sadly at her daughter and said quietly, 'You used to have such tiny little feet.'

Life with Ana was hardly exciting, and Norma Jeane had, as yet, nothing like a social life – but at least the girl felt secure with Grace's aunt. As ever, she returned to what was 'home' with no sense of family.

But as she entered eighth grade, beginning in autumn 1939 at

Emerson, her social life began to change, specifically because her body shape did, too. And her interest in classes – cooking, office practice, elementary Spanish and mathematics – suddenly faded into virtual oblivion, like a child's watercolour exposed to the sun. As if someone had thrown a switch over the summer and autumn, Norma Jeane, as 1939 drew to a close, had grown to her full adult height of five feet five and a half inches. And there was a figure emerging – pertly rounded breasts, which she exhibited (without a brassiere) beneath a tight tan sweater ('and without an under-blouse, which was a no-no,' added Gladys Phillips).

Because there was no money for new clothes, her blue skirt was rather too tight about the hips, and Ana could alter it only so much. But the girl was resourceful: she bought an inexpensive pair of boy's trousers, wore a back-to-front cardigan for a completely different (and more alluring) look on top, and in one week that autumn caused such a sensation that (trousers being forbidden to girls) twice she was sent home to pour herself back into the tight skirt – which of course had exactly the same effect. She was no longer 'Norma Jeane the String Bean' (an alternative classmate sobriquet to 'The Mouse').

'Suddenly, everything seemed to open up,' she said later of that time.

> Even the girls paid a little attention to me just because they thought, 'Hmmm, she's to be dealt with!' I had to walk to school, and it was just sheer pleasure. Every fellow honked his horn – you know, workers driving to work, waving, and I'd wave back. The world became friendly.

More than friendly, it was positively, energetically responsive. And Norma Jeane was ready to co-operate with the new geniality that attended her. The bus fare from Nebraska Avenue to Emerson was only five cents, but she preferred to walk to school, surrounded by two, three or more boys arguing over who would carry her books and lunch-bag. And it was the same in the afternoon.

'Physically, she developed earlier than most of us, and she had no shame about displaying her figure,' according to Gladys Phillips.

Her body just seemed to show through that sweater. And it was unusual for girls to wear bright red lipstick and makeup to school, but Norma Jeane did. This led some of the girls to consider her indiscreet, which she wasn't – but of course they were jealous. There was nothing vulgar about what she wore, but when her name was mentioned in class, boys smiled and raised their eyebrows, and sometimes you'd hear some of the boys humming 'Mmmm*mmmm*!' – I'll never forget it! Suddenly she just seemed to stand out in a crowd.

It was as if her childhood dream of adorers all round her had in a way come true. After years of Grace's tutelage, Norma Jeane knew how to attract attention with cosmetics; but now, aware of her figure and the new, frankly sexual allure she suddenly projected, she rose early in the morning, devoting hours to primping before school. Once there, according to Gladys Phillips, Norma Jeane stood for a long time before the mirror in the girls' lavatory, brushing her light brown hair again and again, running her fingers through every curl. It was said that every time a girl entered the washroom, there was Norma Jeane Baker, refreshing her makeup.

She was indeed trying to rise above a confused and confusing past; refining her appearance before the mirror, she was reshaping, in a way 'covering up' and dismissing the forlorn and abandoned child – refashioning herself into someone new, as Grace often reminded her. And the means to do this were ready to hand, for in Los Angeles there were more colourful, experimental, dramatic, inexpensive cosmetics than anywhere in America. At weekends Hollywood Boulevard was crowded with hawkers, distributing free samples of new lipsticks, rouges, face powders, eye-liners and colognes. At thirteen, then, Norma Jeane Baker bacame immediately aware of her ability to attract and to fascinate, and this she wished to do in an innocent way, without the threat of scenes such as she had with Doc and Jack. She may have felt that this was all she had to offer; no one had seemed to regard her opinions or feelings terribly much, so her body was meant to be praised, prized – just as by the worshipful adorers of her childhood dream.

She was not, as each of her schoolmates testified, an unusually beautiful girl; there was nothing striking about her hair or features. But she radiated, as Mary Baker Eddy said in quite another context, 'animal magnetism'.

It must be stressed that in 1939 such a display of candid, forthright sensuality was not seen as an announcement of sexual availability – although she seems to have been regarded (according to Gladys Phillips) as 'a bit racy'. Even as she attracted attention, there was neither promise nor threat. She was in control.

High school sex was not, after all, the commonplace it later became. Birth control pills were unknown, the simplest contraceptive devices for men and women were not easily available (in fact, they were still officially illegal under the Pure Food and Drug Act of 1933), and there was widespread fear of venereal disease – for which in 1939 antibiotics like penicillin were not yet refined for general public benefit. A furtive kiss on a back porch at night, necking in a borrowed car way up on Mulholland Drive, with the city lights twinkling below: that was the extent of sex for the vast majority of Los Angeles adolescents. The fantasies of some high school boys may have smouldered at the sight of a 'whoo-whoo girl', and movie ads talked of hot-blooded passions, but the only fires raging out of control that winter blazed in the newsreels chronicling the outbreak of war in Europe. As Gladys Phillips and others recalled, there was the occasional rumour about one or another 'bad' girl or 'wild' boy, but there were no such tales about Norma Jeane.

She was, in other words, at last beginning to live up to Grace's expectations of her, for at Emerson Junior High School during the winter of 1939–40, she began to be something of a star. The school was a large, impersonal factory, and she did what she could to be noticed. Long neglected by those to whom she had the right to look for security, she was even now 'performing', pretending to be a siren when in reality she was a naïve adolescent simply yearning for a little applause.

Norma Jeane wanted desperately (her classmates Phillips, Underwood and Losman recalled) to be liked, admired and even respected by them – but there were no opportunities to realize those goals at home. Ana's sedate, cramped quarters on Nebraska Avenue, without a telephone or space to receive guests, denied Norma Jeane the chance to extend invitations to classmates for an after-school glass of lemonade, or to enjoy her Glenn Miller records on the wind-up portable Victrola which Grace had given her for Christmas. 'Norma Jeane was really awfully nice and sweet,' Gladys Phillips said, 'but she also seemed a little pathetic, because she was constantly ashamed of her background.'

During the summer of 1940, Norma Jeane, aged fourteen, blossomed even more fully. She had one colourful print blouse which she adapted to several outfits. Tucked into her blue skirt, it was proper enough for Sunday services with Ana; worn outside her trousers, it was comfortable for riding with a boy on the handlebars of his bicycle; tied high above her waist, it exposed her midriff. She would stop traffic and turn heads when she went to the popular Westwood hangouts – Tom Crumpler's, a popular soda parlour across from the Westwood Village movie theatre; Mrs Grady's, on the south-east corner of Westwood and Wilshire Boulevards; Albert Sheetz, where she also met boyfriends who bought her Coca-Colas and hovered for hours; and the Hi-Ho drive-in, a little bit cheaper and a trifle less tidy. At the Hi-Ho, boys looking for trouble could find it without too much difficulty.*

* According to Gladys Phillips Wilson, 'She never went to fancy places or country clubs because the rich boys just didn't date her. They probably wanted to, because she was a dish, but it wasn't done.'

It was apparently at the Hi-Ho, that summer of 1940, that Norma Jeane first met an older Emerson student named Chuck Moran – a wisecracking, rebellious fellow who borrowed cars (sometimes without permission) to take girls on dates to Ocean Park Pier, between Venice and Santa Monica. Popular with the boys because he was a natural leader and a good athlete, and with the girls because he was a freckle-faced redhead quick to flatter and sweet-talk, Chuck favoured Norma Jeane that summer. She was shapely, she laughed at his jokes and smiled back at his winks, and she seemed shy – a combination of qualities he found irresistible. When she walked into a soda parlour, Chuck Moran called out, 'Here comes the *Mmmm* Girl!'

Several times that summer, Moran squired Norma Jeane in his father's old jalopy, and they often drove out to the dance hall at the Pier, where Lawrence Welk led his orchestra while actress Lana Turner and her husband, the bandleader Artie Shaw, danced the night away. Later, she recalled long, hot summer evenings at the Pier:

> We danced until we thought we'd drop, and then, when we headed outside for a Coca-Cola and a walk in the cool breeze, Chuckie let me know he wanted more than just a dance partner. Suddenly his hands were everywhere! But that made me afraid, and I was glad I knew how to scrape [i.e., fight back] with the best of them – life at the orphanage [and with Doc and Jack] taught me that. Poor Chuck, all he got was tired feet and a fight with me. But I thought, well, he isn't entitled to anything else. Besides, I really wasn't so smart about sex, which was probably a good thing.

That she 'wasn't so smart about sex' and had no dubious reputation among her schoolmates is further indicated by a notation in the school newspaper's prophecy ('A Peek into the Future') that Norma Jeane would one day be 'the smiling and beaming Chairman of the Beverly Hills Home for Spinsters'. This report appeared despite the fact that she was no wallflower, was quite adept at the rumba and the conga and, by graduation time, was 'doing something really modern, The New Yorker' – considered the most sophisticated, languorous new dance to reach California.

Moran's charm somehow kept him out of trouble both with the police (regarding cars he 'borrowed') and with the families of several Emerson girls (whom he often failed to deliver back home until dawn). His dates with Norma Jeane ended when classes resumed in September 1940: she was back at Emerson for ninth grade, and he was off to the tenth, at University High School.

In the group photograph of his graduating class, students smile attentively, trying to look dignified for posterity. But there is Chuck Moran, impolitely raising the middle finger of his left hand toward the camera. The reaction of school authorities and parents when this managed to slip past proofreaders can only be imagined. In any case, Chuck sent Norma Jeane a card on Valentine's Day for the next two years. Dismissed from senior high school eighteen months later for misconduct, Moran then vanished briefly before volunteering for army service. He was shipped off to war, where he was killed a month after his twentieth birthday.

Before 1940 ended, Norma Jeane at last had a friend her own age. Another of Doc Goddard's daughters, Eleanor, arrived to live with her father and Grace on Archwood Avenue, Van Nuys. At the same time, Ana Lower began to suffer from severely impaired circulation and other cardiovascular problems, and so Norma Jeane returned to the Goddards and befriended Eleanor, always called by her nickname Bebe.

Just six months younger than Norma Jeane, Bebe Goddard was a winsome, pretty girl who turned fourteen a week before Christmas. She was also brave – as she had to be, for her childhood was truly appalling. When she was eighteen months old, her parents divorced. For a time she and her siblings lived with their mother, but then Mrs Goddard became mentally ill, and dangerously so. 'It was tragic,' Bebe Goddard recalled years later. 'She was a true sociopath – no conscience, no knowledge of right and wrong – charming and believable when she wanted to be, but then she turned suddenly violent and menacing.' Booted hither and thither from relatives to strangers to a dozen foster homes all over Texas, Bebe matured, caring for her brother and sister while enduring and somehow surviving the most dreadful insecurities and the apparent indifference of her father until 1940.

It is important to detail these unhappy events in Bebe's early life, for much of what Marilyn later claimed to be *her* childhood history was actually Bebe's. The legend of her twelve or thirteen foster homes, the whippings, the near-starvation – all these were borrowed from Bebe's past and conveniently grafted on to her own when they became helpful in winning press and public sympathy. 'What I told Norma Jeane that winter made a great impression on her. She felt enormous pity for me, and we became friends very quickly.'

The two girls were full of fun and vitality. With exactly the same height, weight and hair-colour, they shared clothes and makeup, and Grace was ever vigilant with cosmetic advice. For the first time in her life, according to Bebe, Norma Jeane developed an unfettered sense of mischief and learned to laugh: 'Everyone adored her. She had such a sense of fun.'

Norma Jeane continued to attend Emerson Junior High until her graduation from ninth grade in June 1941. Her final grades in Spanish, Social Living, science and physical education were unimpressive, and she nearly failed Rhetoric and Spoken Arts because so often fear of seeming verbally inept and socially unacceptable paralyzed her throat and silenced her.

But in Miss Crane's journalism class she showed a remarkable aptitude and humour. The name Norma Jeane Baker often appears that year in the school newspaper, *The Emersonian*, for she was a contributor to the 'Features' columns. Given her later success (especially in a certain film), it is interesting to note that she provided this little story for the paper:

After tabulating some 500-odd questionnaires, we have found that fifty-three percent of the *gentlemen prefer blondes* [*sic*] as their dream girl. Forty percent like brunettes with blue eyes, and a weak seven percent say they would like to be marooned on a desert island with a redhead ... According to the general consensus of opinion, the perfect girl would be a honey blonde with deep blue eyes, well molded figure, classic features, a swell personality, intelligence, athletic ability (but still feminine) and she would be a loyal friend. Well, we can still dream about it.

She was in fact writing a description of herself – mostly as she was, but with some qualities she longed to develop.

One of these was better speech. Notwithstanding Norma Jeane's increasing popularity and her growing sense of her power to attract and charm, there was a basic insecurity she never overcame. This had recently been exhibited by her poor performance in Rhetoric and Spoken Arts, in which her teacher Mr Stoops was driven nearly to distraction by her shyness and anxiety about public speaking. As the teacher cajoled and the student grew ever more reticent, there developed an unfortunate sequel – Norma Jeane's lifelong tendency to stutter. As a member of the school newspaper staff, she was asked to be class secretary, 'and I'd say, "M-m-m-minutes of the last m-m-m-meeting." It was terrible.'

But just as she could exploit a meagre wardrobe to superb advantage, so did Norma Jeane turn a slight impediment to her social benefit. She is listed among only a few young men and women singled out for a class alphabet in June 1941: 'A for Ambitious: John Hurford ... G for Glamorous: Nancy Moon ... R for Radical: Don Ball ... V for Vivacious: Mary Jean Boyd,' and – at her own witty insistence – simply 'M-m-m-m: Norma Jeane Baker'. In and out of school, she was the 'Mmmm' girl. Capitalizing on her stammer, she linked it to the sound she heard the boys mutter. Vulnerable, cautious and shy she always was – but sufficiently resourceful to turn a liability into an asset.

*

Norma Jeane spent her first term of tenth grade (sophomore year, beginning September 1941), at Van Nuys High School, which was closer to the Goddard house than University High in West Los Angeles. Her report card was even less distinguished here than at Emerson. She found it difficult to apply herself to academic matters, for Norma Jeane was distracted by the presence of a handsome, five foot ten, brown-haired, blue-eyed young man with a thin, rakish moustache. His name was James Dougherty, and his family occupied a house just in front of the Goddards' bungalow, set back a way from Archwood Street in Van Nuys.

Born in Los Angeles on 12 April 1921, Jim Dougherty at twenty had a very different reputation from Chuck Moran. The youngest of five children in a family that had endured hard times during the Depression, he had once lived in a tent in Van Nuys, working long hours as a fruit-picker before he and his parents could afford to rent a small bungalow. At Van Nuys High, he acted in school plays, starred in the football team and won election as student body president. He also found time to contribute to the family's income by doing odd jobs – shining shoes, making sandwiches in a delicatessen and assisting in a local mortuary, work he continued after graduation. He deferred his chance to attend college on a football scholarship in order to help his mother and siblings.

By late 1941, Jim was working at Lockheed Aircraft, driving a snappy blue Ford coupé and dating several girls; in fact he was particularly serious about one named Doris Drennan until she dropped him because, as she said, 'You couldn't support me.' When he met Norma Jeane that year, Jim was working the night shift at Lockheed (among his fellow-workers was a beefy, heavy-lidded chap named Robert Mitchum) and living so close to Van Nuys High that his mother Ethel and her friend Grace Goddard asked him to drive Norma Jeane and Bebe home from school. (They now had further to travel, for the Goddards had moved in October to Odessa Avenue, into another small house owned by Ana Lower.) That year, Bebe suffered several illnesses that kept her out of class, and Jim remembered that

Norma Jeane seemed to take advantage of the daily opportunity 'to sit a little closer to me'.

For Norma Jeane, Jim was (as she later said) 'a dreamboat' most of all because of his moustache ('she was fascinated by it', according to Dougherty); indeed, it must have reminded her of Gladys's mysterious boyfriend, of Clark Gable and of Errol Flynn, and it made him look both older and distinguished. 'What a daddy!' Norma Jeane said significantly to Bebe after arriving home from school one afternoon.

As for Dougherty: 'I noticed she was a pretty little thing, and she thought I looked angelic in white shirts, but she was only a child so far as I was concerned, and five years was a great difference in our ages.' Admired chauffeur he was willing to be, but serious dating seemed out of the question.

Neither Jim, his mother nor Norma Jeane fully estimated Grace Goddard, who now assumed the role of Dolly Gallagher Levi, the Yonkers matchmaker. She swung into action as soon as she saw the proverbial stars in her ward's eyes, 'expertly maneuvering [Norma Jeane] into my awareness', as Dougherty realized later. A few days after the shock of Pearl Harbor and America's precipitous entry into the war, Grace asked Ethel Dougherty if Jim would escort Norma Jeane to a Christmas dance at Adel Precision Products, where Doc was then employed. Jim agreed, as he later said, partly because he was flattered by Norma Jeane's adoration and partly because his romance with Doris Drennan had not survived the two challenges of her move to Santa Barbara and his inability to support her.

The Christmas party was a major moment in the relationship. During the slow dances, Norma Jeane leaned against Jim (as he recalled 'extra close, eyes tight shut, and even Grace and Doc saw that I wasn't just being Good Neighbor Sam, so to speak. I was having the time of my life with this little girl, who didn't seem or feel so little any more.'

But Grace, eager to accelerate Norma Jeane's advance to womanhood, abetted the process. She paid for the girl to go to movies with Jim; she suggested they hike in the Hollywood Hills; they took boat rides on Pop's Willow Lake; and occasionally they drove north to Ventura County, visited Jim's sister Elyda, and drove out to Lake Sherwood. Grace packed picnic lunches for them and so, with the help of both makeup and her friend Ethel Dougherty, Jim found himself happy to spend weekends with the pretty, admiring and undemanding Norma Jeane.

Frequently in the evenings, the couple parked on Mulholland Drive, on the crest of the Santa Monica Mountains. According to the later testimony of both, their intimacy remained chaste: 'She very neatly held things in check' was Jim's summary. They talked of the war and of school, and Norma Jeane told Jim quite frankly that she was born illegitimate; this evoked neither his pity nor repugnance. He drew her closer, and she rested her head on his shoulder as the car radio, crackling with static, picked up the season's hit tunes: 'Don't Sit Under the Apple Tree' . . . 'That Old Black Magic' . . . 'Moonlight Becomes You'. Most of all, Norma Jeane liked to hear Frank Sinatra crooning 'I'll Never Love Again' and 'Night and Day'. She was 'awfully sweet to be with', as he said; she was more physically developed than most fifteen-year-olds (and was made up to resemble a smart young thing); she seemed to rely on Jim's strength; and she admired everything he did.

At the start of the new year 1942, Adel Precision announced that Doc Goddard was to be transferred to their West Virginia plant as East Coast Head of Sales. 'To tell the truth,' Bebe said years later, 'he had just been messing around, trying to be an actor and tinkering with all sorts of things – so finally he knew he had to settle down. He was a hell of a salesman, and at last here was a good promotion at a steady job.' Grace and Bebe would accompany him, but not Norma Jeane, whom they could not afford to keep. Grace informed her of this quite matter-of-factly one morning but added that she was 'working on something wonderful' for her.

Whatever Grace's secondary plans, this was devastating for

the girl, who immediately perceived that she was once again simply an expendable commodity. As Dougherty confirmed,

> her respect for Grace altered from that moment on. It seemed to her like another rejection, that she was being tossed out of another foster home . . . Grace had told Norma Jeane that she would never feel insecure again, and now the poor girl felt that Grace had gone back on her word.

The first sequel occurred immediately after, in late January. Ana Lower's health had somewhat improved, and so as the second term of sophomore year began and the Goddards prepared to move, Norma Jeane returned to Ana on Nebraska Avenue and attended University High School, an attractive, Spanish-style building at the corner of Westgate and Texas Avenues. During February and March (with Grace and Ethel's constant encouragement), Jim continued to date Norma Jeane, chugging through the Sepulveda Pass or negotiating the tortuous drives through the canyons linking the Valley to the West Side; the Los Angeles freeways were not even on the drawing boards.

For the rootless and rejected fifteen-year-old Norma Jeane, Jim Dougherty's attention was welcome. She had, after all, no sense of herself – no parental background with or against which to grow, no emotional harbour to which she could unfailingly return; she effectively lacked every normal ingredient of a teenager's life except school and a rapid physical development that outpaced her psychological growth.

At University High, some of her classmates noted a change in Norma Jeane's personality: 'she was loud,' according to classmate Tom Ishii. 'She talked loud, and some began to consider her wild.' But anyone aware of her life that spring of 1942 would not have been surprised that concentrated attention from a handsome, older man inevitably fed her ego. Both her emotionally deprived past and her uncertain present were factors encouraging her dependence on Jim as Norma Jeane prepared for the Goddards' departure (which also meant the absence of her new friend Bebe). To complicate matters further, it was clear by March that Norma Jeane's residence on Nebraska Avenue would have to be temporary, for Ana fell ill again with heart disease.

The question came not from Jim or Norma Jeane – not even from Grace, who was too crafty to pose it herself. Ethel Dougherty approached her son with a blunt proposition: 'The Goddards are going to Virginia, and they're not taking Norma Jeane. She can't stay with Mrs Lower, and that means she goes back to the orphanage until she's eighteen.'

'I'm listening,' Jim said.

'Grace wants to know if you'd be interested in marrying her. She turns sixteen in June' – the legal age in California.

'The thought ran through my mind,' Dougherty said later, 'that at sixteen she was far too young for me. I had no thought of marrying her at the time, and I really wouldn't have . . . but I agreed to it because I was going into the service soon and I figured she'd have a home with my mother. And of course I thought she was an adorable girl who was fun to be with. I didn't really think much beyond that. And Norma Jeane went along with the idea.'

But she did so only because she had no choice: as she later said, she married Jim 'so that she wouldn't have to go back to the orphanage'. In mid-March, two days after the Goddards left California for West Virginia, Norma Jeane shocked her teachers and classmates by informing them she was leaving school to get married that June; from that day she was no more to be seen in class and so her formal studies ended in the middle of her second year of high school. This aborted education later haunted her, causing an inferiority complex others would be only too glad to exploit.

It might be too severe to judge Grace and Ethel's motives as calculating; at the same time, their manipulation of Norma Jeane cannot easily be excused. They effectively communicated to her the dangerous notion that her liberation and sustenance were connected to life with a man. Also, the forthcoming marriage was another neat parallel to Grace's obsession, the transformation of Norma Jeane into Jean Harlow: at sixteen Harlow had withdrawn from high school to marry a handsome twenty-one-year-old socialite named Charles McGrew.

'Grace McKee arranged a marriage for me,' Marilyn Monroe said years later. 'I never had a choice. There's not much to say about it. They couldn't support me, and they had to work out something. And so I got married.' It later seemed, she said, 'like a dream that never really happened. It didn't work out – just like Jean Harlow's didn't work out. I guess we were too young.'

Too young indeed, despite the promptings of Grace, who simply ignored the girl's age and concentrated on the role. Even the teenager's innocence was blithely dismissed, as Jim recalled. One afternoon he, his mother, Norma Jeane and Grace were sipping Coca-Colas. Suddenly the girl asked haltingly if she could marry Jim 'but not have sex'. The question was not so much naïve as, more likely, designed to force everyone to reconsider the imminent marriage. But Grace leaped in with an answer: 'Don't worry. You'll learn.' This reply might have been no different had Norma Jeane expressed anxiety about an algebra test.*

Her hesitations were not merely sexual. 'After all, I had never seen any marriage work out,' she said perceptively years after, and in that regard she was on the mark. Della, Gladys, Ana, Grace, Ida and Olive provided only examples of failed marriages and the emotional inconstancy of spouses.

As for Dougherty, he 'tried to make her feel desirable and worthy of everyone's respect and admiration. But by doing so, I may have been undermining my own future with her.' He took her shopping to select a ring before remembering the custom of asking her to marry him – a mere formality in this case, since the decision had already been made for her. Almost distractedly,

---

* Norma Jeane once asked Ana Lower about sex, and she was simply handed an ancient manual. *What Every Young Lady Should Know About Marriage* was a book so coy and evasive that its hottest topic concerned ironing a man's shirts.

she accepted, and with the cast and the scenario ready, a date was set for the event.

On 1 June 1942, Norma Jeane turned sixteen. The following Sunday, she and Jim found a one-room bungalow in Sherman Oaks, at 4524 Vista Del Monte. Despite the tiny quarters, they agreed to sign a six-month lease; the owner offered to supply a new 'Murphy bed', which could be easily retracted into a wall cabinet and enlarge the living space. Their few possessions were moved in before the wedding.

The final preparations bore marks of inconsistencies and evasions of truth which of themselves seem negligible but which actually reveal the tissue of insecurity in which the marriage was wrapped. The invitations were sent by 'Miss Ana Lower' for the wedding of her 'niece, Norma Jeane Baker', but on the marriage certificate the bride signed 'Norma Jeane Mortensen'. She wrote that she was the daughter of 'E. Mortensen, birthplace unknown' and of a woman named 'Monroe, born in Oregon'. She did not supply her mother's first name; like all her relatives and even the Goddards, Gladys did not attend. Lester and Ida Bolender said they would drive up from Hawthorne, although they disapproved of both the wedding and its setting.

At eight-thirty on Friday evening, 19 June 1942, the ceremony was performed by a nondenominational minister named Benjamin Lingenfelder, at the home of Mr and Mrs Chester Howell (friends of Grace's), at 432 South Bentley Avenue, West Los Angeles. Everything was slightly surreal and improvised. A girl Norma Jeane knew only slightly at University High was her matron of honour; Jim's brother Marion was best man, and Elyda's little son Wesley bore the ring on a velvet pillow. The groom recalled how his bride 'liked the winding staircase in the front hall, just like in the movies. But she was shaking so she could hardly stand.' Jim, too, was somewhat unsteady – 'feeling a little undone, because my brother had given me a double shot of whiskey before I arrived.'

A modest reception was held at a nearby restaurant, where a showgirl entertaining another wedding party dragooned

Dougherty on to a makeshift stage for a dance. But when he returned to his table, he found his bride 'not very happy. She thought I'd made a monkey out of myself, and I did.' About four in the morning, the newlyweds arrived home in Sherman Oaks.

Within and beyond all the details, tasks and tensions of the wedding day, Jim Dougherty retained one memory clearer than any other: his bride 'never let go of my arm all afternoon, and even then she looked at me as though she was afraid I might disappear while she was out of the room.'

Chapter Five

'I'm the captain and my wife is first mate,' Dougherty said of marriage; accordingly, his wife should be 'content to stay on board and let me steer the ship.' But from the beginning of the arranged marriage between the insecure, virginal Norma Jeane and the confident, experienced Jim, there were signs of occasional mutiny, and eventually the subaltern jumped ship.

Much later, the captain's two logs appeared: selective, biased, abounding with clarifications of chronology and intimate details but teeming with improvised dialogue and imaginative reconstructions of events. For years they provided the only available chart of the matrimonial voyage – until the discovery of transcribed conversations during which both captain and first mate confided very different accounts of a journey that was headed for shipwreck from the first day.*

James Dougherty always publicly insisted that 'there were never any problems with our marriage ... until I wanted a family and she wanted a career.' Such comments for the record reflected his conventional understanding of marriage as dominated by the husband and his wish to present a rosy picture of

---

* The two published accounts consist of a 13-page article ('Marilyn Monroe Was My Wife', which appeared in the March 1953 issue of *Photoplay*, pp. 47–85); and a later 142-page book that expanded that article, *The Secret Happiness of Marilyn Monroe* (Chicago: The Playboy Press, 1976). Under the name of Dougherty's sister Elyda Nelson, there also appeared 'The True Life Story of Marilyn Monroe', published in the December 1952 issue of *Modern Screen*. According to her brother, this ghost-written article was based on anecdotes provided by him and was much dramatized by the editors.

the first of the three marriages each of them contracted. But he was often more forthright about the thornier aspects of the union. 'I wouldn't be married to another movie actress for anything in the world,' he said. 'She had only one thing on her mind – to be a star – and she gave up everything for it. I think Grace had a lot to do with it.'

As for Norma Jeane, she later said, 'My marriage didn't make me sad, but it didn't make me happy, either. My husband and I hardly spoke to each other. This wasn't because we were angry. We had nothing to say. I was dying of boredom.'

For about six months, from June to December 1942, the Doughertys lived in their one-room rented cabin in Sherman Oaks. Here, sixteen-year-old Norma Jeane tried to rise to the unrealistic demands of being a suitable housewife for a twenty-one-year-old, independent man. She asked few questions, accepting the role of sexual companion and housekeeper enjoined on her by Grace and now expected of her by Dougherty. But this seemed to her very different from the earlier plan proposed – for her to replace Jean Harlow – and the shift in her prospects confused Norma Jeane. 'I really didn't know where I was, or what I was supposed to be doing,' she said later.

Later, Dougherty had to admit,

She was so sensitive and insecure I realized I wasn't prepared to handle her. I knew she was too young, and that her feelings were very easily hurt. She thought I was mad at her if I didn't kiss her good-bye every time I left the house. When we had an argument – and there were plenty – I'd often say, 'Just shut up!' and go out to sleep on the couch. An hour later, I woke up to find her sleeping alongside me, or sitting nearby on the floor. She was very forgiving. She never held a grudge in her life. I thought I knew what she wanted, but what I thought was never what she wanted. She seemed to be playing some kind of a part, rehearsing for a future I couldn't figure out.

Transcribed in 1952 but not included in the final published version of the 1953 article 'Marilyn Monroe Was My Wife', this forthright statement provides a clue to the basic psychological gap that separated the couple. It is also an important corrective to the image of a delightful, carefree, passionate young bride artfully but somewhat disingenuously presented in Dougherty's short book.

For one thing, he realized at once that he was more her father and protector than her husband. 'She called me "Daddy". When she packed my lunch for work, there was often a note inside: "Dearest Daddy – When you read this, I'll be asleep and dreaming of you. Love and Kisses, Your Baby."'

But Dougherty was a gregarious chap who had many friends, played games, loved to go out and thought that flirting with pretty girls at dances and parties was harmless and permissible. She, on the other hand, was friendless, had few social skills, was nervous about embarrassing them both in public, and became jealous, angry and frightened of being abandoned if he paid attention to any other woman. He preferred to save a portion of his income, but she asked for extra cash and spent it prodigally – especially on gifts for him such as expensive Van Dyke cigars and new shirts, as if she could buy his devotion from his own paycheck.

Crucial differences in their sensibilities were immediately evident that summer. Since the shooting of her beloved dog Tippy a decade earlier, Norma Jeane had been extremely sensitive about the mistreatment of animals. 'She loved them all and was always trying to pick up strays,' according to Eleanor Goddard; as Grace had pointed out, the same was true of Jean Harlow, who throughout her life had a menagerie of dogs, cats and ducks. Hence when Jim returned one evening with a dead rabbit ready for skinning, she was unable to bear the sight and became almost hysterical. The idea of eating the poor animal was repugnant beyond description.

Related to this, he complained that 'she couldn't cook for ducks'. Deficient in the kitchen and lacking any preparation for ordinary household tasks, Norma Jeane was constantly anxious, terrified of displeasing her husband and therefore perhaps of being sent away – to where she knew not. No wonder she clung to his arm so insistently on her wedding day.

She was, therefore, prone to culinary miscalculations. She overseasoned percolated coffee with salt; whiskey was served undiluted, in twelve-ounce tumblers; there were endless helpings of mixed peas and carrots, because she had once been told foods should have a pleasing colour combination; and she did not know how to cook fish when her husband returned with a Sunday catch. When Norma Jeane once brought a trout to the table virtually raw, her husband muttered sarcastically, 'You ought to *cook* dinner once in a while,' which elicited the tearful reply, 'You're nothing but a brute.' There followed a terrific argument that ended only when he pushed her, fully clothed, under a cold shower. 'I went out for a walk, and when I came back she'd cooled off.' Such treatment quite naturally increased her feelings of incompetence and her fear of abandonment.

As for their intimate life, Dougherty was often publicly rhapsodic: 'Our life ws idyllic, sexually and otherwise.' Consistent with this, there is attributed to him the description of Norma Jeane as an insatiable nymphet who, while riding in a car, would suddenly shout to her husband, 'Pull off the road here! Pull off here!' demanding instant sexual intercourse and redefining the term autoeroticism. Neatly concocted by imaginative editors at the Playboy Press eager to serve the later tabloid image of the eternally sexy Marilyn Monroe, such anecdotes are not to be found in Dougherty's more discreet notes for his memoir.

More significantly, this sort of assertion is wildly at odds with her private conversations with friends. To director Elia Kazan she later confided that she did not enjoy 'anything Jim did to me – except when he kissed me here,' whereupon she gently touched her breasts; after he was satisfied, Jim usually fell asleep, leaving her awake, confused and discontent. She spoke frankly with other friends, too, about her marriage to Dougherty – in artless but thoughtful recollections, unconcerned with self-justification, much less retribution:

> Of course I wasn't very well informed about sex. Let's just say that some things seemed more natural to me than others. I just wanted to please him, and at first I found it all a little strange. I didn't know if I was doing it right. So after a while, the marriage itself left me cold.

To be sure, Dougherty was never cruel; but in his youthful ardour, manly egoism and spirit of independence, he was equally unprepared for the demands of marriage. As he admitted in his franker moments,

> I used to stay out and shoot pool a lot with my buddies, and this hurt her feelings. I shouldn't have done that, I know. She cried easily when I left her alone, which maybe I did too much.

Far from finding security with a 'daddy' during the first year of her marriage, Norma Jeane quickly learned that in a crucial way her new relationship to this man bore a familiar pattern: she again felt nonessential.

'Her mentality was certainly above average,' Dougherty added privately. 'She thought more maturely than I did, because of her rough life.' But given his attitude toward marriage in general (and this marriage in particular), he may have resented Norma Jeane's maturity: hence his distance from her, and his occasional, unwittingly callous attitude. He had considered the union as a favour to a sweet and attractive girl – and 'an enchanting idea' for himself; he also intended to secure a home for her with his mother when he went to war.

But however innocent and even benevolent, these are of course not the best motives for matrimony – a commitment for which he, as well, was apparently too emotionally callow. They both seem to have been aware of this complex of issues, for they mutually and firmly agreed on a crucial matter: they would not have children. In any case, Norma Jeane, little more than a child herself, was 'terrified of the thought that I would become pregnant . . . Women in my family had always made such a mess of mothering, and I was still getting used to being a wife. Becoming a mother was something I thought of as far off in the future.' Aware of the problems in their union (and of his eventual departure for military service) as well as their increasingly different perspectives, Dougherty was blunter: 'I insisted on birth control.'

For a few months in early 1943 they lived at 14747 Archwood Street, Van Nuys, the home of Dougherty's parents who were living for a time outside Los Angeles. Jim continued to work at Lockheed, where his fellow-worker Robert Mitchum noticed that Dougherty brought the same lunch to work each day: a cold egg sandwich.

'Your old lady makes you the same sandwich every day?' Mitchum asked.

'You ought to see my old lady!' Dougherty replied.

The response was pure Mitchum: 'I hope she looks better than your egg sandwich.'

A few days later, Dougherty brought a snapshot of his wife. Mitchum allowed that she bore no resemblance to the lunch. When Marilyn and Mitchum met a few days later, he thought she was 'very shy and sweet, but not very comfortable around people'.

When Dougherty's parents returned to Archwood Street in mid-1943, the young couple moved for several months into a house on Bessemer Street, Van Nuys. Here for the first time they enjoyed some social life with other couples: a young artist and his fiancée, an accountant, two medical students and their wives. Norma Jeane asked these friends to add their own phonograph recordings to hers for several evenings of dancing. And then, to Jim Dougherty's astonishment, there was an almost instantaneous transformation of Norma Jeane, from demure housewife to natural performer. She loved to dance, she cut in to go from man to man, she giggled and gyrated tirelessly. Jim grew jealous as the male guests became transfixed by her energetic allure, for as Jim's sister Elyda recalled, 'She was just too beautiful. She couldn't help it that men's wives looked at her and got so jealous they wanted to throw rocks!' That summer of 1943, as Dougherty recalled, they often went at weekends to the beach at Santa Monica or Venice, where Norma Jeane attracted attention 'because,' said Jim, 'she wore a bikini that was two sizes too small!'

While living in Van Nuys, Norma Jeane adopted a stray collie to whom she became much attached, naming him Muggsy and devoting hours each day to grooming and bathing the dog and training him. Otherwise she spent much of the day taking similar care of herself, trying out new cosmetics, taking long baths and scrubbing her face many times with soap and water to prevent blemishes and (she believed) to improve the circulation. It seemed that in her constant effort to improve her appearance she was attempting to achieve the impossible ideal of universal acceptance – to be noticed as beautiful, striving even harder towards that goal than she had in high school. 'She was a perfectionist about her appearance,' Dougherty recalled. 'If anything, she was too critical of herself.'

This is not surprising, for Norma Jeane still had no close women friends. The only companions with whom she felt comfortable were her husband's young nieces and nephews, toddlers for whom she loved to baby-sit, bathing them, washing their clothes, playing with them, reading to them. 'Just her presence in a room seemed to keep them content,' Dougherty observed. On the other hand, he remembered that he often saw a forlorn and distracted gaze on her face when he returned home – as if she had feared he would not.

Although Dougherty's job at Lockheed was considered essential for defence and could have maintained his deferment from active service, he longed for overseas duty with his buddies. But Norma Jeane, praying for an end to the war, implored him to wait a while longer – not to leave her in 1943, but to join the Merchant Marines at home. After a few weeks of boot camp on Santa Catalina Island, he was ordered to supervise a company of rookies at its Maritime Service Training Base, where his wife and Muggsy joined him before the end of 1943.

Twenty-seven miles offshore in San Pedro Bay, Catalina is a mile longer than that distance, and eight miles across at its widest point. In 1919 the chewing-gum magnate William Wrigley began to develop the island as a resort, and there he built a great casino and promoted deep-sea fishing and other recreational activities. A popular tourist spot since the 1930s, Catalina remained largely undeveloped in 1943, when its year-round population consisted solely of several hundred retired folk. Connected by schooner, ferry and helicopter to the mainland, its only inhabited town was Avalon; the rest of the island, with its roaming bison and goats, its mountains, canyons and inlets, offered a view of unspoiled California. Primitive though it has always been, Catalina was nevertheless the place chosen by movie moguls Cecil B. DeMille, Joseph Schenck, Louis B. Mayer and Samuel Goldwyn for the first theatre acoustically engineered for sound films. Across the channel they came in their luxurious yachts, to preview and discuss their various achievements.

But with the outbreak of World War II, Catalina was closed to the public and became a military training ground. The Hotel St Catherine (named after the same saint as is the island) was used as a cooking school for service chefs; the Yacht Club was converted into classroom space; the Coast Guard trained at Two Harbors; the Office of Strategic Services (forerunner to the Central Intelligence Agency) set up shop at Toyon Bay; and the Signal Corps built radar posts at Camp Cactus. The Merchant Marine Corps, to which Jim Dougherty reported, was head-quartered in Avalon, whence recruits went forth to exercises, scaling the seacliffs and mountain summits and cutting through the dense forest underbrush in preparation for more hostile conditions overseas. On Catalina Island during 1943 and 1944, the Dougherty marriage, too, became an often tangled conflict to be warily negotiated.

'We got along real well as long as she was dependent on me,' Dougherty said significantly years later. But that year, at seventeen, his wife slowly began to re-evaluate both her husband's dominance and her own unimportance.

Spending half his monthly salary for rent, Dougherty moved his gear, his wife and their dog into an apartment set on a hillside in Avalon, where his job was to train Marine Corps recruits. 'There was a scarcity of women, of course,' he recalled,

> and that's where the trouble with men began. She was jealous whenever I ever talked about my old girlfriends, but I had more reason to be jealous of her that year on Catalina. Norma Jeane realized very well that she had a beautiful body and knew men liked it. She took Muggsy for walks wearing a tight white blouse and tight white shorts, with a ribbon in her hair for a touch of colour. It was just like a dream walking down the street.

And so it appeared to the scores of military men, for whom Norma Jeane enjoyed disporting herself in 'skimpy bathing suits', according to Dougherty: 'Every guy on the beach is mentally raping you!' he complained. But she could not understand his attitude: she did not wear bikinis by day and tight sweaters at night to seduce men, but simply because (as Dougherty had to admit later) 'she realized what she had, didn't think it was bad, and didn't mind showing it off.' She also intended to keep it, and so from a military instructor named Howard Carrington (a former weight-lifting champion), she began to learn to use barbells and dumb-bells to improve her figure and posture. Just as no other female on the base was quite so natural and unashamed in displaying her body, so Norma Jeane was eager to undertake a rigorous programme of physical fitness with gymnasium equipment normally used only by men.

One evening that winter Stan Kenton's famous band came to entertain on the island. Girlfriends, volunteers and wives were ferried over from the mainland, and the vast Catalina Casino ballroom was alive with gaiety, couples crowding on to the dance floor with an encircling outdoor loggia affording splendid moonlit views of the sea and the town. Beer and cocktails were available, but Norma Jeane drank only ginger ale and root beer; she was still in a way Aunt Ana's non-tippling Christian Scientist 'niece'.

But during the seven-hour gala Dougherty had only one dance with his wife, who was by far the most popular partner of the evening. He recalled standing on the sidelines, hearing the men remark on his wife's charms. 'I'll admit I was jealous, not proud of her,' he said years after they divorced.

And then, with the music and dancing still in full swing, Dougherty suddenly announced to his wife that they were departing.

'I'll go home with you, but I have a mind to come back,' she said. 'I'm having a good time!'

'But where will you sleep, Norma Jeane?'

'What do you mean?'

'Well, if you leave me at home to come back here, you don't have to bother coming home again!'

He won this round, but his wife had an amusing and potent riposte. Soon after the dance, he returned early one afternoon from headquarters to find the apartment door uncustomarily locked. When he knocked and called to her, Norma Jeane answered, 'Is that you, Bill? Oh, just a minute!' Dougherty then announced himself. 'Oh, sorry!' she replied. 'I didn't think you were coming over so soon, Tommy!' From within, there was much thumping, the apparent sounds of furniture being moved, and (so Dougherty was convinced) muted conversation. With no rear door for a lover's swift escape, he thought he had caught her in a compromising situation, all his worst fears finally confirmed, his jealousy justified.

Almost crazed with rage, he shouted again – and then his wife opened to admit him, a wide grin on her face. She was alone, wrapped in a bath towel because he had interrupted her shower. His unwarranted anger had demonstrated that he could be unreasonably, childishly suspicious – that he did not trust his wife. And it was trust that she required more than anything to guide her securely through the shoals of young adulthood. Her retaliatory joke may also have unwittingly revealed more serious feelings: it is not hard to imagine that she would indeed have wished to be with another man, even if 'Bill' and 'Tommy' were only momentary fantasies.

But in a way Dougherty was right when he said that his wife was dependent on him; whatever her inchoate longings, she had no one else on whom to rely, and she was miserable when, in spring 1944, he was sent to the Pacific and South East Asian war zones. 'She begged me not to go,' he recalled,

> and when I said I had no choice, she begged to have a baby – a child would be her way of having me with her. But I knew that a baby would be very hard for her, and not only financially. She really wasn't up to being a mother. I said we would have children later, after the war.

Whatever her mixed feelings about him and their marriage, Dougherty's departure revived the old feelings of abandonment. 'She wanted something, *someone* she could hold on to all the time,' Dougherty remembered – as he did her tears and anguish the day he left.

Now the wife of a soldier overseas, Norma Jeane went to live with her mother-in-law at 5254 Hermitage Street, North Hollywood. Ethel Dougherty worked in nearby Burbank, as a nurse at the Radioplane Company, a plant owned by the English actor Reginald Denny, who developed the first successful radio-controlled, pilotless aircraft for antiaircraft training. By April 1944, Ethel had found a job there for Norma Jeane, too – the unpleasant task of spraying a foul-smelling varnish on fuselage fabric (working in the 'dope room', as it was called), but it provided a steady income. With major footholds in both aircraft and defence industries, the Southern California economy was booming during the war and there were jobs for thousands of women.

Life with her mother-in-law was reasonably comfortable and undemanding, but Norma Jeane longed for the companionship of her husband. Paradoxically, it must be admitted that she may have missed him because he was not always the most attentive and sensitive companion. Norma Jeane, in other words, was one of many who often continually seek a neglectful or even unwittingly hurtful mate, in an effort to find the earlier situation of rejection and to correct it by reversal. It was a pattern that would deepen and be repeated in the years to come.

Norma Jeane wrote to Grace in West Virginia (on 15 June 1944) describing her life at that period. Later, she allowed that she had sweetened the account of her marriage out of loyalty to her husband and a deeply rooted desire to please Grace Goddard:

> . . . Jimmie has been gone for seven weeks and the first word I received from him was the day before my birthday. He sent a cable night letter by Western Union saying, 'Darling, on your birthday I send you a whole world of love.' I was simply thrilled to death to hear from him.
>
> I have never really written and told you of our married life together. Of course I know that if it hadn't been for you we might not have never been married and I know I owe you a lot for *that* fact alone, *besides* countless others . . . I love Jimmie in a different way I suppose than anyone, and I know I shall never be happy with anyone else as long as I live, and I know he feels the same towards me. So you see we are really very happy together, that is of course, when we can be together. We both miss each other terribly. We shall be married two years June 19th. And we really have had quite a happy life together.

I am working 10 hrs. a day at Radioplane Co., at Metropolitan [later Burbank] Airport. I am saving almost everything I earn (to help pay for our future home after the war). The work isn't easy at all for I am on my feet all day and walking quite a bit.

I was all set to get a Civil Service Job with the army, all my papers filled out and everything set to go, and then I found out I would be working with *all army fellows*. I was over there *one* day, there are just too many wolves to be working with, there are enough of those at Radioplane Co. without a whole army full of them. The Personnel Officer said he would hire me but that he wouldn't advise it for my own sake, so I am back at Radioplane Co. and pretty content . . . *

  With much love,
    Norma Jeane.

During a summer holiday in 1944, Norma Jeane (then eighteen) took her first journey out of California, visiting Grace at her temporary job at a Chicago film lab. Grace's departure from West Virginia had been necessary, according to Bebe, because although Grace was working regularly, 'she had developed a drinking problem, [which was] not surprising. All my father's wives had that, probably because one of his own chief occupations was whooping it up every day, and they joined him.'

Norma Jeane also visited Bebe in West Virginia, and then she proceeded to Tennessee for a brief stay with her half-sister Berniece Baker, now married and a mother. Of this last visit nothing is known: the daughters of Gladys scarcely knew each other, and although they had hoped to become friends, their desires were inhibited by long absences; reunions were invariably somewhat awkward, despite mutual goodwill.

* Norma Jeane was in fact rated as 'above average' by her supervisors at Radioplane.

Returning to California, Norma Jeane resumed her work at Radioplane, where her new assignment was inspecting and folding parachutes, which she found not much more interesting than spraying glue. Her salary was still the national minimum wage: she was paid twenty dollars a week for sixty hours' work. Belatedly, Norma Jeane wrote to thank Grace for the gift of a new dress and for her hospitality during the Chicago visit; the letter, dated 3 December 1944 and posted just before Dougherty was due home for Christmas leave, included an important reference to the fact that Norma Jeane was sending Grace money from her paycheck:

> I certainly hope Jimmie will be home for Christmas, it just won't seem right without him. I love him so very much, honestly I don't think there is another man alive like him. He really is awfully sweet.
>
> I shall send you more money a little later.
>
> I can't ever tell you how much the trip did for me, I shall be grateful to you Grace *forever*. I love you and Daddy [i.e., Doc Goddard] so much. I sure miss you Grace.
>
> With love,
>
> Norma Jeane
>
> P.S. Tell everyone at the studio 'hello.'

Dougherty's time at home during the Christmas-New Year holiday of 1944–5 was a happy break from her routine. Norma Jeane continued to cling to him, and as the time drew near for him to leave, an odd thing occurred.

According to Dougherty, Norma Jeane suddenly announced that she was going to telephone her father, a man she had neither met nor ever contacted. She placed a call, announcing her name and the fact that she was Gladys's daughter. But very quickly she replaced the receiver and told Jim that the man had simply hung up on her. Was he Norma Jeane's father? Had she reached the right man?

For years, the call was believed by everyone just as she

described it. But even if we are prepared to believe the heartless indifference of a man to his daughter, there are several problems. First, she admitted it was not a Mr Mortensen she called, but she never told Jim the man's name or where he lived. Second, there is no evidence that Gladys (if she knew) ever discussed her daughter's paternity, and Grace never openly speculated. Third, Dougherty never heard the man's voice, nor did Norma Jeane provide details of the call's destination. In every respect, the episode was repeated identically at least twice in the ensuing seven years: each time Norma Jeane attempted to contact her father, the gesture was made in the presence of someone on whose sympathy and support she greatly relied: in this case, she asked Dougherty to hold her in his arms for several hours.

There is a strong possibility, in other words, that this was one of Norma Jeane's 'pretend games' to evoke pity and elicit comfort. Just as later, so now: whenever she feared being abandoned, she presented herself as a lost, rejected child. In fact, she *was* misbegotten, at a time when society still imputed a considerable stigma to bastardy. To the end of her life, long after she had admitted the fact, she bore her illegitimacy with dignified humiliation. In the final analysis, it matters not whether she ever made honest attempts to contact a man she said was her father; indeed, this may have been one of her most convincing performances. But it is significant that at certain moments when she was frightened of being abandoned, she 'called her father'. Bona fide or note, the moment had its effect: she needed to remind others of a primary childhood loss, of a frightful void in her life, a desertion that had left her for ever wounded. 'Comfort me,' her actions said.

'In her rational mind,' as Dougherty said, 'she knew I had to go back to overseas duty ... but she considered my shipping out as another rejection.' Her feelings of loneliness and dismay did not endure, however, and not long after his departure for the Pacific again in January 1945, Norma Jeane left Radioplane. She had seen the possibility of a very different life.

*

The previous autumn, after returning from her cross-country journey, she was at work inspecting parachutes when a crew of photographers from the Army's First Motion Picture Unit arrived at the factory. Their task was to photograph women on the assembly line, contributing to the war effort in various strategic capacities. But these were to be no typical documentary shots of weary girls in overalls. The 'shutterbugs', as the photographers were called, were to return with snapshots for commercial as well as military magazines: good prints and some silent movie shots of the most attractive ladies, carefully posing to show that the country's loveliest were busy patriots.

Among the camera crewmen was twenty-five-year-old David Conover, whose first meeting with Norma Jeane, late in 1944, was described in her letter to Grace dated 4 June 1945.*

> ... The first thing I knew [the photographers] had me out there, taking pictures of me ... They all asked where in the H— I had been hiding ... They took a lot of moving pictures of me, and some of them asked for dates, etc. (*Naturally I refused!*) ... After they finished with some of the pictures, an army corporal by the name of David Conover told me he would be interested in getting some color still shots of me. He used to have a studio on 'the Strip' on Sunset [Boulevard]. He said he would make arrangements with the plant superintendent if I would agree, so I said okay. He told me what to wear and what shade of lipstick, etc., so the next couple of weeks I posed for him at different times ... He said all the pictures came out perfect. Also, he said that I should by all

---

* Conover (who was despatched to his task by his superior officer, Ronald Reagan) wrongly stated in his memoir *Finding Marilyn* that they were first introduced on 26 June 1945; in fact there had been at least a dozen meetings during the seven months before then, as Norma Jeane's letters to Grace reveal. Alas, *Finding Marilyn* abounds with inaccuracies, unconscionable reams of fabricated dialogue and imaginatively concocted events. Conover (1919–83) was a talented photographer but a patent fabulist, too.

means go into the modeling profession ... that I photographed very well and that he wants to take a lot more. Also he said he had a lot of contacts he wanted me to look into.

I told him I would rather not work when Jimmie was here, so he said he would wait, so I'm expecting to hear from him most any time again.

He is awfully nice and is married and is *strictly* business, which is the way I like it. Jimmie seems to like the idea of me modeling, so I'm glad about that.

By the spring of 1945, Norma Jeane was quickly becoming known as a photographer's dream. Co-operative, eager and good-humoured, she tossed her curly chestnut hair, flashed her blue-green eyes, smiled brightly and gazed unblinkingly at the camera, holding even an awkward stance with no display of impatience or discomfort. For Conover as for other cameramen, something fresh and lively in Norma Jeane seemed to spring to life just before the shutter clicked or the film rolled. It was as if she were flirting with the camera, connecting to anonymous admirers, offering herself as fully as she knew how, and winning new adorers, just as in her childhood dream. With the lens aimed at her, she was learning how to fix its glance on herself.

'There was a luminous quality to her face,' Conover said years later, 'a fragility combined with astonishing vibrancy.' And he could not recall any other model so self-critical, nor one who so acutely scrutinized every contact sheet, every negative and print for the tiniest fault: 'What happened to me here?' she asked repeatedly, or 'This is awful, where did I go wrong?' Dissatisfied with anything less than perfection, she was in a way logically extending to the presentation of herself the Bolenders' injunctions to excellence and Grace's preparations for her to become a heroically famous star. Earnest, grave about her appearance, ready with detailed questions about the camera, lighting and the various types of film stock, Norma Jeane Dougherty wanted every image of herself to be brilliant. And alluring, too, for she also wore a sweater that was a size or two small for her ample proportions (36-24-34 in August 1945), and tightened a pair of braces across a horizontally striped shirt, the better to emphasize her firm breasts (which she also uplifted in a half-brassiere).

From June to mid-summer 1945, David Conover continued to photograph Norma Jeane Dougherty in California, from Barstow to Riverside, from Death Valley to Bakersfield. Some of the results were used for army literature, some he gave to his model. Then, by early autumn, two more major developments had occurred.

First, Ethel disapproved of her daughter-in-law's conduct: the girl, Mrs Dougherty said, was simply idling around with young photographers like Conover. 'Mom froze a bit when she began to figure my wife was throwing me a curve,' Jim said later. Ethel complained that Norma Jeane's aspirations to be a professional model were inappropriate for a married woman, soon to be a mother when Jim returned from service. Mother Dougherty also disliked the girl's independent social life. A Hungarian actor named Eric Feldari escorted Norma Jeane to a Hollywood swimming party that summer at the home of the actor Robert Stack, who recalled her wearing 'a white bathing suit, which she filled beautifully ... I remember that she appeared to be shy and somehow on the outside of everything taking place at the party. I tried to be a good host, and every time I asked if she wanted anything, she said, "No, everything is fine."'

Eventually, Norma Jeane had a surfeit of Ethel's disapproving stares, and so she moved back to Nebraska Avenue, West Los Angeles, where she lived in the lower half of Ana Lower's duplex. From his mother, Jim must have received bulletins of his wife's new interests, for he wrote to Norma Jeane that 'all this business of modeling is fine, but when I get out of the service we're going to have a family and you're going to settle down. You can only have one career, and a woman can't be two places at once.' At this time her letters to Jim, formerly so frequent, ceased; she regarded the marriage as virtually dissolved, his temperament and expectations of her detrimental to her blossoming career and his attitude distasteful. 'As far as I was concerned,' she told friends a decade later,

> this meant the marriage was in trouble. If you love someone, don't you want them to be happy? to do something they like and they're good at? All I wanted was to find out what I was. Jim thought he knew, and that I should've been satisfied. But I wasn't. That marriage was over long before the war ended.

In witness whereof, according to David Conover, she offered herself to him in a brief affair that blazed throughout that hot summer of 1945.

The second development occurred on 2 August 1945, when (at the suggestion of Conover and another photographer) Norma Jeane applied for acceptance to the Blue Book Agency. In Hollywood there were thousands of girls who wanted to be models, and as many models yearning to be movie stars. One of dozens of agencies founded to nurture such aspirations, the Blue Book was owned and strictly supervised by the formidable Emmeline Snively. She was a short, proper Englishwoman in her late forties who always wore a hat and, with her septuagenarian mother Emma as a frequent visitor, ran the business with a peculiar combination of suspicion and humour, white-glove propriety and a clear-eyed, sometimes cynical realism about the moral and financial perils of a model's life. With their Old World formality unsuited to casual Los Angeles, Emma and Emmeline Snively were straight from the pages of *Nicholas Nickleby*.

From 1937 to 1943, Miss Snively had directed her so-called Village School in Westwood, which (as her catalogue testified) 'specialized in training girls for photographic and fashion modeling'. In January 1944, she moved to quarters in the Ambassador Hotel on Sunset Boulevard, where she expanded her operation and became The Blue Book Agency, a business that (in the words of her new brochure) 'grooms girls for careers

in motion pictures, photographic modeling and fashion modeling, [with] personalized instruction in charm and poise, success
and beauty and personalized development' – exactly what
Norma Jeane believed she required. At the time there were
about twenty models on Miss Snively's roster; according to
Lydia Bodrero (later Reed), also at Blue Book during 1945 and
1946, many of them longed to become film stars because at that
time models were not well paid in Los Angeles. Post-Snively
success meant graduation to a movie contract or moving to New
York, where models were more handsomely paid.

And so from August through the autumn of 1945, the Blue
Book had a new student-client. The receptionist's notes indicated Norma Jeane's height (five feet five), weight (118 pounds),
measurements (36-24-34, size 12), hair colour (medium blond:
'too curly to manage, recommend bleach and permanent'), eyes
(blue) and 'perfect teeth' (at least for modeling: they were a
pleasing white, but she also had a slight overbite that later required correction). Norma Jeane paid a $25 fee for her picture
to be included in the Blue Book catalogue, and said she could
'dance a little and sing'.

During the first few weeks, Norma Jeane was scrupulous in
attending fashion modeling classes with Mrs Gavin Beardsley,
makeup and grooming with Maria Smith, and posing instructions with Miss Snively herself. The cost of the catalogue
photograph and the $100 fee for the courses were charged
against an assignment obtained immediately for Norma Jeane.
The Holga Steel Company had an industrial show at the Pan-
Pacific Auditorium that September, and Norma Jeane was paid
a total of $100 to work as a hostess for ten days.

'I don't think that kid had ever been inside a first-class hotel
before in her life,' Snively said years later.

She kept glancing around at things, like it was a new world
. . . But I thought I could make her into something quite mar-
ketable in a short period of time. She was a clean-cut,
American, wholesome girl – too plump, but beautiful in a

way. We tried to teach her how to pose, how to handle her body. She always tried to lower her smile because she smiled too high, and it made her nose look a little long. At first she knew nothing about carriage, posture, walking, sitting or posing. She started out with less than any girl I ever knew, but she worked the hardest . . . She wanted to learn, wanted to be somebody, more than anybody I ever saw before in my life.

After the industrial show, two days of posing for a Montgomery Ward clothing catalogue and four days at a Hollywood fashion show, it was clear that Norma Jeane's forte was not modeling clothes but rather appearing in glamour poses for advertisements: it was herself, not what she wore, that made the impression, that sold the goods. Later, she admitted the reason:

> The problem, if you can call it that, was my figure. Miss Snively said nobody was paying attention to the clothes because my dresses or blouses or bathing suits were too tight. In other words, they were looking at me, and to hell with the clothes.

Snively sent Norma Jeane out to editors to pose for magazine covers and to photographers and advertising agencies. The results were immediate and stunning, and by the spring of 1946 Norma Jeane Dougherty (sometimes billed by Snively as 'Jean Norman') had appeared on no fewer than thirty-three covers of magazines like *U.S. Camera*, *Parade*, *Glamorous Models*, *Personal Romances*, *Pageant*, *Laff*, *Peek* and *See*.

Her mentor caught the slightly fey aspect of Norma Jeane's personality – the girl who giggled easily, who took her work seriously but somehow gave the simultaneous impression that there was something vastly amusing about what she was doing.

'When you stop to think about it,' she said years later,

it's kind of funny. You smile for the camera, you hold very

still, you act as if you're having a good time – but it's a day when you're really having terrible cramps. I guess I shouldn't say this, but sometimes modeling seemed so phoney and fake I just had to laugh. They thought that was great, they had a great smile from you, and they just snapped away, thinking that, well, I was having a good time. Sure, sometimes it was fun. But modeling can also be a little crazy. I once asked why I had to wear a bathing suit for a toothpaste ad. He looked at me as if I was some kind of crazy!

Lydia Bodrero Reed recalled that Norma Jeane was 'very serious, very ambitious and always pleasant to be with. There was only one problem for her. She did so many covers that for a while she was considered overexposed – the magazine and advertising people had seen so much of her that after a year she couldn't get much work.' According to Bodrero, there was another danger for a model, a different kind of overexposure. 'Miss Snively warned us never, ever to appear "undraped" (as she called it) – nude photography, we were told, was the kiss of death for a model.'

For Norma Jeane, Snively had an additional particular recommendation: that she lighten her brown hair. Whereas a brunette would always emerge darker in a photo (and, Snively believed, would bring a dusky hue to everything), a blonde could be photographed in any wardrobe and in any light. She reminded Norma Jeane that, in the words of the play, gentlemen prefer blondes; she also pointed to Betty Grable and, before her, to Jean Harlow.

Accordingly, that winter Snively despatched her to a photographer named Raphael Wolff, who just happened to be an old friend of Doc Goddard. He agreed to use Norma Jeane in some shampoo print advertisements, but only (and almost certainly in collusion with Snively) if she would dye her brown hair. Soon she was sitting nervously at Frank and Joseph's, a popular movie colony salon, where a beautician named Sylvia Barnhart supervised the straightening and bleaching to a golden blond.

The maintenance of this coiffure would require regular repetitions and a lifetime of meticulous care – especially later, when the colour was made even lighter, to glazed and haloed blond and eventually to shimmering platinum.

That winter the trio of Snively-Wolff-Barnhart brought closer to reality Grace's long cherished hope that in her precious Norma Jeane there would one day be completed the fantastic recreation of Jean Harlow. And when the Goddards moved back to California from West Virginia that summer, no one was more thrilled than Grace with Norma Jeane's new image. But Jim Dougherty returned to California, too (from his overseas service), and he saw more changes than simply his wife's hair colour. She was particularly excited about a short silent film that the Blue Book Agency had just made of her. Smiling directly into the lens in medium closeup shot, she modelled a swimsuit, walked in a summer sundress, smiled and waved at the camera. It had been, she told him, the most exciting day of her life thus far. Despite Norma Jeane's earlier report that Jim had approved her modelling aspirations, he was now unimpressed with the results.

Chapter Six

'We got along real well as long as she was dependent on me.'
Thus did Jim Dougherty summarize his first marriage.

When he had first left for military service, his last sight of
Norma Jeane could have been a scene from a sentimental wartime movie. His devoted child-bride had clung to him at the
harbour; she then waited tearfully, waving a pink scarf as his
ship glided slowly from shore and out into San Pedro Bay
before slipping over the horizon.

But when Dougherty returned eighteen months later in
December 1945, anticipating a joyful Christmas reunion with
her and his family, there was no emotional dockside greeting.
Years later he recalled:

> She was an hour late. She embraced me and kissed me, but it
> was a little cool. I had two weeks off before resuming ship-
> board duties along the California coast, but I don't think we
> had two nights together during that time. She was busy
> modeling, earning good money. It was my first inkling of her
> ambition.

Speaking of the same time, he added without conviction, 'It
never occurred to me that she was unfaithful.' That statement,
in the light of what he soon learned, is incredible. Dougherty
was surely canny enough to see the danger signals: his wife's
emotional distance, her evident career aspirations – and, the day

after his arrival, her departure for the Christmas holidays to work with a handsome stranger.

André de Dienes was thirty-two, a blue-eyed, muscular Transylvanian immigrant. After spells as a darling of café society in Rome, Paris and London, de Dienes arrived in Hollywood; there he was much in demand because of his talent with a camera, his burly attractiveness and both a manner and an accent that seemed to unite the sinister allure of Bela Lugosi with the Byronic charm of Charles Boyer. That autumn, Emmeline Snively had arranged a meeting between de Dienes and Norma Jeane. According to Snively, 'she still seemed a scared, pretty, lonely little kid who wore mostly fresh white cotton dresses and wanted somebody, somewhere, to think she was worth something.'

De Dienes began simply. He positioned her, shoeless and smiling, along a stretch of Route 101 outside North Hollywood: despite the blinding sun, she gazed unblinkingly into the shutter. The results of this session were more than encouraging, for there was Norma Jeane, pert in pigtails, a red skirt dotted with white stars and a striped jersey – like a sporty hitchhiker, heedless of traffic, sunburn and a photographer who knew how to get what he wanted. He then took her into a grassy field, removed the ribbons from her hair, exchanged the tight shirt for a frilly white apron and borrowed a newborn lamb from a nearby field: now she was the farmer's daughter, unworldly but somehow ripe with what de Dienes called 'naive but disturbing charm'.* There followed another quick change of clothes, her hair was tied back on her neck, she donned a pair of blue jeans and a red blouse was knotted just under the bosom for a peek-a-boo midriff: she perched on a fence and smiled at the camera as if she were about to enter a barn. Daisy Mae was beckoning to every Li'l Abner in America.

When Norma Jeane showed these photographs to Jim, he

---

* One of these shots appeared on the cover of *The Family Circle* magazine for April 1946.

manifested frank indifference: 'So far as I was concerned, she was turning into another human being. She showed me the pictures, her new dresses and shoes – as if I cared about such things. She was proud of her magazine covers and her new popularity at Blue Book, and she expected me to be, too. She wanted a career.' She was, in other words, no longer the dependent castaway; she was now a young woman with ambition, and this was unacceptable to the sturdy, macho marine.

Just before Christmas, to the horror of Ana Lower and Ethel Dougherty (not to say the simmering indignation of the abandoned husband), Norma Jeane left for another, longer journey with de Dienes. 'The truth is,' she said years later, 'that I began the trip with only business in mind [de Dienes paid her a flat fee of two hundred dollars]. But André had other ideas.' By this time, due no doubt to Dougherty's apathy, Norma Jeane's zeal and de Dienes's ardour ('I longed to make her my mistress'), she was hurled again into romantic jeopardy. 'The plain truth is that she was exploited by André,' according to the actor Alex D'Arcy, who knew the photographer. 'He was a thoroughly crazy creature who let her think he was indispensable to her.'

André and Norma Jeane first stopped at Zuma Beach, where he clicked away as she tossed a volleyball, waded into the surf, sported a two-piece bathing suit and ran along the shore. Then they headed for the Mojave Desert, where only the simplest outfit was needed to suggest the link between two types of natural beauty. From there they proceeded north through Yosemite, then on to Nevada and Washington. André's ardour was not cooled as he photographed his model on the snowy slopes near Mount Hood, but when they stopped at a cabin or motel at night, Norma Jeane at first kept the relationship platonic and insisted on separate rooms: 'She needed a really good night's sleep to look her best the next day [and so] she asked me to be good.' For the present he endured, affecting the gloomy dissatisfaction of a rejected suitor even as he slid notes under her door. 'Come to me,' he scrawled. 'We'll make love. You won't be disappointed.'

But a telephone call Norma Jeane put through to Grace Goddard set in motion a chain of events that eventually brought the
model to her photographer's bed. Gladys was then living in
Portland, Oregon, and Grace arranged for mother and daughter
to meet.

The reunion between the two women after more than six
years was predictably awkward; it was also unbearably sad for
Norma Jeane. After the San Francisco clinic found that she was
no danger to herself or others, Gladys had been given $200 and
two dresses, and after nearly a year of wandering alone around
the Pacific Northwest (often finding shelter with the Salvation
Army), the poor woman took a room in a seedy hotel in downtown Portland. Long accustomed to being treated like a
mentally ill incompetent, Gladys had lost the ability of normal
socializing; anorexic and impassive, her appearance terrified her
daughter, who had arrived with gifts and who gave, that afternoon, a sterling performance.

She embraced her mother, who was completely withdrawn as
she sat rigidly in a wicker chair; she then showed Gladys some
of André's pictures and gave her a bag of candy. But Gladys displayed neither gratitude nor pleasure. She could not even
manage to reach out and touch her daughter, and after a long
and awkward silence (during which de Dienes paced nervously
nearby) Norma Jeane knelt at her mother's feet.

And then for a moment the cloud of separation seemed to
part. 'I'd like to come and live with you, Norma Jeane,' Gladys
whispered. This frightened Norma Jeane, who scarcely knew
her mother and, foreseeing the end of her own marriage, shrank
from the thought of being burdened with Gladys's care. Just
then, André spoke up, saying that he was going to marry
Norma Jeane after she divorced, and that they were going to
move to New York. Norma Jeane tried to interrupt him, to correct his expectations, but he announced abruptly that they had
to leave the hotel. 'I'll see you soon, Mama,' Norma Jeane said.
Fighting tears, she kissed her mother, left her address and telephone number on the table with the gifts and quietly withdrew.

Back in André's car as they headed south toward home, she wept inconsolably.

Throughout her life, Norma Jean was haunted by the thought of Gladys, who outlived her by twenty-two years. As she later said, there had never been a chance for a normal mother-daughter relationship, and the fear of sharing a family mental illness compounded the pointed resentment her childhood memories evoked. The actress Marilyn Monroe never took the risk of permitting a situation in which Gladys could again reject or withdraw from her. But this engendered a pattern with motherly women in her life: need clashed with fear, and to forestall pain she often rejected others first. Ashamed and avoiding reminders of her past, she tried in vain to forget her mother, although from afar she covered Gladys's material needs when she could.

That evening Norma Jeane and André stopped at a country inn. There, just as she had sought comfort in Jim's arms after the (real or feigned) rejection by her father, so now she reached out to another strong, older man. 'In my dreams I had explored her body,' de Dienes wrote tremulously years later; 'reality far surpassed my imagination . . . [and then] I realized she was crying.' The tears, he saw, bespoke only Norma Jeane's happiness, her pleasure, her relief after the tensions with Dougherty and the difficult reunion with Gladys. She was certainly not mired in remorse, for throughout the rest of the journey she was 'playful and provocative' (thus de Dienes), an energetic, eager lover who played peek-a-boo with sheets and nightgowns and who teased before satisfying. Of that night, and of this brief affair in early 1946, Norma Jeane later said nothing.

Apart from the obvious physical attractions of de Dienes and the fact that he was an older man (like Dougherty, a kind of surrogate father), he had – like Conover – won her over simply because he was a photographer. The men behind the still cameras in these early years were like the later cinematographers, producers and agents. They could present her to the world literally in the best light; she needed them, was grateful to them, felt she owed them and repaid them with herself, the reality whose image they were promoting and capturing for anonymous others.

This was the beginning of an important pattern in her life, for she was excited by the act of being photographed. 'Making love' to the camera is both satisfying and safe: one may fantasize anyone or everyone, but the moment is unthreatening. This is not so uncommon among models and actors, whose desire to be seen, recognized, approved and accepted, whose longing to please and to gratify others, is at the foundation of their craft.

In this regard, she was very like Jean Harlow, who flirted (sometimes outrageously) with photographers. At an outdoor session with the photographer Ted Allan, for example, Harlow was once handed a fishnet to throw over a white dress. She promptly stripped naked and stood wearing only the fishnet. 'Isn't this better?' she asked Allan, who later thought that Harlow 'figured that if I were turned on, I'd take better pictures. I realized then that she always needed something personal – that feeling of being liked. It made her feel secure.' Norma Jeane was not so different from the woman who had been constantly set before her as an idol.

Observed and admired for her body, each wished to please the gazer, to gratify those who desired her. Sex for Norma Jeane became the logical extension of a character trait within her from childhood and throughout her school years: it was a simple attempt to win approval. The girl who dreamed of worshippers before her nakedness could now give herself in the flesh, could gratify their adoration. To Norma Jeane this was not a matter of immodesty or immorality, nor did she ever seem to feel guilty.

Norma Jeane returned to Los Angeles a more experienced young woman, and this must have been evident in her manner. She found a furious husband who demanded that she make a choice between him and her career. She argued that she had no reason to be a housewife when there had been no husband around for two years; besides, she insisted, what was wrong with modelling? The answer to that was twofold: Dougherty wanted a sedate housewife, not a glamour-queen-in-the-making; he also wanted children. A new cold war infected the Dougherty household that spring of 1946, especially when his wife 'nearly went berserk – she thought she was pregnant.' Perhaps they both thought to question the paternity; in any case, the onset of her period resolved the matter.

In late January, Jim was recalled to duty in the Pacific, where the Merchant Marines helped to transport men and supplies back to Europe and America after the Allied victory; he said that he expected her to have become wiser by the time he returned later that year.

When she heard that Norma Jeane was alone, Grace occasionally invited her to Van Nuys for a meal or a weekend visit. But Norma Jeane invariably declined. This may have been partly a desire to further her independence from the past, but there was another more ominous reason for her distance. By 1946 the older woman was a seasoned alcoholic, sometimes inappropriately giddy and verbose, frequently gloomy and remote. Like Gladys, Grace too was now unpredictable.

From her small apartment beneath Ana Lower's, Norma Jeane went out to work as a model. Emmeline Snively now had a wide variety of photographs to circulate round the offices of Los Angeles artists and photographers, and her telephone rang almost daily with offers.

In February, Norma Jeane posed for the Scottish photographer William Burnside, who was struck by 'the lost look in the middle of a smile' and, like Conover and de Dienes, was charmed by her co-operation and her alacrity to please. 'A kiss took weeks to achieve,' Burnside said years later; from there it was a short route to closer intimacy. First she loved the camera, according to Burnside: 'it soothed her'; then she loved the man who held it. But Norma Jeane was no rapacious starlet offering sex as barter to advance her career: Burnside remembered 'her shyness and sense of insecurity. She did not like to be touched too soon. One could not even think of sexual conquest by force.'

Norma Jeane herself was undergoing a rapid transformation. The awkwardness, the concern for acceptance, the occasional stutter and the hesitation were still there, but now she was giving herself – simply visually, to the camera, or frankly sexually, to the photographer. In the case of Burnside, and perhaps others, a professional's talent secured her gratitude and her gratitude was expressed with her body. But Burnside soon ended their romance. She sent him a lyric:

> I could have loved you once, and even said it
> But you went away,
> A long way away.
> When you came back it was too late
> And love was a forgotten word.
> Remember?

In February and March 1946 she posed for the artist Earl Moran and for the photographer Joseph Jasgur, and in both cases her relationship was very warm but strictly platonic. Moran paid her ten dollars an hour, photographing her in a variety of dress and semi-dress: as a bathing beauty in skimpy two-piece swimsuits; drying herself after a bath; bare-breasted, hanging up her lingerie to dry. From these snapshots he drew charcoal and chalk pictures which he sold to Brown & Bigelow, the major calendar-art company in America. 'She liked to pose,' Moran said years later. 'For her it was acting, and emotionally she did everything right.'

Jasgur, a celebrity photographer known for his contributions to *Silver Screen*, *Photoplay* and the *Hollywood Citizen-News*, agreed to Emmeline Snively's request for test photos of Norma Jeane. On the afternoon of 10 March he opened the door of his Hollywood studio apartment to find 'a shy girl, nothing like a typical model, all breathless and anxious'. She was also over an hour late, which surprised him, for it seemed incompatible with her obvious earnestness about her career; he later thought her unpunctuality was related to 'her uncertainty that she was presentable or acceptable'.

Norma Jeane told Jasgur that she had no money to pay for the photographs and that she lacked even the price of a good meal – surely an exaggeration given her full work schedule that winter. But Jasgur was a friend of Snively, and while the first negatives dried that evening he bought her supper. Their sessions continued throughout that month – atop the Hollywood sign and at Zuma Beach, where he took colour as well as black and white photos, capturing her friskiness as she drew hearts on the wet sand.

Laszlo Willinger also made some extraordinary photos of Norma Jeane that year.

> When she saw a camera – any camera, she lit up and was totally different. The moment the shot was over, she fell back into her not very interesting position. But she had a talent to make people feel sorry for her, and she exploited it to the best of her ability – even people who had been around and knew models fell for this 'Help me' pose.

With her husband away and the circle of her acquaintances widening, it would not have been surprising to find this pretty, lonely nineteen-year-old available to a sharp admirer. But the situation was quite different. The actor Ken DuMain, as well as Norma Jeane's colleague Lydia Bodrero, remembered that Snively's models often double- and triple-dated with friends in the spring of 1946. Evenings with Norma Jeane might include a movie and a ride out to the beach, or a few hours dancing at a club. She did not have a reputation for easy virtue, although she did go out with several young men more than once. DuMain recalled escorting her to a Sunset Strip nightclub she especially liked, 'where a female impersonator named Ray Bourbon attracted crowds of admirers. She loved this sort of thing and was great fun to be with. There was also an innate sweetness and decency about her that no atmosphere or joke could alter.'

Even had she been so inclined, the opportunities would have been short-circuited by a new and awkward circumstance in her life. Piteous letters from Gladys arrived almost daily in Norma Jeane's mailbox that spring, begging to come and live with her. She would be no trouble, she promised; she would find a job. In April, Norma Jeane sent cash to cover the journey and soon they were sharing the one bed and two small rooms on Nebraska Avenue. This would be Norma Jeane's last brief and ineffective attempt to establish a relationship with her mother.

Such was the domestic situation Jim found when he returned on a brief furlough in April. Arriving at the apartment, he found Gladys staring at him blankly: it was clear, as he recalled years later, that by this time Gladys was not able to care for herself. But neither could her daughter assume such a responsibility.

The precise nature of Gladys's mental and emotional problems remains vague, for the few medical reports remaining among family records are inconclusive. On the one hand, she was alert, aware of her surroundings and her identity, and she was not violent; she did not suffer from hallucinations, paranoia or frank schizophrenia. However, there was a retreat from the ordinary business of living; she seemed, in other words, unable or unwilling to maintain ordinary human relations, much less steady employment: in general terms, she seems to have suffered a loss of affect. 'She wandered,' Eleanor Goddard recalled, 'and she was unpredictable. She was docile, but she was not "there".' Years later, more sophisticated medical examinations might have located a biochemical imbalance or even a benign tumour; psychotherapy might have disclosed chronic, treatable phobias or a guilt complex; and drug treatment may have provided help. But in 1946 there were no human or financial resources for Gladys.

The immediate corollary of her living with Norma Jeane was clear: there was no room for three, and so after only a few moments Jim departed to spend the two-day leave with his mother. After their earlier disputes over her career and his plans for their future, he interpreted Gladys's presence as a convenient way for Norma Jeane to prepare for a separation. She was 'calculating', it seemed to him. 'She had made sure that Gladys would be living there on Nebraska Avenue, that her mother would have my place in the only bed in the apartment.' But this assessment may have been too harsh: unaware of Gladys's earlier request in Portland, he felt resentful, summarily excluded from contact or conversation with his wife about their marriage. To him, Gladys seemed simply 'a woman without much emotion', not to say an unwelcome intrusion. He returned to Merchant Marine duty without seeing Norma Jeane again.

In late April, Gladys entered a Northern California clinic, where her daughter struggled to send money to provide supplements for her mother's basic care. Such contributions never ceased, although Norma Jeane's primary concern was now her career.

During early 1946, she spoke several times with Emmeline Snively about the possibility of working in the movies. Conover, de Dienes, Burnside and Moran had told her that this was not a vain hope, that she was a natural for the studio 'stables' of starlets. Annually, hundreds were tested and signed low-paying contracts. Sometimes they were cast in bit parts, a handful were trained and groomed for small speaking roles and, for the very few fortunates, there was eventual graduation to supporting player status.

Among these aspirants, only a minority became stars. The studios knew that public taste was fickle and that great success rarely endured. Apprentices had to be available, a pool of 'talent' from which producers could select the new starlets. Among the accepted qualifications to begin work with a studio, however, one was unwritten but taken for granted. The unmarried young woman was more favourably regarded for possible advancement in the system: pregnancy, after all, could cost a studio enormous sums if a picture had to be cancelled or recast during production. Eager starlets had to be ready for a variety of sacrifices.

These facts of studio life were impressed on her not only by Snively and photographers but also by Grace, whom Norma

Jeane met at least once in April. The Dougherty marriage would have to be formally terminated if Norma Jeane hoped to be groomed for stardom. Grace had arranged Gladys's initial hospitalization; she manoeuvred her guardianship of Norma Jeane; she decided the girl's stay at the orphanage. She had brokered the marriage to Jim Dougherty, and now she could abet its dissolution. Indeed, as Jim had said, 'Grace had a lot to do with everything.' And so, on 14 May, Norma Jeane was shipped from Ana Lower to another of Grace's aunts, a 69-year-old widow named Minnie Willette who lived most conveniently at 604 South 3rd Street in Las Vegas, where divorces could be obtained almost as easily as entrance to the local gambling casinos.

Two weeks later, on duty near Shanghai, Dougherty received a letter with a Nevada postmark: a lawyer named C. Norman Cornwall announced that Norma Jeane Dougherty had filed for divorce. 'First she thought she had security with me,' Dougherty recalled thinking at that time, 'and now she figures a studio contract can provide it better. There are a thousand and one girls who can sing and dance and look good, and she wants to be in the movies. Well, good luck to her.' Jim at once wired the appropriate government office in Los Angeles to cease sending monthly payments to his wife.

By the end of June, he was back in California, where Ana Lower gave him a telephone number. But Norma Jeane was not with Minnie: she was in Las Vegas hospital, under treatment for a mouth infection. At first Dougherty did not recognize her deep voice on the telephone – a tone due not to her medical condition, as he learned at once. 'They tell me I have to lower my tone if I'm going to be in the movies,' she said candidly, adding at once: 'The nurse brought me a letter a few days ago. Why did you cut off my allowance?'

'Look, kid,' Dougherty replied with equal candour, 'this is the way it goes. You don't pay for anything unless you're getting it.' When she went on to say that she did not want to lose him, that they could still 'date' and that she was merely being practical about her career, he was adamant. 'She thought we could live together without being married,' Dougherty said years later, 'that we could go on just as before.' Unsure of her future, she was attempting a safe middle ground.

'Are you crazy?' Jim asked. 'I want a wife and kids. You want a divorce, we'll get a divorce. Then it's over.'

And so it was. Charging Dougherty with the typical generic assertion of 'extreme mental cruelty that has impaired the plaintiff's health', Norma Jeane filed a suit for divorce that was uncontested by her husband. At two o'clock on the afternoon of 13 September 1946, Norma Jeane and Minnie appeared for a final hearing before District Judge A. S. Henderson in Las Vegas. After stating her name and Nevada address, the plaintiff answered a few questions put to her by her attorney:

'Is it your intention to make [Nevada] your home and permanent place of residence?'

'Yes.'

'Has that been your intention since your arrival in May?'

'Yes.'

'You intend to remain here for an indefinite period of time?'

'Yes.'

'You have stated that your husband treated you with extreme cruelty without just cause or provocation on your part. Will you tell the Court some of the acts upon which you base this cruelty charge?'

'Well, in the first place, my husband didn't support me and he objected to my working, criticized me for it and he also had a bad temper and would fly into rages and he left me on three different occasions and criticized me and embarrassed me in front of my friends and he didn't try to make a home for me.'

'What effect did this have on your health?'

'It upset me and made me nervous.'

'So much so that you cannot live with him under the conditions and enjoy good health?'

'Yes.'

'Is a reconciliation possible?'

'No.'

After less than five minutes in court, Judge Henderson slammed his gavel, saying, 'A decree of divorce is granted' even as he rose from his chair. The marriage was dissolved at that moment. James Edward Dougherty countersigned the decree two weeks later, giving Norma Jeane Dougherty her freedom and his 1935 Ford coupé. They neither met nor spoke again. 'I married and was divorced,' she told a reporter four years later. 'It was a mistake and he has since remarried.' That was her last public statement on the matter.

Her testimony notwithstanding, Norma Jeane might have found herself charged with perjury, for she had not in fact lived there without interruption from 14 May to 13 September, as the divorce law required. During the summer she had slipped quietly back to Los Angeles, where Emmeline Snively had contacted her friend Helen Ainsworth. A severe, 200-pound agent familiarly known as 'Cupid', Ainsworth managed the West Coast office of a talent agency known as the National Concert Artists Corporation. As a favour to her old friend Snively, Ainsworth arranged an introduction for Norma Jeane with an executive at the Twentieth Century-Fox Studios on Pico Boulevard in West Los Angeles.*

Precisely at the appointed hour, ten-thirty on the morning of Wednesday 17 July 1946, Norma Jeane arrived at Ben Lyon's office. Then forty-five, Lyon had a long stage and screen career behind him, most notably as the hero of the picture firmly establishing Jean Harlow's career – Howard Hughes's production of *Hell's Angels* in 1930. Lyon and his wife, actress Bebe Daniels, had lived in England during World War II (during which he served with distinction in the Royal Air Force), and on their return to America he was instantly engaged by Fox as recruiter of new talent and director of casting. He handed Norma Jeane a section of the script for *Winged Victory* and

---

* Anticipating some kind of movie work for Norma Jeane, Snively had encouraged her to sign a contract at Ainsworth's National Concert Artists Corporation, which she had already done on 11 March 1946.

asked her to read a few lines; in Fox's 1944 wartime melodrama, the words had been spoken by Judy Holliday, another slightly breathless blonde with great potential for comedy. Nothing is known of this first meeting, nor of Norma Jeane's reading, but Lyon asked her to return for a film test.

And so on 19 July 1946, Norma Jeane was led to one of the sets being built for a new Betty Grable picture, *Mother Wore Tights*. There she was introduced to the great cinematographer Leon Shamroy (who had won Academy Awards for *The Black Swan, Wilson* and *Leave Her to Heaven*); to veteran makeup artist Allan Snyder (who supervised the cosmetics for, among others, Fox's major stars Betty Grable, Gene Tierney, Linda Darnell and Alice Faye); to director Walter Lang (known for glossy, popular entertainments); and to wardrobe designer Charles LeMaire. Lyon had summoned four of the studio's best technicians for the test scene.

But contrary to popular belief, this was no simple task. 'She'd been modeling,' recalled Snyder, 'and so she came to us knowing everything about everything, or so she believed. I remember thinking that here was a very determined and ambitious girl, despite her obvious nervousness.' Norma Jeane demanded that Snyder apply heavy makeup, which was entirely inappropriate for a Technicolor test, and when Shamroy saw this he put down his large cigar and bellowed Snyder's nickname: 'Whitey, what the hell have you got on that face? We can't photograph her that way! Take this girl downstairs, wash the damn stuff off, do her face the way you know it ought to be and bring her back up!'

Her anxiety, and what Norma Jeane knew was her tactical error, at once caused her to stutter and perspire, and (as often throughout her life) embarrassment and fear of failure caused red blotches to emerge on her face. To her great relief, she was then told this would be a silent test: she would be presented for the approval of production chief Darryl F. Zanuck only on the merits of her appearance. She was given a series of simple commands, the small crew of miracle workers set to their task, a hundred-foot roll of Technicolor stock was put in the camera and Lang cried 'Action!'

There was silence on the set. Wearing a floor-length crinoline gown, Norma Jeane walked back and forth. She sat on a high stool. She lit a cigarette, stubbed it out, rose and walked toward a stage window. A remarkable transformation occurred: while the camera was in operation, she showed not a trace of distress; her hands were steady, her movement unhurried, poised; she seemed the most confident woman in the world. Most memorable, her radiant smile evoked smiles from the bystanders.

'When I first watched her,' Leon Shamroy said five years later,

> I thought, 'This girl will be another Harlow!' Her natural beauty plus her inferiority complex gave her a look of mystery ... I got a cold chill. This girl had something I hadn't seen since silent pictures. She had a kind of fantastic beauty like Gloria Swanson ... and she got sex on a piece of film like Jean Harlow. Every frame of the test radiated sex. She didn't need a sound track – she was creating effects visually. She was showing us she could sell emotions in pictures.

Either during that weekend or on the following Monday, the film was screened for Zanuck, whose approval was necessary if a contract were to be offered. As it happened, he was not particularly zealous about Norma Jeane. For one thing, she had never acted anywhere – not a single role, even on an amateur night, nor had she ever had an acting lesson. Zanuck, who personally preferred brunettes like Linda Darnell, also felt that Betty Grable supplied enough blond sex appeal for the studio. In any case, he did not see the same radiance that excited his colleagues. But there was no financial risk in deferring to Lyon and Shamroy. The studio's legal department was instructed to draw up an agreement, and on Tuesday afternoon, 23 July, Helen Ainsworth appointed her colleague Harry Lipton to represent the new client on behalf of National Concert Artists.

Norma Jeane was offered a standard contract without exclusions, exceptions or emendations. Her guaranteed salary, paid whether she worked or did not, was to be $75 a week for six months, with the studio's option to renew for another half-year at twice that amount. Her fate would be determined not so much by her talent as by the interest she might evoke from the ninety-person press and publicity staff at the studio. These 'flacks', as they were called, aroused public curiosity about players, planted stories in newspapers and fan magazines and kept the attention of the most influential columnists of the day: Hedda Hopper and Louella Parsons, Walter Winchell and Sidney Skolsky. They, along with *Photoplay*, *Modern Screen*, *Silver Screen* and other slick publications were courted and cajoled to advance the careers of certain actors. Their power was literally unlimited.

However modest the deal and uncertain the future, Norma Jeane was thrilled – as she was at the first mention of her name in a Hollywood gossip column, on 29 July. Hedda Hopper's syndicated roundup of movie news included this item:

> Howard Hughes is on the mend.* Picking up a magazine, he was attracted by the cover girl and promptly instructed an aide to sign her for pictures. She's Norma Jean [*sic*] Dougherty, a model.

Hughes was, of course, too late. On 5 September, *Variety* printed her name for the first time, reporting under the 'New Contracts' column that she was one of the two young women signed by Fox.

At the age of twenty, the new potential starlet was a year too young to sign a binding contract in the State of California. Grace was still her legal guardian, and so, despite the awkwardness and irregularities in their relationship, Norma Jeane

---

* On 7 July, producer and aviator Hughes had crash-landed one of his planes in Beverly Hills and sustained severe injuries.

again had to turn to her. Grace McKee Goddard had been at the centre of every major moment in Norma Jeane's life: her departure from the Bolenders to live with Gladys; Gladys's subsequent confinement in asylums; the details of Norma Jeane's material welfare and her sojourn at the Orphans Home; her time with cousins in Compton; her return to the Goddards and the shock of being left behind when they moved East; her marriage to Dougherty and the arrangements for her divorce. Sometimes the girl had felt like an unnecessary adjunct, a dispensable if charming object in her guardian's life. But just as often, she had been infused with a sense that she bore within her an idealized self, a lustrous new Harlow to whom professionals now also favourably compared her. Grace had indeed been the great manager of Norma Jeane's life, and dependence on Grace had been the pattern of that management (as it had been with Dougherty). But subordination wearies human relations, and the long history of subordination must have rankled with a young woman who was quickly learning how much she could achieve on her own, with energy, a certain coy, girlish expertise – and with her body.

However much Grace's protection, obsessions and manipulations evoked a tangle of conflicting feelings, Norma Jeane had known more critical history with her than with anyone. Grace knew her as no one did – and in a sense Grace, trapped in a bleak and loveless marriage from which alcohol was no escape, now depended on Norma Jeane to make something come out right, to realize her own dream. When Grace, with an unsteady signature, wrote her own name on the Fox contract below Norma Jeane Dougherty's, she was simultaneously justifying her past authority and releasing the object of it into an unpredictable but inevitable autonomy. She was in effect signing a warranty for Norma Jeane's maturity in a way she had not with the Dougherty marriage; she was permitting herself to become nonessential, a player in the past who might not be retained in the future.

Just days before the contract was countersigned (on 24

August 1946), Norma Jeane was summoned to Ben Lyon's office. Only one detail remained to be adjudicated: the matter of her name. Dougherty, Lyon said bluntly, would have to be changed, for no one was sure whether it should be pronounced 'Dok-er-tee' or 'Dor-rit-tee' or 'Doe-rit-tee' or perhaps even 'Doff-er-tee'. Did she have any preference for a surname? Norma Jeane did not hesitate: Monroe was the name of her mother's family, the only relatives of which she could be truly certain. (Like Jean Harlow, she was also choosing her mother's maiden name for her own.) Lyon agreed: Monroe was a short, easy name, as American as the name of the president who bore it.

The matter of a first name was not so simple. 'Norma Jeane Monroe' was awkward, and 'Norma Monroe' was almost a tongue-twister. At first they decided on 'Jean Monroe', but she was unhappy with that. She wanted to change everything if we were going to change anything, and while Lyon thought, she spoke of her background. She had never known her father . . . her foster father was a demanding, abusive man . . . in high school she was called the 'Mmmm' girl.

Lyon leaned forward in his chair:

'I know who you are, you're Marilyn!' he cried, adding later, 'I told her that once there was a lovely actress named Marilyn Miller and that she reminded me of her.'

The connection was a logical one for Lyon to make as Norma Jeane sat before him recounting her history, afraid she might lose this chance over their inability to find a suitable name. Lyon had thought of Marilyn Miller not only because, like the girl before him, she too had blond hair and blue-green eyes. Lyon had been in love with Marilyn Miller many years earlier, and he had been engaged to marry her before he met Bebe Daniels. He knew that as a child Miller had been deserted by her father and then had a stepfather who was a tyrant. She had become a Broadway musical comedy star during the 1920s (in such hits as the trio *Sally* [1920], *Sunny* [1925] and *Rosalie* [1928]); she had also enjoyed a brief success in films. Then, after three marriages, a failing career and increasingly wretched health, she died in 1936 at the age of thirty-seven. Ben Lyon said he was gazing at the virtual reincarnation of Marilyn Miller – and, he had to agree with Shamroy, of Jean Harlow.

Norma Jeane Dougherty was not immediately convinced: Marilyn (originally a contraction of Mary Lynn) sounded strange, artificial. Lyon reminded her that since World War I, it had been one of the most popular first names for American girls because of Marilyn Miller.

'Say it,' Lyon urged her quietly.

'Mmmmmm,' Norma Jeane tried, stuttering for just a moment.

And then they both had to laugh.

'That's it – the "Mmmmmm Girl!"' Lyon cried, clapping his hands. 'What do you think, sweetheart?'

She smiled. 'Well, I guess I'm Marilyn Monroe.'

Chapter Seven

The movie studio claiming the professional services of a hopeful novice named Marilyn Monroe traced its origins to Wilhelm Fried, a Hungarian immigrant who had operated a penny arcade in Brooklyn at the turn of the century. By the end of World War I he had changed his name to William Fox, and shortly thereafter founded a film corporation, moved West and was producing, leasing and exhibiting films in Hollywood. Among the stars who worked for him were Theda Bara, prototype of the enigmatic *femme fatale*; Annette Kellerman, the champion swimmer; cowboy Tom Mix; the sweetly vulnerable Janet Gaynor, who won the first Academy Award as best actress; and, in the early 1930s, the precocious tot Shirley Temple.

But by 1935, the Depression and a serious accident had altered Fox's fortunes. He declared bankruptcy, and his Fox Film Corporation merged with Twentieth Century Pictures, a company established two years earlier by the movie mogul Joseph M. Schenck (ex-husband of Norma Talmadge) and Darryl F. Zanuck, who had been production chief at Warner Bros; Schenck became board chairman of the new 20th Century-Fox, Zanuck vice-president in charge of production. By 1943, Zanuck was the only one of the trio who had not served a prison term for tax fraud, bribery or illegal union payoffs.*

* The on-screen emblem, the studio advertising and the lot's marquee always identified the company as '20th Century-Fox', but for legal reasons the contracts, documents and stationery had to designate it as 'Twentieth Century-Fox'. In 1984, the hyphen which since 1935 had marked the merger was removed.

Marilyn Monroe joined the studio during the highest grossing time in its history, when the success of *Laura, The House on 92nd Street, A Tree Grows in Brooklyn, The Keys of the Kingdom* and *Leave Her to Heaven* had recently brought in over $22 million. The company was renowned and respected for its technical brilliance, for a series of successful glossy musicals, literate thrillers, gripping dramas and an impressive roster of stars and directors.* But the first television sets were being marketed to American households, and a sharp drop in profits was about to affect all the studios.

The corporate fortunes depended largely on decisions made by one man who dominated the company for thirty-five years. In 1946, Nebraska-born Darryl F. Zanuck was forty-four, a short, sharp-minded, domineering, gap-toothed bundle of energy whose manner is perhaps best summarized by his habit of snapping at his staff: 'Don't agree with me until I'm finished talking!' He had been a screenwriter at Warners from 1923 to 1933, where his credits included several Rin Tin Tin adventures; indeed, Zanuck personally supervised the dog's successful transition from silent to sound pictures.

The image of Zanuck held by screenwriter Ernest Lehman is equally vivid and compelling: he remembered Zanuck as a loud man with a big cigar who strode around the lot with a riding crop in his hand. 'Zanuck had an aide who threw paper balls in the air for him to swing at with the crop while he walked. One day the man was fired, and the story circulated was that he had struck Darryl out!' Lehman remembered also Zanuck's lengthy script conferences and involvement in every aspect of production.

Since he had taken over Fox's operations (at 10201 Pico Boulevard, a ten-minute ride from where Marilyn lived and went to school), the volatile Zanuck was known to treat human colleagues with the same condescension he levelled on canines.

* Among the most popular contract players were Don Ameche, Anne Baxter, Alice Faye, Henry Fonda, Betty Grable, Carmen Miranda, Gregory Peck, Tyrone Power, Gene Tierney and Loretta Young; directors included Henry Hathaway, Elia Kazan, Anatole Litvak, Joseph L. Mankiewicz and Otto Preminger.

Like many movie executives whose power could easily make and unmake careers, he exercised austerity in business dealings but indulged himself personally; this was especially so during early evening conferences with hopeful starlets – meetings that sometimes included very personal business indeed. Zanuck was, according to his good friend, the screenwriter Philip Dunne, 'an energetic and promiscuous lover [but also] a genius in judging character. Like all great executives, he knew when to coddle, when to bully and when to exhort.'

Zanuck's achievements as producer were indisputably impressive and won the studio more than thirty-two Oscars.* In 1946 he was producing the award-winning film about anti-Semitism, *Gentleman's Agreement*, directed by Elia Kazan. But Zanuck was also supervising other scripts, budgets, casting, editing and the final cut of almost fifty pictures annually, as well as authorizing every new studio contract; he approved more films for Technicolor production than any studio in town; and he attracted new directors while retaining veterans. Zanuck worked with remarkable independence of the company president, his former colleague Spyros Skouras, whom he had known at Warners and Twentieth Century; conversely, Skouras, chief financial officer of Fox, relied heavily on Zanuck's creative instincts.

As for Marilyn Monroe, Zanuck scarcely noticed her: she was merely one of many contract players on the lot, and when casting for pictures he turned over her photograph quickly and without interest. Still, Marilyn now had a regular income, and in September she opened a bank account. But the year ended without a single assignment – not even a bit part in a crowd scene. 'She was very serious about wanting to work,' according to her agent Harry Lipton, who added that she did not agree with those who thought it was a fine job that paid without performance. Although not required to report to the studio every day,

---

* Among the best known Zanuck films up to 1946: *The House of Rothschild, Alexander's Ragtime Band, Jesse James, Young Mr Lincoln, Drums Along the Mohawk, The Grapes of Wrath, Tobacco Road* and *How Green Was My Valley*.

she did so, as Allan Snyder recalled. Still living with Ana Lower, Marilyn took a bus or rode a bicycle, visiting the Fox wardrobe department to learn about period and contemporary costumes, fabrics and foundation garments. She asked questions of everyone with knowledge she coveted, anyone experienced who would give her a five-minute presentation on lighting, the moving camera, speech and diction.

'Desperate to absorb all she could', said Snyder, Marilyn also wanted to know the proper makeup techniques for black and white and for colour cinematography. Known throughout the film industry (and later in television) for his technical brilliance in preparing actors' makeup for a wide variety of roles, Snyder quickly became a mentor to the young apprentice. She trusted him, relied on his professional guidance and was grateful for his patience in demonstrating the secrets of movie cosmetology – although she had no assignment and he had a busy schedule.

'I could see at once that she was terribly insecure, that despite her modeling she didn't think she was pretty. It took a lot of convincing for her to see the natural freshness and beauty she had, and how well she could be used in [moving] pictures.' Snyder was touched by Marilyn's conspicuous lack of self-confidence, her childlike wonder at the enchantments and transformations possible through movie crafts. He also saw a determination and an ability to meet the weekly disappointment of 'no call' – even as she persisted in learning all she could about something of which she knew nothing. Like Shamroy and Lyon, Snyder saw a rare, luminous quality in her, something vague and indefinable, a woman's experience and a child's needs. He had a deep and abiding friendship with Marilyn Monroe uncomplicated by romance for the sixteen years from the first day of her career to the end of her life.*

---

* Years later, Snyder summarized the process of making up Marilyn Monroe: a light base, then a highlight under the eyes and out, over and across the cheekbones. This was followed by a toning to the eyeshadow, running lightly out toward the hairline, an outline in pencil round the eyes, brows slightly pointed to widen her forehead, a toning underneath the cheekbones, and delicate shadings

Others at Fox during late 1946 and early 1947 saw her fervour for a job and her eagerness to be included in studio activity; for Marilyn, an assignment would signal acceptance within a circle from which she felt excluded. John Campbell, a staff publicist, recalled that she haunted the press offices daily, wearing a tight sweater and asking about publicity procedures. Campbell found her friendly and did not wish to be rude, but there was no mandate from the front office about her, and so to the publicists she was a bit of a nuisance.

But she was not so to the Fox still photographers, who were often asked to provide magazines, newspapers and advertising agencies with glossies of attractive contract players. For them, Marilyn happily posed in the tiniest bathing suits or a negligée almost as transparent as cellophane. Predictably, the most daring shots could not be used, but in the meantime neither the photographers nor their subject had any complaints. With typical cunning, the Fox publicists created copy that was charmingly variant: one picture of Marilyn in a two-piece swimsuit graced the *Los Angeles Times* on 30 January 1947, with the hilarious headline, 'Baby Sitter Lands in Films'. The accompanying blurb, excising two years from her age, explained that this '18-year-old blond baby sitter walked into a studio talent scout's home' and was at once on the road to stardom. This would, however, be no short route.

In February 1947, Fox exercised the right to renew her contract for six months, and several days later she finally received a casting call. Marilyn Monroe's first film role was as a high school girl in a minor picture called *Scudda-Hoo! Scudda-Hay!* Wisely retitled *Summer Lightning* by British distributors, the Technicolor picture concerns a farming family with half-brothers battling over how best to raise mules.* For several days in March, Marilyn reported to the studio, where she was directed by F. Hugh Herbert in two scenes that contributed

according to costume and lighting. Lipstick colours varied; later, CinemaScope presented fresh challenges.

* The American title refers to farmers' shouts when they goad mule teams – the equivalent of the standard 'Giddee-yap!' for horses.

nothing to a fatally tedious narrative. In one sequence, she was photographed with another starlet in a rowboat: this was entirely removed from the final cut of the film. The second scene survived, in which she can be glimpsed and heard for only a second – walking swiftly behind leading lady June Haver and eight-year-old Natalie Wood and calling to Haver, 'Hi, Rad!' Only the most alert viewer could have noticed the uncredited Marilyn Monroe, who is offscreen before Haver can reply, 'Hi, Peggy!'*

Her inchoate career was not consolidated by her second film for Fox. In May 1947, Marilyn breezed through three short scenes in *Dangerous Years*, a drearily earnest melodrama about juvenile delinquency. As a waitress named Eve at a teenage hangout called the Gopher Hole, she takes no nonsense from the boys. When one invites her for a date after work, she replies that he cannot afford it; moments later, the same cocky lad orders sodas for himself and another girl, boasting to Eve/ Marilyn, 'I said I had money!' She looks him over with cool scorn, tosses her long blond hair and with a baritone sassiness worthy of another Eve (the actress named Arden) cuts him down to size: 'Yeah, and now you blow it on two Cokes!' Her confident acerbity provides the only laugh in an otherwise turgid, verbose film that was soon forgotten. *Dangerous Years* (in which 'Marilyn Monroe' was the fourteenth name in the opening credits) was released in December 1947, four months before *Scudda-Hoo! Scudda-Hay!*

Neither picture helped her or the producers, and in August 1947 the studio did not renew Marilyn's contract. 'When I told her that Fox had not taken up the option,' recalled Harry Lipton, 'her immediate reaction was that the world had crashed around her. But typical of Marilyn, she shook her head, set her jaw and said, "Well, I guess it really doesn't matter – it's a case

* Perhaps thinking of her initials and her self-appointed sobriquet as the 'Mmmmm Girl', Marilyn wrongly stated (on Edward R. Murrow's television interview *Person to Person* in 1955) that her first lines in any film were 'Mmmmm' in *Scudda-Hoo! Scudda-Hay!*, 'but they were cut'.

of supply and demand."' However fervent her desire for success, she was a realist who recognized that she was part of an underbooked team of contract players. When the studio's fiscal revaluation called for the dismissal of a certain number of unprofitable employees, she was among them. Her last paycheck, $104.13 after deductions, was dated 31 August 1947.

Unemployment did not leave her idle, however. Since January, the studio had been sending some of its young actors over to the modest quarters of the Actors Laboratory (on Crescent Heights Boulevard, just south of Sunset), where playwrights, actors and directors from Broadway had a California showcase for their work. In January, Marilyn had seen at the Actors Lab a one-act play by Tennessee Williams called *Portrait of a Madonna*, in which Hume Cronyn directed his wife Jessica Tandy; much revised and expanded, the play opened in New York the following December as *A Streetcar Named Desire*.

Throughout 1947, Marilyn attended informal classes, read plays and studied scenes with an impressive group of experienced actors from New York. This contact was crucial not only for her exposure to the theatre and some of its most controversial and intelligent exponents: her time at the Actors Lab also introduced her to social and political issues that later determined several important choices in both her career and her personal life. 'It was as far from *Scudda-Hoo* as you could get,' she said later. 'It was my first taste of what real acting in real drama could be, and I was hooked.'

Most important, these months evoked new aspects of her maturing character that would constantly be threatened throughout her life. In Marilyn Monroe there was a deep conflict, for she was torn between the performer's desire for approval and acceptance and a craving for learning and serious artistic achievement. Ashamed of her aborted schooling, she was always attracted to educated men and women from whom she might learn about literature, the theatre, history and social issues. In addition, there was in her nature a deeply felt concern for the poor, the weak, the abandoned and disenfranchised – people with whom she always identified both in life and in stories. All these longings and concerns came together in 1947 through the actors she met at the Lab and the kind of drama they championed.

The Actors Lab was a spinoff of the Group Theater in New York. Under its founding directors Harold Clurman, Cheryl Crawford and Lee Strasberg, the Group – and its leading play-wright of social protest, Clifford Odets – offered plays championing the plight of the poor, plays with sharply left-wing messages against capitalism. Although after a decade the troupe formally disbanded in 1940, its members continued to be vital forces in the development of American theatre, and during the following decade several of the Group's actors (Morris Carnovsky and his wife Phoebe Brand, J. Edward Bromberg and Roman Bohnen) tutored students, led scene studies and presented plays for Los Angeles students and theatregoers.

It is impossible to overestimate the impact of Marilyn's exposure to these New York theatre people, to the plays studied and presented and to a company of professionals that was somewhat ragtag but dynamic and full of new ideas. Over ten months in 1947, under the tutelage of Phoebe Brand and her colleagues, Marilyn read and studied – however casually, incompletely and irregularly – at least portions of the following plays that had earlier been offered by the Group Theater in New York:

■ *1931*, by Claire and Paul Sifton, a play first produced that very year, which explored the problems of an unemployed labourer and his girlfriend who finally join Communist sympathizers in New York. Marilyn learned that the New York production had starred Carnovsky, Bromberg, Brand and Odets – a quartet she met one evening that June after a reading of the play.

■ *Night Over Taos* (1932) by Maxwell Anderson, about a revolt against land-grabbers. This play had, in addition to the same cast as *1931*, an actress named Paula Miller who was soon to marry the play's original director, Lee Strasberg. The Strasbergs would eventually become the two most influential people in her acting career.

■ *Men in White* (1933) by Sidney Kingsley, about an idealistic young doctor's struggle to come to terms with the world of conventional medicine; to the same cast as the previous two was added a young actor named Elia Kazan. Marilyn already knew of him because he had been at Fox when she arrived, directing *Gentleman's Agreement*. At the Actors Lab, he was spoken of in almost reverential terms, as a genius of the theatre and cinema, an accomplished actor, director and producer. Then thirty-eight, he had returned to New York and was co-founding a new school, the Actors Studio. Kazan and the Studio would also be significant in her personal and professional life.

■ *Awake and Sing!* (1935) by Odets, in which the identical cast played a Bronx family struggling to survive the Depression; at the finale, the hero becomes a left-wing agitator. Years later, she recalled that she wept at the play's 'crazy, destroyed family, and especially at the suicide of that kind old grandfather', who may well have made her think of her own family and of Tilford Hogan.

■ *Weep for the Virgins* (1935) by Nellise Child, in which Phoebe Brand and Paula Miller, under Cheryl Crawford's direction, played members of a San Diego family trying to escape the drab environment of a fish cannery during the Depression.

■ *The Case of Clyde Griffiths* (1936), by Erwin Piscator and Lena Goldschmidt, in which Brand, Carnovsky, Bohnen and Kazan reinterpreted Theodore's Dreiser's novel *An American Tragedy* in terms of the American class struggle.

135

■ *Golden Boy* (1937), in which the same players (again directed by Strasberg) presented Odets's drama of a man's choice between a career as a violinist or a prizefighter.

In her discussions of this play, Phoebe Brand suggested to the students that this career conflict was present in every serious actor, in every serious artist – indeed, in Odets himself, who was torn between the serious demands of writing for Broadway and the lucrative business of writing for Hollywood. 'She asked us to read his play *Clash By Night*, which had starred Tallulah Bankhead on Broadway,' Marilyn recalled. 'It was one of the few plays I thought I could do, because there was the part of a girl who reminded me of myself.'

As Marilyn attended classes, studied and asked questions, the same themes resurfaced (social discontent and the plight of the disenfranchised poor) and the same names recurred – Odets and the Strasbergs; Cheryl Crawford; and Elia Kazan. For the present, she came to know only Phoebe Brand and her husband Morris Carnovsky; at the Lab, Carnovsky was habitually late for rehearsals and tutorials while his wife constantly enjoined punctuality on their students.

For Marilyn, a child of the Depression, these plays and discussions had a force and relevance unlike the movies she had acted in, had seen produced at Fox or in movie theatres.

All I could think of was this far, far away place called New York, where actors and directors did very different things than stand around all day arguing about a closeup or a camera angle. I had never seen a play, and I don't think I knew how to read one very well. But Phoebe Brand and her company somehow made it all very real. It seemed so exciting to me, and I wanted to be part of that life. But I'd never even been out of California.*

---

* She had, of course, travelled outside California several times before.

To the staff at the Lab, Marilyn seemed shy and self-conscious. According to Phoebe Brand, 'she did all her assignments conscientiously' but made no great impression:

> I remember her for her beautiful long blond hair . . . I tried to get through to her and find out more about her, but I couldn't do it. She was extremely retiring. What I failed to see in her acting was her wit, her sense of humor. It was there all the time – this lovely comedic style, but I was blind to it.*

The Actors Lab was Marilyn's first introduction to acting as a disciplined and demanding enterprise requiring serious application. Her two roles at Fox had been throwaways, and as she knew from observing others in production, film actors had to remember only a line or two of dialogue at a time. While a day on a movie set could extend to ten or even twelve hours (and the work-week to six days in 1947), the actual working time was brief. Actors were late, lights had to be readjusted, cameras were temperamental, script rewrites were demanded: in such a collaborative medium, executives were delighted if a day's work produced four minutes of finished film. (The novelist F. Scott Fitzgerald, who had worked in Hollywood, once described movie-making as an enterprise in which very many people stand around for a very long time, doing absolutely nothing.)

Practitioners of stagecraft, on the other hand, read, memorized and broke down scenes for analysis, discussed them with the director and designer and, it seemed to Marilyn, generally immersed themselves in a much less lucrative and far more demanding profession. 'Movie stars were paid better, and of course the people at the Actors Lab made no secret of how much they resented that,' Marilyn said, adding that she felt a

---

* No records have survived of the class assignments or scene studies at the Actors Lab, and Marilyn never listed those few in which she appeared.

conflict very like that in Odets's *Golden Boy*: should she aim for art or for stardom?

Because she did not want to return to modelling (much less to any other job), Marilyn would not have been able to attend classes at the Actors Lab – even to feed, clothe and house herself after she was dropped from the Fox roster – had it not been for a chance encounter with a generous couple in early August.

This occurred at an annual celebrity golf tournament at the Cheviot Hills Country Club, just across the boulevard from Fox. For the event, pretty young contract players were invited to carry actors' clubs and bags, making themselves agreeable to the likes of Henry Fonda, James Stewart, John Wayne and Tyrone Power. Two weeks before her contract expired that summer, Marilyn was one of the caddies sent over with the studio's compliments.

She was assigned to John Carroll, a handsome, six-foot-four, forty-two-year-old film actor whose virile good looks were often compared to those of Clark Gable or George Brent. Carroll, a wealthy man who had made wise investments, was married to Lucille Ryman, director of the Talent Department at Metro-Goldwyn-Mayer. Her responsibilities included finding new men and women with star potential (she had signed up Lana Turner, June Allyson and Janet Leigh), then obtaining good scripts for them and supervising their drama, dance, fencing and diction classes at the studio. The Carrolls were also known and admired for helping (with both counsel and cash) several young, impecunious apprentices who showed some promise of movie talent.

Years later, Lucille clearly recalled that Marilyn wore a tight sweater and white flared shorts to the tournament – but that she was unable to manage Carroll's heavy golf bag and simply carried a few clubs, occasionally striking attractive poses for the benefit of the attending press. Along with Marilyn's obvious allure and her evident awareness of it, Lucille Ryman saw a certain childlike simplicity, 'the look of a lost waif'. Her sexiness, her delight in herself and her ability to attract attention were somehow neither offensive nor impertinent. 'She was such a cute little number,' according to Lucille. 'I remember thinking, "Oh, this poor little child, this stray kitten."'

At the end of the day, everyone gathered for drinks round the club bar, and finally Marilyn – the object of considerable male attention – quietly announced to the Carrolls that she had no transport home, and that she had not eaten since the previous day. Lucille had to attend a play downtown that evening with a studio colleague, so she suggested that John and Marilyn should go out for supper before he drove her home.

Which they did, according to Lucille. Later, John told his wife the dialogue that accompanied his delivery of Marilyn to her apartment. This was not at Nebraska Avenue, but at a seedy place in Hollywood to which she had moved in June. She invited him to come in, but he replied that he was tired after the long day and eager to return home.

'But how can I thank you if you don't come in?' Marilyn asked. John understood the offer but declined it.

'She made a play for him very quickly,' according to Lucille, 'but there was one very important quality about John she didn't take into account: he did not like such overt behavior.'

Lucille did not think Marilyn was right for MGM: 'She was cute and sexy, but she didn't have the leading lady quality that Mr Mayer was signing up in 1947.' Nevertheless, the Carrolls invited her to dinner in early September. Marilyn told them how serious she was about her career and how much she loved the Actors Laboratory; she added that she was an orphan with no money, and that she had to leave Nebraska Avenue when her Aunt Ana went into a hospital and new tenants took over the house.

Marilyn then added quite calmly that she put all her money into classes, rent and auto maintenance, and that she got food by offering herself for quick sex with men in cars on side streets near Hollywood or Santa Monica Boulevard. 'She really did this for her meals,' according to Lucille. 'It wasn't for cash. She told us without pride or shame that she made a deal – she did what she did, and her customer then bought her breakfast or lunch.' This period of her life she also discussed a few years later with her acting teacher Lee Strasberg: 'Marilyn was a call girl . . . and her call-girl background worked against her.'

Before the Carrolls could comment, Marilyn told them that she was terrified of returning to her little apartment. Attempting to cash her last Fox paycheck, she had asked a Hollywood policeman if a local bank might help, although she had no account there. He asked her name and telephone number and cashed it for her; money in hand, she thanked the policeman and left. That night, the same man broke into her apartment and tried to attack her; he fled by a rear door only when Marilyn shrieked so loudly a neighbour came to the front. 'I don't know,' Marilyn concluded. 'I have to have a place to sleep. And I have to eat and have a car and pay my way at class. I suppose I'll have to go on working the Boulevard.' She paused again. 'I've decided to change my name. To Journey Evers.'

The Carrolls were authentic Good Samaritans, and at once they took action. They lived most of the time at their Granada Hills horse-breeding ranch in the San Fernando Valley, but they also had a top-floor apartment in town at the El Palacio, an elegant Spanish structure at the north-east corner of La Cienega Boulevard and Fountain Avenue. So that Marilyn could continue to attend classes and be available for auditions when Harry Lipton called – without having to 'work the Boulevard' – the Carrolls invited her to live rent-free in the apartment's second suite. As Lucille recalled, 'She said she was raped at nine and had sex every day at the age of eleven, all of which she later admitted was untrue. It was a way of getting us to take her in, to keep her off the streets of Hollywood, and it worked.' Marilyn Monroe was a vulnerable soul, to be sure; but she was also shrewd enough to know which tales evoked a sympathetic reaction from this or that person.

According to their records, the Carrolls gave her cash all that September (eighty dollars on 2 September; fifty on the fifteenth; another eighty on the twenty-sixth and seventy-five on the twenty-seventh). That autumn, they asked their representative,

Albert Blum, to draw up a letter of agreement. They would pay to 'Journey Evers, also known as Norma Jeane Dougherty' the regular sum of $100 weekly, 'for personal management'. Should she find employment through Blum or the Carrolls, she could repay the money and ten per cent would be duly paid to her agent Harry Lipton. Gladys's daughter had never known such generous support.

Things happened quickly that September. On the twenty-first, Lucille noticed a casting call for a student performance of the 1940 comedy *Glamour Preferred*, to be presented at the Bliss-Hayden Miniature Theater (later the site of the Beverly Hills Playhouse) on Robertson Boulevard. She immediately telephoned Lila Bliss and her husband Harry Hayden, who welcomed Lucille's protégés to classes and allowed them to perform onstage without charge because Lucille occasionally brought one of the students over to MGM. The Haydens met Marilyn and days later cast her (with considerable aptness, remembering her invitation to John Carroll) in the supporting role of a Hollywood starlet whose seduction of a glamourous leading man is foiled by the man's sensible and superior wife.

The month's run of this amateur production was scheduled to begin on 12 October, but rehearsals were stymied by Marilyn's chronic lateness and her apparent inability to memorize lines. As Lucille learned after a long discussion with her, both problems arose from the girl's fear of dressing ineptly (she changed clothes several times before leaving the apartment), from a dread of looking unacceptable (she retouched her makeup for hours) and from her terror of failure. In fact she knew the dialogue perfectly, but she stuttered and paused so much that she threw the other student players into total confusion. Marilyn finally managed to stumble her way through two performances which were mercifully unreviewed by the Los Angeles press.* A few

* Several students routinely undertook the same role, each of them appearing in repertory so that different performances could be later compared in class discussions. Other film actors who occasionally appeared at Bliss-Hayden were Veronica Lake, Jon Hall, Doris Day, Craig Stevens and Debbie Reynolds.

years later, she said that it was a terrible play in any case, and that she only took the role from a sense of obligation to the Carrolls. Her statement did not justify her unpunctuality, but her critical assessment was on the mark: *Glamour Preferred* had sunk from sight after an original Broadway run of eleven performances; it was (but for Bliss and Hayden) vanished into oblivion.*

As the autumn passed, the Carrolls found themselves indulgent surrogate parents to Marilyn, who was now begging to spend weekends with them at their ranch so she would not be alone. Lucille and John valued some privacy, however, and they had many tasks as their ranch expanded. One evening Lucille arrived at the apartment to find Marilyn hovering over an array of twenty-five brassieres, on which she had spent an entire week's allowance. Into each bra Marilyn was packing a wad of tissue, so that her breasts would seem to protrude more perkily. 'I sat her down,' Lucille remembered, 'and told her this was all very silly.' Marilyn's reply was simple: 'But this is all anyone ever looks at! When I walk down Hollywood Boulevard, everyone will notice me now!'

In November, the Carrolls received a telephone call at the ranch one Friday evening. Marilyn said in a nervous whisper that a teenage Peeping Tom had climbed a ladder and was looking through her bedroom window. The Carrolls knew that no ladder would reach to the third floor, that this was simply Marilyn's ploy to avoid loneliness and to join them at the ranch. But her recent mention of walking down Hollywood Boulevard alarmed them as much as the fantasy about a Peeping Tom, and Lucille feared that their little stray kitten might become a permanent alleycat; that never having known the secure love of a father at home, Marilyn might seek endlessly for affirmation

---

* After its 1940 premiere, one New York critic wrote that 'joke after tired joke is laboriously lifted from its sarcophagus and spun out of its winding sheet until the stage is crowded with verbal mummies' (*New York Post*, 16 Nov. 1940).

from men who wanted nothing more than a few moments with her body. At twenty-one she was still drifting, even as she longed for professional and personal stability, and so by December Lucille was welcoming Marilyn every weekend at Granada Hills.

At the same time, Marilyn sought constantly to have the Carrolls' devotion reaffirmed, to be reassured they would not abandon her, for they were indeed surrogate parents. But her conduct was not always appropriate. Around the Carroll home she dressed scantily, slept nude with her door open, and generally scandalized John Carroll's mother, who was also visiting. By early 1948, as Lucille Ryman Carroll summarized the situation years later,

> Marilyn had become a problem for us. She called me at my office, and John at the studio, as often as four times a day, even though we repeatedly asked her not to. We were in a trap we had unwittingly stepped into. Finally, we had no control over her: she controlled us.

Part of the control was exercised in her blunt disregard for schedules (her own and others') and her occasional affectation of a mysterious and elusive attitude. After waiting hours for her to arrive at the ranch on several Friday evenings, the Carrolls received a call: 'This weekend I'm going to be with some people,' she said vaguely. There was no need for mystery: 'Being with some people,' according to Lucille, 'meant she was going to be with a photographer for two or three days. The following Monday we found her room littered with photos of herself she studied day and night.'

But then Marilyn got the strange idea that her life with the Carrolls was about to alter dramatically. 'Somehow,' according to Lucille,

> because John rather than I had invited her out to the ranch one weekend, she thought this was going to be the beginning

143

of an affair with him. She came to me and said, 'Lucille, I want to ask if you'll give John a divorce. I don't think you love him – if you did you wouldn't work so hard at your job, and you'd be with him every night instead of going out to shows and screenings. And I think he loves me. He didn't say he does, but he's so patient and he helps me so much. He couldn't do that if he didn't love me.'

Lucille's answer was delivered calmly: if John wanted a divorce he had only to ask for it. When Marilyn went back to John, he explained that his feelings were strictly those of a mentor, that all he wanted was to assist her career and to help her materially. 'And the amazing thing,' according to Lucille, 'is that Marilyn didn't seem bothered by this at all. She wasn't heart-broken, as if a great love were being denied her.' In fact, she may well have been relieved. With such a background as Marilyn had, she was ill equipped to read ordinary social signals, and many of them were subjected to a reading through the lens of her need for masculine acceptance and affirmation.

After five months of caring night and day for Marilyn, it was clear to the Carrolls that, as Lucille said, 'we were in too deep and had to get out'. The social life in which they often included her was soon to provide help in that direction. At a party in February 1948, John introduced Marilyn to a businessman named Pat De Cicco, who was successful with a product called Bon Bons, candy-sized ice cream confections marketed chiefly at movie theatres. De Cicco had become a friend of Fox's executive producer Joseph Schenck, whom Marilyn had met briefly on the studio lot.

Schenck's Spanish-Italian Renaissance mansion at 141 South Carolwood Drive was the setting for legendary Saturday night poker games, to which he and his friends invited attractive young women to keep the highball glasses full and the ashtrays empty. De Cicco asked Marilyn to join him the following Saturday. And so it happened that the former Fox starlet was reintroduced to the present Fox mogul. 'I was invited as an ornament,' Marilyn said, 'just someone to brighten the party.' She did – especially for Schenck, who (as Lucille Ryman Carroll knew within days) 'went for Marilyn like a million dollars'.

Schenck, then sixty-nine, had a long and influential career. He and his brother Nicholas, childhood Russian émigrés to New York, had owned some drugstores and operated amusement parks before their association with Marcus Loew, executive of a theatre chain that became the parent company of MGM. Nicholas remained with Loew, but in 1917 Joe became an independent producer, successful with, among others, the films of his wife Norma Talmadge; his brother-in-law Buster Keaton; and the comic Roscoe ('Fatty') Arbuckle. By 1948, Joe Schenck had been at various times board chairman of United Artists, president of Twentieth Century Pictures and then board chairman of Twentieth Century-Fox where he was still a major power. Bald, with large features and penetrating grey eyes, his severe mouth belied a keen sense of humour and good business sense, both of which were epitomized by advice he gave a friend: 'If four or five guys tell you that you're drunk, even though you know you haven't had a thing to drink, the least you can do is to lie down a little while.' Accustomed to deferential treatment, he could be crude and demanding or gentle and helpful, depending on what opinion he thought someone had of him.

Marilyn was not the only young woman present that Saturday evening; there were other models, starlets and pretty young things hoping for an entrée to a movie career or advancement in it. Besides distributing drinks and cigars, some were willing (not to say expected) to provide more intimate services for one or another of the card players during a break in the game. That evening, Marilyn remained close to De Cicco and tried gracefully to ignore the host's suggestive glances.

Next day, a limousine was despatched to bring Marilyn to a private dinner with Joe Schenck – an invitation she knew it would have been folly to refuse. 'What do I do after dinner when he gets around to what he really wants?' she asked Lucille, who suggested the reply she often gave her MGM starlets: 'Tell him you're a virgin, saving yourself for the right man.' Late that night, Lucille was awakened by an agitated Marilyn, whispering into a private phone from Schenck's home: 'He knows I've been married! *Now* what do I tell him?' The evening ended, perhaps predictably, with Marilyn's submission.

Later, she told Lucille and a few other confidantes that this was the first of many times she had to kneel before an executive, a position not assumed in prayerful supplication. She wanted desperately to work, to succeed as a movie star, and she accepted the fact that sometimes employment conditions are negotiated privately, not in an agent's office. 'Marilyn spoke quite openly of her affair with Schenck,' recalled Amy Greene, later a close friend. 'He helped her career and she provided what she was asked to provide.'

Inveterate womanizer though he was – and Marilyn was only one of many conquests – Joe Schenck did not toss her aside, and in fact she grew quite fond of him. Although he had an agreement with Zanuck not to press for girlfriends to be given preferential treatment, Schenck called his poker buddy Harry Cohn, head of Columbia Studios. In late February, Marilyn arrived at Cohn's office at the corner of Sunset and Gower. One of the most feared and disliked men in the history of Hollywood, Cohn had been responsible for moulding the career of a dancer named Margarita Cansino, who became Rita Hayworth. He was willing to offer Marilyn a six-month contract at $125 a week beginning on 9 March. There was, however, one condition – and not the one she at first expected.

The following week, her hairline was permanently heightened by electrolysis and, after several applications of hydrogen peroxide and ammonia, the basic brown of Marilyn's cheaply dyed blond hair was entirely stripped away. The mirror showed her a woman more and more like the favoured star of her childhood, Jean Harlow. 'So gentlemen prefer blondes, do they?' Harlow asked rhetorically, gazing in a hand mirror in the 1932 film *Red Headed Woman* – and then she turned to the camera, smiled and replied, 'Yes, they do!'

Harry Cohn was no gentlemen, but he preferred Marilyn blond. Having approved her new look, he despatched her to three studio offices. After Max Arnow in the Talent Department had compiled a page of statistics on this latest contract player and the men in publicity had arranged for some trial photographs, Marilyn arrived at the cosy cottage of Columbia's drama coach, a formidable lady named Natasha Lytess who had interests far more serious than dying hair.

Chapter Eight

'She was like an explosion always happening or about to happen – the most volatile woman I've ever known,' said the journalist Jane Wilkie about Natasha Lytess, Marilyn Monroe's drama coach for six years.

In 1948, Natasha was about thirty-five, tall and thin, with grey-streaked, short-cropped brown hair; angular and hyperkinetic, she sometimes resembled a frantic stork on the lookout for trouble. Born in Berlin (not Russia, as she claimed to avoid anti-German sentiment when she emigrated), Natasha had studied with the great director Max Reinhardt, acted in repertory theatre and married the novelist Bruno Frank. With the rise of the Nazis, the couple moved to Paris and thence to America, where they joined a throng of refugee artists, many of whom settled in Los Angeles.* During World War II, Natasha had small roles in two Hollywood films, worked with Samuel Goldwyn's contract players as a drama coach and then accepted the offer of a similar position at Columbia Studios. Her husband returned to Germany in 1947, leaving her to raise their infant daughter alone.

* Among the most notable: architect Walter Gropius; designer Marcel Breuer; philosophers Hannah Arendt, Paul Tillich, Herbert Marcuse and Claude Lévi-Strauss; conductors Otto Klemperer, Fritz Reiner, George Szell, Erich Leinsdorf and Bruno Walter; composers Arnold Schœnberg, Erich Wolfgang Korngold, Kurt Weill and Paul Hindemith; writers Bertolt Brecht and the Mann brothers (Thomas and Heinrich); scientists Albert Einstein, Hans Bethe and Edward Teller; film-makers Billy Wilder, Fred Zinnemann, Fritz Lang and Detlef Sierck (later Douglas Sirk).

Autocratic and severe, Natasha impressed executives and actors alike, often intimidating them with her linguistic fluency, her knowledge of the arts and literature and her stern correction of young actors she considered inferior to those she had known abroad. However accurate her assessment of their limitations, her condescending tone with players could hardly be justified: her general demeanour suggested that she might have been an exotic baroness, exiled in Hollywood.

Natasha's personality was perhaps best typified by handwritten letters to friends and students, in which her sentences were littered with words underlined and exclamation points scattered like comic-strip punctuation. Everything was a matter of the gravest significance, and in private sessions with actors just as in meetings with producers and directors, she brooked neither argument nor opposition. On the studio lot her name evoked respect but not warm sentiments, and her austere, spinsterish manner was abrasive to men and women alike. Only the grudging admiration of Harry Cohn and the insistence of a few immigrant directors kept her on the payroll; had the contract players voted, she might have been back at MGM, begging for uncredited roles as a foreigner of indeterminate origin.

But her manner only veiled a searing disappointment. Natasha had aspired to a great stage career, but in Los Angeles there had been only film work (and not much of that) and her accent and somewhat forbidding appearance limited the available roles. In her subsequent position as drama coach she had to abandon hopes for herself and work for the success of younger, more attractive and less talented actors. From the first day, there were danger signals in her relationship with Marilyn.

In unpublished interviews and memoirs of her years as Marilyn's teacher and occasional housemate, Natasha spoke with barely concealed bitterness – and not only because of the tangled and unhappy finale of their relationship. From their introduction, she resented Marilyn's beauty and appeal even while she admired and tried to refine it. This conflict was attended by the most poignant development, for very soon the teacher was desperately in love with her student – a nearly fatal passion for Natasha, but a neat convenience for Marilyn, who knew instinctively how to turn another's devotion to her own best advantage while ignoring or deflecting whatever sexual advances she disfavoured.

At their first meeting (10 March 1948), Marilyn was captivated by Natasha's experience and erudition, recognizing a woman from whom she could learn a very great deal. She told Natasha about her time at the Actors Lab, and Natasha responded with a little lecture on the Moscow Art Theatre, on the great actor and theoretician Konstantin Stanislavsky, and on Anton Chekhov's influence on modern drama. 'Not very much of what she said that day stayed with me,' according to Marilyn.

She was like a waterfall, pouring out impressions and images. I just sat there watching her expressive hands and flashing eyes, and listening to her confident voice speak about the Russian soul. She told me what she'd been through and made clear how much she knew. But she gave me the impression I was something special, too.

For her part, Natasha was not so impressed:

Marilyn was inhibited and cramped, and she could not say a word freely. Her habit of barely moving her lips when she spoke was unnatural. The keyboard of the human voice is the gamut of emotion, and each emotion has its corresponding shade of tone. All this I tried to teach Marilyn. But she knew her sex appeal was infallible, that it was the one thing on which she could depend.

'There were days,' Marilyn said later, 'when I couldn't figure out why she kept me on as a student, because she made me feel so shallow and without talent. Very often it seemed that to her I was one of the hundred neediest cases.'

By pointing out only Marilyn's deficiencies Natasha paradoxically contributed to Marilyn's conviction that her body, her sexual allure and prowess were her chief (indeed, her only) resources. Moreover, between teacher and student there was a wide cultural gap, one that Natasha exploited in order to exert a kind of psychological control over Marilyn – a subtle mechanism not at all uncommon in the disappointed lover. Thus the dynamics of a complicated Pygmalion-Galatea relationship were at once set in place.

'I took her in my arms one day,' Natasha said, 'and I told her, "I want to love you." I remember she looked at me and said, "You don't have to love me, Natasha – just as long as you work with me."' Both women were being honest, but only one would feel the agony of a hopeless passion. Natasha's pain could have sprung straight from the pages of a Russian novel, for her love had a tragic quality should could neither satisfy nor sever. 'She was in love with me and she wanted me to love her,' was all Marilyn later said on the matter.

Not long before her death, Natasha spoke more freely:

I wish I had one-tenth of Marilyn's cleverness. The truth is, my life and my feelings were very much in her hands. I was the older [woman], the teacher, but she knew the depth of my attachment to her, and she exploited those feelings as only a beautiful younger person can. She said she was the needy one. Alas, it was the reverse. My life with her was a constant denial of myself.

Natasha was correct. Dependent on Natasha though she appeared to be, Marilyn had an independence and a strength as well, an ingrained ambition that overcame countless disappointments, lonelinesses and setbacks. The sad truth is that Natasha Lytess was more profoundly dependent on Marilyn and Marilyn's need of her, and therein may lie the reason why she endured six years of emotional crisis. Even as she was doomed to frustration, Natasha loved so deeply she could not bring herself to the action that would have freed her – separation from Marilyn.

As it happened, their first week of acting and voice lessons coincided with Ana Lower's death from heart disease on 14 March; she was sixty-eight and had been in miserable health for over two years. Four days later she was cremated, and her ashes were interred at the Westwood Memorial Park, near the home Ana and Norma Jeane had shared. According to James Dougherty, Marilyn was not present at the final tribute: she was so afraid to miss a class with Natasha that she said nothing about Ana's death. Only much later did she tell her mentor that Grace's aunt was 'the one human being who let me know what love is' – words that must have been agony for Natasha to hear.

The daily tutorials in breathing and diction had an immediate and not entirely felicitous effect on Marilyn's speech and her subsequent reading of lines before the camera. Because Natasha had a mania for clarity, she forced Marilyn to repeat every speech until each syllable fairly clicked and then to move her lips before speaking. She was especially fierce on the sharpness of final dentals, and so Marilyn had to recite over and over such sentences as 'I did not want to pet the dear, soft cat' until every 'd' and 't' was unnaturally stressed and each word distinct from those preceding and following.

Unfortunately, this exercise quickly ossified into a strained and affected manner of onscreen speech it would take years (and eventually a new coach) to overcome. The exaggerated diction, the lip movements before and during her lines, the overstated emphasis on each syllable – all the verbal tics and peculiarities for which Marilyn Monroe was often vilified by critics – came from the tutelage of Natasha Lytess. And although it would soon be evident that Natasha's method could work well for comic roles, her next drama coach would have to work double time to relax Marilyn's speech patterns for serious, more mature parts. In life, however, there was nothing of the breathless, slightly overwrought sensibility that characterized Marilyn's speech onscreen.

Like many forlorn and unrequited lovers, Natasha seized every opportunity to be near the object of her devotion, forming, training and influencing her beyond the exigencies of film acting technique. 'I began to feed her mind,' she said years later, adding that she introduced Marilyn to the works of poets and composers. According to Natasha, Marilyn was indeed no intellectual, but was rather 'a mental beachcomber, picking the minds of others and scooping up knowledge and opinions'. Natasha thus provided a cultural stimulation Marilyn had never known. Emotionally, however, the two women were ever at cross-purposes, locked in a collusion of half-met needs.

By late spring 1948, Marilyn was receiving a regular studio paycheck; still, the Carrolls continued their allowance to her so that she could have extra private sessions with Natasha. And by this time, as Lucille recalled, Marilyn had resigned her avocation as a boulevard hooker. On 9 June, Lucille arranged for Marilyn to live at the Studio Club, 1215 North Lodi Street in Hollywood, a two-minute walk from the Los Angeles Orphans Home. A Spanish-Moorish complex with an open courtyard and palm trees in profusion, the Club was a residential hotel for young women aspiring to careers in the arts, and the superintendents managed it like a college dormitory or a branch of the YWCA. There were strict curfews, and gentlemen could visit only in the open atrium-style public lounge. Lucille paid in advance the $300 rent for six months, and Marilyn moved into room number 334.*

With her salary and allowance, she treated herself to a new Ford convertible for which she arranged monthly payments; an expensive, cumbersome professional hair dryer; a lavish supply of cosmetics; books; a phonograph; and recordings of classical music. 'I felt like I was living on my own for the first time,' she

---

* The Studio Club was at various times the residence of many successful actresses, among them Evelyn Keyes, Linda Darnell, Donna Reed, Dorothy Malone and Kim Novak.

said later. 'The Studio Club had rules, but the women in charge were nice, and if you came home after they locked the doors at ten-thirty, a smile and apology would usually be enough to satisfy them.' The supervisors were, in other words, too smart to ask the right questions.

But Columbia had no such reticence in enquiring about fees spent on contract players who were paid but not working on pictures. Talent department chief Max Arnow was often the first to receive calls from the studio's accountants, and he received one in June relative to Marilyn Monroe. Within days, Arnow told Natasha there would be one less student on her roster by the end of the month, for they would not subsidize her private classes at the studio. 'Please don't do this,' Natasha pleaded. 'She's doing well. She loves the work, and I'm sure I can build her up for you.' That same day, Natasha rang Harry Romm, who was producing a B-picture called *Ladies of the Chorus*. Yes, Romm said, a major role was still uncast.

By early July, after an impressive audition at which she sang one of the film's songs, Marilyn was hired; the picture was made on the cheap in ten days. She had the role of Peggy Martin, a chorus girl whose mother (played by Adele Jergens) tries to dissuade her from marrying a handsome socialite – a union that can only end in disaster, mother insists, just as hers once did because of 'class differences'. In the tradition of Hollywood's democratic approach to everything including romantic musicals, the one-hour picture ends happily with the triumph of true love (if not of narrative honesty or social reality).

With her long, flowing and silky hair redyed a glistening blond and styled like Rita Hayworth's, Marilyn brightened a dull and cliché-ridden script. Although Natasha's supervision had rendered her speech too deliberate and her gestures so over-rehearsed they frequently seemed mechanical, Marilyn seemed to glow – especially in scenes with her leading man (Rand Brooks) whose character's nervousness merely encourages her to take charge of the situation. A raised eyebrow, a sudden drop in voice and there was a strong undertow of feminine wiles to her characterization. Especially in her two songs ('Anyone Can See I Love You' and 'Everybody Needs a Da-da-daddy'), Marilyn revealed she had more talent than the film required. For the first time, she sang in a film – and very well, too, with a mellow, slightly smoky quality, an intriguing fusion of girlish innocence and womanly enterprise.

Her fellow-players liked her, and there was talk around the lot that Marilyn was someone to watch at work. According to Milton Berle, who met her that year, there was no phony artifice about her, no airs or affectation. She wanted very much to be a star, he recalled, 'but first of all she wanted to be somebody to herself.' Adele Jergens agreed that Marilyn was fiercely earnest about *Ladies of the Chorus*, eager to make herself agreeable by arriving on the sound stage early with her lines word-perfect for every shooting call. 'She told me very tearfully she had lost her mother, and that, just like the chorus girl of the story, she knew what social ostracism was like. Marilyn was the sort of girl you instinctively wanted to protect, even though she obviously had brains and probably didn't need much protection.'

In this Jergens was quite correct, for during rehearsals for *Ladies of the Chorus*, Marilyn had met and speedily fallen in love with the studio's music arranger and vocal coach, Fred Karger. Ten years older, Karger at thirty-two was a handsome, blond-haired Lothario, placid and polite with colleagues but since his recent divorce bitter toward women. Some provided him with fawning comfort, however, and at that time he lived comfortably in a rambling house with his mother, his young daughter, his divorced sister and her children – an extended family to which Marilyn quickly became attached. To Natasha, Marilyn confided that 'the only security I hope for is to be married, and Freddy is the man of my dreams.'

On 9 September 1948, with *Ladies of the Chorus* completed, Marilyn's contract at Columbia expired and no renewal was offered – a repudiation Cohn and Arnow may well have regretted the following month, when she received a favourable notice in the trade publication *Motion Picture Herald*. 'One of the bright spots [in *Ladies of Chorus*] is Miss Monroe's singing,' wrote the critic Tibor Krekes. 'She is pretty and, with her pleasing voice and style, she shows promise' – hardly a rave, but nevertheless a gratifying first review. It did not, however, alter Cohn's decision. His major star was Rita Hayworth, just as Fox had Betty Grable and MGM had Lana Turner; none of them was listening to Harry Lipton or Lucille Ryman when they spoke of a potentially sensational new movie star named Marilyn Monroe with unusual qualities and the determination to have them recognized. 'Under Marilyn's baby-doll, kitten exterior, she [was] tough and shrewd and calculating,' was Lucille's assessment. But this was not enough to get her career moving at a more rapid rate. No one saw her comic potential, no one assessed her instinctive flair – perhaps partly because of the cliché about attractive young blondes.

There was, then, a second hiatus in her career without prospects of advancement. According to Lucille, this encouraged Marilyn in an ingenious but eventually futile scheme to quit the Studio Club for ever and to move in with the Kargers, the better to abet her prospects of marriage – not to replace employment, but in fact to work for it within the sunnier atmosphere of a loving family. Therefore when Fred drove her home after their first date, she directed him not to the Studio Club but to a grimy, flea-infested Hollywood tenement (recently abandoned by another Columbia starlet); this, she said gloomily, was all she could afford. Briefly, the plot worked, and for three weeks she lived with the Kargers on Harper Avenue, south of Sunset Boulevard.

This deception, like those she tried with the Carrolls, was another little scenario, the invention of a shrewd young woman who was quickly learning when to adopt a dramatic pose: if it were lacking at key moments, Marilyn would provide it from the present or contrive it from the past. But there is also something slightly pathetic about such conduct, and touchingly childlike about her longing to be part of a family. Yet Fred's mother and sister liked her enormously, and this affection she exploited, attaching herself again to a surrogate family and helping with chores to prove she would be a good wife for Fred and stepmother to his daughter.

But after three days the Studio Club rang up Columbia's talent department to ask her whereabouts, and the next afternoon Fred delivered her back to the Club. 'He said that because I lied about this, he couldn't trust me with anything,' Marilyn said later. 'He didn't think I would be a good example to the children in his family. It made me feel pretty rotten.' Given Marilyn's psychological needs and Karger's refusal to meet them, both of them seem to have overreacted. The event did not prevent their romance from lasting until the end of 1948, but Karger thenceforth insisted that marriage to Marilyn was not in his plans.* 'This made her miserable,' according to Natasha. 'Many times after she had been with him there were tears in her eyes.' Predictably (indeed, wisely), Natasha's advice was that Marilyn ought to end the liaison.

Whereas Karger's emotional distance kept the affair essentially physical and limited Marilyn's expectations, he did not at all restrain himself professionally in his efforts on her behalf. In addition to voice training, he advised her on wardrobe and etiquette, counsel she immediately followed. That winter, Fred also took her to the orthodontist Dr Walter Taylor and paid for the correction of an overbite and for her teeth to be bleached: they had looked fine for modelling photographs, but movie cameras were another matter. By the end of the year, after she had worn corrective braces and retainers, the contour of her upper jaw was more even and her smile brighter. For this improvement, Marilyn offered herself to Fred all the more importunately. He accepted her embraces but continued to reject any talk of matrimony.

For all the specific assistance, there remains the brutal paradox that the Monroe-Karger affair was characterized by an

---

* He later married Jane Wyman, whom he divorced, remarried and again divorced; at the time of his death in 1979 there was yet another Mrs Karger.

abusive quality that was sadly consistent with her history. She confided to Natasha at the time (and three years later to Elia Kazan) that Karger was constantly critical of her, that he derided her wardrobe and speech and said that her only real talent emerged when she was in bed. Precisely because Karger's low appraisal coincided with her own, she was drawn to him almost obsessively. Ever longing to reverse his estimation, to prove herself decent and worthy of love, she effectively debased herself, begged for endorsement and always made herself sexually available. And the more he acted the superior with a lightly veiled contempt, the more she tried to win him over. Father figure, lover and artistic mentor, Karger offered everything Marilyn thought she longed for. Remote and condescending, he was also the familiar man of her life history. In this regard (just as with Dougherty), she became a little girl eager to ingratiate herself, to please, to win the love of a protective older man. Likewise, Natasha – who so patiently longed for her – was the woman from whom Marilyn desired maternal support; in the cases of both Karger and Lytess, however, the relationships were doomed by almost immeasurable inequality of feeling. Marilyn loved Fred far more than he desired her, while Natasha desired Marilyn much more than she was loved in return.

Thanks to the Carrolls, Marilyn's unemployment that autumn of 1948 did not mean penury. They did, however, insist that she continue her lessons with Natasha (for which they paid) and that she audition for roles at the Bliss-Hayden Theater.

On her way to one tryout in October, a happy accident occurred. Never a particularly cautious or observant driver, she smashed into the rear of a car on Sunset Boulevard and immediately a crowd gathered. Neither she nor the other driver was injured, but Marilyn – wearing red spiked heels and a red and white polka-dot sundress two sizes too small – caused a minor sensation. Among the bystanders was a former Associated Press cameraman named Tom Kelley, then an independent photographer noted for superb work that often included Hollywood's most photogenic models. When Marilyn said she was late for an important meeting and had no money for a taxi, Kelley gave her five dollars and his business card. She thanked him, called Harry Lipton to deal with the accident and raced off to her appointment. The meeting with Kelley augured more favourably than the audition, which did not have a happy outcome.

Nor did her affair with Fred Karger, which by Christmas was seriously foundering. 'Marilyn was beginning to see how she was hurting herself with him,' Natasha said a few years later. 'She was in love with somebody who was treating her miserably, as a convenience. All the time, she was so nice to his family and to his daughter. Marilyn would have loved to marry him, even though he was impossible. She thought love would change him. I hoped she would somehow be distracted from this relationship.'

Natasha's wish was granted, but not as she expected. At a New Year's Eve party given by the producer Sam Spiegel, Marilyn was introduced to Johnny Hyde, executive vice-president of the William Morris Agency and one of Hollywood's most powerful representatives. Before the night was over, Hyde was besotted, and not with liquor. During the first week of January 1949, he prevailed on Marilyn to accompany him on a short vacation to Palm Springs, where he spoke of her career prospects and took her to bed. From that night, Johnny Hyde was desperately in love. But Marilyn was not, and when she next saw Natasha and told her the news, her teacher shrugged and muttered the old French idiom – *Un clou chasse l'autre*: One man goes and another takes his place.

Karger's successor could not have been more different. That season, Marilyn was twenty-two, Johnny Hyde fifty-three. Born Ivan Haidabura in Russia, he emigrated to America at the age of ten with his family, a troupe of acrobats. Never strong in childhood and often unwell as a young man with various cardiopulmonary ailments, Johnny became an agent in New York and proceeded to Hollywood in 1935, where he succeeded as an astute developer and manager of talent; among his many clients were Lana Turner, Betty Hutton, Bob Hope and Rita Hayworth. Barely five feet tall, with sharp features, thinning hair and a generally sickly appearance, he was nothing like a glamourous industry denizen. He was none the less very much respected and wielded considerable influence. Although a husband and father, Johnny was never deterred from a brief romance or a quick conquest – even by a serious heart condition for which, by his fifties, he was under weekly medical observation.

From the night he met Marilyn, Johnny Hyde became a victim of a fierce sexual obsession with this new, formidably young mistress. For her part, Marilyn loved Johnny as if he were her lost father. She learned from him, and especially since she was not progressing as Harry Lipton's client, she wanted to benefit from Johnny's representation – a shift easily accomplished when Hyde bought out her Lipton contract. Within weeks, Johnny was devoting virtually his entire professional and personal time to her.

Before spring turned to summer 1949, Johnny left his family. Determined to make Marilyn the second Mrs Hyde, he brought her from the Studio Club to live with him in a rented house at 718 North Palm Drive, Beverly Hills. To avoid press problems, however, she agreed to maintain a tiny one-room apartment at the modest Beverly Carlton Hotel, 9400 Olympic Boulevard, where she received mail and professional notices. According to Elia Kazan and Natasha Lytess, Marilyn insisted that she would not marry him although she continued to manifest her gratitude sexually. Her rejection of his proposal and concomitant offer of wealth only made him more persistent: 'I'm not going to live long, Marilyn,' he told her repeatedly. 'Marry me and you'll be a very rich woman.' This did not alter her decision, for according to her own code she would not wed someone with whom she was not in love. Also, in refusing Hyde's offer of marriage Marilyn was the more realistic partner, foreseeing the contumely that would otherwise have been directed at her: she would be called a gold-digger, not only romancing for her career but even marrying a man known to be gravely ill.

About the same time, according to one of Marilyn's later associates named Peter Leonardi, Hyde urged her to have a Fallopian tubal ligation. 'Johnny Hyde knew that in Hollywood the girls have to go to bed a lot,' said Leonardi. 'It was before the [availability of the contraceptive] pill, and he just didn't want her to be encumbered with children.' Marilyn at first agreed to be sterilized but then decided against it. 'She never had it done,' according to Dr Leon Krohn, her gynaecologist. 'And the rumors of her multiple abortions are ridiculous. She never had even one. Later there were two miscarriages and an ectopic pregnancy requiring emergency termination [of a pregnancy], but no abortion.'

At twenty-two, Marilyn was eager for both professional success and a decent, honourable life. 'He was willing to act as my agent even though the only coat I had was a beat-up polo coat,' she said, 'and I went to interviews without stockings before it was fashionable, because I couldn't afford any . . . [Johnny] inspired me to read good books, to enjoy good music, and he started me talking again. I'd figured early in life that if I didn't talk I couldn't be blamed for anything.'

Seasoned in the established ways of Hollywood's bartering, she sought recognition and approbation through and from those she could attract. In the case of Johnny Hyde, Marilyn felt singularly essential to someone's happiness – perhaps more than ever before – because of his physical frailty. To this her finest instincts responded, and she submitted to his sexual demands, although without any pleasure or satisfaction of her own: 'I knew nobody could help me like Johnny Hyde,' she confided to Natasha. 'But I felt sorry for him, too, and he was crazy about me. I never lied to him, and I didn't think it was wrong to let him love me the way he did. The sex meant so much to him, but not much to me.' Such sentiments are not those of a callous predator.

Like many such entanglements, however, the affair was not

without a dark and dangerous undertow created by the lovers' differing perspectives and expectations. Marilyn was absolutely faithful to him for over a year, ignoring repeated invitations from both the influential Joe Schenck and from the more attractive Fred Karger, who apparently had jealous second thoughts. Despite her constancy, Johnny referred to Marilyn in her presence as a 'chump' – his word for a mindless woman of easy virtue – just as he referred to almost all women as 'tramps and pushovers'. Like Karger, Hyde could be openly abusive: once again, she was drawn to a man who berated her because his evaluation matched hers.

This complex of reactions was directly related to her work as model and actress. During her time as Norma Jeane with the Bolenders, Gladys, Grace McKee and Jim Dougherty, she was constantly required to rise to others' expectations to such an extent that her own desires and the natural emergence of her own personality, her conduct and appearance, were managed by others. Karger had paid for dental work because he disapproved of her overbite, and now Hyde went further. He arranged for a Beverly Hills surgeon named Michael Gurdin to remove a slight bump of cartilage from the tip of her nose and to insert a crescent-shaped silicone prosthesis into her jaw, beneath the lower gum, to give her face a softer line. These alterations account for the different appearances she presents in films after 1949. Eager to be acceptable, and to win the approval she so desired, smiling prettily for photographers, working towards movie stardom – these were logical strategems for one primed to please.

Capitalizing on Marilyn's natural sexiness, Johnny Hyde was quick to introduce his new girlfriend to the independent producer Lester Cowan, who was investing some of Mary Pickford's money in a Marx Brothers farce. With the opening credits 'Introducing Marilyn Monroe', *Love Happy* went before the cameras in February 1949 with a cameo role quickly devised for her – a simple addendum for the Marxes, whose films were grab-bags of wacky improvisation. Bug-eyed and leering, Groucho had the role of a private detective: answering a tap at his door, he admits Marilyn, who slinks into his office wearing a strapless, iridescent gown.

'What can I do for you?' asks Groucho, turning to the audience to add, 'What a ridiculous question.'

Placing a seductive hand on his shoulder, she purrs, 'Mr Grunion, I want you to help me.'

'What seems to be the trouble?' asks Groucho, with the trademark roll of his eyes and lift of his thick brows.

As Marilyn then strolls away from him off-camera, she replies, 'Some men are following me.'

'Really?' Groucho continues, eyeing her departing figure. 'I can't understand why!' End of less-than-a-minute cameo.

'It's amazing,' was Groucho's comment to the press after filming. 'She's Mae West, Theda Bara and Bo Peep all rolled into one!' For a single afternoon of work, Marilyn was paid $500, plus an additional $300 for promotional photographs. More than half this sum was dispensed in gifts for the Karger women and a gold watch for Fred. She also sent a gift to the Carrolls, who soon after, aware of her connection with Johnny Hyde, rightly decided that they no longer had to throw good money after bad. Their subsidies ceased that spring of 1949, when Marilyn told them she had used their allowance to guarantee the repayments on her convertible.

Love Happy was Marilyn's fourth film, but in spite of two years of studio apprenticeship and a year's study with Natasha, her career was going nowhere and stardom seemed very remote – perhaps not even a realistic goal. No one but Johnny and Natasha, who were surrogate parents replacing the Carrolls, took much notice of her.

Whatever the mixed results of her dramatic exercises with Natasha, the teacher's cultural influence cannot be exaggerated, for in an important way Lytess – and Johnny, too – confirmed Marilyn in her love of Russian culture and literature, an interest first sparked at the Actors Lab. Natasha was more academic about it than Johnny, but after a few whiskies he, too, spoke of the great Russian writers and recited a few lines from Pushkin and Andreyev. That year, Marilyn began a long, painstaking trek through sections of Russian poetry. 'I began to see hope for her,' Natasha wrote of that year.

> She had no discipline, and she was lazy, but I pounded at her. When she came unprepared for a lesson, I was furious. I berated her as I would my own daughter. And always Marilyn would look at me as though I were betraying her.

The clash of wills and attitudes in Natasha – nurturing but severe, generous but tyrannical – was difficult for Marilyn to comprehend, for she was ever sensitive to criticism and needy of endorsement. And if she was aware of Natasha's quiet disapproval over her increasing reliance on Johnny, Marilyn gave no indication at the time. 'Natasha was jealous of anyone who was close to me' was her laconic comment a few years later; she did not elaborate.

Otherwise, the early months of 1949 were spent with Johnny (at his convenience) and with Natasha (at Marilyn's); there seem to have been no other people of consequence in her life, and no contact with those in her past. Natasha corrected her speech and gestures and Johnny broadened her political sensibility. His discussions of the Tsar's last days, the drama of the 1917 Revolution and his belief that there was a core of hope at the centre of Communism were Marilyn's first education in global politics: 'she was intrigued by it all,' according to Natasha, 'and she began to reflect his political attitudes,' which were not, it seems, much more than casual conversations that expressed both his innate love of Russia and his appreciation of democracy. What Marilyn most appreciated, however, was Johnny's defence of serfs and outcasts, the poor and the disenfranchised.

This liberalism struck a resonant chord in her own empathetic nature, perhaps partly because of her own background. The socially conscious plays to which she had been introduced at the

Actors Lab, the fiery culture represented by the melodramatic Natasha, the slightly boozy romanticism of Johnny Hyde – in love with Old Russia but aware of its need for reform – all these introductions to the Russian soul touched Marilyn deeply. Often, she told Natasha, she read a Tolstoy short story while playing a record of Tchaikovsky's 'Nutcracker Suite'. However incongruous the combination, no one could fault her longing for total immersion when she was drawn to learning.

In fact she was beginning to develop an entirely new attitude to herself and her life. Communication with those in her past, represented by Grace, was increasingly rare. There is, for example, no record of her reply to a note from Grace on 20 April, informing her that Gladys, during a temporary leave from a state hospital, had married a man named John Stewart Eley. Of this brief marriage nothing is known, nor would there be further personal communication between mother and daughter; Marilyn continued to send small sums to Gladys, however (which later increased with her own improved lot).

Although Marilyn was not to be deterred from her goal of movie stardom, there were no offers forthcoming after *Love Happy*. She insisted on paying her rent at the Beverly Carlton and, except for the cost of evenings out with Johnny, supported herself with the residue of her fee from *Love Happy*. Contracted to travel for a nationwide promotional tour for that film in July 1949, she was idle until then. And so, because she had some extraordinary expenses – books and car payments among them – she decided to look into her cache of photographers' business cards. There she found the address of Tom Kelley, the man who had come to her rescue the day of her Sunset Boulevard traffic accident.

Kelley's studio was at 736 North Seward, Hollywood; there, amid an array of cameras, lights, furniture, props, plastic trees and painted backdrops, he worked on assignments from advertising agencies. With the help of his wife Natalie and his brother Bill, Tom Kelley produced some of the most aesthetically pleasing camera art of that time, distinguished by imaginative lighting, dramatic angles and, within the limitations of commercial photography, innovative approaches to the presentation of humans with products.

In early May, Marilyn arrived unannounced at the studio with her portfolio, wearing exaggerated makeup, a revealing white blouse, red spiked heels and a tight red skirt that restricted her natural walk. She was not the all-American girl of the Conover or Jasgur photos but a model eager for work. Yes, Kelley said, there was a quick job available: another model had called in sick and he had a shoot scheduled for a beer advertisement. Natalie Kelley guided Marilyn to a dressing-room, adjusted her makeup and handed her a one-piece swimsuit and a colourful beach ball. 'I think I see something here,' Tom said when they emerged.

Within two weeks, the makers of Pabst beer had a new poster ready, and their advertising agency told Kelley she was the prettiest model he had ever used, whoever she was. To Natalie and Bill, Tom confided that he agreed, but he did not entirely understand how the results were achieved. With the right makeup, Marilyn was attractive enough in person. But when she posed, something flashed from her an instant before the shutter winked, and Marilyn on film radiated sex appeal.

On 25 May, Kelley contacted Marilyn through the message desk at the Beverly Carlton. The beer poster had caught the eye of a man named John Baumgarth, a Chicago calendar manufacturer, who asked Kelley if his new model would be willing to pose for an upcoming number. The idea was for a nude photo artfully rendered. Since she had already posed bare-breasted for Earl Moran and was quite casual about partial nudity both at home, on beaches and in photographers' studios, Marilyn accepted at once. Two nights later, on 27 May 1949, she returned to Kelley's studio and signed a release form as 'Mona Monroe'.

Kelley, thirty-seven and calmly serious about the assignment, put one of Marilyn's favourites on his portable record player: Artie Shaw's famous rendition of 'Begin the Beguine'. A red velvet drape was spread on the studio floor, and for two hours Marilyn posed nude, moving easily from one position to another as the photographer, perched ten feet above her on a ladder, clicked away. Obediently, she turned this way and that . . . arched her back . . . faced the camera . . . stretched in profile.

Among dozens of shots, only two clear portraits survived: 'A New Wrinkle' was the Baumgarth Company's designation for her naked profile against a casually rumpled drape and 'Golden Dreams' the title for a full-breasted pose of Marilyn with her legs discreetly angled for decency's sake. Baumgarth paid Kelley $500 for all future publication rights; of this Marilyn received $50 for the session. She never met Kelley again.

Three years later, the photographs became world-famous, and to deflect scandal Marilyn orchestrated a brilliant campaign to exploit conduct that Hollywood and the entire country would otherwise have found unacceptable from a celebrity. She was hungry at the time, she said – out of work, awaiting a movie assignment. Alternatively, she would claim that her car had been repossessed by the finance company, and how could she look for work in Los Angeles without a car? (This excuse was quickly dropped: overdue payments for an expensive new convertible would not go down well with the public.) In any case, the setting was private, the photographer's wife was present. Art photos were taken. What could be wrong? Nothing was, but some of the details, suggested later by her mentors, contradicted the facts.

Quite simply, Marilyn posed nude because it pleased her to do so. The shy girl who tended to stutter during first takes on a movie set remembered (or was creating) the dream of her childhood: she was naked and unashamed before her adorers. Proud of her body, she often paraded unclothed at home; indeed, a casual visitor to Palm Drive might glimpse her naked passing from bedroom to bath or swimming pool to cabana. 'I'm only comfortable when I'm naked,' she told reporter Earl Wilson. Yet in her nudity she was both innocent and calculating. Like her appearance in *Love Happy*, the calendar presented her as a body; this was all that seemed to matter to anyone.

Marilyn's antecedent was again her own exemplar Jean Harlow, of whom Edwin Bower Hesser had taken famous photographs in 1929 in Griffith Park, Los Angeles. Draped in diaphanous chiffon beneath which she was naked, Harlow was captured in nymphlike attitudes, just as she had posed in nothing but a fishnet for Ted Allan. The Hesser pictures so infuriated her first husband that he divorced her: this was the final insult, he charged, from a woman whose display of her body was as well known in life as in her films. 'Can you see through this dress?' Harlow asked in *Red Headed Woman*. 'I'm afraid you can, dear,' a woman replied. 'Then I'll wear it!' announced Harlow with a triumphant smile.

More than any other portraits of a nude woman in the history of photography, those of Marilyn Monroe taken in 1949 became virtual icons, everywhere recognizable, ever in demand. Landmarks in the union of art with commerce, the photographs have appeared on calendars, playing cards, keychains, pens, clothing, accessories, linens and household items; for decades, entrepreneurs have become wealthy by claiming or purchasing rights to their dissemination. 'Golden Dreams', for one example, provided the first issue of *Playboy* magazine with its centrefold in December 1953.

Because of Kelley's craftsmanship, there is nothing prurient about the photographs; rather, in her frank carnality, there was a kind of classic composure, the presentation of artless femininity. Nervous in person, Marilyn was immediately self-possessed when naked before the lenses and beneath the lights. And so the resulting voluptuousness is natural rather than indecent. Desirable, she seems invincible; childlike, she emanates adult repose; nubile, she portrays an innocence that appeals to both men and women. Nudity has rarely been so sublimely rendered photographically as in the results of the Kelley-Monroe session that May evening in 1949.

Chapter Nine

By contrast with her work for Tom Kelley in May, Marilyn Monroe was mostly overdressed during late June and early July 1949.

Lester Cowan was not only the producer of *Love Happy*, he was also an expert promoter who knew that movie premieres benefit from nothing so much as the presence of a shapely, sexy blonde. Thus Marilyn's contract required a personal appearance tour that summer on the film's behalf: she was the most attractive thing about the picture, although her appearance onscreen was minimal. Cowan provided Marilyn with a fee of $100 weekly for five weeks, plus publicity escorts in each city and cash for a new wardrobe. 'I bought the nicest things I could find in Hollywood's department stores,' she recalled. 'Nothing cheap or daring. Johnny and Natasha had told me I should travel like a lady, which I suppose they thought I wasn't. So I bought a couple of wool suits and sweaters, high-necked blouses and a jacket.'

Unaware that summers in Chicago and New York are ordinarily more uncomfortable than in Southern California, Marilyn found her outfits unseasonably warm when the city temperatures soared past ninety and the humidity over seventy. In Manhattan, she endured only four photo sessions and two brief personal appearances before dashing out to replace her woollen clothes with air-conditioned summer dresses – backless, sleeveless and mostly frontless. News cameras whirred and clicked constantly, and with typical piquant contrariness she offset the revealing dresses with elegant white gloves.

All through the tour, Marilyn was 'the observed of all observers', as Ophelia said of Hamlet, and as such she artfully combined her modelling and movie experience with what she had learned from Natasha and Johnny. 'Her shrewdness was evident in her knowledge of the correct thing to say at the right time,' Natasha said. 'Relating to people, she had an innate sense of what was proper.' Marilyn waved, smiled and tossed kisses through the air to crowds; she signed autographs as they entered theaters for advance screenings of *Love Happy*; she visited a crippled children's hospital ward.

The point of these appearances was simply to advertise the picture. Routinely, movie stars were presented like visiting royalty: they were movie queens and princesses but, it was implied, also just plain folks and always, *always* concerned for the little people. But with Marilyn there was an egregious difference: she lingered with sick and handicapped children longer than with the starstruck public or joggling reporters. In Oak Park, Illinois, and Newark, New Jersey, she made schedule-bound publicists frantic when she insisted on meeting every child in a state orphanage and even man and woman in a clinic for the disabled poor. There was no false compassion in the visits; in fact she discouraged photographers from documenting these detours.

In her hotel rooms at night, Marilyn pored through the dense chapters of novels by Marcel Proust and Thomas Wolfe, and sections of Freud on dreams. Then, after a few hours of reading, she ran up telephone charges during nightly conversations with Natasha, to whom she put endless questions to supplement her education. Most of all, she wanted to discuss the character of Grushenka (accent on the first syllable, Natasha insisted) in *The Brothers Karamazov*. Johnny Hyde had first compared her to Dostoevsky's lusty, complex character; perhaps not very seriously, he had even mentioned it as a suitable role for Marilyn in MGM's projected film, then being written by Julius and Philip Epstein. She took the remark with utter gravity and was soon almost obsessed by the girl's dissolute past and her open, generous heart. Alternately crafty and empathetic, Grushenka becomes, by loving Dmitri Karamazov, purer and less selfish, and at the end of the novel she is redeemed by her own sublime sacrifice. (It would be interesting to speculate on Johnny's identification of himself and Marilyn with the Dostoevsky characters.) 'It was the most touching thing I'd ever read or heard of,' she said later. 'I asked Natasha whether it would make a good movie. She said yes, but not for me – yet.'

Her calls to Johnny were not quite so literary: he humoured her when she spoke of the Russian classics, wanting most of all to know if she was faithful to him. He had no reason to worry. By coincidence, André de Dienes was in New York on assignment that summer. He located Marilyn at the Sherry-Netherland Hotel and whisked her away to the Long Island shore on Saturday morning. 'She had the presence and ease of an established star,' he recalled years later. 'She was radiant.' And so his photographs document her that summer day as she cavorted on the beach in a one-piece, white bathing suit, her long blond hair tangled and wet. Marilyn skipped, she danced, she jumped and waded in the waves, she sat on the sand and drew silly designs, she twirled a dotted parasol. She was Sabrina or Ondine, a water nymph bewitchingly sprung into life.

To the photographer's chagrin, she was also faithful to Johnny and rejected de Dienes's attempt that evening to reignite an old romance. Marilyn added that she had an important interview scheduled for the next morning, and she wanted to prepare carefully, for she knew the reporter would ask what she was reading and what were her nonprofessional interests.

But Marilyn's great expectations of the press were quickly demolished when she kept that appointment. On Sunday 24 July, Earl Wilson came to the Sherry-Netherland Hotel on assignment to meet 'The Mmmm Girl', as the publicity men now referred to her. Some people can't whistle, Marilyn said, 'so they just say "Mmmm".' Wilson, who found her 'a pretty dull interview', simply consulted the publicity kit for his column and filed an unimaginative report. Marilyn Monroe, he wrote, was an unknown twenty-one-year-old from Van Nuys (she was actually twenty-three), 'with a tiny waist, a 36½ bra line and long, pretty legs'. Such were Wilson's profoundest observations: she was treated as a woman 'who could make no claim to acting genius', as Wilson snidely noted in his column, ignoring that so far she had had little chance to demonstrate much of anything. When she spoke of serious matters and motives during the interview Wilson was indifferent, like studio moguls who saw only another sexy blonde and, unlike still photographers, took no time to see that the radiance was accompanied by a real flair for comedy.

Back in Hollywood by early August, Johnny took Marilyn to an audition at Fox, where after singing a few bars of a popular song and posing in a short skirt, she was hired (for one film only, without a continuing contract as before) to play a scene as a chorus girl in a musical western. In August she worked a few days on the uninspired trifle called *A Ticket to Tomahawk*, in which her single number – as one of four girls singing and dancing their way through 'Oh, What A Forward Young Man!' – reveals her exuberant abilities as a high-stepping dancer and an estimable singer. Because she had been reduced to virtual invisibility in *Scudda-Hoo! Scudda-Hay!*, this was effectively her first Technicolor appearance; she required, as makeup artist Allan Snyder recalled, less work than the others but was seen to greater effect – resplendent in her yellow outfit. But just as the film swung into production, Fox had a crashing failure on its hands with another colour, comic western – *The Beautiful Blonde from Bashful Bend*, with their principal blond leading lady Betty Grable. The timing of *A Ticket to Tomahawk* was therefore inauspicious, and neither casting nor production executives watched the picture or Monroe's appearance with much interest.

In fact news of the studio's indifference reached the cast

while they were filming, and everyone, Marilyn included, seems to have become bored with the project. One afternoon she arrived half an hour late for a simple exterior long shot, prompting the assistant director to complain, 'You know, you can be replaced.'

'You can be replaced, too,' Marilyn replied coolly, 'but they wouldn't have to [hire a replacement and] reshoot you.'

Then, in early September 1949, the pace of life quickened as Marilyn met two men who would be among the closest and most influential people in her life. That year, Rupert Allan was a thirty-six-year-old writer and editor for *Look* magazine whose responsibilities included arranging interviews and photoessays featuring stars actual and potential. Born in St Louis and educated in England, he was a tall, courtly gentleman, literate, witty, and much appreciated for his discretion and loyalty. Not long after he met Marilyn, Rupert changed professions, becoming one of the most respected personal publicists in Hollywood; his client list included Marlene Dietrich, Bette Davis, Gregory Peck, Deborah Kerr and Grace Kelly, for whom he eventually served as Consul General of Monaco when she became Princess Grace. In Hollywood's social circles, it was considered a great coup to be invited to dinner at the home of Rupert Allan and his mate Frank McCarthy, former aide to General Patton and later a movie producer (of the 1970 film bearing the general's name).

It was to the Allan-McCarthy residence on Seabright Place, high up a winding canyon in Beverly Hills, that (thanks to Johnny Hyde) Marilyn was invited one evening in early September to meet a team of New York photographers preparing a photoessay on Hollywood starlets. Among the cameramen was the second person Marilyn met that year who would alter the course of her life.

In 1949, Milton Greene (born Greenholtz) was quickly acquiring a reputation as one of the country's most talented fashion and celebrity photographers. 'They showed me a portfolio with the most beautiful pictures I'd ever seen. I asked, "Who took these?"' Introduced to Greene, Marilyn said, 'Why, you're nothing but a boy!' Replied Milton, unfazed, 'Well, you're nothing but a girl!'

Twenty-seven and divorced, he was a short, dark-haired and intense man who immediately impressed Marilyn with his knowledge of his craft. He spoke of 'painting with the camera', of colourful and fantastic ideas for celebrating women on film. Always fascinated by his profession and eager to know how he might benefit her, Marilyn attended Milton as if there were no one else present. 'I said I had a busy schedule, but I would pose for him all night.'

In a way, she did. Marilyn and Milton left the gathering and spent that evening and the next morning at what Milton referred to as his 'West Coast house'. This, as it happened, was a room at the Chateau Marmont Hotel on Sunset Boulevard, where a romance blossomed during the remaining brief time of Milton's Hollywood visit (which conveniently coincided with Johnny Hyde's week-long vacation alone, in Palm Springs). By 14 September 1949, Milton had returned to New York, without taking a single picture of Marilyn.* On that date he received a telegram at his Lexington Avenue studio, boldly addressed 'to Milton (Hot Shutter) Greene':

> Milton Greene, I love you dearly
> And not for your 'house' and hospitality merely.
> It's that I think you are superb –
> And that, my dear, is not just a blurb.
>   Love,
>   Marilyn.

Because both were firmly committed to pursuing their careers

---

* Greene's time would come later. Meanwhile, for *Life* magazine's issue of 10 October 1949, Philippe Halsman photographed seven starlets and an ex-model for a photoessay called 'Eight Girls Try Out Mixed Emotions'. Marilyn, incorrectly described as having appeared in only *Love Happy*, was captured 'seeing a monster . . . hearing a joke . . . embracing a lover . . . tasting a drink'. Only the laugh looks credible; only Marilyn had a subsequent career.

in cities three thousand miles apart, neither had any expectation of a reunion after this ten-day summer tryst.

A young, healthy, intelligent lover like Milton Greene, no matter how transient in her life, was a welcome diversion. Some of Marilyn Monroe's chroniclers, without evidence, have claimed there were many such lovers in 1949 and 1950; in fact, Milton Greene was the only dalliance during her relationship with Johnny. Marilyn was (as she told Rupert Allan) 'sad to see Milton return to New York'.

But there was little opportunity for romantic dejection. John Huston, who had just won Academy Awards writing and directing *The Treasure of the Sierra Madre*, was casting a new picture called *The Asphalt Jungle*, a low-key *film noir* about spiritually lost men and women, society's losers involved in an unsuccessful jewel theft. Still to be cast was the part of Angela Phinlay, young mistress to a middle-aged, crooked lawyer; by the end of October, MGM had signed Marilyn for it. This would be her fifth film assignment, and one that significantly altered her fortunes. W. R. Burnett, who wrote the novel on which Huston based his script, described Angela as 'voluptuously made; and there was something about her walk – something lazy, careless and insolently assured – that was impossible to ignore.'

Among the many canards commonly recited about Marilyn's career, few have had such strong but bogus currency as the means by which she won this role. Huston's autobiography summed up the fiction accepted everywhere: typically, he assigned to himself the credit for recognizing Marilyn's talent and casting her immediately after Johnny Hyde brought her to the studio for a brief audition. According to Huston, 'When she finished, Arthur [Hornblow, the producer] and I looked at each other and nodded. She was Angela to a "T".' But Marilyn got the part under quite different circumstances, as both the MGM archives and their talent director, Lucille Ryman Carroll, testified.

Hyde indeed brought Marilyn to Hornblow and Huston.

'But she was just awful,' Hornblow recalled. 'She had heard we were looking for someone very sexy, so she had dressed accordingly, over-emphasizing her figure at every point.' Convinced that only her body would land her the role, she seemed to Hornblow 'a nervous little girl half scared to death'. She read a few lines for Hornblow and Huston and departed with Johnny.

Huston had already decided on his choice for the role, a blond actress named Lola Albright. But Lucille told Huston that Albright (following her success with Kirk Douglas in a picture called *Champion*) was receiving $1500 a week; the role of Angela was a small one paying at most a fifth of that. Why not reconsider Marilyn? Huston was adamant and stalled, testing at least eight other starlets he knew MGM would reject. At the same time, Lucille agreed with Johnny that Marilyn could indeed play Angela 'to a "T"'.

At last Lucille forced the issue. Huston, a flamboyant horse-fancier, had a team of Irish stallions he boarded and trained at the Carroll ranch. Accomplished writer and film-maker though he was, Huston was also a playboy, an inveterate gambler and a notorious roustabout who rarely took his debts seriously. That year he was $18,000 in arrears for payments to the Carrolls. On a Sunday afternoon in September, they invited Huston out to the ranch, where Carroll said quite bluntly that if Huston did not allow Marilyn another test he would sell the stallions outright and collect the money due. The matter was quickly resolved in Marilyn's favour.

Next morning, Lucille telephoned the hair designer Sidney Guilaroff and alerted general manager Louis B. Mayer that an important test was scheduled for Wednesday afternoon. 'For the better part of the next three days and nights we rehearsed,' according to Natasha – and with good results, for Mayer was duly impressed with Marilyn's reading on the set and said so to Huston and Hornblow, who reluctantly accepted what was virtually a command decision. 'She impressed me more off the screen than on,' Huston said. 'There was something touching and appealing about her.' Not until Marilyn's leap to stardom a

Norma Jeane's grandmother, Della Hogan Monroe, 1926. From the collection of Eleanor Goddard.

Gladys Monroe Baker with baby Norma Jeane, aged two: Santa Monica Beach (1928).

Baby Norma Jeane Baker (centre) with her foster mother, Ida Bolender, Hawthorne, California, summer 1926. From the collection of Eleanor Goddard.

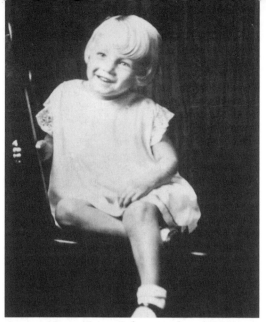

ABOVE *Norma Jeane Baker, age three (1929).*

BELOW *Norma Jeane Baker, age 15, with her classmates: ninth grade, Emerson Junior High School, Los Angeles, June 1941. From the collection of Gladys Phillips Wilson.*

Grace and Ervin Goddard on their wedding day, 1935. From the collection of Eleanor Goddard.

ABOVE LEFT *First appearance as a model, age 19 (1945). Photo by David Conover; copyright T.R. Fogli.*

ABOVE RIGHT *Norma Jeane Baker's wedding to James Dougherty, Los Angeles (May 1942). Photo by Axel Fogg.*

LEFT *Posing for a magazine ad (1946). Photo by André de Dienes.*

Posing for artist and photographer Earl Moran (1946). From the collection of Mickey Song.

With her drama coach Natasha Lytess (1949).

With agent Johnny Hyde, Palm Springs (1949). From the collection of Mickey Song.

As 'Miss Cheesecake of 1951.' with Edward G. Robinson. From the collection of Mickey Song.

In her first leading role, as the psychotic baby-sitter in Don't Bother to Knock (1952). From the archives of Twentieth Century-Fox.

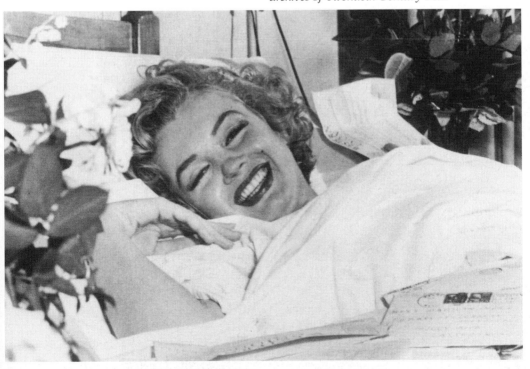

Recovering from her appendectomy (1952).

ABOVE *Preparing for the interior closeups in* River of No Return *(1952)*.

BELOW *As the nearsighted Pola in* How to Marry a Millionaire, *with David Wayne (1953)*.

OPPOSITE *With Betty Grable at a premiere (1953)*.

With Jane Russell at Grauman's Chinese Theater, after immortalizing their handprints in the famous forecourt (1953).

Wedding day, San Francisco (1954).

few years later did Huston express much enthusiasm for her talent as well, and then, typically, he took credit. Some of it, of course, belongs to the gifted cameraman Hal Rosson – who, Marilyn learned, had been briefly married to Jean Harlow.

During the filming of *The Asphalt Jungle* that autumn, Marilyn asked that Natasha be present on the set to coach her. 'It was the first evidence I'd seen of her courage,' Natasha said, 'for no director takes kindly to the idea of a drama teacher who might interfere with his work. But Huston agreed, and so for the first time I worked exclusively with Marilyn.' The results were impressive – not because of, but despite Natasha's presence. As Huston and Hornblow recalled, Marilyn glanced over toward her coach after each take: a nod or shake of Natasha's head indicated her approval or dissatisfaction. Had the role been larger, Huston surely would not have endured the intervention, for Natasha made Marilyn self-conscious and exacerbated her anxiety. (In the finished film, at the end of her first scene she may be glimpsed glancing toward her coach as she walks off-camera.) Yet despite her dependence on Natasha, Marilyn's performance in *The Asphalt Jungle* is remarkable and delineates an important moment of growth in her abilities.

The first of her three brief appearances occurs twenty-three minutes into the story, when, like a napping kitten on a sofa, she glances up to see her Sugar Daddy. Half-smiling, half-fearful, she asks softly, 'What's the big idea, standing there and staring at me, Uncle Lon?' As he embraces her before sending her off to bed with a goodnight kiss, there is a rueful look on her face, the weariness of a kept woman who has stayed with an older man only for the material benefits. In seventy-five seconds of screen time, Marilyn etched a character both pitiable and frightening.

In her second scene, she played Angela even more naïve and carnal. Wearing a black strapless gown, she is at one moment morose at the thought of being abandoned, then exuberant when she learns she may be sent on a luxurious cruise: 'Imagine me on this beach with my green bathing suit,' she says breathlessly to her lover. 'Yipes! I almost bought a white one, but it wasn't quite extreme enough. Don't get me wrong! If I'd gone in for the *extreme* extreme, I'd have bought a French one! Run for your life, girls, the fleet's in!' In a single take after one rehearsal, Marilyn assumed the right balance between gold-digging insistence and girlish high spirits.

Moments later, in her final scene, she has her greatest range in the picture. First angry at a policeman's intrusion, she is then a frightened child, caught in her lies to the police for the alibi she gave her crooked paramour. In two and a half minutes and after only two takes, Marilyn created Angela not as a cartoon-like simpleton but a voluptuary torn between fear, childlike loyalty, brassy self-interest and weary self-loathing.

In *The Asphalt Jungle*, she moved effectively from movie model to serious actress in a brief but crucial role. But perhaps because her character was seen for a total of only five minutes in the picture's two hours, the name 'Marilyn Monroe' appeared onscreen not at the opening but at the end of the picture, eleventh among fifteen. 'There's a beautiful blonde, name of Marilyn Monroe,' wrote Liza Wilson in *Photoplay*, almost alone among reviewers. 'She makes the most of her footage.' Otherwise, there was silence over a role Marilyn for ever after considered one of her best. 'I don't know what I did,' she told Natasha after completing her last scene, 'but I do know it felt wonderful.' Her coach, the sort of mentor who considered explicit praise dangerous for the student's ego, indicated only that Marilyn had performed competently.

The new year 1950 began with an unsettling mixture of anticipation, pride and disappointment.

Natasha now emphasized gestures. 'Body control, body control, body control!' she intoned liturgically, as if she were addressing herself and her own suppressed desires. Meantime, Johnny badgered production supervisors to employ Marilyn wherever possible. In January, she was rushed into a tedious little Mickey Rooney picture at Fox called *The Fireball*, in which she appeared for a few seconds as (of all things) a roller derby groupie.

The assignment was memorable only because she met a Fox studio hairdresser named Agnes Flanagan, a kindly, mothering soul who would many times in the years to come groom her hair. Marilyn often visited the Flanagans and their two children, intermittently attaching herself to them as a family member. As Agnes recalled just before her death in 1985, she had to be careful when telling Marilyn about a piece of clothing or something she admired, for usually the item would appear at her home next day. This prodigality continued right up to 1962, when Marilyn sent Agnes a duplicate of a garden swing she had admired. Such spontaneous acts of generosity were typical, even when Marilyn's finances were limited; throughout her life, in fact, she regarded money as something to spend on people she liked.

Roles in two more minor, forgettable pictures followed later that season, at MGM. In *Right Cross* she spoke less than twenty words and was again uncredited, flashing briefly across the screen as Dusky Le Doux, characterized in the script as 'a new model' with the same implication as she was termed a 'niece' in *The Asphalt Jungle*. At a cocktail lounge, she is approached by a stranger (played by Dick Powell) who invited her to his apartment for a home-cooked dinner and promises, 'If you're good, I'll tell you the recipe,' to which she replies sarcastically, 'I know the ingredients.'

Then, in early spring, Marilyn was pitchforked into an odd movie that quickly vanished before turning up in Australia years after her death. *Home Town Story* was an industrially-financed paean to postwar American corporate ingenuity. Marilyn appeared briefly as Iris, the receptionist in a newspaper office who has no patience with the unwelcome leering of her boss.

Despite Johnny Hyde's strong recommendation of her to MGM after these two cameos, production chief Dore Schary did not offer a deal for more work. His excuse was that the studio had Lana Turner under contract and therefore no need of

179

a rival blonde; to colleagues like Lucille Ryman Carroll, he expressed a quaint moral outrage at the Hyde–Monroe affair. By April, Marilyn could count nine movie roles in three years, none of them enough to bring her closer to stardom. *Ladies of the Chorus* was already a forgotten second feature, and *The Asphalt Jungle*, despite some critical acclaim, was too bleak to win much popular favour.

When not studying with Natasha, Marilyn posed for pinups in evening gowns or swimsuits, scoured the trade dailies and was seen on the movie colony's dinner-party circuit with Johnny, with whom life became increasingly difficult as his health became ever more fragile. Despite this, he refused to limit himself, escorting Marilyn to an endless round of social and corporate events, presenting her proudly as valuable and available talent. More poignantly, Johnny also wanted Marilyn known around town as his fiancée, the desirable young woman he still hoped to marry.

Fearful of displeasing or alienating her, Johnny acted the nervous, besotted lover, taking action perilous in his condition: with the ardour of a twenty-year-old, he was often breathless and in pain after trying to satisfy what he presumed were her sexual needs. However, as she confided to Lucille, Marilyn felt that Johnny might indeed be more disadvantageous than beneficial to her career, and that marriage would effectively ruin her reputation beyond repair. Despite the imprecations of Johnny's friends, she was unyielding. 'It would be ridiculous to pass myself off as Mrs Johnny Hyde,' she told Rupert Allan flatly, adding, 'I'd be taken less seriously than I am now.'

And that was indeed her primary goal: to become more than an agent's mistress and curvaceous window-dressing in minor movies. Natasha had taught her that there was a difficult and demanding craft to be mastered if one were to become an accomplished actress; that Marilyn had to work constantly on clear diction and understated movement. Johnny was more businesslike in his counsel: Marilyn needed only the right project and producer, and the camera could do the rest by capturing her unusual combination of childlike innocence and luminous sex appeal. So far as the art of acting was concerned, he insisted this was an admirable occupation but one not usually necessary to achieve stardom.

In the movies, appearances counted most of all, and they were magically altered by lights and lenses, makeup and camera angles, platforms and costumes. Short actors could appear tall; soft voices could be corrected; a mistake could be rectified simply by repeating the scene. Wonders were performed at the editor's bench, in the sound booths, in the printer's laboratory.

There were, then, quite different attitudes held by Marilyn's two counsellors. Natasha emphasized classic diction and under-stated movement; Johnny said that was all very good but Marilyn should above all keep her figure. Ironically, these different attitudes coincided perfectly with the conflict prevalent throughout Marilyn Monroe's life – her desire to transcend her background and early experience, and the inclination to exploit the limitations it imposed. Johnny saw what she was; Natasha emphasized what she might become.

Although Marilyn had neither the discipline nor the habit of intellectual focus, she was eager to supplement her education. One day while she was browsing in a Beverly Hills bookstore with Rupert Allan, she purchased a few art books, from whose pages she clipped reproductions of works by Fra Angelico, Dürer and Botticelli. These she attached to the walls of the kitchen and bedroom at Palm Drive, and by her bedside she set a framed photograph of the great Italian actress Eleanora Duse, about whom Marilyn knew little except her pre-eminent place in theatre history; Natasha, meanwhile, spoke in reverent tones of Duse as a role model for every serious actress.

Among the books Marilyn scooped up that afternoon was one on the Renaissance anatomist Vesalius, whose artistic renderings of human musculature at once fascinated her. Soon she resumed the regimen of physical exercise she had undertaken on Catalina Island, lifting weights to improve her strength and bust-line. 'She took it all so seriously,' according to Rupert Allan,

> that before long she was comparing Vesalius to photographs of other stars and to herself. She insisted, for example, that she didn't want broad shoulders like Joan Crawford. Of course she also knew that she had a good body, and she longed to know how best to develop and exploit it for her career.

In addition, Marilyn could be seen jogging through the service alleys of Beverly Hills each morning – an activity (like weight-lifting) not commonly undertaken by women in 1950.

For a time that spring, claiming that she was harmful to Johnny's health, Marilyn left Palm Drive and stayed in her official residence at the Beverly Carlton Hotel – a one-room efficiency apartment with cinder-block walls. But her reason for this relocation was not entirely altruistic. Longing to work, she had contacted Joe Schenck and was invited to his home for several evening meetings. In 1950, few starlets were more ambitious than Marilyn, bedazzled by the prospect of glamour and success and willing to dance to the tune of someone able to help achieve them.

In this regard, there is an emotional pattern running through the entire life of Marilyn Monroe like a leitmotif. So limitless was her need for the kind of approbation promised by celebrity, so bereft of the supports of normal life and so primed was she for the acting profession, that she was willing to sacrifice almost anything for it. Although Marilyn Monroe cannot accurately be described as promiscuous or lewd (much less nymphomaniacal), at times she offered her body as well as her time and attention to a man who might help her.

Screenwriter Nunnally Johnson, for one, alluding to her relationship with Schenck, regarded Marilyn as one of the 'eager young hustlers' around town. 'Almost everybody thought I was trying to hoodwink them,' she said privately in 1955, a pivotal year in the transformation of Marilyn Monroe from an 'eager young hustler' to a mature woman. 'I guess nobody trusts a movie star. Or at least this movie star. Maybe in those first few years I didn't do anything to deserve other people's trust. I don't know much about these things. I just tried not to hurt anybody, and to help myself.'

Of course she knew very much indeed, at least by a kind of street-wise (or studio-wise) savvy, and her words are both a significant self-assessment and a contradiction of the conventional understanding that she lacked ability to reflect. In 1950 she knew well that she was regarded as an 'eager young hustler', and in some ways she was. But she was also aware that exploitation is usually a two-way street – that she was being used by others. Hollywood is not alone in its network of human manipulation, although there it is often raised to the level of a high art. Johnny adored Marilyn and longed to regularize their relationship, but she was grateful and made herself available to him virtually on demand. Likewise Joe Schenck, soon to prepare the way for her next job, was a beneficiary of her favours. 'Joe sponsored women,' said producer David Brown, who began his long and prestigious film career as executive story editor at Fox in 1951. 'He prepared them for other men and other lives and possibly even marriage. He took care of them and their careers, and shall we say he asked for a little consideration along the way. Certainly he was an important influence in Marilyn's career.' In her way Natasha, too, benefited: she was being paid a small stipend by Marilyn, who promised to keep her as personal drama coach on her next films and whose ego, at least, Marilyn gratified by her very dependence.

There were, however, drawbacks to it all. Until late in her life, the energy required to develop and sustain the icon called Marilyn Monroe was so fierce and constant that outside the frontiers of her career she had no friendships, and her life was often barren of female comradeship. Healthy peer relations require some sense of a responsive self, but Marilyn always considered herself inferior and unworthy; and so – not because she was inordinately selfish – she was separated for much of her life from an important source of human communion. And by a savage irony, this in turn fostered the vicious cycle of what seemed to be her calculated exploitation of others.

As with acquaintances like Agnes Flanagan, just so with agents, directors and producers: Marilyn felt that she had to barter for affection – not only of individuals, but to acquire the endorsement of millions. There were often distressing results to this habit, for at twenty-three she trusted neither the affections of others nor her own talents. This effected an emotional solitude, for she nurtured the highest professional aspirations while doubting her ability to be accepted as a woman on her own terms. The intensity of her desires clashed with her deepest emotional and spiritual needs. She was someone with a vivid inner life whose desire for recognition caused an outer-directed life: in this regard, Marilyn Monroe may indeed be the ultimate movie actress.

Marilyn's connection to Schenck was valuable, and Johnny Hyde decided to use it to her best advantage. In early April he took her to meet the writer and director Joseph L. Mankiewicz, who had just won an Oscar for his screenplay of *A Letter to Three Wives* and was preparing a new film to be produced by Zanuck. Tentatively titled *Best Performance*, this would be a piquant, wise and penetrating story about a successful forty-year-old stage actress and her young rival. Sharply amusing and rich in characterization, the script treated the perennial and extraordinary jealousies, fears and ambitions of theatre folk. By production time that spring it was called *All About Eve*.

There was a small but significant role just right for Marilyn, as Johnny knew when he read the script and as Mankiewicz, too, recognized at once: the part of 'Miss Caswell', an alluring novice in the theatre, eager, apparently not terrifically talented but willing to ingratiate herself with older gentlemen (like critics and producers) for the sake of her career. A more refined version of *The Asphalt Jungle*'s Angela, Miss Caswell is referred to as 'a graduate of the Copacabana School of Dramatic Art'. She was to appear briefly in only two scenes, but because her character highlighted that of Eve, it was central to the picture's concerns.

Mankiewicz had interviewed other actresses but felt Marilyn 'had done a good job for John Huston [and had a] breathlessness and sort of glued-on innocence right for the part.' With his approval and Hyde's powerful support, Marilyn was signed for a week's work at $500. However temporarily, she was back at Fox.

Her two scenes took more than a month. First there was location shooting in the lobby of the Curran Theater, San Francisco, where outside street sounds necessitated later redubbing of the conversation among herself, George Sanders and Bette Davis; this was followed by a complicated party sequence back at the studio.* Mankiewicz recalled that Marilyn appeared on the set with a copy of Rilke's *Letters to a Young Poet*, but that he had to explain the identity and background of the German poet and his place in literature. Had someone recommended the book to her? No, Marilyn replied: she had read so little that she was confused by how much learning was still ahead of her. 'Every now and then I go into the Pickwick [Bookshop, then in Beverly Hills] and just look around. I leaf through some books, and when I read something that interests me, I buy the book. So last night I bought this one.' Then, with almost childlike guilt, she asked, 'Is that wrong?' No, he replied, that was much the best way to choose books. It seemed to Mankiewicz that 'she was not accustomed to being told she was doing anything right.' Next day, Marilyn sent him a copy of the book.

George Sanders, with whom Marilyn had all her dialogue, agreed that she was

very inquiring and very unsure – humble, punctual and untemperamental. She wanted people to like her, [and] her

---

* For the lobby sequence, Marilyn (with the approval of Zanuck and Mankiewicz) chose an item from her own wardrobe, a clinging sweater-dress that had also shown her figure to good advantage in *The Fireball* and *Home Town Story*.

conversation had unexpected depths. She showed an interest in intellectual subjects which was, to say the least, disconcerting. In her presence it was hard to concentrate.

Sanders had the clear impression that Marilyn would be an enormous success because 'she so obviously needed to be a star' (very like Eve). But he added that she had little of the social grace often required of the savvy starlet – just as Mankiewicz remembered that she seemed to him at the time the loneliest person he had ever known. On location in San Francisco, the cast and crew invited her to join them for meals or a drink and she was pleased, 'but somehow she never understood or accepted our unspoken assumption that she was one of us. She remained alone. She was not a loner. She was just plain *alone*.'

Marilyn's performance in *All About Eve* was just what the script required. In her strapless white gown and elegant coiffure, she moved and spoke with a kind of confident, understated seduction. But the role did little more than advance her as a type of appetizing garnish, too brief and too like that of Angela, and she was unremarked by critics. Johnny's expectation that Zanuck would be persuaded to sign her to a long-term contract was temporarily dashed, for Zanuck still saw nothing remarkable.

Despite the disapproval of his colleagues at the William Morris Agency, Johnny continued to act as if Marilyn was his only client. He placed her in what would be her only commercial, a television spot for motor oil. ('Put Royal Triton in Cynthia's little tummy,' Marilyn purrs to a service-station attendant.) He also invited the journalist Fredda Dudley to feature Marilyn in a *Photoplay* story, 'How A Star Is Born', published that September. Marilyn was, according to Dudley, 'soft-spoken, tentative and liquid-eyed. She looked as wild and terrified as a deer. If anyone moves quickly, she'll bound over the fence.' Always fearful of interviews and disinclined to press conferences, Marilyn nevertheless realized their necessity. But she never became accustomed to them and avoided questions whenever possible; her shyness and her occasionally recurring stutter disinclined her to impromptu statements even at private parties.

That autumn – 'because I wanted to improve my mind and learn how to deal better with people in groups' – she enrolled in a non-credit evening course in world literature at the University of California at Los Angeles. Appearing without makeup and in blue jeans she bought at an Army-Navy store, Marilyn seemed more like a shopgirl than an ambitious studio starlet. Her classmates remembered nothing remarkable about her in class except for the jeans, which were not ordinary apparel for women in 1950. But the instructor, Claire Seay, recalled that Marilyn was attentive and modest; Marilyn enjoyed the course and attended faithfully every Tuesday for ten weeks.

Also that autumn, Marilyn economized by accepting an invitation from Natasha (who now had a modest income from private students) to share her tidy, one-bedroom apartment in an attractive duplex on Harper Avenue, a few steps north of Fountain in West Hollywood. There, Marilyn slept on a living-room day-bed, helped care for Natasha's daughter Barbara, read books, studied plays and generally demolished Natasha's neatness. She also brought along a female chihuahua named Josefa – after Schenck, who had given it to her in June for her twenty-fourth birthday – and on this tiny creature Marilyn lavished (so it seemed to Natasha) inordinate time, attention and money. 'She fed Josefa expensive calf's liver and bought her a quilt to sleep on. But the dog was never house-trained, there was excrement all over the place, and Marilyn could never face cleaning it up.'

When Natasha complained of this unsanitary mess, Marilyn simply looked hurt: 'her eyebrows shifted, her shoulders drooped and there was a look of unbearable guilt on her face. The simplest correction she took for a sentence of damnation.' Contrariwise, as Natasha pointed out to Marilyn, she took exceptionally good care of herself, washing her face constantly to prevent clogged pores, taking long baths and spending what little money she had on monthly trips to the dentist to ensure she had no cavities. 'Natasha, these are my *teeth*!' she cried when asked if these appointments were not excessive.

Nevertheless, because she loved her and because Marilyn 'was a channel for what I had to give and the future looked bright for both of us' – an optimism perhaps not warranted by current circumstances – Natasha sustained the inconveniences, coped with Josefa and worked with Marilyn at night on scene-study. Preparing for whatever film role might come next, the two women devised a complex code, a set of hand signals similar to those of a baseball catcher and pitcher. When Marilyn dropped her voice too low there was one gesture from Natasha, another if she thought Marilyn was standing inappropriately for the scene, still another if Marilyn seemed to lose inner poise.

'I signalled to her if she turned too soon, or if a turn had been "empty" because it hadn't been motivated by proper thought about herself and the character.' Marilyn found the emphasis on motivation and thought confusing, for Natasha seemed to require an intellectual process her student found intimidating. John Huston never spoke of motivation, Marilyn said, nor did Joe Mankiewicz. But Natasha insisted that no real acting – like the craft practised at the great Moscow Art Theatre – was possible without considerable mental effort.

And so to the application of this exercise, attempting to understand a character's motivation and its conjunction with something in her own past, Marilyn applied herself with much fervour. It was a development that prepared her for important instruction later – and also for a decade of argument with film directors, who were generally hostile to such introspection. More significantly, this approach was unwise counsel: Marilyn was already an introspective, sensitive, shy and insecure young woman who constantly second-guessed herself. Over the next four years, much of the spontaneity necessary for her to give a convincing performance would be siphoned away by an excess of analysis.

*

Studying at school and at home, Marilyn found time for occasional visits to Joe Schenck while ignoring Johnny Hyde for several weeks that autumn. She telephoned occasionally but did not visit, and this carelessness offended even Natasha, who threatened to deliver her personally to Palm Drive if she did not see the ailing Johnny. By November he was working on her behalf mostly by phone from his bed, to which he was now restricted by heart disease. However Johnny felt, he devoted himself completely to opening possibilities for Marilyn; with such efforts he still hoped to make her Mrs Hyde, even on his deathbed.

But it was not only Joe Schenck who occupied Marilyn's time and attention. Ambitious to meet everyone who could help her, she went to the legendary Schwab's Drugstore, at 9024 Sunset Boulevard, where the movie reporter Sidney Skolsky maintained an office.*

Just over five feet tall, Skolsky was a bright, energetic man of Russian Jewish descent with the gift of recognizing talent; he was, in other words, rather like Johnny Hyde. Born in 1905, he had worked as a New York press agent in the 1920s for, among others, the impresario Earl Carroll, for whose nightclub entrance he invented the famous illuminated motto, 'Through these portals walk the most beautiful women in the world.' Skolsky then became an entertainment reporter – first for the New York *Daily News*, then for William Randolph Hearst's syndicated newspapers, which included the New York *Post* and the Hollywood *Citizen-News*. Settling in Los Angeles permanently as a movieland reporter, he coined the word 'beefcake' to describe male 'cheesecake', invented the phrase 'sneak preview' and devised the idea of private screenings for the press before public premieres. 'He had a tendency to latch on to blond ladies like Betty Grable, Carole Lombard and Lana Turner, whom he

* In his memoirs, Skolsky claimed in 1975 that he first met Marilyn at a studio drinking fountain; her account of going directly to Schwab's to meet him was supported by Natasha Lytess, Lucille Ryman Carroll and Rupert Allan (and, earlier, by Skolsky himself).

dubbed The Sweater Girl,' recalled Skolsky's daughter, Steffi Sidney Splaver.

Skolsky's Hollywood news column went deeper than those by Louella Parsons and Hedda Hopper, for he regularly provided readers with inside information about the technique and business of film-making, not merely with titbits of gossip about movie stars' lives and loves. Hypochondriacal, fearful of everything from dogs and cats to swimming, Skolsky also suffered from mysterious depressions. 'Marilyn found a kindred soul in my father,' Steffi added. 'They were both like frightened puppies, both brighter than they knew, and of course Marilyn had a weakness for fatherly, intellectual Jewish men.'

Later a sometime movie producer (of, for example, *The Jolson Story* and *The Eddie Cantor Story*) and always a man who had enormous influence with studio publicists, Skolsky was a colourful eccentric who maintained a comfortable office on Schwab's mezzanine, whence he regarded the action below, the arrivals and departures of customers famous and unknown, like Florenz Ziegfeld regarding the stage from his tower-office above the theatre. The reason for the drugstore setting was elementary: Schwab's quietly provided their pill-addicted tenant with whatever compounds he required or wished to sample. Throughout the 1950s, drugs later known to be perilously habit-forming were far more readily available than subsequently, there was no stigma attached to continual use, nor was there yet strict government regulation of dangerous barbiturates, amphetamines and narcotics. Skolsky received mail and telephone calls at Schwab's, where – because driving a car was on his list of phobias – he could easily find someone he knew to squire him around town. It was widely known, for example, that among his chauffeurs was no less a star than Marlene Dietrich, who knew the importance of Sidney Skolsky's friendship.

When not hitching lifts or testing new prescriptions, Skolsky could often be found at his favourite studio, Twentieth Century-Fox, where he managed to obtain free lunches and haircuts and where he counted among his confidants senior Fox publicists like Harry Brand and Roy Craft. 'Do you think I'll ever get my picture in one of these magazines?' Marilyn asked Sidney coyly one afternoon at Schwab's. He knew very well that she had already achieved this goal, but he also sensed her sincerity and saw a touching vulnerability beneath it.

'From then on we were friends,' Skolsky wrote years after her death.

She was always seeking advice, [although] Marilyn was wiser than she pretended to be. She was not the ordinary blond actress-starlet you could find at any major studio ... She appeared kind and soft and helpless. Almost everybody wanted to help her. Marilyn's supposed helplessness was her greatest strength.

Although Skolsky's attachment to Marilyn was beyond question and widely known (by his wife and children and soon by all Hollywood), the relationship never crossed the boundary of platonic, paternalistic friendship.

'He had confidence in me from the start,' Marilyn said. 'I used to talk with him for long periods at a time. I always felt I could trust him, tell him anything.' And so she could. The day they met, she told Sidney how she had been compared to Jean Harlow, that as long as she could remember Harlow had been set before her as an exemplar and ideal. Sidney thought this was neither an impertinent aspiration nor an impossible goal. He had known Harlow and recognized immediately that the two women had a rare combination of ambition and humility, typified by their statements, even at the height of their fame, that they wanted to *become* actresses.

Meanwhile, Johnny Hyde's time at home seemed to improve his health somewhat, especially after Marilyn visited him in late November. On 5 December, after more than a year of representation by Johnny without the usual written client-agent agreement, Marilyn signed the standard form of the Screen Actors Guild contract with the William Morris Agency for three years. Two days later, Johnny told Marilyn that he had used every influence, called in every personal and studio debt at Fox, and had at last arranged a screen test for her there. At stake was not only a six-month deal, a role in a picture called *Cold Shoulder* and perhaps one or two others, but also very possibly a long-term studio contract.

Marilyn was thrilled. At once she raced to tell Sidney, who gave her three sleeping tablets so that the anxiety of preparing would not exhaust her before the test. Then she began to work with Natasha, who read the short scene she was to play, judged it rubbish, sighed and set to work moulding a credible performance.

On 10 December, wearing the same flattering sweater-dress she had worn in *The Fireball, Home Town Story* and *All About Eve*, Marilyn enacted the short, dramatic scene as a gangster's moll. Richard Conte was the actor drafted to play the tough; years later, he recalled that she was completely focused and intense, and that Natasha stood nearby for encouragement.

'I came to tell you that you can't stay here, Benny,' Marilyn said, facing the camera, her voice tense with panic appropriate to the scene. 'If these gorillas find you here, what happens? You can't take such a chance!' Conte's character, apparently believing she has led him into a trap, raises his hand to strike her. 'Go ahead,' Marilyn responds tremulously. 'It won't be the first time I've been worked over today. I'm getting used to it.' A moment later, with the camera catching the glint of real tears in her eyes, the scene fades.

As it happened, Fox never produced *Cold Shoulder*, and Johnny was told that at the moment there was only one small role that Zanuck considered suitable for Marilyn – that of a secretary in a comedy called *As Young As You Feel*, scheduled for production the following month. The offer was accepted.

It was Johnny's last deal. On 16 December he left with his secretary for a rest in Palm Springs, and, at his request and with his money, Marilyn continued on to Tijuana with Natasha for Christmas shopping. Without waiting for the twenty-fifth,

Marilyn spent almost all her available cash on a gift she saw Natasha admiring – an ivory cameo brooch framed in gold. While they were on this expedition, Johnny suffered a massive heart attack and an ambulance rushed him back to Los Angeles. When Marilyn finally caught up with him, on the evening of Monday 18 December, he had been dead several hours.

Johnny Hyde had no opportunity to resolve with Marilyn the bitter tension that underlay his unrequited love, and she had no chance to express her gratitude. 'I don't know that any man ever loved me so much,' she said in 1955. 'Every guy I'd known seemed to want only one thing from me. Johnny wanted that, too, but he wanted to marry me, and I just couldn't do it. Even when he was angry with me for refusing, I knew he never stopped loving me, never stopped working for me.'

His estranged wife and children asked that Marilyn be excluded from the services at Forest Lawn, but she and Natasha – both veiled and giving stellar performances – convinced guards that they were family servants. An hour after everyone had departed, Marilyn stepped quietly to the graveside, reached out to the flower-covered bier and plucked a single white rose, which for years she kept pressed and preserved in the pages of a Bible. Contrary to the established account that she became frenzied at the ceremony, shouting Johnny's name and throwing herself on the coffin, Marilyn was in fact the picture of dignified grief, as even Natasha admitted. 'I saw something in her I had not before that afternoon,' Natasha recalled. 'Remorse, perhaps – repentance, a terrible sense of loss – call it what you will.'

Marilyn sat a long while at the cemetery until, at twilight, attendants gently asked her to leave. During the next month, at work and at home, she frequently broke down weeping, grieving as much for herself as for indefatigable, lovestruck Johnny. Without his dedication to her welfare, without his protection and adoration she felt the terrible loss of an ally, a father and a tender friend. There had been sudden absences and abrupt changes in her life before, of course – her mother's departure, her move into the orphanage, her arranged marriage, the death of Ana Lower and of the dog Josefa late that autumn – but nothing cut so deeply as Johnny's passing.

Within days (hours, Marilyn once claimed), she received a call from Joe Schenck, offering his condolences – and, should she require it, his home, where guest quarters awaited her pleasure (and, presumably, his). 'Joe Schenck was mad for her,' said Sam Shaw, who met Marilyn that winter soon after Johnny's death. A New York photographer, he was often commissioned to design advertisements for Fox productions and to take still photos on the set. 'Long before she was a major star, Joe Schenck was her benefactor. If she was hungry and wanted a good meal, or sad and wanted a good cry, she called him.'

One morning around Christmas time, Natasha found Marilyn asleep, a bottle of pills from Schwab's at her bedside. She then noticed the residue of a gelatine capsule at the corner of Marilyn's mouth and, fearing the worst, became hysterical, which at once roused the sleeping beauty. Without a drink of water, Marilyn explained, she had tried to take a single pill and had then fallen asleep while it slowly dissolved in her mouth.

'Natasha often accused me of overreacting,' Marilyn later told Milton Greene. 'But this time she took the prize. I never went along with all that romantic stuff about following your loved one into the grave. I remember that when Johnny died I felt miserable, I felt guilty, and I had a lot of feelings to sort through – but, oh baby, I sure didn't want to die.' And then she added with a radiant, grateful smile, 'The fact is, he had made certain that I had nothing to die for.'

And much to live for, she might have added. Johnny had arranged for Marilyn a unique holiday gift she much anticipated: an agreement, through Fox publicist Harry Brand, that the studio would present her as their promising young actress in a New Year's Day movie-star feature in *Life* magazine. Wearing a black dress and long black gloves, she had been photographed in profile, a deep décolletage justifying the caption 'Busty Bernhardt'. Her future is assured, ran the accompanying two-sentence caption, for 'just by standing still and breathing she can bring men running from all directions. And after small but pungent roles in *Asphalt Jungle* and *All About Eve*, her studio is convinced she will be a fine dramatic actress too.'

Those words had been written by Johnny, expressing his faith and her hope. But in their offices on Pico Boulevard, Zanuck and his colleagues were not in fact planning to make Marilyn Monroe a 'fine dramatic actress'. After all, why should a busty blonde aspire to anything like the level of Bernhardt?

Chapter Ten

On 5 January 1951 the lease on Natasha's Harper Avenue apartment expired. She chose to buy a small house in Hollywood, and so Marilyn moved again to the Beverly Carlton, to be closer to Fox, she said, and to have more privacy. But Natasha was unaware of the complexities of mortgages and bank loans, and soon she was a thousand dollars short of the cash needed to close her deal. When Marilyn learned this, she arrived at Natasha's door with the money next day. 'It wasn't until much later that I learned how she had gotten it,' Natasha said. 'She had sold a mink stole Johnny Hyde had given her. It was the one really good thing she owned,' and the only item that had any material or sentimental value. The money was like the Christmas cameo – a gift for someone who, despite the complex intensity of the relationship, was a mother to Marilyn.

That year, Marilyn Monroe met three men who would be variously important to her: a famous director; a playwright who for the moment passed only quickly across the horizon of her life; and a drama teacher who affirmed both her attraction to the Russian artistic traditions and to the playwright. Before these introductions, however, she again gave one of her most effective performances: the attempt to contact her long-lost father.

Within two weeks of Johnny's death, the incident that had first occurred with Jim Dougherty was repeated. Marilyn telephoned Natasha one morning. 'She said she had just learned the identity of her natural father,' Natasha recalled, unaware of the earlier telephone call in Dougherty's presence, 'and she wanted

196

me to drive with her to visit him.' And so Marilyn set out with her surrogate mother, apparently to meet her real father. They drove down towards Palm Springs and then further into the desert before Marilyn asked Natasha to stop the car at a service station while she telephoned ahead to assure a welcome. She returned and told Natasha they must return to Los Angeles: her father, she said, had refused to see her. But as with Jim, there were no details; Natasha could not recall a name for this man, and there was no verification of any contact then or later. In a way, the day fulfilled its purpose: Natasha showered Marilyn with more gentle attention, gave her more time for preparing the role she was to begin, made her feel like a welcome and secure child.*

Almost at once life accelerated and intensified its pace, although despite a long-term contract at last ready for her signature at Twentieth Century-Fox that spring, Marilyn's movie work was still confined to stereotyped dum-blonde roles. Her fame increased and her allure was more widely celebrated, but she was essentially a sexy ornament, tossed into roles any pretty starlet might have performed equally well. *The Asphalt Jungle*, *All About Eve* and brief appearances in a trio of tedious pictures in 1951 suggested talent as well as seductiveness. But neither Hollywood nor America was much interested in the conundrum of a beautiful young woman who might have more to offer than physical charms.

As Young As You Feel neatly summarized the problem, and the production of it made her miserable. Based on a story by Paddy Chayefsky, the picture concerns a sixty-five-year-old businessman forced into retirement who impersonates the active, elderly president of the parent company in order to change the system of age discrimination. This was the first time her name appeared above the title (sixth in a list), but nothing else was remarkable as Marilyn undertook the role of Harriet, a

---

* In his memoirs (pp. 220–22), Sidney Skolsky described an identical outing with Marilyn.

seductively distracting secretary. Allan Snyder as usual did her makeup and was a calming presence; 'she was frightened to death of the very public that thought her so sexy,' he said at the time. 'My God, if only they knew how hard it was for her!' Especially in this case, for nothing could compensate her disappointment for the silliness of the role in a picture that benefited no one.

That January she was, therefore, depressed about more than the death of Johnny Hyde, which most people saw as her only grief. 'She can't stop crying,' complained the director Harmon Jones to his friend Elia Kazan, whose fame as a stage director and co-founder of the Actors Studio had now extended to Hollywood with his films of *Gentleman's Agreement*, *Pinky* and Tennessee Williams's *A Streetcar Named Desire*. 'Every time I need her,' Harmon continued, 'she's crying. It puffs up her eyes!' Marilyn had to be sought out in some dark corner of the sound stage, where she sat in utter dejection, perhaps more for her life's prospects than for Johnny.

Dedicated as he was to the craft of directing for stage and screen, Kazan was also (as he frankly detailed in his published memoirs) most energetically committed to sexual escapades, and he came to the set that day specifically to visit Marilyn, whom he had met casually once before in the company of Johnny Hyde. 'She hadn't even gone out with anyone [since Johnny's death],' he recalled, 'so I wondered if I shouldn't look the girl up . . . All young actresses in that time and place were thought of as prey, to be overwhelmed and topped by the male. A genuine interest, which I did have, would produce results.' His randy expectations were quickly fulfilled. She accepted a dinner invitation and soon – while Kazan remained in California directing the film *Viva Zapata!* – he succeeded in his goal.

'All during production,' recalled Sam Shaw,

Marilyn had a big romance with Kazan, and because she was idle much of that spring, she and I and Kazan often drove out to the Fox ranch, where he was directing the picture. Usually we stopped off at some roadhouse or other on the return trip in the evening, had a beer, played the jukebox and danced.

At such times, Shaw added, no one was a gayer or more congenial friend than Marilyn. 'Everybody knows about her insecurities, but not everybody knows what fun she was, that she never complained about the ordinary things of life, that she never had a bad word to say about anyone, and that she had a wonderful spontaneous sense of humour.'

Marilyn found Kazan, then forty-two and married, a sympathetic listener (which he called the real 'technique of seduction') and a man of dazzling intelligence. For his part, he considered her 'a simple, decent-hearted kid whom Hollywood brought down, legs parted', a girl with no knowledge except her own experience, who sought her self-respect through the men she was able to attract – mostly those she allowed to abuse her because their contemptuous attitude to her coincided with hers.

The affair continued thoughout that year. At first, the lovers met in Marilyn's small apartment, but then she made a down payment on a baby grand piano she had painted white, a replica of the chic instrument that once meant so much to her and her mother on Arbol Drive, and which Grace had eventually sold. This made her single room even more cramped, and so she often spent the night with Kazan at the home of agent Charles Feldman and his wife, the actress and photographer Jean Howard. Mornings, Kazan simply donned a white robe and drove Marilyn back to the Beverly Carlton, the top of his convertible lowered as they sang and laughed through the morning mists of Coldwater Canyon.

This may have been the first uncomplicated, satisfying love affair of her life. Marilyn was not deterred by her awareness that there was no possibility of marriage – that fact, indeed, seemed to free her. As for Kazan: 'Marilyn simply wasn't a wife,' he wrote later. 'Anyone could see that.' Rather she was 'a delightful companion'.

The introduction to Feldman through Kazan had an immediate professional benefit. Because Johnny had neglected other clients to devote himself to Marilyn, the William Morris Agency was disinclined to represent her after his death. They did conclude the standard negotiations on her behalf with Fox, but their indifference was plain when, in March, the papers were ready for signing but remained on the Morris desks for three weeks. So it happened that (although the agency continued to receive a portion of her agent commissions), Marilyn went over to the Famous Artists Agency, the company headed by Feldman, a dignified, courtly man who, with a man named Hugh French, managed her career for the next several years.*

The Fox contract was standard. Marilyn's salary, guaranteed for forty weeks of the year and paid whether she worked on a film or not, would be $500 a week for the first year, with the studio's right to renew. Should they choose to do so, she would receive $750 weekly for the second year; $1250 for the third year; $1500 for the fourth; $2000 for the fifth; $2500 for the sixth; and, if she was still at Fox in 1957, $3500 weekly for the last year.†

For seven consecutive years, Marilyn Monroe would be obliged to work only for Twentieth Century-Fox and in whatever roles they assigned. At the end of each year, the studio could unilaterally and without reason cancel the contract and dismiss her; they could at any time loan her out to another company and earn a major profit by so doing (although she would continue to receive only the amount then due from Fox). Furthermore, she was prohibited from accepting any other profitable employment (including theatre, radio, television or

---

* Three years were necessary to resolve the matter of Marilyn's agreement with the Morris office. She was not actively represented by Famous Artists until 12 March 1953 and did not sign a contract with them until March 1954 – not long before that relationship, too, was terminated.

† For decades it was erroneously reported that Marilyn's Fox salary was contracted to peak at $1500 weekly. In fact that was her salary when she walked out on her contract in 1955; had she remained, the increments would have been as scheduled here.

recordings), even if she was not actively working on a film with Fox. Such were the seven-year contracts to which most actors in the American motion picture business submitted – an indentured servitude that gave all practicable rights to the film companies and few to the performers. This was a procedure that endured until the demise of the studio system itself, a radical overhaul towards which Marilyn Monroe would make a major contribution.

But when she signed the contract (which took effect on 11 May 1951), Marilyn was somehow able to obtain an important privilege. Darryl Zanuck, who still considered Marilyn no great addition to his roster and had simply bowed to gentle pressure from Schenck, Hyde, the Morris office and Skouras, agreed to engage Natasha Lytess as her drama coach, and even to employ her wherever possible with other contract players. Natasha at once went on the Fox payroll at $500 per week (with annual increases), and Marilyn paid her an additional $250 for private tutorials. And so there was the ironic situation for which Natasha never felt embarrassment, nor Marilyn jealousy: the actress was paid less than the teacher. But she was as indifferent to Natasha's income as to her own: 'I'm not interested in money,' she said. 'I just want to be wonderful.'

With the Fox contract in place, it was appropriate for the studio to send its prettiest players to the annual rites of spring. Thus it happened that Marilyn made her first and only appearance at the Academy Awards ceremony on 29 March, where she presented the Oscar for best achievement in sound. She wore a deep lavender, off-the-shoulder chiffon gown borrowed from the Fox wardrobe, but as she was preparing to go onstage she noticed a small tear in the fabric. Bursting into tears, she wailed that she could not possibly appear, but an attendant rushed to her side and remedied the situation while other young ladies from Fox doctored her makeup and braced her spirit. Finally, almost speechless with stage fright, Marilyn managed to approach the podium and confer the statuette (coincidentally, to Thomas Moulton, for *All About Eve*).

*

When Elia Kazan wrote in his memoirs of the day he met the lachrymose Marilyn Monroe on the set of *As Young As You Feel*, he failed to add that he had a companion – Arthur Miller, whose original screenplay *The Hook* Kazan hoped to direct. This was to be a politically sensitive story of honest Brooklyn waterfront workers revolting against exploitative racketeers. Like Kazan, Miller remembered Marilyn's subdued manner that January day at the studio. But he also recalled that when they shook hands 'the shock of her body's motion sped through me, a sensation at odds with her sadness amid all this glamour and technology and the busy confusion of a new shot being set up.'*

Next day, at Kazan's invitation, Marilyn accompanied the two men on a visit to the office of Harry Cohn, who was considering *The Hook* for Columbia Studios (and who did not immediately recognize his former contract player). This meeting set in motion a series of events effecting the abandonment of the film, and the reasons for this were important to what soon became an evolving relationship with Arthur Miller.

At Cohn's insistence, the script was turned over to Roy Brewer, head of Hollywood's stagehand union and a personal friend of Joe Ryan, leader of the International Longshoremen's Association. Soon after, Brewer informed Cohn that he had asked the Federal Bureau of Investigation to read *The Hook*, which was immediately labelled inflammatory and dangerously anti-American (perhaps even treasonous) at a time when the Korean War required problem-free shipping of men and arms to Asia. Brewer also announced that unless Miller's script was changed to make Communists the villains and anti-Communism the dominant theme, every theatre receiving a print of *The*

---

* According to Kazan (p. 408), Miller's first meeting with Marilyn occurred when Charles Feldman gave a dinner party for the playwright some time later that winter. But Sam Shaw and Rupert Allan, among others, endorse Miller's account of the earlier introduction. Kazan's entertaining and sumptuously self-revealing autobiography often synthesizes, rearranges and wholly confuses dates and facts: he states, for example, that Marilyn was under contract to Harry Cohn when he and Miller took her along to Columbia Studios next day.

Hook would have its union projectionist ordered off the job. In this matter, Brewer himself was the more 'anti-American', the more seditious of freedoms guaranteed by the Constitution. Miller withdrew his screenplay rather than conform to such absurd demands, and this single act of artistic integrity at once won him Marilyn's admiration.

Her affinity for the weak was frequently remarked. She felt enormous empathy for crippled children, for whom she had upset her publicists' tour schedules, and more than once she inconvenienced others by stopping to attend a lame or stray animal. The sight of a homeless drunk on Hollywood Boulevard, the account of a black actor denied admission to a theatre or restaurant, the plight of those at the fringes of conventional society (like her mother) – all these brought her to the point of tears and elicited a practical and sometimes monetary response. Now Arthur Miller seemed to her a champion of the lost and wounded, of those without a voice to speak for them, and so he won her esteem. In the soil of such sentiments love would soon take root, but the opportunity for its full flowering would require five years.

When they met, Marilyn was twenty-five, Arthur ten years older. Born in Harlem in November 1915, he and his family had endured all the hardships of the Great Depression. After working in a warehouse following high school graduation, he attended the University of Michigan, where he won a playwriting award. By the time he met Marilyn he was married to his college sweetheart, Mary Grace Slattery, with whom he had two children. His work included a Broadway failure (*The Man Who Had All the Luck*), a successful novel about anti-Semitism (*Focus*) and then fame and awards for two successful plays, *All My Sons* (1947) and *Death of a Salesman* (1948). With Tennessee Williams and Eugene O'Neill, Miller was considered one of America's great dramatic talents. Bespectacled, tall and slender, he projected a shy, somewhat diffident manner some labelled intellectual. But Miller's interests from the 1940s on were never merely (or even primarily) bookish: although committed to certain social and family themes, he was an athletic, outdoor type who enjoyed sports, gardening and carpentry more than conversations about aesthetic theory; that came later, when it was expected of him.

During the weeks after their first meeting, while Kazan and Marilyn ignited romantic sparks privately, Miller often joined them on visits to writers and composers. The trio browsed through bookstores, packed picnic lunches, and drove to the shore and through canyons. Arthur felt 'the air around her was charged' and that people in her company were touched 'not only by Marilyn's beauty but by her orphanhood – she had literally nowhere to go and no one to go to.' For ever after, he recalled the apprehension on her face when she read, as if her educational shortcomings would rouse mockery. He felt 'something secret . . . a filament of connection' begin to shimmer between them and, disinclined to infidelity, resolved to leave Los Angeles with all despatch.

Years later, Arthur Miller's prose became florid, almost fragrant whenever he recalled his early meetings with Marilyn Monroe. The sight of her in 1951:

> was something like pain, and I knew I must flee or walk into a doom beyond all knowing . . . [In] my very shyness she saw some safety, release from the detached and centerless and invaded life she had been given. When we parted [at the airport] I kissed her cheek and she sucked in a surprised breath. I started to laugh at her overacting until the solemnity of feeling in her eyes shocked me into remorse . . . I had to escape her childish voracity . . . her scent still on my hands . . . This novel secret entered me like a radiating force, and I welcomed it as a sort of proof that I would write again . . . [She] had taken on an immanence in my imagination, the vitality of a force one does not understand but that seems on the verge of lighting up a vast surrounding plain of darkness.

Typically, Natasha produced a deglazed version. 'She fell in love with him and he fell in love with her, no doubt about it,' according to Natasha. 'They never went to bed that year, but she told me excitedly that this was the sort of man she could love forever.' As for Arthur, he admitted that 'if I had stayed, it would have had to have been for her. And I didn't want to do that. So I just took off and left. But she sure did unsettle me.'

Kazan also knew that the couple had fallen quite chastely in love: of this he was convinced by her rhapsodic talk of Miller even while she was in bed with Kazan. She admired Miller's work and his ethics, she hung up a photograph of him, she was disturbed by his unhappy marriage to Mary Grace Slattery. 'Most people can admire their fathers,' Marilyn wrote in one of her rare letters to him over the next four years, 'but I never had one. I need someone to admire.' Replied Miller, 'If you want someone to admire, why not Abraham Lincoln? Carl Sandburg has written a magnificent biography of him.' The day she received this letter, she purchased the Sandburg book and a framed portrait of Lincoln. They remained with her for the rest of her life.

Kazan, on the other hand, soon departed – but not before Marilyn told him she thought she was pregnant with his child, which as it happened she was not. 'It scared hell out of me. I knew she dearly wanted a child . . . [but] she was so obsessed with her passion for [Arthur] that she couldn't talk about anything else . . . Like any other louse, I decided to call a halt to my carrying on, a resolve that didn't last long.' By summer 1951, the Kazan–Monroe romance was history.

That spring and early summer, Marilyn played the role of a provocative blonde in a film called *Love Nest* – this time she was an ex-WAC who becomes one of many tenants in a Manhattan brownstone owned by a former war buddy, now married. Once again, she was mere embellishment, an item tossed in from left field to brighten a pallid script.

In his column of 2 May, Sidney Skolsky duly celebrated her work, noting that when Marilyn removed her dress to prepare for a shower scene the set was so crowded and quiet 'you could hear the electricity'. For another sequence, she walked on to the set wearing the prescribed two-piece polka-dot bathing suit that had 'hardly enough room for the polka dots', as one wag observed. Leading lady June Haver remembered that 'the whole crew gasped, gaped and almost turned to stone.' But Marilyn was less inhibited about nudity than acting, and her scene was at once graceful and seductive. Jack Paar, with whom she had another brief scene, thought her shyness betokened arrogance and selfishness, yet he had to admit that even in a bit part 'she grabbed the entire picture.' And reporter Ezra Goodman, otherwise rightly ignoring the nonsense of *Love Nest*, praised Marilyn as 'one of the brightest up-and-coming [actresses]'.

Yet despite the endorsement of press and colleagues (and Marilyn's friendships with Schenck and Skouras), Zanuck continued to ignore her potential as a comedienne. She was not advanced to a leading role until later that year, when a Fox stockholder meeting in New York buzzed with talk of the blonde who ignited even a damp comedy like *Love Nest*. Their enthusiasm coincided with a New York *Times* review of *As Young As You Feel*: 'Marilyn Monroe is superb as the secretary,' wrote Bosley Crowther. Bit by little bit, her presence was being recognized; eventually even Zanuck would have to defer to popular demand. She was showing the world the face of a new kind of ingenue, a fully developed woman with the candour of an innocent child taking artless delight in the reality of her own flesh. In a way, of course, she was becoming trapped by an image in whose manufacture she had wholeheartedly co-operated since her modelling days. But her life, both professionally and personally, was stalled.

That autumn, apparently through friends of Natasha Lytess, Marilyn met and began to take supplementary private drama classes with the actor and acting coach Michael Chekhov, nephew of the Russian playwright Anton Chekhov and a former colleague of Konstantin Stanislavsky at the Moscow Art Theatre. Then sixty, he was the kindliest mentor-father in her life thus far, and still another of Marilyn's connections to the Russian tradition so prized by the Actors Lab and Natasha. Highly valued as a teacher in Europe and England, he had worked with such theatrical luminaries as Max Reinhardt, Feodor Chaliapin, Louis Jouvet and John Gielgud. During World War II, Chekhov settled in Hollywood, where, among other movie roles, he was best known for his superb portrait of the elderly psychoanalyst Dr Brulov in David O. Selznick and Alfred Hitchcock's *Spellbound*. When he met Marilyn in 1951, he was putting the final touches to his classic book *To the Actor: On the Technique of Acting*, and this became Marilyn's Bible for the next several years.

'Our bodies can be either our best friends or worst enemies,' said Chekhov to Marilyn on their first meeting. 'You must try to consider your body as an instrument for expressing creative ideas. You must strive for complete harmony between body and psychology.' Doubtless some of the ideas Chekhov expounded were reminiscent of Natasha's slightly breathless emphasis on feeling with the body what she felt in her soul. But with Chekhov there was a difference: whereas Natasha always seemed impatient with Marilyn (because of her own repressed libidinous anger), Chekhov took time and put Marilyn through a series of quiet exercises radically different from the atmosphere of a movie set or a session with Natasha. Her body, he said – that instrument considered merely an object by so many – must be converted into a sensitive membrane, a conveyor of nuanced images, feelings and impulses of the will.

Perhaps the most important training Chekhov offered was in encouraging Marilyn to move outside her own frame of reference. Enlarge the circle of your interests, he advised her: thus she would more and more be able to assume the psychology of other characters without imposing on them her own viewpoint. This was basic Moscow Art Theatre philosophy, although it would be reworked as something quite different by Lee Strasberg a few years later.

The exercises were intense, yet oriented toward simple goals.

Chekhov asked Marilyn to spread her arms wide, to stand with her legs far apart, to image herself becoming larger and larger. She was to say to herself, 'I am going to awaken the sleeping muscles of my body. I am going to revivify and use them.' Then she was to kneel on the floor, to imagine herself becoming smaller, contracting as if she were about to disappear. This was followed by stretching exercises, routines to modulate breathing (and therefore natural diction) – all designed to increase her sense of freedom, which Chekhov felt had been much restricted in her.

Through this new freedom, her teacher said, Marilyn would eventually be emptied of herself and changed – *possessed*, he said – by a dramatic character. 'Merely discussing a character, analyzing it mentally, cannot produce the desired effect of transforming the actor into another person,' he stressed. 'Your rational mind will leave you cold and passive. But as you develop an *imaginary body* [by which he seems to have meant a use of creative imagination and a kind of physical humility] your will and feelings will want to be another character.' But Marilyn was most of all gripped and excited by Chekhov's sense of 'creative individuality', a sense of imaginative autonomy that would enable her to become more than she had ever been – the transcendence of a limited self for which she had so longed.

She had not discussed with Chekhov anything of her private life and must, therefore, have felt something like an especial benediction when Chekhov required her to read *Death of a Salesman* and a week later read from his own manuscript about 'artists of such magnitude as Arthur Miller and Elia Kazan and their magic. This is native American as well as human tragedy.'

Chekhov's manner and methods seemed to Marilyn quite wonderful – but they were also rarefied, sometimes almost mystical. Inevitably, when asked to report to him on her thoughts and exercises at home, she froze with fear, unable to bear the possibility of disappointing him despite his gentle manner. At this time, her fear of failure became increasingly neurotic, her terror of embarrassing herself and others unreasonable, and she developed the nearly frantic desire to do everything perfectly, as Ida Bolender had once urged.

In an odd way, then, the seriousness of her intent was having unfortunate side-effects, for whereas Natasha's unremitting quest for perfection had turned Marilyn's natural speech into self-conscious and exaggerated diction, Chekhov's sessions made her even more terrified of presenting herself as unacceptable. He asked her to read a dense book called *The Thinking Body*, by Mabel Elsworth Todd, and although she tried for several years to understand its teachings and theories on the interconnection between anatomy, psychology and emotions, she felt poorly equipped to comprehend its idiosyncratic language (as have many readers before and since).

Herein lies ones of the most touching paradoxes of Marilyn Monroe's life and career: the professional means offered to raise her self-confidence had the opposite effect. She could never quite handle the analytic approach to role-playing to which she was exposed, nor could she reach the intellectual standards others set for her. But Marilyn was so charmingly docile, appealing and grateful for every morsel of education and information, that every influential person tipped the issue into a kind of control, however benevolent. She felt more, not less intimidated as she worked harder.

The efforts required made Marilyn ever more self-conscious and unfree in acting and effected a kind of paralysis. Instead of seeking the role within herself, Marilyn was urged by her teachers to seek herself in the role, and in so doing she was thrown back on her own insecurities and insufficiencies. With each project, she became more frightened, an anxiety-ridden performer convinced she could never please teachers or directors – a woman who, if she ate breakfast before coming to work, threw it up before she went on the set.*

* According to the reporter Louella Parsons, Marilyn vomited just before airtime on the several occasions she was a guest on her radio programme – a reaction surely betokening nervousness and not her reaction to Parsons's show (cf. Louella O. Parsons, *Tell It To Louella* [New York: Putnam's, 1961], p. 225).

In fact, it was remarkable that in the end she achieved so much with such mediocre scripts. Somehow she found the strength to pass from complete inexperience to mere competence to polished expertise in a specific kind of light comedy in the style of Billie Burke and Ina Claire. But Marilyn's opportunities were for ever limited by the studio system and the roles assigned her, by often well-meaning but over-academic advisors, by her own emotional fragility and finally by poor health. The first, immediate result was an unfortunate and eventually chronic unpunctuality.

In July, for example, she was over an hour late for an interview with Robert Cahn, who was writing the first full-length national magazine feature story on Marilyn Monroe (it eventually appeared in *Collier's* on 8 September 1951). 'She is particularly concerned with looking her best and spends hours at the make-up table,' Cahn wrote. 'No matter how much advance notice she is given, she is always late. "I'll be just a minute" can range from twenty minutes to two hours.' That comment notwithstanding, the article was unexpectedly laudatory and perceptive, thanks to gentle pressure exerted by the studio publicist Harry Brand.

But Cahn also helped enshrine the conventions of the Marilyn myth by buying wholesale the inflated stories given him by Fox and by the actress herself. 'She's the biggest thing we've had at the studio since Shirley Temple and Betty Grable,' Brand said at the time.* He then added some details of his staff's imaginative concoctions, items calmly put out to the press from time to time to sustain the public's interest in Fox's stars: 'With Temple, we had twenty rumours a year that she was kidnapped. With Grable, we had twenty rumours a year that she was raped. With Monroe, we have twenty rumours a year that she has been raped and kidnapped.'

According to Sidney Skolsky, who helped Marilyn and Harry

---

* This was of course true, but it was also virtually an indictment of Zanuck's low estimate of Marilyn.

Brand (and later the writer Ben Hecht) create the dramatic legend, the truth was more pedestrian. 'How much of the story about her bleak childhood is actually true, I really can't say,' Sidney said years later in a rare moment of understatement.

But she was not quite the poor waif she claimed to have been. When I first met her, she was supposed to have lived in three foster homes. As time went on it became five, eight, ten, because she knew it was a good selling point.

As Skolsky realized, Marilyn didn't know who she was, but she knew what she ought to be. Aware of the elements of good movie story-telling, she felt her biography, too, should have the elements of a good movie. The following year, this would begin to take the shape of a literary exercise for which she would help provide the basis and Skolsky and Hecht the language.

In almost storyboard detail, Cahn described Marilyn's stunning appearance at a studio dinner party, and her placement at the right hand of Spyros Skouras. Her measurements were of course duly noted, but then Cahn discussed her childhood and indicated just how eager audiences were to see more of her.

Since *The Asphalt Jungle* and *All About Eve*, fan mail for Marilyn was pouring into the Fox Studio at the rate of two or three thousand letters each week – more than for Susan Hayward, Linda Darnell, Betty Grable, June Haver, Tyrone Power or Gregory Peck. Since January, the press department had sent out more than three thousand photographs of her to newspapers. The army newspaper *Stars & Stripes* proclaimed her 'Miss Cheesecake of 1951', and in Korea servicemen made her pinup photos the choicest wallpaper. As Marilyn said a few weeks before her death, 'The studio didn't make me a star. If I am one, the people did it.' And Cahn added, 'Like a famous predecessor, Jean Harlow, Marilyn's name is rapidly becoming the current Hollywood definition of sex appeal . . . [and Fox executives] hope they have another Harlow.' After visiting Marilyn's apartment, Cahn added that this platinum blond had real (not studio-manufactured) literary interests: he saw on her book-shelf volumes of Whitman, Rilke, Tolstoy, Sandburg and Arthur Miller, with bookmarks and notepaper peeping out between the pages.

At the same time, Rupert Allan was putting final touches to a similar (though much briefer) story for *Look* magazine. He, too, noted that for their interviews she was

> terribly late. She arrived an hour past schedule, then departed to freshen her makeup and change her clothes. Everything was delayed until she finally settled down, and even then she was nervous as a cat. Marilyn was never happy with herself. A new self-consciousness had gripped her, and if she picked up a hand mirror, she saw a host of flaws she felt she had to disguise.

Rupert's article was a great success. He and his colleagues added fourteen photos of Marilyn (reading, weight-lifting and jogging as well as posing for stills from her films) and he proclaimed that she had 'the brightest star potential among blondes since Lana Turner'. In Skolsky's column a week later, the comparison with Turner continued, to which he added the comment that Marilyn had Joan Crawford's intelligence and social power. (This was dubious praise at best, since Crawford never finished fifth grade, made no pretence of anything other than what is called street wisdom, and was to most people more intimidating than lovable.*)

That summer Marilyn appeared in what she may have considered her unlucky thirteenth film, *Let's Make It Legal* – perhaps the most arid, humourless picture of her career despite its presentation as a comedy. In the altogether unnecessary, brief role of a blond gold-digger, she appeared for less than two

---

* Marilyn was the cover story for *Quick* magazine (19 November 1951), which designated her 'The New Jean Harlow' – as did *Focus* for that December, also designating her fair competition for Turner, Grable and Hayworth.

minutes but had third billing after the title credits. 'Nothing happened easily for Marilyn,' recalled Robert Wagner, another young Fox supporting player in the picture who would have better fortune later. 'It took a lot of time and effort to create the image that became so famous.' In *Let's Make It Legal*, there was much effort but little effect.

Because they liked her and had to make a virtue of necessity, F. Hugh Herbert created the role and I. A. L. Diamond the script with special attention to Marilyn's personal history. Another character first describes her as 'the girl who won a beauty contest as Miss Cucamonga and has a contract to model. She's down here [in Los Angeles] posing for cheesecake and trying to better her life', which she does by chasing a handsome plutocrat on the golf course – shades of John Carroll. Then, in her final seconds onscreen, she is nothing so much as Joe Schenck's dinner guest: the setting is a men's poker party, and Marilyn pours drinks and wins the game; the ambitious model has made herself agreeable to those in power. In each scene she wears some of Fox's most revealing outfits, and although her role is only a decorative one, she provides the comedy's only light moments. So agreed the critics, who for the most part found the story 'indifferent' but Marilyn 'amusing'.

There was nothing droll about the next picture (her fourth in 1951), an adaptation of Clifford Odets's play *Clash by Night*, directed by the formidable German immigrant Fritz Lang. For this, Marilyn was loaned out to RKO since Fox had no immediate plans for her. The scenario of *Clash by Night*, set among fishermen and canneries in Monterey, California, tells of an unhappily married woman (Barbara Stanwyck) who, after an affair with a cinema projectionist (Robert Ryan) returns to her fisherman husband (Paul Douglas). Marilyn was cast as Peggy, a girl who works as a sardine packer and is engaged to Stanwyck's brother (Keith Andes).

According to a letter of acknowledgement from the film's producer Jerry Wald to Sidney Skolsky, Marilyn landed the part only because Skolsky championed her to the point of manic coercion. For this browbeating, Wald was forever grateful: Marilyn attracted moviegoers to this stark and static picture and her performance enlivened an otherwise sordid, dreary business.

Her success was not achieved easily, however, and the production was an ordeal for herself and her colleagues. To begin with, as Sidney and Natasha clearly recalled, Marilyn was so nervous during production that – as with the radio show – she vomited before almost every scene, and red blotches appeared on her hands and face. Only powerful determination drove her on to the set. 'Hold a good thought for me,' she whispered time and again to her coach and her patron as she went, shivering with fright, to film a scene.

Marjorie Plecher, who supervised her wardrobe on *Clash by Night* (and who later became Mrs Allan Snyder), recalled that Marilyn's quest for perfection led many to think of her as difficult. 'Every element had to be just so – not only in her performance, but also in wardrobe and props. She didn't think the costume jewellery engagement ring given her for the part was right, but she liked mine – so that's the one she wore in the picture.'

Marilyn required all the goodwill she could muster. Fritz Lang, who did not suffer actors' idiosyncrasies easily, summarized the young co-star *tout court* as 'scared as hell to come to the studio, always late, couldn't remember her lines and was certainly responsible for slowing down the work.' Most of all, Lang resented the interference of Natasha, a daily presence on location and in the studio. 'She fought Lang to have me there,' according to Natasha. 'I was glued to her, working in her tiny dressing room all day long. She was so nervous she missed many of her lines, and then Lang took her on like a madman.'

But especial kindness was extended to Marilyn by Barbara Stanwyck, an actress already well established and willing to be patient with an anxious newcomer touted as a potential star. 'She wasn't disciplined and she was always late,' according to Stanwyck, 'but there was a sort of magic about her which we all recognized at once.' When reporters, newsmen and visitors came to watch filming of *Clash by Night*, Marilyn was the object of their attention: 'We don't want to talk to [Stanwyck or the two leading male actors],' Lang recalled hearing more than once. 'We want to talk to the girl with the big tits.' Proud as ever of her body, Marilyn was none the less resentful that the press wanted only pictures and spicy anecdotes about her life and her boyfriends: she much preferred to discuss her career, a topic the reporters resolutely avoided as if it were tangential. Robert Ryan recalled that this journalistic attitude depressed her and made her fearful that she would certainly not last very long as a serious apprentice.

Released in 1952, *Clash by Night* earned Marilyn several favourable notices. Alton Cook, writing in the New York *World-Telegram and Sun*, rightly proclaimed her performance in *Clash by Night* worthy of citation: 'a forceful actress [and] a gifted new star, worthy of all that fantastic press agentry. Her role here is not very big, but she makes it dominant.' And so she did, investing Peggy's few scenes with a combination of brash carnality and skewed masochism: when her fiancé threatens her (not entirely playfully) with strangulation, she punches his jaw. The gesture gives him and the audience second thoughts about this submissive sexpot.

Before 1951 was history, Marilyn was back at her home studio. Theatrical exhibitors had seen a rough cut of Lang's film, and word quickly circulated at Fox that their loaned-out player ought not to be so lightly assessed or casually employed. In the New York office, studio stockholders asked Spyros Skouras when Fox would put Marilyn in a new picture; he, in turn, put the same question to Zanuck. At last the issue had to be faced.

In fact, there was a dramatic property available – an adaptation of a Charlotte Armstrong thriller about an unstable young woman who has lost her lover in a wartime plane crash. Released after several years in an asylum, she is hired as a babysitter in a hotel. There, she is pushed to the brink of madness again when she fantasizes that a rude, exploitive hotel guest (played by Richard Widmark) is her dead beloved: he tries to push his advantage with her and the poor girl spins out of control, endangering herself and the child in her care.

This was Marilyn Monroe's first leading part in a serious feature film.* Finally titled *Don't Bother to Knock* after much studio dithering, it was the project to prove that Marilyn Monroe could tackle and succeed in something other than a pretty *comprimario* role. And so she did, despite a script threaded with clichés, a production budget that must have established a new low in Hollywood, and a director even more contemptuous of Marilyn than Lang (the Englishman Roy Baker, who snarled unintelligible orders when he was not downing mugs of strong tea).

Zanuck required a screen test before formally assigning the role. 'Natasha, I'm terrified,' Marilyn said breathlessly, arriving at her coach's home without warning late one night. Filled with her typically conflicting feelings of longing and terror, she threw herself on Natasha's patience, and they worked with only brief intervals for two days and nights. 'I didn't think she was ready for so demanding a role,' Natasha admitted years later, 'but she made such a beautiful test that even Zanuck had to write her a glowing note.' She was even more impressive in the film, which was shot rapidly and in continuity. Baker printed the first take of every scene despite Marilyn's protests; hence *Don't Bother to Knock*, as completed in early 1952, represents Marilyn's acting in flashes of astonishing improvisation. 'Actually, I had very little to do,' Natasha added. 'She was terrified of the entire project, but she knew exactly what the role required and how to do it. I simply tried to infuse her with some confidence.'

From her first appearance, entering through the revolving door of a New York hotel, Marilyn's portrait of Nell Forbes is that of a fearful doe, unsure of herself and her place in society.

* *Ladies of the Chorus* was a so-called B-picture, a second feature; by 1951, it was also a forgotten film.

Wearing a plain grey dress, black cardigan and matching beret, she has a dislocated glance and demeanour, as if she were a war orphan or a displaced child. Everything about her appearance is muted, her hair scarcely brushed, only a touch of makeup on her face: there is nothing glamourous about this woman, only the beauty of marred porcelain.

In the hotel suite where she cares for a young girl, she pours on cologne, then tentatively clips on her employer's earrings and bracelet. Gazing in a mirror, she slowly smiles – but her pleasure turns to fear when the noise of an aircraft draws her to the window; she gazes out, a tear gliding down her cheek; a haze of memories overcomes her. In these closeups, as in extreme long shots when Widmark watches her across the hotel courtyard, Marilyn acts with the surest of gestures, her hands and shoulders poised with the right balance of fear and expectation.

In fact her performance never falters. Everything in her gaze at Widmark, whom she insists is her lamented fiancé, conveys a fierce but tender plea for refuge, and in finely modulated phrasing her long speech becomes affectingly piteous. 'I'll be any way you want me,' she says in a hoarse whisper, her voice almost breaking, 'because I belong to you. Didn't you ever have the feeling that if you let somebody walk away from you, you'd be lost – you wouldn't know which way to turn, or have anybody to take their place?'

Marilyn made of Nell not a stereotypical madwoman but the recognizable casualty of a wider urban madness, a kind of representative personality for all the fragmented characters seen elsewhere in the hotel. As she said her lines that winter ('When I was in high school, I never had a pretty dress of my own'), she may well have thought of her own girlhood; when she spoke of the character's loneliness in an Oregon asylum, the memory of her visit to Gladys in Portland may have come to mind. Her performance had extraordinary density and subtlety, and the result is a fully realized portrait: a woman psychologically wounded by war, emotionally broken by loss – one who has attempted suicide but longs deeply for a reason to live. In her last scene, surrounded by a crowd of staring hotel guests, she seems a frightened animal; led away, she glances wistfully at Widmark, reconciled to his estranged girlfriend Anne Bancroft. 'People ought to love one another,' she says, giving the line the reverence of a prayer. Of her talent for subtle dramatic acting there could no longer be any doubt. When the film was released the following summer, the trade journal *Motion Picture Herald* hailed her as 'the kind of big new star for which exhibitors are always asking', and *Variety* declared Marilyn a 'surefire money attraction'. She was, added the New York *Daily Mirror* 'completely in charge of her role'.

'We had a hell of a time getting her out of the dressing room and on to the set,' as Richard Widmark put it years later. 'At first we thought she'd never get anything right, and we'd mutter, "Oh, this is impossible – you can't print this!" But something happened between the lens and the film, and when we looked at the rushes she had the rest of us knocked off the screen!' Anne Bancroft, Jim Backus and others were equally enthusiastic about Marilyn's acting.

Marilyn's reaction to the praise of her colleagues was a bemused and sincere modesty: so far as she was concerned, the performance could have been much better. Congratulated and comforted by Aline Mosby, a United Press correspondent she trusted, Marilyn simply said: 'I'm trying to find myself now, to be a good actress and a good person. Sometimes I feel strong inside but I have to reach in and pull it up. It isn't easy. Nothing's easy. But you go on.' And then she added: 'I don't like to talk about my own past, it's an unpleasant experience I'm trying to forget.' Studying with Chekhov and Lytess, creating a new image for herself, playing difficult and demanding roles like Nell Forbes – these were mechanisms by which she could escape those unhappy experiences. To become 'a good person' meant, however, that Marilyn longed to be a new and different person, and in 1952 this goal became virtually an obsession with which studio publicists were only too happy to co-operate.

Secretive about her past though she was, Marilyn could never forget its most poignant facts – her unknown father and estranged mother. As 1952 began, she set up a plan for a woman named Inez Melson to act as her business manager and as Gladys's guardian. From Marilyn's income a regular contribution was made towards the care of her mother, whom Inez visited several times each month in the various state hospitals where she lived. Mother and daughter had not met in five years, nor had there been any exchange of telephone calls or letters. More to the point, Gladys was never discussed, for Fox's publicists had long followed Marilyn's lead and declared the actress an orphan. And so for the present Gladys Monroe remained a woman on the fringes of her daughter's memory, a shadowy figure who was a potential cause of shame, someone Marilyn assisted only privately.

In 1952, she had no less than three addresses – furnished apartments on Hilldale Avenue in West Hollywood and two blocks from that, on Doheny Drive; and then a comfortable suite at the Bel-Air Hotel in the rustic, secluded setting of Stone Canyon. Then as ever, Marilyn seemed a rootless soul who felt she belonged to no one; it was her unstated (and perhaps unacknowledged) aim, therefore, to belong to everyone.

There would always be surrogate parents, and in 1952 those roles were neatly filled by Natasha Lytess and Michael Chekhov. This pointed up Marilyn's renewed desire to play Grushenka in a film of *The Brothers Karamazov*, for in so doing she could become the adopted Russian daughter of this exotic Russian 'couple'. And because they were convinced it was possible, Chekhov and Lytess encouraged her – as did Arthur Miller, to whom she wrote. He had been 'dazzled by the richness of *The Brothers Karamazov*', he wrote, since his college days.

But Marilyn could be recalcitrant and unco-operative, selfishly late for appointments and presumptuous of others' generosity. When Michael Chekhov told Marilyn that her lateness upset his schedule and that perhaps they should suspend tutorials, he received an irresistible letter:

Dear Mr Chekhov:
Please don't give me up yet – I know (painfully so) that I try your patience.
 I need the work and your friendship desperately. I shall call you soon.
 Love,
 Marilyn Monroe.

Chekhov was won over on the spot.

As for Natasha, she was left in a kind of emotional limbo with Marilyn, who wanted to be protégée, daughter and generally the most important person in Natasha's life – but on her own terms, and without regard for the pain she must have known this caused. Such a situation Natasha sustained not only for the income and influence but also because she was still in love with her wounded but increasingly proficient student.

Following *Don't Bother to Knock*, Zanuck again put Marilyn in two undemanding and decorative roles. First she was a shapely, dumb blond secretary in the farce *Monkey Business*, in which scientist Cary Grant invents a youth potion. Then, in the anthology comedy *We're Not Married*, she appeared for about five minutes as a wife and mother who wins a 'Mrs Mississippi' beauty contest only to learn that her marriage was technically illegal and she can after all bill herself as 'Miss'. The role was created, according to the film's writer Nunnally Johnson, only to present Marilyn in two bathing suits.

 Allan Snyder, as usual making up Marilyn for *Monkey Business*, agreed with the director Howard Hawks that rarely had an actress seemed so frightened of coming to the set. But when she finally arrived, according to Hawks, the camera liked her; it was odd, he added: 'The more important she became the more frightened she became ... She had no confidence in her own ability.' Snyder, who had by this time been working with her for almost six years, understood: Marilyn was simply terrified that she didn't look good enough.

She knew every trick of the makeup trade – how to line her eyes, what oils and color bases to use, how to create the right color for her lips. She looked fantastic, of course, but it was all an illusion: in person, out of makeup, she was very pretty but in a plain way, and she knew it.

A crisis interrupted the filming of *Monkey Business* and pre-production of *We're Not Married*. On 1 March 1952, Marilyn's persistent abdominal pain and fever were diagnosed by Dr Eliot Corday as appendicitis. She begged him to delay an operation, and for several days she lay in Cedars of Lebanon Hospital while antibiotics allayed the infection. After a week, Marilyn returned to work without surgery.

Her request did not betoken any dedication to the two films, which she would happily have forsaken; on the contrary, she had a very personal concern. In early February, Marilyn had been introduced to a world-famous baseball player, and by the end of the month they were dating steadily. 'But we're not married!' she told an enquiring reporter who suspected monkey business.

Chapter Eleven

When Marilyn Monroe met Joe DiMaggio in early 1952, she was twenty-five, he was thirty-seven. Inner conflicts and constant fears notwithstanding, she was becoming the most famous star in Hollywood history. He had recently retired.

Joseph Paul DiMaggio, the eighth of nine children and the fourth of five sons, was born to Sicilian immigrants on 25 November 1914 in Martinez, a small town in Northern California. A year later the family moved to San Francisco, where Giuseppe DiMaggio had better prospects for the crab fishing that supported his family; his boat, the *Rosalie* (named in honour of his wife) was docked at North Beach.

Young Joe was raised in a strict Catholic household where discipline, modesty and self-sacrifice were taken for granted, and where family devotion, schoolwork and attendance at the Church of St Peter and St Paul circumscribed the DiMaggio children's activities. Joe's parents constantly enjoined on him the importance of good manners and honest work; they also warned against allowing anyone to take advantage of him. No one must think the DiMaggios unworthy as they worked into the American mainstream.

From the age of six to eight, Joe had to wear awkward, heavy leg braces to correct a mysterious congenital ankle weakness. This period reinforced his personality as a somewhat withdrawn boy as well as his determination to excel at something physical. Free of the braces, he was soon playing baseball with his brothers Vincent and Dominic; born just before and after him, they were already talking about becoming professional ball-players and eventually realized their goal.

Like many children of immigrants, Joe was raised to be proud of his Sicilian heritage, but he was also somewhat embarrrassed by it and longed to be thoroughly, successfully American. Marilyn Monroe, too, had been discomfited by her early history and worked to overcome its effects, and this became one of the bonds between them. They were both shy but attractive teen-agers, reserved with the opposite sex but clearly appreciative of stares and compliments. Joe preferred baseball, and at fourteen helped a boys' club team win a championship.

By sixteen, Joe had reached his full height of an inch over six feet, and although wiry thin (his adult weight never topped 190 pounds), he was strong and naturally graceful. Like Marilyn, he left high school in tenth grade – not to marry, however, but to work in an orange juice bottling plant to help support his large family. At weekends and during every free daylight hour, he was in a park playing baseball. Before his eighteenth birthday, he was being paid to do just that as a shortstop with the San Francisco Seals, and by 1935, at the age of twenty-one, he was batting .398 under the guidance of his manager and friend Lefty O'Doul.

The following year Joe signed a contract with the New York Yankees, for whom he was very soon the all-star right-fielder and the most publicized rookie in twenty-five years. His salary was the princely sum of $15,000, most of which he spent to move his family to a comfortable house on Beach Street. He also invested in a seafood restaurant on Fisherman's Wharf ('Joe DiMaggio's Grotto'), began to wear expensive suits, drove a Cadillac and was seen in San Francisco and New York in the company of pretty showgirls. By the time he was twenty-two Joe DiMaggio was a folk hero, at a time when America, deep in a Great Depression, desperately needed idols and paragons. Admired by men, worshipped by schoolboys, desired by women, he was a powerful, smooth man whose impassive expression on and off the field made him all the more attractive and intriguing.

Like Marilyn, Joe was a serious, decent and respectful colleague at work; like her, too, he relished the results but not, it seemed, the effort. As friends and teammates found, Joe never seemed to play baseball for the joy it gave him: it was a matter of achievement, of pride and (unlike Marilyn's motivation) he played for the money. In 1938, for example, he began the season late after holding out for a higher salary than the $25,000 he had been offered (and which he finally accepted). Similarly, on 2 August 1939, in the ninth inning of a Yankee game against Detroit, he caught a fly ball almost five hundred feet from home plate, so remarkable a feat that reporters celebrated it and virtually ignored the fact that the Yankees lost the game. 'I didn't let myself get excited,' was Joe's typical comment. Indeed, he never seemed to rejoice in his good fortune, even when he was three times hailed Most Valuable Player in the American League. Remote and (some reporters said) aristocratic, Joe DiMaggio at twenty-five physically rather resembled the new pope, Pius XII.

But with obvious differences. In 1937, voted one of the best-dressed men in the country, Joe had a bit part in the movie *Manhattan Merry-Go-Round*. Also in the cast was a good-humoured blond showgirl named Dorothy Arnoldine Olsen. On 19 November 1939 they were married.

Joe told the press they would live in San Francisco in the winter, on the road with the Yankees during the ball season; Dorothy said she preferred Los Angeles and New York. He wanted a family woman like his devoted mother and his doting sisters; Dorothy wanted a career. From the start, then, compromises had to be negotiated. During the 1940 ball season, the DiMaggios rented a Manhattan penthouse on West End Avenue. Very soon thereafter, she began to complain to friends that he was out most evenings at sports clubs and restaurants with his cronies, a habit he saw no need to modify when Dorothy became pregnant in early 1941, nor when their son, Joe Jr, was born on 23 October. The marriage was a rocky business by 1942, although such matters were not typically found in the press, which had far more important world issues to report.

When his batting average sank in 1942, Joe's fans became confused and his wife more dissatisfied, and he abandoned his $43,500 salary. In February 1943, Joe enlisted in the Army Air Force. Assigned to supervise physical training units, he served on the baseball battlefields of California, New Jersey and Hawaii, spending much of the time in hospital with stomach ulcers.

By the time of his discharge in September 1945, his wife had won an uncontested divorce; she married a New York stockbroker the following year. Although Joe made some attempts at reconciliation with Dorothy after her second divorce in 1950, he continued to live off-season in his family's San Francisco home, where his unmarried sister Marie cooked, cleaned, sewed and attended his every household need; otherwise, he lived in New York hotels. 'Joltin' Joe' DiMaggio, returning to the Yankees, was a lonely, melancholy figure, apparently not much cheered by the historic $100,000 salary he was paid. He was, however, a steadying and influential presence on the team, often playing against doctor's orders.

But some part of his personality seems to have become fixed in a kind of quiet, adolescent stasis, for his friendships with women were mostly transient, cool and uncomfortable for both after his divorce. Almost paranoid that people wanted to exploit his fame, Joe frequently complained that 'everybody who calls me wants something'. As Allan Snyder recalled, Joe could be very difficult in social situations – especially those involving Marilyn – surly and suspicious of everyone's words and deeds.

Joe's favourite New York hangout was Toots Shor's restaurant, a clubby male preserve one woman called a gymnasium with room service. There, an atmosphere of jokey machismo prevailed; most conversations involved sports, girls and the comic pages. Over the years, regulars included Babe Ruth and Jack Dempsey, Damon Runyon and Ernest Hemingway, the columnist Bob Considine and George Solotaire, a rotund, loquacious fellow who ran the Adelphi Theater Ticket Agency. He could procure for Joe a choice show ticket and could broker a date with an attractive showgirl. George is credited with coining the word 'dullsville' to describe a boring play and 'splitsville' for divorce; it is tempting to believe that this talent sprang from his success, for he moved up from Brownsville (a poor section of Brooklyn) to Bronxville (a wealthy part of Westchester). Lefty O'Doul and George Solotaire were among Joe's lifelong buddies.

In 1949, after heel surgery, Joe DiMaggio fell into a deeply depressive anxiety that made him, as he said, 'almost a mental case', and from which he emerged more taciturn and antisocial than ever – and more determined to prove himself valuable. Playing against the Boston Red Sox (who had won ten of their previous eleven games), DiMaggio hit four home runs in three games. 'One of the most heart-warming comebacks in all sports history,' as *Life* magazine put it, made him 'suddenly a national hero ... even among people who never saw a game in their lives.' He played in 139 games in 1950, hit .370 in the final six weeks, scored 114 runs and hit three home-runs in a single game.

But by the summer of 1951, repeated injuries and ailments had taken their toll, and one reporter summed up the prevalent opinion that Joe on the playing field was 'very slow. He can't pull a fast ball at all. He can't run and he won't bunt.' That year, a few weeks after his thirty-seventh birthday – suffering from arthritis, ulcers, calcium deposits on his throwing elbow and bone spurs on his heels – Joe DiMaggio retired. Two days later, on 13 December 1951, he signed a contract to act as host of a New York television show before and after every Yankee home game – a job for which his camera-shyness did not well suit him. Nevertheless, he was paid $50,000, and his role as a spokesman for various products assured that he would be a rich man for the rest of his life. Careful with his money, he had already developed a substantial investment portfolio. As the elder statesman of sports with a team of worshippers at Toots Shor's, Joe was considered even by those close to him as a 'loner ... aloof from locker-room highjinks, impassive, never speaking ill of other players but tense and variable.'

Shy and restless that winter of 1951–2, Joe wanted to meet Marilyn Monroe after he saw a news photograph of her posing sexily in a short-skirted baseball outfit, aiming to hit a ball. Taking this image for a real-life interest, he learned from a friend that the statuesque blonde was a swiftly rising movie star; never mind, he said, he wanted to meet her. Introduced at an Italian restaurant on Sunset Boulevard (after she had kept him waiting for two hours), Joe found that she had never attended a baseball game and knew nothing about the sport. For his part, suspicious of Hollywood and its concomitant adoration of what he believed to be phoney glamour, Joe had no interest in movie-making.

This mutual indifference alone might have scuttled any possibility of romance, but chemistry accomplished what conversation could not. Marilyn liked this quiet, tall and handsome man whose continental manners she took for a kind of courtly deference.

> I was surprised to be so crazy about Joe. I expected a flashy New York sports type, and instead I met this reserved guy who didn't make a pass at me right away. I had dinner with him almost every night for two weeks. He treated me like something special. Joe is a very decent man, and he makes other people feel decent, too.

He was free with his counsel, and Marilyn heeded every word attentively. She must avoid Hollywood fakes and phonies, he insisted. She must be wary of reporters. She must earn as much money as she could and save most of it. All this she heard, but little of it seemed as important as his calm, paternal advocacy and his attractive physique.

A passionate romance was ignited that February, and the press soon duly noted the closeness between two of America's most publicized celebrities. He agreed to attend the final day's shooting of *Monkey Business*, which he did more reluctantly than she attended her first baseball game. 'Joe is looking over

Marilyn Monroe's curves,' reported Sidney Skolsky archly, 'and is batting fine.'

The attraction is not difficult to understand, and not only because of the considerable physical charm each projected.

Both of them knew the requirements of careers that depended on their bodies, and both were proud of their sex appeal. As her liaisons with Karger, Hyde and Kazan (and her attraction to Miller) demonstrated, Marilyn invariably preferred a parent-figure to a mere Lothario. She found in Joe a strong, silent defender, a man willing to protect and love her without any deflection of will or attention. Just as important, with him Marilyn moved into a wider circle of popular acceptance – beyond moviegoers to the level of association with a national hero.

On his side, Joe responded to this beautiful blond showgirl who might double as a devoted mother and homemaker; that, after all, had been his type of woman since he chose Dorothy, although (not strange to relate) he had had little success finding a replacement. But in Marilyn he was choosing a newly cele-brated, sexy woman at precisely the time her star was rising. Although her public image was seductive and exhibitionistic, he believed that Marilyn wished to settle down and have a family. He would have the most glamourous housewife in the world. 'It's like a good double-play combination,' Joe said.

Both Joe and Marilyn were characterized by a wariness about accepting love. He constantly articulated and enjoined on her the danger of being exploited, and to this she responded at once. In this regard, both of them believed that their value derived en-tirely from their public success. But in an important way their apparent similarities did not augur well. Joe's triumphs were in the past, and he was living on their interest; Marilyn had not even reached the brightest point of her career.

There were disparities evident at the outset, but nothing (so it seemed) that could not be finessed. Joe had an Old World view of women, who should be modest and – it was taken for granted – obedient to their men. Proud of Marilyn's beauty, he liked her to be admired, but from a decent distance, and any hint of attraction (even friendship) between Marilyn and another man immediately roused an almost irrational jealousy. In addition, he told her, there could be no better career than wife and mother: would she not consider retiring, too, so they could have a family and a private life? On this she would make no promises, saying only that yes, raising a family was her fondest dream.

Accustomed to a tidy Italian home, Joe was almost obsessively neat; Marilyn, like many busy and distracted performers, was sloppy to the point of genius. Joe was an earnest, loyal man in many ways perhaps emotionally repressed and distant from his own feelings; Marilyn was often hyperkinetic and gravid with possibilities. She had to live in Los Angeles, he preferred San Francisco. He devoted considerable time to money matters, she gave them scant attention. For the time being, these seemed negligible points of contrast. And further smoothing the relationship was Marilyn's easy camaraderie with Joe's twelve-year-old son, with whom she was both buoyant and generous, encouraging visits to his father but never attempting to supplant Dorothy.

Natasha was a different matter, as might have been expected. That February there was evident a mutual antipathy between coach and lover such as can perhaps only be recognized by rivals. 'She got really jealous about the men I saw,' Marilyn said a few years later. 'She thought she was my husband.'

As for Natasha: 'I first met him when I went to her apartment on Doheny one evening,' she recalled. 'I disliked him at once. He is a man with a closed, vapid look. Marilyn introduced us and said I was her coach, which made no impression on him. A week later I telephoned her and Joe answered: "I think if you want to talk to Miss Monroe" – Miss Monroe! – "you'd better call her agent."'

At once, Marilyn herself played the canny mediator. The following day she went to Fox and asked that Natasha be engaged as the company's chief drama coach. This request was immediately granted and Natasha had a two-year-contract, for the studio was both eager to please Marilyn and glad of the chance to ensure that her mentor would have other duties and not always be present on a Monroe picture. But her efforts at peace-making and her inability to comprehend possessiveness took a toll that month. William Travilla, her costume designer at Fox, recalled Marilyn weeping behind the set of *Monkey Business*. She felt inadequate for everyone, she said; no matter how she tried, she was disappointing those she loved. Not so her audiences, Travilla replied, and at once Marilyn was cheered.

He proved quite right within days. Because it had been reported that she had seriously begun taking voice lessons with studio musician Hal Schaefer, Marilyn was asked to sing as part of an entertainment programme at Camp Pendleton, south of Los Angeles. There she brought thousands of soldiers to their feet with her expert, smoky rendition of a song called 'Do It Again'. Marilyn left no doubt to what the title pronoun referred, delivering a sexual summons complete with little moans of longing and pleasure as she invited someone to 'Come and get it, you won't regret it.' Her tone was unwavering and languorous, her breathing perfectly controlled; it was as if her own mind was racing from the studio to the bedroom. Never had so telling a hush fallen over a makeshift outdoor theatre as that day at Camp Pendleton. Moments later, there was almost a riot of applause and a stampede towards the stage.

The song, composed by George Gershwin and written by B. G. DeSylva, had originally been sung by Irene Bordoni in the 1922 Broadway show *The French Doll*. After Marilyn recorded it on 7 January 1953, it was only hers and every fantasy lover's. Even the embargo on its sale added to the value, for it was often pirated at high costs admirers willingly paid. Years later, at last in commercial release, 'Do It Again' remained one of the most amusingly erotic songs ever recorded.

Wearing a cashmere sweater and a tight skirt, Marilyn was completely at ease away from directors and coaches, cameramen and press officers. Her humour was sharp, her manner with the men exactly right. They whistled and stomped, cheered and clapped. The master of ceremonies came onstage to thank her, adding that she looked just fantastic and was the most beautiful sweater girl they had ever seen at Pendleton. Without a pause, Marilyn turned to her audience: 'You fellows down there are always whistling at sweater girls,' she said into the microphone. 'I don't get all the fuss. Take away the sweaters and what have you got?' And with that, as she must have expected, a tumult arose. Her quickness did not desert her backstage. When an impertinent journalist asked if she was not wearing falsies, as she did in the movies, she replied: 'Those who know me better, know better.'

Marilyn Monroe was quickly becoming the most publicized woman of 1952, and any doubt about her essential strength, her ability to confront a crisis and to turn it to her advantage was dispelled by her management of the calendar scandal.

About 1 March the press department at Fox received the news that the photograph of the nude woman circulating round the country on the John Baumgarth Company's 1951 calendars had been reprinted (such was the demand) for 1952. Now that Marilyn at least partly clothed was being seen more frequently in movies, magazines and newspapers than ever before – especially since she was socially connected to the great DiMaggio – she was soon identified as the bare figure of 'Golden Dreams'. And so Harry Brand, Roy Craft and the entire press staff at Fox had potential national ignominy at the studio gates.

No American movie star had ever been proved to have done anything comparable, although there were the usual rumours. Hollywood traditionally dealt in playful innuendo and ingenious provocation, but since the introduction of censorship in 1934 the studios had been forced by moral watchdogs, acting with the hearty approval of the government, to deny stardom to anyone who threatened the nation's purity by something as wicked as posing nude for a photo. The year was 1952, after all, the era of Senator Joseph McCarthy's demented warnings: at any moment, Russians would be creeping over the windowsills of America's homes – an invasion entirely due, he and his supporters warned, to the national collapse of morals. Still in the throes of the great Allied victory, the United States was in a kind of schizoid adolescence, perhaps inordinately proud of being 'the leader of the Free World', which meant not only the obvious great freedoms but also the fact that America was the richest nation with the most weapons.

At the same time, Hollywood studios bowed to the pressure of a few self-appointed vigilantes like Joseph Breen and his cronies at the Motion Picture Production Code. They happily did business with organized criminals on one day and the next took a magnifying glass to scripts and finished prints, excising from movies any visual or verbal implication of human activities typically conducted in bedrooms and bathrooms. Even the screen-time for a kiss was regulated, and married couples never shared the same bed (unmarried couples, of course, did not exist). It was, in other words, an era of false morality and dangerous repression, much assisted by groups like the Legion of Decency, whose name alone indicated its self-righteous Victorianism. This vigilante group, operating with the benediction of America's Roman Catholic bishops, did nothing to advance the cause of tolerance (much less art or Christianity): their opponents, the Legion implied, were unprincipled libertines. Until the group was whisked away by more tolerant breezes in the Church more than a decade later, their nervous, institutionally celibate executives could condemn a film for using the word 'virgin' (in *The Moon Is Blue*); thus they were in the curious position of disallowing a word which was hallowed by daily use in prayer. But that movie, a sharp and satirical adult comedy, was widely boycotted because of the condemnation, for if the Legion sneezed, Hollywood caught cold. With such astonishing cultural double standards (not to say moral hypocrisies) was American life fairly replete in the 1950s.

The men at Fox were terrified that March, and telephones jangled hourly with calls between executives in New York and California. Marilyn was summoned to the front office, shown 'Golden Dreams' and asked if the rumours were true. Without hesitation or embarrassment she nodded yes, 'athough I really thought that Tom [Kelley] didn't capture my best angle.'

For years after her death, many men and women took credit for dealing with the matter, but it was Marilyn herself who devised the successful strategy by which crisis was averted and her image untarnished – indeed, much enhanced – by this disclosure.

An interview had been scheduled for the following week with United Press International correspondent Aline Mosby. Marilyn dutifully answered questions and posed for a photo. She then asked Mosby to remain with her alone and, lowering her voice to a conspiratorial whisper, she said, 'Aline, dear, I have a problem, and I don't know what to do.' Marilyn reached for a facial tissue and dabbed at her eyes, where tears had already formed.

A few years ago, when I had no money for food or rent, a photographer I knew asked me to pose nude for an art calendar. His wife was there, they were both so nice, and I earned fifty dollars I needed very bad. That wasn't a terrible thing to do, was it? I never thought anybody would recognize me, and now they say it will ruin my career. I need your advice. They want me to deny it's me, but I can't lie. What shall I do?

On 13 March 1952 the story broke in the Los Angeles *Herald Examiner* under Aline Mosby's headline, 'Marilyn Monroe Admits She's Nude Blonde of Calendar'. Condemnation, as Marilyn had rightly predicted, was forestalled by throwing herself like Little Nell on the mercy of the press and the public. Within days, the story was picked up by every wire service, magazine and newspaper in the country and many in Europe.

Marilyn had turned potential personal and professional disaster into conquest, gaining with this single deed unprecedented access to the press and a favourable publicity siege for herself and Fox that neither could ever have bought. She also orchestrated a brilliant exposure – not of her nakedness but of her candour and apparent purity of heart, and she created a moving and credible little drama of difficult early days (an element irresistible to just about everyone). Advertising her body and her sexuality in the frankest possible way, she simultaneously appeared to be as innocent as a cherub in a Renaissance painting. For weeks she humbly met the press, a grown-up ragamuffin straight from the pages of Dickens, an innocent whose body only a pervert could denounce. For her former plight she begged understanding – not, it must be noted, forgiveness. She presented herself as an honest working girl who had come up from a poor and bitter situation: surely people would sympathize with that? The Salvation Army, had they press representatives, could not have devised a better scheme to win support for a street urchin or a fallen woman. She was not ashamed, she said repeatedly and emphatically.

I've been on a calendar. I don't want to be just for the few, I want to be for the many, the kind of people I come from. I want a man to come home after a hard day's work, look at this picture and feel inspired to say 'Wow!'

Marilyn indeed made herself 'the biggest news of the day', as the reporter Joe Hyams said. And so she was. She appeared on the cover of *Life* magazine's 7 April issue, photographed by Philippe Halsman, wearing an off-the-shoulder white dress, her eyes half-closed and her mouth slightly open; typically, she was posed as if almost quivering with her trademark blend of innocent surprise and sexual availability. The air of intimacy was highlighted by positioning her in a corner, wedged between a cabinet and a door.

Halsman had photographed her for *Life* earlier, with other aspiring starlets; now he found her much less self-conscious than before, and surrounded by exercise equipment, by photographs and by serious books (Shaw, Steinbeck, Ibsen, Wilde, Zola and the Russian novelists) and treatises on art (the works of Goya, Botticelli and Leonardo). As he worked, her every move and gesture was a mixture of conscious and unconscious appeal to men – 'the way she giggled, the way she stood in the corner flirting with the camera and especially the way she walked.'

'Marilyn Monroe: The Talk of Hollywood', proclaimed the *Life* cover. The inside story showed a small reproduction of the nude calendar photo next to one of her (fully clothed) at home, dreamily listening to classical music: thus the most traditionally American weekly magazine was approving Marilyn Monroe. She was receiving 5000 fan letters a week, *Life* reported, adding that 'Marilyn is naive and guileless but smart enough to have known how to make a success in the cutthroat world of glamour.' After a résumé of her childhood – with the appropriate arabesques – the article concluded that 'with all Hollywood at her feet . . . a possible future project for Marilyn is a film biography of Harlow': exactly what she and Sidney told *Life* they were planning to produce. Throughout the year, she was frequently called 'the successor to Harlow', a designation quietly circulated by Marilyn and Sidney themselves.

Henceforth, the content of every interview she gave and story she approved was magnificently contrived – not to hoodwink, but to advance herself and to contradict the prevailing Hollywood hypocrisies. As for the slightly fictitious tints (she was not either hungry or homeless when she posed for Kelley), Marilyn always believed those points to be incidental.

At this time, with waves of adoration, forgiveness and pity washing over her, Marilyn began to see more of Sidney Skolsky, who urged her to continue the embellishment of the legend and helped her to do so. 'If anything was "wrong" in a star's biography,' as producer David Brown said, 'it could be changed by the Publicity Department, or by a star's prudent mentor. Names were changed, ages, birthplaces, new parents were assigned – anything was possible to serve the mythmaking.'

One of the hoary anecdotes devised about the early life of Norma Jeane involved the incredible story of a madwoman (sometimes named as her mother, frequently her grandmother, often a neighbour) who, when Norma Jeane was one year old, attempted to suffocate her with a pillow and had to be forcibly removed. This grotesque fiction seems to have been inspired by her recent film *Don't Bother to Knock* (not yet released), for in its climactic moments Nell binds and gags a little girl, nearly suffocating the child. Blurring the distinction between her real self and her movie self, she made herself the victimized child of the movie.

Marilyn thus assumed the difficult task of sometimes justifying her life by dramatizing it. 'My childhood was like this movie, which you can see later this year,' she was saying. 'But I survived.' Just as she acquitted herself of a charge of pandering by claiming she was photographed nude because she was hungry and almost homeless, so with the fabricated stories she accumulated about her childhood (fourteen foster homes, for example). The lost little girl who was in fact *part* of her own real self was becoming the *single* vital element endearing her to the world.

As Marilyn had predicted to Natasha, Joe sternly disapproved of the nude calendar, by then in print all over the world. He perhaps did not discuss this with her, but for much of late March and early April (while he was preparing his broadcast season with the Yankees), he did not contact her quite so frequently. He broke his silence, however, to rush to her side when yet another revelation about Marilyn's past made news that spring. Contrary to her earlier accounts of an orphaned childhood, the press learned that her mother was indeed alive – in fact she was sufficiently well to have been released from the state hospital at Agnew and was working temporarily as an aide at a private nursing home called Homestead Lodge on Colorado Boulevard, in the Eagle Rock section of Los Angeles near Pasadena. But because it had been years since Gladys had lived anything like a normal life, her behaviour was erratic (especially around other psychiatric patients).

The matter surfaced on the death of a man named John Stewart Eley, to whom Gladys was briefly married during this time. An electrician who lived in West Los Angeles, he died there of heart disease at the age of sixty-two on 23 April 1952.

At about this time, Gladys wrote to her daughter, addressing her by her new name:

Dear Marilyn,
   Please dear child, I'd like to receive a letter from you. Things are very annoying around here and I'd like to move away as soon as possible. I'd like to have my child's love instead of hatred.
   Love,
   Mother.

The letter, which Marilyn kept to the end of her life, cut her to the heart; she had not shown Gladys any ill will. But she refused to visit her, despite Inez Melson's transmission of Gladys's requests; nor, it seems, would she ever contact her mother in any way. That Marilyn acted so denotes another paradox in her complex character. She helped her mother, but from a distance – by writing cheques, making arrangements for her care and, eventually, by providing for her in a trust fund. But in 1952, Marilyn seems to have reached a point in her life when all her energies and talents were devoted to the creation and maintenance of an entirely new person, and it was as this new person that she wished to act – more, to become. Gladys was a reminder of an unhappy past, a family history which, she had been told by Grace McKee Goddard, was full of dark and dangerous illnesses which could be inherited. Better to be a new person with a new, fresh identity – the new Jean Harlow, perhaps, or just Marilyn Monroe.

'I knew there was really nothing between us,' she said defensively of her mother a few years later, 'and I knew there was so little I could do for her. We were strangers. Our time in Los Angeles was very difficult, and even she realized that we didn't know each other.' And she concluded this statement – one of her rare discussions of her mother – with the telling words: 'I just want to forget about all the unhappiness, all the misery she had in her life, and I had in mine. I can't forget it, but I'd like to

try. Whan I am Marilyn Monroe and don't think about Norma
Jeane, then sometimes it works.'

Much of Marilyn Monroe's own psychological suffering in
years to come would derive from her inability to forget; and
much of the psychotherapy failed to deal directly with her guilt
and its aftermath.*

With the revelation that Gladys was alive, the studio for the
second time that year had to devise a way of coping with the
press and with public opinion. Once again, Marilyn was summoned to the executive offices, and once again she found a way
to deflect resentment of the previous falsehoods and turn the
issue to her own advantage. The columnist Erskine Johnson was
invited to receive an exclusive interview. 'Unbeknown to me as
a child,' Marilyn said with uncharacteristically antique vocabulary (the speech was written by Sidney Skolsky),

> my mother spent many years as an invalid in a state hospital. I
> was raised in a series of foster homes arranged by a guardian
> through the County of Los Angeles and I spent more than a
> year in the Los Angeles Orphans Home. I haven't known my
> mother intimately, but since I have become grown and able to
> help her I have contacted her. I am helping her now and want
> to continue to help her when she needs me.

To this she added, in a July letter to the editor of *Redbook*, that
she had

> told the story the way I knew it as a child, and even since
> knowing of her existence, I have tried to respect my mother's
> wish to remain anonymous ... We have never known each

* On 28 October 1952, noting that Gladys did not 'get a complete [Christian
Science] healing,' Grace Goddard wrote to MM urging that her mother be trans-
ferred either back to the hospital at Agnew or to the Rockhaven Sanitarium in
Verdugo City. As usual, Grace's counsel was followed: the following 9 February
Gladys was moved to Rockhaven, and thenceforth Marilyn paid the monthly fee
of $250 for her care.

other intimately and have never enjoyed the normal relationship of mother and daughter. If I have erred in concealing these facts, please accept my deepest apologies and please believe that my motive was one of consideration for a person for whom I feel a great obligation.

What she meant by her mother's wish to remain anonymous is unclear. All that can be known for certain about Marilyn's attitude to Gladys is that fear made her seem callous. Resenting her past, she tried to cloak it.

More to the point, her illegitimacy had to remain hidden. 'Marilyn's father was killed in an automobile accident,' wrote Johnson, 'and her mother subsequently suffered a nervous breakdown.' Little else concerned the studio executives, glad to have the question of Marilyn's maternity settled because that year a number of women had stepped forward claiming they were her mother.

Although Marilyn appeared for only a minute in another Fox anthology movie in 1952, she was billed as the star when it was released. *O. Henry's Full House* begins with 'The Cop and the Anthem', in which an amusingly pompous vagrant, played by Charles Laughton, tries vainly to have himself arrested in order to assure a warm bed and food for the winter. For his last effort, aware he is being watched by a patrolman, Laughton approaches Marilyn, a well-dressed streetwalker, to proposition her. But he whispers that he cannot afford to give her money or buy her a drink and, touched by her beauty and simplicity, offers her his only possession – his umbrella: 'for a charming and delightful young lady,' he says, tipping his bowler hat. As he hurries away, she gazes at him with a long, sad gaze. The policeman approaches: 'What's going on here? What's happening?'

'He called me a lady!' she says in grateful astonishment, and as the scene fades she begins to weep – for herself rather than for him, it is implied. This was one of the most touching moments in Marilyn's screen career – a perfect vignette delicately acted.

In addition to his frequent Los Angeles trips to play umpire for Marilyn with the press, Joe attended her and during an incident that earned her even more sympathy. Two Los Angeles sharpies were arrested and charged after it was proved that photographs of a nude woman they peddled were indeed of Marilyn. It seemed that every week of her life was newsworthy: every relationship, every part of her history, everything past, present and possible, especially now that she was seen and photographed so often with Joe. Rumours of imminent marriage swirled in and out of Hollywood.

On 18 April, Marilyn's option was, to no one's surprise, exercised by Fox: she would receive $750 a week for the year beginning 11 May – one of the lowest salaries then paid any important star. She had not yet officially signed with Feldman and Famous Artists; her status with the Morris agency was still unclear; and even if representatives had gone to seek redress and a new contract in light of her increased value to the studio, their chances would have been slim. A seven-year contract was in full force, and there was nothing to be done about it.

After months of intermittent distress, she had her appendix removed on 28 April at Cedars of Lebanon Hospital. When Dr Marcus Rabwin lifted the hospital linen to begin surgery, he was astonished to find that Marilyn had taped a hand-written note to her abdomen, a plea that revealed her terror of infertility:

Dr Rabwin – *most important* to read before *operation!*
Dr Dr Rabwin,
Cut as little as possible. I know it seems vain but that doesn't really enter into it. The fact that I'm a *woman* is important and means much to me.
Save please (I can't ask you enough) what you can – I'm in your hands. You have children and you must know *what* it means – *please Dr. Rabwin* – I know somehow *you will!*

Thank you – thank you – thank you. For Gods sake Dear Doctor *No ovaries* removed – please again do whatever you can to prevent large *scars*.
Thanking you with all my *heart*.
    Marilyn Monroe.

Rabwin, slightly disarmed, thought it a good idea to have a gynaecologist present during the surgery, and so Dr Leon Krohn was brought in to assist. From that day, he became Marilyn's specialist, caring for her during a lifetime of chronic menstrual and reproductive problems. On 6 May, Marilyn was back at home with only a small scar and, she happily told Joe, her ability to conceive intact. During Mary she recuperated at the Doheny Drive apartment, but before the end of the month, because fans had learned her address and were besieging her with mail (and unwanted visits), she decided, with Joe's help, to move into a small suite at the Bel-Air Hotel.

In 1952, Marilyn Monroe for the first time engrossed universal attention. From the calendar to the news of her mother and her relationship with Joe; from the release of no fewer than five films (*Clash by Night* in June, *We're Not Married* and *Don't Bother to Knock* in July, *Monkey Business* and *O. Henry's Full House* in September and October); from her frequent appearances in Sidney Skolsky's column to her presence on magazine covers and in news stories at least thrice weekly and sometimes more – never before, perhaps in the history of the world, had someone other than a great ruler or head of state received such celebration. Pictures, interviews and news of Marilyn Monroe flowed in an uninterrupted cascade.

On 1 June she turned twenty-six and was informed by Fox that a colour film test made a week before had been approved. She was already scheduled to appear in a Technicolor picture that summer – *Niagara*, a thriller to begin immediately with location shooting at the Falls. Now it was announced, on her birthday, that in the autumn she would have the plum leading role in *Gentlemen Prefer Blondes*, a musical comedy based on stories, a book, a silent film and a Broadway musical by Anita Loos. Marilyn landed the second role, originally planned for Betty Grable, because of her increasing popularity; because at her contracted weekly salary she came much cheaper than Grable; because she was ten years younger than Grable; because, after hearing the unreleased recording of 'Do It Again', Zanuck was persuaded she could handle the musical numbers; and perhaps most of all because she was championed for the role by Jule Styne, who wrote the Broadway songs, including what would become Marilyn's signature tune, 'Diamonds Are a Girl's Best Friend'.

On 8 June, Marilyn left a farewell note for Sidney at Schwab's and flew to New York. Sharing the news with his readers, he observed on 10 June, 'My, how fast the months go – and the calendars!' Two days later, his entire column was devoted to a résumé of her life and career.

By this time, she and her co-stars in *Niagara* – among them Joseph Cotten and supporting players Jean Peters and Max Showalter (then known as Casey Adams) – were enduring the sounds and furies of both Niagara Falls and Henry Hathaway, a director not known for his friendliness to actors. He was leading them through a script by Charles Brackett, Walter Reisch and Richard Breen about a tortured former mental patient named George Loomis (Cotten), who is to be murdered in a plot hatched by his wantonly voluptuous wife Rose (Marilyn) and her young lover Patrick (Richard Allan). While the cataract rages, so do everyone's passions: George is mad with jealousy, Rose seethes with lust, and Patrick is hot to kill for his mistress. At the finale, the plot is foiled by George, who kills the lover and Rose before going over Niagara Falls to his own death.

To the surprise of many, Marilyn and Hathaway worked seriously and cordially together, although she was terrified during production in New York and California that summer: 'She never had any confidence,' according to the director, 'never sure she was a good actress. The tragedy was that she was never *allowed* to be.' Somewhat to the contrary, however, *Niagara* permitted her just that latitude, and her portrait of Rose, generally disregarded because of the camera's emphasis on her walk and her nakedness under the bedclothes, is convincingly sluttish. There is nothing of the breathless, innocently sexy, comic ingenue here – only the surly, selfish tart, confident of her power to seduce and destroy, her voice coated with contempt for a weak and ineffectual husband who refuses to help himself.

Joseph Cotten found Marilyn easy to work with and a genial colleague. 'If you wanted to talk about yourself, she listened. If you wanted to talk about her, she blushed. A rather lost little girl, I found her to be.' As for her lateness, Cotten recalled Marilyn replying to the unit manager, 'Am I making a picture or punching a time clock?'

Like Nell Forbes in *Don't Bother to Knock*, Marilyn's portrait of Rose is entirely at odds with the safe, sexy beauty with whom Fox and America's audiences felt comfortable. In these two films, Marilyn's appeal is dangerous; she cannot be trusted; her allure is deadly. From these pictures it was only a slight turn of type to the coy, manipulative dumb-when-convenient gold-diggers of *Gentlemen Prefer Blondes* and *How to Marry a Millionaire*, roles which made her even more determined to escape typecasting. Yet in *Niagara* she had a little more to do: indeed, this was the film that established her stardom.

In an early scene, arriving at the tourists' community party in Niagara Falls wearing a tight red dress, Marilyn as Rose reclines languidly and hums a few measures of the song 'Kiss', which she has requested. She is at once the incarnation of every male fantasy of available sex, and every young man in the sequence turns away from his date, stupefied by this force of nature. 'Kiss' and the more innocent gathering are then aborted when Rose's husband smashes the record. This moment was improvised on the set at the last minute, when studio watchdogs, after an outraged representative of the Woman's Clubs of America visited the shooting, felt forced to proclaim Marilyn's singing too suggestive.

In the fully preserved recording of the Lionel Newman/ Haven Gillespie song (unreleased until years after her death), Marilyn's significant gifts as a singer are evident. There is, in her sureness of pitch and breath control, in the silkiness and calmness of her approach to each phrase, a certitude of winning her request; she makes, in other words, the stereotypical 1950 love lyrics both credible and enticing: 'Kiss me . . . thrill me . . . Hold me in your arms . . . This is the moment . . . ' One hears in her smoky vibrato the influence of Ella Fitzgerald (whose recordings she studied nightly at home), and even the dynamics of contemporary singers like Julie Wilson, Jo Stafford and Doris Day. But this is no mere pastiche: had her complete catalogue of recordings been commercially available in the 1950s, Marilyn Monroe would have been hailed as one of the finest balladeers of her time.

Henry Hathaway called Marilyn 'the best natural actress I ever directed', an assessment not generally shared by critics (although *Time* and *Newsweek* took note of her growing dramatic abilities). Her nuances of expression, her impatience and her lusty bravado throw this Technicolor *film noir*, about mismatched couples at romantic Niagara Falls, into a state of constant anxiety. Desire, her performance implies, is as perilous as proximity to the torrent. It was also, as Allan Snyder recalled, the film in which she accidentally learned her famous hip-swinging walk. The crew was shooting her as she walked a long distance away from the camera, but the uneven cobblestone street threw her high heels off, and the result was a seductive swivel she used for ever after.

For Hathaway, she was

marvelous to work with, very easy to direct and terrifically ambitious to do better. And *bright*, really bright. She may not have had an education, but she was just naturally bright. But always being trampled on by bums. I don't think anyone ever treated her on her own level. To most men she was something that they were a little bit ashamed of – even Joe DiMaggio.

Hathaway was right. Over weekends in June and July, Marilyn sped to Manhattan to be with Joe, who was broadcasting for the Yankees. Both at the stadium and in the television studio, Joe was nervous and unsure of himself with microphone and camera, forcing himself to interview players, awkwardly reading cue cards and beer commercials. But he would not accept any advice from Marilyn, who had a few tips of her own – breathing exercises she learned from Natasha, a few moments of inner focus counselled by Chekhov.

'A lot of guys used to hang around that [television] studio just to see her,' according to Yankee player Phil Rizzuto. 'She'd sit in the stands before the games and talk to some of the players. They were kids and just liked the idea of going home and telling their friends they knew a movie star.' This did not at all please Joe, however, who disliked the attention others paid to Marilyn as much as he resented her low necklines and tight skirts. 'Joe loved her,' Rizzuto said. 'I know that.' But the problem was that Joe was 'a jealous guy, and he didn't like all the men looking at her.' One might as well have asked the waters of Niagara to cease falling.

But Marilyn knew how to dilute resentment. For propriety's sake, she suggested that they book two separate rooms at the Drake Hotel; they used only one. In public, the lovers were seen at expensive restaurants like Le Pavillon, and they signed autographs everywhere. 'It's the seventh inning stretch in the Marilyn Monroe-Joe DiMaggio love game,' Sidney Skolsky reported. But the event was destined for extra time.

Back in Hollywood for studio work on *Niagara* while Joe had to linger in New York with the Yankees, Marilyn was urged by Hathaway to quit the Bel-Air Hotel. He also advised her (in vain) to give up the lessons with Natasha Lytess, which he felt did nothing but make Marilyn feel more inferior and more self-conscious. Then, for a few scenes in *Niagara*, Hathaway asked her to wear her own clothes, but she replied without embarrassment that she possessed only slacks, sweaters and one black suit, which she bought for Johnny Hyde's funeral. 'That's why I have to borrow clothes from the studio when I go out,' Marilyn explained. 'I don't have any of my own.'

The reason was simple economics. Of her $750 salary, Marilyn took home less than $500 after taxes. From this she paid ten per cent to William Morris, almost $200 weekly for drama, diction and singing lessons, at least $50 or $60 a month to Inez Melson, and more for Gladys.

Returning to California in late July, Joe asked Marilyn to meet him in San Francisco, where he introduced her to his family. There she picked up the cues that a DiMaggio woman was an expert in the arts of housewifery – cooking, sewing, ironing, housekeeping. To Joe and to reporters Marilyn subsequently said that being a homemaker was the one job to which she longed to devote herself. 'I think I'll reach some real stature when I have a family,' she added.

Before summer's end, Joe asked her to consider abandoning moviemaking: did it not, after all, cause her only anxiety? This she was not prepared to do, but neither was she willing to disconnect herself from him. And so she asked for time. This only made DiMaggio more persistent. 'I didn't want to give up my career,' she said later, 'and that's what Joe wanted me to do most of all. He wanted me to be the beautiful ex-actress, just like he was the great former ballplayer. We were to ride into some sunset together. But I wasn't ready for that kind of journey yet. I wasn't even thirty, for heaven's sake!'

Ensuring her ongoing primacy in the national press, Marilyn continued to surprise. With no advance advertising, for example, she made her live radio debut on the 'Hollywood Star Playhouse' that summer, reading with poise and conviction a role in an unexceptional one-act play. On 26 October she was heard on ventriloquist Edgar Bergen's radio show, trading wisecracks with Bergen's characters Charlie McCarthy and Mortimer Snerd.

She also risked frightening the horses. To the columnist Earl Wilson she gave the new information that she wore 'nothing, but nothing at all – no panties, slips, girdles or bras' beneath her outerwear, a custom very rare in 1952. 'I like to feel unhampered,' she explained. Accounts of her undress ran throughout the rest of the year. At a benefit baseball game in Los Angeles, for example, a group of actresses wore jerseys and shorts, 'but La Monroe showed up to toss the first baseball of the game in a tight dress with absolutely nothing on underneath.' About this same time, photographer George Hurrell had a session with Marilyn at the studio. 'She did the same routine that Harlow did,' he recalled. '[She arrived] wrapped in something and, all of a sudden, let it fall. I presume the idea was to get you going. Well, they were exhibitionists.'*

Equally daringly, on a promotional tour for *Monkey Business* that summer Marilyn wore a dress cut so revealingly from shoulder to navel it was quite evident she wore neither slip nor brassiere. The film's national premiere was in Atlantic City, New Jersey, and so studio publicists arranged with officials of the Miss America Pageant for Marilyn to be the first female Grand Marshall of the parade.

When this news circulated, a branch of the United States government wanted to benefit from her visit, too. On Monday 1 September, Marilyn was asked to pose with uniformed servicewomen as part of an advertising drive to recruit more ladies into the armed forces. Flanked by several of them wearing regulation dark suits and ties, Marilyn smiled broadly in her low-cut white summer dress with red polka-dots. Because the photographer insisted on snapping the picture from a balcony and asked Marilyn to lean slightly forward, her ample bosom appeared all too prominently, perilously close to total exposure in the resulting picture. Three hours after United Press International had wired it round the country, an army official ordered the picture withdrawn and Marilyn cancelled from the recruiting campaign. 'This picture might give parents of potential women

---

* In 1929, Jean Harlow arrived on a Hollywood movie set wearing a black crocheted dress 'with not a stitch on under it', according to the director Arthur Jacobson. 'You couldn't tell whether she had put it on or painted it on' (see David Stenn, *Clara Bow* [New York: Doubleday, 1987], p. 179).

recruits a wrong conception [of military life],' said an unidentified officer with absolute gravity. Marilyn fired off a reply at once: 'I am very surprised and hurt.'

Next day, 2 September, she was even more boldly semi-dressed when leading the Miss America parade. For days there were loud shockwaves and indignant announcements from some church and women's groups as newspapers across the country showed a beaming Marilyn, wearing a wispy black item with little here, less there, nothing much anywhere and a neckline that plunged to the waist and threatened to keep on going. The result was predictable: she had more attention than any of the contestants. 'People were staring down at me all day long,' she said innocently a few days later, 'but I thought they were admiring my grand marshall's badge.' After Joe met her in Los Angeles and angrily expressed to Marilyn his fierce disapproval of such public displays, she summoned a reporter: 'That dress was designed for eye level,' she said, 'not for photographers who stood on a balcony and shot downward. I'm embarrassed and hurt.' Sidney Skolsky helped to calm the troubled waters, too: 'Photographers stood on a high platform and shot down,' he wrote indignantly. 'What did they expect to see?'

Such bold exploits, designed to shock and therefore attract attention, are often typical of performers, who require publicity to maintain their careers; but all actors are to some extent exhibitionists, some more literally so than others. Nor is this need for attention inconsistent with an acute shyness or reticence in private life; an actor's true nature, after all, is very often wildly variant from the public persona.

In this case, 'Marilyn Monroe' was indeed becoming a carefully calculated role she assumed: an audacious, luxuriantly sensuous woman with ever blonder (and eventually white platinum) hair and moist lips, smiling for crowds and singing saucily for thousands. In a way, the role of Marilyn Monroe fulfilled and released a part of her that, she said, had dreamed of nudity and the adoration of masses since childhood. Since she began to speak of that dream at this time in her life, it may indeed have been a case of *post hoc ergo propter hoc.* The increasing danger, however, was that while dedication to a film career sometimes endorsed and enhanced her self-image, it long prevented her from achieving a solid inner basis from which to live; that which she so fiercely desired, in other words – to portray other people convincingly – was a hindrance for one who had little sense of her own identity.

Although she was not hesitant to appear nearly naked for certain public events throughout her life, Marilyn was hereafter seen less frequently at Hollywood nightclubs, parties, restaurants and premieres than any actress of her time and fame. She was available and admired on screen, in magazines and newspapers, but people seldom saw her in person, and only a handful of other celebrities met her at intimate gatherings. A notable exception was her presence at a party given by Fox at the home of bandleader Ray Anthony in late 1952. The occasion celebrated Anthony's recording of the song 'Marilyn', by Ervin Drake and Jimmy Shirl. She delighted the guests by playing the drums under Mickey Rooney's direction.

Otherwise, there were two reasons for her social reticence: first, while she was comfortable being the focus of a crowd's attention, singing, smiling or waving, Marilyn was hesitant to speak in public. She always hated impromptu interviews and press conferences, for which she felt unprepared, and she was fearful of appearing stupid or socially inept and therefore unacceptable. In addition, by restricting her Hollywood personal appearances, she was effectively making herself the celebrity of celebrities, fascinatingly enigmatic for movie folk as well as the world at large.

Clothes occupied much of her time that autumn. While interior sequences, retakes and dialogue redubbing for *Niagara* remained to be done at the studio, Marilyn set herself an important task. Joe heartily agreed with Henry Hathaway that her wardrobe needed major attentions, and he accompanied her, providing advice and expressing opinions as she purchased blouses, dresses and suits from startled clerks in Los Angeles clothing stores.

The general astonishment at one store derived not so much from the presence of celebrities shopping (a common enough occurrence in Los Angeles, after all) but from Marilyn's choice of tightly fitted trousers below an equally clinging blouse leaving a bare midriff. In the dressing-room of another store, she shocked an employee in attendance when, about to try a sleeveless white dress with a plunging neckline, she removed her jeans and sweater and stood stark naked.*

As she may have expected, this brought loud disapproval from Joe, and more than once that autumn there were news reports of 'some estrangement' and a 'rift' separating America's favourite unmarried couple. This was all the more rumoured around 1 October, when Joe left town after what Marilyn later termed 'a lot of name-calling [by Joe].'

Thus it happened that Marilyn (who never liked to shop alone) asked Natasha to accompany her. On the afternoon of Saturday 4 October the two women went to Jax, a store on Wilshire Boulevard, where Marilyn selected several pairs of lounging trousers, shirts, blouses and accessories and wrote a cheque against her account at the Bank of America for $313.13. Beneath her signature, she added her current address: 2393 Castilian Drive, where she and Joe had taken a two-month sublease to avoid the annoying reporters surrounding them so often at the Bel-Air Hotel.†

---

* A similar story was told by designer Ceil Chapman when Marilyn visited New York during a break from shooting *Niagara*: a saleswoman at Saks Fifth Avenue was angry with Chapman 'for bringing in a girl who was trying on things without underwear or stockings' (see Earl Wilson, *Show Business Laid Bare* [New York: Putnam's, 1974], p. 65).

† These details would not be remarkable but for the outrageous claims made by one of the strangest fans ever to have met Marilyn Monroe. While filming scenes at Niagara Falls that summer, she was asked by a twenty-five-year-old visitor from Ohio named Robert Slatzer to pose with him for snapshots. For such impromptu photos and importuned autographs, no public figure was ever more generous and co-operative with admirers and strangers than Marilyn, nor was any more exploited before or since her death. But in this case she unwittingly contributed to Slatzer's fame. There is no convincing evidence that Marilyn Monroe and Robert Slatzer ever again met, and there are neither letters, additional photos nor any documentation of a relationship between them. Years later, however, one

Before the end of 1952, Marilyn was at work on the twentieth

of the most preposterous claims in American popular history was launched.

In 1972, with Marilyn conveniently unable to contradict him, Slatzer approached journalist Will Fowler with a short, incomplete article in which Slatzer speculated that Marilyn Monroe's death was caused by a political conspiracy – a popular hypothesis in the light of the rumours then swirling round the assassinations of President John F. Kennedy; his brother, Attorney General Robert F. Kennedy; civil rights leader Martin Luther King, and others. 'Too bad you weren't married to Monroe,' Fowler said, unimpressed with Slatzer's proposal. 'That would *really* make a good book.' Soon after, Slatzer contacted Fowler again, saying he had forgot to mention that he had indeed been married to Marilyn. 'Slatzer made a career of being a pretender,' according to Fowler, 'selling gullible talk show producers who don't do their research very well with the deception that he was married to Marilyn. He was never married to her. He met the star only once, in Niagara Falls . . . He never met Marilyn before or since.' Eventually, Fowler withdrew from the project. (See Will Fowler, *Reporters: Memoirs of a Young Newspaperman* [Santa Monica: Roundtable Publishing, 1991], n.p.; also Will Fowler to DS, 9 April 1992).

Nevertheless, Robert Slatzer proceeded and eventually published *The Life and Curious Death of Marilyn Monroe* under his own name. Among the most persistent but injudicious of his assertions is his absurd claim that he spent the weekend of 3–6 October 1952 with Marilyn Monroe in Tijuana, Mexico, where they were married on 4 October. This marriage, according to Slatzer, was annulled a few days later because she was 'afraid of Joe, of what the studio would say, and of Natasha Lytess, who was very jealous and possessive and who had a tremendous influence over her' (Slatzer, p. 166). Quite apart from the fact that Marilyn was in Los Angeles that entire weekend, Slatzer could never produce a written record of the union or its dissolution: the marriage paper, he reports, was burnt by a *petit fonctionnaire* in Tijuana.

It is important that, since the publication of Slatzer's book in 1974, there has not been a single witness to attest the truth of his marriage. A man named Noble Chissell once said he had been present at the event, but before he died Chissell admitted to Will Fowler that he was 'just trying to help out a friend' with the false attestation (see Fowler, n.p.). Moreoever, Chissell told photographer Joseph Jasgur that Slatzer had promised him a much needed one hundred dollars to support the lie. Allan Snyder, one of Marilyn's closest friends and confidants, was with her on every film throughout 1952. 'I never believed Slatzer married Marilyn,' he said. 'There was no proof of it, and there was always something that suggested to me it never happened' (Snyder to DS, 3 July 1992). Kay Eicher, to whom Slatzer was married from 1954 to 1956, has always laughed heartily when the Monroe-Slatzer marriage is mentioned: among many others, she confirmed that he met her only once, at Niagara Falls, when the impromptu snapshot was taken. 'It's the one photo he's always using to tell his story,' according to Eicher. 'He's been fooling people too long' (see Eicher in *The Star*, 1 Oct. 1991. Slatzer did film of her career and her sixth that year – the Technicolor musical comedy *Gentlemen Prefer Blondes* (written by Charles Lederer), which for ever enshrined her in memory as the luscious, nubile gold-digger, apparently witless but in fact shrewd about the ways of men, misers and millionaires. 'I thought you were dumb!' remarks the father of her rich boyfriend. 'I can be smart when it's important, but most men don't like it.' This crucial piece of dialogue (as the script assistant's notes reveal) was inserted at Marilyn's direct suggestion: as usual, she understood the part better than anyone, and her addition is her own sly riposte to the prevailing sexism of the 1950s. In *Gentlemen Prefer Blondes*, Marilyn was Lorelei Lee, and Jane Russell was cast as her wise-cracking brunette side-kick Dorothy Shaw. (At her contractual fee of $1250 per week, Marilyn received about

not, of course, claim to have been married to Marilyn until long after her death, which was a wise choice: her immediate contradiction might otherwise have killed a great enterprise.)

But the 'marriage' was not sufficient drama for Slatzer, who also claimed to have been Marilyn's most intimate confidant until her death – the man who knew and kept all the secrets of her career and her love life. It was a bold assertion, for not one of Marilyn's friends, relatives, business associates, colleagues, spouses or lovers could ever recall meeting him (much less Marilyn ever mentioning him), nor is he to be found in any of her personal telephone or address books; indeed, not one of her intimates ever heard of Robert Slatzer during her lifetime or after her death – not until the appearance of his book. Worst of all, however, has been Slatzer's influence on Marilyn Monroe's chroniclers. The nonsense about a love affair between her and Robert F. Kennedy, and Slatzer's accusations that Kennedy was directly involved in her death, owed much to the improvisations of Slatzer. For years – in print and on television talk shows – Slatzer turned an enormous profit. He also furthered his claims of intimacy with Marilyn by selling photographs he claimed to have taken of her in 1962 on the set of her last, unfinished film, *Something's Got to Give*. But the negatives and contact sheets for the photos he sold prove that those pictures were taken not by Slatzer (whom no one can recall visiting director George Cukor's closed set) but by James Mitchell, Fox's still photographer assigned to the production. Few have profited so richly and undeservedly as Slatzer, whose claims could otherwise be ignored except that he and a few cronies have greedily created a nefarious industry that has persisted for decades, and one by which reputations have been gravely, deliberately and systematically vilified. On this entire matter, see the Afterword: *The Great Deception*.

$15,000 for the picture; Jane Russell was paid $150,000. She was still subject to the terms of her contract, and the tangled skein of her relationship with the Morris and Famous Artists agencies had not yet been unravelled.)

Lorelei and Dorothy sailed from America to Paris; they meet millionaires; they work in a nightclub; they cope with various silly misadventures surrounding Lorelei's weakness for rich men and her fragile fidelity to her wimpish fiancé; and the stars save a thin story from total collapse by sheer energy in several song and dance numbers (which really ought to be designated 'strut numbers').

Most notable, however, was Marilyn's legendary rendition of the song 'Diamonds Are a Girl's Best Friend', by Jule Styne and Leo Robin. Surrounded by dozens of men in black tie and tails, Marilyn fairly shimmers in Travilla's pink strapless gown against a garish red cyclorama. Like the other musical numbers, the sequence was directed not by Howard Hawks (whose métier was not musical comedy) but by the respected choreographer Jack Cole. But Marilyn did not really dance: she skipped, ran, leaped, strolled, pointed, threw her arms about and was whisked here and there by a platoon of men as she caresses ropes of diamonds and rhapsodizes over the erotic appeal of 'Tiffany's . . . Cartier's . . . Speak to me, Harry Winston!!!' This was a parody of greed-as-sex, legitimized in 1953 (so the studio and critics thought) by its own amoral cuteness. The number succeeds in spite of itself and remains the most frequently shown piece of Monroe footage because Marilyn played it for high-class satire.

On this number Marilyn worked tirelessly, as if she knew the sequence would endure as a kind of national icon: according to the actor Ron Nyman (one of the team of adoring chorus men in the 'Diamonds' sequence), she was very much liked on the film, but her shyness hindered the kind of immediate warmth Jane Russell projected. In addition, when Marilyn insisted on something (a retake, an alteration to the number, a conference with Natasha), she got it ('when she put her foot down, it was down,' as Nyman said). Musical director Lionel Newman recalled the recording sessions, for which Marilyn insisted on singing with the orchestra – an unusual practice for film recording, which usually depends on voice overdubbing of prerecorded music. She also asked for eleven takes, agonizing to get the song perfectly. 'She was damned sure of what she wanted,' according to Newman, '[but] the men in the orchestra adored her. She was always congenial, courteous, not temperamental, and never forgot to thank everyone who worked with her.'

Marilyn (perhaps the least materialistic movie star in history) performed 'Diamonds Are a Girl's Best Friend' as if it were a kind of satire. Hers is an unreal cupidity, as her winks and smiles attest. 'I feel as though it's all happening to someone right next to me,' she said of the resulting notoriety when the picture was released. 'I'm close, I can feel it, I can hear it. But it really isn't me.' ('There wasn't a real thing about her,' said Hawks. 'Everything was completely unreal.') For this sequence, Marilyn prepared with almost manic ferocity, according to Jack Cole. Hal Schaefer, Fox's chief music coach responsible for developing and arranging the picture's score and coaching Marilyn privately, agreed. 'She loved to sing, she sang well, and she just adored her idol, Ella [Fitzgerald]. The most important influence on Marilyn's vocal art was in fact a recording I gave her called *Ella Sings Gershwin*, for which there was only Ellis Larkin's piano accompaniment.'

The role of Lorelei Lee fixed Marilyn in the world's consciousness as the exaggeratedly, dishily seductive blonde – all body; no thought; little feeling; all whispery, high voice and no sensibility. Impossibly lacquered, moistly cosmeticized, she is at once a kind of winsome Kewpie Doll and a clear peril to a man with money. Defined by avarice, Lorelei Lee on paper is little more than a buxom cartoon. Marilyn, however, made her the satirical icon of a decade. 'My great ambition,' she said that winter, 'is to have people comment on my fine dramatic performances, [but] I also intend to concentrate on singing and comedy parts.'

She was, however, of clearly divided mind, whether to aspire to such high dramatic roles or to concentrate on musical comedy. Of this time, she later said:

> I had to get out, I just had to. The danger was, I began to believe this was all I could do – all I was – all any woman was. Natasha and everybody else was talking about how convincing, how much of me must have been in this role, or how much of the role was in me. I knew there was more I could do, and more that I was. Nobody was listening to me.

'She wants to be a star so much she aches,' said Sidney Skolsky during the making of this elaborate movie, which took from November 1952 to February 1953. This desire was frankly admitted by Marilyn herself: 'I want to be a big star more than anything. It's something precious.'

But the intensity of her desire was not quite so evident to those who observed her chronic lateness and her terror of beginning to work even when she finally arrived on the set of *Gentlemen Prefer Blondes*. Natasha Lytess hovered, Allan Snyder gently encouraged, Howard Hawks (his direction unhampered by subtlety) cajoled, co-star Jane Russell befriended Marilyn. Still, she hesitated to show herself on the sound stage for both small scenes and complex musical numbers. Lorelei Lee was dedicated to the proposition; Marilyn Monroe was committed to every detail of her craft. Any man with a bankroll was fair game to her movie character; anyone who would increase her confidence and refine her art was a friend to Marilyn.

'She was terrified,' according to Jane Russell, always known as an amiable, calm and courteous professional; she attributed Marilyn's anxiety to her 'desperate, *desperate* desire to be a star'. To help calm Marilyn's nerves, Jane invited her to informal religious discussions held at the home of fellow-Christians that winter; for her part, Marilyn gave Jane a book on Sigmund Freud. 'Neither of us converted the other,' according to Marilyn. Jane quickly recognized that Marilyn was 'far more intelligent than people gave her credit for', and she admired Marilyn for remaining long after the day's shutdown to work with Jack Cole – and then arriving next morning with 'no makeup, tangled hair and blue jeans', Jane recalled, 'for dance rehearsals that were hard, sweaty work.' Marilyn was, as Cole added, quite aware that she had no dance technique,

> that she was just a terribly pretty girl whom all this had hap-pened to, and all of a sudden she was a star, she was going to have to go out and do it and everybody was going to look at her. And she was just terrified! She knew that she was not equal to it. What made her not show up at the studio was that she couldn't sleep [from fear] . . . She would get into makeup and comb her hair 'just one more time' because she was so frightened of coming out. And she was such a little girl she didn't know how to apologize.

Not much help was provided by the ubiquitous Natasha, who was now directing her on the set immediately after she had received points from Hawks. Marilyn shielded her eyes against the bright lights after each shot, looking for her coach's appro-val. When Hawks could no longer endure this interference, he followed the actions of Fritz Lang and removed Natasha from the sound stage, but Marilyn reacted by simply arriving later and later. Natasha was readmitted within a week, and Hawks continued to find her 'the most frightened little girl [who] didn't think she was good enough to do the things she did. But [when] she got out in front of the camera, [it] liked her.'

According to Jane, Marilyn nevertheless always seemed a little angry or unhappy. Much of the distress had to do with the increasing tension between Joe (who visited the set two or three times, only to be ignored because of all the dither about Marilyn) and Natasha (whom Joe saw at the centre of the storm, and as a more important person to Marilyn – at least profession-ally – than himself).

The imminent stardom, which everyone felt was sure to fol-low the release of *Niagara* and *Gentlemen Prefer Blondes* in

1953, did not, however, convince Marilyn she could sustain it, much less grow as a good actress. 'I'm really eager to do something else,' she told a reporter during production that autumn. 'Squeezing yourself to ooze out the last ounce of sex allure is terribly hard. I'd like to do roles like Julie in *Bury the Dead*, Gretchen in *Faust* and Teresa in *Cradle Song*. I don't want to be a comedienne forever.' Nor was she much gratified when critics, typically, stressed only her looks in assessing *Gentlemen Prefer Blondes*.

As if to prove the seriousness of her higher aspirations, Marilyn took a cue from Natasha, who saw an item in the *Los Angeles Times*. Natasha's old friend and mentor Max Reinhardt had died in 1943, and now his first wife was about to auction 178 of his *Regiebücher*: production notebooks with his markings concerning action, timing, scenery and cuts. These materials would be wonderful additions to Marilyn's library, said Natasha, doubtless eager for access to them herself.

And so on Wednesday 3 December the two women rushed off to the Goldenberg Galleries in Beverly Hills. After the bidding rose beyond a few hundred dollars, Marilyn battled for the prize against the rare book dealer Jake Zeitlin, who was acting on behalf of the University of Southern California: their Doheny Library already housed more than three thousand items in its Reinhardt Collection, and the university was eager to complement the archives. The sums had reached thirteen hundred dollars.

'Thirteen twenty!' called Zeitlin.

This amount was repeated from the podium, and there was a pause.

'One thousand three hundred and thirty-five!' cried Marilyn deliberately, thus winning the collection.

Like Notre Dame's football team that season, Marilyn had won a victory against the University of Southern California; also like Notre Dame, the victory did not make her very popular when the matter was trumpeted in the newspapers during the next week.

On 5 December the university's librarian, Lewis Stieg, announced that he hoped Marilyn would donate the collection to the Doheny Library. Through reporters, she replied that so valuable a collection, she now realized, should be available to all drama students; she was considering Harvard and Stanford, among others, as the appropriate repository. To further his cause, Stieg then asked Marilyn to join him in a choice viewing location on the fifty-yard-line at the Rose Bowl game on New Year's Day. She declined.

A few weeks later, Marilyn received a letter from Reinhardt's son Gottfried: 'Surely you will understand, dear Miss Monroe, that aside from monetary expenditure, these books belong to [me] and not to you.' Following a gracious agreement from Marilyn, he was about to send her a cheque when the auctioneer informed him that she had neither collected nor paid for the books; payment, therefore, was due directly to the Galleries. The materials then went to Gottfried.

On a chilly Christmas Eve, Marilyn returned alone from a studio party to her rented suite at the Beverly Hills Hotel. Unlocking the door and switching on the lights, she was surprised to find Joe, reaching up to place the last silver ornament on top of a lavishly decorated tree. There was champagne in a silver ice bucket, and logs blazed cheerfully in the fireplace. It was, she told friends later, her merriest Christmas ever.

Chapter Twelve

1953

Early in the new year 1953, Marilyn and Joe made a pact. She would not wear such revealing dresses as to embarrass him in public; he would try to be more patient with her and more polite to Natasha, with whom there was a mutual sharp antipathy. 'Marilyn,' she said one evening, 'this man is the punishment of God in your life' – hyperbolic even by Natasha's standards.

Scourge or no, Joe squired Marilyn to restaurants throughout the winter, Sidney Skolsky describing them in his 9 February column as 'still very much a combination'. His remark was ironic, for that very evening, *Photoplay* magazine honoured Marilyn Monroe as Hollywood's 'Fastest Rising Star'. Her escort was not Joe but the hastily corralled Sidney.

The reason was simple. To an award ceremony in the dining-room of the Beverly Hills Hotel (where she lived that season), Marilyn had decided to wear a gold lamé dress designed for her by Travilla. This was a saucy, seductive, body-hugging number she had worn in *Gentlemen Prefer Blondes* – a floor-length gown with a deep-plunging neckline, which had been seen only in a momentary long shot. 'She had to be hand-sewn into it,' Travilla recalled, adding that he begged her not to wear it. 'You're too fat for it at the moment, Marilyn! It's too tight – people will laugh!' But she was adamant, telling Travilla that she had just learned 'a trick to lose weight quickly – colonic irrigation, an enema that washes water out of the system and immediately shows in lost inches.' This drastic and potentially harmful way to lose weight became a regimen with Marilyn for the rest of her life. 'She had two sessions of colonic irrigation that day,' Travilla recalled, although for all that she was happy to fill the dress tightly.

After Joe saw the dress and the absence of brassiere, slip or underwear beneath the costume that afternoon, he departed angrily. In his column next day, Sidney discreetly informed his readers that Joe 'had to go to San Francisco for a few days' – no doubt to cool off in the northern air and to take comfort in the simple decencies of his family.

As she may well have expected, Marilyn had no competition for attention as she glided into the hotel's Crystal Room that evening, wearing the skin-tight gold dress 'that looked as if it had been painted on', as columnist Florabel Muir reported next day.

With one little twist of her derriere, Marilyn Monroe stole the show . . . The assembled guests broke into wild applause, [while] two other screen stars, Joan Crawford and Lana Turner, got only casual attention. After Marilyn every other girl appeared dull by contrast.

And with that, the formidable Joan Crawford swung into action. A star since the year of Marilyn's birth, she met her potential rival with no sporting good cheer. To the contrary, she summoned the press and publicly denounced Marilyn's 'burlesque show', advising that 'the public likes provocative feminine personalities, but it also likes to know that underneath it all the actresses are ladies.' And then, with almost religious solemnity, Crawford added: 'Kids don't like [Marilyn] . . . because they don't like to see sex exploited. And don't forget the women. They won't pick [a movie] for the family that won't be suitable for their husbands and children.'

Obviously the forty-nine-year-old star was relying on Hollywood's (and the country's) short memory, for as Billie Cassin and then as the young Joan Crawford she had literally jumped to fame by dancing the Charleston nude on speakeasy tabletops, and then by appearing in a number of blue movies. Nor would she have been pleased, that February night, to be reminded of a statement she made in her wild twenties: 'One thing that makes for healthy American girls is a small quantity of clothing.'

But not for Marilyn the pithy rebuttal or the handy reference to Crawford's past. Just as when she had been denounced because of her busty appearance next to America's sedate servicewomen, she quietly disarmed the enemy: 'The thing that hit me hardest about Miss Crawford's remarks,' she told Louella Parsons and the nation, 'is that I've always admired her for being such a wonderful mother – for taking four children and giving them a fine home. Who better than I knows what that means to homeless little ones?' It is unlikely that Marilyn knew of Crawford's way of mothering – an appalling severity later detailed in a book by one of the unfortunates she adopted. But never mind: Marilyn the waif, with a canny appeal to her own benighted past, conquered once again.

In 1953, perhaps only in America could the matter of a young woman's dress become front-page news – a sudden Southern California storm in an otherwise temperate climate. But moral support was forthcoming. 'Marilyn's the biggest thing that's happened to Hollywood in years,' said Betty Grable, who had been Fox's great audience draw during the previous decade. 'The movies were just sort of going along, and all of a sudden – zowie! – there was Marilyn. She's a shot in the arm for Hollywood!'

So much was true, and Grable was personally friendly toward Marilyn. But in fact the studio publicity department wrote those words just as the two blondes, with the brunette Lauren Bacall, began work on *How To Marry a Millionaire* in March. An expensive Technicolor comedy, it was designed as Fox's attempt to make CinemaScope as effective for intimate films as for their biblical epic *The Robe*. The new wide-screen process and Marilyn Monroe: these were Fox's two major defences against the increasing defection of audiences to television. Just as with Technicolor, stereophonic sound, 3-D, Cinerama (and even a mercifully short-lived contraption called Smell-O-Vision or AromaRama), studios tried to provide by gimmickry what was often lacking in strong adult stories with coherent narrative construction.

The result of this rush to draw audiences also meant that roles could be specifically written (more often, simply sketched) for popular stars. The clever writer and producer Nunnally Johnson had already provided Marilyn and Fox with her episode in *We're Not Married*; now he was ready to oblige both by presenting her, Grable and Bacall in what was essentially a fashion show. Based on two tired old plays, the title *How To Marry a Millionaire* summarized its plot about three gold-diggers who pool their resources, rent a Manhattan penthouse and set about capturing rich husbands.

Although for her sleeping scene Marilyn caused a stir (as she had during *Niagara*) by wearing nothing underneath the sheets, she was as usual paradoxically terrified to step clothed before the camera. When she was finally able, however, an intensity occurred – 'a love affair nobody around her was aware of,' according to her director, Jean Negulesco. 'It was a language of looks, a forbidden intimacy . . . The lenses were the audience.' And they responded by the hundreds of thousands. Before the summer, Marilyn was receiving more than 25,000 fan letters weekly and *Redbook*, following *Photoplay*, bestowed on Marilyn yet another award – 'Best Young Box Office Personality'. All this notoriety and the unimaginable fame did not, however, turn her head; she affected no airs, demanded no privileges. She remained herself; as she had said, it all seemed to be happening to someone else.

Never had Natasha been less necessary to Marilyn's performance than in *How To Marry a Millionaire*, but the actress seemed 'under the spell of her dramatic coach', as Nunnally Johnson recalled. 'By this time,' added Marilyn's co-star Alex D'Arcy, 'Natasha was really advising her badly, justifying her own presence on the set by requiring take after take and simply feeding on Marilyn's insecurity. "Well, that was all right, dear," she often said to Marilyn, "but maybe we should do it one more time."'

The standard manoeuvre ensued during shooting that spring. First, Marilyn demanded retakes of every shot until she saw the nod of approbation from Natasha, who was at last banished by the exasperated producer and director on 13 April. Then, claiming an attack of bronchitis, Marilyn failed to appear for work next day. Finally, Natasha was reinstated – and at a higher salary. 'Monroe cannot do a picture without [Lytess],' her agent Charles Feldman wrote in a memo to his staff after visiting the film set. 'The coach threatens to quit unless she is compensated in a substantial manner.'

But also typically, this capitulation was well rewarded. As the myopic Pola, Marilyn had the least onscreen time of the pretty trio, yet she gave a comic performance worthy of Harold Lloyd or Charlie Chaplin, crashing hilariously into doors and walls when not wearing her glasses.* The camera also captured brief moments of real sweetness, for Pola (very like Marilyn herself, as Johnson doubtless intended) is an insecure young woman, fearful of rejection and dependent on the kindness of friends.

Marilyn's droll rendering of near-sighted Pola was her first important comic role, and with it she joined a short list of women who successfully combined humour and sexual allure: Mabel Normand, Clara Bow, Marion Davies, Colleen Moore and Jean Harlow made up nearly the entire pre-Monroe list; Carole Lombard and Lucille Ball were highly attractive women, to be sure, but their films stressed lightning comic antics rather than sexiness. In fact most comediennes were defiantly plain –

---

* The picture is spiced with lines rewarding the movie buff. Modelling a luscious orange bathing suit at a fashion show, Marilyn enters as a hostess comments, 'You know, of course, that gentlemen prefer blondes – and this is our proof of it!' Similarly, Bacall protests a fondness for much older men: 'Look at that old fellow what's-his-name in *The African Queen* . . .' – a reference, of course, to her husband Humphrey Bogart (twenty-five years her senior).

those like Louise Fazenda, Marie Dressler and Fanny Brice. With the success of *Gentlemen Prefer Blondes* and *How To Marry a Millionaire*, Marilyn conjoined a carefully planned comic timing to the appealing accidents provided by nature. With these films, too, she learned how much could be communicated by adopting Jean Harlow's trademark humming of the simple sound 'Mmmmm' to suggest just about anything, and her ability to stand quite still and overwhelm the presence of every other moving actor in a scene.

Some of the nuances in her performance may well have derived from classes she attended that spring at the Turnabout Theater: Michael Chekhov introduced her to the famous mime Lotte Goslar, who trained actors in certain aspects of subtle movement and body language. During the production of *How To Marry a Millionaire*, Marilyn went to group sessions with Goslar. Her shyness, however, precluded her engaging in exercises with classmates or improvising with them more than once or twice, and so she attended only infrequently.

Despite Marilyn's idiosyncracies, even Lauren Bacall, no cheerful martyr to the tardiness of fellow-players, had to admit that there was 'no meanness in her – no bitchery. I liked her. She said that what she really wanted was to be in San Francisco with Joe DiMaggio in some spaghetti joint.' Marilyn also endeared herself to Betty Grable, who had been passed over for the role of Lorelei Lee. When Grable's daughter was hurt while horse-riding, Marilyn telephoned frequently, offering help and comfort – 'and she was the only person to call', according to Grable. ('Honey,' she said warmly to Marilyn one day during production, 'I've had mine – now go get yours.')

Similarly, Alex D'Arcy recalled trying to calm Marilyn's fears of inadequacy by inviting her to dine out one evening and praising her acute comic timing. 'I looked into those famous liquid eyes,' he recalled, 'and saw only a little scared child. I had to avert my gaze to hide the twinge of pity I felt.' Try though they might, the Hollywood press could not find titbits concerning professional jealousy during the production of either *Gentlemen Prefer Blondes* or *How To Marry a Millionaire*.

*

The 'little scared child' was lonely when Joe travelled on business for much of that spring. DiMaggio's paternalistic criticisms had become as familiar as his slightly condescending protectiveness, and his absence seemed to summon the abandonment she had felt earlier – in her childhood and when Jim Dougherty shipped out during the war. Typically, Marilyn turned to her surrogate papa, Sidney Skolsky, for comfort and companionship. She chauffeured him to his appointments when she had no shooting call and accompanied him to the occasional Hollywood wedding (Sheilah Graham's), to a nightclub opening and to a party for visiting royalty (the King and Queen of Greece, who turned up in Hollywood that autumn).

But Marilyn felt forsaken if separated from Sidney for ten minutes, as happened at a party given by the actor Clifton Webb. Desperately, she followed Judy Garland from room to room. 'I don't want to get too far away from you – I'm scared,' Marilyn said – to which the equally insecure Garland replied, 'We're all scared. I'm scared too.' Marilyn was also tense and self-conscious when Sidney squired her to a sneak preview of *Gentlemen Prefer Blondes* early that June; displeased with her own image on the screen, she seemed to enjoy only scenes without her.

No such anxiety was evident on 26 June, when Monroe and Russell signed their names and placed their hands and feet in wet cement on the forecourt of the Chinese Theater on Hollywood Boulevard – the very place where Gladys and Grace had pointed out the marks of other stars almost two decades earlier. Dressed in matching white polka-dot summer dresses, the blonde and the brunette joined a long list of movie stars who for thirty years had accepted Sid Grauman's invitation to this awkward act of movieland exaltation.* That evening, Skolsky

---

* The tradition began when Mary Pickford and Douglas Fairbanks accidentally stepped into freshly poured cement in front of the theatre, and Grauman, leaping to assist them, asked the stars to make a virtue of necessity and add signatures to footprints. Marilyn's were not far from those of Jean Harlow, who had obliged Grauman on 29 September 1935.

took the two stars to dinner at Chasen's restaurant, an autograph hound's delight where even the normally blasé kitchen staff slipped into the dining-room to watch Monroe and Russell tuck in to their steaks and fried potatoes. For an entire week, the day's events were detailed in words and pictures on the pages of every major American newspaper and magazine, which gave them as much coverage as the coronation of Queen Elizabeth II that same month and even more than the highly publicized engagement of that glamorous couple, Senator John F. Kennedy and Miss Jacqueline Bouvier.

By early summer, Fox had given Marilyn her next assignment. Following the unjust rejection of her touching, subdued performance in the unpretentious and underrated *Don't Bother to Knock*, the studio had put her in leading roles against a mighty waterfall (in *Niagara*), on a luxury liner and in a pasteboard Paris (in *Gentlemen Prefer Blondes*) and in a Manhattan penthouse (in *How To Marry a Millionaire*). It was perhaps inevitable that eventually she would be cast as a saloon singer in a western.

Like the previous Technicolor extravaganzas, *River of No Return* was full of impressive scenery and special effects; it was also, alas, a bundle of clichés, and neither the splendour of the Canadian Rockies nor Marilyn's maturing beauty could redeem ninety minutes of celluloid ennui.

The first problem (about which she complained to Fox at once) was the tiresome story of an ex-prisoner cowboy who finds his lost little boy in the care of a mining-camp singer. Deceived by her greedy boyfriend, the trio – Marilyn, beefy Robert Mitchum and winsome little Tommy Rettig – are left amid the glories of nature to battle the perilous rapids of the eponymous river; Indians who are out for any white scalp they can find; a hungry bobcat; and fortune hunters who appear out of nowhere with rifles and threats. After negotiating their route on a flimsy raft along the final stretch of water, they come to town and to a final shootout that will make of them a happy little family.

This was Marilyn Monroe's twenty-second film and her fifth leading part, but Twentieth Century-Fox still had no idea what to do with her. The truth is that, whatever special qualities she brought to them, any actress could have played her roles: for they required little more of her than to pose picturesquely, walk seductively, gaze blankly and sing a few songs that fed male fantasies and confirmed the cherished belief that pretty blondes are both dumb and venal. Object though she did, Marilyn was constrained to abide by her contract, and she fervently devoted herself to music rehearsals. As the performer Kay in *River of No Return* she was required to deliver four songs, which she did with admirable panache – a torch song ('One Silver Dollar'); a bawdy backroom ballad ('I'm Gonna File My Claim'); a tune to amuse a boy ('Down in the Meadow'); and the title number. Thirty years after her death, this quartet was at last commercially released as part of Marilyn's complete recordings, too late to have rightly celebrated her as a first-rate vocalist independent of an arid movie but permanent confirmation that she was capable of far more than was asked. As so often, her moments onscreen provide the picture's only interest.

The second problem with *River of No Return* was the choice of director. Viennese-born Otto Preminger was trained as a lawyer and aspired to a judgeship; but he turned to film-making (most notably of *Laura* in 1944), in which he was reputed to act not only as jury but also executioner with his casts and crews – a dictatorial man who could reduce even the hardiest actors to sobs. This turgid western was an assignment for Preminger as for Marilyn, but one for which he was culturally unfit, and this pitched him into an unmellow humour from the start.

At the centre of the production's problems that summer was Natasha, who was 'trying to direct [the picture]', according to Marilyn's agent, Charles Feldman. 'I pleaded with [Marilyn] to relax and speak naturally,' recalled Preminger, 'but she paid no attention. She listened only to Natasha ... and rehearsed her lines with such grave ar-tic-yew-lay-shun that her violent lip movements made it impossible to photograph her ... Marilyn was putty in [Natasha's] hands.'

Those hands could be tenacious, as Natasha herself unwittingly admitted: 'Marilyn,' she said one day in Canada, 'you don't care about me, only my work with you. If you didn't need me, you wouldn't know how to spell my name.' To such desperate statements it is almost impossible to reply, nor could Marilyn find one satisfactory to Natasha. 'Marilyn thought there was some magic in Natasha,' said Robert Mitchum years later. 'She felt she needed someone other than a director, preferably a woman, to tell her when she did something right.'

The tension was not helped by the sheer physical demands placed on Marilyn, who had (both on location and in the studio) to cope with real and recreated rapids. Paul Wurtzel, chief of Fox's special effects department, recalled that Marilyn was subjected to considerable rough treatment – gallons of water thrown at her for take after take on the raft, to mention just one difficult sequence. 'We put her through a lot on that film, and there was never one complaint. She knew what the picture required, and once we got her on her marks she was a pro. The whole crew adored her.'

Dominated by her coach, longing to please her director and (thus Robert Mitchum) fearful of going before the cameras because she was terrified of being judged, Marilyn nevertheless shone in the final cut. There was something inconsonant about her as a nineteenth-century performer in the crude wilderness: her tight jeans, stylish blouse and perfect makeup were absurdly anachronistic. At the same time (as in *Niagara*), she was both the startling exponent of unpredictable nature and a figure in stark contrast to it. Her best moments have the ingenuous, direct appeal springing from her amalgam of tenacity and softness: singing on a makeshift stage in a mining camp; collapsing with chills and hunger in the forest; seeing the futility of her long affair with a handsome but nasty manipulator; realizing her love for quiet, protective Mitchum and his brave little boy.*

---

* 'I wouldn't accept *River of No Return* [as an assignment] today,' Marilyn said in 1955. 'I think I deserve a better deal than grade-Z cowboy movie in which the act-

Her achievement was all the more remarkable because, as Mitchum, Wurtzel and Snyder recalled, Marilyn rarely had a moment to herself, either in Canada or back in the studio. Publicists arranged a constant stream of interviews; Zanuck or one of his minions telephoned her daily to recite Preminger's complaints about Natasha; and Joe, anxious about false rumours of a flirtation between Marilyn and Mitchum, arrived with his friend George Solotaire. The threatening eddies and the chilly Canadian nights were easy to sustain by comparison with the emotional squalls swirling around her.

Snyder recalled one quiet, important moment. On a train to location shooting, he and Marilyn were admiring the spectacular scenery when he said, 'Here are the Canadian Rockies, Marilyn. If you're really in love with Joe, why don't you get out of the movie business? The two of you could move up here, build yourselves a beautiful house, settle down and have kids.' She thought for a moment. 'Whitey, I know all that,' she said sadly, 'but I can't do that – I just can't.' She did not elaborate.

While Marilyn worked days, Joe fished, hunted and then waited at Becker's Bungalows in Jasper, Alberta (where the cast and crew were also housed), and at the Mount Royal Hotel in Banff when the company moved there. They could live together at times like this, but whenever there was talk of marriage she was even more uncertain than just before a movie scene. As Snyder recalled, 'Joe could be very hard to get along with – surly and withdrawn – and he was awfully jealous. Marilyn liked to invite a few people for coffee or a drink at the end of the day, but when Joe was around the mood was dark. He hated the movies and everything to do with them.'* Joe's only practical purpose was the star's comfort, especially after she turned her ankle in Jasper National Park on 19 August – a minor incident that brought a famished press back in full force, as if she

---

ing finished second to the scenery and the CinemaScope process. The studio was [backing] the scenery instead of actors and actresses.'

* The press, however, saw only undiluted bliss in the Monroe-DiMaggio affair: even the New York *Times*, on 12 July, was delighted to report their 'long-time romance'.

were moribund, to document her hobbling about on crutches and behaving bravely.

Location shooting in Canada was completed at the end of August, and on 1 September, Marilyn, Joe and the company returned to Hollywood for interior scenes at Fox. When the plane landed in Los Angeles, a throng of over a hundred reporters and photographers pushed forward, shouting questions, jostling for pictures and – rare for newsmen – applauding her wildly. Robert Mitchum had to exert all his considerable brawn to protect her from injury. 'She thought they were cheering for someone else,' he recalled.

By a fascinating coincidence, that week a historic book was published: Dr Alfred R. Kinsey's *Sexual Behavior in the Human Female*, which was even more controversial than his earlier companion volume, *Sexual Behavior in the Human Male*.

There was important news in the world that summer: the armistice ending the Korean War and the first return of American troops in early September; the controversy surrounding the execution of the alleged spies Ethel and Julius Rosenberg; the rantings of Senator Joseph McCarthy (who madly accused former President Truman of deliberately supporting Communism); the bloody Soviet crackdown against anti-Communist demonstrations in East Berlin and Russia's announcement that it had the hydrogen bomb.

But of equal importance to both the media and to the American people was Dr Kinsey's published research, the first serious scientific studies of sexual activity in the United States. The mere fact of its contents and availability virtually divided a country still mired in Puritanism, still in a kind of perpetual adolescence, incapable of confronting its collective *id*. Marilyn Monroe and *Gentlemen Prefer Blondes*, which opened nation-wide in July, were popular manifestations of precisely what Dr Kinsey was exploring and exactly what movie audiences both longed for and deeply feared.

From 1942 to his death in 1956, Kinsey, a zoologist, was director of the Institute for Sex Research at the University of Indiana. In 1948 he published *Sexual Behavior in the Human Male*, the first academic study of sexual activity in America and a surprise bestseller. Kinsey and his staff interviewed more than 5000 American males, of whom they asked detailed questions about their frequency of marital and extramarital intercourse, petting, masturbation, homosexual experiences and incidents of bestiality. When the book appeared in stores (and only a few public libraries), many municipal police departments tried to confiscate copies – just as women's groups and church societies had tried to interfere with interviews and suppress the publication. Shocking as the inquiry was, it was equalled by the news that the National Research Council and the Rockefeller Foundation had provided funding for the study. Millions claimed it was a filthy book and many shrugged it off as unnecessary and really quite boring; there is no count available on how many copies were borrowed, loaned, stolen and smuggled into schoolbags.

Then, more than 12,000 interviews and five years later, came *Sexual Behavior of the Human Female*, just when Marilyn Monroe was appearing daily in newspapers, weekly in magazines and constantly (or so it seemed) on the neighbourhood movie screens. Many civic and religious leaders attacked both Kinsey and Monroe as if they were directly, commercially linked, but neither could be controlled or contained. Marilyn cavorted her way through 'Diamonds Are a Girl's Best Friend' while the Institute for Sex Research organized and interpreted questionnaires, films, literature and art, thus attempting an interdisciplinary study of sex and sexual practices. In 1952, just when the scandal had broken over Marilyn's calendar poses, the United States Customs Office was suing the Institute for importing foreign erotica. Such works, after all, were carefully controlled by the authorities, lest the purity of the American mind be contaminated by unseemly considerations of matters sexual.

The Kinsey reports were designed to be read: although they extended to 800 pages, the format and contents were simple. After detailing their methodology, there were dispassionate, clinical lists of results. No consideration was allowed for either bravado or false humility, but the essential veracity of the reports was supported by the anonymous nature of the interviews and the frankness of the subject matter.

The 1948 study of men focused on the variety and frequency of heterosexual and homosexual activity, while in 1953 the women's study calmly dwelt – to the horror of millions in America – on the female orgasm. Equally appalling to many was Kinsey's sober insistence that no particular type of sexual activity could be called 'more normal' than any other type; on the contrary, he said, sexual activity runs a gamut of procedures and 'outlets'. Normality, in other words, is the province of legislatures and social customs.

The coincidence of the Kinsey reports with Marilyn Monroe's rise to stardom and her firm entrenchment within it was mutually reinforcing: for the first time, academic inquiry was taking seriously the most delicate aspect of popular awareness and that which required the most stringent regulations. Like Marilyn, Kinsey punctured the pretences of Puritan-Victorian moralism about desire (not to say female aggressiveness) that still persisted – in Hollywood through the Motion Picture Production Code and the Legion of Decency, and throughout the country in civic, school and church groups.

Of particular relevance to American life in general, and to the beginning of a widespread backlash against the sexual openness of characters represented by Marilyn Monroe, was the discovery that women's sex lives had changed dramatically since World War I. By 1950, Kinsey reported, more than half of the country's women were not virgins at the time of marriage; fully a quarter of married women had extramarital affairs; and, most astonishing of all, women were indeed *enjoying* sex. The American female, in other words, was leading a life quite different from the presumptions of American men. This claim was so sensational that Kinsey's publisher, who printed a first run of 500 copies, soon sold more than 250,000.

The week Marilyn's plane touched down in Los Angeles, *Time* magazine was trumpeting news of 'K-day' and detailing the contradictory reactions to Kinsey's publication by both press and public, for the book was dividing people as much as the morality of Marilyn's costumes and Lorelei's motives in *Gentlemen Prefer Blondes*. The New York *Times* buried the story of the Kinsey controversy in a remote inside page, while the Philadelphia *Bulletin* prepared a 3300-word report which it finally killed, fearful (as it said in an explanation to its readers) of giving 'unnecessary offense to many in [our] large family of readers'. The Chicago *Tribune* was less confused, dismissing the report as 'a real menace to society', while the Raleigh *Times* offered free copies. Perhaps predictably, Europe yawned: Italian newspapers mentioned Kinsey only briefly or ignored him altogether, while Paris expressed surprise that anyone could be surprised. Meanwhile, in American nightclubs, where any word connoting sexual intercourse was forbidden, the word 'Kinsey' was used as a code substitute to avoid obscenity charges. In 1953, straightforward discussion of sex could perhaps be found only in Kinsey's books, medical and psychiatric seminars and high school locker-rooms.*

In fascinating ways, then, Marilyn Monroe's rise to the height of stardom coincided with the Kinsey report on women and when America itself was in the throes of a kind of adolescent confusion about sex. She replaced the bawdy, wisecracking Mae West and the sparkling allure of Jean Harlow (both phenomena of the 1930s) with something at once adult and childlike.

---

* As if on cue that same September, calendar distributors and playing card manufacturers were reshipping in record numbers the image of Marilyn Monroe nude. Hot on their trail were the police, who in several cities raided shops, confiscating calendars as if they were dangerous chemicals. One hapless Los Angeles businessman, Phil Max, made headlines round the country that year when he was arrested and fined after placing 'A New Wrinkle' in the window of his camera store on Wilshire Boulevard.

Although in herself she transcended America's fantasies by a constant effort at self-perfection, Marilyn simultaneously represented those fantasies. She was the postwar ideal of the American girl, soft, transparently needy, worshipful of men, naïve, offering sex without demands.

But there was also something quietly aggressive in her self-presentation as a frankly carnal creature; thus by a curious congruence, her sexual impact both matched and resisted the cultural expectations of 1953. Vulnerable and frightened though she was (and often appeared to be onscreen), there was also something tenacious and independent about her. And perhaps most disturbing of all to a culture in such turmoil, she made overt sexuality seem respectable. The ladylike Audrey Hepburn and Grace Kelly received the Academy Awards, but Marilyn was everywhere mobbed and constantly heard the cheers of thousands.

At the same time, this unwitting pioneer had to be presented by the studio mostly as one of life's contingencies – little more than a dumb blonde (and thought so by the country) in order that she could charm without challenge. Men could appreciate her without feeling she had triumphed over them, and women could sense that she was no threat at all. Her admirers yielded to her without handing her a victory – or even, finally, any respect at all.

But because she seemed to be a woman with a strong sense of her body's power, she was an exponent, a summary of the post-war American woman Kinsey reported – and like Kinsey's woman, she could not yet be taken seriously. In this regard, it is perhaps easier to understand America's obsession with her during her life and since her death, for in considering Marilyn Monroe, the culture had somehow to confront both the reality of a responsive yet independent woman as well as the threat she posed to both sexes, the unfulfilled dreams and the personal (not merely sexual) maturity both longed for and feared in the American woman.

This entire amalgam of desire and confusion about Marilyn

and her problematic presence was in a way symbolically represented in her live television debut on 13 September. As a guest on Jack Benny's comedy show, she portrayed herself in a dream sequence on a ship's deck. But when Benny awoke there was only a large, unattractive woman at his side – who is then miraculously transmuted into Marilyn Monroe. 'She was superb,' according to Benny. 'She knew the hard-to-learn secret of reading comedy lines as if they were in a drama and letting the humor speak for itself.' Her Fox contract prohibited cash compensation for this performance, but Marilyn could accept a new black Cadillac convertible with red leather interior which she proudly sported around town for the next two years.

As usual, one of her tasks in the new car was to chauffeur her friend Skolsky, who continued to stand in for the occasionally absent Joe DiMaggio. That autumn, Marilyn and Sidney were seen at Ciro's cheering Johnnie Ray; in such surroundings, even the celebrities acted like fans and begged for her autograph. 'Success has helped The Monroe,' Skolsky noted. 'But she hasn't lost that rare combination of being part of the crowd as well as aloof at the same time.'

This remark went perhaps deeper than he intended, for during her recent history Marilyn had (rather like royalty) cultivated both an involvement with people and a distance from them. A singular example of this paradox occurred when she learned on 28 September of the death of Grace McKee Goddard, who after several years of chronic alcoholism and crippling strokes took her life at the age of fifty-eight by means of an overdose of the barbiturate phenobarbital. When Grace was buried at the Westwood Memorial Park on 1 October, Marilyn was not among the mourners.

Her absence had less to do with a shyness of crowds than the fact that for years there had been virtually no communication between the two women. Grace, who had effectively planted the seed of Marilyn's career, had shaped its destiny, groomed and encouraged young Norma Jeane, had been excluded from the realized success and was never present at the celebrations of stardom. After an exchange of a few warm letters in the early part of Norma Jeane's marriage to Dougherty, subsequent correspondence was only sporadic, concerned mostly with the care and lodging of Gladys.

Marilyn's withdrawal was at least partly the result of Grace's retreat into a haze of alcohol and drug dependence – a condition that so frightened Marilyn on two visits in 1949 and 1951 that she avoided meetings thereafter. In this regard, Grace may have reminded her of the gradual loss of Gladys. In effectively cutting off relations with Grace, Marilyn avoided being rejected again by the one who had once before abandoned her by marrying her off and departing to West Virginia.

In a sad way, Marilyn's distance from Grace was the ironic fulfilment of the distance Marilyn had once felt from Gladys – a void Grace had both filled and exploited. Making Gladys's daughter her own, she had set in motion the schedule of her own eventual rejection, for at the end Grace had succeeded only too well in transforming her friend's child into a creature of her own fantasy. She had also arranged Norma Jeane's marriage and participated in its dissolution, sending her to stay with her Aunt Minnie so that a quick Nevada divorce would expedite the first contract with Fox. Married for years to a shiftless, womanizing tippler and suffering both illness and addiction, Grace could no longer endure the complete loss of meaning in her own life as she watched Marilyn's thrive.

Denied participation in the career for which she felt responsible – and perhaps in some unadmitted way burdened with guilt for the separation between Gladys and her daughter – Grace saw death as her only refuge. When she was found lifeless on a fragile cot in her Van Nuys bungalow, the undramatic finale had in some ways the contours of classical tragedy. There lacked only a recognition scene and the catharsis of articulated pity for a woman driven and ultimately destroyed by that wildest of American furies, the savage quest for stardom's empty affirmation.

By the time she was twenty-seven, all the women Marilyn

Monroe had known as role-models had come to unfortunate ends. It is not surprising, therefore, that she turned again to Natasha Lytess as a surrogate mother and spent more time with her.

Although she did not attend the gala event, Natasha helped select a studio gown for the premiere of *How To Marry a Millionaire* on 4 November. Before the screening, Nunnally Johnson and his wife Dorris invited to their home for drinks and a buffet supper Marilyn, Lauren Bacall and her husband Humphrey Bogart. Vivacious, laughing and radiantly beautiful, Marilyn was also edgy with excitement over the imminent reception of the film. Unaccustomed to liquor, she downed three beakers of bourbon and soda and headed for the theatre, amiably supported by the notorious imbiber Bogart – her gait as much restricted by her tight dress as by her tight confusion. The waiting crowd, however, saw only their beloved Marilyn and repeatedly roared her name as an array of celebrities arrived. Dressed in platinum-coloured silk with shining beads, she was indeed the cynosure of all eyes. That night, as Jean Negulesco recalled, Marilyn felt 'she had proved to everyone (and herself) that she could stand any competition.'

Marilyn's entrance into the theatre, reported a trade journal, defied everything 'since Gloria Swanson at her most glittering', but a few snide comments from her contemporaries did not escape her attention. 'This is just about the happiest night of my life,' she said. 'It's like when I was a little girl and pretended wonderful things were happening to me. Now they are. But it's funny how success makes so many people hate you. I wish it wasn't that way. It would be wonderful to enjoy success without seeing envy in the eyes of those around you.'

She may well have been thinking of Natasha Lytess as much as of any proximate star rival. Coach and occasional, unofficial dresser she may have been, but Natasha was also (thus Marilyn) 'going quite made and asking [my] attorney to give her $5000 to cover medical costs about to be incurred by surgery. I am completely fed up with her and now realize that she is an extremely tricky woman. But,' she added kindly, 'I don't want her to lose her job at Fox.'

There were, it seems, three reasons for this sudden shift in attitude. First, after twenty films under Natasha's tutelage, it was clear that not one of Marilyn's colleagues had ever approved of the coach's tactics or appreciated her interference. At last the complaints had accumulated beyond Marilyn's ability to ignore them. Second, Marilyn was quite simply gaining in confidence; third, she wished to please Joe. By late 1953, according to Marilyn's new agent Hugh French, Lytess's days were 'numbered, and in the long run that surely must be a good thing for Marilyn.'

The end of the Marilyn–Natasha symbiosis, which would actually require two more years for its official rupture, was applauded by no more than Joe, who after almost two years of courtship at last obtained Marilyn's consent to marry him. At the same time, he was resentful of her attachment to Hollywood in general as much as to Natasha in particular, and he constantly urged Marilyn to quit moviemaking altogether – or at least to improve her financial status in the business, which was his only level of interest in it. On 1 December, for example, after a meeting with Marilyn, Feldman's colleague Ray Stark drafted an inter-office memorandum to the effect that DiMaggio had 'convinced Marilyn not to do any more Fox pictures until she can negotiate a better contract.'

Joe could not have realized that there were soon to be identical suggestions from Marilyn's old acquaintance, the photographer Milton Greene, who would add to his counsel the idea of a bold new venture. He arrived in October with his new bride Amy, a former Richard Avedon model who subsequently worked as an executive fashion consultant.

Since their brief fling in 1949, Milton (now thirty-one) had left *Life* for *Look* magazine and had become one of the most sought-after celebrity photographers. One of his assignments in 1953 was a series on Hollywood stars, and that summer he took nine portraits of Marilyn as she strummed an antique mandolin and then half-reclined, casual and relaxed in a short, provocative black caftan. When Milton's photographs were published in the 17 November issue of *Look*, Marilyn sent him a dozen roses in gratitude.

But there was more. Milton also listened to Marilyn complain of the studio system, of her absurd salary ($1500 a week) considering the great sums her films were making for Fox, and of her boredom with roles like Lorelei, Pola and Kay. He suggested that they consider forming their own production company, to raise finance, choose subjects and directors, and bring their best creative efforts to bear on Marilyn's future. And so there was set in motion a crucial turn in Marilyn's professional life and, as she and Milton began to speak quietly with their attorneys, a complicated task that would transport her from Hollywood for over a year and help to alter for ever the tradition of actors' long-term contracts to studios. From Milton Greene, in other words, she was hearing the counsel, the concern and the offer of representation no agent had given her since the death of Johnny Hyde.

At this time, the Greenes and Marilyn became fast friends – primarily because, according to Amy, Milton saw a potential in her that no one else had, and she began to rely on him. He had rendered her sublimely in still photographs: what might they not accomplish together as producers of films specifically made for and starring the most famous woman in the history of entertainment?

On 21 November 1953, Joe left Los Angeles for San Francisco, where he began to make quiet plans for their wedding. Marilyn, meanwhile, kept her counsel and when ordered to report for ten days of difficult interior retakes on the dreaded *River of No Return*, 'she cooperated to the fullest', as the vigilant Hugh French was pleased to observe.

Everyone had good reason, therefore, to expect that Marilyn would comply with Fox's order for her to report on 15 December for her next assignment – a silly affair called *Pink Tights*, a remake of Betty Grable's 1943 film *Coney Island*, about a schoolteacher-turned-music hall crooner. But this stereotypical role was only one of the last straws in the burden of Marilyn's resentment against Fox. Nor was she mollified by the news that Frank Sinatra would co-star, for she also learned that he would be paid $5000 a week, more than three times her salary.*

At a quarter to midnight on 23 December, as studio executives wondered how to bring pressure on her for being a week late to work, she boarded Western Air Lines flight 440. Booked as Miss Norma Dougherty, she paid $15.53 for a cheap seat in the rear of the aircraft and stowed a small overnight bag with one suit, a skirt and two sweaters. But lavish Christmas gifts from Joe (among them a mink coat) awaited her in San Francisco.

---

* Her resentment of this discrepancy may have motivated her blunt 'reservations' about Sinatra's recent album when she spoke with Dave Garroway on the 'Today' television show early in 1954: otherwise, she always spoke with highest praise for him.

Chapter Thirteen

JANUARY – SEPTEMBER 1954

Marilyn Monroe's career spanned sixteen years. During the first eight, 1947 to 1954, she appeared in twenty-four productions; during the second half, from 1955 to 1962, only five. For years this diminution in professional activity – never caused by any loss of her worldwide popularity – was put down to laziness, alcohol and drug addiction and psychological problems that led at last to an almost blithe self-destruction.

It is true that Marilyn could be capricious and self-absorbed: with her emotional and psychological needs, she did well to be concerned with sorting the real from the specious requirements. Professionally, this often led her to be remiss in her duties, chronically late and apparently unconcerned for the welfare of her colleagues. But these faults were never deliberate, and anyone who knew her attested that whenever she was confronted with the turmoil her bad habits caused, Marilyn was truly contrite.

As for chemical dependence, Marilyn was never an alcoholic: in fact, she had little tolerance for liquor, as the premiere party for *How To Marry a Millionaire* demonstrated. A few evenings of overindulgence make for good gossip, but not an accurate diagnosis of alcoholism. More serious was her addiction to sleeping pills, which began innocently in early 1954 during a period of routine insomnia due to jet lag. The pills were cheerfully handed out to her in generous free samples from Sidney Skolsky, who had unlimited access to them at Schwab's.

Chemical dependence was poorly understood as late as the

1960s; it was also something Marilyn's colleagues, employers and friends did little to correct. Barbiturates to sleep, amphetamines to stay awake, narcotics to relax – in Hollywood, these were as plentiful as agents, and could easily be obtained through the studio front office. Bookshelves are heavy with horror tales of film stars' lives imperilled or destroyed by careless physicians working for uncaring studio executives who ordered whatever was necessary to get a performer through a production. Errol Flynn, Judy Garland, Tyrone Power, Montgomery Clift, Richard Burton, Elizabeth Taylor – the list of names stretches from the days of silent films to the time of music videos. Sidney shared his supplies with Marilyn ignorant of the dangerous effects: he even boasted in his column that he offered her whatever she needed whenever she was ill or even irritable – that Joe called Marilyn and Sidney 'pill-pals, not pen-pals'.

Yet of all movie stars, Marilyn Monroe's reputation has suffered the most – perhaps because of her fundamental benevolence, her youth, her simplicity, her patent longing to belong. Such a woman, to whom the fantasies and hopes of an entire culture were attached, was not allowed weakness. She had to be as perfect as her onscreen beauty, her strength as unmarred as her face, the blond halo a sign of inner perfection. The culture, in other words, asked more of Marilyn Monroe than perhaps of anyone in its popular history. And because she was a woman, she seemed to fail twice as badly, to disappoint infinitely more than the tipsy chaps at the bar or the roués sneaking in and out of Beverly Hills bedrooms.

But she was always a sign of contradiction, and so in a way the public wanted her to fail. She evoked forbidden desires, she represented the full flourishing of unabashed sexual femininity. In 1969, the drug-induced death of Judy Garland, never a sex symbol, elicited pity. But Marilyn Monroe, it was implied, was receiving only fair retribution when, it was erroneously reported, she died of an accidental (or intended) overdose. But this idea of her failure and collapse, which has taken on the status of conventional wisdom, cannot be supported by facts.

Marilyn Monroe worked less frequently in films during the last eight years of her life not because her powers were failing but because they were being refined, because she tried to work more often and more deeply in life – and in this enterprise she succeeded remarkably often against appalling odds. The most artificial, expensive and undisciplined entertainment form in history was not the best place for a woman whose childhood melded into an adolescence founded on the enforced models of aspiring to stardom and entering a premature marriage.

To be sure, Marilyn's benighted past led her to crave the *effects* of stardom: the applause, the wide field of anonymous adoration so often mistaken for personal love. Equally evident is the fact that she had neither the background nor temperament for the discipline serious acting requires. Famished for respect, endorsement and simply a reason to believe in her own worth, she was ripe for the inconstant but well-oiled machinery of Hollywood. Ironically, by her own co-operation she had become something deeply artificial – Marilyn Monroe The Superstar – and of this she was acutely if inarticulately aware in her twenty-eighth year.

Marilyn's actions throughout 1954 were an attempt to demonstrate her seriousness of purpose by daily deeds rather than grand gesture, public apology or self-defence. During this year, she moved quickly, openly defying her studio, then marrying, travelling abroad for the first time in a one-woman show and finally abandoning the troubled marriage and quitting Hollywood for New York.

First she stood up to the studio. Suspended by Fox on 4 January 1954 for failing to appear on the set of *Pink Tights* and denied her normal income until she returned to fulfil her contractual obligations, Marilyn instructed her attorney, Loyd Wright, to tell the press that she was 'not fighting over money. The whole trouble hinges on the fact that the studio has refused to let Marilyn look at the script. She wants to be sure it's a good one for her.'

On two counts, this was an interesting position to publicize:

first, because at stake was indeed her salary – only a fraction of what less popular actors earned despite her status as one of the top five money-making stars in the world; second, although she had no right of script approval, she knew that studios often invited important actors to review a script – the unilateral imposition of one could result in a disappointing performance. It was, in other words, in producers' own interest to find scripts that appealed to their employees. In the case of Marilyn, Fox thought it best to keep her in the successful rut of the last several pictures without consulting her first, while she (and, for different reasons, Joe DiMaggio and Milton Greene) wanted major changes in the direction of her life and career.

Of *River of No Return* and *There's No Business Like Show Business*, Marilyn said a few years later,

> I was put into these movies without being consulted at all, much against my wishes. I had no choice in the matter. Is that fair? I work hard, I take pride in my work, and I'm a human being like the rest of them. If I keep on with parts like the ones [Fox] has been giving me, the public will soon tire of me.

As for *Pink Tights*, she was adamant: 'I read the script and didn't like it. The part isn't good for me. It's as simple as that. Of course I'd like a salary adjustment, but right now I'm more interested in getting a good script so I can make a good picture.'

On Pico Boulevard this brought men close to panic, for Fox stockholders and New York executives were beginning to jam the telephone lines, urging that this unfortunate and potentially disastrous situation be corrected with all despatch. But Zanuck, less courteously than she, took as hard a line as Marilyn: 'I couldn't believe she'd be this crazy. We've got a $2,200,000 production planned; the script is completed to our satisfaction and we are not obligated to send it to her [which he already had done]. The picture is written and designed for her.' And so, for the first two weeks of 1954, the battle lines were drawn and no quarter given.

In this matter, Marilyn was again taking a page from the life of Jean Harlow, who fought for years to overcome her image and play a wider variety of roles. She, too, went on strike for a better salary, a new contract, more artistic freedom and more serious pictures, goals in which she was encouraged even by the most studio-subservient Hollywood magazine, *Photoplay*. In January 1934, exactly twenty years before Marilyn's adventure, Harlow got her new contract with Louis B. Mayer – a deal that would at first pay her $3000 a week (at the height of the Great Depression) and ultimately twice that.*

Nor was the Harlow connection lost on the press when news of the Monroe-DiMaggio wedding filled headlines worldwide. 'Marilyn herself is a girl full of surprises,' noted *Time*. 'She is also the most talked about new star since Harlow.' *Life* agreed: she was 'the inheritor of a tradition founded by Jean Harlow.' Anticipated for two years but announced only an hour in advance, the marriage was somehow not perceived as anticlimax: it was the union of two of the most adored (and poorly understood) Americans of the century. After a stormy courtship, everything subsequent happened with astonishing swiftness, from the ceremony itself through the short term of the marriage.

Self-promotion was second nature to Marilyn, and she saw the value of first informing a publicist at Fox: she telephoned Harry Brand from San Francisco, at 1.30 PM on 14 January. Then she stepped into the City Hall chambers of Municipal Judge Charles S. Peery, where bride and groom signed the register: Joe stated his age accurately as thirty-nine; she gave her true legal name (Norma Jeane Mortenson Dougherty) but took three years from her age and wrote twenty-five. Wearing a dark brown broadcloth suit with an ermine collar, she then stood by Joe's side, three orchids shaking slightly in her hand as she promised to 'love, honor and cherish' – the absence of a vow to

* Similar studio wars were ignited by feisty, determined performers such as Bette Davis, Katharine Hepburn and Olivia de Havilland.

'obey' duly noted by the reporter permitted in chambers. Several relatives and friends of Joe were witnesses; Marilyn had no loved ones present. When the orchids quickly withered in the warmth of her hand, she turned to Joe: if she died before him, would he place flowers at her grave every week – just as William Powell had done at the grave of his beloved Jean Harlow? Joe promised.

Attempting a hasty retreat from the judge's chambers, the DiMaggios were mobbed by two hundred reporters and photographers and more than three hundred fans admitted to City Hall. The newly-weds were forced to submit to flashbulbs and questions, to kiss for the camera, then to kiss again.

How many children did they plan? 'I'd like to have six,' replied Marilyn. 'One,' said Joe.

Where would they live? 'Here, San Francisco,' said Joe. 'I'm going to continue my career,' said Marilyn, adding after a glance from Joe, 'but I'm looking forward to being a housewife, too.'

With that, Joe almost growled, 'Let's go.' He took Marilyn's hand and hurried towards a rear staircase. They took a wrong turn into the Assessor's Office, crashed into a score of autograph hounds on two staircases and finally reached Joe's dark blue Cadillac outside. He raced the engine and they sped away, ignoring the last question about their honeymoon location.*

By late that afternoon, they had driven south to the town of Paso Robles, where Joe took a six-dollar room at the modest Clifton Motel, insisting on a double bed and a television set. 'It usually rents for seven-fifty,' said the motel owner, Ernest Sharp, 'but this is the off-season.' Days later, he told the press that Marilyn was 'radiant' but Joe 'solemn and tired'. He had, Sharp concluded, overheard Joe say to his bride enigmatically, 'We've got to put a lot of miles behind us.'

Next morning, Marilyn telephoned Loyd Wright for news

---

* Among cities worldwide, London was pre-eminently excited by the wedding. 'Marilyn weds', announced the *Daily Express* in a banner headline. 'Oh, what a housewife!' exclaimed the *Daily Sketch*. 'I'm yours for keeps, Joesey boy', the *Daily Mirror* improvised.

and messages; apparently as a gesture of goodwill on her marriage, Fox had lifted the suspension. She was back on payroll and respectfully asked to return to work on 20 January for *Pink Tights* rehearsals. But Joe was adamant: his wife would not appear in a movie scantily clad and portraying a woman of easy virtue. Her wedding vow formula notwithstanding, Marilyn obeyed. When she had not presented herself at work by the twenty-sixth, business considerations prevailed and the suspension was again imposed. Leaving Paso Robles on 15 January, the DiMaggios drove further south, past Los Angeles to a hideaway near Palm Springs, where Joe demanded that their room be changed when he could not get first-rate reception on the television set.

Retired Joe might have been, but he was eager to retain his star status. Before the marriage he had agreed to accompany his old friend and mentor Frank 'Lefty' O'Doul and his new bride Jean to exhibition baseball games and rookie training sessions in Japan. Marilyn, longing to be the loyal wife, decided to travel with him – even at the risk of further antagonizing Fox.

Just past midnight on 29 January the DiMaggios and the O'Douls prepared to depart for Tokyo on Pan American's flight 831. Wearing an uncharacteristically matronly and dour black suit softened only by a leopard-skin choker, Marilyn arrived at San Francisco Airport with her right hand hidden in a mink coat. When one of the pressmen noticed a splinted and taped thumb peeking out, an embarrassed Marilyn was at once interrogated.

'I just bumped it,' she said awkwardly. 'I have a witness. Joe was there. He heard it crack.' When pressed for details, she turned away coolly and became silent. This was the first indication, to the press and to their friends, that the union had a dark side. Signs of violence would surface with alarming frequency during the next eight months, and they were curiously reflected by Marilyn's ambiguous sobriquet for Joe – 'my Slugger' – although as she often said, she had never seen him play baseball.

The subject of the broken thumb was quickly changed by Joe, who was ordinarily silent during encounters with the press. He said Marilyn would visit army hospitals in Japan, where many American soldiers who had fought in Korea were recuperating. 'Yes,' said added weakly, 'I hope to do that.' Asked if she would soon return to movie acting, she replied simply, 'I don't know. I'm under suspension.'

'We're not concerned about that now,' said Joe, escorting his wife away from the reporters. 'We're on our honeymoon.' The departure had not quite so gay an atmosphere, however.

A stopover in Honolulu provided little rest. A mob of fans pushed on to the tarmac screaming 'Marilyn!', sweeping round her and tearing at her clothes and hair. Amid her growing panic, six policemen rushed forward to escort the couple to a waiting lounge. 'Airport officials,' reported United Press International on the spot, 'said it was the most enthusiastic greeting given a movie star in years.'

On 2 February they arrived in Tokyo, where (as *Time* reported) Joe again 'went virtually unnoticed as Japanese by the thousands swarmed to meet his bride. Marilyn's fans pressed so thickly about the arriving couple that both were forced to scramble back into the airplane, escaping later through its baggage hatch.' At the Imperial Hotel, two hundred police were summoned to restore order as Marilyn's devotees – demanding a glimpse of her or at least a photograph of her room – caused a riot, fell into fishponds, jammed themselves in revolving doors and broke plate glass windows. Unwilling to disperse until she waved to them from a balcony, the crowd shouted until Marilyn reluctantly agreed to appear, saying she loved her public but this was going too far: she was being treated 'like I was a dictator or something'.

According to Lefty O'Doul, this was the first time Joe appreciated just how much Marilyn's celebrity exceeded his. And with this realization, Joe became surly. He would permit her to leave the hotel only to attend the ball game with him: 'No shopping, Marilyn. The crowds will kill us.' She did not argue, but O'Doul saw that she resented being given orders.

As for Joe, his resentment blazed even hotter next morning, at the only press conference arranged in his honour. All the questions were directed at Marilyn, who with almost Zen-like composure had to produce spontaneous replies to the most intimate questions:

Did she agree with the Kinsey report? 'Not fully.'

Did she sleep naked. 'No comment.'

Was her walk natural? 'I've been walking since I was six months old.'

What kind of fur was she wearing? 'Fox – and not the Twentieth Century kind.'

Did she wear underclothes? She shot a withering glance at the translator and replied caustically à la Rose Loomis (in *Niagara*), 'I'll buy a kimono tomorrow.' It is not hard to imagine Joe's reaction when the Tokyo press dubbed his wife 'Honorable Buttocks-Swinging Actress'.

As if it had been sketched for a television comedy, the DiMaggio situation became even more complex the following day, 3 February. Just as Joe tried to separate Marilyn from press and public, an invitation arrived from General John E. Hull's Far East command headquarters. If necessary government clearances and USO status could be obtained, would Miss Monroe like to visit American troops still stationed in Korea – perhaps to entertain them with an improvised one-woman show? With Joe and Lefty scheduled for days of baseball and nights of meetings with Tokyo's sports reporters, Marilyn considered this an excellent suggestion – in the great tradition of those performers who went to sing for the men in uniform. Joe, however, was adamantly opposed, and according to two friends, 'the marriage seemed to go wrong from their honeymoon, [when] some general asked her to go to Korea . . . Marilyn looked at Joe. "It's your honeymoon," he said, shrugging. "Go ahead if you want to."' She did. On 8 February, Marilyn received USO Entertainer Serial Number 129278 and her clearance papers for Korea.

For four days beginning 16 February, Marilyn, accompanied by Jean O'Doul and army entertainment officer Walter Bouillet, travelled by plane, helicopter and open jeep to ten wintry sites where more than 100,000 soldiers and 13,000 marines welcomed her with deafening roars and prolonged applause for a dozen performances. In two days alone, her audiences included grateful troops of the 3rd, 7th, 24th and 40th army divisions – 60,000 men. Most of them had never seen a Monroe film, for they had been in service since her rise to stardom. But they knew her photograph, the calendar, the snapshots, the thousands of pictures in newspapers and magazines.*

At each stop, Bouillet alighted first, like a sideshowman about to produce a rabbit from his hat. Then, instead of a furry white bunny, out popped Marilyn, eyelashes fluttering, kisses flying from her mouth to her palm, then blown over the hillside teeming with uniformed soldiers. She wore clam-tight olive drab trousers, a windbreaker and dazzling rhinestone earrings before changing into her show gear: heedless of biting winds and freezing temperatures, she wore a tight-fitting lavender dress she kept as a memento for the rest of her life. On makeshift stages Marilyn sang, among other songs, 'Diamonds Are a Girl's Best Friend' and 'Do It Again'. The temperature may have risen some few degrees as she sang the second song, whose lyrics only seemed to question the title of the first.

'There were seventeen thousand soldiers in front of me,' Marilyn told Ben Hecht a few months later:

and they were all yelling at me at the top of their lungs.

I stood smiling at them. It had started snowing. But I felt as warm as if I were standing in a bright sun . . . I've always been frightened by an audience – any audience. My stomach pounds, my head gets dizzy and I'm sure my voice has left me.

But standing in the snowfall facing these yelling soldiers, I

---

* The premiere issue of *Playboy* magazine in December 1953, which featured Marilyn on the cover and at the centrefold, was not easy to obtain and unavailable on news stands. It remained a valuable collector's item, more reported than owned or even seen.

felt for the first time in my life no fear of anything. I felt only happy.

One of her accompanists, a pianist named Al Guastafeste, recalled her lack of star attitude: 'She was Marilyn Monroe, but she didn't seem to realize it! If I made a mistake, she said she was sorry. When she made a mistake, she apologized.'

Her sixth audience was composed of 10,000 Dutch, Thai and American troops. Flanked by two tanks onstage, Marilyn was asked by a presiding officer how she felt. 'Safe,' she replied, and the crowd roared with laughter. But she could be serious, and there was no doubt to chroniclers of the tour that Marilyn's intentions were indeed earnest.

'She gave us the feeling she really wanted to be there,' recalled Ted Cieszynski, on duty with the Army Corps of Engineers as photographer for the Public Information Office. He had a front-row seat for her performance at K-2 airbase at Tae-Gu.

This wasn't an obligation she had to fulfill, and it wasn't a self-promotion. Of all the performers who came to us in Korea – and there were a half dozen or so – she was the best. She showed no nervousness and wasn't anything like a dumb blonde. When a few of us photographers were allowed to climb up on the stage after her show, she was very pleasant and cooperative and told us how glad she was to be with us. She took her time, speaking with each of us about our families and our hometowns and our civilian jobs. It was bitter cold, but she was in no hurry to leave. Marilyn was a great entertainer. She made thousands of GIs feel she really cared.

Marilyn knew that she was the object of ten thousand male fantasies, yet somehow she wanted to communicate that it was not desire she wished to arouse but understanding. 'This is my first experience with a live audience,' she told a crowd as she prepared to depart in a helicopter after her last performance, 'and my greatest experience with any kind of audience. It's been the best thing that ever happened to me.' Later, she added:

> I felt I belonged. For the first time in my life, I had the feeling that the people seeing me were accepting me and liking me. This is what I've always wanted, I guess. Please come visit us in San Francisco.

The chopper blades whirred and Marilyn turned to climb aboard. Smiling gallantly and (said an eyewitness) with tears in her eyes, she called her farewell:

> Goodbye, everyone. Goodbye, goodbye – and God bless you all. Thank you for being so nice. Hold a good thought for me!

The importance of these four days cannot be overstated. Far from Hollywood, Marilyn had given brilliant, spontaneous performances (happily, they are preserved on news film). This she did, free not only of her husband's critical appraisal but also away from the scrutiny of her drama coach, directors and executives who always reinforced her conviction that she was not good enough or that she lacked real skills. Instead of being paralysed with anxiety as was often the case on the set, she found an outpouring of love from enthusiastic audiences. 'When I went to Korea,' she told Sidney Skolsky later, 'I wan't nervous, not one bit. I didn't break out with red blotches on my arms or chest or anything. I was perfectly at ease.'

Her potentially disastrous live performances went extremely well because she was allowed to be spontaneous, to be herself. And whereas a Hollywood set exacerbated her painful self-consciousness and caused her to forget and stumble on her lines, in Korea she never missed a word. Nor was she required to analyse every gesture, but simply to sing boldly and with feeling. Like orphans and disabled children to whom she related so well, the anonymous soldiers were in a way the perfect antidotes to the famous ballplayer, the overbearing director, the name or the face that asked too much of her.

Back in Tokyo, Marilyn rushed to Joe like an excited child, telling him she had never felt so accepted. 'It was so wonderful, Joe! You never heard such cheering!' But Joe, ever the realist, seemed not to care. 'You never *heard* such cheering, Joe!' she repeated.

There was a pause, and he looked away. 'Yes, I have,' he said calmly.*

The marriage was already deeply troubled by the time Marilyn and Joe returned to San Francisco on 24 February. When the annual *Photoplay* Awards for the previous year's best performances were announced, Marilyn was the winner again, this time for her work in *Gentlemen Prefer Blondes* and *How To Marry a Millionaire*. But when she went to Los Angeles to pick up the prize, her husband did not accompany her and again Sidney filled in as escort. 'Joe hates crowds and glamour,' she told him, unable to conceal her disappointment in her husband's indifference. Nevertheless, when she entered the Beverly Hills Hotel dining-room on 8 March, the earlier scene there was repeated. Wearing a dazzling white satin sheath cut low from the shoulders, Marilyn looked somewhat different, and it took some reporters a while to notice that her hair had been re-coloured from honey blond to a brilliant halo of platinum. Like Harlow, Marilyn now undertook to have as much white in her life as possible – not only her hair and her wardrobe, but her furnishings as well. Everything she chose was calculated to dazzle, as if she could again win from her public the adoration she was denied at home.

After the ceremony, Marilyn and Sidney had a nightcap in her suite. And then, for perhaps the first time, she stunned him.

---

* Skolsky told the story somewhat differently. 'Joe, did you ever have ten thousand people stand up and applaud you?' Joe's voice was 'as unemotional as a pair of discarded spikes. "Seventy-five thousand," he answered quietly' (Skolsky, p.213).

'Sidney, do you know who I'm going to marry?'

'Marry? What are you talking about?'

'I'm going to marry Arthur Miller.'

'Arthur Miller! You just got home from a honeymoon. You told me how wonderful Joe was, how happy he made you, and what a great time you had! Now you tell me you're going to marry Arthur Miller. I don't understand.'

'You wait. You'll see.'

There is no evidence of a reunion or correspondence between Marilyn and her favourite playwright, but this was one fantasy she intended to realize.

Prolonging her stay at the Beverly Hills Hotel that March, Marilyn took the advice of Charles Feldman and Hugh French that there would be superb publicity and perhaps a respectable income from a movie star autobiography, a genre just appearing on literary horizons. Marilyn agreed, on the understanding that a first-rate ghost writer would be required, someone with whom she could speak freely about her past; she also demanded approval of the contents.

Marilyn's agents quickly contacted Jacques Chambrun, agent for the prolific journalist, novelist and screenwriter Ben Hecht; that spring a deal was struck. Marilyn and Hecht, who had met cordially during production of his script for *Monkey Business*, scheduled meetings several times weekly – often, at her insistence, with Sidney Skolsky ready to chime in. Hecht wrote quickly (in those days before convenient tape recorders), and before the end of April a first draft of her autobiography was ready. 'Marilyn wept and wept for joy at what I had written,' Hecht wrote to Chambrun.*

---

* Speed was one of the qualities that made Hecht so attractive to Hollywood, and even a partial list of his achievements indicates that quality did not suffer for it. After receiving the Oscar for *Underworld* in 1929, he wrote (or doctored, without credit) more than 200 screenplays, among them *The Front Page* (with co-author Charles MacArthur), *Queen Christina*, *Twentieth Century*, *Nothing Sacred*, *Wuthering Heights* and *Whirlpool*. He was also, although uncredited, a major contributor to the final script for *Gone With the Wind* and he wrote or rewrote many Alfred Hitchcock films, among them *Foreign Correspondent*, *Spellbound*, *Notorious*, *The Paradine Case*, *Rope* and *Strangers on a Train*.

The result had a strange and tangled history, for the book was not finally published until 1974, after the deaths of both star and writer. *My Story*, as it was titled, contains imaginative anecdotes created in 1951 and 1952 by Marilyn and Sidney; life-stories told that spring of 1954 by Marilyn and Sidney to Hecht; heavily re-drafted portions of an unauthorized serialization of the Hecht manuscript which were published in the London *Empire News* from May to August 1954 (a serialization illegally sold by Jacques Chambrun without the approval of Monroe or Hecht); and the final reworking of the text in the early 1970s by Milton Greene and an unknown writer or writers engaged by him.

Hecht's draft, preserved among his papers at the Newberry Library in Chicago, contains no account of some of the most commonly believed moments in the life of Marilyn Monroe – the actual childhood rape, for example. According to the writer's widow, the disorganized and incomplete 168-page type-script submitted to the *Empire News* was not the work of her husband, but was prepared under the supervision of the shrewd (not to say unethical) Chambrun, whom Hecht subsequently fired for multiple acts of misrepresentation, unauthorized publication and downright theft of income due to his client.

By careful comparison of the published version with the un-published Hecht draft, it is clear that none of the first sixty-six pages of *My Story* was composed by Hecht at all. As internal evidence, there are Rose Hecht's detailed notes to Folder Twelve of her husband's papers, as well as a comparison with the corpus of Hecht's work: the vocabulary and diction of *My Story* in these sections bear scant resemblance to anything ever written by Ben Hecht. For external evidence, there is the absence of Hecht's completed *manuscript* as opposed to the *typescript* of these pages, both of which he always personally approved. The various typed versions (even those not of Hecht's provenance) found their way into the Hecht papers simply because Chambrun, when fired, was required to return to Hecht's attorneys everything relative to his work. 'Sit down and try to think up something interesting about yourself,'

Hecht said to Marilyn when they began their task. She did, he did, Sidney did (and later Milton Greene did).

As part of the task, Marilyn telephoned her old friend Lucille Ryman Carroll, asking her to welcome Ben Hecht and to be entirely frank about Marilyn's early days in Hollywood. 'But you're married to Joe now,' said Lucille, surprised. 'Surely you don't want me to tell Hecht *everything*! This will be the end of your career *and* your marriage.' But Marilyn insisted, perhaps because she hoped Hecht would indeed print the entire truth, thus simultaneously assuring ever fresh controversy for herself as well as precipitating what Lucille feared, the end of her marriage to Joe. The calendar he had ruefully accepted as a momentary aberration on Marilyn's part; her days on the Boulevard would surely be difficult to justify. Hecht knew what could be published in those more discriminating days, and the more incandescent details of Marilyn's life 'walking the boulevard' were entirely omitted. Alas, the entire Monroe–Hecht enterprise collapsed that June, when Hecht learned that his agent had sold extracts from the manuscript – much of it doctored by Chambrun himself – to the London *Empire News* without the permission required of himself and Marilyn. Skolsky, however, was not prepared to let a good thing entirely evaporate: he quickly drafted a little book about Marilyn that received her endorsement when it was published serially in newspapers and between covers later that year. (The first book about her was a slim volume of under a hundred pages, news items stitched together into a narrative by Joe Franklin and Laurie Palmer and published in 1953.)

But by this time Marilyn had other concerns. She rented a house at 508 North Palm Drive, Beverly Hills (Jean Harlow had lived at 512), and a reluctant Joe agreed to move from San Francisco to live with her there – at least part-time, for by the end of May she was back on a movie set. Of this he did not approve, but nor did he wish her to work without some sort of supervision.

Although Feldman had been representing Marilyn unofficially and without contract since the death of Johnny Hyde, the

William Morris agency legally had rights to a percentage of her earnings until the end of 1953. With that deal now expired, Marilyn signed with Famous Artists at last, on 31 March 1954, just as Feldman and French were concluding the terms of her reconciliation with Fox.

Marilyn's arrangement with the studio was straightforward, although it, too, would soon be open to question and become the basis for a complicated battle when she left Hollywood later that year. For the present, however, things looked manageable. Fox agreed to drop their demand that Marilyn appear in *Pink Tights*. Instead, if she would play a supporting role in the musical *There's No Business Like Show Business*, they would give her the leading role later that year in the film version of George Axelrod's Broadway hit *The Seven Year Itch*, to be directed by Billy Wilder.

Marilyn was back on salary at $1250 weekly, but only until August 1954 when a new seven-year deal would commence (on much the same terms as before). There would also be a bonus of $100,000 for *The Seven Year Itch*, although this was never put in writing, was never entirely paid, and became a bargaining chip when she next defied Fox and (they claimed) reneged on her contractual obligations.

A singular cause of contention was Marilyn's insistence that the studio pay for her drama coach (Natasha), her choice of music coach (Hal Schaefer) and her dance director (Jack Cole) for *There's No Business Like Show Business*. These concessions she won, but Fox still feared losing the world's biggest star; they demanded, therefore, that her time of suspensions (two periods from January to April) be added to her current contract before the new seven-year deal took effect in August. Thus Marilyn would have to be available for another film – a clear reflection of their anxiety that she would repeat the ploy of absenting herself. Little did they know at the time that this demand would have disastrous consequences for them.

Because *The Seven Year Itch* would be co-produced by Wilder and Feldman (who had a particularly good relationship with Fox and many clients there), Marilyn realized that once again she would be making other people rich without being given either creative control or fair financial compensation. At the same time, she was in fact planning a longer absence than anyone expected. Throughout 1954, letters and telephone calls were exchanged between her attorney, Loyd Wright, and Milton Greene's attorney, Frank Delaney – both men eager to find financial backing for a new venture to be called Marilyn Monroe Productions. This was all discussed in remarkable secrecy, for had Fox learned of her plans, the contract might well have been legally invalidated by evidence of her contrary intentions.

Marilyn spent most of April and May in San Francisco, where she and Joe lived with his sister Marie and others of his family. As before with the Kargers, Marilyn tried to attach herself to a family, longing to find what had been denied in childhood. But the idea of Marilyn as a simple housewife is ludicrous, as are fantasies of her scrubbing the stove top, sewing booties for children-to-be and tasting to see if the pasta is perfectly *al dente*.

She returned to Hollywood in late May and worked daily with Hal Schaefer and Jack Cole for her numbers in *Show Business*.* Shooting began on 29 May, with Natasha, at Marilyn's request and to Joe's annoyance, back on the set and very much in her life again. He was jealous, too, of the time his wife had with Schaefer, a handsome, polished bachelor with whom Marilyn spent long hours at the studio, often into the evening. For weeks Marilyn ignored Joe's jealousy over this, and (as she later said) Joe ignored her completely: they seemed, in fact, like mere roommates who met occasionally at Palm Drive.

There's No Business Like Show Business was little more than a CinemaScope excuse for overdesigned musical numbers by Irving Berlin, the sequences vaguely stitched together by the

---

* That year, Henry Hathaway had hoped to direct a film of Somerset Maugham's novel *Of Human Bondage*, to star James Dean and Marilyn. Zanuck would not even discuss so serious a project for her.

story of a terribly sweet family of Irish vaudevillians (Ethel Merman, Dan Dailey, Mitzi Gaynor, Donald O'Connor and Johnny Ray). Marilyn had the superfluous supporting role of a hat-check girl who falls in love with one of them and proves she can sing, pose and posture. But she and the film sink in an extravagant cuteness of bloated production values, excessively fussy costumes and saccharine pieties including everything from little homilies on sobriety to discourses on performers becoming clergymen.

Throughout the filming that summer, Marilyn was ill with bronchitis (the lingering effects of a virus she had picked up in Korea), anaemia and, for the first time, serious side-effects of sleeping pills, which made her groggy, moody and weepy on the rare mornings she appeared on time for shooting calls. The director Walter Lang and the other cast members were annoyed and alarmed when Marilyn repeatedly arrived confused, shaky and unprepared. According to Natasha,

At night she would do scenes beautifully with me in a rehearsal, but the following morning she had forgotten the words entirely. 'You don't know how unhappy I am,' Marilyn said. And that was all she said, but the company working with her was driven half insane by the delays.

There was, her coach noted, 'this conflict between her laziness and her ambition'. But even Natasha had to admit that more than an indictment of sloth was at stake here; she spoke dolefully of how Marilyn

called me at two or three in the morning that spring when DiMaggio was being so filthy to her, when he beat her. She couldn't stand being treated that way. I talked to her for hours, until my hand was clammy on the telephone. She knew she could call me at any time, and that spring she did.

This reliance on Natasha explains an otherwise odd occurrence on 14 June, when Marilyn telephoned Hugh French and insisted that Natasha be kept on the Fox payroll with an increased salary. When studio executive Lew Schreiber flatly refused this request, Marilyn threatened to resign from moviemaking for four years. This provoked a series of hastily called meetings between Marilyn, Zanuck, Feldman and French. Natasha got her rise. Having won that victory, Marilyn went further. She refused to sign the new Fox contract for *The Seven Year Itch* unless she was guaranteed her choice of dialogue, vocal and dance coaches on all forthcoming pictures. She insisted (said the inter-office memoranda at Famous Artists) that she was 'tired of having to fight the studio when all she was interested in was getting great parts'.

Natasha was not the only confidant of this bitter stage in Marilyn's marital life: the Greenes, among others, were told of it later in excruciating detail, as were Elia Kazan, Arthur Miller and Lee Strasberg. At the same time, an increasing reliance on barbiturates was Marilyn's defence against the realization that she had indeed contracted an ill-advised marriage: more than anything, she needed and desired to sleep – not only to prepare for the next day's schedule, but also to avoid confrontations with Joe. Placid with strangers and acquaintances but condescending and often bitter toward women, he was not the right husband for her at that time of their lives; he was, in fact, very like Fred Karger, and Marilyn's submission was much like a repetition of that earlier affair.

More poignantly, she was repeating the pattern of trying to form an alliance with a man who really had a low opinion of her, who derided her wardrobe and took it for granted that he knew what was best for her. Once again, the relationship confirmed her own pathetic self-esteem, and with Joe the motif of manly condescension took a more overtly abusive quality – perhaps because, according to the paradox of such relationships, he did indeed love her in his fashion.

It was perhaps inevitable, then, that Marilyn would again seek emotional satisfaction elsewhere, and she found it in the gentle, patient Hal Schaefer, her musical director during *Gentlemen Prefer Blondes* and *River of No Return*. He returned to work with her on *Show Business* at her insistence, and she later saw that he was given onscreen credit for his work with her – an achievement so highly regarded that Schaefer was loaned to Warner Bros to work with Judy Garland in *A Star Is Born* (although, alas, without the appropriate credit).

Schaefer was a kind and untemperamental man who guided Marilyn through four songs for *Show Business* and several more she recorded for RCA that year. Very soon there were such widespread rumours of a romance between teacher and student that DiMaggio spoke only of his resentment. 'It's ridiculous that Mr DiMaggio could be any more jealous of me than he is of other people working with Marilyn,' Schaefer said, perhaps un-wisely. 'She's a wonderful girl and kind to us all. I'm embarrassed about the whole thing.' Such statements did nothing to diminish either the gossip or Joe's fuming.

And then a dreadful thing occurred. On the evening of 27 July, Schaefer had an appointment with Sheila Stuart, another actress-singer he was coaching, at the home of the studio lyricist Harry Giventer. When Schaefer failed to arrive, they made several phone calls to his home, his office and mutual friends, but without success. Concerned because they knew of the Marilyn–Hal affair (or at least the rumours of it), they decided to drive to his bungalow at Fox, where at four in the morning they found him sprawled on the floor, unconscious. Giventer and Stuart rode with Schaefer in an ambulance to Santa Monica Hospital, where emergency gastric lavage saved him from an overdose of Benzedrine and Nembutal, washed down by a potentially lethal liquid later identified as typewriter cleaning fluid. On this both police and hospital reports were unambig-uous. As for the situation that precipitated this unfortunate incident, no one ever elaborated. At her husband's insistence, Marilyn may have told Hal it was necessary to end their intense relationship, whatever its nature; it has also been suggested that anonymous callers had threatened Schaefer.

Giventer and Stuart confirmed that although Marilyn was not Hal's only visitor during his recovery, she was the most constant. In fact, someone had called her at once, for Marilyn arrived just as Hal was wheeled into the emergency room, accompanying him as far as she was allowed, clinging to the stretcher and crying repeatedly, 'It's okay, baby – it's Marilyn – I'm here – it's okay.' At the request of Fox's publicists, the press considerately but not convincingly reported Schaefer's illness as nervous collapse due to overwork: the story occupied so much space for so long, however (and Giventer and Stuart gave such adamant denials of anything really *serious*), that no one believed the event was anything but the result of a romance somehow gone tragically wrong.

The columnist Louella Parsons adored Marilyn, never accepted rumours of the troubled marriage to Joe and was the last to believe its rupture. She usually wrote of her rhapsodically, as if she were Hollywood's very own Joan of Arc battling the treacherous enemies of capricious fame and fickle studios; she also heaped purple prose on Joe. But Parsons knew of the Marilyn–Hal business, and she informed her readers that Joe was 'very unhappy when Marilyn went to the hospital many times to see Hal Schaefer when he was critically ill . . . He was just as jealous of Marilyn's relationship with Natasha Lytess, whom he once ordered out of their house.' Whatever the precise nature and extent of Marilyn's relationship with Hal Schaefer, it was so revived at the time of her divorce from Joe that their friends believed it was an importing contributing factor. And events following the divorce proved them right.

On their work, Schaefer was candid. 'She had very little self-esteem,' he said years later.

But at the same time she was a quite complicated woman with a sure grasp of what she wanted to accomplish. By this time, despite her insecurities, she was no longer hiding behind the music. I was with her all the time in the recording studio, and there was very little intercutting, editing or overdubbing. She trusted me, and we became quite close. I had been warned to stay away from her, not to socialize. I was gentle and considerate with her, which seemed to mean everything, and she warmed to this.

The admonition to distance himself was delivered indirectly, from Fox colleagues and Marilyn's agent, but the implication was clear: Joe did not suffer any rival gladly.

But Schaefer found it impossible to resist Marilyn's non-musical overtures, both to work and to friendship. To compensate for what she considered this 'stupid part in a stupid picture [*Show Business*]', Marilyn made a series of recordings for RCA, among them a stingingly bittersweet rendition of 'A Fine Romance', whose revised lyrics fairly described the swift decline of her own marriage: 'a fine romance with no kisses . . . my heart's not made of plastic, that's why I'm so sarcastic . . .'

This number was completed in only two takes one summer afternoon with seventeen musicians under Schaefer's leadership. 'Breathe from your stomach, Marilyn,' Hal told her before they started, and she seemed at once to relax. He smiled: 'Forget about your chest.' Schaefer coaxed her to a high B-flat, then to a husky low D-flat. 'I won't be satisfied,' she told him, 'until people want to hear me sing without looking at me.'

Perhaps more than any other recording, 'A Fine Romance' conveys the range of her alternately brash, tender, wistful, seductive, angry emotions that year – indeed, as Schaefer said, she was 'a complicated woman'. But for reasons that remain unclear, the song was not released until years after her death – despite RCA's sale of more than 75,000 copies of 'I'm Gonna File My Claim' (from *River of No Return*) during the first three weeks it was available that summer.

The role of Vicky, hastily added to the final script of *Show Business*, seemed to Marilyn very like the studio's revenge: it was a throwback to the unnecessary earlier parts, merely an inelegant gloss on Lorelei Lee. One of her numbers especially, 'Heat Wave', defied the censors with its photographic emphasis on Marilyn's parted legs, abdomen and crotch as she bumped and ground: 'We're having a heat wave, a tropical heat wave – it isn't surprising, the temperature's rising – you certainly can can-can . . .' Seen years later, this is not so much camp entertainment as a dreary omen of ever bolder, more tasteless performance styles to come from others decades later. 'Miss Monroe's wriggling and squirming are embarrassing to behold,' ran a typical view of this number. She fared somewhat better, despite an absurdly plumed and spangled costume, singing 'After You Get What You Want, You Don't Want It'. Marilyn's interpretation, according to Irving Berlin, showed him for the first time the sexy subtext of the song.

Her achievement was all the more remarkable because Marilyn was that day in a state of extreme nervous anxiety – a condition detailed by Skolsky in his column on 9 June. That same week her attorney had to appear in court to answer charges of reckless driving filed against her by a man named Bart Antinosa, whose car was hit from behind by Marilyn as she drove along Sunset Boulevard on 21 May. Antinosa asked $3000 in damages; the court, after conferring with his repair shop, awarded him $500.

Only a few cast members and choreographer Jack Cole knew, however, that Marilyn's vulgar shenanigans in 'Heat Wave' were the invention of Natasha Lytess: 'I had a code with her, a certain gesture to indicate she should let go of certain muscles. They thought I was a Svengali.' The code gesture remained unknown for years, until Rita Moreno (also working at Fox that year) revealed it in 1991: 'If Marilyn wasn't doing what Natasha wanted, Natasha pointed to her own crotch. This was the signal that Marilyn's performance wasn't coming from the right place!'

Joe and his friend George Solotaire were present on 27 August, the day Marilyn filmed the 'Heat Wave' dance. After perhaps the fifteenth take, she ran to embrace him, but he pulled back as if she were a cobra; there was no welcome, no encouragement for her. Soon she was recalled before the camera, and after five minutes of watching her cavort suggestively in a skin-tight, two-piece outfit – and watching the usual crowd on a movie set ogle her – he stormed out, muttering about movies in general, about Jack Cole, about Hal Schaefer: no one nearby was uncertain of his opinions.

Anxious and embarrassed, Marilyn at once lost the musical beat, fell out of step, forgot her lines and, perspiring heavily, slipped and fell. From another corner of the sound stage, Sidney Skolsky jumped to her rescue. While she regained her composure and had her makeup and hair retouched, he introduced her to two other studio guests: a sixteen-year-old actress, Susan Strasberg, and her mother Paula, wife of the director and drama teacher Lee Strasberg of New York's Actors Studio.

Marilyn had known of the Strasbergs ever since her days at the Actors Lab in Hollywood. As Paula Miller, Mrs Strasberg had acted in *Night Over Taos*, which Marilyn had studied; and Lee had been set before Marilyn by the Carnovskys and by Kazan as a valuable teacher for a serious actor. 'I've heard so much about your husband,' Marilyn told Paula that day at Fox. 'I've always dreamed of studying acting with Mr Strasberg.'* Paula replied that Marilyn would be welcome to visit the Actors Studio whenever she came to New York. That idea must have seemed all the more appealing placed alongside *Show Business* and the obvious dissolution of her marriage.

Like Jean Harlow, Marilyn was never happy trying to be a tidy and effective homemaker. This role Joe demanded of her, but in vain, for she had neither the time nor the inclination for such chores. Harlow and Hal Rosson had also contracted an unwise marriage, and within a year they were divorced, incompatible lifestyles being cited as the major factor corroding the union. 'I kept thinking of her, rolling over the facts of her

---

* While she was having an affair with Elia Kazan, during the filming of *Viva Zapata!*, Marilyn had met and socialized with the star, Kazan's protégé Marlon Brando. He had studied with Strasberg and held him in high regard. In 1954, Brando was also working at Fox (on *Désirée*), and one day at lunch he again recommended Strasberg and the Studio to her.

life in my mind,' Marilyn said later. 'It was kind of spooky, and sometimes I thought, am I making this happen? But I don't think so. We just seemed to have the same spirit or something, I don't know. I kept wondering if I would die young like her, too.'

There were deeper differences, and they had to do with their belief in what constituted a marriage. For Joe male supremacy was all: he could never accept that she wanted to continue working as an actress, that she refused to retire, that she wanted to invite friends to their rented home. And she could not understand his shame at her frank enjoyment of her body and her pleasure in others taking pleasure in admiring it. There were, finally, serious storm warnings coming from rumours about Hal Schaefer – that Marilyn's late evenings were not always or only spent rehearsing, recording or singing. In this regard, Joe's jealousy and suspicion may not have been without foundation, but Marilyn always spoke of Hal only as a musical mentor.

Meanwhile, Joe's mistress was television: he preferred sports events, but just about anything would suffice to amuse him. Marilyn's tastes were more ambitious. She craved excitement, company, live diversions; she wanted to see plays, attend concerts. She bought books and longed to discuss poetry and plays with Joe. These left him cold, and he saw no reason to go out and present themselves to 'phonies', who just wanted to exploit them and stare at them. The old differences were there, and constant togetherness made them sharper. That spring, she gave him a gold medal for his watch chain, inscribed with a maxim from Saint-Exupéry's *The Little Prince*: 'True love is visible not to the eyes, but to the heart, for eyes may be deceived.' Joe's response: 'What the hell does *that* mean?'

The DiMaggios did have in common a tough, street-smart outlook and a suspicion about people's loyalties. In addition, neither had completed high school, and they both longed to rise above their humble backgrounds by fame and achievement. There was a fierce physical desire binding them, too, but this had been satisfied for two years and could not lighten every sacrifice and burden of normal married life.

Joe DiMaggio never spoke on the record about Marilyn Monroe, never expressed a word of praise or pride about her, never spoke to historians, journalists or biographers either before or after her death; indeed, he rarely allowed her name to be mentioned even by his closest friends. In contrast, Marilyn was always open in her respect for Joe – before, during and after the marriage – and she often seized opportunities to praise his appearance. 'He has the grace and beauty of a Michelangelo [figure],' Marilyn had said early on. 'He moves like a living statue.' As it happened, this turned out to be prophetic praise, for very soon Joe's attitude was one of stony indifference. 'He wouldn't speak to me for days at a time,' she said later that year. 'I asked him what was wrong, but he said, 'Stop nagging me.' I was permitted to have no visitors unless I was sick.' They were, after two years of romance, deeply bored with one another.

'When I married him, I wasn't sure of *why* I married him,' Marilyn confided later to friends. 'I have too many fantasies to be a housewife.' Part of the reason for making it legal seems to have been pity for Joe's grief over the death of a brother, who had drowned in 1953. Joe had wept for days, turning to Marilyn for comfort, and this had given her a brief sense that she was of importance to him. For her part, she wanted the stability and protection of this strong, silent father-figure.

But she could not be satisfied by television, baseball games or variety shows, and when Joe ignored her for them she was thrown straight back to her condition of early childhood neglect. Joe was almost twelve years older, dominant, apparently serene, a man to take control – he was also, ironically, the absent father of Norma Jeane's youth, the fantasy man she loved and longed to win over.

To please Joe, she had to be, from the beginning, a docile child playing at being a married woman – much as she had been with Jim Dougherty. She tried to conform to these expectations, but in so doing she was repeating the situation of her first marriage. Joe wanted Marilyn to be for him only, but this she resented: she also needed to please the crowd. Irving Berlin was

quite right: 'after you get what you want, you don't want it.'
She had wanted to be protected, not possessed.

On the other hand, Joe may have had his fantasies. One might
reasonably ask to what he was attracted if not the woman he had
known? To whom did he wish to commit himself after a two-
year affair if not the Marilyn Monroe who was by this time even
more a public figure, less easy to control? He seemed at times to
resent his wife because she *was* available to him. He distrusted
what he could possess and worshipped what eluded him: thus
his lifelong attraction (outside marriage) to transient showgirls
and, even after their divorce, his unfailing interest in Marilyn.
Happy in the pursuit of control, he may have felt he had found
the ultimate fantasy in Marilyn, as she felt she had found one in
him. But for him, too, Irving Berlin's words were a fair description.

Perhaps Joe also believed he could change her, could 'retire'
the mythic Marilyn as he had retired Joltin' Joe. He, too, was
victimized by fame; he, too, had little identity except as a star,
and this he jealously guarded. There was, then, a fateful rivalry
between husband and wife. A traditionalist, he resented her income, fame and independence: Joe wanted his wife at home,
nicely subordinate. And very near the core of their incompatibility was the fact that he looked to the past for his glory, for
the public valuation of his image and compensation for it, while
Marilyn looked to the immediate present and the future.

But she could only do so with the emotional perceptions imposed by her past. Always attempting to be someone better than
she believed herself to be, ever yearning to become the accepted,
deeply and permanently loved one, Marilyn tried constantly to
rise to others' expectations. She learned to play billiards with
Joe on their honeymoon, but her enthusiasm was feigned; she
went fishing with him in San Francisco, but this she found painfully tiresome, she tried to learn the fine points of baseball and
the details of a television Western series, but none of this engaged her. She had been so accustomed to making herself over
to please others – Grace Goddard, Jim Dougherty, Fred Karger,

Johnny Hyde, Natasha Lytess – that she assumed the role of 'Mrs DiMaggio' automatically.

Throughout 1954, Marilyn Monroe's schedule might have seemed daunting to a marathon runner: everything was happening with breathless speed even as the tensions in her private life grew more unendurable. She completed *There's No Business Like Show Business* at the end of August and at once began location work in New York on *The Seven Year Itch*.* Marilyn's role was that of a nameless Manhattan girl, the unwitting temptress of a nervous married neighbour, played by Tom Ewell, whose wife is away on holiday. They flirt, they talk, he worries, but the filmscript ends with virtue preserved (unlike the play, which did not have to cater to the Motion Picture Production Code).

Everyone connected to *Itch* was working with all despatch: George Axelrod, finishing the adaptation of his play for the screen; Billy Wilder, meticulously planning the texture and mood of each scene; and designer William Travilla, completing sketches for all ten of Marilyn's outfits in one weekend. The one he designed for a scene of *The Seven Year Itch* is among the most famous costumes in movie history: a simple halter-front, écru-coloured summer dress with sunburst pleats, the skirt to be blown high by a blast of cool air propelled through a sidewalk grating as a subway train roars below.

On 8 September, Joe bade farewell to Marilyn, who boarded the night flight for New York and arrived at eight-fifteen next morning. Harry Brand's publicity department had assured that five hundred airport employees were informed of her arrival. In defiance of the flat-chested, loose-fitting shift dresses decreed by Dior that season, Marilyn left the plane in a form-fitting woollen dress. She posed on a platform and chatted happily

---

* Because of her exclusive contract with RCA Records, Marilyn's voice could not be heard on the released soundtrack recording of *There's No Business Like Show Business* (the voice was Dolores Gray's). Marilyn did, however, record the songs for separate release by RCA.

with reporters until police pushed back the throng and escorted her to a limousine. Then she was whisked off to six morning interviews, a luncheon with magazine reporters and a press conference at the Daily News Building.

The media were kept duly alerted throughout the week. On 13 September, a thousand spectators attended the first of two outdoor New York scenes. These could of course easily have been photographed on the Fox lot, but that would have sacrificed fantastic publicity (which was the entire point of this journey to New York). Every newspaper and magazine carried feature stories and interviews, and the accountants at Fox were already guessing the extent of the forthcoming profits on *The Seven Year Itch*.

And so as crowds cheered and were then asked to keep silence, Marilyn leaned out a window of 164 East Sixty-first Street, shouted 'Hey!' and tossed a pair of shoes to Ewell. 'Hi!' she cried gaily. 'I just washed my hair!' Cut. Retake. Retake. Print. And that was that. It seemed too easy. But according to George Axelrod, who was present during production, Marilyn was as usual terrified when the moment of filming arrived. This was the moment when her image would be captured for ever; this was the means by which she would be seen, assessed, accepted and appreciated (or not), and therefore loved and remembered (or not). Unlike photographs, over which she always demanded the right of approval, Marilyn had to beg directors for take after multiple retake in order to reassure herself, which she never could. She was bright and witty, Axelrod recalled, and she had a natural intelligence and sense of humour, none of which she trusted. 'But although she was full of aspirations and frantic to succeed, she had no technical vocabulary about acting or filmmaking, and that gave her "protectors" the advantage over her. They taught and encouraged her – although not too much, or they'd have been out of work.'

But Marilyn also adored the attention of the crowds, and when she was adored the exhibitionist came to life – and perhaps never more vividly than from one to four o'clock on the chilly morning of 15 September. The famous skirt-blowing scene was to be filmed outside the Trans-Lux Theater, on Lexington Avenue at Fifty-second Street, and the press and public were again given notice. Several hundred professional and amateur photographers had gathered, and by midnight they were joined by almost two thousand bystanders eager for as much of Marilyn as they could glimpse. Wilder's assistant announced the procedure: if everyone would co-operate by remaining behind barricades so the scene could be shot, the camera would then be pulled away and every photographer could snap away to his heart's content.

What ensued was promptly dubbed by columnist Irving Hoffman 'the shot seen round the world. Marilyn stood over the grating, special effects chief Paul Wurtzel controlled a huge fan below the street, and Marilyn's white dress flew up, revealing (as planned) white panties but no underskirt or half-slip. The photographs appeared worldwide. For two hours, the crowd roared, she smiled, she giggled, she waved, she co-operated with everyone. Twice she requested a brief break, stepping into the theatre to warm herself with a cup of coffee, for the strong wind machine and the cool night air gave her a chill. 'She was shaking like hell that night and caught a virus,' recalled Tom Ewell. But like Jean Harlow, Marilyn was never remote from her public and never affected the glamorous aura of an otherwordly visitor.

The event was the canny idea of the photographer Sam Shaw, who had been friendly with Marilyn since 1951 and was working on assignment from co-producer Charles Feldman to document the making of *Itch*. From the time of preproduction he had in mind the skirt-blowing scene as the logo for the entire picture. 'The location work on Lexington Avenue,' he said years later, 'was of course for the sake of publicity. Everyone knew it would have to be photographed again back in the studio.' Wilder and Wurtzel confirmed this plan in advance, aware that the closeups would have to be reworked later simply because there was too much ambient noise to record dialogue. In fact most of the still photographers from that night reveal more than is in the finished film of *The Seven Year Itch*: in the final scene as completed at Fox, Marilyn steps over a grating, a blast of air lifts her skirt just to knee level, and the camera discreetly cuts to her face as she looks around, grateful for the cool breeze. Disney could not have supervised it more delicately.*

But there was nothing amusing in what followed.

The previous afternoon in Beverly Hills, Joe had received a call from his old friend the columnist Walter Winchell, who advised that quite a spectacle was about to occur on Lexington Avenue. Joe caught a plane for New York that night. But by the next evening he was exhausted and, indifferent as always to moviemaking, he decided to await Marilyn's return at the St Regis Hotel bar. Winchell arrived and, taking a cue from Othello's Iago, tried to create a good story for his column by urging Joe to join him on Lexington Avenue. But Joe refused: 'It would make her nervous, and it would make me nervous, too.'

'Oh, come on, Joe. I have to be there. It might make some copy for me.'

'No, you go, Walter.'

But Winchell prevailed, and the two men arrived to see what Winchell expected and Joe feared most of all. As his wife's skirt flew up again and again and the crowd shouted approval, he turned furiously to Winchell: 'What the hell's going on around here?' Billy Wilder recalled 'the look of death' on Joe's face as he and Winchell hurried back to the hotel bar. One might reasonably ask why it had not occurred to Joe that many people on Lexington Avenue that night (not to say countless others) had certainly seen much more of Marilyn on the calendar.

Later, shouts and screams were heard from the DiMaggios' suite. Natasha, in the adjacent room, went to investigate but was turned away by Joe. Next morning, she and Gladys Whitten,

---

* Disney would not, however, have approved of a line in this scene that had to be cut because of censors' objections. 'Don't you wish you could wear skirts?' Marilyn asks Ewell as the breeze refreshes her. 'I feel sorry for you men in your hot pants.'

Marilyn's hairdresser on the picture, confronted an appalling sight: 'Joe was very, very mad with her,' Gladys recalled, 'and he beat her up a little bit. There were bruises on her shoulders, but we covered them with makeup.'

That afternoon, 16 September, the DiMaggios returned to California. Two weeks later, Marilyn filed a petition for divorce.

Chapter Fourteen

OCTOBER 1954 – JANUARY 1955

Marilyn Monroe's chronic inability to arrive on time for work was usually due to a variety of fears: that she was insufficiently prepared or that her appearance was unworthy of the camera. But most of all she was afraid that she would be rejected for a poor performance, that once again (as in her childhood) she would be sent away, unwanted, disapproved, unloved. Thus too, if corrections or suggestions were offered by a director, he had to speak with the utmost delicacy and gentleness to avoid Marilyn breaking down in sobs of remorse for her mistake; many shooting days were so lost during her career.

But her four-day absence from the Fox lot during the last two weeks of September 1954 had a quite different cause. The fateful night on Lexington Avenue and at the hotel, followed by the long flight to Los Angeles next day, left her weary to the point of illness, and in fact she was put to bed with a heavy cold that verged on pneumonia. The thirty-five-day schedule for *The Seven Year Itch* ran to forty-eight, and the film was not completed until November. Her co-star Tom Ewell recalled that Marilyn repeatedly apologized during their kissing scenes: 'I hope you don't mind the smell of the medicine I've taken today.'

Against doctor's advice but to Billy Wilder's delight, she did manage a few days at the studio between 18 September and 1 October. 'I knew she was trying,' said Ewell, 'and I liked her for that alone.' Like everyone on the production, he was sympathetic to the problems in her private life; and like Fox's chief executives, he knew that Marilyn alone would make or ruin the picture's chances for success. 'Others could give you a good, funny performance,' Zanuck wrote to Wilder on 20 September, 'but nothing could make up for Marilyn's personality in this film.' This was more warning than instruction, as Wilder well understood.

Not unexpectedly, there were problems: she had, after all, to render a completely rounded comic performance at a sad and painful time in her own life. If she were to be on the set in the morning, Marilyn required regular doses of sleeping pills from the studio physician, Lee Seigel, and these she supplemented with handouts from Skolsky. 'I have to sleep,' she told Sam Shaw. 'My fans want me to be glamorous. I won't let them down.'

Meanwhile, her marriage was in utter disarray and for it the untidy, shabby house on Palm Drive was a metaphor; the kitchen and laundry were untended, beds unmade, unfinished food left lying around. This neglect of basic tidiness was inevitable for a woman so busy, preoccupied, unhappy and habitually disorganized as Marilyn, although it is intriguing to speculate on why no one ever thought to engage a housekeeper. Cleanliness was next to godliness for Joe but next to impossible for Marilyn.

'When you got her to the studio on a good day, she was remarkable,' Wilder recalled, 'even though that creature Lytess was still lurking and Marilyn depended on her approval for everything. I didn't like it, but I went through anything to get the scenes right.' And so he did, against terrific odds. *The Seven Year Itch*, forced to comply with the moral requirements of the Code and the Legion of Decency, ended by being a static movie, enlivened only when Marilyn is onscreen – especially in the hilarious send-up of television commercials. The story, alas, lacks any payoff, and its treatment of a married man's moral dilemma often sounds just plain silly instead of being credibly comic.

The pleasant gloss of the film owed much to what Wilder has called Marilyn's flesh impact – she looks on the screen as if you could reach out and touch her, she's a kind of real image, beyond mere photography. But there's something else, too. She had a natural instinct for how to read a comic line and how to give it something extra, something special. She was never vulgar in a role that could have become vulgar, and somehow you felt good when you saw her on the screen. To put it briefly, she had a quality no one else ever had on the screen except Garbo. No one.

'I wanted so much to do something right in my art when so much in my life was going bad,' she said soon after. And so she did, although she of all people never appreciated the result. Marilyn astonished the crew one day late that September. Accustomed to long delays because normally she stuttered for the first word or two of a line and retakes were required, the crew dreaded filming a sequence near the end of the film, a long and difficult scene in which Marilyn had to explain to Ewell why she finds so ordinary and unromantic a man exciting and why his wife should be jealous. Axelrod and Wilder fully expected Marilyn to need several days to get the lines down. To their astonishment, she did it perfectly in three minutes and a single take, 'letter perfect and with an impact that made everyone on the set applaud.'

Moments later, Marilyn explained to her writer and director that the scene worked for her simply because she believed every word of it, and because it seemed so close to her own experience. Heard years later, the scene has a touching simplicity and sweetness of spirit:

Ewell: Let's face it. No pretty girl in her right mind wants *me*. She wants Gregory Peck . . .
Marilyn: How do you know what a pretty girl wants? You think every pretty girl is a dope. You think that a girl goes to a party and there's some guy – a great big hunk in a fancy striped vest, strutting around like a tiger – giving you that

'I'm so handsome, you can't resist me' look – and from this she is supposed to fall flat on her face. Well, she doesn't fall flat on her face. But there's another guy in the room – way over in the corner – maybe he's kind of nervous and shy and perspiring a little. First you look past him, but then you sort of sense that he's gentle and kind and worried, that he'll be tender with you and nice and sweet – and that's what's really exciting! Oh, if I were your wife, I'd be jealous of you – I'd be very, very jealous.

[*She kisses him.*]

I think you're – just – elegant!

On 27 September, not two weeks after the DiMaggios returned to Palm Drive, Joe departed for New York and Cleveland to broadcast the World Series. For the next few days, Marilyn was in constant contact with her old friend Mary Karger Short (Fred's sister), the first to learn of the DiMaggios' separation.

When he returned to Beverly Hills on Saturday 2 October, Marilyn told Joe she had asked an attorney to draft divorce papers. In addition, she told Darryl Zanuck, who left instructions that Joe was to be barred from entering the Fox lot. Joe, believing that Marilyn could be placated and a crisis averted, said nothing and simply moved from the upstairs bedroom to the downstairs den, maintaining a dignified, aloof silence.

But that night neighbours heard a terrific fight at 508 North Palm. Mrs John C. Medley, concerned, was on the alert for violence: she was one of several neighbours who saw Marilyn, dishevelled and wrapped in a fur coat, leave the house and walk for hours along the street and through the service alley to the rear of Palm Drive.

Early Monday morning, Marilyn's actions revealed that while her pain may have been acute, her stamina and survival instincts were stronger. Publicity-conscious as ever, and eager again to turn something potentially embarrassing into something positively beneficial to the image of Marilyn Monroe, she telephoned Billy Wilder to say she was ill and unable to report for work. Immediately thereafter – just as she had from San Francisco on 14 January – she called Harry Brand. Speaking quietly, as if in confidence, she said that she had retained Jerry Giesler, the most public criminal lawyer in Hollywood, known especially for defending celebrities in delicate cases. Giesler would represent her in what she hoped would be a swift, un-complicated and uncontested divorce. Remain calm, Brand told her: he would manage everything. Such was the position, power and presumption of studio press agents that they were told of and then managed news of births, marriages, divorces, illnesses and deaths involving the more incandescent denizens of Holly-wood.

Crack ex-reporter that he was, Brand mustered the troops. He dashed off a quick announcement to the news wire services that the world-famous marriage was ending 'because of incom-patibility resulting from the conflicting demands of their careers', which must have amused everyone who knew that Joe was all but fully retired from just about everything except during World Series time. Brand then mobilized his platoon – Roy Craft, Frank Neill, Chuck Panama, Mollie Merrick and Ray Metzler – and gave each a list of major newspapers, re-porters and columnists. Within seven minutes, each of twenty Los Angeles news outlets was 'the first' to know the story.

The news was trumpeted worldwide next day, 5 October, and that morning more than a hundred reporters and photographers pitched camp on the lawn of 508 North Palm Drive. Inside, Giesler sat with Marilyn, who was in bed, sedated by Leon Krohn. She signed a one-and-a-half-page document pleading for divorce and alleging that in the eight months of her marriage she had suffered 'grievous mental suffering and anguish, all of which acts and conduct on the part of the defendant were with-out fault of the plaintiff.'* The complaint stated that the

---

* Giesler informed the press that this was standard vague legal diction and could refer to anything as 'common as political differences'.

couple separated on 27 September, when Joe went East, that there would be no request for alimony, that there was no community property to be divided. Giesler then descended to Joe and handed him the papers, informing him that he had ten days in which to contest the divorce before a default decree could be obtained. Joe said nothing, pocketed the papers and resumed watching television.

And now a brilliant little suspense drama was enacted for the benefit of the press. Giesler left the house, saying to reporters only that there was no possibility of a reconciliation but that the divorce was amicable – in testimony of this, he added that Miss Monroe was ill with a virus and that Mr DiMaggio was thoughtfully preparing soup for her. Perhaps next day there would be further news and even an appearance of the principals.

By the morning of 6 October movie cameras had been set up on the lawn of 508 North Palm Drive. Huston or Hitchcock himself could not have improved on the melodramatic scene as a grey mist lifted and the hazy California sunshine broke through. At ten o'clock there was much scurrying as Joe swiftly left the house with his luggage, attended by his friend Reno Barsocchini. The two men climbed into his Cadillac (a duplicate of Marilyn's), and Joe said that he was heading for San Francisco: 'It is my home and always has been. I'll never come back here.' In fact he did not proceed at once to San Francisco but instead remained in seclusion for six weeks at the home of Leon Krohn, who had befriended both him and Marilyn. According to the doctor, Marilyn telephoned Joe every night at Krohn's home.

At 10.55 that morning, she appeared. Wearing a form-fitting black jersey sweater in striking contrast to her blond tresses, a black leather belt, a black gabardine skirt and black pumps, she seemed bound for a funeral. Leaning for support on Giesler's arm, Marilyn made her way to the newsmen's microphones. At her side in a moment was Sidney Skolsky, who turned to newsmen and announced, 'There is no other man,' which of course was taken to mean that there certainly was. Giesler shot him an angry glance and seized control.

'Miss Monroe will have nothing to say to you this morning,' he began. 'As her attorney, I am speaking for her and can only say that the conflict of careers has brought about this regrettable necessity.'

The press would naturally not permit Marilyn to depart silently. But in response to a volley of questions she said in a choked, hoarse voice, 'I can't say anything today. I'm sorry. I'm so sorry.' And then she broke down and sobbed, resting her head on Giesler's shoulder and patting her eyes with a white handkerchief. From there she went not into the house but to a car, which took her first to Dr Krohn's office on North Roxbury Drive and then to the studio. Two hours later, she was back home and in bed.

Reactions were solicited immediately. Natasha Lytess, gloating, told the press:

> The marriage was a big mistake for Marilyn and I feel she has known it for a long time. Things like this just don't happen overnight. It is best this way . . . Now at last it will be possible for Marilyn to develop her talent to the fullest. In this girl we have a potentially great dramatic star. Her recent experience was a handicap to fulfillment of this goal. Now that is all behind her.

As for Joe's resentment of Marilyn's screen image and dress, Natasha added disingenuously, forgetting that she shared his objections:

> Some people are small enough to resent things that bring success to others, you know. They quarreled a lot. Marilyn kept hoping for the best, but Mr DiMaggio never could consider her feelings.

Discussing the divorce only briefly with a few friends, Marilyn was succinct with Michael Chekhov: 'Joe is a sweet guy, but we don't have much in common,' and not long after, she confided bluntly to Susan Strasberg, 'Bored – he bored me.'* Later she elaborated a little:

> He didn't like the women I played – he thought they were sluts. I don't know what movies he was thinking about! He didn't like the actors kissing me, and he didn't like my costumes. He didn't like anything about my movies, and he hated all my clothes. When I told him I had to dress the way I did, that it was part of my job, he said I should quit that job. But who did he think he was marrying when he was marrying me? To tell the truth, our marriage was a sort of crazy, difficult friendship with sexual privileges. Later I learned that's what marriages often are.

Promptly at nine o'clock on the morning of 7 October, Marilyn was back at work on *The Seven Year Itch*, looking very cheerful, as Billy Wilder recalled. 'I feel alive for the first time in days,' she told him. 'Had a wonderful night's sleep, too.'

As for Joe, he retreated moodily from view. 'I can't understand what happened,' he said, clearly hoping she would drop the divorce complaint. 'I hope she'll see the light.' He then added, probably with unintentional condescension, 'I think [Marilyn] is a good kid – young and naive – but I think she is being misled by the wrong friends.'

On 26 October, Joe made a bold attempt to win back his wife by seeking the mediation of Sidney Skolsky. They went to Palm Drive, where Joe begged her to reconsider. 'But Marilyn's determination was always like iron,' Sidney recalled. 'Her mind was set on divorce.'

Next day, Sidney accompanied Marilyn and Jerry Giesler to Santa Monica Court. Her attorney, as Sidney recalled with some astonishment, 'told Marilyn how he wanted her to act for

---

* Skolsky agreed with this blunt assessment: 'Joe DiMaggio bored Marilyn. His life-style added up to beer, TV, and the old lady – the wife who ran third to *Gunsmoke* or *The Late Show* and a can of beer, night after night after night. She couldn't settle for that – not even with an all-American hero' (Skolsky, p.225).

the reporters and cameramen. He worked like a good film director, explaining every mood and expression he wanted. Giesler
got a flawless performance from Marilyn' – perhaps because
there could be no retakes.

Meticulously and formally dressed in a black dress with a
scooped neckline, a black hat, contrasting white leather gloves
and white pearls Joe had given on her birthday, Marilyn made
another grand movie-star appearance. At only twenty-eight, she
was living the most public year of her life, turning everything
into a press and publicity event, creating and offering new facets
of herself even as she discovered them.

'Your Honor,' she said calmly to Judge Rhodes, in a statement transcribed worldwide,

> my husband would get in moods where he wouldn't speak to
> me for five to seven days at a time – sometimes longer, ten
> days. I would ask him what was wrong. He wouldn't answer,
> or he would say, 'Stop nagging me!' I was permitted to have
> visitors no more than three times in the nine months we were
> married. On one occasion, it was when I was sick. Then he
> did allow someone to come and see me.

And then she added words which may not represent the truth;
in any case, they contradict much that she told friends and the
press:

> I offered to give up my work in hopes that would solve our
> problems. But even this didn't help.

Then her voice broke:

> I hoped to have out of my marriage, love, warmth, affection
> and understanding. But the relationship was mostly one of
> coldness and indifference.

Natasha wished to appear as witness, but Marilyn wisely refused. To the stand, therefore, came the calm business manager
Inez Melson:

Mr DiMaggio was very indifferent and not concerned with
Mrs DiMaggio's happiness. I have seen him push her away
and tell her not to bother him.

In less than eight minutes, her interlocutory divorce was
granted by Judge Orlando H. Rhodes; the final decree would be
effective in exactly a year.

But Joe remained fiercely jealous, as was evident from a
bizarre event that he and his friend Frank Sinatra engineered
nine days later.

Since mid-October, Joe had retained a private detective to
follow Marilyn (evidently in the hope of finding evidence
against her), and the end of his marriage did not terminate the
contract. On the evening of 5 November the detective told Joe
that he had followed Marilyn, variously disguised, to the same
address several times: 8122 Waring Avenue, which happened to
be the residence of Sheila Stuart, the actress and student of Hal
Schaefer who with Harry Giventer had found him ill in his
office. Summoned by the detective, Joe arrived on the scene
and, enraged, wanted to break into Stuart's apartment to find
what Marilyn was doing and with whom.

The detective advised a few minutes' caution, and he in turn
summoned Sinatra, who arrived at the corner of Waring and
Kilkea with a crew of men. Some of them then approached the
apartment complex and together broke through a tenant's
door.* There was an ear-splitting scream, and the private eye's
flashlight found someone: a thirty-seven-year-old woman
named Florence Kotz sat upright in bed, terrified, clutching her
nightgown and bedclothes round her and shrieking for help,

* Accounts differ: Sinatra maintained he waited in a car nearby, and he went to
court to contest the evidence of the private eye, Philip Irwin.

323

which soon arrived. The gang might have been able to shoot straight, but they could not locate the door of Sheila Stuart, a few yards distant. The commotion roused Sheila, Marilyn and another guest, who scurried away while the mêlée continued. Soon after, Marilyn's car was found parked at 8336 De Longpre Avenue, where she had rented an apartment after leaving North Palm Drive.

This was known for years as the night of the 'Wrong Door Raid'. Florence Kotz sued Sinatra and DiMaggio for $200,000, and the case went to court. Sinatra denied being a participant, and after four years the case was dismissed in California Superior Court when Sinatra's attorney Milton Rudin arranged an out-of-court payment to Florence Kotz of $7500. As for Sheila's guests, DiMaggio always insisted they were Marilyn and Hal Schaefer; to no one's surprise, both of them denied these allegations.*

On 4 November, Marilyn completed principal photography on *The Seven Year Itch* and Charles Feldman gave a dinner party in her honour at Romanoff's restaurant in Beverly Hills, inviting eighty guests to celebrate her forthcoming hit. This was not only a generous and friendly gesture: Feldman had two other reasonable motives.

First, the gala evening was Feldman's response to Darryl Zanuck's increasing complaints about Marilyn's absences, her lateness during production, and the necessity of multiple takes

---

* The so-called Wrong Door Raid was widely reported in the press on 6 and 7 November, although Sinatra's representatives were at the time able to keep his and DiMaggio's names out of the stories: see UPI and AP wire service reports for those dates. But *Confidential* magazine (vol. 3, no. 4 [September 1955]) broke every detail of the story, and it is both interesting and important to note that the State of California later instituted an investigation of the magazine's methods, practices and results. The result of the inqruiy, presumably much to DiMaggio's and Sinatra's chagrin, cleared *Confidential* and in fact stated that they were 'quite zealous in checking out and documenting their reports to the public . . . As well, the activities of detectives [engaged by the magazine] were well within the rigorous code of regulations prescribed by the state for their business.' See *New York Times*, 2 March 1957, p.19.

when she misread her dialogue. These were ridiculous objections, Feldman insisted: the day Marilyn completed work on *Show Business* she went to New York for location work on *Itch*. Her divorce took her out for almost a week, but when she returned she worked fifteen consecutive days: 'she has been most cooperative – this girl is really a sensational actress.' He added that as Zanuck well knew, twenty takes or more were not unusual by a meticulous film-maker. William Wyler routinely wearied actors by doing sixty or more, and Elia Kazan often submitted Marlon Brando and Vivien Leigh to dozens of takes before he got what he wanted for the film of *A Streetcar Named Desire* (which Feldman had produced for Warner, and which won several Oscars).

Feldman's second reason was not quite so public. Marilyn was making quiet little noises about leaving Hollywood. Her lawyers were concluding lengthy examinations of her deals with Fox and finding loopholes by which her contracts could be declared null and void. This was being undertaken so that she and Milton Greene could form Marilyn Monroe Productions, to make films they would control from first day to last, and on which they could realize not only a vaster income than her Fox salary but also a handsome tax break. As part of the deal, it was also known that Marilyn was going to leave Feldman for new agents, the men at the Music Corporation of America, familiarly called MCA (with whom she signed on 26 July 1955).

'I feel like Cinderella,' Marilyn said when she arrived at Romanoff's, wearing a brilliant red chiffon gown borrowed from the studio wardrobe. Clark Gable danced with her, Humphrey Bogart poured her a drink, Clifton Webb spread some sharp gossip, and Sidney Skolsky got material for weeks of columns. Zanuck attended, as did Jack Warner, Claudette Colbert, Samuel Goldwyn, Gary Cooper, Billy Wilder, Susan Hayward and Loretta Young. Marilyn knew, commented Sidney Skolsky in his column a few days later, 'that the so-called elite of the town had finally accepted her. Marilyn had never felt she belonged. She had gained her fame because of her popularity with the fans,' but always felt neglected by Hollywood. 'I have come up from way down,' Marilyn said later. Most memorable for her that evening was her introduction to Clark Gable. 'I've always admired you and wanted to be in a picture with you,' she said while they danced.

'I ran *Gentlemen Prefer Blondes*,' replied Gable, 'and I told my agent you have the magic. I'd like to do a picture with you, too.' And so they would, but under circumstances not quite so pleasant as that evening.

Radiant and happy despite her exhaustion, Marilyn charmed everyone. Told by George Axelrod and Darryl Zanuck that after seeing the first seven completed reels of *The Seven Year Itch* they thought she was magnificent, Marilyn replied, 'It's because of Billy [Wilder]. He's a wonderful director. I want him to direct me again, but he's doing the story of Charles Lindbergh next, and he won't let me play Lindbergh.'

Each day of 1954 continued to be filled with complex business and personal relationships, and with minor but uncomfortable health problems. At seven o'clock in the evening of Sunday 7 November, Marilyn arrived (three hours late) at Cedars of Lebanon Hospital 'for correction of a female disorder she has suffered for years', said her surgeon, Leon Krohn, referring to the procedure he performed next day in an attempt to correct her chronic endometriosis.

The press documented her stay in hospital, with special attention to the fact that Marilyn was delivered to the hospital by Joe, that he was the only visitor during her five-night stay, and that he was present all day, every day, through dinner and each evening. On Tuesday he brought a bottle of Chanel No. 5 to her fifth-floor room, and this set off widely reported rumours of a reconciliation. 'There's no chance of that,' Marilyn said firmly on Wednesday, 'but we'll always be friends.'

On Friday 12 November, Marilyn was permitted to return home, and because Joe had briefly returned to San Francisco she asked Mary Karger Short to help her leave hospital. Intrusive, infamous pictures were taken that day of a wan, dishevelled

Marilyn almost weeping as she tries to hide her face from a herd of insolent photographers. But these reflect not (as often maintained) emotional breakdown but the simple fact that she had hoped she might slip away unnoticed by using the hospital's rear freight elevator. With her hair unbrushed and without her usual cosmetics, she did not wish to be seen, much less photographed – thus her distress when the boys from the *Daily News* leaped out at her.

But she did not obey the doctor's orders to rest. The next evening Joe was back in Los Angeles, and the couple dined at the Villa Capri, where they had met almost three years earlier. The first to honour his forthcoming fortieth birthday on 25 November, Marilyn presented him with a gold watch.

Sidney continued to squire Marilyn during November to social events, however, and that month they were seen at the Tiffany Club, the Palm Springs Racquet Club and the Hob Nob Club. And one evening, Marilyn Monroe made history in a new, unexpected fashion.

In the 1950s, Hollywood nightclubs did not invite non-white artists to perform, and when she learned that agents for her idol Ella Fitzgerald had been denied any discussion of an engagement, Marilyn personally called the owner of the Mocambo. 'She wanted me booked immediately,' Fitzgerald remembered, 'and if he would do it, she would take a front table every night I was there. She also told him – and it was true, due to Marilyn's superstar status – that the press would go wild. The owner said yes, and Marilyn was there, front table, every night.' With this, Marilyn Monroe placed herself firmly in the vanguard of a controversial support of civil rights – a concern that would become intense in the years to come as she read, asked questions, challenged lawmakers and learned about one of the shabbiest prejudices in American life.

That same season, a different sort of culture came into her life in the person of the English poet Edith Sitwell, whom Marilyn met at a Hollywood tea and to whom she expressed her own sincere interest in poetry. Dame Edith said that if Marilyn ever came to London she would be pleased to invite her to luncheon.

*

Everything seemed to accelerate towards the end of 1954. Milton Greene arrived in Los Angeles with preliminary papers for the formation of Marilyn Monroe Productions, thenceforth familiarly called 'MMP' by everyone. Just as she was taking the unpopular step of supporting the rights of minorities, so another kind of rebellion was evident. Weary of being typecast by unimaginative studio executives, offended by the prospect of another seven years of servitude at Fox and aggrieved at the absence of the verbally promised but still unpaid $100,000 bonus for *The Seven Year Itch*, she longed for better stories and scripts, more ambitious roles and the right to choose her projects and her directors.

Such demands were not to be taken seriously in Hollywood, but just as she had broken nightclub rules, so now Marilyn was ready to fight with Zanuck, Skouras, stockholders and critics. Aware of her power and prestige, with the success of the Romanoff party still fresh in her mind, she chose this time to make a break. She knew the studio needed her to promote *Itch* the following spring, and she knew she was America's biggest star. Marilyn was ready for a major gamble – and one with enormous risks, for there was no guarantee she could in fact survive without the machinery she had come to detest.

Perhaps nobody but photographer Milton Greene could have preserved Marilyn's career by paradoxically taking her away from Hollywood. Apart from brief spells at Columbia and MGM, she had been Fox's chattel since 1947, and now she felt her own seven-year itch. No longer willing to be treated capriciously by a boss or a husband, she was attracted to Milton not only because he photographed her brilliantly, but because he was not an industry figure. He had no more sense of how to make a movie deal than she, and no idea, either, of the intricacies of production control, budget or the thousand details of film-making. In a way, their partnership was a blind endeavour, but she would have it no other way. Part of her wanted not to be a sexy starlet but a serious actress; part of Milton Greene, did not want to be a popular photographer. 'He, too, wanted to rise above his past,' said his close friend, the writer and publisher Michael Korda. 'He wanted to be a stage producer, a movie producer, a mogul – almost anything other than what he had done already.' At twenty-eight and thirty-two, Marilyn and Milton were primed for adventure.

The enterprise briefly succeeded, at least in part because it took Hollywood by surprise. Milton Greene and his attorneys Frank Delaney and Irving Stein could manoeuvre deals because the West Coast movie people did not take seriously those on the East Coast they considered ignorant *arrivistes*. MMP was thought to be a typical bit of Marilyn's fey daydreaming, like her occasional statements that she would like to play Grushenka in a film of *The Brothers Karamazov*.

At the same time, Marilyn felt that Charles Feldman's friendship with Zanuck put her at a disadvantage. Famous Artists and Feldman did more business and had more clients at Fox than any other agency in town, and this did not go down well with her. Suspicious of almost everyone connected with the studio, she left Feldman – casually breaking that contract, too, even though she owed him $23,350 advanced to her as a personal loan; at the encouragement of Milton Greene, she now went over to MCA.* There, agency president Lew Wasserman saw to it that she would be managed on both coasts: by himself and his colleagues in California, and by Jay Kanter and Mort Viner in New York.

Feldman, ever the gentleman, chose not to enforce his contract with a volatile and unhappy client; he did, however, insist on being repaid the money she owed him, although it would take five years for him to collect. As for Wasserman and company, Marilyn knew he was the most powerful agent in the business. He had already negotiated a historic deal for James Stewart by which the actor waived a portion of his salary for a percentage of a film's profits. This was the origin of the so-

---

* Feldman had advanced Marilyn money to buy story rights for a project never realized; to pay Natasha; to pay her attorneys; and to commission an original screenplay.

called percentage deal, which revolutionized actors' fees, eventually enabling them to be producers as well and creating the phenomenon of the hyphenate – the actor-producer-writer-director becoming the ultimate jack-of-all-Hollywood trades.

As for Marilyn, she felt that thus far she had

> never had a chance to learn anything in Hollywood. They worked me too fast. They rushed me from one picture into another. It's no challenge to do the same thing over and over. I want to keep growing as a person and as an actress, and in Hollywood they never ask me my opinion. They just tell me what time to show up for work. In leaving Hollywood and coming to New York, I feel I can be more myself. After all, if I can't be myself, what's the good of being anything at all?

The fear that she was not indeed herself, that there were major parts of her person unknown and unexplored, was her central concern for the rest of her life.

In 1955 she set for herself several tasks – as producer, acting student, analysand – which suggested her desire to try a very different persona than 'Marilyn Monroe', whom she all but abandoned that year. If this were mere caprice, or a series of shallow 'experiences' to which she gave herself in lieu of serious pursuits, it would be easy to label her as many did: an immature, self-absorbed, lazy dilettante. But in fact she was nothing of the kind. At twenty-eight, much of her experimentation was a legitimate kind of self-exploration that would only later become permissible for people of post-college age in American culture; in the 1950s, uniformity and the aspiration to stability were set forth as prime national virtues, and by one's early twenties a respectable person was expected to have achieved a passport into some aspect of the commercial scramble. Honest enough to admit that she was neither familiar nor comfortable with an identity she poorly understood and had in fact not yet achieved, Norma Jeane/Marilyn for a year disposed of The Monroe and became a frank wanderer into new realms.

In this regard, her lifelong obsession with mirrors was not simply the sign of an actress's narcissism. Colleagues at work and friends at home often found her before a wall of mirrors, or seated at a three-panelled vanity table as if it were a sacred triptych; she gazed not in dreamy, mute adoration but in ruthless assessment, studiously refashioning and recreating, ever dissatisfied with the image she beheld. Constantly dressing and undressing, reviewing, repainting, drawing once again the lip and brow lines, washing and recommencing the application of a new look on a new face, she lived in a perpetual state of self-criticism, ever trying and retrying to focus some unrealized image of an unfinished self.

As she embarked on the search for a new Marilyn, the men at Fox were rightly alert to their own best interests and wise enough to find mechanisms to sustain them. For an entire year, from the end of 1954 to Marilyn's signature on a new Fox contract at the end of 1955, Greene's lawyers dealt with Fox's.

The eventual collapse of the traditional studio system and its ownership of actors owed much to her tenacity and to the success of efforts exerted by her, Greene and his attorneys. Marilyn Monroe was Fox's prodigal daughter, to be sure, but ultimately she was enthusiastically welcomed home and very much on her terms. It was as before a relationship of mutual benefit, for Marilyn and Milton needed Fox's money and they needed her to bring them profits.

As for the personal association between the star and her new partner, it had its fantastic side. Neither Monroe nor Greene were remarkably articulate, both depended on spokesmen, and in conversation there were often long pauses with mysterious non sequiturs. Of the hundreds of transcripts of meetings between Marilyn Monroe and Milton Greene, most suggest they might have been playlets drafted by the young Harold Pinter.

Marilyn travelled East, staying with the Greenes for Christmas 1954 and planning a life in New York that was to include regular attendance at Broadway plays and study with Lee Strasberg at the Actors Studio. She would, she said, leave the details of business and financial matters to Milton, his lawyers and accountant. Thus with the new year 1955, everyone's hopes were high with artistic expectations and friendly trust; even personal problems might have easy resolutions.

Marilyn spent a good deal of time quietly with the Greenes at their home on Fanton Hill Road in Weston, Connecticut, during the next twenty-eight months. Since his city childhood, Milton had wanted a country home, and from its origins as a stable the house was enlarged over the years and became one of the most charming and architecturally admirable in the area. The stable became the living-room, with a two-storey vaulted ceiling and a large fireplace. There were guest rooms, a large country-style kitchen and a photographer's studio.

The Greenes brought Marilyn into the many social and professional circles of their life. 'With us she had something entirely new,' Amy recalled,

> and that was a structured life in an organized house. She had her own little room when she visited. But most of the time we were in the New York social whirl. We were invited everywhere and were doing everything. She wanted to become an educated lady, but she also wanted to be a star. That was a conflict. But in the beginning she was very happy, functioning well, fighting Zanuck, feeling her oats.

Jay Kanter, one of her New York agents at MCA, agreed. 'Marilyn seemed to me very free that year, animated, enthusiastic, looking forward to serious work. She liked being out of the Hollywood film business. It was a time full of promise and she seemed to me to be taking hold of a new life.'

On the evening of Friday 7 January, part of that new life was publicly announced. Milton gathered eighty pressmen, friends and potential investors in MMP at Frank Delaney's home on East Sixty-fourth Street. Every Manhattan columnist and every reporter of any status was present except Dorothy Kilgallen and Walter Winchell, both of whom had been excluded by Milton 'because of their general hostility toward Marilyn'. The star as usual was an hour late, finally arriving all in white, wearing a borrowed ermine coat, a white satin dress and her hair a new shade of subdued platinum; she resembled nothing so much as a reincarnation of Jean Harlow. 'She really wanted to *be* Jean Harlow,' according to Amy.

> That was her goal. She always said she would probably die young, like Harlow; that the men in her life were disasters, like Harlow's; that her relationship with her mother was complicated, like Harlow's. It was as if she based her life on Harlow's – the instant flash, then over.

In a calm voice, Marilyn formally announced that evening the establishment of her new company, with herself as president and Milton Greene as vice president. 'We will go into all fields of entertainment,' she said, 'but I am tired of the same old sex roles. I want to do better things. People have scope, you know.' When asked how this related to her status at Fox, Delaney interrupted: she was no longer under contract to Fox.

Delaney's quiet, brief remark reached executives on Pico Boulevard before their working day was over; reacting with perhaps predictable shock, they called their own press conference. Marilyn Monroe was most certainly legally bound to work for them, it was announced – and for four more years. That, it seemed, was that. But of course it was not, and over the next several weeks the discord was daily served up in the nation's papers.

After the press party, Marilyn told the Greenes she wanted to continue the celebration at the Copacabana, where Frank Sinatra was singing. That would be impossible, Amy Greene said: Frank's show had been sold out for weeks. 'Never mind,' Marilyn replied. 'If you all want to hear Frank, follow me.' She scooped up her ermine wrap and led the contingent of party-goers to the Copacabana, where Milton suggested they enter through a rear door and ask to see Angelo, the maître d'hôtel.

Within minutes, additional tables and chairs were pushed on to the nightclub floor. Sinatra, distracted, stopped singing and the room was hushed. There in front of him, shimmering in white, was Marilyn, who had just raided through the wrong door but was in the right place. Sinatra had to smile, he winked at her, and the show resumed. 'So we couldn't get in?' Marilyn whispered to Amy. 'I stand corrected,' her friend replied. 'She knew,' Amy said years later, 'precisely the power and influence she had.'

When he said Marilyn was no longer bound to Fox, Delaney had spoken neither cavalierly nor without grounds. He had taken careful count of the days Marilyn was put under suspension in early 1954, and of the time when Fox was obliged to exercise their option for *Show Business* and for *Itch*. Late by a few days in renewing that option and remiss in putting on paper the single verbal guarantee of a $100,000 bonus for *Itch*, the studio was technically in arrears; in addition, they had relied on Feldman to get Marilyn to sign two relevant documents, but she had cannily avoided doing so. Furthermore, as Delaney pointed out to all who would listen, 'it seems legally impossible that Mr Feldman could have become both Miss Monroe's agent *and* the producer [of *Itch*] without a separate agreement and the consent of Miss Monroe.' This made *Itch* separate from the rest of Marilyn's deal, a situation never put in writing. Delaney, therefore, could claim that *de facto* the production of *The Seven Year Itch* terminted the Monroe–Fox contract of 1951.

By happy accident for MMP, someone at Fox mentioned to someone at *Variety* that 'Miss Monroe had indeed made [*Itch*] under a new agreement which gave her a substantial salary increase.' This bit of publicity aided the MMP cause immeasurably: according to California law, publication of such a statement meant that Marilyn now had no furthur obligations to Fox until a new contract was negotiated. At the same time, she received a letter from Fox in which it was casually admitted that her 1951 contract was effectively terminated by oral agreement when they began *Itch*. 'It is the damndest letter you ever saw, and a lawyer's dream' wrote Irving Stein, 'because seldom does an opponent make so good a record of an oral arrangement. I am convinced that Twentieth had best bargain realistically or they will lose a diamond mine.' For the moment, things were almost hilariously favourable for MMP.

As might have been predicted, sabres were at once duly and loudly rattled in the offices of both Fox and Greene. First of all, the studio suspended Marilyn – an empty threat, as she was still being paid her weekly salary because *Itch* was officially still in production and required her presence for a few final retakes in Hollywood that January. But she would be further penalized, Fox announced, if she did not remain for her next assignment, *How To Be Very, Very Popular* – which, because she was to have the role of a stripper, Marilyn had no intention of accepting.

Duly fulfilling her obligations for *Itch*, Marilyn and Milton flew to Hollywood on Sunday 9 January and next day she was at the studio for the final shots. 'You're looking good,' said Billy Wilder in welcome. 'Why shouldn't I?' replied Marilyn. 'I'm incorporated!' The first picture of her new company, she said somewhat proleptically, might be the life of Jean Harlow.

Back in Manhattan, MMP's wiry, hyperkinetic corporate lawyer Irving Stein was hard at work. An honourable man thoroughly dedicated to the success of the new company, Stein was an old friend of Greene's attorney Frank Delaney and had been brought in as counsel for the new venture. He worked tirelessly for them, frequently without regular pay, for MMP had no income until Milton remortgaged his Connecticut home that spring to help provide seed money and daily operating expenses – such as the cost of Marilyn's New York apartment.

Stein proved his worth at once, urging that in case Fox should attempt to lawsuit Marilyn ought to make herself a legal resident of the State of Connecticut (which, as an additional benefit, had no income tax). Accordingly, before the end of January she applied for a driver's licence and registered to vote there. Just as important, Stein realized the significance of Marilyn's continuing relationship with Joe DiMaggio, who had visited her in New York during the Christmas holidays – indeed, had stayed with her at least one night at her hotel.

Irving Stein saw the relationship from a strategic viewpoint: it could either present a difficulty or become an advantage for the business simply because Marilyn was obviously not emotionally free of Joe. 'It might be fatal for us,' Stein noted in his corporate diary on 27 January, 'since Joe is inducing pressure to have Marilyn return to California.' And then, significantly, he added: 'Leave her alone and we're in trouble.' Four days later, he wrote himself a reminder: 'Get Joe DiMaggio to talk to Frank [Delaney]. Milton and Marilyn had a row in [the] car coming down from Conn[ecticut]. We must know DiMaggio!' On 2 February, his corporate notes indicate that he told Delaney it was appropriate to relay to Marilyn news of Fox 'only while DiMaggio was in town'.

This was not difficult, for wherever Marilyn went, Joe was sure to follow. When she and Milton travelled to Boston to visit a potential contributor to MMP, Joe popped up at their hotel, and so she abandoned Milton and spent five days with her ex-husband in Wellesley, Massachusetts, at the home of his brother Dominic. The press was delirious with rumours of a renewed love match.

'Is this a reconciliation?' asked a newsman, interrupting their dinner at a Boston restaurant.

'Is it, honey?' asked Joe sweetly, turning to his ex-wife.

Marilyn hesitated a moment. 'No, just call it a visit.'

The man Milton and Marilyn had travelled north to visit was a wealthy dress manufacturer named Henry Rosenfeld, a New Yorker whose business had brought him to Boston that month. A legendary figure in fashion, he had founded a company during World War II with the idea that wealthy women could wear inexpensive clothes that would nevertheless be as chic as designer models. At that time his spare, casual shirtwaist

About to sing for American troops in Korea (1954). Photo by Ted Cieszynski.

Singing 'Diamonds are a Girl's Best Friend' for the troops in Korea (February 1954). Photo by Ted Cieszynski.

Arriving at an army outpost in Korea to entertain roops (February 1954). Photo by Sakamoto; opyright T.R. Fogli.

Recording for RCA Records (1954).

ABOVE *With her good friend and makeup artist Allan Snyder, on the set of* There's No Business Like Show Business *(1954). From the collection of Allan Snyder.*

BELOW *On location in New York for* The Seven Year Itch – *a shot arranged for the press but not included in the film (1954). From the collection of Chris Basinger.*

OPPOSITE *Lexington Avenue, New York: filming* The Seven Year Itch *(1954). The actual skirt-blowing shots were eventually recreated in the Hollywood studio.*

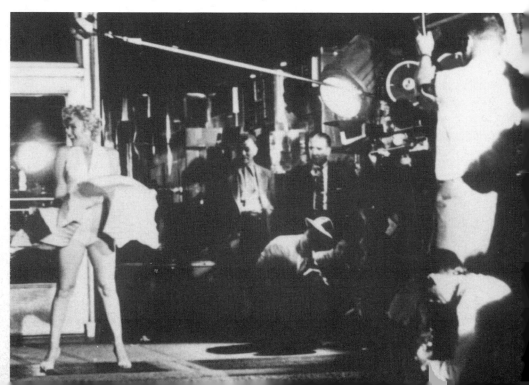

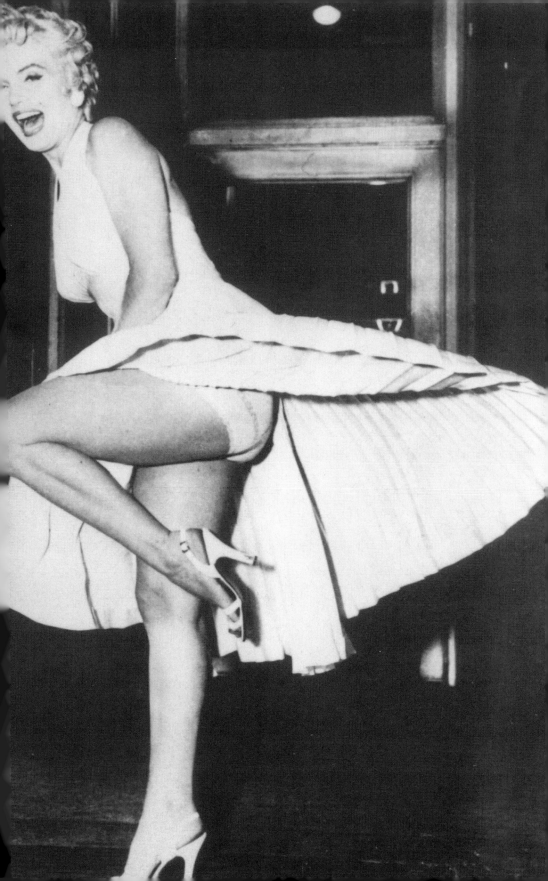

With her mentor and mythmaker, columnist Sidney Skolsky (1954).

At the premiere of The Seven Year Itch *on Marilyn's 29th birthday (1955).*

ABOVE *With Tom Ewell in* The Seven Year Itch *(1954). From the collection of Greg Schreiner.*

OPPOSITE *At the New York press conference announcing the production of* The Prince and the Showgirl *(1956): revealing the broken strap she had carefully prepared.*

ABOVE *The Strasbergs – Lee, Paula and Susan.* UPI/Bettmann Archive.

RIGHT *With partner and co-producer Milton H. Greene, arriving in Los Angeles.*

RIGHT *As Cherie in* Bus Stop
*(1956). Photo by Milton H.
Greene.*

BELOW LEFT *Press conference
(1956).*

BELOW RIGHT *Los Angeles,
spring 1956. Photo by Milton H.
Greene.*

During production of The Prince and the Showgirl, *London (1956). Photo by Milton H. Greene.*

The Millers in California (1956). Photo by Milton H. Greene.

In Chicago promoting Some Like It Hot *(1959), with reporter Mervin Block (right). From the collection of Mervin Block.*

dresses, for example, sold for eight to ten dollars and were hailed by office girls, actresses and society ladies alike; by 1955, his annual volume had leaped to $80 million. Dubbed the Bronx Christian Dior, Rosenfeld had developed many professional interests, and Milton hoped to make film production one of them. This attempt failed on the grand scale, but for several months Rosenfeld provided small sums for MMP's operating expenses, and there were rumours (impossible to corroborate) that Marilyn used her charms in private to convince Rosenfeld of the seriousness of her company's venture.

At the same time, very many people – Sam Shaw, Elia Kazan, Cheryl Crawford and Milton's own team – believed that the company's principals had resumed their own affair. Certainly the photographs Milton took of Marilyn during 1954 and 1955 are some of the most seductive and erotic ever rendered by any cameraman. In some, like the diffused, so-called 'Black Sitting', in which she seems like a Berlin vamp circa 1928, she wears little more than fishnet stockings, a kind of teddy and a hat, her expression and attitude oddly distracted, almost madly, intoxicatingly carnal.

For years, Amy Greene firmly denied that Marilyn and Milton were lovers; she claimed that she of all people would have known of such an involvement. But Amy had to admit that 'Marilyn was a homewrecker, although she didn't want to be,' and that Milton was a cagey and elusive man, given to excesses and indulgences he often seemed unable or unwilling to control. After the Monroe–Greene partnership was dissolved, however, Marilyn spoke quite freely to others (her publicist and confidant Rupert Allan, for one) of her ongoing liaison with Milton throughout his marriage. Since the time of André de Dienes, a confident and persuasive photographer was perhaps the single most powerful, irresistible aphrodisiac to Marilyn Monroe.

Also in January 1955, Milton leased a suite for Marilyn at the Gladstone Hotel on East Fifty-second street near Lexington Avenue. There she could meet the press, be available for interviews and take advantage of whatever New York activities seemed helpful. She would also be close to Milton's studio at 480 Lexington Avenue, where business meetings and photo shoots were frequently scheduled. Marilyn quickly learned, as she said on national television in April, that if she slipped on dark glasses and a scarf, wore an old coat but no makeup, she could stroll around New York quite untroubled, without even being recognized, much less importuned for autographs. 'Marilyn Monroe', after all, would surely be a knockout if one were ever to turn a corner and meet her fact-to-face, and the effort of being Marilyn Monroe was not something to which she dedicated herself in 1955.*

Instead, she had more serious concerns. Marilyn decided to take up Paula Strasberg's offer to meet her husband and to visit the Actors Studio. Shy of simply telephoning for an appointment, Marilyn turned to two of Strasberg's former colleagues, Elia Kazan and producer Cheryl Crawford, who were both preparing for the premiere of Tennessee Williams's new play *Cat on a Hot Tin Roof.* They provided a recommendation, and she set off to meet the most famous and controversial drama teacher in America. The introduction of Monroe and Strasberg was the start of a relationship both personal and professional that was as important as any in her life and that endured until her death.

Lee Strasberg, then fifty-four, was born Israel Srulke in 1901 in Poland. He came to America in 1909 and grew up among the immigrants of Manhattan's Lower East Side, a materially poor but culturally rich community. In his early twenties he trained as an actor with Richard Boleslavski, the Russian director who had worked with Konstantin Stanislavsky at the Moscow Art Theatre. Then in 1931 (renaming himself Strasberg), he co-founded the legendary Group Theater with Cheryl Crawford

---

* One day that February, she was leafing through an issue of *Variety* and found an advertisement taken by RCA for two of her songs from *There's No Business Like Show Business.* Alongside the titles was her portrait in a circle, with a phonograph arm placed provocatively, like a hand, across her upper, unclothed chest. She burst out laughing.

and Harold Clurman. With the Group he was actor, producer and director as well as supervisor of training, and here he began to develop an approach to acting which was called The Method. Quitting the Group in 1937 after arguments about The Method's principles, Strasberg worked independently and in 1951 was named artistic director of the Actors Studio, four years after its founding by Kazan, Crawford and Robert Lewis.

The Studio was a place where actors met to explore, a kind of theatrical laboratory where performers tried out characterizations before an audience of colleagues, took chances, made mistakes, were mocked and encouraged by their peers. Most of their work was never seen by the public, only by members. There were no formal classes; members simply arrived at Strasberg's twice-weekly sessions (Tuesdays and Fridays from eleven to one), perhaps rehearsing at other times privately with moderators or coaches – or, if they were among the chosen few, with Strasberg himself at his home, where they were charged the absurdly low price of thirty dollars a month for three sessions each week. Attendance at the Studio sessions was by invitation only, based on an audition before Strasberg.

A short, slight, intense and severe man who was an absolute authoritarian within his domain, Strasberg affected a distant, rather stern manner with many of his students as well as with his opponents (among the latter were other important drama teachers: Herbert Berghof, Sanford Meisner and Stella Adler). 'We were like converts to a new religion,' said the actor Eli Wallach of the Studio's early days. 'We didn't understand anyone else's acting except our own. Everyone else was a pagan.' Early members of the Studio (no one was called a student) were in deadly earnest about its superiority, according to Shelley Winters, another attendant from the start. 'We were dedicated to the idea of great theater. We all thought we would do Shakespeare plays and marry each other.'

Strasberg himself was something of a sign of contradiction. His legion of admirers and devotees emphasized his ability to dissect a performance down to the smallest gesture and the

339

slightest pause, illuminating every element that helped and hindered true characterization. Less enthusiastic were those who observed his tyrannical manner, his emotional coldness with all but those few favourites, and the intimate nature of some of his improvisations. 'He some times got into areas that were better left to a psychiatrist,' remembered Anne Jackson, a member who did perform Shakespeare and who married Eli Wallach.

'Lee was enshrined' at the Studio, according to Elia Kazan, who added that for years Strasberg

> noticed that actors would humble themselves before his rhetoric and the intensity of his emotion. The more naive and self-doubting the actors, the more total was Lee's power over them. The more famous and the more successful these actors, the headier the taste of power for Lee. He found his perfect victim-devotee in Marilyn Monroe.

Briefly, The Method according to Strasberg was based on several indisputable doctrines.

First, the task of the actor is not merely to imitate but to reproduce reality through the use of 'emotional recall' or 'affective memory'. Because of this, the actor's behaviour onstage must be psychologically sound, motivated by a single purpose based on one's unique personality. To ensure that the character and the play are lifelike and spontaneous, improvisation is encouraged during rehearsals (and even in some cases during performances). And over all these principles is an almost mystical commitment to the art of acting and to the truth it can reveal.

Because of Strasberg's emphasis on true emotion based on the actor's personal history, he urged that anything preventing access to the inner life be confronted forthwith – endorsing psychotherapy, he became a kind of analyst-doctor to his students. After Marlon Brando's celebrated performance in *A Streetcar Named Desire* and his equally celebrated term of psychoanalysis, the link between acting and therapy was firmly and respectably established. 'It made me a real actor,' said Brando, praising Strasberg's Method (although he also studied with Stella Adler, whose approach was quite different). 'The idea is you learn to use everything that happened in your life in creating the character you're working on. You learn to dig into your unconscious and make use of every experience you ever had.'

This angle led to an array of actors subsequently accused of being nothing but jumbles of tics and habits, looking ever more deeply into themselves and overloading performances with personal problems. George C. Scott, who acted in Strasberg's critically lacerated production of *Three Sisters* in 1963, derided much of his director's tactics, his preference for wounded, mannered and dependent performers, and later referred famously to 'Lee-you-should-excuse-the-expression-Strasberg.'*

In the days when Kazan was the premier teacher at the Actors Studio, the emphasis of The Method was on action and emotion, with grave fidelity to the text of the play and the integrity of the character. But with Strasberg's ascendancy, there was a shift to the dredging and prodding of sense memories and individual history, which led to a certain hyperemotionalism about which Robert Lewis made the apt comment, 'Crying, after all, is not the sole object of acting. If it were, my old Aunt Minnie would be Duse!'

Among the most respected opponents of everything Strasberg represented was none other than Laurence Olivier, who believed that acting was a matter of carefully prepared technique and the accumulation of external details from which a character emerges. Reflection on one's personal history seemed to him inconsistent with the actor's goal of reproducing not his own but

* Among scores of famous actors at the Studio for various lengths of time: Anne Bancroft, Marlon Brando, Ellen Burstyn, James Dean, Robert De Niro, Robert Duvall, Sally Field, Ben Gazzara, Julie Harris, Dustin Hoffman, Anne Jackson, Patricia Neal, Paul Newman, Al Pacino, Geraldine Page, Estelle Parsons, Sidney Poitier, Eva Marie Saint, Kim Stanley, Maureen Stapleton, Rod Steiger, Eli Wallach, Shelley Winters and Joanne Woodward.

the playwright's intentions. Once, surrounded by devotees of The Method, Olivier fulminated:

> All this talk about The Method, The Method! *What* method? I thought each of us had our own method! . . . What they call 'the Method' is not generally advantageous to the actor at all. Instead of doing a scene over again that's giving them trouble, they want to discuss, discuss, discuss. I'd rather run through a scene eight times than waste time chattering away about abstractions. An actor gets a thing right by doing it over and over. Arguing about motivations and so forth is a lot of rot. American directors encourage that sort of thing too much.

He was referring, he said without apologies, to Lee Strasberg. Olivier's hesitation notwithstanding, Strasberg was not a crackpot who attracted only or even primarily neurotic dependents. Fine actors by the dozen came to Strasberg at the Studio, which in 1955 moved from shabby, cramped quarters on West Fifty-second Street to an abandoned Greek Orthodox church at 432 West Forty-fourth Street, between Ninth and Tenth Avenues.

Strasberg was himself far too fine an actor not to realize (and on occasion to admit) that great acting, like every true craft or art, has something ineffably mysterious about it – that in great acting, the actor virtually vanishes behind the role; that actors can indeed utilize their own frailties to create a character – and that good actors will directly and invariably do so. Attracted especially to the young, to stars, to the ill and to the emotionally fragile, he took on with especial concern those with acute sensitivities. He also insisted – and here he was often on dangerous ground – that some students were not good candidates for The Method unless they underwent a systematic unblocking of feelings, a prolonged and parallel exploration of hitherto hidden mines of the past – specifically, through psychoanalysis.

This was the enterprise that he enjoined on Marilyn Monroe, making it a condition of her dramatic training when she visited him in early February 1955. 'My father wanted,' according to his daughter Susan,

> to arouse everything undealt with, everything repressed about her past, and to tap all her explosive energy. To bring all that up, he said she'd have to work on it in a formal, professional setting . . . Marilyn was drawn to my father because although she had little formal education, she understood human nature and at once agreed with his suggestion. Human nature, especially her own, fascinated her. They were really destined to meet and work together.

Marilyn agreed, for she wanted everything in her life to begin afresh. Without knowing it, Natasha Lytess was from that day dropped for ever from her life and career.

Marilyn, Lee said, simply had to open up her unconscious. In a general way, this was sage advice, and it had a certain intellectual allure for her; in other respects it was disastrous. Any depth work must be undertaken in a person's own time and rhythms, not under duress, not out of respect for a guru, not as an object lesson or as a passport to a tangible goal. Marilyn's early life was a tangle of loss, deprivation and abuse, some of it acknowledged, some not so. And while certain people are crippled, severely limited by not confronting repressed feelings and memories, others cannot or will not do so except at the cost of enormous personal pain. It is axiomatic that each inner life has its own integrity, that there are guidelines but no absolute rules for attaining psychological health and maturation. Accordingly, there are concomitant risks when an inappropriately enforced system of exercises or a formula of exploration is enjoined on someone too vulnerable or impressionable to make an independent judgement. And this was the clear and present danger when Marilyn set off to seek a psychiatrist of whom Lee Strasberg would approve – and who, she also needed to be sure, would not alienate her from Milton Greene and their new business venture.

Her choice was no surprise. Within two weeks, Marilyn began to travel three, four and often fives times a week from her sixth-floor suite at the Gladstone to 155 East Ninety-third Street, to the consulting-room of a psychotherapist named Dr Margaret Hohenberg, who for several years had been treating Milton Greene.

'Milton did more than recommend Hohenberg to Marilyn,' according to Amy. 'He actually brought her to Hohenberg, although he was at first skeptical because he thought that as two women they wouldn't get along.' A large, stout, fifty-seven-year-old Hungarian immigrant whose white hair was bound in tight braids, Margaret Herz Hohenberg began a rigorous course with her new patient. She had studied medicine in Vienna, Budapest and Prague, worked in hospitals for the insane and then specialized in psychoanalysis before coming to New York in 1939 and beginning private practice. 'I like talking to her' was all Marilyn said to Amy.

The year 1955 was therefore to be the year in which 'Marilyn Monroe', the glamorous, sexy, Technicolor star, was indeed put aside; neglected, too, was the image of Jean Harlow that had been so controlling an element. The replacement was almost a female version of Brando, as Marilyn affected the theatrical fashion of the serious actor she aspired to become: on the side-walks and streets of New York she wore blue jeans or plain trousers, sweatshirts and only the merest touch of makeup, if any at all. But within there was only a chrysalis, something still childlike. No longer presenting to the world a painted face, a manufactured product, she wished somehow to be (as it is called) a real person, and to do so, she started as if with a clean slate.

Even in this enterprise, Marilyn was somehow stymied, for in place of artifice there was a new, subtler peril. She now thought that she was independent, that she was doing something for her-self and by herself alone, not to please others. This was the most poignant illusion of all.

Chapter Fifteen

The idea, Lee Strasberg and Margaret Hohenberg told Marilyn, was that her confused childhood, her inability to sustain friendships, her suspicion that others wanted only to use and discard her, her obsession with pleasing others – all these need not destroy her: they might yet become part of the vocabulary and technique of a new art. As she had said,

> I had teachers and people I could look up to – but nobody I could look over at. I always felt I was a nobody, and the only way for me to be somebody was to be – well, somebody else. Which is probably why I wanted to act.

But there was too much pressure on her to succeed, too many goals set before her, too much business responsibility to bear. Where there should have been space and time to learn about herself – which was her reason for quitting Hollywood in the first place – now there was only urgency.

This was evident almost at once, for Marilyn became agitated, tense and unable to sleep. A doctor was summoned, she was given sedatives and barbiturates and told not to maintain quite so busy a schedule of therapy, meetings and outings for the next few weeks. Then, on 28 February 1955 – just days after Marilyn had begun psychotherapy – Irving Stein came to her suite at the Gladstone for a business meeting: they discussed the best ways to continue discussions concerning a new contract with Fox, and Marilyn said she would have to discuss everything with Joe DiMaggio. 'It seemed to me,' Stein wrote in his corporate notes,

that [the] entire tone of our conference changed with Milton's arrival. Her attention was diverted from me and directed to Milton. She scarcely looked at me and seemed reserved in her answers, as though she were editing them for Milton's benefit. This [was] especially so in answering questions involving Joe D ... Conference extremely unsatisfactory from time Milton came ... [I] telephoned the doctor, [who] asked me to again impress on Marilyn the necessity for cutting down on her activities.

The notations are significant from several viewpoints.

First, Marilyn's meetings with Dr Hohenberg put into a new perspective her relationship with Milton, whom she loved, needed and respected. But sharing his therapist also gave a new twist to the game, for now she had to please both the man who was supporting her and helping her to define a new career and the woman who was helping *him*. She was once again in a position of subordination, forced into the role of grateful child bound to please. That this conflict became intense, evoking all kinds of muddy confusions, was revealed in her agitation and sleeplessness. 'The tone of the conference changed with Milton's arrival' suggests that Marilyn also feared that he was discussing her in his sessions with Hohenberg just as she was discussing him. The further complication was the intermittent presence of Joe. Fearing Milton's resentment of this, she was 'editing her answers for Milton's benefit'. Dangerous weeds of suspicion were sprouting in what was to have been the new field of her career.

Second, resorting to medication, which only clouded her mind when she sought clarity, was an easy balm but complicated her therapy and disconnected her from those with whom she was to collaborate in serious matters. Margaret Hohenberg seems not to have been told of these drugs, although it would have been unlikely for her not to see their effects and to enquire appropriately. There is no evidence the therapist worked in consultation with one of Marilyn's physicians (a Dr Shapiro) who was simply summoned by her to provide sedative tablets for a famous patient he was told was in some kind of crisis.

From this time to the end of Marilyn's life, there would be just such a lack of communication between therapists and physicians – some of them more benevolent, better qualified, less manipulative than others, but all of them acting independently. Each saw Marilyn Monroe as his or her responsibility; each had a proud, proprietary claim; each readily assumed the superior role from which Marilyn, in her quest for independence and maturity, ought to have been freed. But she was, after all, simply too valuable a patient.

Third, at the age of twenty-nine she had behind her only the many experiences of life in the business of entertainment, not much of which helped her to grow up, and all of which sent her reeling back on her appearance, her prettiness, the dedication to surface glamour.

'My problem,' she said at the time,

is that I drive myself. But I do want to be wonderful, you know? I know some people may laugh about that, but it's true . . . I'm trying to become an artist, and to be true, and [I] sometimes feel I'm on the verge of craziness. I'm just trying to get the truest part of myself out, and it's very hard. There are times when I think, 'All I have to be is true.' But sometimes it doesn't come so easily. I always have this secret feeling that I'm really a fake or something, a phony . . . Joe understands this. He'd had a very difficult time when he was young, too, so he understood something about me and I understood something about him, and we based our marriage on this.

And then Marilyn added that her feelings of inadequacy sprang from the old, impossible identification of one's best work with

347

perfection – the goal set before her from the days of the Bolenders to the days of moviemaking and now, in the move to serious acting:

> My one desire is to do my best, the best that I can from the moment the camera starts until it stops. That moment I want to be perfect, as perfect as I can make it . . . Lee says I have to start with myself, and I say, 'With *me*?' Well, I'm not so important! Who does he think I am, Marilyn Monroe or something?

As those last sentences indicate, she was perhaps saved from desperation not by therapy but by her extraordinary ability to cut through the anxiety with a leavening humour, a gentle self-mockery and an awareness that 'Marilyn Monroe' was indeed not the deepest part of the self she sought and perceived she was becoming.

For a time, Marilyn sought relaxation in reading and museums. One afternoon in early March, she scoured shops in lower Manhattan and returned to her hotel with two sacks of books, among them Shaw's *Letters to Ellen Terry* and *Letters to Mrs Patrick Campbell*, Richard Aldrich's biography of his wife Gertrude Lawrence, James Joyce's *Ulysses* and a copy of the typescript for Noël Coward's comedy *Fallen Angels*, which was on Broadway that year with Nancy Walker and Margaret Phillips.

Continuing her interest in matters cultural, Sam Shaw and his wife dined with Marilyn and Joe several times that season, and after Marilyn mentioned her interest in poetry Sam arranged a meeting with the poet and novelist Norman Rosten and his wife Hedda. Thus began a close friendship that lasted until her death, with Norman acting as a kind of New York cultural mentor and Hedda, eventually, as Marilyn's Manhattan secretarial assistant. The Rostens were initially attracted to her, Norman recalled, because of her simplicity and honesty. Looking nothing like the movie star, she arrived at the Rostens' Brooklyn home with

Sam, who mumbled her name in such a way it sounded like 'Marion'. Hedda asked her guest's occupation, and when she said she was preparing for classes at the Actors Studio, Hedda asked what plays she had done.

'Oh, I've never been on the stage. But I have done some movies.'

'What was your movie name?'

And, as Norman Rosten remembered, 'in a timid voice' came the reply: 'Marilyn Monroe'. Not long after, Norman took Marilyn to a Rodin exhibition, where she was deeply moved by *The Hand of God*, a depiction of lovers emerging and embracing in the curved shelter of an enormous palm.

Yet Marilyn's timidity had its obverse in her full awareness of the effect and meaning of her stardom. 'When she came to visit us in Brooklyn Heights,' Norman Rosten said years later, 'she always insisted on helping out with the dishes. She wanted very much to be regarded as a regular person, one of the family, you might say. But she never could quite let you forget that she was a movie star.' There were, at such times, gently melodramatic sighs, unexpected withdrawals into a dreamy silence, prolonged sessions before Hedda's mirror, adjusting makeup and letting it be known how important her appearance was to her and, presumably, to everyone present. This co-existed with another presentation, that of the scrubbed, disguised Marilyn preferring to go unrecognized as she walked the streets of Manhattan.

That spring, Milton decided that Marilyn's status required a more elegant venue than the Gladstone Hotel. The actress Leonora Corbett, who had appeared on the London stage in the 1930s and then in the first New York production of Coward's *Blithe Spirit*, was seeking a six-month tenancy for her one-bedroom suite on the twenty-seventh floor of the Waldorf Towers, and a deal was hastily made. Soon the Rostens and the Shaws joined the Greenes in a champagne toast to Marilyn's fashionable new address.

There was another reason for celebration, although one not clear to anyone but Marilyn. As it happened, Norman Rosten had been a college classmate of Arthur Miller, and quite by chance Marilyn had been reunited with the playwright through the Rostens. Since their introduction four years earlier, Miller had written the prize-winning play *The Crucible*, based on the Salem witch trials of 1692 – a situation he linked with the tawdry investigations of so-called subversive activities in the 1950s. Soon to open in autumn 1955 was *A View from the Bridge*.

A year younger than Joe, Miller was to turn forty that year; Marilyn was twenty-nine. His life was in some turmoil, although this was belied by his placid manner. Like Joe, his tall, gaunt frame and apparent humourlessness gave him a certain grave authority; like Joe and Jim, he was athletic and loved the outdoor life of hunter and fisherman. But Miller also represented for Marilyn the serious theatre to which she was devoting her new life.

While he admitted his somewhat faddish youthful dabbling in Communist social theory, Arthur had come to it late, after other writers (Hemingway, Wilson, Silone, among others) had abandoned mid-twentieth-century Russian Marxism as intellectually and socially sterile. He was much regarded in the 1950s as the dramatic conscience of American society, for his work was plainly concerned with moral and social issues affecting families after the war. But he was no cool theorist; American playwrights tend not to be. Eugene O'Neill, Tennessee Williams, William Inge, Arthur Miller, Robert Anderson and later David Mamet, John Guare, David Rabe and August Wilson (to name but a few) write not academic theses but works rooted in memory and feeling, plays for actors and audiences that provide affective understanding of recognizable human dilemmas.

In this regard, Arthur's first wife was more of an intellectual and a theorist. Mary Grace Slattery was a liberal Catholic and an editor intensely interested in the politics of the thirties, forties and fifties. She provided her husband with creative stimulus as well as economic support, working during the early years of their marriage as a waitress until he was firmly established. (It has even been suggested that from the experiences of *her* father, an insurance salesman came the inspiration for *Death of a Salesman*.)

But as he detailed later in his autobiography, the demands of Arthur's work that year were ineluctably linked to Marilyn's reappearance in his life, 'and the resulting mixture of despair for my marriage and astonishment with [Marilyn] left little room for concentration' on preparing for forthcoming productions. Only two or three quiet suppers with the Rostens and one or two evenings alone with Marilyn were necessary for their friendship to develop into a love affair. 'It was wonderful to be around her,' he said years later. 'She was simply overwhelming. She had so much promise. It seemed to me that she could really be a great kind of phenomenon, a terrific artist. She was endlessly fascinating, full of original observations, [and] there wasn't a conventional bone in her body.'

But this did not mean Joe DiMaggio was out of the picture; for perhaps the only time in her life, that spring Marilyn maintained simultaneous intimacies – with the man who had been her husband and the man who was about to be. The trick was to keep each unaware of her meetings with the other, and this required some slick negotiating.

However thrilling his new love, Miller feared that he 'might be slipping into a life not my own,' which was an anxiety well founded. He was not quite sure what he wanted, for while he did not wish to end his marriage to Mary Grace Slattery – however deeply troubled and unsatisfying it had become – 'the thought of putting Marilyn out of my life was unbearable.' Marilyn found herself in something of a quandary, too. She was not at all ready to give up a grand passion simply because the man was married. At the same time, she was revaluating everything in her past, and although Arthur was physically attractive, intellectually stimulating and parentally tender, and although she desired him perhaps more completely than any man before, Marilyn had no intention of encouraging a divorce.

Quite the contrary: she urged him not to end his marriage on her account. For the present, she would be content to have him as occasional lover. This edge of detachment, perhaps predictably, made Arthur Miller all the more ardent a pursuer. But the truth is that he needed as much endorsement as Marilyn, for he was in the first throes of a terrible struggle with right-wing ideologues out to destroy him for being (so they thought) a Communist sympathizer who advocated overthrow of the government, a man whose life's work, daring to be critical of certain hoary myths about American supremacy, was treasonous. 'I had lots to do,' Marilyn told Amy later. 'I was preparing for a new stage in my career. But Arthur didn't have much to look forward to. In a way, I felt sorry for him.' And in a way she may have empathized with his contest for freedom, the right to criticize and the desire for artistic expression without interference from authorities: these were, after all, trademarks of her own relationship with Fox.

Political storms were gathering darkly on the horizon. Miller had a temporary break in his friendship with Kazan, who cooperated with the authorities asking the names of those who had once belonged to fashionable left-wing groups interested in things Russian and particularly in the historical and cultural roots of the Russian Revolution; Miller refused to follow Kazan's lead. Not at all interested in the tricky webs of intrigue, Marilyn was none the less sympathetic to his plight, although she also avoided taking sides – Kazan or Miller, and how might Strasberg, that champion of Russian-based acting theories, regard the matter?

Yet somehow her professional admiration and support of Kazan remained firm. At the premiere of his new film *East of Eden* on 9 March, an event benefiting the Actors Studio, she and Marlon Brando volunteered as ushers. Two weeks later, she and the Greenes attended the premiere of Tennessee Williams's *Cat on a Hot Tin Roof*, directed by Kazan. Both works stirred considerable controversy.

Not every event did, however. Opening night of the Ringling Brothers circus at Madison Square Garden, on 30 March, was a benefit for the Arthritis and Rheumatism Foundation. Among all the stars who turned out none was more visible or roaringly approved by 18,000 spectators than Marilyn: in a little scenario designed by the impresario Mike Todd (with Milton Greene supervising), she made a grand entrance in a tight, sexy outfit of feathers and spangles, riding on an elephant painted shocking pink. 'It meant a lot to me because I'd never been to the circus as a kid,' she told the nation a week later.

The forum for that comment was Marilyn's interview with Edward R. Murrow, whose television programme *Person to Person* offered an apparently casual but carefully rehearsed visit to celebrities. After weeks of preparing for the technical challenges of broadcasting a live show from the Greene home in Connecticut, the interview was at last scheduled for 8 April. But as airtime drew near, Marilyn became distraught, believing that her light makeup and simple outfit made her look wan and dowdy alongside petite, dark-haired Amy. When a CBS cameraman tried to calm her, saying she looked fabulous and that millions of Americans would fall in love with her on the spot, Marilyn became very nearly paralysed with fright: this was unlike a sound stage, there was no rehearsal, no possibility of a retake. But then the producer said quietly to Marilyn, 'Just look at the camera, dear. It's just you and the camera – just you two.' And with that she was reassured and made an admirably unaffected presence.

When Murrow asked the purpose of MMP, Marilyn replied directly that wished 'primarily to contribute to help making good pictures . . . It's not that I object to doing musicals and comedies – in fact, I rather enjoy them – but I'd like to do dramatic parts, too.' She also thanked those who had contributed so much to her career, singling out John Huston, Billy Wilder, Natasha Lytess and Michael Chekhov. Marilyn's appearance at the time was thought unglamorous and awkward, perhaps because she was such a refreshing change from the prevalent artifice: she answered questions briefly and unself-consciously, never taking the spotlight for herself or jockeying to be the star of the sequence.

As for Milton, his time during 1955 was divided between his photographic studio, where he tried to conduct business as usual, and meetings with Irving Stein, Frank Delaney and Joe Carr, his accountant. MMP desperately needed cash for such basic operating expenses as Marilyn's hotel bills and support, as well as 'seed money' for whatever project they hoped to realize. To Milton fell the responsibility of finding wealthy patrons, which was a futile endeavour. And so it became all the more necessary to recognize the flag of truce waved towards him by the men at Fox. Throughout 1955, the terms of the new contract between MMP and Fox were painstakingly negotiated.

From early April, with Marilyn's presence in New York more widely known, she was besieged with requests for appearances. The Arthur P. Jacobs Company, headed by the man of that name, had a public relations staff in New York and Los Angeles and was signed as Marilyn's publicity consultants. Jacobs and his colleagues on both coasts – John Springer, Lois Weber, Rupert Allan, Patricia Newcomb – constantly sorted through literally hundreds of demands each week for Marilyn's presence at interviews, benefit appearances, charity appeals and award dinners.

But because Marilyn insisted on her regular hours with Dr Hohenburg and her private sessions with Strasberg, she strictly limited both her meetings with reporters and the photo sessions necessary to keep her before the public. An exception was made for the photographer Eve Arnold, whose images of Marlene Dietrich had so impressed Marilyn. 'Imagine what you could do with me!' she told Arnold. Charming photos were taken of her as an autodidact, reading James Joyce's *Ulysses*; conversely, Arnold presented another aspect of her – in a leopard-skin, crawling through muddy marsh grass like a primal, predatory animal.

The search for identity could be a surprisingly ambiguous adventure, and in a way the closer Marilyn got the harder it was to grasp. Sometimes, she had to dress formally for business and social engagements, and Amy Greene often assisted her in selecting the proper additions to her frugal wardrobe. Shopping with Amy or with Hedda Rosten, Marilyn wore dark glasses, a scarf or a hat, no makeup – but disguised though she was, she wanted desperately to be recognized. She had, therefore, to take certain measures. As Norman Rosten recalled, Marilyn hired a limousine to take her shopping, drawing down the blinds to ensure that when she stopped passers-by would know that someone who mattered was about to alight.

Amy Greene recalled a day of shopping in Fifth Avenue's department stores. Marilyn began as usual in her *incognito* mode, completely unrecognized by customers and clerks. But as they went through the stores and aisles, Marilyn gradually put aside, piece by piece, the outfit she wore, until finally she tore off a wig and her dark glasses, rushed into a dressing-room and emerged as Marilyn Monroe, to the astonishment and excitement of everyone at Saks Fifth Avenue. Discarding the camouflage was a two-fold gesture: Marilyn wished to remove the disguise, the mask that hid her from her public, and to emerge as herself. But what she then revealed was in fact the *manufactured* Marilyn about whom she had such ambivalent feelings. Without that, she feared she had no real identity; trying to escape her false persona, she was simultaneously afraid of losing it. Similarly, Susan Strasberg and a friend recalled Marilyn angry and withdrawn when a taxi-driver did not recognize her.

That same season, Stanley Kauffmann was editing a book of Sam Shaw's photographs of Marilyn during *The Seven Year Itch*. 'She wore a sweatshirt and slacks. There was a bit of a belly. The knees were slightly knocked. Her hair looked tired.' But when Kauffmann showed her a picture he wanted to include, of her looking tired after a long day on the set, Marilyn was adamant in her refusal. 'When people look at me, they want to see a star.'*

---

* For all the boldness and the ambiguity of her adoption of disguises, there was still the fundamental crisis of identity, to which Marilyn even referred jokingly. When Susan once said she was in conflict about something and that she felt she had another voice clamouring inside her head, Marilyn remarked, 'You have only one voice? I have a whole committee!' (Susan Strasberg to DS, 3 June 1922.)

Marilyn Monroe

About this time, Marilyn began to refer to herself in the third person. Susan Strasberg recalled walking with her when she noticed a group of fans awaiting her return at the Waldorf. 'Do you want to see me be her?' she asked Susan. Momentarily confused, Susan then saw something remarkable: 'She seemed to make some inner adjustment, something "turned on" inside her, and suddenly – there she was – not the simple girl I'd been strolling with, but "Marilyn Monroe", resplendent, ready for her public. Now heads turned. People crowded around us. She smiled like a kid.'

Similarly, Sam Shaw could never forget Marilyn repeatedly speaking of herself in the third person. Referring to a scene in *Itch* or to a photograph of herself, she said time and again, 'She wouldn't do this . . . Marilyn would say that . . . She was good in this scene.' Truman Capote wrote of finding Marilyn sitting for a long while before a dimly-lit mirror. Asked what she was doing, Marilyn replied, 'Looking at her.' Eli Wallach, walking with her one evening on Broadway, recalled Marilyn without makeup or distinctive clothes, suddenly stopping traffic and attracting attention. 'I just felt like being Marilyn for a minute,' she said, and there was the magnetism. It was as if an image flashed through her mind – a daydream of someone glamorous, remote and almost half-forgotten named Marilyn Monroe – and for a moment she reassumed that image. But she knew that Marilyn Monroe was only a part of herself; thus she could associate with 'Marilyn Monroe', but she rarely identified with her. She had co-operated in the creation of the image and was willing to present what agents, producers, directors and the public wished. Danger, emotional confusion, a crack in relationships: these occurred only when she tried to steer her life's course entirely by the chart of fame mapped out for Marilyn Monroe, with no reference to the deeper, private self within.

In therapy, she was urged to keep a notebook of random thoughts, or a diary, but this she never did, as she confided to friends. Twice Marilyn purchased notebooks with marbled covers but they remained blank, for she did not have the necessary, elementary discipline and she was ashamed of what she considered her atrocious spelling and punctuation. But occasionally she scrawled notes on scraps of paper. That year, with the evocations suggested by her analysis and then her drama classes, Marilyn's jottings show the concerns of her inner work:

'My problem of desperation in my work and life – I must begin to face it continually, making my work routine more continuous and of more importance than my desperation.'

'Doing a scene is like opening a bottle. If it doesn't open one way, try another – perhaps even give it up for another bottle? Lee wouldn't like that . . .'

'How or why I can act – and I'm not sure I can – is the thing for me to understand. The torture, let alone the day to day happenings – the pain one cannot explain to another.'

'How can I sleep? How does this girl fall asleep? What does she think about?'

'What is there I'm afraid of? Hiding in case of punishment? Libido? Ask Dr H.'

'How can I speak naturally onstage? Don't let the actress worry, let the character worry.'

'Learn to believe in contradictory impulses.'

More frequently, Marilyn transformed some of her feelings into poems – 'rhythms' might be a better word, images of what she felt and feared in her twenty-ninth year.

Night of the Nile – soothing –
darkness – refreshes – Air
Seems different – Night has
No eyes nor no one – silence –

except to the Night itself.

Life –
I am of both your directions
Somehow remaining,
Hanging downward the most,
Strong as a cobweb in the wind,
Existing more with the cold frost
than those beaded rays
I've seen in paintings.

To the Weeping Willow

I stood beneath your limbs
And you flowered and finally
clung to me,
and when the wind struck with the earth
and sand – you clung to me.
Thinner than a cobweb I,
sheerer than any –
but it did attach itself
and held fast in strong winds
life – of which at singular times
I am both of your directions –
somehow I remain hanging downward the most,
as both of your directions pull me.

But unlike many amateur poets, Marilyn never took her odes
too seriously, as shown by one in particular that has an airy
humour and natural gravity worthy of e.e. cummings or
William Carlos Williams:

From time to time
I make it rhyme,
but don't hold that kind
of thing
against

me –
Oh well, what the hell,
so it won't sell.
What I want to tell –
is what's on my mind:
'taint Dishes,
'taint Wishes,
it's thoughts
flinging by
before I die –
and to think
in ink.

From the first day they worked together in private sessions in the Strasberg apartment at 225 West Eighty-sixth Street that spring of 1955, Lee gave Marilyn the strongest paternal-professional guidance of her life – a kind of total psychological mentorship that soon provoked the resentment of both Milton Greene and Arthur Miller. Lee fully agreed with and encouraged Marilyn's resentment of movies in general and Fox in particular, for he believed their abuse of good actors and writers was standard operating procedure. This disaffection was based on his own experience, for in 1945 that studio had denied him the opportunity to direct *Somewhere in the Night*, which he had co-written with Joseph L. Mankiewicz. Opinionated and pugnacious, Lee had been released from his studio contract and returned to the East Coast, where, according to Susan, life was very difficult for the four Strasbergs (Lee, Paula, Susan and her younger brother John). 'My father was terribly frustrated and had fights with the wrong people, but he also had an ability to inspire others' – which led his former partner Cheryl Crawford to send him acting students. Kazan then asked him to take over the supervision of the Actors Studio from Robert Lewis.

Because at first she was frightened to speak and participate in open class exercises, Marilyn was invited to the Strasberg home – an emotional minefield, according to Susan, where Paula had subordinated her own career, her wishes and the life of her entire family on the altar of Lee's supremacy.

Then seventeen, Susan Strasberg (who had already appeared importantly in two films, *Cobweb* and *Picnic*) was about to have a great success on Broadway as Anne Frank. Susan felt an immediate empathy for the frightened, vulnerable Marilyn, 'despite the mask of celebrity she put on and took off at will. She told us more than once, "Hollywood will never forgive me – not for leaving, not for fighting the system – but for winning, which I'm going to do."' Because Marilyn was soon another member of the Strasberg family – having meals at their kitchen table and often staying overnight – Susan had the chance to see her tough core. Underappreciated by studio executives, Marilyn nevertheless knew how to use her past, combining it with both her beauty and her essential sweetness of spirit to project a childlike attitude that almost everyone found irresistible.

But Lee and Paula devoted so much time and attention to her that Susan 'was convinced there was no love or energy left for me, and I felt guilty for even feeling that way, because I saw how lonely Marilyn was. She really had nobody she felt she could trust completely – not one person.' Lee became Marilyn's father while Paula became her mother, nursemaid, coach – and keeper of the pills. One night, Marilyn was so desperate for sleep after a Strasberg party that she combined sleeping tablets with one glass too many of champagne: dazed and unable to walk, she crawled to Lee and Paula's bedroom, scratching at the door while Susan watched, frozen with fear.

'Don't you ever feel anxious? Don't you have anxiety attacks?' she asked friends in sober moments. When told these were common feelings, sometimes especially in actors, she replied quietly. 'But you're not in my position. When you're on a film you've got to look good in the morning so you've got to get some sleep. That's why I take pills.'

This habit was, contrary to the usual idea of Marilyn, nothing like an attempt at self-destruction; much less was she a psychotic personality. In addition, it must be stressed that she was also doing what very many people did in the 1950s – and perhaps pre-eminently those in the arts. The abuse of pills was not only the habit of sensitive playwrights like Tennessee Williams and William Inge, and self-indulgent actors like Tallulah Bankhead and Montgomery Clift: it was an accepted part of the artistic life. 'Our family doctor gave me sleeping pills when I was seventeen,' recalled Susan.

People mixed champagne and pills all the time, to increase the effectiveness of the pills. As for Marilyn, she had the burdens of her fear, her timidity, her insecurity and her unusually agonizing monthly periods that rendered her literally incapable of moving.

Marilyn's use of hypnotics and barbiturates (she never took amphetamines, marijuana or intravenous drugs) had begun innocently enough with Sidney Skolsky's unlimited free samples. By 1955, the occasional imprudent combination of pills and wine disturbed what little routine she had and made her strident, moody and lethargic next day.

However embracing of her, the Strasberg family was far from the ideal one for Marilyn. Lee was prone to rages and Paula to hysterical fits and threats of suicide, while by a certain sad irony these gifted, overbearing parents depended for several years on the talent, success and income of their daughter for financial survival. 'Our household,' Susan said, 'revolved around my father, his moods, his needs, his expectations and his neuroses. He was teaching people how to act, but that was nothing compared to the drama in our house ... Our entire family were intimate strangers.' Her brother Johnny was convinced that 'it was hard for anyone to have a relationship with [Lee] if you weren't a book, a record, a cat or Marilyn.'

An unintentionally negligent father, Lee lavished on Marilyn the attention he denied his children: more than once, when Susan approached him to discuss something in her personal life, he replied, 'I'm not concerned with that except as it relates to your work.' Marilyn, on the other hand, received private tutorials when she wanted them and gentle nurturing when she was depressed, unhappy or insecure. This Lee did because he seemed genuinely to believe in her raw, untapped talent (not apparently because he was in love with her, although he may have been). The strong bond between them was their mutual hunger to be respected by the mainstream from which they had deliberately withdrawn.

There was another common link, and that was the Russian aesthetic to which Marilyn had earlier been exposed by Carnovsky and Brand, Lytess and Chekhov. The Strasbergian Method and the exercises utilizing Russian plays and poetry were for Marilyn part of a logical continuum that included her association with Arthur Miller, whose left-wing sympathies coincided with those of the Strasbergs. Marilyn's attraction to the outcast and disenfranchised led her to love the characters in Miller's recent plays, and even to identify with them. Lee and Arthur were in a way becoming complementary halves of father and lover, teacher and guide. 'When I have problems, I like to talk to Lee.' With him, she felt protected, endorsed, welcome for the first time in a circle she respected. Grateful, she lavished gifts on his family – much to the annoyance of Milton, whose allowance to her she freely spent.

When she began to attend the group sessions at the Studio that summer, Marilyn was at first too frightened to speak. A young aspirant named Gloria Steinem one day asked Marilyn if she could imagine playing a scene before so impressive and confident a group. 'Oh, no,' was the reply. 'I admire all these people so much. I'm just not good enough. Lee Strasberg is a genius, you know. I plan to do what he says.'

Those orders sometimes required private rehearsals with classmates. Telephoning one young man to whom she had been assigned for a scene study, Marilyn announced herself:

'Hi – it's me, Marilyn.'

Joking, he asked, 'Marilyn who?'

'You know,' she said quite seriously, 'Marilyn? from class?'

Perhaps it was the humility of the most famous woman in the class that made accomplished actresses like Kim Stanley – who that year had a huge success in the lead of William Inge's play *Bus Stop* – affirm that 'anybody who had any largeness of spirit loved Marilyn. And she won us all . . . She had something about her that made you love her. She didn't do anything at first; for a long time she just sat and watched.' Frank Corsaro, a fellow-student at the time and later artistic director of the Studio, recalled that Marilyn's 'endeavour to develop herself as an actress was a serious one. She was invariably late, but she listened and observed the critiques with a steadfast gaze.'

When she did speak, Marilyn had something to say. One day the young playwright Michael Gazzo suggested that a scene written by George Tabori was not quite clear. Marilyn leaned forward intently, then tentatively raised her hand, was recognized by Lee and said in a soft voice that she believed this was the point of the scene: the situation *at that moment in the play* was unclear to the character; confusion was the dominant 'through-line' Lee was after in the rehearsal. He allowed that she was right on the mark. On another occasion, a sympathetic interviewer asked her favourite authors. When Marilyn replied that she was reading Kafka's *The Trial*, her observation was acute: 'I know they say it's a kind of Jewish thing about guilt – at least that's what Mr Arthur Miller says,' she said, 'but I think it goes beyond that. It's really about all men and women – this sense that we've fallen or something. I suppose that's what they mean by Original Sin.' These were not the statements of a dilettante, but of one who discussed what she liked, tried to read critically and to consult interpretive texts.

By mid-May, Marilyn was a regular observer at the Studio, sitting quietly at the rear of the room. At the same time, a 52-foot-high photograph of her was lifted into place over Loew's State at Forty-fifth and Broadway. 'That's all they're interested in,' she said ruefully to Eli Wallach as they walked past the theatre that was preparing for the opening of her new film.

On 1 June she was every inch Marilyn Monroe, attending the

premiere of *The Seven Year Itch* and afterward accepting the applause of an audience that included Grace Kelly, Richard Rodgers, Henry Fonda, Margaret Truman, Eddie Fisher and Judy Holliday. Over the next few weeks, the picture opened across the country, and once again Marilyn was the most popular, most photographed, most documented person in America – more so even than President Eisenhower. She was also earning a fortune for Fox: *Itch* was (in the language of *Variety*) the summer's hottest ticket, grossing over $4.5 million. For this Billy Wilder as producer-director received half a million and a share of the profits, and Marilyn's agent, co-producer Charles Feldman, received $318,000 and the same additional guarantee. Marilyn, still awaiting her $100,000 bonus (which was eventually paid), had so far received only her weekly salary. Thus Greene and company were negotiating even more fervently with Fox for a new contract – not only because they could not operate much longer without it, could not buy literary properties or set up a production company – but also because they knew Fox, too, had strong incentive to keep their best product and not give cause for litigation.*

Joe DiMaggio was her escort for the premiere, coincidentally on her twenty-ninth birthday, and after the screening he was the host at a party for her at Toots Shor. 'We're just good friends,' she told the press. 'We do not plan to remarry. That's all I care to say.' At the same time, she was redoubling her time with Arthur Miller, taking long walks in lower Manhattan, dining at the Rosten home and, more privately, at the Waldorf. There Joe tracked her to discuss Arthur. 'Marilyn was afraid of Joe,' according to her publicist Lois Weber,

physically afraid. He was obviously rigid in his beliefs. There

---

* However much Hollywood marketed Marilyn and sex, it continued to reward elegance: the Oscars in 1953 and 1954 were handed to Audrey Hepburn and Grace Kelly. Even later, her extraordinary work in *Bus Stop* and *The Prince and the Showgirl* was ignored by colleagues: Marilyn, who had the temerity to have spent a year away from Hollywood, was not even nominated for an Academy Award.

must have been a great ambivalence in his feelings toward her ... There were times she made it clear he had hurt her very badly, maybe even struck her in some jealous rage.

Rupert Allan's impressions were identical: 'Marilyn told me that Joe had been a great friend to her after the divorce, but that while they were married he had beaten and abused her and believed her unfaithful.' This renewed relationship with Joe made Milton Greene more concerned than ever that Marilyn's diverse loyalties might sabotage his grand design for a lucrative new contract with Fox.

Early that summer, one particularly insensitive reporter in the New York press pool observed that Lee Strasberg had supplanted Milton as Marilyn Monroe's mentor. This caused considerable tension at ensuing meetings of MMP and, around, 1 July, Milton urged Marilyn to join him and Amy on a trip to Italy. ('How do we meet with Marilyn while Milton is away?' asked Frank Delaney plaintively in a call to Irving Stein.) She could not be persuaded to leave New York, giving both her classes and her regular attendance at Broadway plays as the reason for remaining. She had also accepted an invitation from the Strasbergs to join them for weekends at a rented beach house on Fire Island, not far from Manhattan.

By this time, Marilyn had come to depend on Lee and Paula. Sometimes as often as twice or three times a week she arrived at their apartment in the middle of the night, sleepless and dishevelled, complaining that her sleeping pills – for which she was developing a tolerance – were ineffective. That summer her nightmares, loneliness, the awful work of talking over and over in psychotherapy about her childhood, her absent parents, her early marriage, her resentment of Grace Goddard, her time prostituting herself, her resentment against Fox – the remembrance of all these took a fearful toll on her sensitivity and diminished rather than abetted her confidence.

In addition, Marilyn was growing ever more suspicious of the Greenes, of her professional relationship with Milton and her personal one with Amy. She felt inferior, she felt ignored in business decisions, she was weary of her own solitude. Milton and his partners could not seem to finalize a deal with Fox, and Marilyn began to wonder if she had made a mistake in leaving Hollywood. All this she poured out to the Strasbergs in the small hours, drinking champagne when Paula offered tea, finding more pills in their cabinets until she finally drifted off to sleep at five or six in the morning.

Thus 1955, in many ways a year of valuable discovery and precious learning, was also the time when Marilyn swallowed too many pills and too much champagne. Amy recalled this as a time when Marilyn was constantly on and off a diet, on and off pills. 'One day she gave me a bottle of sleeping pills and asked me to keep these for her: if she asked for them, I was to give her an argument. I told her she'd come to the right person. But soon she cajoled and begged me, and Milton insisted I give her the pills.'

As usual at that time, such drugs were not difficult to obtain, and physicians kept Marilyn and Milton supplied. 'Miltowns [a popular tranquillizer] were handed out like candy,' as Amy recalled. It seemed everyone had unlimited supplies of pills – and soon Milton was as much a wreck because of them as Marilyn. Pharmaceutical companies gave doctors free pills, and some doctors gave too many free samples to patients, keeping them frequent visitors to their offices. 'It was an awful cycle,' Amy added. 'Milton's brother was a doctor, and we had tons of pills – anything we wanted, uppers, downers, it was all available.'

In this regard, Marilyn's time with Hohenberg seems to have been unfruitful. The more anxious Marilyn became, the more separate she felt from Milton and resentful of him and his therapist, as Irving Stein and Frank Delaney noted in separate memoranda throughout the year. How could Milton function when she could not? How could he, too, take pills and visit Hohenberg and yet despatch his tasks? How deeply and how long would she feel disengaged from others, from life? Inner work invariably entails a dark and painful period, a classic night of senses and spirit, but Marilyn could not find any sustaining light or hope during that year that had promised to be so golden.

One weekend at the Strasberg beach house that summer, Marilyn stood naked in the moonlight while Susan, sharing her room, watched fascinated, admiring the resilience, buoyancy and glow of Marilyn's skin. 'I wish I were like you,' said Susan.

'Oh, no, Susie,' Marilyn replied. 'I wish I were like *you*! You're about to play a great part on Broadway – Anne Frank – and people have *respect* for you. No, no – I have none of those things.'

That same summer, Marilyn surprised the town of Bement, Illinois, by accepting an invitation to celebrate their centenary, to open an art show and to speak about her favourite president, Lincoln, of whom a new bust was to be unveiled. To accompany her and to document the journey, she invited the photographer Eve Arnold, who recalled that Marilyn 'had a great sense of showmanship and self-promotion', and this apparently negligible summertime event in rural America was not to be slighted. 'I'm going to bring art to the masses!' she said with a laugh.

The trip took her away from New York for just one day. The citizens of Bement were beside themselves with adoration, taking amateur snapshots and obtaining autographs of the great movie star, and Marilyn loved it all. According to Arnold, Marilyn always knew instinctively where the camera was placed, played to it, made love to it, got proof of her existence from the still photograph, not the movie's flickering image. In the presence of the camera as a worshipping audience, a transformation occurred automatically: Marilyn's breasts were thrust forward, her abdomen was drawn in, her rear end swivelled, a smile and a glow illuminated her face. Her skin, as Susan had remarked, had something like a translucent glow, and a fine mist of down on her face captured a kind of halo, a nimbus of light round her: photographs seemed to canonize her, to offer a creature almost ethereal as well as sensual.

She was experienced enough to know just how much she needed great photographers like Greene and Arnold, those who memorialized her in images, supporting the myth and illusion that propelled people into cinemas. 'She was pleased if you liked her most recent motion picture,' recalled John Springer of the Jacobs office, 'but if you talked about her recent magazine cover or photo layout, she really came alive with pleasure.' And so she did in Bement, smiling, waving, meeting grandmothers, holding infants in arms – always aware of the beloved camera but also of the people who would cherish her, perhaps for ever after.

Returning to New York and to weekends with the Strasbergs and the Greenes, Marilyn saw more of Arthur Miller, just as *A View from the Bridge* was preparing for its premiere. This she attended at the Coronet Theater on 29 September, when she met the playwright's parents for the first time. Not long after, Marilyn sat in the kitchen of Isadore and Augusta Miller's Brooklyn home, wearing no makeup and only a plain grey skirt and a high-collared black blouse. 'This is the girl I'm going to marry,' Arthur told his parents. No one thought he was very serious, for there had not yet been any open talk of divorcing Mary Grace.

Marilyn also visited Norman and Hedda Rosten. At their beach house she was once mobbed to the point of near-drowning when swimmers besieged her, but she laughed off the event, ever grateful for the attention. Champagne and caviar, prized because they were not the stuff of waifdom and orphanages, became her favourite foods that year. And poetry, however dense, nourished her immediately, even before someone began to offer an exegesis or she consulted a critical text. Rosten remembered her reading aloud with great feeling a selection from Yeats, making the words her own, as she did a photo opportunity or a movie role:

For everything that's lovely is
But a brief, dreamy, kind delight.
O never give the heart outright . . .

When she finished, her host added, there was in the room almost a reverential hush no one dared interrupt. There seemed to be a tacit understanding not only of Yeats's wisdom but of the words' aptness for her who had just read them.

That autumn there were scenes from plays by Anton Chekhov at the Actors Studio, and Lee loaned Marilyn several recordings of Tchaikovsky, Scriabin and Prokofiev – all of it adding to Marilyn's established love for Russian culture. In these interests Arthur indulged and encouraged her, and so when she learned that season that her much loved Michael Chekhov had died in California, Marilyn asked Arthur to read aloud with her some passages from *The Brothers Karamazov*, as a kind of private memorial. Chekhov had been the first to encourage her to undertake the role of Grushenka, and that evening Arthur promised to write a screenplay of the novel for her.

Expanding this cultural predilection, she went to hear the Russian pianist Emil Gilels at Carnegie Hall on 11 October. When introduced, he said to Marilyn, 'You must visit Russia one day. Everyone there would like to see you.'

'I would love to,' Marilyn replied, 'and some day I will. Right now I'm reading Dostoevsky.'

In fact she had already made a fateful decision. During her visit to Bement, Carleton Smith of the National Arts Foundation had asked if she would like to travel to Moscow to lead a contingent of American artists discussing an exchange of Western and Russian culture. No time was necessary for Marilyn to accept, and at once she took the necessary step of applying for a Russian visa. But the typical bureaucratic delays intervened – and a good thing, for she could not at this time abandon MMP and the growing prospects for an imminent deal and a return to work.

At the same time, Marilyn was known as the companion of Arthur Miller, whose every statement was noted by the Federal Bureau of Investigation. Thus, beginning in 1955, a formidable file on Marilyn Monroe also began to accumulate in Washington – records of which she was never aware during her life. They represent some of the most ludicrous waste of paper in history.

As documents later declassified revealed, the FBI, the CIA and the office of the Attorney General were in 1955 vigilant to the point of obsession regarding the travels of those thought to be dangerous to the national interest by virtue of past Communist sympathy – which was sometimes all but 'proven' by anyone's affinity for Russian culture. Marilyn's FBI file meticulously tracked her departure from Hollywood, her relocation with the Greenes in Connecticut, her friendship with Arthur Miller, her studies at the Actors Studio and her request to travel to Russia. J. Edgar Hoover demanded that every attempt by Marilyn to leave the country be carefully monitored – travels with or without Miller, and on whatever apparently personal business. The nation just might be thick with Russian spies masquerading as movie stars.*

At the same time, Marilyn's relationship with Arthur had effectively ended all rumours of a reconciliation with Joe. 'I expect our divorce to become final within about a month,' he told reporters glumly when he arrived in Paris that summer. The final decree dissolving the marriage became effective on 31 October 1955. 'I never should have married him,' Marilyn told Amy Greene. 'I couldn't be the Italian housewife he wanted me to be. I married him because I felt sorry for him, he seemed so lonely and shy.' She 'felt sorry' for Arthur, too, and these feelings – however much based on her wish to be needed, not merely desired – are important elements towards understanding why she contracted marriages that seemed unsuited to her talent and temperament.

In the autumn, the lease at the Waldorf Towers expired, and MMP took another half-year lease for her at 2 Sutton Place.

---

* Curiously, however – perhaps because it required express approval of the Attorney General – there was no extensive security check conducted on Marilyn during 1955.

From here she went to classes and therapy as usual but also intensified her theatre-going: during the 1955 and early 1956 season she saw, among other plays, Paul Muni in Jerome Lawrence and Robert E. Lee's *Inherit the Wind*; Susan Strasberg in *The Diary of Anne Frank*; and Edward G. Robinson and Gena Rowlands in Paddy Chayefsky's *Middle of the Night* (about which there were brief but fruitless discussions for her to play in a film version). Escorted by Marlon Brando – with whom she was often seen at theatres, restaurants and returning late to Sutton Place – she also attended several film premieres, among them a December gala for *The Rose Tattoo*.

At a benefit supper after that screening, Marilyn was introduced to an actress she had recently seen onstage – but one she was in no hurry to meet. In October she had attended the opening night of George Axelrod's first comedy after *The Seven Year Itch*, a farce called *Will Success Spoil Rock Hunter?* (which was being presented even as the author was writing the screenplay for *Bus Stop*). The leading lady of *Rock Hunter* was Jayne Mansfield, a buxom platinum blonde manufactured to capitalize on Marilyn's popularity.

More to the point, the play was a hilarious satire on the idea of an American screen goddess named Rita Marlowe who forms her own production company. 'You all start out by saying you want to write about the *real* me,' says Rita to a journalist, 'the shy lonely girl I really am. But then you always end up by writing the same old things. How I don't wear underpants. My divorce . . .' The play, from first scene to last, was a *pièce-à-clef* about Marilyn Monroe.

As the curtain rises, Rita Marlowe has just divorced a legendary sports figure named Bronk Brannigan, a character prone to violent assertions of his rights over Rita. She is attended by her masseur, just as Marilyn regularly engaged her good friend, the actor and physical therapist Ralph Roberts, for such treatments. Similarly, there are references throughout the play to the major professional players in Marilyn's life: Sidney Skolsky, the William Morris Agency, Charles Feldman, MCA, Billy Wilder and Darryl Zanuck – and the journalist without experience who joins forces with Rita is a clear reference to Milton Greene, novice producer. There is also a playwright named Michael Freeman – a double of Arthur Miller – who has written a work called *No Hiding Place Down Here* (which has a plot satirizing *A View from the Bridge*).

Marlowe (an obvious annexation of the names Marilyn and Monroe) is a silly, empty-headed cipher who dresses scantily both at home and work and has pretensions to act absurdly inappropriate roles (Joan of Arc, for example). Rita is also considering a neorealist film script based on a play about a psychiatrist and a hooker – at which point Axelrod was getting dangerously close to the documentary genre.

All sexual energy, Rita cannot remember the name of a magazine from one moment to the next, but her stupidity does not prevent a happy ending: a playwright in Hollywood and the journalist transplanted there both return to New York, rejecting the artifice and regaining their souls in the bargain. The play, which ran successfully for 444 performances, did not seem to Marilyn as amusing as it did to theatre audiences. With no further comment, she said flatly to Axelrod several months later, 'I saw your play.' He did not ask her to elaborate.

As the year drew to an end, there was a major snowfall in New York and wild flurries of activity in the offices of Milton Greene and of his attorneys. For one thing, Frank Delaney left the services of Milton and MMP when he sensed Marilyn's inexplicable loss of confidence in him. Irving Stein added Delaney's duties to his own.

On another issue, Marilyn's occasional hairdresser Peter Leonardi falsely claimed that she and Milton had promised to set him up in business at his own salon; he brought the matter to deposition and then foolishly tried to bribe a settlement out of court by taking as hostage several of Marilyn's fur coats. Irving Stein's corporate notes from 6 October to 9 November, when the matter was resolved, record significantly that the entire matter – more reminiscent of a Feydeau farce than the dealings of a serious corporation – was to have been adjudicated not by attorneys or police, but by Marilyn's psychiatrist, Dr Hohenberg. Stein referred to her in his notes as 'Marilyn's psycho'.

The influence of Dr Hohenberg on the day-to-day decisions of Marilyn's business life seems to have grown like Topsy: 'Milton telephoned to say the psychiatrist vetoed Marilyn's seeing Peter [Leonardi] . . . and that Marilyn should not submit to the demands of everyone who insisted upon seeing her.' Why it should have been necessary for Greene or anyone else to obtain Dr Hohenberg's approval, or even to involve her in business and legal matters, is not easy to know, but that she made herself virtually indispensable to Milton and Marilyn was obvious. And that they were in no position to act independently – much less to regulate their mutual, increasing reliance on barbiturates – further suggests that perhaps they required treatment other than what Margaret Hohenberg was prepared to provide.

But the principals of Marilyn Monroe Productions were to end 1955 and begin 1956 in good spirits, whatever the attendant psychological problems. After all the fussing and feuding between Fox and MMP – much of it merely keeping lawyers and agents busy with reams of paper – a contract was ready for Marilyn to sign.

Its principal provisions provided at last the tardy bonus of $100,000 for *Itch*; $100,000 per future film and $500 weekly during production for maid service and other expenses. She had to appear in only four films for Fox over the next seven years, and they would be projects whose subject, director and cinematographer she could approve; she could make one picture at another studio for each she made with Fox; and she could record, be heard on radio and appear on half a dozen television programmes annually; she would also have the benefits of a tax shelter, for her own corporation would pay out her salary.* In regular monthly cheques to MMP, Fox would pay Marilyn a

---

* At the time, the top corporation tax was 53 per cent, while the top personal income tax was 88 per cent.

gross annual salary of $100,000, and Milton would receive $75,000.

The year ended as it began, with a champagne party – this one held privately and quietly, at the Greenes' home as midnight tolled on 31 December. To make it altogether a happy new year, they had just decided on the company's first two projects, each based on a play. Marilyn was to appear in a film of William Inge's Broadway hit *Bus Stop* for Fox, and with Laurence Olivier in a movie version of Terence Rattigan's *The Sleeping Prince*, to be produced in London.

'I'm beginning to understand myself now,' she said at that time. 'I can face myself more, you might say. I've spent most of my life running away from myself, but after all, I'm a mixture of simplicity and complexes.' There would be ample and dramatic opportunities offstage, during the coming year, for all this to be tested.

Chapter Sixteen

1956

'There is persuasive evidence that Marilyn Monroe is a shrewd businesswoman,' proclaimed *Time* magazine on 30 January 1956, detailing the terms of her new contract with Fox, as if it had been the easy victory of a one-woman operation. *Time* also reported that she would soon be on her way to Hollywood to begin *Bus Stop*.

It was indeed a busy season. On 5 February, Laurence Olivier, his agent Cecil Tennant and the playwright Terence Rattigan arrived in New York for meetings with Marilyn about *The Sleeping Prince*, which Olivier had played in London with his wife Vivien Leigh in 1953. In 1954, Hugh French had suggested to Marilyn that the role of an American chorus girl who falls in love with a Middle European royal roué was perfect for her. As she began to choose her own projects, Marilyn had kept Rattigan's play in mind and wanted no other than Olivier for her prince – precisely, she said, because it was so wildly improbable a pairing of actors and because it might help her achieve greater respectability as an actress. For his own benefit, Olivier asked to co-produce, direct and act as co-star, a demand to which MMP finally yielded after an avalanche of cablegrams between them and Olivier that winter.

On Tuesday 7 February, Olivier, Tennant and Rattigan met Marilyn at Sutton Place, after waiting the usual hour-and-a-half. 'But then she had us all on the floor at her feet in a second,' recalled Olivier, for whom punctuality was indeed the courtesy of theatrical kings. 'She was so adorable, so witty, such incredible fun and more physically attractive than anyone I could have imagined, apart from herself on the screen.'

Two days later at noon, a press conference was held in the Terrace Room of the Plaza Hotel, where more than 150 reporters and photographers gathered. As if this was to be the announcement of a presidential candidacy or a papal election, the event had something faintly surrealistic about it: not for this group the attitude that 'it's only a movie', as Alfred Hitchcock so often said. No, this would be more than that: it would be an *event* uniting a great English classical actor with America's (indeed, the world's) greatest sex symbol – an unlikely alliance, indeed.

At last there arrived the solemn, dark-suited Olivier; the quiet, dignified Rattigan; and Marilyn, in a low-cut, black velvet dress designed by John Moore. Only two shoulder straps, thin and frail as cooked spaghetti, kept her from sudden indecency.

The questions were typically tiresome:

'Sir Laurence, what do you think of Miss Monroe as an actress?'

'She is a brilliant comedienne, and therefore an extremely good actress. She has the cunning gift of being able to suggest one minute that she is the naughtiest little thing, and the next minute that she is beautifully dumb and innocent.'

'Marilyn, how do you feel about working with Sir Laurence?'

'He has always been my idol.'

'Is it true you want to play *The Brothers Karamazov*? Do you think you can handle it?

A flash of irritation crossed her face. 'I don't want to play the brothers. I want to play Grushenka. She's a girl.'

'Spell that name "Grushenka", Marilyn,' someone dared.

'Look it up,' she snapped.

The reporters turned back to Olivier, asking two or three more prosaic questions about Hollywood, his salary, his control over American stars.

And then it happened. As if to smile for a photographer, Marilyn leaned forward and one of the straps of her dress broke.

There was a moment of silence, then the popping of enough flashbulbs to blind an army in battle. She smiled, calmly asked for a safety pin and then bent forward while the strap was re-attached to the back of her dress. 'Shall I take my coat off, boys?' Olivier asked puckishly. 'Does anybody care?' The strap broke twice more before the conference was disbanded.

'The strap breaking was deliberately, brilliantly pre-arranged and carefully maneuvered in advance while she was dressing,' recalled designer John Moore. Eve Arnold, photographing Marilyn that day, agreed: 'Before we went downstairs, she said to me, "Just wait and see what's going to happen." ' The result was another Monroe coup – and her picture on the front page of several New York dailies. She may never have needed publicists.

But less risky and risqué photographs were also produced that winter. Cecil Beaton arrived from London, following her around her apartment with a camera while she romped, squealed with childish delight, leaped on to a sofa, put a flower stem in her mouth and puffed on it as though it were a cigarette. He found her 'artless, high-spirited, infectiously gay'.

Otherwise, for the first two months of the new year, Marilyn continued her wintry New York retreat, touring the streets of Brooklyn Heights with Arthur Miller, visiting the old haunts of writers and artists and listening adoringly as Arthur told stories of his boyhood. That winter, according to Sam Shaw (who photographically documented the lovers' New York wandering), 'Brooklyn became Nirvana to her, a magical place, her true home.' But Nirvana is a fantasy, and magical places are generally restricted to venues like Disneyland. The Monroe–Miller association, which she deemed 'heavenly', had to be lived out firmly on earth, and from the start it was burdened with terrible disadvantages.

For one thing, Miller was entering on what would be a difficult time in his own creative life – just as Marilyn was about to re-enter her professional life with fresh and astounding success, giving that year the two great performances of her career. The situation was oddly reminiscent of her and Joe. Second, arch-conservative political groups, operating unchecked and at the instigation of some pressmen and under government sponsorship, were about to make their nastiest skirmishes against Arthur.

'There are all sorts of police gazette stories about Marilyn and her "Red Friends",' noted Irving Stein in his corporate notes for MMP on 6 January 1956. Indeed, there were several right-wing writers hostile to anyone like Miller who had even a vaguely liberal spirit, and in 1954 he had been refused a passport to attend a production of one of his plays in Belgium. The columnist Louis Budenz often sniped at Miller, whom he labelled a 'concealed communist', and the reporter Vincent X. Flaherty was even sillier: 'Teenage boys and girls worship Marilyn. When Marilyn marries a man who was connected with Communism, they can't help but start thinking Communism can't be so bad after all!'

But the most vituperative voice against the playwright belonged to none other than Joe DiMaggio's buddy Walter Winchell – who was an eager news-gatherer for J. Edgar Hoover, director of the FBI, to whom he regularly wrote friendly notes beginning 'Dear John'. On 12 February, days after Miller and his wife announced they were soon to be divorced, Winchell broadcast to the nation a story planted by Hoover himself – that 'America's best known blond moving picture star is now the darling of the left-wing intelligentsia, several of whom are listed as Red fronters.'

By this time, Arthur was certainly among the two or three most famous Americans scrutinized (and soon to be indicted) by government sub-committees obsessed with rooting out the threat to national security, for a violent overthrow by Moscow-directed Communists was presumed imminent. Hoover's men had kept a file on Miller since his college days, when he had liberal social interests; he then supported the American Relief Ship for Spain; he was classified as unfit for World War II military service because of any injury (which certainly seemed unpatriotic to the Bureau); and he was a member of the

American Labor Party. By 1944, agents were frankly spying on Miller, and in 1947 they found most suspicious his weekly attendance at a seminar of writers organized by an editor at the venerable publishing house Simon & Schuster, where writers gathered to counterattack the extreme right-wing propaganda disseminated by the media.

Miller's professional achievements did little to stem the FBI's surveillance. His first Broadway success, *All My Sons* (1947) concerned an engine manufacturer who knowingly sells defective parts to the Air Force; this the FBI labelled 'party line propaganda'. In 1948, a savagely Red-baiting newsletter called *Counter-Attack* openly called Miller a Communist, just as the FBI disapproved of his support for the new state of Israel. Even more absurdly, in 1949 the FBI became drama critics, condemning *Death of a Salesman* as 'a negative delineation of American life . . . and [a play that] strikes a shrewd blow against [national] values.' But most alarming of all for Hoover's agents was Miller's support of a Bill of Rights seminar that openly criticized 'the police state methods of certain Army and FBI officials'.

When the Monroe–Miller marriage was subsequently rumoured to be inevitable, Winchell went further: 'the next stop [for Miller] is trouble. The House Un-American Activities Committee subpoena will check into his entire inner circle, which also happens to be the inner circle of Miss Monroe – and all of them are former Communist sympathizers!'

This sort of nonsensical vilification was common – symptomatic of the paranoia that swept America in the 1950s, washed into homes in regular waves of hysteria by vicious gossips like Winchell. At once the agents of the FBI grabbed their dark glasses and notebooks and began compiling data on the travels of Marilyn and her friends the Greenes, who were for a time seen as potential subversives, too. But government snoops could report only that 'Miss Monroe, after completing her next assignment in the motion picture *Bus Stop*, will return to New York before her scheduled journey to England to make a motion picture with Laurence Olivier.' This they might have taken from Hedda or Louella – or even from those other meticulous but very different agents, the ladies and gentlemen at Arthur P. Jacobs Company, who issued regular statements of Marilyn's departures, arrivals and professional plans. The only exclusive revelation provided in advance to Washington was erroneous, for they believed her Los Angeles address was to be the Chateau Marmont Hotel; by coincidence, that is where she installed Paula Strasberg during the production of *Bus Stop* (and where Marilyn had clandestine weekends with Arthur during April and May).

Neither columnists nor government agents went so far as to see any dark significance in one event that February. Norma Jeane Mortenson (as she usually signed herself) at last legally became Marilyn Monroe. On 12 March she swore, 'I am an actress and I found my name a handicap. I have been using the name I wish to assume, Marilyn Monroe, for many years and I am now known professionally by that name.'

There were three other important formalities to certify, and they were quickly despatched. After some grumbling from Milton – delivered, as usual in such delicate matters, through the mediation of Irving Stein – Marilyn assigned to Milton not the fifty-one per cent in MMP he had requested, but two per cent less, reserving control for herself. Had *Time*'s editors known this, it would have been their best evidence that she was indeed a 'shrewd businesswoman'.

Second, Marilyn's agents at MCA (in this matter monitored by chief executive Lew Wasserman himself) urged Greene and Stein to 'shoot for the best deal, a quality distributor' for MMP's forthcoming productions. Wasserman suggested Warner Bros for the Olivier film. 'Be conservative,' Wasserman cautioned Milton, 'for if you reach for the moon and miss you will destroy Monroe Productions.' You deal with the distributors, Milton responded to Wasserman in several notes and calls. Good idea, replied Wasserman, adding ominously, 'There are already uninvited cooks in the kitchen. Be careful. MMP has the flair for public relations, so we [i.e., Greene, Monroe and Wasserman] will tell the studio what to do.' The cooks, presumably, were studio executives elsewhere offering deals disapproved by Wasserman, whose corporate and political influence at this time (not to say in the decades to come) cannot be overstated.

Third, there was the matter of Marilyn's will, which she signed on 18 February and, as such things do, tells much about her sentiments early that year. Presuming an Estate valued at $200,000 (an arbitrary figure based mostly on hopes for the future), her bequests were: $20,000 to Dr Margaret Herz Hohenberg; $25,000 to Lee and Paula Strasberg; $10,000 to Mrs Michael Chekhov; $100,000 to Arthur Miller, 'to be paid however is best for him tax-wise'; sufficient cash to cover sanitarium expenses for Gladys Baker Eley for the rest of her life (but not more than a total of $25,000); $10,000 to the Actors Studio; and $10,000 for the education of Patricia Rosten, daughter of Norman and Hedda.* The signing complete, Irving then asked Marilyn if she had an idea for her tombstone inscription: 'Marilyn Monroe, Blonde,' she said, tracing lines in the air with a gloved finger and adding with a laugh '37-23-36.'

Just before she departed for Hollywood and *Bus Stop*, Marilyn gathered up her courage and prepared to act onstage with Maureen Stapleton in part of the bar room scene from Eugene O'Neill's *Anna Christie*. 'This was really a brave thing for her,' said Stapleton years later.

> She could have chosen a role that wasn't too well known, so that her performance could have been criticized only on its own merit. But to do *Anna Christie*, something that's been done by a dozen wonderful people – Garbo included! This meant that everyone in a professional audience came with an idea of how it should be done.

* This will was twice revised.

Marilyn was terrifically serious while they rehearsed, added Stapleton, a Broadway leading lady then best known for her success in Tennessee Williams's *The Rose Tattoo*: 'I found her intuitive, bright and attentive, though I could see she was absolutely terrified of this new experience.' Once, after concluding a rehearsal at the Studio, they shared a taxicab, arriving first at Marilyn's apartment. Because they were so emotionally drained, the matter of sharing the fare took on the proportions of a scene from O'Neill himself. 'Look,' Stapleton finally said, 'if you don't get out of this cab and go home and just let me pay, I'm finished with you *and* the scene!'

Distressed, Marilyn alighted, kept her money and watched the taxi depart. When Maureen entered her apartment soon after, her telephone was ringing. 'You really don't want to do the scene with me, do you?' Marilyn asked, her voice wavering. A few minutes were needed for the reassurance that Maureen was still a good friend and colleague and very much wanted to do the scene with Marilyn.

The night of the performance, 17 February, Marilyn was nervous to the point of collapse, terrified she would stumble or forget her lines as she so often did before a camera. Maureen suggested that Marilyn put a copy of the script on a table, an acceptable custom at Studio workshops. 'No, Maureen – if I do it this time I'll do it for the rest of my life.'

Anna Christie was a good role for Marilyn, for the character is (thus the text) 'a blond, fully developed girl of twenty, handsome but now run down in health and plainly showing all the outward evidences of belonging to the world's oldest profession.' She comes to a waterfront saloon in New York, sinks wearily into a chair and utters the opening line made immortal by Garbo in the 1931 film version – but spoken that night at the Actors Studio with a breathless urgency that made Anna pathetic as well as hardboiled:

Anna: 'Gimme a whisky – ginger ale on the side – and don't be stingy, baby.'

After a friendly exchange with tough Marthy (Stapleton),

Anna speaks of her childhood in words O'Neill could have written especially for Marilyn – and which those who attended the performance thought were delivered with almost painful authenticity:

'It's my old man I got to meet, honest! It's funny, too. I ain't seen him since I was a kid – don't even know what he looks like . . . And I was thinking, maybe, seeing he ain't ever done a thing for me in my life, he might be willing to stake me to a room and eats till I get rested up. But I ain't expecting much from him. Give you a kick when you're down, that's what all men do.'

Of that evening, Marilyn said not long after,

I couldn't see anything before I went onstage. I couldn't feel anything. I couldn't remember one line. All I wanted was to lie down and die. I was in these impossible circumstances and I suddenly I thought to myself, 'Good God, what am I *doing* here?' Then I just had to go out and do it.

The result, according to most people present, was astonishing. Anna Sten found her 'very deep and very lovely, giving and taking at the same time – and that's a very rare quality.' Kim Stanley remembered that spectators 'were taught never to clap at the Actors Studio, like we were in church, but it was the first time I'd ever heard applause there.' As for Lee and Paula, they were ecstatic, and later at their apartment – while Marilyn wept over what she considered her unworthy performance – they hailed her as the greatest new talent of the decade, which she must have realized was glitteringly hyperbolic. This sort of praise she rightly rejected, but something in her wanted to believe it, and that caused damage enough, as events would soon disclose.

Robert Schneiderman, on the teaching staff at the Studio at the time, recalled that Marilyn was 'often brilliant when she performed [in scene studies], but when she finished a role she would collapse in tears, although she was told she had been right on target or sustained a character perfectly. Marilyn had low self-esteem but she was really an excellent actress and constantly strove to be better.'

On 25 February, Marilyn returned to Hollywood for the first time in over a year, accompanied by Amy and Milton Greene, their two-year-old son Joshua and Irving Stein. At Los Angeles International Airport, Marilyn calmly and wittily fielded questions about her new company and, so it seemed, her new life: 'When you left here last year you were dressed differently, Marilyn,' began one reporter. 'Now you have a black dress and a high-necked blouse: is this the new Marilyn?' Resting a black-gloved hand on her chin, she needed no time to think: 'No, I'm the same person – it's just a new dress.'

She and the Greenes then proceeded to a rented house at 595 North Beverly Glen Boulevard in the Westwood section of Los Angeles, very near the University of California and close to Fox, where the interiors of *Bus Stop* were scheduled after location shooting in Phoenix, Arizona and Sun Valley, Idaho. For leasing a nine-room home belonging to Mr and Mrs Sidney Lushing, MMP paid $950 per month.

Four days later there was a more serious public appearance, although it, to, had its lighter moments. On 21 November 1954, a Los Angeles police officer had cited Marilyn for driving along Sunset Boulevard without a licence, but because she was in New York she had failed to appear in court that winter. Now that the matter was to be settled, dozens of reporters, photographers and television cameramen greeted her and Irving Stein at the Beverly Hills City Hall.

'You may have the idea that this is good publicity,' rumbled Judge Charles J. Griffin, warming to his momentary place in the sun.

'I'm very sorry,' Marilyn replied in a clear voice. 'It isn't at all the kind of publicity I want.'

'Well,' continued the Judge, 'it isn't the type that will win you an Oscar.' He continued somewhat loftily, making a little speech about laws being for everyone, the true nature of democracy – almost everything but an exegesis of the Gettysburg Address. At last, somewhat more gently, he concluded: 'I would suggest, Miss Monroe, that in the future I would much rather pay to go and see you perform than have you pay to come and see me.' Irving paid the $55 fine, and they departed. Outside, she could not resist answering a few questions: 'I couldn't get a word in edgewise in there!' she said. 'Apparently the judge didn't know I've been away for a year. But don't get me wrong, boys. I don't really believe in ignoring traffic citations.'

In all these appearance, people noted a new Marilyn, a woman more poised, with more self-confidence and assurance than before: so much was confirmed by a number of reporters to whom she granted interviews in February and March, among them writers for *McCalls, Modern Screen, Harper's Bazaar, The Saturday Evening Post, Movieland* and *The Toronto Star.* 'She seemed content and more serious than ever before,' according to Allan Snyder, with whom she had a happy reunion. But her manner on a movie set remained to be assessed.

The usual personal dramatic scenarios continued. Informed of Marilyn's return to Los Angeles, Natasha Lytess tried desperately to contact her. A dozen telephone calls and several hand-delivered letters came to Beverly Glen within the first week of Marilyn's return, but she ignored them, having quietly replaced Natasha with Paula Strasberg just as she had dropped Famous Artists and signed on with MCA. But here there was a poignant twist, for Natasha had been stricken with cancer and was no longer able to work at Fox. Entirely dependent on her work with private students, she hoped to resume with Marilyn.

Marilyn's lack of response confused and hurt Natasha deeply, and then, on 3 March, she received a telephone call from Irving Stein:

I identified myself as Marilyn Monroe's lawyer and instructed her firmly not to call Marilyn Monroe or visit or attempt to see Marilyn Monroe. These instructions must be obeyed to avoid trouble. Natasha, whom I'd never met, called me 'Darling' and asked if I'd listen. The following are exact quotes: 'My only protection in the world is Marilyn Monroe. I created this girl – I fought for her – I was always the heavy on the set. I was frantic when I called the house and she would not speak to me. I am her private property, she knows that. Her faith and security are mine. I'm not financially protected, but she is. Twentieth told me on Friday, "You don't have your protection any more, we don't need you." . . . But my job means my life. I'm not a well person. I would like very much to see her even with you if only for one half-hour.' I told her no. Marilyn wouldn't and didn't intercede and we didn't want to speak to or see her. I told her she must not call Marilyn or I would have to use other means to stop her.

'In Marilyn's powerful position,' Natasha said a few years later, 'she had only to crook her finger for me to keep my job at the studio. Had she any sense of gratitude for my contribution to her life, she could have saved my job.' With this statement it is impossible to disagree, for however thorny the relationship had been, Natasha was always available to Marilyn.

In great emotional and physical pain, Natasha arrived unannounced at Beverly Glen on 5 March. Lew Wasserman, present for a meeting with Milton, answered the bell, 'barring my way, his arms stretched across the doorway. "Your engagement with the studio," he said, "is none of Miss Monroe's concern."' Natasha glanced up, and there at a second-storey window was Marilyn, looking down at her without expression. 'It was the last time I ever saw her,' Natasha said not long before her death. 'Between us there was always a wall, and communication was impossible. I have wondered many times that I still care.' To everyone's astonishment, Natasha Lytess outlived Marilyn, but after a long and bitter struggle she succumbed to cancer in 1964.

That Marilyn ignored so humble a plea, that she could have dictated a recommendation and did not, that she turned away from one who had negated herself to cater to Marilyn – all this remains a conundrum, an uncharacteristically inclement act of her life. But Natasha was, after all, a mother figure like Grace Goddard, and once again Marilyn – even while she was trying to create an entirely new life with a new set of colleagues – was perhaps primarily motivated by the subtle desire to reject Natasha before Natasha (by dying) withdrew from her. The entire scenario recalled the term of Grace's relationship with Marilyn. Perhaps out of guilt for her unkindness to Natasha, Marilyn at once contacted Inez Melson, who was charged with the supervision of Gladys's care, and then she called the office manager at Rockhaven Sanitarium. Her payments for Gladys's care were indeed arriving regularly through Inez – $300 a month.

As the starting date for *Bus Stop* approached, Milton Greene assumed the burden of details and finalized the production schedule. For a man without an hour's experience in such matters, he learned quickly and for the most part expertly. In all his tasks he was much assisted by Irving Stein, who ran interference with Marilyn: for the moment, she was indifferent to everything except what would affect her performance. But she also felt Milton's assumption of so much responsibility gave him control of MMP – its long-range plans as well as daily decisions, and this aroused her suspicions.

For the present, however, Marilyn devoted her energies to working with Paula – relying on her guidance as they broke down the script of *Bus Stop* scene by scene, analysing every line and preplanning every gesture. Sometimes Paula was able to encourage her with gentle reassurance; at other times, Marilyn would be drained and tearful after an hour with Paula, convinced she could never rise to expectations. Yet whereas with Natasha originality was often blocked from Marilyn's rehearsals and performances, Paula drew out moments of real inspiration.

Marilyn Monroe

First of all, Marilyn perfected a flawless Texas-Oklahoma twang for Cherie, the dance-hall 'chantoosie'. This would be her chance to be taken seriously in a major film, as she knew: nothing would be left to accident, nothing improvised. Milton had worked out the look of the picture and the texture of each scene as he worked on the script; Milton, too, designed Marilyn's makeup -- an almost ghostly white pallor for a woman who sings and dances through the night, sleeps most of the day and rarely sees sunlight.

Longing to repeat her early success in *The Asphalt Jungle*, she had asked for John Huston, but he was unavailable. Typically, Lew Wasserman stepped in and settled the problem quickly. He contacted Joshua Logan – a large, Falstaffian man, brilliant, imaginative, neurotic, deeply troubled by insecurity and by his lifelong efforts to suppress and then to conceal his homosexuality. Logan was one of the two or three most honoured Broadway directors, famous for staging *South Pacific* and *Mister Roberts*, among other hits. More recently, he had directed the film of *Picnic*, which featured a memorable performance from Susan Strasberg, the daughter of his old friend Lee. 'But Marilyn can't act!' Logan objected when Wasserman offered him the job. Consult Susan's father, Wasserman retorted.

'I have worked with hundreds and hundreds of actors and actresses, both in class and in the Studio,' Lee intoned gravely when Logan asked, 'and there are only two that stand out way above the rest. Number one is Marlon Brando and the second is Marilyn Monroe.'

Logan accepted the assignment only on the condition that, although he liked Paula, he would not suffer her interference directly on the set. After all, he had a reputation for being able to work with the most vulnerable and tortured actors (Margaret Sullavan and Henry Fonda, among others). Paula could coach Marilyn to their hearts' content in dressing room and trailer, at night and at meals, but she was not to be seen near the set or the camera. His injunctions were soon ignored – and a good thing, too, for Paula's 'interference' turned out to be inspired coaching: the differences in Marilyn Monroe's acting, beginning with this performance, are everywhere evident.

Yet for all her benefits to Marilyn, Paula's contributions were sometimes undermined by her husband, who first demanded that Paula receive a fee of $1500 per week. 'Marilyn is too emotionally weak to handle this sort of thing alone,' Lee told Milton in Marilyn's presence. 'She *needs* Paula.' There was no quicker way to diminish Marilyn's confidence, but there it was: Milton balked, Irving fumed and Fox complained, but Marilyn insisted and Paula Strasberg was paid $1500 a week, more than any member of the crew, any designer or the composer – and more than most American film actors. Lee Strasberg made it clear (as had Natasha) that Marilyn's new strength derived from his tutelage, transported to her through Paula: to move out on her own now would be unthinkable.

This was the effect of living in the Beverly Glen commune as well, for with Marilyn there was a thin line separating the situation of a supportive extended family from that of her lifelong feeling that she was the *puella aeterna*. Marilyn may have been at her creative peak, but it was not to Lee's advantage for her to believe that.

As some might have predicted, this spelled trouble. Marilyn worked with Paula late into the night, on location and back at the studio; then, emotionally strained beyond exhaustion, she could not sleep. Milton kept her supplied with the barbiturates she needed, importing them from various doctors in Los Angeles and New York in whatever quantities were necessary. The result was not surprising: often in the morning, Marilyn looked as wan as Cherie and was difficult to awaken, much less deliver on time to the set. Logan was forewarned of this and, alone among her directors, cleverly arranged alternative camera shots for almost every morning.

Much of this was the strategy of the former Marilyn. But with the maturity and resourcefulness of the new came an occasional imperiousness, an attitude that, since she was president of her company, she ought so to act. It was a mask, a new way of covering her old fears, but crew members were often hurt and confused. Nor did the chemical effects of nightly dependence on sleeping pills enhance (much less stabilize) her mood.

With these strains and tensions, the company arrived in Phoenix on 15 March, where the annual rodeo provided setting and action for important sequences, and where Marilyn met her leading man, a young stage actor named Don Murray who was appearing in his first film. She was not a friendly player with Murray, perhaps because she was older (though only three years) and terrified of appearing so, but also because (said Milton in a note to Irving) 'she wants to let everyone know whose show this is.' Throughout the filming, Marilyn passed notes to Joshua Logan, to George Axelrod and to Paula Strasberg, fearful that Murray would make her look foolish and that Hope Lange, a younger blonde in a supporting role, would make her look unattractive. 'Like a child,' according to Murray, 'she said and did things impulsively, from a self-centered viewpoint. When she thought I'd ruined a scene of hers, she continued the action as rehearsed, taking her costume and hitting me across the face with it. Some of the sequins scratched the corner of my eye and she ran off. But she wasn't deliberately mean.'

Besides these obvious, sometimes crude ways of demonstrating her supremacy on the set, it was in important ways artistically Marilyn's show, too, and here the other side of her rose magnificently to take control. When the designer showed her a showgirl's costume that was simply too glamorous, made for Technicolor, CinemaScope and the possibility of an Oscar, she knew it was not at all in character. Marilyn insisted on something shredded, worn, at once paltry but provocative. She rummaged through the wardrobe department, found a torn and moth-eaten item, then poked holes through fishnet stockings and designed a brilliantly shabby outfit that evoked Logan's blissful admiration.

As filming progressed, Milton's initial strategy was to forbid access to Marilyn – which for the press and their colleagues created terrific problems. 'Milton seemed to want complete control over her,' the photographer William Woodfield recalled, 'and we had to devise all sorts of odd means to shoot her – long focuses through a hotel window, two-hundred-millimeter lenses on cameras under bleachers and tricks like that.'

According to the journalist Ezra Goodman, who was for ever stymied in his attempts to reach Marilyn, she was 'surrounded with intrigue and a coterie of advisors headed by Milton Greene who [ran] interference for her and [did] their best to gum up the works where a reporter is concerned. No one gets to Monroe without first clearing through him.'

On 18 March in Phoenix, Marilyn and Milton argued loudly over MMP absorbing the cost of Lee Strasberg's visit to the production. Immediately after the discussion, she was called to film a portion of the rodeo sequence and suddenly fell from a six-foot ramp. Dazed and in momentary shock before writhing in pain, she lay very near to Milton, who as usual was constantly taking still photographs of every scene. 'He just kept clicking away with his camera without moving to help her,' as Axelrod recalled. 'I was a photographer before I was a producer' was Milton's reply when George asked why he did not rush to her aid. Perhaps because of the general tensions associated with film-making, Marilyn and Milton also engaged in a heated debate over the forthcoming presidential election, an argument which production assistant David Maysles and Irving Stein noted through March and April with decreasing patience.

From the hundred-degree desert heat of Phoenix the company travelled to the Idaho mountains, where amid snowdrifts and sub-zero temperatures they managed to complete a few scenes in Sun Valley during five days beginning 26 March. When they returned to Los Angeles, the leading lady and several of her supporting players (Arthur O'Connell, Betty Field and Hope Lange) were suffering from a nasty virus. On 5 April Lee Seigel, the studio physician, ordered Marilyn home to bed, and Logan tried to work around her. But her condition worsened, by the twelfth she had a high fever and acute bron-chitis, and after consultation with another doctor, Siegel ordered Marilyn into hospital. The company shut down for a week.

The same day that Marilyn entered St Vincent's, Arthur Miller entered a cottage at Pyramid Lake, forty miles from Reno, where he began the two-month residency requirement necessary for a quick divorce. Several nights later, Marilyn tele-phoned from her hospital room, desperate and weeping. 'I can't do it, I can't work this way. Oh, Papa, I can't do it,' she cried. She tried to explain the difficulties she was having: 'I'm no trained actor, I can't pretend I'm doing something if I'm not. All I know is real! I can't do it if it's not real!' Arthur listened anxiously.

'I want to live quietly,' Marilyn continued. 'I hate it, I don't want it anymore, I want to live quietly in the country and just be there when you need me. I can't fight for myself any more.' In his memoirs, Miller added, 'I saw suddenly that I was all she had.' This was not a caution to him, however: on the contrary, it seemed only to propel him closer to the resolve of marriage, confirming him in the role of healer: 'We would marry and start a new and real life . . . her pain was mine.'

Yet for all her stated dependence on Arthur, Marilyn had grave doubts from the start about any rush to the altar, and she still begged him not to break up his family to marry her. Marilyn was of divided mind: she wanted to be with Arthur in the country and she longed for a simple life. But if this seemed like a fantasy by Thornton Wilder she knew that too had a dark underside: *Our Town* is full of compassion for lives darkened, stifled and derailed. Thus Marilyn – even while she thought she wanted to retire – also wanted to wrok, to be respected as a serious adult, to transform a messy past into an ordered future.

At the same time, she was especially needy of comfort during filming, and so she did not hinder Arthur from visiting her every weekend in Hollywood (on which journeys he technically jeopardized his divorce procedure). As Amy Greene remem-bered, Logan began to dread Mondays, knowing that Marilyn would be unable to work after a weekend with Arthur at the Chateau Marmont Hotel – whither (without their knowledge) the FBI tracked the lovers.

'She was a wreck after those weekends,' according to Amy. 'She couldn't bring Arthur to see us, he couldn't leave the hotel, and then suddenly, on Sunday night or Monday morning, he slipped back to Nevada. Of course this left her confused, guilty, lonely – and all of that brought on a cycle of pills and sickness.' In a way, the situation was far easier for Arthur, who seemed to Marilyn always calm, composed and in control of the situation.

Whereas George Axelrod had reworked the film of *The Seven Year Itch* for Marilyn and satirized her and her crowd in *Will Success Spoil Rock Hunter?*, the screenplay for *Bus Stop* was written, said Logan, 'expressly for her, and [he] let the entire story be guided by his feelings for her . . . The girl was half Inge and half Monroe.' And despite all the problems during production, from the core of strength that underlay Marilyn's fragility she created an extraordinarily rich, moving and convincing portrait.

The story is simplicity itself: a virginal Montana cowboy (Murray) goes to Phoenix for the rodeo and meets a girl from the Ozarks (Marilyn) with whom he immediately falls in love. She resists but is eventually touched by the boy's sweetness, naïveté and innocence – the qualities she lacks and fears he would require of her. The predictable happy ending unites them.

From her first appearance, a tired, abused showgirl fanning herself against the heat of a summer night, Marilyn's Cherie transcends the limitations of the character and the story. Her performance has obviously been thought out, planned with attention to every detail, but nothing seems calculated. Gone is every Lytess-inspired hesitation and every overworked mannerism. 'I've been tryin' to be somebody,' she says in her first moments, and we hear the person behind the role. 'I can't quit now – it took me too long to get this far!'

Her rendition of 'That Old Black Magic' in a rowdy bar room

presented Marilyn with a delicate assignment, for the song had to be badly sung: this is a girl with pretensions beyond her abilities, after all. Her singing, therefore, is a small miracle – a touching combination of Cherie's nervous energy and minor talent, her shyness and unrealistic hopes, her longing and her fear. Pulling up her long gloves, trying to be heard over men guzzling beer and playing cards, she gives a brilliantly terrible performance.

But it is in her long speech on the bus that Marilyn gave shape and substance to the character, somehow reaching into herself with a wistfulness that never seems self-indulgent: the character's hopes collide with her fragility in one of the great performances of the decade. In a voice poised between tremulous confession and a great ache of longing, she spoke of Marilyn as well as of Cherie, and this gave her the truth she so immediately conveyed:

> I've been goin' with boys since I was twelve – them Ozarks don't waste much time – and I've been losin' my head about some guy ever since . . . Of course I'd like to get married and have a family and all them things . . . Maybe I don't know what love is. I want a guy I can look up to and admire. But I don't want him to browbeat me. I want a guy who'll be sweet with me. But I don't want him to baby me, either. I just gotta feel that whoever I marry has some real regard for me – aside from all that lovin' stuff. You know what I mean?

She ensures that we do.

When the pictured opened on 31 August the critics were reaching for superlatives. Typical was the *New York Times* review: 'Hold on to your chairs, everybody, and get set for a rattling surprise. Marilyn Monroe has finally proved herself an actress in *Bus Stop* . . . [She is] the beat-up B-girl of the [Inge] play, down to the Ozark accent and the look of pellagra about her skin, and [there is] the small flame of dignity that sputters and makes of her a rather moving sort.' *The Saturday Review of Literature* added that in this film Marilyn 'effectively dispels once and for all the notion that she is merely a glamour personality.'

Logan – who quickly became her adoring director – proclaimed Marilyn

> one of the great talents of all time, and the most talented motion picture actress of her day – warm, witty, extremely bright and totally involved in her work. I'd say she was the greatest artist I ever worked with in my entire career ... Hollywood shamefully wasted her, hasn't given the girl a chance. She has immense subtlety, but she is a frightened girl, terrified of the whole filmmaking process and self-critical to the point of an inferiority complex.

At the end of May, *Bus Stop* was complete and Marilyn prepared to return to New York, where Arthur was soon due to return from Nevada. Her departure from Hollywood was delayed, however, when President Sukarno of Indonesia requested an introduction to her. Almost fanatically devoted to American movies and American actors – 'I go to three or four Hollywood movies a week!' he boasted – Sukarno was in Los Angeles touring movie studios and addressing the Association of Motion Picture Producers. To make his journey really memorable, he told the press, he would like to meet Miss Marilyn Monroe. There was much scurrying to telephone booths, and hours later Miss Marilyn Monroe was dragooned for a diplomatic command appearance on 1 June – her thirtieth birthday. She later recalled Sukarno's charm and courtesy, adding that 'he kept looking down my dress, although you'd think with five wives he'd have enough.' By this time, she had enough of just about everything, and after the presidential introduction Marilyn collapsed into bed. It was her thirtieth birthday.

Finally, Marilyn departed on 2 June; the Greenes remained to pack and close up the house on Beverly Glen. This was no easy task, for the tenants had been a messy and careless lot during their three-month stay, and it looked as if the house had been taken over by an unusually high-spirited and reckless fraternity.

'The Greenes have lost or misplaced the inventory,' wrote Al Delgado of MCA to his colleague Jay Kanter.

> This is quite serious because this is an expensive house with expensive furnishings and the inventory is probably over forty pages long. When the owners of the house return, I feel that Milton will have trouble and may possibly have a lawsuit on his hands ... I will do everything in my power to rectify the condition of some of the furnishings and feel very badly about the whole thing, as the house was in perfect condition when they moved in.

For months there followed an angry exchange of letters, invoices and threats of legal action. The matter was still being adjudicated that autumn, when Irving Stein had to deal with the owners, who were due reimbursement for many damaged and destroyed items in their home: two electric blankets; six pillows; eight sheets; five wool blankets; ten chair slipcovers; a $300 invoice for carpet and furniture cleaning; an unpaid telephone bill for the same amount; more than a dozen smashed cups, saucers, glasses and antique crystal goblets; three broken lamps; three sets of curtains; and two pieces of outdoor furniture. In addition, workmen had to remove the heavy black fabric Marilyn had nailed against the windows of her bedroom, for the slightest exterior light roused her from sleep, pills or no.

The causes of such exceptional ruin are not easy to explain (nor did anyone attempt a justification): surely one puppy and two-year-old Joshua could not have accomplished so much unaided. But the house was also Milton's studio, and he and Marilyn were, as Amy conceded, 'intense and excessive. When they loved and hated, it was with all their being. When they drank and drugged, they did so with great passion.' The demolition job seems to have been the combined result of wild parties, an overburdened photographer trying to cope with multiple new responsibilities, an occasionally unstable movie star and an atmosphere in which there was a prodigal consumption of alcohol and drugs.

On 11 June, Arthur Miller was granted a Reno divorce, and the next day he joined Marilyn in New York. At once, the press camped outside 2 Sutton Place South, following the couple when they went to dinner at the home of Arthur's parents in Brooklyn.

A week later, Marilyn telephoned Irving Stein to announce that she wanted to redraft her will, leaving everything she owned to Arthur. 'I told her about the possibility of a prenuptial agreement, but she said she didn't want one,' Irving noted in a memorandum dated 19 June. 'She also asked about obtaining film rights to Miller's literary properties.' Marilyn did not, however, forget her mother: the revised will left seveneighths of her property to Arthur, the balance for Gladys's care.

With good cause, Milton was alarmed: what did these issues portend for the future of Marilyn Monroe Productions? To what extent did she intend to bring Arthur into the corporation? To what extent might Arthur desire or even *demand* association with MMP? That year, his only professional prospect was a forthcoming London production of *A View from the Bridge*, which he was expanding from one act to two. Jealous though he may have been, Milton suspected that Arthur's love might be alloyed with financial self-interest: Miller had, after all, considerable alimony to pay and very little income. But these were not matters Marilyn would discuss with Milton, and from this month a net of suspicion surrounded them all, with Marilyn at the centre of a fierce battle for control.

There were other concerns, too, for Arthur was summoned to appear in Washington before the House Un-American Activities Committee to answer questions about his Communist Party affiliation. But this Committee had a problem of which Arthur was then unaware, and which they were scrambling to resolve. They had no proof of any treasonous activities by Arthur Miller – much less could they come up with 'a live witness that can put him in the Party, [or even] a photostat of Miller's Communist Party card.' Ironically, when HUAC staff director Richard Arens turned for help to J. Edgar Hoover (working through the mediation of Hoover's aide Clyde Tolson), he was told that the FBI had no such data – this despite the efforts of Hoover's friend Walter Winchell, who had tried to summon anti-Miller support by proclaiming that 'Marilyn Monroe's new romance [is] a long-time pro-lefto.' With further irony, this would have exactly the opposite effect.

On 21 June, Arthur left Marilyn and his parents, went to Washington, sat before the HUAC and made several important statements. He admitted that although he had attended Communist party writers' meetings four or five times in the 1940s and signed many protests in the last decade, he was never 'under Communist discipline'. Calmly and articulately, he also said: that he had indeed denounced HUAC when it was investigating the 'Hollywood Ten' (a group of writers blacklisted for what were considered dangerous political beliefs); that he had opposed the Smith Act, which outlawed advocating the overthrow of the government, for 'if there is a penalty on advocacy, if it becomes a crime without overt action, then I cannot operate and neither can literature: a man should be able to write a poem or a play about anything'; and that he would not provide HUAC with the names of those he saw at meetings a decade earlier. 'The life of a writer is pretty tough,' he said, 'and I don't want to make it tougher on anyone. I'll tell you anything about myself, but my conscience will not permit me to use the name of another person.' He concluded that he believed it would be 'a disaster and a calamity if the Reds ever took over this country,' and that he had long since abandoned any connection with Communists or belief in their principles.

Arthur's statements appeared in print all around the country and – much to Marilyn's delight – he became something of a maverick hero in the fight against censorship and repression. But immediately there was the threat of a contempt citation, spearheaded by Congressman Francis E. Walter, who claimed that 'moral scruples do not constitute legal grounds for refusing to answer a Congressional investigator.' Walter's cronies were quick to agree: 'No question about it,' said Congressman Gordon H. Scherer flatly. 'Miller is clearly in legal contempt.'

During these fantastic proceedings, there was a recess during which two things occurred, each of them more surprising and more welcome to newsmen than what had just transpired within chambers.

First, Representative Walter had an idea. He informed Arthur's lawyer, Joseph Rauh, that the entire hearing and the possibility of a contempt citation would be dropped 'provided Marilyn agreed to be photographed shaking hands' with Walter. This condition Arthur at once rejected and denounced, and so on 10 July a contempt citation against him was issued in Congress by a vote of 373 to 9.

Arthur himself had something to say. During the hearing, he had asked for his passport to be returned to him so that he could travel to England that summer for a production of his play – 'and to be with the woman who will then be my wife'. Reporters shouted the obvious question, and then Marilyn Monroe, who was seated before a television set in New York, heard Arthur say, 'I will marry Marilyn Monroe before 13 July, when she is scheduled to go to London to make a picture. When she goes to London, she will go as Mrs Miller.'

The announcement surprised her more than the country. 'Have you heard?' she asked Norman and Hedda Rosten, whom she telephoned almost hysterically. 'He announced it before the whole world! Can you believe it? You know, he never really asked me. We talked about it, but it was all very vague.' To Amy Greene, Rupert Allan and others she added with unveiled sarcasm, 'It was awfully nice of him to let me know his plans.'

The contempt citation would take a year to adjudicate, but in the meantime Arthur Miller's passport was granted (not for the then normal term of two years, but for six months only, beginning 6 July). A lover – especially the fiancé of America's favourite beauty – simply could not be dangerous to the United States, for Communists were not romantics, now, were they? On the contrary, a serious man affianced to Marilyn Monroe legitimized the public's adoration of her, just as her acceptance of him made Arthur Miller somehow less threatening and toned down his role as a controversial figure. His announcement had made him – well, simply a man in love wishing to take his bride on honeymoon. Just as in a Marilyn Monroe movie, love was conquering all. For the moment it could be forgotten that in the committee hearings he was raised to almost heroic status among liberal-thinking Americans confronting the Orwellian spirit of the times.

'Arthur was learning from Marilyn,' as Susan Strasberg noted. 'In one day, he was already a master of the media.' Cameras, microphones and reporters – not to say his presumption of Marilyn's response – would conteract anything a crew of zanies could do to him. For his courageous stand in Washington, 'she admired him from that day,' according to Rupert Allan, 'although his tactic for the wedding announcement greatly distressed her. And in Marilyn's case, admiration was always linked to love. She thought he was a great writer. But I'm sorry to say that at that moment I think he used her.'

Dr Hohenberg, still wielding enormous influence over every aspect of her client's public and private life, approved the marriage (as Irving Stein noted, perhaps with some astonishment, in a corporate memorandum dated 22 June) and advised Marilyn to go right ahead and meet the press. Of course she would marry Mr Miller, Marilyn announced, putting aside her reservations. But from 22 June until the marriage date (which they would not divulge), Marilyn pondered. Her imminent departure for London to make a film with the formidable Olivier was one challenge, the wedding another.

Life was, therefore, suddenly filled with another set of claims on Marilyn's courage, talents and self-awareness. No one permitted her to go just a bit more slowly, to think things out for herself over an arc of time. Certainly she was eager to prove herself, to feel she had passed from childish dependencies to adulthood. But there was no one who encouraged the necessary apartness and reflection. The fortunes of many – their self-interest, career, future and fame – were allied to that of a talented, sensitive, highly-strung thirty-year-old.

Marilyn was poised to marry a man who very much appealed to her desire for self-improvement. But his tendency to lecture her and to be the wisdom-figure fed her sense of inferiority. Try though he might, and love her though he surely did at the outset, many who knew them realized that Arthur Miller was soon wandering into the dangerous territory of suppressed disdain, effected (however subtly) by his assumption of moral and intellectual superiority.

In this regard, Marilyn was again replicating the life of Jean Harlow, whose second marriage was to cameraman Harold Rosson, sixteen years her senior. They were soon divorced, and Harlow took up with actor William Powell, nineteen years older. '[Jean] was always anxious to increase her knowledge,' said her friend Maureen O'Sullivan, 'and she felt she could learn a lot from Powell.' Marilyn and Jean each contracted three marriages, and each longed to be a serious actress, to transcend the common presumption that they were only sexpots. That Marilyn was at least generally aware of these parallels is clear from her continued discussions with Milton Greene, throughout 1955 and 1956, of how they might somehow produce a film about Harlow's life – with or without her old ally Sidney Skolsky, with whom she had originally discussed the project and whom she had now replaced with Milton.

Marilyn Monroe and Arthur Miller promised to meet the press at his home in Roxbury, Connecticut, at four o'clock on Friday 29 June. But first they were to have a quiet lunch with Miller's parents at the home of his cousin Morton, a few miles distant. A crew of reporters and photographers was gathering at Miller's home on Old Tophet Road meanwhile, supervised by Milton.

But one team heard of the family lunch at Morton's and decided to steal a march on their colleagues. Mara Scherbatoff, a Russian princess in exile who was New York bureau chief for *Paris Match*, asked her companion to drive her over to Morton's for some advance pictures and perhaps even a pre-emptive statement. Just before one o'clock, Marilyn, Arthur and Morton emerged from Morton's house, said nothing, leaped into Arthur's car and sped along the narrow, winding route toward Tophet Road, with Scherbatoff and her driver in hot pursuit. But on a blind curve near Arthur's house, the photographer's car hurtled from the road and smashed into a tree. The Princess Mara was thrown through the windshield and hideously injured.

Hearing the crash, Miller stopped his car, and the three ran back to the accident; the sight was so dreadful that Arthur would not let Marilyn come near. They then drove home to telephone for help, Marilyn trembling and pale, leaning on Arthur for support. They had seen enough to know that no one could help, and in fact the aristocrat-reporter died at New Milford Hospital less than three hours later.

But the press conference, held outdoors under a luxuriant tree, was not delayed. Extant film footage, in which Arthur mumbles banal replies to questions and Marilyn seems distracted and less than joyful, must take into account the disastrous prelude. In fact neither of them said much at all, making a hasty retreat to the house after less than ten minutes.

When the last reporter had departed, the casually dressed couple departed with Morton and his wife for the Westchester County Court House in White Plains, New York. Just before seven-thirty that evening, Judge Seymour Rabinowitz pronounced them husband and wife in a four-minute, single-ring ceremony. Not a single member of the press knew, and the newlyweds were able to return to Roxbury without hearing the pop of one flashbulb.

On Sunday 1 July a second ceremony was held at the home of Arthur's agent, Kay Brown, near Katonah, New York. But while friends and relatives gathered for the traditional Jewish marriage rite and a buzz of happy conversation prevailed downstairs and on the lawn, the Greenes were busily attending a nervous Marilyn in an upstairs guest room. She had in fact been withdrawn since Friday, and although Milton and Amy could but privately speculate, he had already put through a call to Irving Stein, advising the lawyer to 'stand by in case of immediate difficulty about Marilyn's marriage.'

The reason for her depression was soon clear to Amy and Milton.

'Do you really want to go ahead with this marriage?' Milton asked Marilyn. 'You don't have to, you know.' Her eyes were glazed with tears, and Amy tried to comfort her: 'We can put you in a car and we'll deal with the guests.' The civil marriage, they guessed, could somehow be annulled before the religious rite solemnized the union.

'No,' Marilyn said quietly. 'I don't want to go through with it.'

But as Milton prepared to attend to this awkward task, Marilyn called him back.

'No, Milton!' she cried. 'We've already invited all these people. We can't disappoint them.'

According to Amy, Marilyn had considered Mara Scherbatoff's death a bad omen for her wedding. 'But she also knew that, omens or not, she had made a terrible mistake in agreeing to this marriage.'

But the cast and crew awaited, and as Marilyn said, she felt sorry for Arthur. The show went on. Moments later, Rabbi Robert Goldberg presided, with Arthur's brother Kermit and Hedda Rosten as attendants. That afternoon, Marilyn performed beautifully, greeting all twenty-five guests, working the party tidily, assuring that everyone had enough cold lobster (rabbi or no), roast beef, sliced turkey and champagne. 'Well,' said George Axelrod, congratulating the Millers and wittily repeating Shaw's famous reply to Isadora Duncan's proposal, 'I hope your children have Arthur's looks and Marilyn's brains.' She laughed heartily, Axelrod recalled, but Arthur was unamused. From the bride's gaiety, no one would have guessed her tortured hesitation.

Before the Millers prepared to depart for London and the production of *The Prince and the Showgirl* (as the film of *The Sleeping Prince* was eventually rechristened by Warner Bros), Arthur put his Roxbury house up for sale, reasoning, with Marilyn's agreement, that later they could begin a new life together in a new home. On 2 July, the *Herald Tribune* carried the notice:

> Playwright and screen star's hideout, 7 rooms, 3 baths, swimming pool, tennis court, terrace, two-car garage, small studio. 4 acres. $29,500 ($38,500 with 26 acres).

A quick sale was made for $27,500 and after a small mortgage and fees were paid, the balance was put in escrow for another property nearby.

That first week of July was full of hard negotiations, all of them Milton's responsibility. There were many legal and commercial matters for him and Stein to settle – among them disputes with Olivier regarding the deal between MMP and Olivier's production company; discussions involving MCA and Jack Warner, who was insisting on control of the film's final cut; and with the British ministry of employment, who were balking at the unusual number of Americans to be imported for this co-operative venture. Also, the Millers asked Hedda Rosten, Arthur's old friend and Marilyn's new one, to join the company as Marilyn's personal secretary, at a generous fee of $200 weekly. Amy Greene, foreseeing trouble because of Hedda's increasing problems with alcohol, advised Milton that here was a perfect example of Marilyn's excessive generosity – not to say her need to surround herself with a battalion of support as she prepared for the challenge of Olivier and an English cast.

But the most outrageous and time-consuming demand of all came from none other than Lee Strasberg, who appeared at Milton's office, asked that Irving be summoned forthwith, and announced the condition for Paula's participation as Marilyn's coach on *Prince*. He would accept nothing less than a guarantee of $25,000 for ten weeks' work, plus expenses and double for overtime. This, Stein quickly figured, would come to about $38,000 – again, much more than most actors were receiving in New York or Hollywood. But as Stein noted in his corporate memorandum,

> Lee doesn't care that this money would really come from Marilyn's pocket. Joe [Carr, MMP's accountant] and Milton carefully explained the shaky finances, but Lee was adamant. He kept emphasizing Marilyn's emotional weakness – and then he said he would be willing to settle for a percentage of the picture! He also wanted George Cukor to direct, not Larry. Paula, he said, is more than a coach – therefore he doesn't care what other coaches get. He absolutely rejects Paula's *Bus Stop* salary.

Lee Strasberg might have been as good an agent as a teacher; in any case, what amounted to his Method-acting portrayal of Budd Schulberg's opportunistic Sammy Glick threw Milton and the company into mild panic. Marilyn simply said that she would yield some of her own weekly income, for Paula *must* be there. She was, although tricky cheque-book manoeuvres were necessary for the remainder of the year so that Paula Strasberg received the salary that paid her, after Monroe and Olivier, more than anyone connected with *The Prince and the Showgirl*. A curious coda to this episode is the fact that the ubiquitous Dr Hohenberg, to whom Milton and Marilyn were still attached, involved herself in the negotiations on behalf of Paula, whom she did not know.

On 9 July, Milton and Irving departed for London as an advance team, and on the rainy afernoon of 13 July, Marilyn and

Arthur followed. The rest of the team – Paula, Hedda, Amy and Joshua – arrived ten days later. When the Millers arrived on the morning of the fourteenth, Sir Laurence and Lady Olivier were at the airport to greet them – along with more than seventy policemen necessary to control a squad of two hundred shouting photographers and reporters. As Arthur recalled, England could have been towed into the ocean without anyone noticing. Whenever Marilyn appeared in public during the next four months, she was invariably mobbed, and it was soon decided that if she went to stores, they would have to be cleared in advance. Just so, if she made a remotely interesting statement it received front page coverage in the London papers next day. On Saturday 25 August, for example, Marilyn decided to go shopping in busy Regent Street, but she was so overwhelmed by adoring crowds that she fainted, police cordons were set up, and she was unable to work next day due to nervous exhaustion and a transient attack of agoraphobia.

As if Milton had not enough budgetary problems, Arthur confided to him his own precarious financial situation that first evening. He was obliged to pay $16,000 a year for the support of his two children; his ex-wife was receiving forty per cent of his income; and he had tax problems and legal fees. Would there be any possibility of integrating his income, which was not much in any case, with Marilyn's? Could he file a joint tax return with Marilyn and MMP? 'Perhaps later on we can deal with this question of [buying rights] to his writings,' replied Irving with some exasperation when Milton took up with him the issue of Arthur's finances. 'That could help him.'

For the rest of the year, MMP tried to find a way that would (Irving noted) 'result in capital gain to [Arthur] and defer income . . . We can also try to get financing and distribution for an Arthur Miller picture, although it will be very difficult . . . He is willing to write a screenplay for *The Brothers Karamazov* for Marilyn, [because] of late he has been extremely conscious of expenses and how they can be charged against MMP as business expenses.' Miller wanted the financial help of MMP, in other words, but as Irving concluded, 'he might not agree that he needs help to bring his *name* before the public.' These discussions proceeded despite the repeated counsel of Miller's friend and agent Kay Brown that 'he ought to stay out of [Marilyn's] career, as she ought to stay out of his.' A complicated scenario was thus in process concerning control of Marilyn's money, career and corportion. The various players – none of them friendly towards one another – included Arthur, Milton and Lee.

The Greenes were installed at Tibbs Farm, Ascot; the Millers had grander quarters at Parkside House at Englefield Green, Egham, near Windsor Park. An hour's drive from London and a little less to Pinewood Studios, Parkside House was a Georgian mansion owned by Lord North (publisher of the *Financial Times*) and his wife, the pianist and actress Joan Carr. Situated in ten lush acres with gardens and convenient bicycle paths, the house featured an oak-beamed living-room, five bedrooms, two baths and quarters for the resident servants. Marilyn was delighted that Milton had arranged for the master suite to be repainted white in her honour.

But during the next four months there was not much time for Marilyn to enjoy the house, London or the English countryside. The day after their arrival, she was hauled off to a press conference at the Savoy Hotel, where two inspectors, a sergeant, six constables and four teams of police had to restrain four thousand fans along the Strand. Marilyn arrived an hour late, wearing a tight, two-piece black dress joined at the midriff with a diaphanous inset. The usual tiresome question-and-answer session followed. Yes, she said, she was delighted to be working with Sir Laurence; and yes, she would like to do classical roles. 'Lady Macbeth, perhaps?' asked a reporter from the provinces. 'Yes, but at present that is just a dream for me. I know how much work I have to do before I could undertake a role like that.' With such grace and modesty, she won over the British press in a single afternoon. According to Jack Cardiff, the cinematographer for her film, Marilyn was everywhere surrounded by such a blaze of publicity that a special pass was issued to everyone working at Pinewood for admittance to the lot.

Cardiff, who photographed such colourfilms as *The Red Shoes, Black Narcissus* and *The African Queen*, came to know and befriend Marilyn during the difficult production of *Prince*. He found her alternately terrified and strong, afraid of facing the public and her fellow-actors but eager to make a hit in this picture.

> Unlike many other leading ladies I'd known and worked with, Marilyn was never bitchy, never used foul language even when the going was rough. Of course there was a kind of psychological dichotomy about her that everyone found somewhat difficult: on the one hand her stated desire to be a serious actress, on the other her lack of discipline, her lateness. I think all this arose from her fear of being rejected, of failing. But behind this vulnerability there was a lot of iron and steel.

On 18, 19 and 20 July, Marilyn submitted to the usual wardrobe and makeup tests for Technicolor, every aspect supervised by Milton, to whose keen eye Olivier grudgingly deferred. The major reason he arranged this deal, Milton told Olivier, was 'to take her out of the sexpot category – to put her in something that required her greatest comedic gifts.' Marilyn's appearance in the film was to him an important factor in her success as a sophisticated comedienne.

But Olivier had his doubts. When he introduced Marilyn to the English cast, he said he was delighted to be working with his old friends Sybil Thorndike and Esmond Knight, whom he had known for decades. Then, in his most charmingly condescending manner, he took Marilyn's hand and said that of course everyone would be patient with her, that *their* methods (nothing like *The* Method, it was implied) would perhaps require some time for her to learn, but they were so *pleased* to have 'such a delightful little thing' among them.* 'He tried to be friendly, but he came on like someone slumming,' Marilyn said later, and in this she was stating only the obvious truth.

To establish his primacy on the set, to counter the enormous influence he feared from Paula (and against which he had been warned by Billy Wilder and Joshua Logan), Olivier took the most patronizing attitude: his co-star he regarded as merely a Hollywood product from whom he would have to exact obedience and obeisance. 'All you have to do is be sexy, dear Marilyn,' Olivier said, and the die was cast. From that moment, as Hedda Rosten reported to Norman, Marilyn became 'suspicious, sullen, defensive'. Even Arthur, who usually sided with Olivier to encourage Marilyn's co-operation, had to admit that the director's arch tongue was too quick with the cutting joke, and that Marilyn felt intimidated by him from the start.

This unfortunate atmosphere was exacerbated by a calamitous event from which her marriage never recovered and which further shook Marilyn's confidence just when she needed it most. As she confided to the Greenes, Susan Strasberg, Allan Snyder and Jack Cardiff, Marilyn found Arthur's notebook open on the dining table at Parkside House and casually glanced at the page. There she read that her husband was having second thoughts about their marriage, that he thought she was an unpredictable, forlorn child-woman he pitied, but that he feared his own creative life would be threatened by her relentless emotional demands. 'It was something about how disappointed he was in me,' she told the Strasbergs,

> how he thought I was some kind of angel but now he guessed he was wrong – that his first wife had let him down, but I had done something worse. Olivier was beginning to think I was

---

* In a letter to Milton from London dated 12 April, Olivier had referred to Marilyn as 'a clever little thing' and 'a dear girl'.

a troublesome bitch, and Arthur said he no longer had a decent answer to that one.

Arthur never admitted he had made such personal observations, but his published memoirs and every interview he granted after her death expressed those sentiments. In a matter of a moment, Marilyn's life with her third husband commenced its slow, tragic decline – within three weeks of the vows, as if justifying her worst pre-nuptial anxieties.

Marilyn was devastated, according to Susan Strasberg, who was with Paula in London: the shock influenced Marilyn's work and placed on her coach an additional burden of motherly nurturing. Even from the first weeks of filming, Allan Snyder added, the marriage seemed strained, the newlyweds distant from each other. 'I think Arthur really likes dumb blondes,' Marilyn said later to Rupert Allan, trying to lighten the pain of this memory. 'He never had one before me. Some help he was.' Sidney Skolsky later summed up the issue: 'Miller looked on Marilyn strictly as an ideal and was shocked to discover that she is a human being, a person, even as you and I and maybe Miller.'

Marilyn and Paula had to endure a rehearsal period, beginning on 30 July – exercises to which Marilyn was unaccustomed; filming finally began on 7 August. As might have been expected after his introduction of her to the cast, there was a frostiness between Marilyn and Olivier, who leaped from behind the camera to act before it. In both stars, anxiety clashed with pride, and there were often dozens of takes for each scene. Olivier, exasperated, gave a direction, only to watch Marilyn walk off to discuss it with Paula and frequently to telephone Lee in New York.

The Strasberg interference very nearly sabotaged *The Prince and the Showgirl*, and Paula was soon sucked into something she did not want, as Susan recalled. But there was a relevant history:

My mother had once been tested for a movie role – that of a

pretty blonde – but she was passed over in favor of Joan Blondell, and in a way I think she was now trying to regain her lost acting career through Marilyn. She was always blamed for Marilyn's lateness, but this infuriated my mother – and what could she do about it? She really wanted Marilyn to succeed. On the other hand, Marilyn used my mother as a kind of whipping girl, someone to take the blame for her own faults.

At the same time, Arthur made no secret of his resentment of the Strasbergs: to him Lee and Paula were 'poisonous and vacuous', and he detested Marilyn's 'nearly religious dependency' on them – perhaps, among better reasons, because he felt his own primacy and influence were thereby compromised. 'She didn't know any more about acting than the cleaning woman' was Arthur's assessment of Paula; she was 'a hoax, but so successful in making herself necessary to people like Marilyn [that] she created this tremendous reputation.' Arthur perhaps failed to see that Marilyn simply had no women friends in her life, and Paula's unalloyed maternal attention was quite simply the best she could get.

Equally, relations between Arthur and Milton became strained. 'Greene thought he would be this big-shot producer and she would be working for him,' Arthur said later. 'But she saw that he had ulterior aims,' by which, presumably, he meant money and prestige. But those aims may indeed have been shared.

Nor was Milton an innocent. Even his MCA agent and friend Jay Kanter allowed that 'it was important for Milton to control her, just as it was for Strasberg and for Miller to control her.' One of the mechanisms for such manoeuvring was for Milton continually to provide Marilyn with whatever drugs she needed (or thought she needed) to get from one day to the next with Olivier. At the time, production assistant David Maysles felt he was 'getting involved in things way above his ability to sustain',

411

as he told his brother Albert: David was referring to the generous allotment of pills that often kept Marilyn in a state near oblivion. These drugs, as everyone knew, were 'wrecking her', as Allan Snyder put it, 'and by this time Milton really wasn't as good for her as he wanted to be. He was a great manipulator, and there were gallon bottles of pills being flown in for her', from none other than Amy and Marilyn's New York doctor, Mortimer Weinstein; on 27 September, for example, Milton wrote to Irving asking that Weinstein send 'two months supply of Dexamyl – *not* spansules – for MM, a dozen or so at a time in small envelopes or parcels, and commence as soon as possible.' As Cardiff said, Milton was brilliant and exhausted with responsibility, but he could be 'a dark, somewhat sinister character who felt he had to keep the show on the road however he could.'*

As if all this were not enough, there occurred a fight over credits: Milton's agreement with Olivier called for 'Executive Producer' status for Milton H. Greene, but by late October, Olivier felt this was inappropriate and took the argument directly to Jack Warner himself. In the first released prints of the picture, Milton was so credited, but later his name was mysteriously and unjustly removed.

None of the many problems could have been much alleviated when Olivier's wife Vivien Leigh arrived – Marilyn's predecessor who had created onstage the role of the American showgirl Elsie Marina. With uncharacteristic lack of consideration (but perhaps with Olivier's tacit or expressed approval), Vivien came to Pinewood to watch a few days of shooting, making no secret of her low estimation of Marilyn.

Thus, not entirely unreasonably, Marilyn was miserable wherever she turned. She felt condescension from her director, betrayal by her husband and a lack of support from Milton, who had to co-operate with Olivier and his staff. All these people she respected and no one, she felt, treated her as an equal. In this environment of complete dependence, she lost her

* For the nature and effects of Dexamyl, see below, chapter 20.

ability to make any concrete decision and constantly second-guessed herself. The result was that Marilyn was pitched back to the conditions of her childhood and adolescence, when every relationship was transitory.

In this regard, her fundamental emotional needs could perhaps never be met by so unreal a career as film acting, for the obvious reason that she had so long assumed a false identity with a false name, hair and image; she invented a new character for each film; and her habitual suspicions about others' loyalties had compelled her to change agents, coaches and advisers – not to mention husbands. Nothing was permanent, nothing rooted, and now there was no one on whom she could rely without question.

In an odd way, her lifelong condition of dependence – the one thing from which no one was willing to free her – was also one of the strongest elements in her appeal to the public. She begged to be embraced; no man or woman could fail to be moved by someone so patently needy and to all appearances inviolable. One reporter who managed a private interview at Parkside House recalled a parade of her courtiers drifting in and out, inserting comments and informing her of their presence. As he departed, Marilyn touched his arm lightly and said with unutterable weariness, 'Too many people, too many people.'

From July to November, then, life was a constant web of intrigue. At various times, all sorts of misadventures occurred: Lee arrived (at the expense of MMP, of course), conferred with Olivier and was tossed out. Paula – on a restricted work visa – eventually went back to New York in the autumn, along with Hedda Rosten, who drank so much she was little help to anyone. Their departures left Marilyn depressed and lonely and soon Milton summoned Dr Hohenberg to London, which meant much expense with little result, for the doctor summarily announced that Milton 'had been wrong to form MMP with Marilyn, and that she did not know how much longer the two partners could work together in an atmosphere of such emotional strain.' Marilyn, of course, saw this as a complete rejection of her professional life by her own psychiatrist.

But Hohenberg had a suggestion for Marilyn, and forthwith whisked her off to meet her old friend Anna Freud, an analyst with a thriving London practice. Marilyn had several therapeutic sessions with Sigmund Freud's daughter.

Things continued to happen quickly and unpredictably. Arthur decided to visit the actors Yves Montand and his wife Simone Signoret in Paris, to discuss a production of *The Crucible* there; he then went on to New York to visit his children. At the same time, Marilyn was convinced that Milton was buying English antiques, charging them to MMP and shipping them to his home in Connecticut. It seemed as if everyone was spending her money – most of all Lee Strasberg, who put through daily reverse-charge telephone calls to Marilyn, reminding her that her only chance of finishing the picture successfully was for Paula to return. Thus Marilyn forced Olivier's hand with the British authorities, and Paula came back to London with a renewed visa.

All during this time, an expensive and complicated colour film was in process – of all things, a drawing-room comedy in which Marilyn Monroe, by some miracle of grace, gave one of the two finest performances of her life. As the production files indicate, she regularly sat in to watch the rough prints of the previous day's work, and both Olivier and Milton had to agree that 'she had some criticisms that were very good, and [she] overtly conveyed her appreciation to Larry.'

While she was performing some of her best scenes in late August, Marilyn learned she was expecting a baby. Later, the pregnancy was always doubted even by those close to the situation like Amy and Allan, but Irving Stein's daily memoranda of telephone calls from London indicate that on 31 August, Marilyn's condition was confirmed by two London doctors. 'Milton told me [by telephone] that she was pregnant but she is afraid she will lose the baby,' noted Irving. He understood Milton's concern, for Irving too had seen, before his departure from London, that 'Hedda and Marilyn were drinking a lot. Hedda is not a good influence on Marilyn, encourages her unreasonableness and evasiveness of truth ... and says she and

Arthur are neither of them ready for children ... Marilyn weeps, saying that all she wants is to finish the picture.' Marilyn lost the baby during the first week of September.

This event was kept secret even from Olivier, who was allowed to believe that Marilyn was simply being moody and intransigent in the absence of Arthur. This ignorance of the facts was no doubt the cause of his resentment of her as a 'thoroughly ill-mannered and rude girl ... I was never so glad to have a film over and done.' Nor, indeed, was she; but her public statements were invariably generous and deferential: 'It was a wonderful experience to work with Olivier. I learned a lot.'

At least two eminent ladies claimed to have learned from her. Edith Sitwell, that empress of all eccentrics, kept her earlier promise and welcomed Marilyn to her home in October. Wearing her usual array of rings on each finger, a medieval gown, a Plantagenet headdress and a mink stole, Dame Edith sat grandly, pouring hefty beakers of gin and grapefruit juice for herself and her guest. During several hours one afternoon, they sat discussing Gerard Manley Hopkins and Dylan Thomas, whose poems Marilyn was reading during sleepless nights at that period. For Dame Edith, Marilyn recited lines from one of Hopkins's *Terrible Sonnets* – 'I wake and feel the fell of dark not day' – saying that she understood perfectly the poet's mood of despair. 'She's quite remarkable!' pronounced Sitwell soon after.

To her pleasant surprise, Marilyn won the appreciation of one of the supporting players, the elderly Dame Sybil Thorndike, one of the legendary actresses of the English stage and the first to play Shaw's Saint Joan on the London stage. After less than a week on the set with Marilyn, she tapped her old friend Olivier on the shoulder: 'You did well in that scene, Larry, but with Marilyn up there, nobody will be watching you. Her manner and timing are just too delicious. And don't be too hard about her tardiness, dear boy. We need her desperately. She's really the only one of us who knows how to act in front of a camera!' Even from Dame Sybil, these remarks did not go down well with Olivier.

*

Whatever Marilyn's insecurities about her marriage, she publicly defended Arthur against the Lord Chamberlain's initial prohibition of *A View from the Bridge*, which was at first banned for its allusion to homosexuality. Outraged by the censorship, Marilyn was among the first to join the Watergate Theatre Club, one of the many small theatre clubs of the time, established to permit uncensored performances to members. This turned out to be somewhat amusing to the English sense of irony, for at the play's premiere at the Comedy Theatre on 11 October, Marilyn's low-cut scarlet gown caused an appreciative riot and almost prevented the curtain from going up. Arthur calmly accepted this, but he began to exert pressure in graver business matters.

The Milton Greene side of Marilyn Monroe Productions was not enthusiastically supporting Arthur's desire to become involved in productions with her, and so Arthur took advantage of a strain in the Marilyn–Milton relationship to attempt greater control of MMP. This he did with some good reason, for things were in a generally chaotic condition. But Marilyn did not appreciate this, and for much of October – not knowing whom she could turn to – she was unco-operative, irritable and even uncordial to her colleagues at Pinewood. She had never been one who could leave her anxieties at the studio gate.

None of this tension was evident to the public, of course; in fact, Marilyn was the golden girl of London that season. *Bus Stop* opened in London a few days after *A View from the Bridge*, and the general attitude of the press was summarized in *The Times* on 17 October: 'Miss Monroe is a talented comedienne, and her sense of timing never forsakes her. She gives a complete portrait, sensitively and sometimes even brilliantly conceived. There is about her a waif-like quality, an underlying note of pathos which can be strangely moving.'

And so, with British favour ringing in her ears, Marilyn Monroe was invited to meet the Queen. The last to arrive even for this prestigious event, Marilyn finally appeared just before the doors were closed at the Empire Theatre, Leicester Square, on the evening of 29 October. Before a screening of the British film *The Battle of the River Plate*, twenty film stars were presented to Her Majesty, among them Brigitte Bardot, Joan Crawford, Anita Ekberg and Victor Mature, but only Marilyn stopped the monarch in her glide down the receiving line. Wearing a dangerously off-the-shoulder gown, Marilyn made a perfect curtsy and clasped the Queen's outstretched hand. Film of the event has survived, showing both women (who were exactly the same age) with somewhat astonished smiles. While Marilyn was in breathless awe at this single moment, Her Majesty's gaze was fixed in astonishment on the famous Monroe breasts, which for the occasion had been taped and pushed forward to even greater prominence.

Even on this occasion, the press reflected the public's adoration: 'Marilyn Monroe, the sleek, the pink and the beautiful, captured Britain,' proclaimed the *Daily Mirror*. The *Daily Mail* marvelled at her 'diplomacy, mischief and bubbling sense of fun'. She was, announced the *Spectator*, 'as intelligent as she was pleasant as she was pretty,' and the *Observer* remarked stoutly that she had earned a 'place in the social history of our time'.

Late in his life, even the formidable Laurence Olivier softened his harsh assessment of the time with Marilyn, whom he never again met. Years after her death, he reflected: 'No one had such a look of unconscious wisdom, and her personality was strong on the screen. She gave a star performance. Maybe I was tetchy with Marilyn and with myself, because I felt my career was in a rut . . . I was fifty. What a happy memory it would have been if Marilyn had made me feel twenty years younger . . . She was quite wonderful, the best of all.'

And so she was. As Elsie Marina, an American showgirl performing with a travelling troupe in London, she catches the wandering eye of the Grand Duke Charles, Regent of Carpathia (Olivier), who has come to England for the coronation of George V in 1911. With him are his teenage son, King Nicholas VIII (Jeremy Spenser) and the Queen Dowager (Sybil Thorndike), mother of Charles's late wife. Very little happens in *The*

Prince and the Showgirl: the Regent fails in a rather blunt seduction scene, realizes Elsie is a pushover for gypsy violins and romantic sweet-talk, and soon finds to his chagrin that they are, contrary to his reputation and intentions, in love. But Elsie is no witless performer. She learns of the young king's plot to overthrow his father and foils both that and a possible catastrophe with the Austro-Hungarian government. At the fadeout, the prince and the showgirl promise to meet again eighteen months hence, but she knows this exceeds even her romantic expectations.

On first or twentieth viewing, it is astonishing to realize how troubled was the production of *The Prince and the Showgirl*. Marilyn's Elsie is from first frame to last a marvellous portrait – alternately feisty and independent, not to be had for the price of caviar and champagne, wise in the ways of monocled playboys and entirely capable of mediating an international crisis. Absent are the distracting, trembling exertions of her lips and chin, and her performance is one of absolute control. In the early supper sequence, for example, while Olivier ignores her to conduct state business, Marilyn munches a midnight supper and downs several glasses of wine, easily stealing the scene right under Olivier's patrician nose. Bored with the Duke, she slowly becomes drunk; the entire sequence is a masterpiece of improvisation, revealing a comic talent in Marilyn Monroe reminiscent of Billie Burke (in *Dinner at Eight*), or of Miriam Hopkins (in *Trouble in Paradise*).

Scurrying to avoid embassy footmen, Marilyn showed an antic agility never exaggerated; awakening to the realization she is in love, half a dozen feelings pass over her face; practising a few steps of her vaudeville routine while waiting for the pompous Regent, she is amused by her own amusement – a girl so joyously alive that dancing is as natural as walking. One looks to Giulietta Masina's Gelsomina and Cabiria in Fellini's *La Strada* and *Nights of Cabiria* to find so perfect a melding of actress with character in a radiant affirmation of life.

There are as well the gentle nods to offscreen history. The

last scene filmed that November was Marilyn's second sequence in the picture, her introduction to Olivier in a lineup of show-girls. Elsie was to bow courteously, and Marilyn and Olivier together – as if to reconcile their differences on the final day of production – devised a moment straight from their first meet-ing: the thin strap of her dress breaks and she cries, 'Oh, don't trouble – I can fix it with a pin.'

From this moment, Marilyn's performance never falters, and her final scene is quietly affecting as she bids him farewell – a wistful, wise Cinderella who has been to the coronation ball but now knows the man of her dreams was only that. It is the gentlest, bittersweet coda, disclosing at last the significance of the long liturgical sequence at Westminster Abbey. Here Olivier had wisely kept Jack Cardiff's camera not on the details of ritual but on the reverent reactions of a showgirl with a won-drous purity of heart. The 'unconscious wisdom' is as patent as the light splashing through stained glass, the presence of grace evident in her eyes as the choir exults. Here the best instinct of director and star finally conquered every obstacle, every painful difference separating them over four months. They were, after all, equally dedicated to achieving a fine finished product. That year, Marilyn's Elsie and her Cherie in *Bus Stop* mark the high-light of her professional life, her achievements brightening an otherwise tangled and confusing year.

On 22 November the Millers arrived in New York. Accord-ing to the ledgers at Warner Bros, Marilyn had worked fifty-four days, Olivier only twelve more, but such were the rumours then and in later years that the general impression was of an irresponsible, drugged actress who could scarcely func-tion. *The Prince and the Showgirl* belies such judgements, and not much publicity was devoted to the fact that the film was completed under budget and required only two days of reshoot-ing.

By the year's end, weary, restless, uncertain of her marriage, her company, her friendships and her future, Marilyn asked Arthur if they might escape for a sunny winter holiday – and so they did, clocking in the new year at a place aptly called Moot-point, a seaside villa on the north coast of Jamaica.

Chapter Seventeen

1957 — 1959

With the new year 1957 Marilyn Monroe began her second long absence from film-making.

Quitting Hollywood in 1954 after *The Seven Year Itch*, she had not returned there until spring 1956, for *Bus Stop*; this was followed by four months in London for *The Prince and the Showgirl*. Following these two extraordinary performances in one year, she tried to lead a private, quiet life – and to assume a different kind of role. Now, married to a world-famous but curiously inert playwright, Marilyn tried out the part of New York Jewish spouse, but this was no more appropriate or comfortable than the previous two.

Yet somehow she seemed to have no choice. Casting about for an identity in 1957, Marilyn was again taking on the role of loyal and supportive mate. Although her repeated attempts to fill it are touching, they were also self-defeating because unrealistic and untrue to herself; such self-abasement was a reversion rather than motion forward.

This return to housewifery, so unnatural for her, was all the more problematic because it was embraced as an alternative – when MMP, her cherished hope for professional independence and control over her destiny, was in a shambles. She was, therefore, desperately assuming a socially acceptable but disastrous role for herself.

With Arthur Miller, the props were sometimes chicken soup, kasha and horseradish, although by a curious irony, this wife-on-leave was supporting her husband financially. Marilyn believed in his talent, but she could see little application of it: irregularly, he worked on his writing, but there was not much to show for it. Arthur, too, recognized something was deeply wrong. 'I was off balance and could no longer confidently predict her moods. It was almost as though the fracture of her original idealization of me in England had left no recognizable image at all' – a tortuous way of admitting that he had hurt her so deeply that she lost confidence in him.

Moreover, his attitude toward her was divided. 'I felt an urgency about making something for her . . . constructing a gift for her' that would celebrate her beauty and complexity. But if he saw her as a kind of tragic muse, he also considered her 'a mere child, an abused little girl'. Elia Kazan believed that Arthur was giving Marilyn 'a rose-tinted view' of her future, that of an elite actress doing serious plays which he would provide. Such was the condescension of a man who found himself, in 1957, in a creative drydock – an unwitting indolence in which Marilyn joined him.

In January, they found a New York apartment for rent on the thirteenth floor at 444 East Fifty-seventh Street, immediately adjacent to her former residence at 2 Sutton Place South. Marilyn, with the help of her designer John Moore, played interior decorator. She had a wall removed and made one large room of two, creating a living-dining area, several walls were mirrored and others were painted stark white, like the ceiling. Everywhere, in fact, there was white: a baby grand piano, a sofa, tub chairs and several pieces of furniture. The place had the look of a movie set from the early 1930s, something reminiscent of Jean Harlow's bedroom in *Dinner at Eight*. But as friends like Norman Rosten recalled, Marilyn never thought the apartment was 'right', and she constantly remodelled, changed furniture, draperies, accessories, *objets d'art* in the country house they eventually bought in Connecticut and the summer cottage they rented on Long Island.

Despite her tendency to hide herself under a headscarf and behind dark glasses, Marilyn was often recognized in her new neighbourhood. Letter carriers and trash collectors greeted her familiarly by her first name. 'I love them for it,' she said. 'Somehow they know that I mean what I do, both when I'm acting on the screen and when I meet them in person.' She loved contact with strangers and neighbours, many of whom were shy of her fame. A young woman who lived nearby regularly recognized her but was too afraid of intruding on Marilyn's privacy to express her admiration. They passed one another for months until one evening, when the woman was wearing a new coat, Marilyn broke the silence: 'You must excuse me for speaking to you, but you look so nice in that coat that I just can't bear not telling you.' The young admirer almost burst into tears.

At the same time, Marilyn's business and personal relationship with Milton Greene was rapidly failing. There were mutual resentments about the problems during production of *The Prince and the Showgirl*; each was suspicious about the other's honesty and candour; they argued about forthcoming projects and over Arthur's increasing involvement; and both partners were ingesting too many kinds of pills. But the major cause of the breakup was Marilyn's violent shift of loyalties to Arthur, who encouraged her to wrest control of MMP away from the man he deeply disliked.

Michael Korda, then a young writer and friend of Milton, knew that Greene, on the other hand, bitterly resented Arthur's managerial attitude over Marilyn and MMP's future; Korda was also aware that Milton's talents were badly affected when he began taking Dilantin, an anti-epileptic drug for which he had no medical need but which was popularly thought to augment energy by increasing the brain's electrical impulses. Dilantin was also supposed to counteract Nembutal and other barbiturates and hypnotics, thus balancing the effect of drugged sleep with artificially induced energy next day: the result was a cycle of catastrophic addictions.

In another, subtler angle, Arthur's assumption of control proved that Milton could no longer control the situation as easily as he had before. Amy Greene, who had been close to

Marilyn since 1954, also saw the pattern emerging in 1957. For her husband's sake, Marilyn felt compelled to break with everything that in Arthur's mind represented Milton: the business of MMP, a certain social life, a choice of films. 'But there was another knot in the problem,' according to Amy. 'Although he didn't mean to, Milton always put Arthur down: "You go away and be a good husband" was his attitude to Arthur. "You go and write a play and let us take care of business." As for Milton himself, everyone who knew his work acknowledged that he had a streak of genius. But he was also a man of frightening excesses and eventually he destroyed himself, and almost his family, too.'

As MMP began to unravel, Marilyn took some comfort in a routine, and for much of 1957 and 1958 it was unvarying. Five mornings each week she visited her analyst; thence she proceeded to something remarkably similar, her private sessions with Lee Strasberg. By coincidence, both mentors now lived at 135 Central Park West.

Marilyn had wanted a new analyst to replace Margaret Hohenberg, who was still counselling Milton. To that end, she telephoned Anna Freud in London, who had a ready reply: in New York was Anna's closest friend since girlhood – Marianne Kris, a doctor whose father had been the paediatrician for Freud's children. And so that spring, Marilyn began sessions with Dr Kris. The relationship, which lasted for four years, was crucial and finally harrowing, sometimes helpful but more often troubling rather than illuminating.

Born in Vienna in 1900, Marianne Rie grew up amid the intellectual excitement of the birth of psychoanalysis. She took a medical degree in Vienna in 1925 and did further study in Berlin, where at Freud's recommendation she was analysed by Franz Alexander; later, when she returned to Vienna, Freud himself completed her psychoanalysis and she married Ernst Kris, an art historian who also became an analyst (as who did not in the Freud–Kris social set). Sigmund Freud called Marianne his 'adopted daughter', and together the Freuds and the Krises fled the Nazis and went to London in 1938. Marianne and Ernst subsequently continued to New York, where she developed a private practice and a specialty: the clinical aspects of Freudian child psychoanalysis.

Ernst Kris had died on 28 February 1957, a few weeks before Marilyn began to visit Marianne, who was glad for the opportunity to work, and as she acknowledged, the more troubled and famous her patients were, the better for her notes and theories. It was quite a coup to have Marilyn Monroe in her consulting room. For her part, Marilyn was pleased to have Kris, with her close connections to the seminal thinkers of psychotherapy: if anyone could help her, she reasoned, Kris could.

At this time Kris was developing a controversial set of principles which, she believed, enabled her to predict a child's psychological development and potential problems. A dark-haired, handsome woman, she was an intense pragmatist who took the approach that children were the key to understanding the human psyche. She held that, as a colleague wrote, 'some of the most important advances in psychoanalysis have come from child psychoanalysis.' Thus, while Kris accepted adults as patients, she always emphasized that one had to see the problems of those adults as based entirely on childhood experiences. Helping adults, in other words, meant in an important way treating them like children. It is worth detailing this background and viewpoint of Marianne Kris because her relationship with Marilyn Monroe was from the start ill-advised.

On the one hand, Marilyn was trying harder than ever to face her 'real self', to put aside the glamorous appurtenances that made for superstar Marilyn Monroe, to face her fears and her memories (as Lee Strasberg insisted was essential for acting) and to become someone good and respectable, which she always doubted herself to be. She wanted a clean slate: marriage to a working playwright, motherhood, then perhaps a return to her art.

There was an obvious peril here. A devout Freudian, Kris (like Strasberg in his private sessions with Marilyn) constantly led her back to childhood. As Marilyn told her friend and publicist Rupert Allan, there was a consistent motif in this therapy: What was her relationship to her mother and father in childhood? What memories were there to be confronted? What resentments had to be faced? If one could understand the past, Kris stressed, one could be free of its tyranny. But Marilyn had never known her father's identity and scarcely knew her mother; her feelings about maternity (and about preparing for it herself) had been shaped by surrogates, from Ida Bolender to Grace McKee to Ethel Dougherty and even to Natasha Lytess and Paula Strasberg.

But analysing the past did not necessarily direct one to the future. Marilyn felt blocked, stymied in her life, in a rut – but no one seemed to acknowledge that her sense of crisis was not necessarily a sign of breakdown, as it was diagnosed; it could be, on the contrary (indeed, it was), an indication that she longed for her life to move to some new, deeper level as yet unrevealed. The Freudian school took seriously the medical model: crisis meant something was wrong and had to be fixed. This is fine so far as it goes, but it simply did not go far enough. And for Marilyn, who always felt it best to put her life right by doing rather than discussing, by action rather than by talk, a weariness often set in. But these were parental authority figures, and so she stayed with the programme.

Isolated and introspective in childhood, she was now asked to focus her attention almost exclusively on that unhappy period. And so she was on a kind of treadmill, repeating over and over with Kris what she had with Hohenberg, and this became self-defeating. Where were the fresh revelations, the new energies generated to move beyond the childhood? Reasoning about it did not resolve it; understanding did not necessarily lead to acceptance, nor to the alteration of the *meaning* of the past that contains seeds of possibility for both present and future.

With Hohenberg, with Kris and later with her last analyst, Marilyn felt 'as if I were going around in circles,' as she told Rupert. 'It was always, how did I feel about this, and why did I think my mother did that – not where was I going, but where had I been? But I *knew* where I had been. I wanted to know if I could use it wherever I was *going!*'

Notwithstanding the insights provided by Freudian principles, their wholesale application to someone like Norma Jeane Mortensen/Marilyn Monroe was futile. Excessive introspection exacerbated her lack of self-confidence. Intuition suffered at the expense of a forced, conscious intellectualism that paralysed her and pushed her further back into herself. There was, therefore, a confusion of realms and realities here, and for Marilyn to attempt an analysis of the past led to an endless cycle first of trying to evoke painful memories and then to find out what they meant. But the memories were vague and disconnected: no wonder, then, that Marilyn continued to tell her friend Susan Strasberg that if she couldn't answer Kris's questions, well, she just made up what seemed interesting. This, as Marilyn must have known, was counterproductive. Too much the vogue in the 1950s, this sort of strict Freudianism was also unhelpful because the system of five sessions weekly fed Marilyn's condition of childlike dependence. It is also curious that Kris, like Hohenberg, seemed unable – over the course of four years – to alleviate Marilyn's increasing reliance on sleeping pills. As for Arthur, he was, as his own family and friends acknowledged, 'too stand-offish' in the matter, 'amazingly thoughtless and unappreciative [of Marilyn]. Art is interested in people, but not in any particular person.'

With a husband who approached her as 'a mere child' and was taking steps to control her business, an analyst who treated her as a girl who had buried her past, and surrogate parents (the Strasbergs) who fancied themselves intellectual guides, it was difficult for Marilyn to find her way to adulthood.

Each day after her session with Kris, Marilyn took the elevator to Lee Strasberg, who led her in a series of sense-memory exercises that required her to feel and act like a child: one day she had to play a hungry baby, another a lonely waif, a confused schoolgirl, a young bride. This was the key to unlocking her 'real tragic power', he said – and she believed him because she needed to: like Hohenberg and Kris, he made himself indispensable to her. As Kazan observed, Lee also turned her against other influences – teachers, directors, even her husband.

The result was predictable: Marilyn began to worry more about herself. Impossibly high ideals were being set before her (she might soon play Lady Macbeth, Strasberg said). 'Lee makes me think,' Marilyn told Norman Rosten, her voice full of awe. 'Lee says I have to begin to face my problems in my work and life – the question of how or why I can act, of which I'm not sure.' She thus had not one but two therapists when she needed not to be enclosed within a prison of self-examination but freed from it.

This was almost pathetically evident in March, when for a Studio class Marilyn was asked to do a scene that included a song. She stood before the group and began to sing in a wavering voice: 'I'll get by as long as I have you . . .' And then suddenly the room was as still as a lake, for Marilyn began to weep. She kept her pitch, focused on the words and music and let the tears fall. Everyone in class felt this was great acting, but Marilyn was simply terrified. She was not performing; she was anxious about Lee's judgement.

As for Arthur and the Strasbergs, Susan recalled the considerable mutual antipathy. 'Whether it was competitiveness or that [Arthur] wanted total control over Marilyn, I couldn't figure out. There seemed to be two kinds of people: those who went for control, like my father and Arthur, and those who went for approval, like [Paula], Marilyn and me.' For the first time, Marilyn's friends began to observe that she was gaining weight, drinking too much and suffering frequent attacks of various viruses.

Around 1 April, Marilyn saw a first print of *The Prince and the Showgirl*. For perhaps the only time in her life, she wrote a lengthy, detailed letter, dictating furiously to her new secretary May Reis, who had once worked for Arthur and who now (because he had no need of her) attended Marilyn. 'It is not the same picture you saw last time [in New York that winter],' she wrote to Jack Warner,

> and I am afraid that as it stands it will not be as successful as the version all of us agreed was so fine. Especially in the first third of the picture the pacing has been slowed and one comic point after another has been flattened out by substituting inferior takes with flatter performances lacking the energy and brightness that you saw in New York. Some of the jump cutting kills the points, as in the fainting scene. The coronation is as long as before if not longer, and the story gets lost in it. American audiences are not as moved by stained glass windows as the British are, and we threaten them with boredom. I am amazed that so much of the picture has no music at all when the idea was to make a romantic picture. We have [shot enough] film to make a great movie, if only it will be as in the earlier version. I hope you will make every effort to save our picture.

This was clearly a sober critique by a seasoned professional, not the raving of an ignorant, mentally confused actress.

But it was also different from her reaction when she saw the rough cut in London, which was virtually the same screened for her now. Her strategy was, according to all the documents in the files of MMP and Warners, to imply that Milton had secretly recut the film – an action that owed much to Arthur's encouragement, as the legal proceedings subsequently documented.

First, she stated that Milton ought to have obviated postproduction problems in working with Olivier and the film editor; second, she insisted that Milton's credit as the film's executive producer was neither contracted nor deserved. But as their MCA agent Jay Kanter recalled, and as the relevant MMP-Warner contract of 1956 clearly indicated, Milton's credit had indeed been formally and firmly contracted before production. And Olivier himself, never one to yield credit he considered rightfully his own, had a change of heart and enthusiastically supported Milton's claim to be listed as executive producer – a status Milton demanded not out of vanity but for his future as a film producer.

Because Marilyn was seeking to sever herself emotionally and professionally from Milton and to ally herself only with Arthur, she disingenuously took up the matter of Greene's credit as her cudgel. While her talent for acting was being refined, her ability to make consistent and sound business judgements was not; nor was she able to admit that her desperate attempt to ingratiate herself to her husband (who was only too willing to take whatever control he could) was at odds with both her knowledge and her intuition about the marriage itself.

On 11 April, Marilyn issued a statement through Arthur's attorney, Robert H. Montgomery Jr, stating that Marilyn Monroe Productions had been mismanaged by Milton, that he had misinformed her of certain contractual agreements and entered into secret negotiations for new deals without her knowledge or consent. She would, therefore, soon announce a new board of directors. As Arthur had pointed out, she had the controlling 50.4% of the company's stock, against Milton's 49.6%.

Five days later, in a meeting at Montgomery's law offices, she calmly announced that MMP's vice-president Milton Greene, attorney Irving Stein and accountant Joseph Carr were forthwith dismissed from her company and replaced by Montgomery; by George Kupchik, Arthur's brother-in-law; and by George Levine, a friend of Arthur who was a city sanitation worker and carpet salesman. As for the matter of Milton's producer status, even Robert Montgomery admitted to his colleague John Wharton that Marilyn was 'absolutely irrational on the subject of Milton's credit'.

Greene's public response was suitably dignified, with a tone of mild hurt and shock:

It seems that Marilyn doesn't want to go ahead with the program we planned. I'm getting lawyers to represent me, [but] I don't want to do anything now to hurt her career. I did devote about a year and a half exclusively to her. I practically gave up photography.

Marilyn was not at a loss for an equally public reply, although the comments, drafted by Miller and Montgomery, were not at all typical of her, nor were the facts accurately represented.

He knows perfectly well that we have been at odds for a year and a half and he knows why. As president of the corporation and its only source of income, I was never informed that he had elected himself to the position of executive producer of *The Prince and the Showgirl*. My company was not formed to provide false credits for its officers and I will not become party to this. My company was not formed merely to parcel out 49.6% of all my earnings to Mr Greene, but to make better pictures, improve my work and secure my income.

The stakes were clear. Because of her expectation of a new life and new career with Arthur Miller, Marilyn had been persuaded that her need for Milton Greene no longer existed. The result was that he was suddenly badly treated by the woman to whom he had devoted his considerable talents. It was true that he had shared and perhaps even encouraged some of her most perilous weaknesses. But he had also enabled her to free herself from studio servitude and form a company in which she had succeeded magnificently by selecting and delivering arguably the best roles of her career. They had discussed plans for the future – among them a film with Charles Chaplin, who was indeed interested. Now everything was sabotaged.

'The truth is,' said Jay Kanter, 'that suddenly Milton was left out in the cold.' And Amy, who was not blind to Milton's mistakes and weaknesses, recalled that Marilyn admitted to her that 'Arthur was taking away the only person I ever trusted, Milton,' but that she felt powerless to withstand him. At the root of it all was the frustration and sadness Marilyn felt over her marriage to Arthur, and much of that feeling she directed against Milton. It was ironic that Marilyn now found herself in the same situation as previously. Just as she had once allowed Milton to appoint his friends as corporate officers of MMP, so now she was allowing Arthur to do the same, but with men far less qualified. Despite her anger and protests, she was exerting no more professional contrl over her destiny in 1957 than she had in 1954.

That anger was fierce in April. At a social gathering, the Millers met Arthur Jacobs and Marilyn (reported Jacobs) 'screamed about me and Jay [Kanter], calling us "shitty friends of that shitty Mr Greene, who got me a psychiatrist who tried to work against me and for Mr Greene!"'

Marilyn Monroe and Milton Greene never met again. Lawyers battled for a year until she finally bought out his stock for $100,000 – his entire remuneration for over two years of work. He returned to work as a photographer, but a bitter disillusionment afflicted him, and in ensuing years he became increasingly addicted to alcohol and drugs. But Milton was always courteous in his public statements about Marilyn:

She was ultrasensitive, and very dedicated to her work, whether people realize this or not. She came through magnificently in *Prince* and she was great in *Bus Stop*. All I did was believe in her. She was a marvelous, loving, wonderful person I don't think many people understood.

As for Irving Stein and Joe Carr, they had no more to do with film production companies. Carr worked for years before his death as a private accountant, and Irving Stein became chairman of the Elgin Watch Company. Approaching home in his car one evening in 1966, he suffered a heart attack, crashed into a tree and was killed instantly; he was fifty-two.

As usual, Marilyn's few public appearances showed her as ever cheerful. Among the charity events she supported was an all-star soccer game at Brooklyn's Ebbets Field, where on 12 May she opened the American-Israel match; wearing open-toed shoes, however, she kicked with such gleeful force that two toes were sprained. She remained for the game without complaining so that she could award the trophy to the victors.

But emotional rather than physical discomfort attended her later that month, when she went with Arthur to Washington for his court appearance on the contempt of Congress citation from the previous year. The formal indictment and the trial date had been handed down in February, and at last Arthur's attorney, Joseph Rauh, was prepared to contest the issue; were they to lose, a possible two-year imprisonment and $2000 fine could be imposed. The trial was held from 13 to 24 May, during which the Millers were houseguests of Joe and Olie Rauh.

'She had no desire to do anything except support her husband,' recalled Olie, 'and she asked questions about the case every day and every evening. She had no movie commitments and seemed not a bit conflicted about it.' Then, when Arthur and Joe left for the hearings, Marilyn 'picked books off our shelves – and every one she chose had something to do with psychiatry.'

On the last day of the trial, as Joe Rauh rested his defence on the grounds that a refusal to answer irrelevant questions was not a punishable offence, Marilyn handled a crowd of reporters brilliantly. She asked Olie Rauh for a glass of sherry, donned white gloves ('because I haven't done my fingernails and one of those women will notice they're unpolished'), saw that her panty-line showed through her white dress, promptly removed the undergarment and stepped out to the reporters, telling them she was in Washington to see her husband vindicated. But on 31 May, after the Millers had returned to New York, Arthur was found guilty on two counts of failing to answer HUAC in 1956. The preparation of an appeal and the final disposition of the case would last another year.

The Millers spent much of the summer in quiet indolence at a rented cottage in Amagansett, far out on Long Island. He tried to work on several projects, while Marilyn walked along the beach, read poetry, visited the Rostens in nearby Springs and made only rare appearances in New York – when, for example, she accepted an invitation to attend the ceremonial ground-breaking for the Time-Life Building.

Marilyn's moods that season were alternately effervescent and depressed; this Miller and Rosten took as a sign of mental instability. It was considered hypersensitive and unrealistic when a wounded seagull reduced her to weeping, or if she stopped her car at the sight of a stray dog wandering a country road. A discussion of the deer-hunting season roused her angry denunciation of blood sports. On the other hand, she enjoyed nothing so much as time spent playing lawn tennis or parlour games with young Patty Rosten, just as she regularly welcomed Jane and Robert, Arthur's children, when they visited their father.

In fact few celebrities donated so much public time as Marilyn to charities benefiting youngsters: that year she sold tickets for and attended, among others, the Milk Fund for Babies and the March of Dimes for children afflicted with polio. She was always relaxed and sympathetic with children, always listened, asked about their needs, wrote down their names and later sent toys and gifts. They were, after all, unaware of her fame, asked nothing of her and allowed her to be, if only for a few moments, a mother. With those she knew better, like Patricia Rosten and the Millers, no demand on her time or attention was excessive. 'She loved children so much,' according to Allan Snyder. 'My daughter, other people's children – she went for them all. If she'd had one of her own to care for, to grow up with, I'm sure it would have helped her immensely.'

Yet Marilyn often suddenly withdrew from everyone to be alone for hours that summer. She had been grievously offended over the verdict handed down in Washington and was anxious about another protracted time of examination, interrogations, meetings with lawyers – and the fees, which fell entirely on her.

She then quietly announced to Arthur one day in July that a doctor had confirmed her pregnancy – news that made her happier than anyone could recall. With this, Arthur noticed 'a new kind of confidence, a quietness of spirit [he] had never seen before'.

But there was to be no term of the pregnancy. On 1 August she collapsed in extreme pain and was briefly unconscious. An ambulance and physician were summoned, and Marilyn was rushed to Doctors Hospital in Manhattan, where it was determined that she had an ectopic pregnancy: the fetus was being formed in a Fallopian tube. The loss of her child that August wounded Marilyn's confidence and sense of maturity, and to Susan Strasberg, among others, she confided feelings of incompetence and worthlessness. Even her body seemed to indict her as unfit for adulthood.

Returning home after ten days, she was determined to prove herself in the role of Arthur's good wife, as if every emotional and physical obstacle presented her with the challenge not merely to survive but to triumph. Concluding negotiations for their new home in Roxbury, Arthur and Marilyn devised elaborate plans for an unlikely replacement for the simple house. While working on the final stages of the Guggenheim Museum, Frank Lloyd Wright was living at the Plaza Hotel, and there he met Marilyn, who had fantasized something grand: she envisioned a vast home, complete with swimming pool, projection booth and auditorium, children's nurseries, a costume vault and a lavish study for Arthur. Wright drew plans, but the cost was enormous and the project was never realized. The Millers settled for the tasks of repairing and updating the existing house.

Something else would be realized, however. Sam Shaw had read Arthur's short story 'The Misfits', published in *Esquire* magazine that year, and he suggested it as the basis for a screenplay. The story concerned three wandering men in the wilds of Nevada who capture wild horses to be butchered for canned dog food; in the story was a woman as rootless and unsettled as they but with an innate sense that life is sacred. This, Shaw argued, could become a serious film, with a role for Marilyn that could confirm her as a major dramatic actress. But Arthur had another idea: why not a rewrite of *The Blue Angel*, the 1930 film that had made Marlene Dietrich an international star? 'Look, Arthur,' Sam countered, 'you wrote a wonderful story – why not do that as a film. It's something original, it's strong, and it's something for you both.'

That autumn, Arthur began working on the scenario for a movie based on his story. As he proceeded, Marilyn read portions, laughing at the humorous moments and reflecting silently on the characters and motifs. She was not sure how the role of Roslyn Tabor, the Reno divorcée who alters men's destinies, would finally suit her, but this hesitation she kept to herself and simply encouraged Arthur to keep writing.

At Christmas 1957, Marilyn was as usual generous to a fault, spending a good portion of her savings on others. Arthur received a new set of the *Encyclopaedia Britannica*. Susan Strasberg unwrapped a Chagall sketch. There were books and records for Lee, and to Paula she gave the necklace of pearls with a diamond clasp, a gift from the Emperor of Japan in 1954 during her honeymoon with Joe. 'She knows how much I love those pearls,' said Paula, moved to tears. 'Look, she gave them to me!' Most extravagant of all was her gift to John Strasberg, then eighteen and, Marilyn felt, an unhappy, often ignored outsider in his own family. To him she calmly signed over the ownership of her Thunderbird, knowing he longed for but could not afford a car.

The first months of 1958 were a time of melancholic strain in the Miller marriage. After several false starts on *The Misfits*, Arthur was pitched into a nervous gloom, and his wife was not adapting to suburban idleness. 'Arthur was writing, writing, writing, but it wasn't worth a damn,' according to Olie Rauh. 'Meantime, she was trying to keep a low profile: he was the important one, she felt, he should write.' Inevitably, Marilyn and Arthur exchanged angry words – sometimes in company, as the Strasbergs recalled. Marilyn knew about and tried to ameliorate the wary suspicions and discomfort preventing good relations between Lee and Arthur, but her negotiations were futile.

More than once, as Susan recalled, Marilyn became tense and hostile when the Millers and Strasbergs visited, and the result was an explosion of anger (often for no apparent reason) directed at her husband, who would leave the room quietly instead of retaliating. Scolded for her bad manners and humiliation of Arthur, Marilyn was struck with remorse: 'If I shouldn't have talked to him like that, why didn't he slap me? He should have slapped me!' That had been her punishment in earlier days, and she expected it now. Even with friends like the Rostens, there was merely 'a façade of marital harmony', as Norman recalled, and Arthur's reaction was frequently to find refuge in sleep – 'hiding', as Rosten added, for he was 'more unraveled than ever'.

Marilyn could not inspire Arthur to better or swifter writing, nor could she give him a child, which was her desire more than his, as he admitted in his memoirs. However she may have thought about it, she seemed to herself an ineffective muse and a failed partner. Her extended professional leave also evoked a scratchy contentiousness, and this led to a period of even more excessive drinking during the first few months of 1958. At least once that March this nearly led to calamity, for at Roxbury she tripped and fell halfway down a flight of stairs, sustaining only a bruised ankle and a cut to her right palm from a broken whiskey glass.

On another occasion, Rosten recalled her sitting alone at a party in her Manhattan apartment, sipping a drink and apparently 'floating off in her own daydream, out of contact'. When he approached her, she said, 'I'm going to have sleep trouble again tonight,' and she thought the drinks would narcotize her. Similarly, friends like her dress designer John Moore recalled her greeting him for a fitting at the apartment on Sunday morning with a sly grin: 'The maid's not here,' she whispered as if scheming, 'so we can put more vodka in the Bloody Marys!'

But liquor often made Marilyn ill, and she had little tolerance beyond one or two modest drinks; she preferred champagne, which did not upset her stomach. But with alcohol, her appetite increased, and with no apparent reason to look her best for Hollywood, she quickly gained even more weight – as much as eighteen pounds above her normal 115. By April, the few photographs she approved for publication showed her in the latest style, a comfortable black chemise or 'sack dress' that afforded neat camouflage. Such an outfit the international press deplored: 'She shouldn't wear it, she looks awful,' reprimanded the Associated Press. John Moore agreed, attempting diplomatically to communicate the joint opinion by showing her a clipping from a German newspaper: in a chemise, it said flatly, Marilyn Monroe looked like someone in a barrel. Her reaction was an amused avoidance of the issue by a delicious non sequitur: 'But I've never even *been* to West Berlin!'

It may also have seemed as if she had never been to Hollywood, which was changing fast and, with its short memory, almost forgetting her. By April 1958, almost two years had passed since she had made a film in America, and during the interval, studio executives were not breathlessly awaiting her return. On the contrary, they created replicas, copycat blondes in wild profusion whom they often outfitted with Marilyn Monroe's earlier wardrobe.*

But Marilyn's agents made certain she was aware of the threat as well as the changes; indeed, by May she was ready to listen to offers to return to Hollywood – not only because she longed to

---

* At Fox, for example, the market on peroxide was cornered by Jayne Mansfield, who wore Marilyn's notorious gold lamé dress from *Gentlemen Prefer Blondes*, while Sheree North inherited her red beaded gown from the same movie. At Universal-International, her tight bodices from two pictures were loaned out for Mamie Van Doren; her form-fitting corset from *River of No Return* was handed over to Corinne Calvet for *Powder River*. Marilyn's white pleated dress from *The Seven Year Itch* swirled round Rosanne Arlen in *Bachelor Flat*, and outfits from

do more than talk to Marianne Kris and listen to Lee Strasberg, but also because the Millers were short of money. She also wanted to apply in her work what she hoped she had learned since 1956. Fearing there might be no purpose in her life, she felt that therapy and acting classes suggested all sorts of avenues, but that everything was theoretical. Now Marilyn longed to 'be up and at it, doing something for a change,' as she told Sam Shaw and Susan Strasberg. She had lost a child, had to abandon plans for a new home, was mired in an arid matrimonial patch and when she gazed in the mirror saw someone still lovely at thirty-two, but slightly bloated, pale and weary. She listened to the men at MCA – Lew Wasserman, Jay Kanter and another colleague, George Chasin.

At first, the agents reported, Fox offered to produce a film of the musical play *Can-Can* for her and Maurice Chevalier; also discussed were a picture called *Some Came Running* with Frank Sinatra and one based on William Faulkner's novel *The Sound and the Fury*. Yes, her agents said, these projects would avoid a reversion to the type of roles she had resented and said she would turn down – women like Lorelei Lee in *Gentlemen Prefer Blondes*, Pola in *How to Marry a Millionaire* and the nameless girl in *The Seven Year Itch*.

Just as they were considering these and other projects, Billy Wilder sent Marilyn a two-page outline of a film he was writing with I. A. L. Diamond, a script based on an old German farce. Titled *Some Like It Hot*, this was to be a wild comedy set in the Roaring Twenties, about two musicians who accidentally witness the St Valentine's Day Massacre. To avoid the killers, the men successfully disguise themselves as women and sign up

several Monroe films were worn by Barbara Nichols in hers. At Columbia, Cleo Moore was taught how to walk like Marilyn, while at MGM, RKO and elsewhere, Barbara Lang, Joi Lansing, Diana Dors and Beverly Michaels had to sit through hours of excerpts from Marilyn's pictures, studying her. Even Sidney Skolsky championed a substitute Marilyn. Most of these women never had a chance to discover if they could do anything other than imitate someone inimitable.

with an all-girl band, among whom is the ukelele-strumming blonde Sugar Kane. The comic possibilities were enormous, Marilyn as Sugar would have several songs and, although it was the kind of role she wanted to put behind her, she had sufficient faith in Wilder's judgement and previous success to negotiate. By late spring, it was agreed that Marilyn would receive $100,000 plus a historic ten per cent of the film's gross profits. This would, she reasoned, by simply an easy, lucrative interval while Arthur completed *The Misfits*.

On the evening of 7 July, Marilyn left Arthur in Amagansett and arrived next morning in Los Angeles, accompanied by her secretary May Reis and by Paula Strasberg. Reporters and photographers remarked on Marilyn's white-blond hair, her white silk shirt, white skirt, white shoes and white gloves. Stepping into Southern California's morning light, she practically blocked out the sun.

Paula was again present, Marilyn said with her usual piercingly honest self-assessment,

> because she gives me a lot of confidence and is very helpful. You see, I'm not a quick study, but I'm very serious about my work and am not experienced enough as an actress to chat with friends and workers on the set and then go into a dramatic scene. I like to go directly from a scene into my dressing room and concentrate on the next one and keep my mind in one channel. I envy these people who can meet all comers and go from a bright quip and gay laugh into a scene before the camera. All I'm thinking of is my performance, and I try to make it as good as I know how. And Paula gives me confidence.

May Reis, then fifty-four, was a highly intelligent, discreet and trustworthy assistant who had been secretary to Elia Kazan and, until 1955, to Arthur Miller. Fatherless at nine, she had cared for her sick mother and grandmother and from adolescence worked to support them and her brother Irving who became a director (of, among other films, the screen version of Arthur's play *All My Sons*). By 1958, she had been attending to Marilyn's secretarial needs in New York for almost three years, answering fan mail at Fifty-seventh Street, keeping her schedule, fielding phone calls and co-operating with Marilyn's agents and publicists. According to her sister-in-law Vanessa Reis, May agreed to travel with Marilyn to Hollywood for *Some Like It Hot* and the next two films 'because May was alone in the world and had no family – and so Marilyn became her existence, her profession, her commitment. She already knew that working for Marilyn was a handful, but May knew that stars are a handful.'

The tasks began that very afternoon, when Marilyn and May were rushed off to a press conference at the Beverly Hills Hotel, with Billy Wilder and co-stars Tony Curtis, Jack Lemmon and George Raft. Fortunately, she would live at the hotel temporarily (for wardrobe fittings, makeup tests and ukelele lessons) and also during interior filming at the Goldwyn Studios. As they approached the first day of production, Marilyn's customary anxieties were much alleviated by news from Washington and New York just when shooting began in early August. In the United States Court of Appeals, Joe Rauh had won a reversal of Arthur's contempt citation, on the premise that Arthur had not been completely informed as to why he had to answer questions in the first place.

At first, good spirits prevailed with Marilyn, her director and her co-stars. For six years, all her films had been shot in Technicolor; because that was now in her contract with Fox, Marilyn naturally expected that *Some Like It Hot* would be a colour picture, too (although this film was for United Artists). But no, Wilder explained, this picture had to be shot in black and white, otherwise the makeup of the two men in drag would be absurdly garish to be convincing. Of this Marilyn was not sure until a quick test shot made everything clear; from that point, the production began with an amiable optimism that made everybody almost deliriously happy.

Wilder also noticed that Marilyn had matured as an actress. 'She has her own natural instinct for reading a line,' according to Wilder, 'and an uncanny ability to bring something to it.' And Paula was helpful. 'There was no question about it,' said Rupert Allan. 'Paula gave Marilyn the security she needed during production – without the unfortunate complications of Natasha.'
For all that, Wilder found that Marilyn

was still not easy to work with. She was constantly late, and she demanded take after take after take – the Strasbergs, after all, had taught her to do things again and again and again until she felt she got them right. Well, now she had us doing things again and again, our nice sane budget was going up like a rocket, our cast relations were a shambles, and I was on the verge of a breakdown. To tell the truth, she was impossible – not just difficult. Yes, the final product was worth it – but at the time we were never convinced there would *be* a final product.

In other words, the camaraderie at the start of *Some Like It Hot* went cold. Jack Lemmon and Tony Curtis, with whom Marilyn had most of her scenes, grew weary and annoyed after the tenth and fifteenth take of the same shot, for Marilyn would cut in the middle of every one, angry or exasperated because she had got a word wrong – or, more often, was convinced she could do the scene better. 'Sometimes this stretched out to three days something we could have completed in an hour,' Wilder added, 'because after every bad take Marilyn began to cry, and there would have to be new makeup applied.' In addition, Marilyn came to the set without having memorized her dialogue, which had to be written on cue cards or taped on props.
Marilyn was a year younger than Lemmon and Curtis, yet she was afraid of seeming much older and was paradoxically anxious that in their farcical drag they would appear like college boys. 'She picked up on anything,' recalled Allan Snyder. 'She'd say her eyebrows were wrong, or her lipstick – anything not to appear out there.' Perhaps even if she arrived late, they would

be grateful that she was there at all. She was living in what her poet friend Norman Rosten called 'Marilyn time'.

'I never heard such brilliant direction as Billy gave her,' said Lemmon, 'but nothing worked until she felt right about it. She simply said over and over, "Sorry, I have to do it again." And if Billy said, "Well, I tell you, Marilyn, just possibly if you were to . . ." – then she replied, "Just a moment, now, Billy, don't talk to me, I'll forget how I want to play it." That took me over the edge more than once. Nobody could remind her she had a professional commitment. She couldn't do it until she herself was ready.'

Tony Curtis was blunter: kissing her, he said, was like kissing Hitler, by which he probably meant it could not possibly appeal to anyone but Eva Braun. 'Well, I think that's his problem,' Marilyn replied airily. 'If I have to do intimate love scenes with somebody who really has that feeling toward me, then my fantasy has to come into play – in other words, out with him, in with my fantasy. He was never there.' But she had to do the scene dozens of times to make her fantasy convincing for herself, and by this time Curtis was glassy-eyed and hoarse with exhaustion – just when Marilyn glowed, melding 'organically', as she liked to say, into the role.

Even as loyal a friend as Rosten had to agree that at such times Marilyn was trouble itself, a difficult woman who brought along the entire baggage of her emotional insecurities. Meanwhile, she justified her demand for multiple takes by saying that with each one she was 'relaxing a little more . . . and I'll go a bit further on the next try.' She did not admit that at the root of the problems was not only her insecurity but also her terror at being back in Hollywood: she was afraid that everything for which she had worked was gone, that with her company now only a nominal tax shelter for her salary, she would once again revert to being misperceived and abused by the very system she had once so courageously abandoned.

By early September, the company was filming on location at a late nineteenth-century Victorian resort called the Hotel del

Coronado, a two-hour drive south of Los Angeles. After a month of strained relations with her colleagues and the unfounded conviction that she was performing poorly, Marilyn had reverted to reliance on massive amounts of barbiturates to sleep. In addition, she sometimes took pills during the afternoon as well, perhaps to anaesthetize her feelings of insufficiency.

Marilyn's gynaecologist, Leon Krohn, was present for much of the production, and he was openly concerned for Marilyn's health. 'It seemed to me,' he said later,

> that she was in a Pygmalion situation: Arthur Miller was trying to make a sophisticate out of her, and I believe this caused her great tension. She often told me how she longed for a child, but I cautioned her that she would kill a baby with the drink and the pills – the effects of those barbiturates accumulated, I told her, and it would be impossible to predict when just one drink will then precipitate a spontaneous abortion.

Marilyn also felt, as she later told Rupert Allan, that in playing the role of Sugar Kane she had reverted to exactly the kind of role that had driven her from Hollywood in 1954.

Marilyn now longed to have the film completed, and in September she typed a note to Norman Rosten: 'I have a feeling this ship is never going to dock. We are going through the Straits of Dire, [and] it's rough and choppy.' In a postscript she added, 'Love me for my yellow hair alone. I would have written this by hand but it's trembling.' She was referring to a favourite poem by Yeats:

> . . . only God, my dear,
> Could love you for yourself alone,
> And not your yellow hair.

For Marilyn, any reason to love her would suffice.

Perhaps because from afar their marriage seemed not quite so troubled, Marilyn longed for Arthur as she had during *Bus Stop*, and she turned to him when she had doubts about a projected photo story. Richard Avedon had photographed her in a variety of costumes and poses for *Life* magazine, in which Marilyn fancifully portrayed Theda Bara, Clara Bow, Marlene Dietrich, Lillian Russell and Jean Harlow. Marilyn was with Avedon as with other photographers, virtually the reverse of herself on a movie set: 'very easy to work with', according to Avedon. 'She gave more to the still camera than any actress – any woman – I've ever photographed, infinitely more patient, more demanding of herself and more comfortable in front of the camera than away from it.'

Arthur contributed a lovingly elegiac and eulogistic tribute to accompany the Avedon pictures, praising Marilyn's ingenuity, her sense of play, 'the spontaneous joy she takes in anything a child does, [and] her quick sympathy and respect for old people . . . The child in her catches the fun and the promise, and the old person in her the mortality.' The best of the lot, he said, was the homage to Harlow, whom Marilyn conveyed 'not so much by wit as by her deep sympathy for that actress's tragic life . . . She has identified herself with what was naive, what was genuine lure and sexual truth.'

But when Marilyn read the draft of his comments, she felt not encouraged but depressed. Why the emphasis on naïveté, on 'lure and sexual truth'? Was that all she had to offer? In this she reacted neurotically, for Arthur's essay is one of the most appreciative and laudatory ever written of her. But ignoring the praise, she seized on the comparison with Harlow. In her own net of insecurities, the reminders of her predecessor's difficult life, her struggle in Hollywood and her untimely death overwhelmed Marilyn, and on Friday 12 September she telephoned Arthur in New York.

Of their conversation nothing can be known. But that evening Arthur wrote to Marilyn of his own emotional problems, and the letter has survived. Addressing her as his 'Darling Girl,' he wrote that she was his ideal, and he then apologized for the things he had not done (perhaps a reference to his lack of material support in their marriage) and for those he had (a possible allusion to the infamous notebook entry). He added that he believed he was making important discoveries in the regular psychotherapeutic sessions he had resumed with a Dr Loewenstein, which he believed was illuminating the blockage in his emotional life. He justified the reservations she had about the *Life* article (which they evidently discussed on the telephone) by stating his belief that his points were good and interesting. The letter concluded with a plea for her love and her understanding of his mental confusion.

The letter is crucial, for its contradicts the general tone and content of Arthur Miller's published memoirs, in which he portrayed himself as the healthy-minded, long-suffering partner of a woman he saw as occasionally sweet and talented, but ever on the edge of madness. In this regard, *Timebends* is a book whose sections on Marilyn are full of condescension for a 'dear girl' and a 'mere child', a disturbed, distracted person mired in a past of her own invention, and a woman from whom he barely escaped with sanity and life intact. Although no autobiography can be expected to provide an objective account of the author's intimacies, this one is remarkably incomplete and selective of the facts in their marriage, and so singularly clouded with self-defence, that it could have been written only by one rooted in his own guilt and remorse.*

The letter of 12 September 1958 helps to correct this one-sided view. She may have been seeking an earthly saviour, as he claimed, but he had been looking for a goddess. As Sidney Skolsky rightly remarked, Arthur may have been shocked to discover that Marilyn was neither his salvation nor the one he

* Notwithstanding any objective valuation of their merit, the playwright's entire corpus of plays and screenplays following his marriage to Marilyn – from *The Misfits* (1960), through *After the Fall* (1964), and up to *The Last Yankee* (1993) – comprises an encoded guide to the network of conflicted feelings about his life with Marilyn Monroe, a complex he seems never to have completely resolved.

hoped could disentangle his own spiritual problems, but that she was needy in her own right. His creative inertia and his admitted emotional background were not her responsibility to resolve, and Norman Rosten was correct when he judged that Arthur was 'more and more living with her in the third person, as an observer, [and] the shadow that had fallen between them in England was increasing, deepening.'

Their telephone conversation alone was not enough to cheer her, for that night Marilyn apparently took one too many sleeping capsules, perhaps with champagne. She was neither dying nor comatose, but, in a reaction typical for one who ingests such a combination, she vomited so violently that Paula had her admitted to hospital for the weekend. Marilyn was back at work on Monday. Later that week, Arthur arrived to comfort her, but also, as his friend Olie Rauh believed, because he was virtually idle in New York: he had submitted the first draft of *The Misfits* to John Huston, whose response to it was favourable and who, they hoped, would direct it.

Arthur's presence was no help at all. Embarrassed by what he considered her lack of professionalism, he was another authority figure Marilyn had to please. In addition, he distressed an already harried production crew by unwelcome interference, which doubtless he thought was part of the support he was offering Marilyn. Nor was his unwittingly superior attitude welcome. Introduced to Wilder and Diamond, Arthur held forth on the differences between classical comedy and tragedy – a professional tactic that endeared him neither to his wife's colleagues nor to her. At the time, Jack Lemmon realized she was 'going through some kind of hell on earth – suffering and still producing that magic on film. It was a courageous performance, really courageous.' She was, he said, always giving everything she had, struggling to do better.

Behind this struggle was the judgement Marilyn felt was constantly being levelled against her by Arthur. To Rupert Allan and Susan Strasberg, Marilyn confided her fear that Arthur regarded her as self-absorbed and unprofessional. In their time, actors like Spencer Tracy and Errol Flynn (among others) shut down filming for a week at a time while they skipped off for their alcoholic binges, and Judy Garland was endlessly pampered with whatever drugs she required; they were but three of countless stars whose conduct, by comparison, made Marilyn seem as alert and punctual as a cadet. In a way, decades of studio carelessness and indulgence were devolving against her: she had not only personal habits to correct but also years of corporate cossetting of stars' whims, which at last – for economic reasons – were no longer quite so blithely tolerated.

Arthur's resentment of Marilyn was obvious to everyone during production. 'There were days I could have strangled her,' said Billy Wilder, 'but there were wonderful days, too, when we all knew she was brilliant. But with Arthur it all seemed sour, and I remember saying at the time that in meeting Miller at last I met someone who resented her more than I did.' Professionally idle, dependent on his wife's income, humiliated by what he saw as her childish caprice and contemptuous of Hollywood in any case, Arthur could no longer tolerate her or the marriage.

But there was another problem, and that autumn the atmosphere on location in Coronado was thick with tensions. 'Arthur told me he would allow Marilyn to work only in the morning,' Wilder recalled.

He said she was too exhausted to submit to outside work in the afternoon sun. 'The morning? She never shows up until after twelve! Arthur, bring her to me at nine and you can have her back at eleven-thirty!' We were working with a time bomb, we were twenty days behind schedule and God knows how much over budget, and she was taking a lot of pills. But we were working with Monroe, and she was platinum – not just the hair, and not just her box-office appeal. What you saw on the screen was priceless.

The reason for Arthur's request was simple: in late October, the

Millers learned that Marilyn was pregnant again. Fortunately, her most strenuous scenes were already shot and the filming of *Some Like It Hot* was completed on 6 November.

By this time, director and star were barely speaking. When *The New York Herald Tribune* sent Hollywood columnist Joe Hyams to interview Wilder, he openly discussed Marilyn's unpunctuality and inability to remember lines. When Hyams asked if he would do another project with her, Wilder replied, 'I have discussed this project with my doctor and my psychiatrist and they tell me I'm too old and too rich to go through this again.' But this was a reaction of the moment: with the passage of time and the enormous success of *Some Like It Hot* – the biggest grossing American film for the first half of 1959 – Wilder praised Monroe's unique gifts and she said it would be a privilege to work for him again. That winter, in fact, Marilyn telephoned Wilder from New York, intending (as she told the film's musical composer Matty Malneck) to offer the olive branch but finally unable to do so. Wilder's wife took the call:

'Audrey?'

'Hi, Marilyn!'

'Is Billy there?'

'No, he's not home yet.'

'Well, when you see him, will you give him a message for me?'

'Of course.'

'Well,' Marilyn said, and then paused. 'Would you please tell him' – she was putting her words together slowly, thoughtfully – 'would you please tell him to go and fuck himself?' A slight pause again, and in a gentler voice Marilyn concluded: 'And my warmest personal regards to you, Audrey.'

But Wilder was not bitter. 'Anyone can remember lines,' he said, 'but it takes a real artist to come on the set and not know her lines and yet give the performance she did!'

Some Like It Hot is essentially a one-joke chase movie stretched on the frame of a story as classical as Shakespeare or the Da Ponte libretti for Mozart, or as Victorian as *Charley's Aunt*: men forced to dress like women cannot disclose their true identities to the women with whom they fall in love. As a variation of boy (as girl) meets girl but cannot woo girl, *Some Like It Hot* might have been little more than a glossy college romp. But Wilder and Diamond, taking full advantage of Marilyn's voluptuous charm, added all the elements of Prohibition-era wildness: forbidden liquor, the sudden leap toward free love and even, in the closing line, an implicit nod toward tolerance of homosexuality. When Joe E. Brown learns that his beloved Jack Lemmon is not, after all, a woman, he smiles and shrugs off the objection: 'Well, nobody's perfect.' But somehow Marilyn's performance was. For all the problems, what survives is a radiantly funny portrait of a ukelele-strumming girl aglow with expectations for the right kind of man to love.

Returning to New York before the end of November, Marilyn was determined to rest during the early stages of her pregnancy. But on 16 December she miscarried; it was the last time she tried to be a mother. Both for sleep and as a tranquillizer, she had been taking Amytal, a brand name of the barbiturate amobarbital, and now she guiltily recalled Leon Krohn's warning, as she wrote to the Rostens: 'Could I have killed it by taking all the Amytal on an empty stomach? I took some sherry wine also.' For weeks she was inconsolable, convinced that the drug abuse she now freely admitted had caused the spontaneous abortion.

The Christmas-New Year holiday was a time of quiet recuperation, and Marilyn entered 1959 in a depression she tried to alleviate by taking sleeping pills as sedatives against tension and anxiety, a practice not generally discouraged by physicians at that time. But Amytal and Nembutal are themselves depressants, and so there was sometimes a vicious cycle of insomnia, drug-induced sleep, a stupefied morning and a vaguely unhappy day endured by taking more pills. Marilyn's sessions with Dr Kris, to whom she resumed regular visits, seemed to provide little comfort or illumination. Kris prescribed the sedation Marilyn requested and, it may be presumed, recorded and monitored the amounts.

There was one particularly uncomfortable side-effect of her drug use: chronic constipation, which she countered by increased reliance on enemas. Since 1953, she had taken one a day before special occasions if she felt bloated, so that she could fit snugly into a form-fitting gown. But by 1959, her enemas had become as casual a habit as a haircut or shampoo and far more dangerous; pharmacy receipts for that year include the purchase of several sets of the necessary paraphernalia.

Marilyn returned to her private classes with Lee and to workshops at the Actors Studio – both of these to Arthur's annoyance, as Susan Strasberg recalled, for there was a widening rift between him and her parents. Marilyn also dutifully read film scripts submitted by her agents – none of them, she replied, either appealing or appropriate; and she worked with Arthur on further improvements to the Roxbury house, the first home she had ever owned with anyone.

Marilyn was no recluse, however, and she was particularly delighted to meet famous writers that year. Carson McCullers extended an invitation to her Nyack home, where Isak Dinesen joined them for a long afternoon discussion of poetry. Carl Sandburg, who had met Marilyn briefly during the filming of *Some Like It Hot*, was also an occasional visitor to her apartment for casual literary discussions *à deux*. He found her 'warm and plain' and charmed her by asking for her autograph. 'Marilyn was a good talker,' according to Sandburg, 'and very good company. We did some mock playacting and some pretty good, funny imitations. I asked her a lot of questions. She told me how she came up the hard way, but she would never talk about her husbands.'

In 1959, Marilyn was not, therefore, the invariably withdrawn, darkly self-absorbed (much less suicidal) enigma of later myth. She had some days when she was (thus Susan) 'restless because she wasn't working', and so she rightly seized every possibility of a happy occasion.

Photographs of her at the New York preview of *Some Like It Hot* in February, and the premiere party at the Strasbergs in March, for example, show a luminous, smiling Marilyn all in white: she looked like cotton candy, someone remarked. On a promotional tour for the film, she was as ever low-keyed and generous with the press. Mervin Block, a reporter for the *Chicago American*, recalled that at a press luncheon at the Ambassador East on 18 March she seemed 'uncomfortable in the presence of so many strangers', but that she was 'patient and cheerful. Even when a nervous photographer spilled a drink all over the front of her dress, she remained calm, showed no anger, didn't act like the great star she was.'

As for their long-planned film of *The Misfits*, John Huston was reading various drafts of the screenplay. Otherwise, Arthur's dramatic works-in-progress were stalled and, as one friendly observer noted, he could not see how to give them a push. His own anxious inertia was ironically highlighted by his reception, on 27 January, of a gold medal from the Natinal Institute of Arts and Letters. In painful times, as Dante wrote, the worst agony is the remembrance of past glory.

On such occasions, Marilyn rose to the moment. She invited Arthur's family to dinner, livened the atmosphere with jokes, and, on request, sang 'Diamonds Are a Girl's Best Friend'. Of Arthur's relatives, she especially loved his father and frequently invited the senior Millers to Fifty-seventh Street. Marilyn fussed over Isadore, devoted a day to preparing a meal he especially liked, offered him little gifts and treated him as lovingly as if he were her own father. If he dozed, she untied his shoelaces and brought a footstool; if he had a cold, she brought soup and a shawl.

Marilyn's fundamental courage and lack of self-pity at this time was most evident in the way she dealt with a marriage in swift decline. As the year and her inactivity progressed, she lost interest in the plans for expansion at Roxbury. 'Empty hours oppressed her,' according to Susan, 'and she seemed bored with the part-time role of country housewife.' Marilyn had hoped to find a literary mentor, father and protector in Arthur, but this was an ideal no man could fulfil; for his part, he had wanted her for his tragic muse, his occupation, and he used her fragility as the excuse for his own literary setbacks. She was his artwork *faute de mieux.* Here, then, were two people once in love but now vainly dependent on Marilyn's public persona and the iconography of fame to keep them together. 'I guess I *am* a fantasy,' she said sadly of this time.

All was not gloomy. On 13 May, Marilyn received Italy's Oscar, the 'David di Donatello' as best actress for *The Prince and the Showgirl*. Four hundred people jammed into the Italian Consulate on Park Avenue where Filipo Donini, director of the Italian Cultural Institute, presented the award. Ten days later, an interesting offer came from her old friend Jerry Wald, who had produced *Clash by Night*. He had another script from Clifford Odets and thought they might revive a successful moment of history with a new Wald–Odets–Monroe project called *The Story on Page One*.

Producer and writer wasted no time in outlining the story for her. The role of Jo Morris, as they described it, was that of an attractive, lonely and disconnected woman, raised by foster parents, unprotected and open to all kinds of abuse. Dependent on men, she nevertheless believes that she has more to offer the world than beauty, and her shrewdness enables her to survive. Intelligent and charming, she longs for love at any cost and, hoping to find a safe harbour from her past, she marries an older man and even tries to have children. But her husband becomes unreasonably jealous and brutal.

The story outline had proceeded only so far when Marilyn replied that she was interested in something from Clifford Odets, but that she would await a completed script; she was also doubtful about the news that Odets was to direct. Most important, as she told Paula, Marilyn recognized that *The Story on Page One* read like an outline of her own life. From the end of May through mid-June, letters, telephone calls and occasional telegrams augured well for *The Story on Page One*. But then Marilyn fell ill. On 23 June at Lenox Hill Hospital, her New York gynaecologist Dr Mortimer Rodgers operated to relieve again the condition of chronic endometriosis and thus her abnormally painful menstrual periods, her unusually severe bleeding and her infertility.*

After she had spent a quiet summer, Marilyn heard again from Jerry Wald, who was back on the wire with another subject, at first called *The Billionaire* and eventually *Let's Make Love*. This seemed an idea full of promise, planned by Wald and Twentieth Century-Fox as a Technicolor, CinemaScope musical comedy with a script by Norman Krasna, who had written comedies for Carole Lombard and Marlene Dietrich; most recently, he had revised his play *Kind Sir* into the successful comedy *Indiscreet* for Ingrid Bergman and Cary Grant. At first, *The Billionaire* was to have been directed by Billy Wilder, whom Marilyn approved but feared would not work again with her; in fact Wilder told Rupert Allan he would be delighted to do just that – but he was already at work on his next script (*The Apartment*). She then agreed with Wald's suggestion of George Cukor, who had directed Greta Garbo, Jean Harlow, Katharine Hepburn, Joan Crawford and Ingrid Bergman, among other important Hollywood ladies. 'He told me not to be nervous,' Marilyn said of her first meeting with Cukor. 'I told him I was born nervous.'

Marilyn was to play an actress named Amanda Dell who performs in an Off-Broadway musical satire also called *Let's Make Love*. This show-within-the-show satirizes the fabulously wealthy French-born, New York businessman Jean-Marc Clément. He decides to visit a rehearsal and, without revealing his true identity, he is hired as an actor – to play himself. Clément falls in love with Amanda, who until the last minute refuses to believe the truth that her co-star is really a tycoon.

Cary Grant, Rock Hudson, Charlton Heston and Gregory Peck turned down the male lead – either because of the song-and-dance routines or because they were unwilling to serve as mere acolytes in a Monroe picture. Wald and Cukor then had

---

* *The Story on Page One* was eventually completed by Odets and filmed with Rita Hayworth in the leading role.

the idea that an authentic French musical star would be the perfect choice and Marilyn, on their recommendation and Arthur's, yielded. Her leading man, appearing in his first American picture, would be none other than Yves Montand, who had played in the Paris production of *The Crucible* and recently had a great success with his one-man show on Broadway. 'I'm sure he accepted for one good reason,' Arthur Miller said years later. 'It meant he was breaking into movies as a leading man opposite Marilyn Monroe' (neither an unwise nor unworthy motive). On 30 September, Marilyn signed to do the picture; negotiations for Montand, which included a paid trip to Hollywood for him and his wife Simone Signoret, were completed before Christmas.

Meanwhile, Fox employed Marilyn as a goodwill ambassador. Nikita Khrushchev's historic tour of America was at its peak that September, and the film industry's banquet in his honour was held on 19 September in the most lavish commissary of them all, Fox's Café de Paris. From her table (where she chatted amiably with Billy Wilder, William Wyler, Joshua Logan and others), Marilyn was summoned to meet the Soviet premier: he smiled, gazed unblinkingly into her blue eyes and shook her hand so earnestly and so long it hurt for days. 'He looked at me the way a man looks on a woman – that's how he looked at me,' she reported proudly. An interpreter conveyed some small talk about *The Brothers Karamazov*, which by then had been filmed with Maria Schell as Grushenka, and Marilyn had only warm words for Schell's performance. Yes, she would like very much to visit Russia, she replied to Khrushchev's invitation. For perhaps two minutes, the Cold War thawed slightly.

In October and November, there were pre-production details: wardrobe fittings, colour tests, meetings with Cukor and scene study with Paula Strasberg, who was included on the team as usual. This time there were also rehearsals and pre-recordings for several songs. According to Frankie Vaughan, the British pop star who played a supporting role, 'She was always on time for rehearsals. There were none of those notorious late starts. When she arrived, everybody smartened up, as if her presence was the light that fell on everyone. Certainly she seemed to me very professional.' These numbers required some basic choreography, and because dancing on-camera made Marilyn more nervous than anything else in a movie, she demanded the help of her old friend Jack Cole, who had trained her throughout the rigours of *Gentlemen Prefer Blondes* and *There's No Business Like Show Business*.

At the same time, an even deeper friendship was established. An actor known as 'masseur to the stars', Ralph Roberts had earned high esteem among theatre and movie folk because of his sophisticated knowledge of physiotherapy and of the special muscular problems often afflicting actors and dancers. He had met Marilyn at the Strasberg home in 1955 when he, too, was both student and close friend of the family. Roberts had acted on Broadway in Jean Anouilh's *The Lark* with Julie Harris and Boris Karloff, and he had trained the actor who played the masseur (a surrogate Ralph Roberts) in the opening scene of *Will Success Spoil Rock Hunter?*

Over six feet tall and ruggedly handsome, Ralph had a solid reputation as a Southern gentleman in the classic mould, soft-spoken, compassionate and courtly. He was also widely read and had refined, multicultural interests. That season he was in Los Angeles, and when Marilyn heard that he had greatly helped Judy Holliday during the filming of *Bells Are Ringing*, she rang him at once. From the day of their reunion, he was 'Rafe' to her: she preferred the British pronunciation. More important, he quickly became her closest friend and most intimate confidant for the rest of her life.

Very soon, Marilyn needed Ralph's support. With the holidays there arrived her co-star, the formidable, smoothly romantic Yves Montand. Under Cukor's supervision, Montand and Marilyn began to rehearse the early scenes of *Let's Make Love*, a movie which bore, as Simone Signoret said, *un titre prémonitoire* – a threatening title.

Chapter Eighteen

1960

'Marilyn was a smiling, bubbling, beautiful hostess. She still has the old glamour, the magic.' So wrote her friend Sidney Skolsky, inspired by a reception Marilyn hosted for Yves Montand at Fox's commissary during the second week of January.

'Next to my husband and Marlon Brando,' she said, offering a toast, 'I think Yves Montand is the most attractive man I've ever met.'

This remark brought polite applause, and heads turned toward the guest of honour, whose English was poor and heavily accented. 'Everything she do is original, even when she stand and talk to you,' he read haltingly from a card. 'I never see anybody who concentrate so hard. She work hard, she do scene over and over and over but is not happy until perfect. She help me, I try to help her.'

At first, this kind of warm collegiality prevailed as well at the Beverly Hills Hotel, that sprawling pink complex of Mediterranean revival buildings on Sunset Boulevard, where the studio installed the Montands in bungalow number twenty and the Millers a few steps away in number twenty-one. After the tensions of the previous year, an uneasy truce seemed to prevail between the Millers: they hoped, Marilyn told friends, that *The Misfits* – his Valentine for her, she called it – might restore their marriage.

Arthur had known the Montands since 1956, and the couples had spent several pleasant evenings together in New York the previous September, when Yves was the toast of Broadway.

Now they dined together each evening when Yves and Marilyn returned from rehearsals. Over spaghetti in one suite or lamb stew in another, Montand practised his English, asking Arthur and Marilyn for help and trying to understand a humourless and badly structured script. Simone, rather more fluent and then between film assignments, described her leisurely days of shopping and her walks around Beverly Hills. Marilyn complained about *Let's Make Love*, which was turning out to have more holes than the wheel of Swiss cheese the Montands kept in their kitchenette: 'There was no script, really,' she said later. 'There was nothing for the girl to *do!*' And Arthur, puffing on his pipe, had to agree that yes, the script pages he read were abysmally unfunny and riddled with clichés.

By the end of January, Arthur was in Ireland, working at John Huston's home on his own revisions for *The Misfits*. Although that script was far from camera-ready, he returned in mid-March for an astonishing reason – to write some scenes for *Let's Make Love*.

In his memoirs, Miller wrote with lofty bitterness that his work on this picture meant 'a sacrifice of great blocks of time ... [for] a script not worth the paper it was typed on' – a task, he said, that he undertook only to give his wife emotional support. His assessment of the screenplay is astute, but the circumstances of his involvement were somewhat different, not to say determinative for the course of the Millers' marriage.

On 7 March the Screen Actors Guild joined the Writers Guild, already on strike against producers and studios, and from that day, every Hollywood production shut down – just when *Let's Make Love* had some of its most pressing script and production problems. The major issue at stake for these unions was additional payments to actors and writers for the television broadcast of their earlier films, from which studios were now realizing huge new profits, and no playwright or screenwriter would break the strike to work on the problematic sequences of this film. But to everyone's astonishment – Marilyn's most of all – Jerry Wald prevailed on Arthur Miller to break ranks.

According to Yves Montand, Miller 'came running [back from Ireland] to rewrite some scenes, pocketed a check [from Fox] and complained about prostituting his art.'

Indeed, Miller was apparently not so mortified at the task as he later claimed: he attended the screening of the dailies, commenting so imperiously that Cukor left the room, and generally playing the experienced playwright who was slumming in Hollywood – an attitude that had caused problems on *Some Like It Hot*. Nonetheless, his fee of several thousand dollars for his contributions must have alleviated whatever agony he felt.

Most significantly, this situation was disastrous for a marriage already in tatters. Sidney Skolsky summed up the matter: 'Arthur Miller, the big liberal, the man who always stood up for the underdog, ignored the Writers Guild strike and rewrote [pages of the script]. Arthur did it silently, at night,' and the result was that 'his wife no longer looked up to him ... Any resemblance he had once possessed, in Marilyn's eyes, to a President assassinated nearly a century ago [Lincoln, to whom she had often compared Miller] had vanished.' Violating his own ethics, Arthur lost Marilyn's confidence for ever: the man whose courage and moral outrage a few years earlier had won her admiration had betrayed his own ideals. 'That was the moment I knew it was over,' she told Rupert Allan, visiting Los Angeles from Monaco. 'Nothing seemed to make sense any more.'

There was much slamming of doors in their bungalow, and the Montands, among others, heard angry voices late into the night. From that time, the production 'was a terrible ordeal for everybody', according to Jack Cole, who added, echoing Billy Wilder, that 'Arthur Miller hated her.'

'There was something terrible happening between them,' recalled Vanessa Reis, 'and the marriage was obviously unraveling. This took a terrific toll on May, who was the soul of discretion and found it painful to watch. One evening, Arthur, Marilyn, May, Rupert Allan and I were about to go out for dinner, but the atmosphere was so tense I left the group.'

George Cukor recognized the anxiety in Marilyn's life, although he did not know the specific causes: he admitted later that he had 'no real communication with her at all . . . and very little influence. All I could do was make a climate that was agreeable to her.'

Some relief was provided by a new friendship as Marilyn worked through the project and tried to keep her private misery from public perception. Considerable emotional support was provided on *Let's Make Love* by Marilyn's new stand-in, the actress Evelyn Moriarty, whose height, colouring and experience earned for her one of the most taxing jobs on film sets – to walk through scenes in advance of the star's arrival, testing and confirming lighting cues and rehearsing with other actors. Cukor had known and liked her work for years and had recommended her for the job, and at once Evelyn – a sensible, patient and good-humoured lady with a wealth of experience and a keen grasp of studio politics – won Marilyn's confidence. From the spring of 1960, the women were good friends.

Perhaps because of her recent, second miscarriage, Marilyn had another kind of camaraderie – with the children of colleagues, the youngsters she welcomed to a sound stage otherwise closed to visitors. Frankie Vaughan introduced his seven-year-old son David to her one day, and as she welcomed him Marilyn said, 'Please come and give me a kiss.' The boy hung back shyly, and Marilyn, appearing hurt, repeated her invitation; still, the boy demurred. 'Suddenly,' as Vaughan recalled, 'she started crying, just sobbing on my shoulder.'

But there were other, pleasanter occasions, as with Vanessa Reis's children. Marilyn invited them to watch a scene being filmed, and later took them back to the hotel for a weekend brunch and a swim. Similarly, Cukor recalled a visit to the set of two young girls he knew whose sister had recently been killed in an accident. Learning of the tragedy, Marilyn asked to be introduced; she then insisted on having her picture taken with the girls, told them how beautiful they were and befriended them in no time.

Nor was her kindness restricted to children. Maggie Banks, an assistant choreographer, recalled that the wife of a company electrician was seriously ill: 'I saw Marilyn hand the man a roll of bills; he started to cry, and Marilyn just hugged him and walked away.' Likewise, Evelyn Moriarty never forgot that Marilyn anonymously donated a thousand dollars to defray the funeral expenses of a crew member's wife. Such acts of generosity she accomplished spontaneously and with no thought of anyone but the recipient.

By late spring, the emotional and professional complications surrounding the filming of *Let's Make Love* seemed insurmountable. Yves Montand realized that he had agreed to play a bumbling, graceless foil to Marilyn. This disappointment he could sustain for the sake of his American movie debut, but the thankless role made him more than ever concerned for his English dialogue, which Cukor had to rerecord entirely. Each day of filming, Montand confided to Marilyn that he was terrified of speaking and acting poorly, of seeming as doltish as his character, and this at once established a bond between them. For perhaps the first time in her career, a leading man had revealed fears identical to her own. Marilyn was right, Yves said: Arthur did not understand her panic about performing – only another actor could. They discussed their shared terror of being mocked and rejected by colleagues, for each had worked hard for a few good roles, and each was married to a more respected artist. A warm bond grew between them, not a sudden rush of adolescent passion. Even Simone Signoret, soon to be immersed in a sordid discharge of tabloid venom, recognized that there had been in Marilyn's life (and were even then) 'a whole succession of people who had taken pains to explain to her that she was anything but an actress ... They thought the starlet Marilyn was cute, but they detested her for becoming the actress Monroe.'

Nevertheless, the burden of the film's success was as usual Marilyn's. According to Jack Cole, Marilyn was well aware of this – and of her limitations. Insecure, afraid of failing herself and her husband, she was as usual late and often absent for scheduled musical numbers, which took half the production time and which, as Cole admitted, he had to improvise for her each day – a task not made easier by her frequent hangovers from sleeping pills. But she was 'never bitchy', he added, agreeing with Jerry Wald that the star was 'not malicious, not temperamental'. She simply regarded her task as overwhelmingly significant for herself and others, and she hesitated to do something for which she felt inadequate. 'Is there anything I can do to help?' she often whispered to Frank Radcliffe, one of the dancers assigned to lift her in the film's musical numbers. 'Am I doing anything wrong?'

The filming of this unfortunate picture aggravated every aspect of Marilyn's insecurity, for she found no support from Cukor's perfunctory direction or Miller's condescending manner. Nor was there any encouragement from the nervous atmosphere on the set, where virtually everyone knew they very likely had a disaster in *Let's Make Love*. The situation evoked all her feelings of inadequacy, further sharpened by the kind of psychological imperative that her therapy had not alleviated, and that is so futile: 'What am I afraid of ?' she scribbled one day on a piece of notepaper, while awaiting a call to the set. 'Do I think I can't act? I know I can act but I am afraid. I am afraid and I should not be and I must not be.' In March, she was pleased, but not infused with fresh confidence, when she received the Golden Globe Award from the Foreign Press Association as best actress in a 1959 comedy or musical, for *Some Like It Hot*.

Marilyn found time to improve her political literacy that year. After reading a sheaf of papers sent to her from Connecticut, she accepted the mostly honorific position of alternative delegate to the Fifth Congressional District. To Lester Markle, a *New York Times* editor she had met in 1959, Marilyn wrote a letter on 29 March that revealed the seriousness of her social concerns that election year. 'What about [Nelson] Rockefeller?' she asked.

He's more liberal than many of the Democrats. Maybe he could be developed? At this time, however, [Hubert] Humphrey might be the only one. But who knows, since it's rather hard to find out anything about him ... Of course, [Adlai] Stevenson might have made it if he had been able to talk to people instead of professors ... and there hasn't been anyone like Nixon before, because the rest of them at least had souls! Ideally, Justice William O. Douglas would be the best President ... and how about Kennedy for Vice President? But they couldn't win, because Douglas is divorced. I don't know anything about Kennedy. Maybe this ticket is hopeless, too. But it would be nice to see Stevenson as Secretary of State.

Now, Lester, on Castro. I was brought up to believe in democracy, and when the Cubans finally threw out Battista with so much bloodshed, the United States [didn't] stand behind them and give them help or support even to develop *democracy*. The New York Times's responsibility to keep its readers informed means in an unbiased way. I don't know – somehow I have always counted on The Times, and not [just] because you're there.

I hope Mrs Markle is well. It's true I have been in your building quite frequently, mostly to see my wonderful doctor [Kris], as your spies have already reported. I didn't want you to get a glimpse of me, though, until I was wearing my Somali leopard coat. I want you to think of me as a predatory animal.

She concluded with 'slogans for late 1960':

Nix on Nixon
Over the hump with Humphrey
Stymied with Symington
Back to Boston by Xmas – Kennedy.

Her essential affability, her desire to enlarge her capacities and to escape her unhappiness, was evident elsewhere, too. Joe Hyams, Hollywood correspondent for the *New York Herald Tribune*, recalled that 'she was bubbly and fun for several interviews that season. Her fear and depression were never apparent, although she must have prepared painstakingly for these meetings, the way she prepared makeup for a scene.' And although Marilyn hated surprise parties, she was grateful when the cast and crew of *Let's Make Love* celebrated her thirty-fourth birthday at lunch on 1 June. That evening, Rupert Allan was host for a casual dinner in her honour at his home on Seabright Place. Marilyn spent most of the evening discussing American drama with Tennessee Williams and his mother Edwina, the legendary lady who had inspired *The Glass Menagerie*.

That spring, Simone Signoret was awarded an Oscar as best actress (for a British picture called *Room at the Top*) and within days left for her next film assignment in Europe. Shortly thereafter, Marilyn and Arthur departed for a weekend with John Huston, to scout Nevada locations for *The Misfits*, now scheduled for late summer. 'I'll miss you,' Marilyn said to Yves, bidding farewell as she climbed into a car. 'What will be, will be,' Arthur muttered. If his remark betokened suspicion of the growing intimacy between Marilyn and Yves, Arthur was dead right.

Marilyn returned to Los Angeles alone, while Arthur remained to work with Huston. One evening in late April, she returned from Fox with a cold and a slight fever. Yves went to her bungalow to ask if he could bring her a drink or supper and, as he recounted in his memoirs, he sat on the edge of her bed, patting her hand tenderly. 'I bent over to kiss her good night, but suddenly it was a wild kiss, a fire, a hurricane I couldn't stop.'

The affair (the effect of her broken union, not the cause of it) began in late April and ended quietly in June. The press learned of the romance in the usual ways, with reporters lurking round the shrubbery of the Beverly Hills Hotel and shamelessly bribing maids and messengers for exaggerated accounts of the lovers' comings and goings; by mid-June, columnists were alluding to divorces and remarriage. As for Marilyn, during the time of the affair she enjoyed Montand's ardour and his company, but most of all she was grateful for the warm attention. Ever the realist, however, she expected nothing more, and there is no evidence for the legend that when the affair was over she was so grief-stricken that she came perilously close to a breakdown. Quite the contrary: she accepted the finale with great dignity, telling the press that although some of her acting partners had said unpleasant things about working with her, Yves had not – 'but is that any reason for me to marry him?' She met the absurd rumours of marriage head-on, effectively deflating them.

Arthur Miller never regarded the affair as significant, for it did not merit so much as a veiled allusion or a footnote in his autobiography. This omission is noteworthy, for even a passing reference to it would certainly have strengthened his case as he catalogued the reasons why his marriage collapsed (as he believed) under the weight of Marilyn's emotional illnesses. Given the lovelessness of the marriage by this time, he may indeed have felt no jealousy at all.

Let's Make Love concluded in June. Only Marilyn's efforts on the production leavened the film, and even they could not redeem it: the film finally sinks under the weight of its own tedium, not to say the egregious lack of imagination in its construction and design.

But Marilyn's rendition of 'My Heart Belongs to Daddy' was a triumph, her platinum hair shimmering against a black background as she seems to breeze through a number that required two weeks of rehearsal. As in the previous trio of films since 1956, her speech is natural, her gestures unmannered and credible, and in another musical number, 'Specialization', her timing is never less than perfect, her phrasing and pauses now instinctively controlled. As Amanda Dell, she was often quizzical, but Marilyn knew how different were confusion and stupidity. 'I liked her very much, whatever our difficulties,' George Cukor said, adding accurately that Marilyn was, after all, 'quite dazzling on the screen, and at the end of the picture very generous to everyone she had worked with.' To Jack Cole especially, Marilyn felt enormously grateful:

> She gave me a little card . . . and inside was a check for $1500, and a note that said, 'I really was awful, it must have been a difficult experience, please go someplace nice for a couple of weeks and act like it all never happened.' It was all very dear. Then two days later I got another card with another check for $500, and the card said, 'Stay three more days' . . . That was her way to say she loved you and didn't want you to feel mad.

By the end of June, Marilyn found herself very much alone, with every variety of sustaining relationship terminated, imperilled or interrupted. Yves returned to his wife in Paris, Arthur to his work with John Huston in Reno, Paula to visit her daughter at work on a film in Europe. At this time, according to Inez Melson, 'there was a childishness about her that made you feel she should be protected from anything that could be harmful to her.'

It was not surprising, therefore, that, during her last month in Los Angeles, Marilyn turned more frequently to one she believed would offer the fatherly, salvific protection she required. On the advice of Marianne Kris, she visited five or six times weekly the Los Angeles psychoanalyst Dr Ralph Greenson, whom she had been seeing irregularly since January.

Like many Hollywood stars with whom he was so popular, whose problems fascinated him and whom he treated in remarkable numbers, Ralph Greenson had changed his name.

Born in Brooklyn on 20 September 1910, Romeo Samuel Greenschpoon was one of twins and the first of four children; his father, then a medical student, insisted that the twin sister be named Juliet. One of the most unlikely of Ralph Greenson's later statements was his assertion that their father loved Shakespeare and romantic stories but was unaware that Romeo and Juliet were lovers who killed themselves. However that may be, the son was fimly convinced that being a premature Romeo with a twin sister Juliet was decisive for his subsequent development.

From childhood, Juliet demonstrated a keen talent for music and became a concert pianist, an achievement Romeo both admired and resented. Her applause, recognition, public acclaim and admiration created an acute sibling rivalry and weighed heavily on him; throughout his life, he attempted (without much success) to excel on the violin. Instead of adopting a musical career, Romeo followed his father, attending college at Columbia University and then the University of Berne, Switzerland, where he took a medical degree in 1934. There he met Hildegard Troesch, whom he married the following year; they had two children, Daniel (later also a psychiatrist) and Joan. While an intern at Cedars of Lebanon Hospital in Los Angeles from 1934 to 1936, he was known as Ralph R. Greenschpoon and then in 1937 legally became Ralph R. Greenson. In 1938 he returned to Europe and underwent Freudian analysis under Otto Fenichel.

After his return to America, Greenson began his military service in November 1942 and was assigned to serve in the medical corps at a veterans' hospital in Canandaigua, New York, until November 1944. The discharge report on Greenson (filed from the Army Air Force Regional Hospital in Scott Field, Illinois, on 21 January 1946) contains an important, detailed clinical summary of a serious incident that occurred in Canandaigua on 13 December 1943. Greenson claimed that while riding in an army ambulance, he suffered a head injury (presumably in a collision), was briefly unconscious and suffered mild amnesia. For several days afterward he exhibited signs of euphoric mania, and when he travelled to Chicago to visit his brother it was determined that Greenson was dragging his left foot and that there was facial nerve damage.

'A private physician was called in,' according to the report. 'The physician advised bed rest and conservatism; however, due to the fact that officer's situation was such as it was, taking American Board of Neurology and Psychiatry [licensing examinations], and due to officer's euphoria, this was not fulfilled.' A Chicago neurologist named Pollack was then summoned, and he found all the classic symptoms of a fractured skull – severe bruising beneath the ear, unequal reflexes in the arms and legs and inability to focus both eyes simultaneously. From the time of the accident, noted the 1946 report, Greenson had completely lost his sense of smell, suffered occasional fits and seizures, exhibited left facial weakness ('quite pronounced at times'), loss of right arm reflexes and faulty co-ordination.

The conclusion of the report was unambiguous: the attending diagnostician hesitated to make any 'definite prognosis as to the future, as often in these cases, very peculiar and unforeseen complications can develop at a later date . . . Other diseases of the nervous system [were observed], manifested by occasional fits secondary to CNS [central nervous system] trauma.'

Disqualified for overseas service, Greenson served as chief of the neuropsychiatric service at the Army Air Force Convalescent Hospital in Fort Logan, Colorado, beginning in November 1944. Promoted to the rank of captain, he then headed the Operational Fatigue Section at the same hospital. Here, he gained the experience he later shared with his friend, the writer Leo Rosten (no relation to Norman), who used the material as the basis for a novel called *Captain Newman, M.D.* In 1945, Greenson petitioned for release from service in order to enter private psychiatric practice in Los Angeles, where (as he claimed in a letter dated 5 December 1945 to military authorities in Washington), there was a community of civilian and veteran psychiatric cases desiring private psychiatric treatment. This request was denied.

Following his discharge in 1946, Greenson (with financial help from a brother-in-law) set up his psychiatric practice in Los Angeles and, in 1947, purchased a home at 902 Franklin Street in Santa Monica, just at the cusp of West Los Angeles. The house had recently been completed after a long construction period by the owners, John and Eunice Murray, who found they could not afford the mortgage; Greenson paid $16,500 for the Mexican-colonial house. Not long after, the Murrays separated (they were divorced in 1950) and Eunice moved to a rented cottage not far from the ocean. The loss of what she called her dream house pitched Eunice Murray into a sense of bereavement so acute that over the years she regularly visited it.

In postwar America, psychoanalysis and psychiatric sessions were very much the vogue – not merely for adults in genuine mental or emotional crisis, but also for those who felt drastic action was needed to resolve life's ordinary demands, and often for those who were merely bored or lonely or self-absorbed and could afford to pay a sympathetic listener. (Chidren who were simply ill-behaved, annoying or precocious were often subjected to long-term therapy, sometimes with disastrous results.) In many large cities across the country, and especially in wealthier communities, daily sessions with one's analyst were a commonplace for those who could afford them.*

Among the board-certified psychoanalysts with medical degrees in Los Angeles County in 1950 was Ralph Greenson, a founding member of the Freudian group known as the Los Angeles Psychoanalytic Society, which had strong personal ties with Anna Freud in London, and with her colleagues in Europe and New York; among his good friends was Marianne Kris, who recommended him to Marilyn Monroe.

---

* The Swedish psychoanalyst Nils Haak wrote extensively on the necessity of high fees, which he (and thousands of colleagues) saw as an integral part of the psychoanalytic process because of the sacrifice involved. The belief that what is cheap is of little value is deeply rooted in human society, Haak argued, adding that the payment of large sums prevent the patient from feeling infantile and the analyst from feeling merely kind and undercompensated for all the sufferings he is asked to attend.

All during the 1950s, Greenson's Los Angeles practice thrived: to his office in Beverly Hills came many celebrities as well as the merely rich of the county's west side, and he cultivated a reputation as a popular lecturer before professionals and layfolk. Greenson was, as his wife Hildi wrote in an introduction to his collected lectures, 'a charismatic speaker who loved teaching, enjoyed his audience and rarely missed an opportunity to engage a group in dialogue.' His manner at such events was perfectly attuned to the entertainment capital of the world: Hildi recalled that

> Romi [short for Romeo] always mounted the platform or approached the lectern with quick, bouncy steps and obvious pleasure ... When I once marveled that he never seemed nervous, his characteristic reply was, 'Why should I be nervous? Just think, these lucky people get to hear *me*' ... His gestures were dynamic and his voice would rise to a passionate pitch or break into a helpless chuckle over his own joke. He gave full vent to his own emotions ... [and] his audience was never bored.

He was, in other words, as much a showman as anything else, in a way (as some colleagues believed) eager for the applause and notoriety once accorded only to Juliet. This at least partly accounts for his increasingly direct involvement in the business of Hollywood. Represented by his brother-in-law, the noted lawyer Milton Rudin (who was married to the younger Greenschpoon sister, Elizabeth), Greenson received a healthy 12½ per cent of the gross receipts of the film version of *Captain Newman, M.D.* – whose title character, as Greenson wrote to Leo Rosten in September 1961, was himself, just as 90 per cent of the patients were based on his own during the war. Greenson was also closely connected to a number of film studios, where he met several executives and producers who became patients; similarly, for his articles and interviews in magazines, he sometimes engaged Leo Rosten as 'producer'.

The catalogue of Greenson's articles and lectures reveals the extent to which he sought more than professional endorsement: he longed to reach the widest possible lay audience, too, and this encouraged him to popularize and even sometimes to trivialize serious issues. Among the titles of his collected lectures were 'Emotional Involvement', 'Why Men Like War', 'Sex Without Passion', 'Sophie Portnoy Finally Answers Back', 'The Devil Made Me Do It, Dr Freud', and 'People In Search of a Family', which (as his wife rightly noted) 'concerned a need Romi found in his patients which echoed his own partly unconscious desire to make people he cared about a member of his family. It was his foster-home fantasy of a haven where all hurts are mended.' Sterner critics believed that many of the papers he wrote were delivered for the purpose of getting attention (and thus new clients) – appeals for applause rather than serious creative work.

Greenson was for years clinical professor of psychiatry at the UCLA Medical School and a training and supervising analyst at the Los Angeles Psychoanalytic Society and Institute. It is no exaggeration to say that throughout his career – apart from whatever benefits he may have offered his private patients – Greenson was known in Southern California as a beguiling performer who kept audiences nicely entertained.

Dr Benson Schaeffer, who was working with autistic children at the Neuropsychiatric Institute during Greenson's tenure at UCLA, expressed the common impression of Greenson after attending a seminar and hearing a public lecture: 'He wanted to amuse and be thought clever. Frankly, I saw no overwhelming depth in the man. He seemed more shrewd and canny than profound.'

'Only later,' said another local colleague, 'was it clear to many of us just how shallow he was' – a judgement readily confirmed by reference to his papers and articles. These are too often popular to the point of frivolity; a cursory reading of the material is sufficient to reveal how much 'pop psychology' this physician generated. Indeed, he might not have won so many

ardent disciples or such fervent respect anywhere but in Hollywood, where to challenge is too often to court disfavour, and to
coddle is to secure virtually undying devotion. Anna Freud's
biographer, who liked and respected Greenson, nevertheless
described him accurately as 'a hard-living man of passionate enthusiasm and even flamboyance, a man for whom
psychoanalysis was – as Anna Freud thought it should be, and
as it was for her entire friendship circle – a way of life.'

This way of life did not preclude presentations of issues that
were frequently sprinkled with appalling generalities unworthy
of a serious therapist and more suited to talk shows:

From 'People in Search of a Family', 1978:

People who search for families try to undo the effects of a bad
family life. It is an acting out to replace the unhappy past with
a happy future. Family life is good for your health.

From 'Misunderstandings of Psychoanalysis', 1955:

Children are complicated and people are complicated. But I
don't feel it is hopeless at all.

From 'Special Problems in Psychotherapy with the Rich and
Famous', 1978:

The movie actor or actress is not a star until he is instantly recognizable not only by his peers but by the world at large . . .
I have found the impatience of the budding star and the fad-
ing film stars to be the most difficult with whom I have tried
to work.

But perhaps most surprising of all was Greenson's contradiction of a fundamental tenet of psychiatry, not to say all medical
ethics and practice: 'Psychiatrists and physicians,' he said (in a
lecture called 'Drugs in the Psychotherapeutic Situation' at the
UCLA Center for the Health Sciences in 1964), 'must be willing

to become emotionally involved with their patients if they hope to establish a reliable therapeutic relationship.' This universally condemned position would be crucial, not to say downright harmful, in the case of Marilyn Monroe.

Like many in his field at that time, Greenson relied heavily on drug therapy as an adjunct to psychotherapy, routinely prescribing (or asking his patients' physicians to prescribe) barbiturates or popular tranquillizers of the day (Librium, for example) in an effort to ease patients' crises or to please them. In this regard, Anna Freud's biographer documented Greenson's treatment of Ernst Freud, Sigmund's son, who suffered severe migraine headaches: he prescribed massive doses of tranquillizers, even at that time too facile a response to a condition whose causes are still poorly understood.

Whatever his private crises and difficulties, Ralph Greenson was the soul of serenity in public. At a UCLA symposium called 'The Good Life', he sat debating with three clergymen when a sudden storm brought a thunderclap and a power failure. Electricity was restored after a moment, and, 'Please note,' he announced triumphantly, 'that I am the only speaker still sitting down.' His wife, touchingly loyal, incongruously wrote that 'his self-assurance had scored a point for psychoanalysis.' Or for egotism.

But of all Greenson's interests, it was the nature and burden of fame that seems to have most intrigued him and celebrities to whom he was most attracted. This was a recurring theme in his life's work, and in 'Special Problems in Psychotherapy With the Rich and Famous', he described his experiences with Marilyn Monroe – a period of his professional and personal life which became an obsession. In this paper, Greenson did not, of course, mention her or anyone else by name: with so many details, that was hardly necessary.

Greenson wrote of a famous and beautiful, thirty-four-year-old actress lacking self-esteem who was already being treated by an East Coast colleague. For her first appointment with him, she arrived half an hour late, with the excuse that she was typically tardy for appointments. In response to his inquiry, she then described her early life, giving special emphasis to Grace's passion for her to be a movie star. Although she had not completed high school, Greenson found her intelligent, with a love of poetry, theatre and classical music. Her husband had undertaken to educate her, she said; for this she was grateful, but the life of the housewife bored her. He then said he would see her regularly at his office or at his home, which, he said, would not attract public attention.

This was an astonishingly illogical suggestion. Access to Greenson's consulting room at his Santa Monica home was through the front door; his family lived there with him, and his young daughter at once noticed the new, famous patient and was subsequently asked to befriend her – hardly a mechanism to deflect attention. In fact, Greenson was pleased and proud to have so celebrated a client, and from late 1960 to the end of her life, one of the terrible miscalculations in his treatment of Marilyn Monroe was the extent to which he brought her into his home and made her a member of his family. Any vigilant psychiatric community or university department would have instantly challenged him on this and threatened professional censure.

His tactic was disastrous: instead of leading his patient to independence, he did exactly the opposite and effectively made her entirely dependent on himself. He was not a Svengali, he told Marilyn's studio colleagues not long before her death, but he was certain he could prevail on her to do anything he wished. His disclaimer notwithstanding, Greenson's words could indeed have been uttered by poor Trilby's mesmeric teacher.

And so, from early 1960, Marilyn Monroe consulted Ralph Greenson five times a week when she was in Los Angeles. 'I was going to be her one and only therapist,' he wrote proudly in a letter to Marianne Kris, describing her as 'so pathetic, such a perpetual orphan that I felt even sorrier and she tried so hard and failed so often, which also made her pathetic.' These sentiments are remarkable, for they betray Greenson's complete lack of professional distance and his dangerous emotional involvement: finding a patient 'pathetic', 'feeling sorry' for her and judging her to have 'failed so often' are phrases more characteristic of a wounded parent or a smug teacher than a sensible counsellor committed to the mental health of his patient.

Even his diction became fractured when Greenson tried to write of Marilyn Monroe, and in time he lost all discretion with her. Nevertheless, in addition to five and eventually seven meetings weekly ('mainly because she was lonely and had no one to see her, nothing to do if I didn't see her'), he encouraged her to telephone each day – a strategy he undertook, he said in his essay, so that she would understand his values and translate them into the things she needed to survive in the world of film acting.

As summer began, Marilyn described herself tersely: 'I'm thirty-four years old, I've been dancing for six months [in *Let's Make Love*], I've had no rest, I'm exhausted. Where do I go from here?'

In fact she already had the answer: to New York for meetings and wardrobe tests for *The Misfits*, which was at last being rushed into production in July after several delays. This she undertook despite a persistent pain in her right side and frequent bouts of severe indigestion that interrupted her uneasily achieved sleep, to which she could return only by taking more sleeping pills. These were easily obtained through several doctors, especially her Los Angeles physician, Hyman Engelberg. He had been recommended to Marilyn by Ralph Greenson, who told him, 'You're both narcissists, and I think you'll get along fine together.' Very quickly, Engelberg fulfilled a specific function for Greenson, who persuaded the internist to 'prescribe medication for her . . . so that I had nothing to do with the actual handling of medication. I only talked about it with her and he kept me informed.' Here, someone might have observed, lay dragons.

On 18 July, en route to Nevada, Marilyn arrived in Los Angeles for a session with Greenson, an appointment with Engelberg and a date with Yves Montand, who was working on a second American film and with whom her relationship was still occasionally intimate.

Two days later, clutching a purseful of medication for pain and insomnia, she arrived in Nevada. There already was her 'family', as she called them – her coach (Paula Strasberg), her masseur (Ralph Roberts), her secretary (May Reis), her personal makeup artist (Allan Snyder), her hairdresser (Agnes Flanagan), an expert at full body makeup (Bunny Gardel), her wardrobe supervisor (Sherlee Strahm) and her driver (Rudy Kautzky, borrowed from the Carey Limousine Company). She would need all this support and more: while the making of *Let's Make Love* had been described as an ordeal, the making of *The Misfits* would be an undiluted horror, not even remotely justified by the final product.

Perhaps no motion picture in history was ever realized without complications: production files are usually chronicles of delays, illnesses, unforeseen difficulties due to weather, sudden changes in the schedules of cast and crew, budget problems, and often uneasy relations between actors and directors, the legendary temperaments of stars and the countless details dependent on a successful interplay of many arts and crafts. The meticulous Alfred Hitchcock foresaw almost every eventuality of the process, enjoyed as much control as any director and suffered no fools gladly, yet towards the end of his life, he expressed his amazement that any movie was ever made at all, by anyone: 'I have lived,' he said, ' in a constant state of astonishment that we ever completed even one picture. So much can go wrong, and it usually does.'

The films of Marilyn Monroe were no exception, and from 1953 her co-workers had to deal with chronic fears that led to habitual lateness. They put up with her unpunctuality because she brought so much effort to her work, because the result was invariably rewarding, and because she was, paradoxically, among the least temperamental actresses: there is no record of a public display of anger against an actor or director, no outburst of pride or contempt. Demanding of producers and technicians only a measure of the expertise she required of herself, she knew what was at stake with each picture; and because, like all performing artists, she knew how much she needed acclaim, she worked ceaselessly to merit public loyalty. This résumé deserves emphasis for a consideration of her twenty-ninth and final film, which asked everything of her except what she was most equipped to give – her unique, highly imaginative talent and a special gift for subtle and sophisticated comedy.

As shooting began, the screenplay of *The Misfits* was far from complete, despite three years of work, several drafts and re-drafts and a detailed outline. Two things were soon clear, however.

First, the film was based on Miller's own experience when he came to Nevada to fulfil a residency requirement for his divorce from Mary Grace Slattery. During those months of 1956, he had met a crew of cowboys who captured mustangs – wild horses once trained for use as children's ponies but now sold for butchering as dog food. For Miller, these men were as much misfits as the animals they considered useless. 'Westerns and the West,' according to Miller, 'have always been built on a morally balanced world where evil has a recognizable tag – the black hats – and evil always loses out in the end. This is that same world, but it's been dragged out of the nineteenth century into today, when the good guy is also part of the problem.' His story and scenario would be, he said, 'about our lives' meaninglessness and maybe how we got to where we are.'

This was perhaps a noble theme, but he lacked the necessary components of a good story: characters with sufficient history or 'back story' to make them credible; a narrative with issues compelling and relevant for an audience; and above all a clear emotional sensibility that would engage and entertain, quite apart from exalted or academic theses. The script, as Miller and Huston continued to hammer away at page after page, was full of grand but disconnected rhetoric about rugged individualism, the contemporary lack of intimacy and communication, the decline of the West and the nature of the American conscience. But a screenplay is composed of more than ideas, and in *The Misfits* very little happens. People wander about, go to bars, drink too much, drive through the desert, go to a rodeo, rope and capture horses – but mostly they mumble arid aphorisms ('Maybe we're not supposed to remember other people's promises . . . Nothin' can live unless somethin' dies . . . I can't get off the ground and I can't get up to God'). There is something tediously literary about the tone of this screenplay.

'This is an attempt at the ultimate motion picture,' said Arthur's friend and former editor Frank Taylor, who was dragooned on to the project as producer. But with such self-consciousness surrounding everyone – and in a setting where summer temperatures peaked at 120° by day – the endeavour was perhaps futile from the start.

The second issue was even more problematic. When Miller began *The Misfits* in 1957, he was a man in love, touched by his wife's emotional alliance with nature, her love of children and animals, her appreciation of gardening, of flowers, and her general sensitivity to life, of which he saw her as a ripe representative. By 1960, his attitude was considerably different. The film to star the writer's wife was now planned as a black and white picture that clearly reflected his bitterness and resentment. For Marilyn Monroe, this was the great betrayal of her life (thus far) – the public exposure of private grief.

The Misfits would reveal Arthur's feelings to all the world, and Marilyn had to convey them – and in no uncertain terms, for Arthur gave her character, Roslyn, dialogue lifted straight from the story of Marilyn Monroe, from childhood to her divorce from Joe DiMaggio and her subsequent meeting with an older man with whom there is only a tentative future. Even the house in which they talk and eat and love is unfinished: it is a replica of the unfinished Miller house in Roxbury, transplanted fictionally to Nevada for the real-life couple about to be divorced. And to play the role of the man who slaughters horses for dogmeat, Miller chose none other than Marilyn's childhood idol, Clark Gable – 'the man I thought of as my father', as she had said since childhood. Miller even abbreviated the actor's name for the character's: Gable was 'Gay'. At the fadeout they drive along a starlit road toward a (possibly vegetarian?) future.

Gay/Gable's sidekick was named Guido, for the actor chosen – Eli Wallach, a friend of Marilyn from the Actors Studio – was famous for his portrait of the Italo-American 'Alvaro' in Tennessee Williams's *The Rose Tattoo*. As the script was rewritten each day, and as Arthur's resentment against Marilyn increased, it was given to Wallach to read the last angry speech against Marilyn/Roslyn:

She's crazy. They're all crazy. You try not to believe that because you need them. She's crazy! You struggle, you build, you try, you turn yourself inside out for them. But it's never enough. So they put the spurs to you. I know, I've got the marks. I know this racket, I just forgot what I knew for a little while.

And the third cowboy, Perce, was to be played by Montgomery Clift, far more addicted to drugs and alcohol than Marilyn, a tortured homosexual whose face had been smashed in an auto accident and who suffered a lifelong neurotic relationship with his mother – and was given lines like 'My face is fine, Mom – all healed up – good as new.' It was just as Taylor predicted (indeed, warned) at the outset: 'Each of the players *is* the person they play.' Even the helpful, devoted masseur Ralph Roberts was handed a cameo, as an alert ambulance driver.

So much was evident from Marilyn's first scene, filmed on 21 July in the cramped bedroom of a Reno boarding house. With the director, cameraman, crew and actors wilting in the heat, Thelma Ritter played Isabelle, a landlady very like Grace's Aunt Minnie (who sheltered Norma Jeane when she came to Reno for her divorce from Jim Dougherty). In the scene, she coaches Marilyn, the forlorn nightclub performer now late for her court

appearance, nervously and hastily applying makeup as she re-
hearses her remarks for the judge.

Marilyn's lines in her first scene are lifted straight from the
pages of the DiMaggio divorce plea:

Ritter/Isabelle: '"Did your husband act toward you with
cruelty?"'

Marilyn/Roslyn: '"Yes."'

Isabelle: '"In what way did this cruelty manifest itself?"'

Roslyn: '"He persistently" – how does that go again?' She
cannot remember the lines.

Isabelle: '"He persistently and cruelly ignored my personal
wishes and my rights and resorted on several occasions to
physical violence against me."'

Roslyn: '"He persistently" – oh, do I have to say that? Why
can't I just say, "He wasn't there"? – I mean, you could touch
him, but he wasn't there.'

From this point, Marilyn gave a performance remarkable for
its acute yet controlled pain.

'At least you had your mother,' remarks Isabelle to Roslyn,
who replies, 'How do you have somebody who disappears all
the time? They both weren't there. She'd go off with a patient
for three months' – an exact summary of Gladys and her last
marriage, to fellow-patient John Eley. None of this could have
been easy for a woman who so carefully masked her private
pain; perhaps it was especially mortifying for her to enact a
scene in which Clark Gable asked, 'What makes you so sad? I
think you're the saddest girl I ever met,' to which she had to reply, 'No one ever said that to me before.' These were, after all,
the very words spoken by Arthur to Marilyn not long before
they married.

Rupert Allan, present for the shooting, recalled that Marilyn
was

desperately unhappy at having to read lines written by Miller
that were so obviously documenting the real-life Marilyn.
Just when she might have expected some support, she was

miserable. She felt she had never had a success. She felt lonely, isolated, abandoned, worthless, that she had nothing more to offer but this naked, wounded self. And all of us who were her 'family,' – well, we did what a family tried to do. But we had jobs connected to the picture, and it was the picture that was her enemy.

Had there been doubt in the minds of anyone on the production (or later in the audience), Miller and Huston made everything clear: on the inside of Gay/Gable's closet door are taped a collection of photographs of Marilyn Monroe in earlier roles and poses: 'Don't look at those,' Roslyn tells Guido. 'They're nothing. Gay just put them up for a joke.' Which did not, to Marilyn, seem very amusing at all.

Sam Shaw, who had been present from the genesis of the project, added that Arthur's great love was for a script he insisted on changing and changing some more, to suit his shifting feelings about Marilyn, while her great love was for the character of Roslyn, for the integrity of the role. 'But the character was just never realized, he never gave it to her. She fought and fought, but Arthur was unyielding, unbending.' Added Norman Rosten, one of Arthur's oldest friends, 'Miller's was the triumph of intelligence over feeling. It may turn out that Miller was less the artist than she.'

If Arthur was asking Marilyn to relive her past, he was also requiring her to prepare for the future. During location shooting, the Millers moved from their shared suite to separate rooms, apparently because Marilyn could not bear what had happened to her role: she had for months been begging her husband at least to make Roslyn a whole character, with speeches that were not mere declamations. By early August, everyone on *The Misfits* knew that the star and the writer were barely speaking, that they did not drive out to the desert or lake locations together, that Paula transmitted messages from one to the other, and that some kind of relationship was developing between

Arthur and Inge Morath, one of the photographers assigned to document the film.

The Misfits was, then, an apt title. No one was surprised that Marilyn, who was given the privilege of a noontime first call on most days, was habitually late even for that, but she had solid, objective reason. Every night, Arthur rewrote entire scenes, handed to her as she went to bed or on awakening – a situation that threw her into panic. 'I have not really helped her as an actress,' he admitted after the fact. Marilyn was confused: 'I never really know exactly what's expected of me.'

By mid-summer, she was in agony, her upper abdominal pain severely aggravated and her ability to digest food impaired: now, before the first take of every day, she was violently sick. Her co-star was her comforter on this picture: as if filling the old father fantasy, Clark Gable was the most patient actor on the team.

On at least one occasion, Gable marched her back to her hotel room, for she was truly, perhaps dangerously ill. 'But I promised John [Huston]!' she cried. 'I said I would be there!' She returned to the crew soon after and did her scene – with Gable leading the applause afterward. He had acted in five films with Jean Harlow and compared them favourably as comediennes, adding that 'Harlow was always very relaxed, but this girl is high-strung, and she worries more – about her lines, her appearance, her performance. She's constantly trying to improve as an actress.'

But there was not much material with which to make that improvement. As Miller rewrote Roslyn, she expressed her dismay at the capture of mustangs and their imminent slaughter not by dialogue or reasoning with the men, but 'by throwing a fit', as she said later.

I guess they thought I was too dumb to explain anything, so I have a fit – a screaming, crazy fit. I mean *nuts*. And to think, Arthur did this to me. He was supposed to be writing this for me, but he says it's his movie. I don't think he even wanted me in it. I guess it's all over between us. We have to stay with each other because it would be bad for the film if we split up now. Arthur's been complaining to Huston about me, and that's why Huston treats me like an idiot with his 'dear this' and 'dear that.' Why doesn't he treat me like a normal actress? I wish he'd give me the same attention he gives those gambling machines.

'I am supposed to work six days a week,' she told a reporter, 'but it's just too much. It takes me two days to recover and regain my strength and spirit. I used to work six days, but I was younger then.' Of this time she said later,

I had to use my wits, or else I'd have been sunk – and nothing's going to sink me ... Everyone was always pulling at me, tugging at me, as if they wanted a piece of me. It was always, 'Do this, do that,' and not just on the job but off, too ... God, I've tried to stay intact, whole.

With the external discomforts of summer in Nevada, the internal turmoil of a collapsed marriage and a diminishing sense of purpose, the inelegance of the script, the shallowness of her role, the macho posturing of John Huston and the meagre reserves of courage she had every day to summon even in the best of circumstances, Marilyn's conduct was remarkable (all protestations from Miller and Huston to the contrary notwithstanding). 'She had considerable anxiety,' recalled Kevin McCarthy, who had the small role of Roslyn's husband, 'but like a wise child she used it.'

Nor, until late August, was Marilyn robbed of her humour and alertness to others' needs. When autograph seekers recognized her one afternoon, she quickly grabbed a player's wig, slapped it on her head and replied to their question with a faked voice: 'I'm Mitzi Gaynor!' Immediately after her stand-in Evelyn Moriarty completed several rehearsals of the cues for Marilyn's screaming scene (in which she berates the men for their inhumane treatment of animals and their contempt for life), Marilyn was waiting with hot tea, honey and lemon for her. And for a scene in which she was to be awakened from a night's sleep by Gable, Marilyn allowed the sheet to drop so far as to reveal one naked breast. 'Cut!' called Huston with a yawn. 'I've seen 'em before!'

'Oh, John,' said Marilyn, 'let's get people away from the television sets. I love to do things the censors won't pass. After all, what are we here for, just to stand around and let it pass us by? Gradually they'll let down the censorship – though probably not in my lifetime.'

Huston was a hard-drinking egoist with, as his daughter Anjelica said, 'a mean streak' that often led him to endanger the safety of his cast. During the filming of *Moby Dick* in 1955, Huston's obsession for realism kept his players amid a perilous storm off the Welsh coast. Leo Genn fell twenty feet in a squall and was placed in a body cast for seven weeks, and Richard Basehart was severely injured when Huston kept his cameras rolling despite thunderous waves.

Even more danger was endured by Gregory Peck, twice near death from his director's demand that he be lashed to the side of a two-ton, ninety-foot-long rubber whale during a rolling fog: the towlines snapped, the channel waves rose to fifteen feet and Peck slipped into the sea. Only a sudden windbreak pulled him out for air – but the fog was so thick no one could spot the actor, who somehow survived. Later, the scene was recreated at the Elstree Studios near London, in an 80,000-gallon tank with sixty-mile-an-hour wind machines. Bound to the sculpted beast, Peck was pummelled by streams of water. 'I want you with your eyes staring open as you slowly come out of the sea on that whale's back,' said Huston.

Always patient and co-operative, Peck took the challenge. 'What I didn't know,' he later recalled, 'was that the winch they were using to rotate the section I was tied to was hand-operated and had once jammed. I could have come up dead, which I think would have secretly pleased John – providing the last touch of realism he was after.' Similar episodes occurred throughout the making of John Huston's films: he was a director often praised for his realism and ability to dramatize literary properties. Gable was aware of Huston's methods when he signed to do *The Misfits*, and over $800,000 of the film's $3.5 million budget was for this actor's salary.

During a career spanning three decades and dozens of films, Clark Gable was proud of rejecting stunt doubles and performing his own heavy-action sequences. His antics in *China Seas* (1935) were typical: where a steamroller comes loose during a scene and threatens the lives of several bystanders, the decision was made to have Gable's stand-in rush forward to secure the machine. But the star announced to his startled director, 'I'm doing this one myself.' And so he did, earning the cheers of cast and crew.

Gable was, then, ready to be dragged four hundred feet by a truck moving at thirty-five miles an hour, to simulate being dragged by a horse. His stunt double could easily have been summoned, but Gable was insistent, ignoring the welts, bruises and cuts that resulted despite his heavy padding. He also repeated several takes in which he was asked to sprint a hundred yards, and his friend Ernie Dunlevie recalled his complete exhaustion for a scene in which he lifted two cement blocks for Marilyn to use as porch steps: 'They must've shot that scene twelve to fifteen times, and it wasn't a fake block.' Montgomery Clift fared ill, too: his hands were lacerated and bleeding after he was forced to throw a mare bare-handed with a rope.

Gable was at first patient – but not with the frank sadism which seemed to prevail during a scene in which a stallion was to attack his double. The director and representatives of both the producers' insurance companies and the Humane Society required a trained roper, and a man named Jim Palen was submitted to the hazardous ordeal of lying on the salt flats in front of a camera while the stallion reared back, hooves smashing down for the take in which Gay was to be battered by the raging animal. For two takes, Palen barely escaped serious injury – and on the third, the horse smashed his face. The man reeled, spitting blood – but when it was clear that he had suffered no broken bones, Huston called for another take. The hardy Gable, hitherto the director's macho sidekick, left the scene in disgust: 'You can all go to hell,' he announced. 'I've got news for you – I ain't no friend of you boys.' Later he told his wife Kay, 'They don't care if they live or die. What surprised me is that no one gave a damn if *I* got killed or not. We were never allowed to take chances when the studios had us under contract. I was curious if Huston would try to stop me. Hell, no – he was delighted!'

In the most appalling heat (even hardy local cowboys were fainting), Huston asked Marilyn for dozens of takes even when she was satisfied after merely several: she was soon convinced that he and Arthur were punishing her for her lateness, for her displeasure with the script, for her open criticism of its structure and characterization – not to say the humiliation she felt at having to play Roslyn. Arthur continued to hand her new pages of script each night to memorize by morning; she was awake through the small hours trying to learn them; and no one was surprised when, nervous and exhausted, she increased her dosages of sleeping pills and could be awakened only after the considerable efforts of Paula Strasberg, Rupert Allan or Allan Snyder.

As *The Misfits* careened toward disaster, it was not Marilyn's intransigence or chemical dependence that imperilled the production: the decisive sabotage was effected by John Huston himself, who was in the grip of serious addictions that endangered everyone on the project. For one thing, he would not stop the chain smoking that gave him a hacking cough, or the drinking that clouded his judgement, and filming was shut down on at least three occasions when he collapsed with bronchitis or the emphysema that compromised his breathing and, years later, eventually killed him.

But another grave matter was neatly summed up by Arthur, his staunchest ally: the director 'had begun staying up all night at the craps table, losing immense sums and winning them back and showing his mettle that way' – and then falling asleep in his chair during filming, unaware, when he awoke, what scene was being played out. 'Chaos was on us all,' according to Arthur. 'But I like to gamble,' said Huston in defence of his habit, as if he were saying, 'I like to go fishing on weekends.' Even to reporters he was similarly blasé: 'Well, I ran into trouble last night. Went downstairs and dropped a thousand.' (His schedule, according to one journalist, had him at the dice tables from eleven at night to five in the morning.)

In his autobiography, Huston was frank about the matter: 'I spent a lot of my nights in the downstairs casino . . . There was mostly craps, blackjack and roulette . . . I had a marvelous time losing my ass one night and winning it back the next.' But losses prevailed, and Huston frequently fell ill from hard living. 'The telltale sign that he was feeling better,' wrote one biographer, 'was his return to the casino.'

Huston's fierce gambling was not, as some have claimed, the director's diversion from the problems of working with a temperamental star. Before Marilyn arrived on the picture, Huston had already established a credit line at the Mapes Hotel casino and was betting hundreds each night. Within ten days his stakes had reached to ten and twenty thousand a night: according to the production's archivist, Huston put all his spare cash on the dice tables, winning, risking, gaining and tossing away enormous sums of money – 'losing steadily but with no apparent regard for how much.' When Marilyn saw that this happened nightly, and that her director was sleeping while she was in turmoil over her performance, the result was predictable: she retreated further. Denied the support of her husband-screenwriter and deprived of rudimentary directorial courtesy, she was a lost soul. She was neither amused nor flattered when Huston invited her to gamble one evening; trying to play the good sport, she shook the dice and turned to Huston.

'What should I ask for, John?'

His reply was typical. 'Don't think, honey, just throw. That's the story of your life. Don't think, do it.'

Chaos continued to bedevil *The Misfits*. Paula Strasberg, who was now being paid $3000 per week, seemed dazed, but no one knew that Paula was in the first stages of the bone marrow cancer that took six years to kill her. As Susan recalled, Paula was already taking massive doses of narcotics, secretly stashed in her carry-all. In fact her only concern was Marilyn's welfare, as even Huston had to agree: 'I think we're doing Paula a disservice,' he told his secretary. 'For all we know, she's holding this picture together.' In an important way, she was, simply by being ever available to Marilyn.

Meanwhile, pills for Marilyn were flown in every other day, supplied by her Los Angeles doctors.* Ralph Roberts and Rupert Allan, who shared the responsibility for soothing companionship with Marilyn, were surprised when Ralph Greenson wrote a prescription for 300 milligrams of Nembutal (trade name for the barbiturate pentobarbital sodium) each night; the normal dose for insomnia, then as later, is 100 milligrams for a maximum of two weeks, after which tolerance develops and the drug's effectiveness diminishes. Serious poisoning and even death can occur after ingesting anything more than two grams.

In addition, local physicians provided supplements – even to the extent of injections. Nor did Miller intervene: 'I was almost completely out of her life by now.' And with these drugs, Marilyn's depression was aggravated, her confusion increased, her speech was often incoherent and her gait unsteady. She suffered dreadful nightmares, her moods vacillated unpredictably, she broke out in rashes – and still Marilyn worked each afternoon. As Rupert Allan remembered, she would step away to perforate Seconal capsules with a pin before washing them down; this method of accelerating the effect could have been lethal.

'It took so long to get her going in the morning that usually I

---

* As Arthur Miller knew, 'doctors had gone along with her demands for new and stronger sleeping pills even though they knew perfectly well how dangerous this was. . . . there were always new doctors willing to help her into oblivion.'

had to make her up while she lay in her bed,' recalled Allan Snyder.

> Girls on the crew would have to put her in the shower to wake her up. All of us who loved her knew that things were coming apart something terrible. We felt an awful despair. And still Arthur continued to make the character of Roslyn worse and worse, and Marilyn knew it.

Yet somehow she managed to complete her scenes, and on 10 August the film was only two days behind schedule.

Then, on 16 August, John Huston dropped $16,000 at the dice table – a loss precipitating one of the most demeaning fictions attached to the life of Marilyn Monroe. The $16,000 brought Huston's total gambling losses to over $50,000, far beyond what the production company of *The Misfits* had agreed to offer as an aggregate sum for casino credit to him and the entire company. At the same time, the cash outlay for the production had been enormous, and when Max Youngstein, vice-president of United Artists, came to visit the shooting, it was clear that Huston had gone too far. At that precise moment, both the Mapes Hotel casino and Harrah's were calling in the debt.

There was only one solution: Huston had to raise quick cash. The alternative was for the production to be indefinitely shut down, for the weekly payrolls could not otherwise be dispensed. Thus began a series of quietly frantic telephone calls from Huston to friends in San Francisco. Filming continued on a day-to-day basis, and for the moment no one was aware of the imminent crisis. Huston had boasted that 'the one great lesson in gambling is that money doesn't mean a goddamn thing,' but he was now disabused of this conviction.

On Saturday 20 August, Marilyn flew to Los Angeles, as she often did when she had a free weekend during production. She consulted Greenson and Engelberg on these visits, obtained her medications and prescriptions and, on at least two occasions, met Montand, then nearing completion of his new film. But he was required at the studio on the twentieth, and they could not meet. This Marilyn understood, and in any case she was preoccupied with the purchase of a new gown for the world premiere of *Let's Make Love*, which was to be held in Reno. That mission accomplished, she slept soundly at the Beverly Hills Hotel and on Sunday morning returned to Nevada, where the premiere had to be cancelled because of a power failure. Ralph Roberts and May Reis had accompanied her on the trip.

The gossips, however, were working at full tilt, and that Sunday, Montand gave an interview to Hedda Hopper in which she pressed him for details about his relationship with Marilyn. 'I think she is an enchanting child,' he responded,

> a simple girl without any guile. Perhaps I was too tender and thought maybe she was sophisticated, like some of the other ladies I have known. I did everything I could to make things easier for her when I realized that mine was a very small part. The only thing that could stand out in my performance was my love scenes, so naturally I did everything I could to make them realistic.

His statement was meant for the benefit of his wife, whom he was soon to rejoin, as Marilyn knew full well; still, they were ungallant words, not to say oozing Gallic condescension.

With the publication of Hedda Hopper's column the following week, there were again headlines about a lurid romance gone wrong; these were imaginatively hooked up to the difficulties on *The Misfits*, and soon newspapers and magazines were trumpeting Marilyn's near collapse over the end of a relationship as well as the hardships of the summer's filming. And this would provide John Huston with his safety net.

As the production files and published history of *The Misfits* make clear, Marilyn was back at work on Monday 22 August, joking with colleagues and apparently refreshed from two consecutive nights of uninterrupted sleep. The next day she worked painstakingly with still photographers, rejecting some prints for publication and approving others; and on the twenty-fourth, twenty-fifth and twenty-sixth she appeared in difficult sequences (at the rodeo with crowds, and in scenes with Gable), all of which required many retakes.

Then, on Thursday 25 August, Max Youngstein informed John Huston that *The Misfits* bank account was dry as the Nevada desert. The director had not come up with enough cash to cover his gambling debts, and filming would have to be suspended for a week until corporate meetings at United Artists in New York and Los Angeles approved additional payments for the production. Huston asked that no immediate announcement be made to the cast; he would, however, inform Arthur and Marilyn, who were investors.

Marilyn took advantage of the shutdown to travel to Los Angeles for a long weekend – to see her doctors; to visit Joe Schenck, who was seriously ill and soon to die; and to attend a dinner party. Huston, who drove her to the Reno airport, seized on her departure for his own benefit. He contacted Greenson and Engelberg, told them of their patient's barbiturate problem and unstable conduct, and asked that she be admitted to a private clinic for a week's rest. The doctors agreed to co-operate. And as an eyewitness recalled, Huston, having put Marilyn on the plane, 'returned from the airport cheerfully humming "Venezuela", and repaired to the casinos where he won three thousand at craps.'

Far from collapsing on arrival, as Huston predicted would happen (and doubtless hoped), Marilyn checked into the Beverly Hills Hotel and attended the scheduled dinner party at the home of Doris Warner Vidor, recently widowed wife of the director Charles Vidor. On Sunday evening, 28 August, she met Greenson and Engelberg, who advised her about the picture's temporary shutdown and counselled a week's rest – but not at the hotel, they said. United Artists' insurance company would cover her stay at a comfortable private hospital, and it is a measure of her willing submission to their persuasive arguments that Marilyn was that evening admitted to the Westside Hospital on La Cienega Boulevard. Huston and company now had time to barter for cash.

Meanwhile, Arthur and *The Misfits* crew in Nevada were unaware of Marilyn's whereabouts.* On Monday morning, the entire company was summoned to a meeting, at which the producer Frank Taylor announced that Marilyn had suffered a breakdown and the film was suspended for a week. 'And with that,' as Evelyn Moriarty remembered,

Arthur Miller got up and stormed out – he knew, as we all did, that this was a ruse. Of course she had troubles, we knew that, too. But Marilyn was being blamed for everything. All of her problems were exaggerated to cover up for Huston's gambling and the terrible waste of money on that production. It was so easy for her to be made the scapegoat.

'When the press learned of Marilyn's "breakdown," of course they created a sensation,' as Ralph Roberts recalled. On Monday, after a call from a lonely Marilyn, he drove to Los Angeles with Lee and Susan Strasberg; May Reis and Rupert Allan were already in attendance there. 'We all went to visit her,' according to Ralph, who remembered that Rupert wished to buy a stack of magazines for Marilyn but did not because her face was on most of them, with lurid stories about her and Yves.

Rupert Allan and Ralph Roberts agreed. Marilyn's confinement to hospital had been accomplished with the co-operation of physicians who danced to Huston's tune, and also saw the personal and financial value in attending their famous patient for a week. To be sure, she had an underlying barbiturate habit that deserved attention, but these same doctors were keeping

---

* Two days later, James Goode wrote in his production diary: 'August 27 – No shooting. Marilyn is ill and has flown to Los Angeles for medical treatment. No one has said why.'

her well supplied with the drugs – actions that even in 1960 were at least careless and at worst downright unethical.

So it was that John Huston's secretary said to Evelyn Moriarty on Monday, 'Don't worry, we'll all be back at work next week' – which they were, on Monday 5 September. Two conflicting realities thus prevailed. On the one hand, Marilyn frequently delayed filming, as did the horses in the film, and the uncertain weather and Nevada's cloudy skies. But on the other hand is the fact that her pill-taking habits were not so critical that she singlehandedly shut down *The Misfits*; in any case, she was for years made to bear the burden of the film's runaway budget, which by then topped four million dollars. Had she in fact been desperately ill, as Huston gave out to the press, how could it be announced on the first day in hospital that she would return promptly in time for filming a week later? Hyman Engelberg himself confirmed that on 29 August: 'My guess is that she will probably be able to go back to work in a week,' he told the press. 'She is just tuckered out.'

As often happens, the enforced rest enabled her to make certain hard decisions. 'She was very brave,' according to Ralph, 'but she didn't want us to do anything for her. She wanted the security of knowing we were with her, but she could do for herself, and she wanted to be well. Under all the frailty was a will of steel.' But at the same time, she was entirely submissive to her therapist, as was soon clear to her closest friends. As Rupert Allan put it, 'Greenson had an amazing amount of control over her life. When she checked into the clinic, he announced in my presence that she would be allowed only one incoming and one outgoing call a day.'

To his credit, Arthur arrived within hours in Los Angeles and attended Marilyn daily until 4 September, when she returned with him to Reno – 'looking wonderfully self-possessed', as he wrote years later; 'her incredible resilience was heroic to me.' But by this time 'we both knew we had effectively parted.'

Until 18 October she was in Nevada completing *The Misfits*. Miller continually rewrote script pages, Huston gambled, and after a warm welcome by the cast and crew Marilyn was work-ing with renewed energy. According to the production diary 'when she was told [about late script changes], she stayed up the entire night preparing the [new] scenes.'

From 24 October to 4 November the final interior scenes and process photography for the film were completed at the Para-mount Studios, Hollywood. There, Marilyn and Clark Gable made a private pact: they would agree to no more last-minute revisions: 'I *know* Arthur's a good writer,' she said plaintively to Huston one evening, 'but I don't want to see another new word he's written. Not for a while, please.' Gable was adamant: exhausted from the months of location work, he flatly refused multiple takes and new pages of dialogue.

On Monday afternoon, 31 October, Henry Hathaway (who had directed her in *Niagara*), saw Marilyn standing alone out-side the Paramount soundstage. Approaching her, he noticed that she was crying. 'All my life,' she said between sobs,

I've played Marilyn Monroe, Marilyn Monroe, Marilyn Monroe. I've tried to do a little better and find myself doing an imitation of myself. I so want to do something different. That was one of the things that attracted me to Arthur when he said he was attracted to me. When I married him, one of the fantasies in my mind was that I could get away from Marilyn Monroe through him, and here I find myself back doing the same thing, and I just couldn't take it, I had to get out of there. I just couldn't face having to do another scene with Marilyn Monroe.

Herein lies one of the most poignant elements in Marilyn's life – and particularly in her life with Arthur Miller.

The teenage wife, the model and starlet had worked tirelessly to become accepted, to be the star Grace McKee Goddard had proposed as her destiny. And so she was, in her twenties, the lacquered blonde of *Gentlemen Prefer Blondes, How To Marry a Millionaire* and *The Seven Year Itch*. But she had finally resented and rejected the artifice of the manufactured Marilyn Monroe, realizing that was itself a role she could assume and put off; that although Hollywood's Marilyn Monroe was indeed a *part* of her real self, there was – so she hoped and for it she worked – a deeper self, however unformed.

She had coveted the vocation of a serious actress, and to that she gave herself fully by leaving Hollywood at the height of her fame, by exchanging the image of the wife of the sports hero for that of the earnest playwright's spouse. Except for her performance in *Bus Stop* in the spring of 1956, which brought her back to Los Angeles for three months, she had stayed away from the studios for four years – from the conclusion of *The Seven Year Itch* to the beginning of *Some Like It Hot*. There was then another absence, over a year, until she returned for the unhappiness of *Let's Make Love*.

To *The Misfits*, so long in preparation, she had attached the greatest hope of her life: that Arthur would fulfil his promise to her. He provided, we must assume, only what he could, but brought forth, alas, only the image of a forlorn and dejected Marilyn Monroe – not the maturing person who had completely altered her acting style, not the performer of increasing range and depth whom Hollywood continued to misperceive and underrate. She was in *The Misfits* only a pale, wan, frightened remnant of the image she had hoped to abandon. 'I couldn't face having to do another scene with Marilyn Monroe,' she said, because she knew she was capable of more, and that the standard-issue 'Marilyn Monroe' was indeed herself changing.

Perhaps only in this context can her performance in *The Misfits* be assessed. In this, her last completed film, she had her most disappointing major role: Roslyn allowed her to be nothing more than a biased caricature of herself, minus the humour, without the liveliness. There are moments of admirable command – her cries of resentment against the capture of animals, the shadings of confusion and dismay that flicker across her face as she rides across the desert. Audiences and critics then as later generally found the film arid and static, although Marilyn was praised by a few veteran admirers for her 'serious, accurate performance . . . Miss Monroe is magic, and not merely a living pin-up dangled in satin before our eyes.' Once again, she gave an exceptional performance in a mediocre film, and in this regard *The Misfits* synthesizes and summarizes her entire movie career. It had been only thirteen years since *Scudda-Hoo! Scudda-Hay!*, and in twenty-nine films she had had less than a dozen leading roles. Neither the films nor the roles were ever as fine as her performances in them, and she knew it.

None of Marilyn's self-awareness, none of her gifts, her courage, her impatience with herself and her patience with others, was inconsistent with personal problems and reliance on sleeping pills. Arthur Miller was right: she *was* something of the life force.

But that, too, is richer than anything so vague and vain as beauty. The medieval mystics would have described her weeping on the studio lot that October day 'the gift of tears' – a moment of epiphany, the crisis in the life of a woman hitherto stymied by a nation's shallow popular image of a merely sexy, pretty girl. Blocked by stereotypes she yearned to forget, she longed to sleep; even this was in a way a desire to annihilate the 'Marilyn Monroe' who had already died in her.

So far, psychiatry had not been much help at all – not only because she was so unclear about her past and future but because she believed she had to give right answers, to please therapists who seemed to know so much, or at least who asked so many intimate questions. When practised without respect for the client's spiritual autonomy, psychotherapy can be counterproductive, especially for those who live double and triple lives as performers, as role-players. In their cases, as Freud himself admitted, life itself can be the superb therapist. Here she was, at thirty-four, the age when very many people reach a crossroads: she had the courage and the inner means to make choices, she had the native intelligence to recognize possibilities beyond the past. The tears that day were not just for the false self – they

At a surprise celebration for her thirty-fourth birthday, during filming of Let's Make Love *(1960).*
From the collection of Vanessa Reis.

With Yves Montand and Arthur Miller (1960).

With Bunny Gardel and Sherlee Strahm, on location in Nevada for The Misfits *(1960). From the collection of Evelyn Moriarty.*

With her secretary May Reis, on location in Nevada for The Misfits *(1960). From the collection of Vanessa Reis.*

With co-star Eli Wallach, on location for The Misfits *(1960). From the collection of Evelyn Moriarty*

Dr Ralph Greenson and his wife at Marilyn's funeral (1962). The Bettmann Archive.

With Clark Gable, during the final days of filming The Misfits *(1960).*

RIGHT *With Joe at Yankee Stadium on opening day of the baseball season (1961). The Bettmann Archive.*

BELOW *Receiving the Golden Globe Award for* Some Like It Hot *(from Rock Hudson, 1961). From the collection of Mickey Song.*

Entering Madison Square Garden for the gala birthday celebration of President John F. Kennedy (1962). From the collection of Chris Basinger.

RIGHT *Eunice Murray (1962). The Bettmann Archive.*

BELOW *In her dressing room rehearsing for* Something's Got to Give, *with Paula Strasberg (1962). Photo by James Mitchell, Twentieth Century-Fox Studios.*

With Wally Cox and Dean Martin during production of Something's Got to Give *(1962). Photo by James Mitchell, Twentieth Century-Fox Studios. From the collection of Evelyn Moriarty.*

During the filming of the nude scene in Something's Got to Give *(1962). Photo by James Mitchell, Twentieth Century-Fox Studios. From the collection of Evelyn Moriarty.*

ABOVE *The last day Marilyn Monroe worked on a film: her thirty-sixth birthday (June 1962), with Henry Weinstein and Eunice Murray.*

OVERLEAF *On the set of* Something's Got to Give, *June 1962.*

were a farewell, a kind of death to everything she wanted to abandon.

In fact, therapy was endorsing her dependencies, not freeing her from them. John Huston's next film was to be about Sigmund Freud, a project in which Marilyn expressed keen interest, and in which Huston was willing to cast her. A few days later, however, she reported to Huston, 'I can't do it because Anna Freud doesn't want a picture made. My analyst told me this.'

There were more serious dependencies. As Ralph Roberts, Rupert Allan and Susan Strasberg ruefully recalled, Drs Greenson and Engelberg made no efforts to wean Marilyn from barbiturates that autumn: 'in fact they provided them,' as Ralph said.

When we came to Los Angeles for the final work on *The Misfits*, there was an understanding that Marilyn would call me, and I went over to May Reis to collect the Nembutal pills the doctors gave her to dole out to Marilyn. These I delivered from May to Marilyn. But soon I said this was silly, and I simply collected them from the doctor directly and brought them to Marilyn. So far as I could see, there was no thought about how harmful all this might be.

That autumn, while completing the studio work on her last picture, Marilyn consulted Greenson seven days a week at his home. His son and daughter knew their father had famous clients; they knew, too, that he cancelled patients at his office to rush home to see one or two of the most celebrated, and that Marilyn was prime among them.

It is astonishing to realize how quickly a mutual dependence was established, and how rapidly Ralph Greenson betrayed every ethic and responsibility to his family, his profession and to Marilyn Monroe, for reasons that would take more than a year to become clear.

The first indication of trouble was Greenson's request that his daughter Joan deliver drugs from a pharmacy to the Miller bungalow at the Beverly Hills Hotel, where he would be treating her: Arthur Miller himself would probably answer the door, Greenson told his daughter. The delivery was made, and the doctor's daughter, then twenty, met Miller and, through the open bedroom door, saw Marilyn in bed, being treated by her father and accepting the medication she had delivered.

Greenson's action constituted a terrible breach of patient confidentiality, a disclosure of patient identity to the physician's own family, and his subtle but clear first attempt to join that family to the client. In addition, there can be no defence or justification for this overt involvement of the psychiatrist's daughter: pharmacies have delivery services, hotels have messengers. Such a cavalier lack of basic professional discretion was only the first instance of Greenson's egregious mishandling of his most famous patient.

From this point to the end of his life he developed a keen interest in 'countertransference', the reversal of dependency from patient to therapist; eventually he used this term to describe his own feelings for Marilyn. In a sense, as this increasingly proprietary and grotesque control of patient by therapist continued, Ralph Greenson substituted the ultimate celebrity, Marilyn Monroe, for his celebrated sister Juliet, whom he loved, admired, protected, applauded and bitterly resented. As for his contention that Marilyn would be less conspicuous visiting his home than his office, that was patently absurd: automobiles crawled past his house each day, waiting for a glimpse of the black limousine Marilyn engaged to transport her around town. More dogs were walked on Franklin Street, more strollers passed by, more tourists pointed and chattered: the Greenson home was becoming a star's stopping place. But the doctor went further, asking his daughter to meet Marilyn when he was delayed, suggesting that Joan take a walk with the star and befriend her.

'I was her therapist,' Greenson said of Marilyn, 'the good father who would not disappoint her and who would bring her insights, and if not insights, just kindness. I had become the most important person in her life, [but] I also felt guilty that I put a burden on my own family. But there was something very lovable about this girl and we all cared about her and she could be delightful.'

Painful as it was, Marilyn knew that autumn of 1960 where she had to begin to make changes. During the last week of October, she told a few friends she had asked Arthur Miller to leave their bungalow at the Beverly Hills Hotel: they would presently make a joint announcement of their decision to divorce. Not long before they married, Arthur had said that 'the sad fact of her life is that she has calculated wrong every time she's made a decision.' The implication was unmistakable: in marrying him, she was doing right. But now, in the early days of an unseasonably damp and chilly California autumn, she had revised the calculation.

On 5 November, the day after *The Misfits* was complete, Marilyn heard the news: Clark Gable had suffered a serious heart attack. He had been a calm, unself-conscious friend during the production, her childhood fantasy father sprung wonderfully to life. 'I kept him waiting – kept him waiting for hours and hours on that picture,' Marilyn said guiltily to Sidney Skolsky. 'Was I punishing my father? Getting even for all the years he's kept me waiting?' Her words had the ring of a psychoanalyst's judgement or suggestion.

By 11 November, she was back in New York, alone in her apartment on East Fifty-seventh Street; Arthur was living pseudonymously at the Chelsea Hotel on West Twenty-third. On that date, their representatives announced an imminent divorce to the press. Five days later, apparently recovering in the hospital, Gable had a second massive attack and died. He was fifty-nine, and his fifth wife was pregnant with his first child. Marilyn was inconsolable when she read gossip column reports: the party line broadcast that it was her antics during *The Misfits* that had killed him. No one bothered to report the terrible exertions to which Huston had subjected Gable; no one mentioned the actor's habit of smoking three packs of cigarettes daily for thirty years.

There were other changes in Marilyn's life, too. May Reis, who had served her and Arthur for years, resigned: the job was, as her sister-in-law Vanessa recalled, simply too demanding for her. Rupert Allan, perhaps the oldest and dearest friend of his one-time client Grace Kelly, had been invited to assist her now that she was Princess of Monaco, and Rupert was spending many months each year abroad. His place as Marilyn's personal press representative was taken by Pat Newcomb, who quickly became a trusted ally to her famous client.

By December, Marilyn had resumed daily sessions with Marianne Kris and classes at the Actors Studio, to which she donated a thousand dolars. As always she shared her good fortunes, and this had been, after all, a banner year: another payment of almost $50,000 for *Some Like It Hot* had just arrived, and twice that, the partial fee for her salary of $300,000 for *The Misfits* (the salary included acting and uncredited co-producer's fee). This landed her in the 90 per cent tax bracket, and in fact at the year's end she was surprised to find herself with very little savings. Her New York Attorney, Aaron Frosch, took no fee for preparing her divorce papers.

At Christmas 1960, spent quietly with the Strasbergs listening to music and sipping champagne, she was a picture of weariness, as Ralph and Susan recalled. Nor were the children of her former husbands forgotten. 'I take a lot of pride in them,' she said of Joe DiMaggio Jr, and of Robert and Jane Ellen Miller, who received Christmas gifts and cards with loving notes from Marilyn. 'They're from broken homes, too,' she told a writer visiting from England, 'and I think I can understand them. I've always said to them that I didn't want to be their mother or stepmother as such – after all their mothers are still alive. I just wanted to be their friend. Only time could prove that to them, and they had to give me time. Their lives are very precious to me.' And hers to them, for they never changed their warm feelings toward Marilyn. Joe's sister and Arthur's father also remained on the friendliest terms with their ex-in-law.

The holidays temporarily lifted Marilyn's spirits – just as the entire country seemed alive with optimism at the end of 1960. A new freshness and vitality prevailed, a sense of youth and humour, of energy and strength of purpose. Marilyn and America were taking their cue, basing their mood, on the brightness, wit and enthusiasm that radiated from President-elect John F. Kennedy.

Chapter Nineteen

1961

'I really am trying to find myself,' she told a friendly reporter, 'and the best way for me to do that is to try to prove to myself that I am an actress. And that is what I hope to do . . . My work is important to me. It's the only ground I've ever had to stand on. To put it bluntly, I seem to have a whole superstructure with no foundation. But now I'm working on the foundation.'

Eager to forget the hardships of *The Misfits* and to counterpoise the end of her marriage with the beginning of a new project, Marilyn and Lee Strasberg proposed a television dramatization of *Rain*, the classic Somerset Maugham story. To her letter informing him of these plans, Maugham replied from his home on the French Riviera; touched and pleased by her desire to be his Sadie Thompson, he said she would be 'splendid' and, with hearty support for the project, he sent his best wishes and admiration.

During January, negotiations for the broadcast at first proceeded smoothly. Fredric March agreed to co-star as the tortured, repressed and angry Reverend Davidson, and his wife Florence Eldridge was to play Mrs Davidson. Contracts were almost settled with NBC, which at the time regularly offered television versions of classic dramas. But Strasberg insisted on directing, and this demand became the sticking point, for network executives were unwilling to sign him. Eager to have Marilyn, they argued against Strasberg and for a veteran film or television director, and Marilyn was offered consultation on their choice.

But at this rejection Strasberg was furious, and with customary loyalty (and perhaps feeling she could acquit herself well under no other director) Marilyn supported her teacher. Lee, otherwise so vocal about actors finding their own ways, did not encourage her to see another; to the contrary, he thought of *Rain* as *their* project and, on their behalf, he later cancelled plans for it.

Lee also figured in Marilyn's new will, a simple, three-page document dated 14 January 1961 that reflected her recent divorce. In it, she left $10,000 each to her half-sister Berniece Miracle and to May Reis, and to the Rostens she bequeathed $5000, specifying that it be used for the education of their daughter Patricia. Her personal effects and clothes were left to Lee Strasberg, 'it being my desire that he distribute these among my friends, colleagues and those to whom I am devoted.' A trust fund in the amount of $100,000 was also established for Gladys and for Mrs Michael Chekhov, to provide a minimum of $5000 annually for her mother's care and $2500 for the latter's. Twenty-five per cent of the residual Estate was left to Marianne Kris, 'to be used for the furtherance of the work of such psychiatric institutions or groups as she shall elect'; and seventy-five per cent was left to Lee Strasberg.*

There was another matter to be adjudicated more immediately: Marilyn's divorce from Arthur. Through their lawyers, they reached a swift settlement. The Roxbury house would be Arthur's, since it had been purchased with proceeds from the sale of his previous home, and there would be no alimonies on either side; there remained only the exchange of a

---

* By the time Marilyn's Estate was finally appraised in 1963, it was valued at $92,781 (or about $375,000 in 1993 dollars). Lee Strasberg's second wife, whom he married after the death of Paula in 1966, was his sole beneficiary when he died in 1982; thus Anna Mizrahi Strasberg, a woman Marilyn never knew, became heir to the bulk of Marilyn Monroe's Estate – which meant primarily income from film royalties and from the licensing of her image on coffee mugs, T-shirts, pens, etc. In 1992, this generated something in excess of one million dollars a year. By this time, Marianne Kris was long dead, and her heirs were the Anna Freud Children's Clinic in London.

few personal items. Arthur signed a waiver of his rights to contest a unilateral filing for divorce.

And so on Friday 20 January 1961, Pat Newcomb accompanied Marilyn and her attorney, Aaron Frosch, on a swift mission to Mexico. At Pat's suggestion, the day of Kennedy's inauguration was deliberately chosen 'because the press and the whole country would be looking at that, and we could slip away and return unnoticed', which indeed they did. On Friday evening, the trio arrived in El Paso, Texas, crossed the border into Juárez, and before Judge Miguel Gomez Guerra Marilyn pleaded 'incompatibility of character' and requested an immediate divorce. This was granted forthwith, they were back in New York by Saturday evening, and from Tuesday 24 January she was no longer Mrs Arthur Miller.

Looking tired and depressed, she was blunt with reporters. 'I am upset and I don't feel like being bothered with publicity right now,' she said on her return – but then she tried to appear cheerful, adding with a rueful smile, 'but I would love to have a plate of tacos and enchiladas – we didn't have time for food in Mexico!' She was, as Pat recalled, trying valiantly despite her evident depression over the formal termination of the marriage. At the same time, Pat knew that 'at the core of her, she was really strong, much stronger than all of us – and that was something we tended to forget, because she seemed so vulnerable, and one always felt it necessary to watch out for her.'

As for her comments on Arthur Miller, Marilyn displayed her customary dignity when publicly discussing former husbands or lovers. 'It would be indelicate of me to discuss this. I feel it would be trespassing,' she said. 'Mr Miller is a wonderful man and a great writer, but it didn't work out that we should be husband and wife. But everybody I ever loved, I still love a little.' Typically, there was no bitterness towards those from whom she felt estranged, even from those she felt had in some ways abused, demeaned or been faithless to her. Marilyn confided only in friends whose discretion she could trust: she had no desire to justify herself before the press. To show her essential goodwill, she attended the New York premiere of *The Misfits* at the Capitol Theater on 31 January. Montgomery Clift was her escort.

But beneath the brave, cheerful public exterior, Marilyn's mood was as dark as the New York winter. *The Misfits*, like *Let's Make Love*, was not well received by most critics, and audiences were puzzled by the story and disappointed with the leading players. By 1 February, after the divorce, the failure of two films, the breakdown of negotiations for *Rain* and no prospects for the work that always somehow sustained her despite its anxiety-provoking aspects, Marilyn was able to find consolation in nothing, and so she told Marianne Kris as well as her friends. Except for her visits to Kris, she stayed at home in her darkened bedroom, playing sentimental records, subsisting on sleeping pills and rapidly losing weight.

Her condition alarmed Marianne Kris, who suggested to Marilyn that she check into a private ward of New York Hospital for a physical check-up and a good rest, with meals served and every comfort provided.

On Sunday 5 February, Kris drove Marilyn to the vast Cornell University-New York Hospital complex, overlooking the East River at Sixty-ninth Street. After freely signing her own admission papers (as 'Faye Miller', to avoid publicity), Marilyn was taken not to a normal hospital room but – as Kris had arranged – to the Payne Whitney Clinic, the psychiatric division of New York Hospital. There, to Marilyn's horror, she was placed in a locked and padded room, one of the cells for the most disturbed patients.

Such an incarceration might cause a perfectly healthy person violent upset and panic: for Marilyn, it was as if she had at last become the heir of the mental illness she believed had bedevilled her ancestors. It all happened so quickly, as she later told Norman Rosten, Ralph Roberts and Susan Strasberg, that she was pitched into a state of extreme shock. She broke down weeping and sobbing, shouting to be released and banging on the locked steel door until her fists were raw and bleeding. She was ignored, and the staff reaction was that here indeed was a psychotic case, just as her physician had attested. Her clothes and handbag were taken away and she was put into hospital garb and threatened with a straitjacket unless she behaved.

A young psychiatric houseman, visiting her cell (it can only be called that) on Monday morning, evaluated her as 'extremely disturbed', which in a sense she was, and as 'potentially self-destructive', a judgement he made after Marilyn smashed a small window in her locked bathroom door in an effort to get to the toilet. As she told the doctor, she felt upset and humiliated – not to say betrayed, as she later told her friends. But the intern merely asked repeatedly, 'Why are you so unhappy?' – as if she were at a luxury resort and not confined against her will in a lunatic asylum. Quite rationally, Marilyn answered, 'I've been paying the best doctors a fortune to find out why, and you're asking *me*?' Such a logical counter is often taken as a challenge, and is not the sort of contradiction most professionals wish to hear.

For two days and nights, she endured this frightening situation. Marilyn, who from childhood hated locked doors and never barred her own bedroom, was almost in a state of total nervous breakdown, and from this point in her life never locked her bedroom door not permitted a key or latch to operate it. Susan Strasberg agreed with Ralph Roberts and Rupert Allan that Marilyn 'always had a means of making a fast getaway even from a studio soundstage whenever she felt the walls were closing in on her. She hated to feel closed in,' at work or at home.

Finally, a sympathetic nurse's aide agreed to give her notepaper and then to deliver a message to Lee and Paula Strasberg, who received it on Wednesday 8 February:

Dear Lee and Paula,
Dr Kris has put me in the hospital under the care of two idiot doctors. They both should not be my doctors. I'm locked up with these poor nutty people. I'm sure to end up a nut too if I

stay in this nightmare. Please help me. This is the last place I should be. I love you both.

Marilyn.

P.S. I'm on the dangerous floor. It's like a cell. They had my bathroom door locked and I couldn't get their key to get into it, so I broke the glass. But outside of that I haven't done anything that is uncooperative.

But the Strasbergs were only friends, powerless to help, much less to order or obtain Marilyn's release. They may well have contacted Kris, who would not have provided any details of Marilyn's condition.

When there was no reply from the Strasbergs by the morning of Thursday the ninth, Marilyn was permitted to make on telephone call. Frantic for help but managing to affect calm, she tried two or three friends but received no answer at their homes. At last she reached Joe DiMaggio in Florida.

Joe and Marilyn had not met for almost six years, but during that time she had remained in contact with his family and asked about his welfare. From 1958, Joe held a $100,000-a-year job as a corporate vice-president for V. H. Monette, Inc., a supplier for military posts. Essentially he was a goodwill ambassador, travelling to army bases worldwide and presiding at exhibition baseball games. During the training season, he coached the Yankees in Florida.

As for his private life, Joe had come close to marrying a woman named Marian McKnight in 1957, but this relationship ended when she was crowned Miss America; otherwise, there was no serious romance in his life. He was, according to family and friends, never out of love with Marilyn: 'He carried a torch bigger than the Statue of Liberty,' said his close friend, the Washington attorney Edward Bennett Williams, whose testimony was typical. 'His love for her never diminished through the years.' 'He loved her a great deal and they had always remained in contact,' agreed Valmore Monette. And so it was to Joe that Marilyn now turned for help.

DiMaggio arrived that evening from St Petersburg Beach and demanded that Marilyn be released from the clinic into his custody the following day. Informed that this would have to be approved by Dr Kris, he telephoned her and said that if Marilyn was not discharged by Friday he would (his words, according to Marilyn) 'take the hospital apart brick by brick.' Kris suggested that Marilyn enter another hospital if Payne Whitney was not to her liking; Joe replied that that would be discussed in due course.

Things then happened quickly.

First, to avoid even the possibility of unwelcome publicity, it was arranged for Ralph Roberts to deliver Marilyn back to Fifty-seventh Street, with Kris literally along for the ride. As Ralph recalled, Marilyn unleashed a storm of protest and criticism against her therapist, and after Marilyn was safely returned home (where Joe awaited), Ralph drove Kris back to her residence. En route, as he recalled, she was trembling with remorse, repeating over and over, 'I did a terrible thing, a terrible, terrible thing. Oh, God, I didn't mean to, but I did.' It may have been the most accurate statement of her therapeutic relationship with Marilyn; in any case, it was the last time she had anything to say, for Marianne Kris was dismissed that day and never saw Marilyn Monroe again.

Second, it was clear to Joe that, whatever her condition when she entered Payne Whitney, she was wretchedly unhappy, shaking and anorexic on her departure. She agreed to enter a far more comfortable and less threatening environment if he would stay at the hospital and be with her daily. At five o'clock on the afternoon of Friday 10 February he helped her to settle into a private room at the Neurological Institute of the Columbia University-Presbyterian Hospital Medical Center. There she remained, regaining her strength, until 5 March.

For years a letter from Marilyn Monroe to Ralph Greenson

was believed lost – a document providing details of Marilyn's state of mind and feeling and her assessment of her life that winter; in 1992, it was at last discovered. The letter was written on 1 and 2 March 1961, from Columbia-Presbyterian, and the sanity, sobriety, wit and maturity of the writer are everywhere apparent. If ever there was any doubt that Marilyn Monroe at this time was a woman who, despite problems, had a clear view of her life, a native intelligence and compassion, it is forever belied by her letter.

Dear Dr Greenson,

Just now when I looked out the hospital window where the snow had covered everything, suddenly everything is kind of a muted green. There are grass and shabby evergreen bushes, though the trees give me a little hope – and the desolate bare branches promise maybe there will be spring and maybe they promise hope.

Did you see 'The Misfits' yet? In one sequence you can perhaps see how bare and strange a tree can be for me. I don't know if it comes across that way for sure on the screen – I don't like some of the selections in the takes they used. As I started to write this letter about four quiet tears had fallen. I don't know quite why.

Last night I was awake all night again. Sometimes I wonder what the night time is for. It almost doesn't exist for me – it all seems like one long, long horrible day. Anyway, I thought I'd try to be constructive about it and started to read the letters of Sigmund Freud. When I first opened the book I saw the picture of Freud inside, opposite the title page and I burst into tears – he looked very depressed (the picture must have been taken near the end of his life), as if he died a disappointed man. But Dr Kris said he had much physical pain which I had known from the Jones book. I know this, too, to be so, but still I trust my instincts because I see a sad disappointment in his gentle face. The book reveals (though I am not sure anyone's love letters should be published) that he

wasn't a stiff! I mean his gentle, sad humor and even a striving was eternal in him. I haven't gotten very far yet because at
the same time I'm reading Sean O'Casey's first autobiography. This book disturbs me very much, and in a way one
should be disturbed for these things, after all.

There was no empathy at Payne Whitney – it had a very
bad effect on me. They put me in a cell (I mean cement blocks
and all) for *very disturbed*, depressed patients, except I felt I
was in some kind of prison for a crime I hadn't committed.
The inhumanity there I found archaic. They asked me why I
wasn't happy there (everything was under lock and key,
things like electric lights, dresser drawers, bathrooms, closets,
bars concealed on the windows – and the doors have windows so patients can be visible all the time. Also, the violence
and markings still remain on the walls from former patients).
I answered: 'Well, I'd have to be nuts if I like it here!' Then
there were screaming women in their cells – I mean, they
screamed out when life was unbearable for them, I guess –
and at times like this I felt an available psychiatrist should
have talked to them, perhaps to alleviate even temporarily
their misery and pain. I think they (the doctors) might learn
something, even – but they are interested only in something
they studied in books. Maybe from some life-suffering
human being they could discover more – I had the feeling
they looked more for discipline and that they let their
patients go after the patients have 'given up.' They asked me
to mingle with the patients, to go out to O.T. (Occupational
Therapy). I said, 'And do what?' They said: 'You could sew
or play checkers, even cards, and maybe knit.' I tried to explain that *the day I did that* they would have a nut on their
hands. These things were farthest from my mind. They asked
me why I felt I was 'different' from the other patients, so I
decided if they were really that stupid I must give them a very
simple answer, so I said, 'I just am.'

The first day I *did* mingle with a patient. She asked me why
I looked so sad and suggested I could call a friend and perhaps not be so lonely. I told her that they had told me that

there wasn't a phone on that floor. Speaking of floors, they are all *locked* – no one could go in and no one could go out. She looked shocked and shaken and said, 'I'll take you to the phone' – and while I waited in line for my turn for the use of the phone, I observed a guard (since he had on a gray knit uniform), and as I approached the phone he straight-armed the phone and said very sternly, '*You* can't use the phone.' By the way, they pride themselves in having a home-like atmosphere there. I asked them (the doctors) how they figured that. They answered, 'Well, on the sixth floor we have wall-to-wall carpeting and modern furniture,' to which I replied, 'Well, *that* any good interior decorator could provide – providing there are funds for it,' but since they are dealing with human beings, I asked, why couldn't they perceive the interior of a human being?

The girl that told me about the phone seemed such a pathetic and vague creature. She told me after the straight-arming, 'I didn't know they would do that.' Then she said, 'I'm here because of my mental condition – I have cut my throat several times and slashed my wrists,' she said either three or four times.

Oh, well, men are climbing to the moon but they don't seem interested in the beating human heart. Still, one can change them but won't – by the way, that was the original theme of *The Misfits* – no one even caught that part of it. Partly because, I guess, the changes in the script and some of the distortions in the direction.

Later:

I know I will never be happy but I know I can be gay! Remember I told you Kazan said I was the gayest girl he ever knew and believe me, he has known many. But he *loved* me for one year and once rocked me to sleep one night when I was in great anguish. He also suggested that I go into analysis and later wanted me to work with Lee Strasberg.

Was it Milton who wrote: 'The happy ones were never born'? I know at least two psychiatrists who are looking for a more positive approach.

This morning, March 2:

I didn't sleep again last night. I forgot to tell you something yesterday. When they put me into the first room on the sixth floor I was not told it was a psychiatric floor. Dr Kris said she was coming the next day. The nurse came in after the doctor, a psychiatrist, had given me a physical examination including examining the breast for lumps. I took exception to this but not violently, only explaining that the medical doctor who had put me there, a stupid man named Dr Lipkin, had already done a complete physical less than thirty days before. But when the nurse came in, I noticed there was no way of buzzing or reaching for a light to call the nurse. I asked why this was and some other things, and she said this is a psychiatric floor. After she went out I got dressed and then was when the girl in the hall told me about the phone. I was waiting at the elevator door which looks like all other doors with a doorknob except it doesn't have any numbers (you see, they left them all out). After the girl spoke with me and told me what she had done to herself, I went back into my room knowing they had lied to me about the telephone and I sat on the bed trying to figure that if I was given this situation in an acting improvisation, what would I do? So I figured, it's a squeaky wheel that gets the grease. I admit it was a loud squeak, but I got the idea from a movie I made once called *Don't Bother to Knock*. I picked up a light-weight chair and slammed it against the glass, intentionally – and it was hard to do because I had never broken anything in my life. I took a lot of banging to get even a small piece of glass, so I went over with the glass concealed in my hand and sat quietly on the bed waiting for them to come in. They did, and I said to them, 'If you are going to treat me like a nut, I'll act like a nut.' I admit the next thing is corny, but I really did it in the movie except it was with a razor blade. I indicated if they didn't let me out I would harm myself – the farthest thing from my mind at the moment, since you know, Dr Greenson, I'm an actress and would never intentionally mark or mar myself, I'm just that vain. I didn't cooperate with them in any way because I couldn't believe in what they were doing. They asked me to go quietly and I refused to move, staying on the bed so they picked me up by all fours, two hefty men and two hefty women and carried me up to the seventh floor in the elevator. I must say at least they had the decency to carry me face down. I just wept quietly all the way there and then was put in the cell I told you about and that ox of a woman, one of those hefty ones, said, 'Take a bath.' I told her I had just taken one on the sixth floor. She said very sternly, 'As soon as you change floors, you have to take another bath.' The man who runs that place, a high-school principal type, although Dr Kris refers to him as an 'administrator,' he was actually permitted to talk to me, questioning me somewhat like an analyst. He told me I was a very, very sick girl and had been a very, very sick girl for many years. He looks down on his patients. He asked me how I could possibly work when I was depressed. He wondered if that interfered with my work. He was being very firm and definite in the way he said it. He actually stated it more than he questioned me, so I replied, 'Don't you think that perhaps Greta Garbo and Charlie Chaplin and Ingrid Bergman had been depressed when *they* worked sometimes?' It's like saying a ball player like DiMaggio couldn't hit a ball when he was depressed. Pretty silly.

By the way, I have some good news, sort of, since I guess I helped. He claims I did: Joe said I saved his life by sending him to a psychotherapist. Dr Kris said that he is a very brilliant man, the doctor. Joe said he pulled himself by his own bootstraps after the divorce but he told me also that if he had been me he would have divorced him, too. Christmas night he sent a forest-full of poinsettias. I asked who they were from since it was such a surprise – my friend Pat Newcomb was there and they had just arrived then. She said, 'I don't know, the card just says, "Best, Joe."' Then I replied, 'Well, there's only one Joe.' Because it was Christmas night I called him up and asked him why he had sent me the flowers. He said, 'First of all, because I thought you would call me to thank me,' and then he said, 'Besides, who in the hell else do you have in the world?' He asked me to have a drink some time with him. I said I knew he didn't drink, but he said occasionally now he takes a drink, to which I replied then it would have to be a very, very dark place! He asked me what I was doing Christmas night. I said nothing, I'm here with a friend. Then he asked me to come over and I was glad he was coming, though I must say I was bleary and depressed, but somehow still glad he was coming over.

I think I had better stop because you have other things to do, but thanks for listening for a while.

Marilyn M.

Joe visited her every day at the hospital, and before her release he went ahead to Florida, whence she had agreed to join him for a few weeks' rest.

On 5 March, Marilyn left Columbia-Presbyterian after a 23-day rest. Six security guards escorted her through a mob of four hundred fans and dozens of photographers and reporters crowding round the hospital entrance; present to help were May Reis (still willing to be helpful in such circumstances), Pat Newcomb and her colleague John Springer, from the New York office of Arthur Jacobs. 'I feel wonderful,' she said. 'I had a nice rest.' Smiling 'as radiantly as an Oscar winner' (thus one reporter on the scene), Marilyn also appeared healthier than ever: she had lost most of the fifteen pounds she had gained during the unhappy summer of 1960 and sported an elegantly casual new champagne-coloured coiffure that matched her beige cashmere sweater and skirt and her identically dyed shoes.

Three days later, she attended the funeral of Arthur's mother at a Brooklyn funeral chapel, where she comforted her former father-in-law and offered condolences to Arthur. 'She had just been discharged from the hospital,' Isadore Miller told a writer later, 'and I was about to enter one myself. When I did, she called me every day after my operation, wiring flowers and phoning my doctor.' Their affection was unaltered by the divorce from Arthur.

By the end of March, Marilyn was with Joe, who left the Yankees in St Petersburg and took her to a secluded resort in Redington Beach, Florida. Here they relaxed, swam, combed the shore for shells, dined quietly and retired early. Once or twice they drove to St Petersburg and watched the Yankees train, and Marilyn thrilled the team by simply being there and cheering them on; Joe was very proud of her indeed. Said his friend Jerry Coleman, 'Joe DiMaggio deeply loved that woman' – an attachment that was quickly becoming mutual once again. Lois Smith: 'The attraction to Joe remained great. Marilyn knew where she stood with him. He was always there, she could always call on him, lean on him, depend on him, be certain of him. It was a marvelous feeling of comfort for her.' DiMaggio was, as Pat Newcomb said years later about that year, 'a hero. Marilyn could always call on Ralph, who was generous with his time and the best friend she ever had. But Joe had the power to come to Payne Whitney and say, "You are leaving here!"'

At the end of April, Marilyn was back in Los Angeles and feeling so well (except for a nagging pain in her stomach and right side) that she told columnists and friends she would soon be back at work on a new film, although what that might be she had no idea. At first she accepted an offer to live briefly at the home of Frank Sinatra, who was away on a European tour; then Marilyn contacted Jane Ziegler, the daughter of Viola Mertz, her former landlady at 882 North Doheny Drive at the corner of Cynthia Street. An apartment had just become available in this same complex where she had rented in 1952. Marilyn moved in some hastily bought furniture – bookcases, a large bed she put in the living-room and a vanity table and wardrobe in the small bedroom.

Visitors like Ralph Roberts and Susan Strasberg saw that the place could have been a hotel room: it lacked personal touches, there were no photographs or awards, merely a few books, a suitcase of clothes and a makeup box. The apartment seemed to be merely a base from which she would dash out to a waiting limousine for errands, for visits to Dr Greenson or Dr Engelberg, or for meetings with an agent, a publicist, screenwriter or producer. As sensitive as ever to ambient noise, Marilyn depended on Nembutal to sleep.

In May she was happy to receive from Clark Gable's widow an invitation to attend the christening of the baby John Clark; this reunion killed the occasional rumour that Kay Gable believed Marilyn's unpunctuality the cause of her husband's death. Then, within days of that happy event, she was admitted to Cedars of Lebanon Hospital, where Dr Leon Krohn again operated to relieve her agonizing, chronic endometriosis.

Back home by 1 June, she dined with a few friends on her thirty-fifth birthday and met a London reporter. 'I'm very happy to have reached this age,' she said. 'I feel I'm growing up. It was wonderful being a girl, but it's more wonderful being a woman.' On 7 June she attended a party in Las Vegas, given by Frank Sinatra for Dean Martin's forty-fourth birthday; also present were (among others) Elizabeth Taylor and her husband Eddie Fisher.

The reason for her presence was simple. It is unclear exactly when Marilyn began a brief, intermittent romance with Frank Sinatra (perhaps as early as two or three rendezvous in 1955 in New York), but the liaison was resumed that June and lasted until late that year. Frank, apparently the more smitten, met Marilyn at his home in Los Angeles, and occasionally in Las Vegas or Lake Tahoe.

'There's no doubt that Frank was in love with Marilyn,' said the producer Milton Ebbins, who knew them both well that year. Ebbins, a friend of Sinatra and vice-president of Peter

Lawford's production company, recalled an incident that revealed Sinatra's infatuation for Monroe. After accepting an invitation to a luncheon for President Kennedy at the ocean-front home of Lawford (who was then married to the president's sister Patricia), Sinatra failed to arrive.

'He has a terrible cold,' said his secretary Gloria Lovell, telephoning the singer's last-minute excuse. (By coincidence, Lovell lived in the same apartment complex as Marilyn.)

'Oh, Gloria, come on, this is hard to believe,' replied Ebbins, who took the call. 'Tell him he's *got* to come. He can't do this to the president!' But the secretary was adamant: Sinatra would not appear. Later, Ebbins learned from Lovell and from Sinatra himself the real reason for the astonishing absence: 'He couldn't find Marilyn!' Ebbins recalled. 'She had been staying at his house for a week-end, and she had gone out for something – shopping or a facial or whatever – and he couldn't find her! It wasn't worry for her safety, he was just that jealous of her whereabouts! To hell with the president's lunch!'

Marilyn resented this proprietary attitude. She liked and admired Frank and felt safe in his company. She would not, however, be possessed by him, for by 1961 Joe really had no competition; Marilyn also knew that despite their involvement Frank followed his own romantic inclinations elsewhere. 'I think he might have married Marilyn if he had the chance,' according to Ebbins. 'After all, for Frank to break an engagement with the president of the United States – and I can assure you how badly he wanted to go there – that was a major thing for him! He could have come to the lunch, departed and found her later. I tell you, he was hung up on this girl!' Rupert Allan, Ralph Roberts and Joseph Naar (a close friend and agent-manager for Lawford) also knew of Sinatra's deep feelings for Marilyn.

But for all that the rumour mills and columnists have over the years made of this relationship, it was, after 1961, essentially a friendship: Marilyn's man was Joe, and it was well known that Frank was involved with, among others, the actress Juliet Prowse.

Throughout that spring, the chronic pain in Marilyn's right side had become sharper, along with more frequent bouts of indigestion. During the third week of June, she asked Ralph Roberts to accompany her to New York, where on 28 June, in agony with digestive tract illness, she entered the Manhattan Polyclinic on West Fiftieth Street – her fifth admission to a hospital in ten months. Doctors diagnosed impacted gallstones and an acutely inflamed gall bladder, the cause of her chronic pain and 'indigestion', which often (as typical of the condition) troubled her at night and unfortunately led her to take more barbiturates.

On 29 June, a successful, two-hour cholecystectomy was performed; back in her room after the operation, Marilyn awakened to see Joe, who had been with her during admission and right up to the time she was wheeled away for surgery. He was with her daily for a week, until family business took him to San Francisco; then, from August to November, he was away on foreign business with Monette. Marilyn remained in constant contact with him.

On 11 July, after receiving a new hairdo from the famous New York stylist Mr Kenneth, Marilyn left the hospital. Outside, two hundred fans and a hundred reporters and photographers waited, crushing around with questions, requests for autographs – and trying to touch her, to tug at her sweater, to be as close as possible to the most photographed woman in the world. 'It was scary,' she said later.

> I felt for a few minutes as if they were just going to take pieces out of me. Actually it made me feel a little sick. I mean I appreciated the concern and their affection and all that, but – I don't know – it was a little like a nightmare. I wasn't sure I was going to get into that car safely and get away!

Pat Newcomb arrived from Los Angeles to help, bringing along the bouncy little gift of a puppy. Marilyn was delighted, saying, 'I think I'll call him Maf Honey, in honor of Frank' – a joke referring to Sinatra's alleged friendships with shady characters.

That month, Marilyn and Ralph drove to the Miller home in Roxbury, where she retrieved a few final possessions. He recalled that day – Marilyn holding an old winter topcoat close to her face and saying, rather like Mama Bear expecting to find Goldilocks, 'He's been with a woman who wears another kind of perfume and who has been wearing my coat,' which Marilyn forthwith tossed into a trashcan. (The woman was, as they both knew, Inge Morath, soon to become the third Mrs Arthur Miller.)

Later, Marilyn told Norman Rosten,

I told [Arthur] when I'd be there, but when I arrived he wasn't. It was sad. I thought maybe he'd ask me in for coffee or something. We spent some happy years in that house. But he was away, and then I thought, 'Maybe he's right, what's over is over, why torment yourself with hellos?' Still, it would have been polite, sort of, don't you think, if he'd been there to greet me? Even a little smile would do.

There was, however, a warmer moment with someone else from Marilyn's past, although one not quite so familiar. Her half-sister, Berniece Baker Miracle, was in New York for a visit, and on a second retrieval mission to Roxbury she accompanied Ralph and Marilyn. This was perhaps the third time in their lives the women had met, and there was little for them to discuss or to share. But Marilyn was genial and complimentary to Berniece, as Ralph remembered: 'Just look at her lovely hair, that beautiful red color – it's just like our mother's.'

In early August, Marilyn decided to return to Los Angeles. Unable to find a New York psychiatrist she liked and unwilling to consider a return to Marianne Kris, she settled on Greenson for permanent therapy. While Marilyn travelled by air to California, she asked Ralph Roberts to drive cross-country with his car, so that over the next few months he could be her companion, chauffeur (driving was still awkward after her surgery) and masseur. This position he was glad to undertake for so close a friend. She leased a room for him at the Chateau Marmont Hotel, less than ten minutes away from Doheny Drive, and they were together (like the most devoted siblings, as Pat and Susan put it) every day from August to November. Ralph helped Marilyn resettle in her apartment; they shopped; he delivered her for facials at Madame Renna's, on Sunset Boulevard; he drove her to Greenson's home for sessions every afternoon at four; and most evenings they barbecued supper on the terrace at Doheny. She called him 'The Brother'.*

Among Marilyn's first requests was that Ralph help to install heavy curtains, similar to those she had in the Beverly Glen house in 1956 – blackout fabric extending almost the entire width of the wall to assure a complete blockage of light.

Marilyn was, according to Ralph, trying to take things slowly at first; her health and stamina returned, and she seemed happy and optimistic. But Ralph, Pat, Susan Strasberg, Allan Snyder and, on his occasional visits to Los Angeles, Rupert Allan, noticed that the more deeply Marilyn entered into her psychotherapy, the more miserable she became. 'At first she adored Greenson,' Roberts recalled,

but it did not seem to any of us that he was good for her. He began to exert more and more control over her life, dictating who she should have for friends, whom she might visit and so forth. But she felt it was necessary to obey.

Marilyn's relationship with her therapist became, during the last year of her life, painfully tangled and complex. By October, Greenson was regularly cancelling appointments with other

* To confuse tourists and fans, Marilyn installed on the doorbell at Doheny Drive the name Marjorie Stengel. Formerly Montgomery Clift's secretary, Stengel had worked briefly for Marilyn in New York after the departure of May Reis.

patients at his Roxbury Drive office and rushing home to meet Marilyn privately. In November she often stayed after her session for a glass of champagne with his family – thus finally obliterating her anonymity as a patient and accepting an intimacy which Greenson offered with monumentally inappropriate nonchalance. Soon she was staying for dinner, sometimes three or four times weekly. Ralph Roberts, who arrived promptly after her hour to return her to Doheny Drive, was more and more frequently dismissed by Greenson, and one or another of the family drove Marilyn home later in the evening. The doctor was, as his wife had mentioned in another context, making a patient 'a member of his family', and thus fulfilling 'his foster-home fantasy of a haven where all hurts are mended.'

But what may have sprung from honourable motives also revealed Greenson's own weakness and had profoundly deleterious effects on his patient, himself and his family: he was swiftly becoming the classic case of the therapist who would himself have benefited from expert counselling. Instead of providing the techniques for Marilyn to find within herself new resources for independence and autonomous judgement, he made her more dependent, ensuring his own dominance. And because he gave her the signal to do so, Marilyn began relying on his family, telephoning Greenson's house at any hour to discuss her dreams, her fears, her hesitation about this script or that appointment and the vagaries of one relationship or another. Treated and addressed like a family member, she acted more and more like one, presuming access at any time and asking Joan Greenson to transport her here and there when Ralph was otherwise engaged. 'He overstepped the usual patient-doctor boundaries,' as his colleague and friend, the psychiatrist Dr Robert Litman said. 'I do not suggest there was anything improper in the relationship, but there was certainly a danger in getting so involved in adopting her and putting her into his family. This put him in an impossible situation.'

Joan and her brother Daniel (both of them college students at the time) knew their father was a strict Freudian, but Greenson told them and his wife that he believed traditional therapy would not be effective in Marilyn's case, that she needed the example of a stable family in order to find one for herself. He found her, he told them, so charming and so vulnerable that only he could save her. Of this overt saviour complex any professional colleague would sternly disapprove.

As for Marilyn, this heightened relationship – which she was in no position to contradict – was at first flattering and satisfying. But Greenson could not replace her need to work, to do something as an actress, and without the compensations of creative activity, she fell into a depression. At this time, she sent to Norman Rosten a lyric expressing her mood of dark doubt for the course of her inner life:

> Help Help
> Help I feel life coming closer
> When all I want is to die.

A part of her, as she told her best friends, rejected the stifling manipulation of her psychotherapeutic situation – but she felt more and more dependent.

Marilyn's complete absorption into the orbit of Greenson's life continued uninterrupted, and on a Saturday afternoon in late November, the doctor took a remarkably selfish step. Asking Marilyn to come to his home for two sessions in one day, he sent her back to Ralph Roberts, who was waiting in the car at kerbside. She was, as Roberts could never forget, deeply upset and weeping. 'Dr Greenson,' she said, 'thinks you should go back to New York. He has chosen someone else to be a companion for me. He said that two Ralphs in my life are one too many. I told him I call you *Rafe* [the English pronunciation of his name]. "He's *Rafe!*" I said, over and over. But he says no – that I need someone else.'

Without argument, Roberts came to the apartment the next afternoon to collect the massage table he used each night for

Marilyn. Gloria Lovell told him she had heard Marilyn weeping throughout the night, that she longed for her friend to remain. In thrall to Greenson, she had no courage or resourse to withstand this extraordinary imposition and rupture of a good and beneficial friendship. Marilyn Monroe's life was not becoming wider and more open to growth, but narrower, more dependent and childish. 'She began to get rid of a lot of people around her who only took advantage of her,' wrote Greenson of this time in Marilyn's life.

The following day, before departing for New York, Roberts came to say goodbye, but he could not rouse Marilyn after ringing for five minutes. Untangling a garden hose, he made as if to water the shrubbery, flowers and plants and then deliberately splashed her apartment. Marilyn pulled back the curtain, opened a window and said, 'I know what you're thinking, but everything's all right.' Yes, she said, she was groggy from too many sleeping pills. But there was a reason. The residents of a nearby house had a wild party the night before, and knowing of their famous neighbour they stood under her window and shouted her name, calling her to join them.

Marilyn never knew the name of the woman who had led this group, nor did they ever meet; she was a former bit-part actress who sometimes used the name Jeanne Carmen. Like Robert Slatzer, Carmen emerged from obscurity many years later to transmute her geographical proximity to Marilyn Monroe into something of a career. Claiming that she was Marilyn's roommate at Doheny Drive, she began, in the 1980s, to invent an imaginative series of scurrilous tales for which there is simply no basis in fact: a wild romance between Marilyn and Robert Kennedy, for example, including indiscreet assignations, joyrides to Malibu beaches and nude swims.

Like that of Slatzer, however, Carmen's name is nowhere to be found in Marilyn's address books, nor did anyone who knew Marilyn ever hear of (much less see or meet) her. Betsy Duncan Hammes, a singer, close friend of Frank Sinatra and Bob Hope and the daughter of a Los Angeles County under-sheriff, was a frequent visitor to her friend Gloria Lovell, who lived across the breezeway from Marilyn and dined several times weekly with her. 'I never heard of anyone named Jeanne Carmen,' said Betsy. 'I know she never lived in that complex, because Gloria and I certainly would have known her, just as we would have known if Marilyn had a roommate.'

But Marilyn's difficulties were just beginning. Also in November, she was summoned for discussions at her old studio, where she had contractual obligations to fulfil: two films, to be specific, at $100,000 salary per picture. Marilyn was not the only bankable Hollywood star to be embittered by the much trumpeted news that Elizabeth Taylor was to receive ten times that amount for a Fox epic called *Cleopatra* which (as everyone also knew) was in a financial and artistic pickle – first at the London production facilities and then in Rome, where its budget had risen to the then comical sum of thirty million dollars, plunging Fox to the brink of bankruptcy. By this time, *Cleopatra* was almost a metaphor for the studio itself, where astounding chaos prevailed.

The company's problems had, indeed, been escalating for years and may be briefly outlined. Buddy Adler had been production chief since 1956, after Darryl F. Zanuck retreated to Europe to work as an independent producer releasing through the studio. An effective and admired executive, Adler died in 1960, at fifty-one. At this crucial time, Fox was reeling from the advance of television, the decline of the old studio system (and the end of the old seven-year contract), the beginning of wildly inflated salaries (Taylor's was a case in point) and an array of nasty power struggles within the executive boards of Fox in Los Angeles and New York.

Also at this time, blame for the unprecedented costs of *Cleopatra* was laid at the feet of studio president Spyros Skouras, who was 'demoted upward', as it were, from president to chairman of the board. The power vacuum was filled, on orders from Fox's New York-based committee of financiers, by a man named Robert Goldstein, who was not especially familiar with the fine points of film production. 'You must have a death wish,' said executive vice-president David Brown candidly to Skouras, who had asked his opinion about this choice. Brown's reply was subsequently reported (by Skouras or some meddler) to Goldstein. 'Not long after,' as Brown added, 'I was at once booted out of the executive vice-presidency for creative operations and my position as a director of the parent company, and suddenly I was a producer!'*

The chaos continued, with reversal following comic reversal: Hollywood sometimes resembles its own best silent two-reel comedies.

First, Fox's board assigned two outside financial experts, John Loeb and Milton Gould, to investigate the company's problems. According to Gould, they travelled from New York to Hollywood, found the studio 'in a shambles, and immediately got Goldstein dismissed'. Although he admitted that he had absolutely no expertise in the business of moviemaking ('My job was to stop the mismanagement of money'), Gould replaced Goldstein with a new executive vice-president in charge of production.

This new man was Peter G. Levathes, an intelligent and sophisticated attorney, once a Skouras assistant and then, after the war, head of the television department at the Young & Rubicam advertising agency in New York. Unaccustomed to the techniques, traditions, demands, details and temperaments of film studio productions, Levathes was an energetic and benevolent man, but perhaps not the wisest choice to head a studio with a $22 million debt. He was, according to director Jean Negulesco, 'a tall, dark man, nervous and with the far-away look of a man with responsibilities beyond his understanding or ability.'

By this time, David Brown was at work on Marilyn's new

---

* As it happened, this was fortunate for Brown and for film history: David Brown went on to produce or co-produce an impressive array of films: *The Sting*, *Jaws*, *Cocoon*, *Driving Miss Daisy*, *The Player* and *A Few Good Men*, to name only a few.

picture, for which he had brought in writer Arnold Shulman to work on a revision of the popular 1940 comedy *My Favorite Wife*, which had starred Cary Grant and Irene Dunne. In the new version, Marilyn (as Ellen Arden), married and the mother of two babies, is seduced by the boss of her husband Nick, a swiftly rising young businessman. Failing this rather sordid little 'fidelity test', she believes she has ruined Nick's chances for success, and, humiliated, she flees to Hawaii and the Far East. But Ellen misses the connecting flight from Honolulu to Japan – a lucky mistake, for that plane goes down in the Pacific. She is reported dead but remains in Hawaii for five years, until longing for her children and the collapse of an affair encourage her to return home. But at this very time, Nick has had her declared legally dead and has just remarried.*

From the start, Marilyn did not want to do this picture, 'but Dr Greenson said it would be good for me', as she reported to Ralph Roberts. Brown, borrowing a song from a Fred Astaire film, quickly settled on the film's title: *Something's Got to Give*. In addition, he engaged George Cukor, who also owed Fox a picture; despite the manifold problems on *Let's Make Love*, Marilyn and George had parted as friends and she approved the choice. But very soon Cukor saw danger signals.

First of all, the scenario was an almost insurmountable challenge, both in construction and character credibility: how, for example, could the comic, the sexual and the sentimental aspects of this story be updated and balanced? As autumn passed, even a sharp and witty writer like Shulman was stymied – by the project as well as by the accumulation of corporate problems at Fox. 'There was nothing they could do right with this thing from the start,' Shulman recalled years later, adding that it was

---

* The 1940 script, by Sam and Bella Spewack, was itself inspired by Tennyson's poem 'Enoch Arden', about a seaman believed dead who returns after a long absence to find his wife remarried. Recognizing her happiness, he does not reveal his identity and subsequently dies of grief. The Spewacks and their successors slyly named the couple of their movie scenario *Ellen* and *Nick* (combined to allude to Enoch) *Arden*.

clear to him (as it was also to David Brown and others) that both the film and Marilyn were to be the targets of blame for an increasing series of management blunders. That winter, Shulman was succeeded by Nunnally Johnson, who had written and produced *We're Not Married* and *How To Marry a Millionaire*.

'Have *you* been trapped into this, too?' Marilyn asked Johnson when they met for a script conference at the Beverly Hills Hotel. As they discussed the problems with the scenario he found that she was 'quick, she was gay, she probed into certain aspects of the story with the sharpest perception.'

At the same time, David Brown was replaced by an unlikely and yet, from one viewpoint, an entirely logical candidate. 'Richard Zanuck called me one day,' Brown recalled, 'and reported that he had just been in an elevator with a man who was carrying the script-in-progress for *Something's Got to Give*. "I'm worried," Dick said. I was, too.'

Henry Weinstein, a New York producer of the 'Play of the Week' television series and an associate producer for the Theatre Guild, had only recently been hired by Fox – 'and Weinstein [thus David Brown] was the studio's instrument to remove me as producer from Marilyn's picture.' The decision was made unilaterally by Levathes, who cabled Spyros Skouras in New York on 10 January: 'The change will become effective this week as discreetly as possible.' Weinstein's appointment to the job had also been championed by none other than Ralph Greenson; he was much admired by the young producer, who knew the psychiatrist socially. Reflecting after the fact, Levathes realized years later 'how much Weinstein and Greenson seemed to need each other'.

'Her therapist said it would be better if Marilyn had someone who understood her and could deal with her, so Henry got the job,' recalled David Brown. 'His appointment made no one very happy. George Cukor, for example, threw an ink bottle at poor Henry on first meeting.' As for Greenson, he obtained for himself a position on the picture as special consultant and counsellor to Marilyn Monroe – not for a large fee, but, to be sure, for a satisfying charge to his ego. This was the closest he came, after his dramatic lecture presentations onstage, to achieving relative stardom.

Everything was spinning out of control, as Nunnally Johnson recalled: 'there was no one at the studio with the strength or intelligence to call a halt to this idiocy.' While he wrote and pre-production began on *Something's Got to Give*, Marilyn turned to the occupation that so often encouraged her: studio photography. Twenty-seven-year-old Douglas Kirkland, then a bright young photographer who would soon be established as one of the finest in his profession, was on the staff of *Look* magazine, then preparing a special quarter-century issue. Elizabeth Taylor, Judy Garland and Shirley MacLaine had been photographed, and Marilyn agreed to a session in November.

Douglas Kirkland met Marilyn Monroe three times and, as he recalled years later, he saw 'essentially a different person each time I met her'. First, he and two colleagues met Marilyn at her apartment. 'She seemed,' he recalled, 'to be paranoid about her privacy, and we were all made to vow we would never divulge where she lived.' Apart from that, he found a cheerful, easygoing woman with no star complex, speaking animatedly and eager to co-operate with the project.

Their next meeting, two days later, was for the shooting session at a photographer's studio, which began at nine in the evening. Kirkland vividly recalled that she seemed 'very white, almost luminescent – this white vision drifted as if in slow motion into the studio. She seemed to give off a glow.' As they had agreed, Marilyn slipped into a bed with silk sheets, then discarded her robe and, from above, Kirkland began to take his pictures. But then she said, 'Let's stop for a minute,' and, turning to the crew – several assistants to herself and Kirkland and some people from *Look* – she said, 'I want everybody to leave. I think I should be alone with this boy. I find it works better that way.'

There was, as he remembered, an extraordinary sexual tension in the room. Kirkland snapped his photos, Marilyn seduced the camera, turned, sat forward, leaned backward. And then she asked him to come down from the gallery above and to sit on the bed with her. Kirkland, married and father of two, continued to work 'even while she was teasing, toying with me, making it very clear what she meant and what she was offering.' After the last photo, he shared a glass of champagne with her, and their colleagues rejoined them.

'This glowing-white woman in white silk sheets had enjoyed playing this game,' recalled Kirkland, 'and even though nothing happened between us, for her something had.' It was just as André de Dienes, Phillipe Halsman, Milton Greene and every photographer had learned: the camera lens was not an inert glass eye, but the eyes of millions. The ultimate sex object, she responded to its stimulative power, it aroused her, and – as the entire impact of her personality was directed at that lens – she ineluctably invited the man present and the men absent.

Their third meeting took place at Marilyn's apartment two days later, when Kirkland returned with the proofs. She wore a scarf on her head, and dark glasses. Alone, she was irritable and aloof and, after some delays, selected ten images she approved; those she rejected she cut up with scissors. Of the one she most preferred, Marilyn said, 'To me, this is the kind of girl a truck driver would like to be in there with, in those white sheets.' A certain blue-collar appeal, he sensed, was what Marilyn sought: the presentation of a woman for the average working man, not the aristocrat. 'If I am a star,' she said soon after, 'it was the people who made me one – not the studio, but the people.'

That Marilyn was alternately cheerful and troubled had a foundation Douglas Kirkland could not have known.

Spending so many hours at the Greenson home on Franklin Street, Marilyn came to appreciate its Spanish colonial charm – the stucco walls, the balconies, the profusion of hand-painted Mexican tiles, the beamed cathedral-ceiling living-room, the home-like kitchen. At this house she dined often after her therapy; here she taught Joan to dance, and here she attended

Greenson's evening musicales. Her love for the house, and her virtual part-time residence there, led Greenson to suggest that Marilyn look to purchase a similar home of her own – nearby. To this idea she was lukewarm, as she was to the idea of the new Fox project. But by this time Greenson was making the decisions. 'I encouraged her to buy the house,' he said later. 'She said she had no interest in remaining in California or making it her residence. She said that after her next picture she would go back to New York, which she considered her permanent home.'

But that statement he made in 1966. In 1961, the task of helping Marilyn find the right house fell to the woman who was engaged as her new companion, replacing in Marilyn's life (so the doctor intended) the devoted Ralph Roberts.

Greenson had told Marilyn to hire Eunice Murray, then fifty-nine, the woman who had sold her home to him fourteen years before. 'The doctor thought the house would take the place of a baby or a husband, and that it would protect her,' according to Eunice, who was perhaps unaware of the impudence and imprudence of such an idea. But this was not the worst of the matter. In Marilyn Monroe's submission to Eunice Murray – there can be no other noun to describe their relationship – Ralph Greenson made perhaps the unwisest choice of his life. Even his wife (not to say every one of Marilyn's friends and colleagues who subsequently met Eunice) described Eunice as one of the strangest creatures in their experience. But from the end of 1961, Marilyn spent very few nights without Eunice Murray nearby: when she had time off, Greenson brought Marilyn to live with his family again, because, he believed, 'there was nobody else around whom I could trust.' This is among the oddest of Greenson's odd remarks, but 'there was nobody else' but Eunice who was so willing to do his bidding with regard to Marilyn Monroe.

The second of two girls, Eunice Joerndt was born in Chicago in March 1902, and when she was very young, her parents – devout members of the Jehovah's Witnesses sect – moved to rural Ohio. An outwardly docile and sweet child, Eunice attended country grade school and at fifteen she was sent off to the Urbana School and Academy (in Urbana, Ohio), an institution steeped in the tradition of the Swedenborgian religion, where her sister Carolyn, four years older than Eunice, was already boarding. The following year the school roster lists Los Angeles as Eunice's home address and Chicago as Carolyn's.

This discrepancy is easily explained. Contacted at their new home in Los Angeles, the parents were told that Carolyn was ill with Spanish influenza and had been put under a physician's care. Enraged at this flagrant defiance of their religious prohibition against medical care, the Joerndts legally disowned poor Carolyn, who thenceforth ceased to exist for them. When this unhappy news arrived, a school housemother temporarily looked after Carolyn.

Eunice escaped the flu and thus virtual orphanhood. But she adored her sister, considering herself (as she said) Carolyn's 'mere shadow'. She was also deeply affected by her parents' violent reaction, and from this time, and with good reason, she began to suffer subtle but distinct signs of emotional disturbance – primarily an inability to differentiate her life from that of her sister and other contemporaries, and an almost paralysing terror of being abandoned. Her formal education ended in 1918, before her sixteenth birthday, apparently because of her emotional and psychological frailty.

The influence of the Swedenborgian religion on the Joerndt girls at Urbana Academy cannot be overestimated. Urged to imitate their founder (the eighteenth-century Swedish scholar, scientist and theologian Emanuel Swedenborg), the forty students were urged 'constantly to engage in thought about God, salvation and the spiritual diseases of men' while undergoing 'instruction in arts and morals'. Set before them as the sublimest goal was marriage, which they believed continued in eternity.

The sisters' close alliance persisted, and in early 1924 they both announced their engagements. Grateful for the benevolence offered by the Urbana community and devoted to the principles of Swedenborgianism, Carolyn married Franklin Blackmer, a prominent Swedenborgian minister who served for six years as president of Urbana College. Carolyn herself taught there from 1921 to her wedding day, and she was a powerful force in the college's life until her death in 1972 – despite the retirement of her husband, a 'controversial, alienating man', as the college's historian candidly described him.

Continuing to identify with her sister, who that year married Reverend Blackmer, Eunice married John Murray, a World War veteran and the son of an equally prominent Swedenborgian minister named Walter Brown Murray. John planned to enter the ministry too, and to that end he attended the Yale Divinity School. But he quit the seminary, was never ordained, and turned instead to his first love, carpentry, which Eunice took for an imitation of the Lord Jesus himself. John Murray eventually rose to become vice-president of the United Brotherhood of Carpenters and Joiners.

Carolyn Joerndt Blackmer devoted her entire life to Swedenborgianism, Urbana, her husband and the little nursery school she opened on campus in 1929, which expressed her love of children and her desire for good early education. By that time, Eunice and John were beginning their own family and eventually had three daughters named Jacquelyn, Patricia and Marilyn. Although Eunice's lack of education prevented her from becoming a teacher, she imitated further her adored sister, to the point of calling herself a 'child nurse' or even, more boldly, a 'nurse' – a designation she continued to assume during her later life in Los Angeles, where she listed herself as such in telephone directories (as an educated, trained professional – indeed, a 'shadow' of Carolyn). Lacking any training or credentials other than the normal school of motherhood, Eunice throughout her life admired her sister Carolyn and her brother-in-law Franklin Blackmer to the point of idolatry; indeed, after the death of Carolyn she married Franklin, who died within the year. Eunice Joerndt Murray Blackmer's life might have served as the true-life basis of a minor nineteenth-century Gothic romance.

Eunice and John Murray's marriage was frankly troubled almost from the outset. He travelled round the country and into Mexico, organizing trade unions and leaving his wife to raise their daughters. They lived at various addresses in Los Angeles and during World War II (in which John was too old to serve) they resided on busy Twenty-sixth Street in Santa Monica. At the same time they began to build a five-bedroom Monterey hacienda on nearby Franklin Street – a house they had planned for years, according to Eunice's later memoir. The home was completed in 1946, but by that time John Murray was virtually an absentee father, and Eunice had no money for the mortgage. This was a grave disappointment for her, and she sold the home to Ralph Greenson after inhabiting it only four months; to maintain a connection to the house, she befriended the buyers and even asked if she might work for the doctor.

Almost at once, he hired her, putting her in the homes of his most important clients as monitor, companion and nursemaid, a position for which she had no training or special capability; she did, however, (as Greenson required), obediently report to him every detail of his clients' private lives. 'It was strictly a financial relationship,' said Eunice's son-in-law Philip Laclair, who married her daughter Marilyn.

> She did it for the money. Her husband [John Murray] left her badly, she had no formal training as a nurse – not even a high school education – but she was a kind woman and became a valuable asset to Greenson. She always followed his orders very closely.

In 1950, after more than a decade of long separations, the Murrays were at last divorced – a moment that perhaps made Eunice feel more than ever a failure, for in terminating a marriage she failed to live out one of Swedenborgianism's essential tenets; she had also failed in her emulation of Carolyn. (John Murray subsequently remarried, moved to New Mexico and died in 1958.) From 1950, Eunice was a lonely woman looking for purpose and comfort, and this she found in her work for Ralph Greenson. Eager to serve a man of authority who was both father figure and carer of souls, Eunice was sent by him to work (as she said) 'in any kind of therapy that seemed indicated', either with clients 'seriously ill with depression or schizophrenia, [or with] others, like Marilyn Monroe, [who] were simply recovering from stressful experiences and needed supportive aid.'

With her famous client Marilyn Monroe, who also bore the name of her youngest daughter, it would have been natural for Eunice to sense a younger version of herself – a shy, confused soul abandoned by her parents, denied education and victimized by unhappy marriages. Here Eunice (by 1961 a grandmother) had an opportunity to revise her own earlier life, to correct what had gone wrong – with the help of the common denominator she shared with Marilyn: Ralph Greenson. From the first day of their meeting at Doheny Drive in 1961, she regarded Marilyn as a recalcitrant child – so Greenson also described her – and as Marilyn's friends soon recognized, Eunice treated her with a certain benign condescension, indicating in her sweet, quiet manner where she should shop and how they should arrange their schedule around Marilyn's daily sessions with Greenson. And Marilyn, accustomed to accepting her doctor's decisions, offered no resistance – for the present. But very soon, as everyone recognized, Marilyn resented Eunice's prying and her obvious function as the doctor's 'plant'.

Among the first to recognize that Eunice was inappropriate for Marilyn was Pat Newcomb, who had almost daily contact with her client, helping to schedule appointments for photographers and reporters as well as facilitating the ongoing discussions with Fox. 'At first,' said Pat,

Marilyn sought her advice because she was supposed to be this wonderful housekeeper Greenson had found for her. But from day one, I did not trust Eunice Murray, who seemed to be always snooping around. I tried to stay out of her way because I just didn't like her. She was sort of a spook, always hovering, always on the fringes of things.

Alan Snyder was also dismayed, frankly describing Eunice as 'a very strange lady. She was put into Marilyn's life by Greenson, and she was always whispering – whispering and listening. She was this constant presence, reporting everything back to Greenson, and Marilyn quickly realized this,' for Eunice could often be overheard telephoning to Greenson the details he desired.

As Christmas approached, Marilyn telephoned Ralph Roberts in New York, telling him she was having a miserable time in therapy but that she still felt her best option was to stay with Greenson. 'She said that she dreaded doing the movie that was being planned for her, that she missed her Manhattan friends, and she asked me to return to Los Angeles with her after the trip she planned to New York early in 1962.' But despite her unhappiness Marilyn was, she told Ralph, looking forward to Christmas: Joe was coming to spend the holidays with her.

DiMaggio arrived in Los Angeles on 23 December, decorated Marilyn's apartment with a tree and stocked her refrigerator with champagne and caviar. On their behalf, Marilyn had accepted an invitation to the Greensons for Christmas dinner; Joe, always shy with strangers, reluctantly agreed to attend. New Year's Eve, however, the former Mr and Mrs DiMaggio spent quietly together at Doheny Drive.

That winter, Marilyn told Ralph and Pat (and presumably Joe) that Mrs Murray was on the lookout for a house in Brentwood, a western section of Los Angeles near Santa Monica and Franklin Street. This was the location Greenson and Mrs Murray thought best for Marilyn. Come to think of it, Marilyn added, it was odd: somehow she could never bring herself to address her housekeeper as anything but 'Mrs Murray', who always addressed her familiarly as 'Marilyn'.

Chapter Twenty

In late January 1962, Eunice Murray found a home for Marilyn Monroe. Ralph Greenson accompanied his patient on her first visit to approve the choice, and she purchased it from the owners, William and Doris Pagen, for $77,500. Marilyn had prudently deferred her income from *Some Like It Hot* and *The Misfits*, and that January she received cheques totalling $225,000; most of this paid past taxes, and then Marilyn put down $42,500 and signed for a 6½ per cent, fifteen-year mortgage with monthly payments of $320. She would take title and possession of her new home two months later.

Contracts were drawn up without problems and with the assistance of her new attorney, Milton Rudin (Greenson's brother-in-law). Rudin expedited the purchase of the house and subsequently managed the transfer of Marilyn's representation from MCA to his own firm. With Greenson, Murray, Weinstein and Rudin in place, both the private and professional aspects of Marilyn Monroe's life seemed safely assured. Only for a moment did she hesitate before signing the escrow papers: 'I felt badly because I was buying a house all alone,' she said later. But encouraged by Greenson, buy it she did, although as Marilyn's friend and stand-in Evelyn Moriarty recalled, 'she was talked into this house – by Mrs Murray and by Dr Greenson, as she told us several times while we were filming *Something's Got to Give*.'

The house was remarkably like a modest version of the

Murray–Greenson home. Near Santa Monica and the ocean, between Sunset and San Vicente Boulevards there is a series of short, dead-end streets off Carmelina Avenue known as the 'numbered Helenas'. At 12305 Fifth Helena Drive was a Spanish hacienda behind a high white wall. Secluded and private, the small (2300 square feet) single-storey house with attached garage and a tiny guest house needed considerable refurbishing, but it had a red-tiled roof, thick white stucco walls, casement windows, a beamed cathedral ceiling in the living-room and arched doorways throughout. The property also featured lush plantings and a swimming pool – all nestled in a quiet cul-de-sac convenient to shopping, to Fox and a mere mile from the Greenson residence on Franklin Street, just around the golf course of the Brentwood Country Club.

A visitor at the front door looked down to see a tile with the Latin motto *CURSUM PERFICIO*, a translation from the original Greek of a New Testament verse.* The threshold gave, without foyer, on to a small living-room; to the left were a kitchen, dining area and small solarium; to the right were three small bedrooms, one facing the front lawn, with a small private bath, and two smaller bedrooms connected by a second bath. As was the custom in many homes built during the Great Depression, there was little closet space – two small cupboards for three bedrooms, plus a linen closet – and none of these had operating locks, as Eunice pointed out. This was bad news to Marilyn's new secretary, a woman in her late fifties named Cherie Redmond. From January 1962, Cherie worked at Doheny Drive; from March, she was at Fifth Helena; and when

---

* The meaning of the original Greek in II Timothy 4:7, and of Jerome's later Latin rendering *Cursum perficio*, is 'I complete the course [or race]'. Centuries later, the verse was commonly used as a motto in European doorways to welcome travellers and pilgrims to places of refuge; it was then taken up and used in homes, the simple equivalent of the modern mat announcing 'Welcome!' Gloomy symbol-seekers have read the motto as Marilyn's prophecy of her death (or worse, her death-wish); in fact, it had been installed by the builder thirty years before.

production on the new film began, she was in daily attendance at Fox.

Cherie wished to secure Marilyn's financial papers, cheques and related private materials in a closet or in one of the small bedrooms – 'but there isn't one door in the place that locks,' as she wrote to her New York counterpart, Hedda Rosten (who was taking care of mail and minor secretarial duties at Fifty-seventh Street). As the next owners after Marilyn discovered, none of the inoperative interior locks were repaired while she was in residence. (Cherie finally had one installed for her small filing cabinet, on 15 March.)*

Just as Marilyn was planning the partial renovation of the new house and the purchase of new, Mexican-style furnishings, she heard the first rumblings of Hollywood talk about an important new man in her life: nothing in the press, of course (that would have been unthinkable in 1962), simply party chatter. In time, the talk became a loud shout, then an uproar.

A passionate love affair between Marilyn Monroe and John F. Kennedy has been assumed for so long that it has achieved as solid a place in public awareness as almost any other event in the man's brief presidency.

But if the phrase 'love affair' describes a protracted intimacy sustained by some degree of frequency, then such a connection between these two is impossible to establish with any of the rudimentary tools of historico-critical studies. In the absence of such evidence, no serious biographer can identify Monroe and Kennedy as partners in a love affair. All that can be known *for certain* is that on four occasions between October 1961 and August 1962, the president and the actress met, and that during *one* of those meetings they telephoned one of Marilyn's friends from a bedroom; soon after, Marilyn confided this one sexual encounter to her closest confidants, making clear that it was the extent of their involvement.

In October 1961, after a photography session for a magazine

* See Chapter 22, footnote, page 643.

story, Marilyn asked Allan Snyder to deliver her to a party at Patricia and Peter Lawford's Santa Monica beach house. The occasion was a dinner party in honour of Pat's brother, President Kennedy, and among the other guests were several blond movie stars – Kim Novak, Janet Leigh and Angie Dickinson, for all of whom the president had a keen appreciation. All contrary allegations notwithstanding, this was the first meeting between Marilyn Monroe and John Kennedy; hearsay about any earlier introduction simply cannot be substantiated. Before this, the schedules of Monroe and Kennedy since his inauguration in January 1961 reveal wide geographic distances between them. That October night, Marilyn was driven back to her apartment by one of the Lawfords' staff.

The second encounter occurred during February 1962, when Marilyn was again invited to a dinner party for the president, this time at the Manhattan home of Fifi Fell, the wealthy socialite widow of a famous industrialist. She was escorted from her New York apartment to the Fell residence by Milton Ebbins, who also saw her home.

The third meeting occurred on Saturday 24 March 1962, when both the president and Marilyn were house-guests of Bing Crosby in Palm Springs. On that occasion, she telephoned Ralph Roberts from the bedroom she was sharing with Kennedy.

'She asked me about the solus muscle,' according to Ralph, 'which she knew something about from the Mabel Ellsworth Todd book [*The Thinking Body*], and she had obviously been talking about this with the president, who was known to have all sorts of ailments, muscle and back trouble.' Ralph clearly recalled not only the origin and details of Marilyn's question but also the ease with which Kennedy himself then took the phone and thanked Roberts for his professional advice. 'Later, once the rumor mill was grinding,' according to Ralph,

Marilyn told me that this night in March was the only time of her 'affair' with JFK. Of course she was titillated beyond

belief, because for a year he had been trying, through Lawford, to have an evening with her. A great many people
thought, after that weekend, that there was more to it. But
Marilyn gave me the impression that it was not a major event
for either of them: it happened once, that weekend, and that
was that.

The fourth and final meeting took place in May 1962, at the
legendary birthday gala for Kennedy at Madison Square Garden, an event that included a party afterwards at the home of
movie executive Arthur Krim and his wife Mathilde, a scientist
later renowned for her great work against AIDS. This May
meeting was the briefest of them all, as the president, his brother
and his family were mobbed by friends, admirers and the press
all evening.

Were Marilyn Monroe's characteristic candour on such matters the only evidence – the fact that she never exaggerated nor
minimized her romantic involvements – that would be weighty
reason to accept her version of the one night of intimacy. There
is, however, good external evidence to support her claim.
Accounts of a more enduring affair with John Kennedy, stretching anywhere from a year to a decade, come from fanciful
supermarket journalists and tales told by those eager for quick
cash or quicker notoriety: those who fail to check the facts of
history and are thus easily despatched as reliable sources.

In fact, there were at least two other famous blond actresses
whose affairs with President Kennedy are far more easily established. Angie Dickinson almost completed her autobiography,
with all details of her affair with the president intact, then
decided to omit the Kennedy affair. But with that excision, her
story apparently lacked drama. On third thought, she withdrew
the typescript, returned the money paid as an advance against
royalties and, having once entered the publishing kingdom,
abandoned all hope for ever. A second blond actress, whose

autobiography was in fact published, simply omitted any mention of her brief affair with the president.

'Marilyn liked [President Kennedy] the man as well as the office,' according to Sidney Skolsky, among the first friends to be informed of the March tryst; he added that she also enjoyed the fantasy that this experience carried – 'the little orphan waif indulging in free love with the leader of the free world.' And as she soon after told Earl Wilson, Rupert Allan and Ralph Roberts, she found John Kennedy amusing, pleasant, interesting and enjoyable company, not to say immensely flattering. As for Mrs Kennedy, as Skolsky added, 'Marilyn did not regard [her] with envy or animosity,' and was aware that her own role in Kennedy's life (like that of other women she knew) was limited to a necessarily shallow transiency.

The posthumous revelations of Kennedy's philandering revealed the impossibility, for obvious reasons, of pursuing any serious romance with one woman. The exaggeration of his 'affair' with Marilyn is part of the myth of King Arthur's Camelot, an image subsequently grafted on to his brief term. There was a need to believe in the tradition of courtly intrigues and infidelities – Lancelot and Guinevere, Charles II and Nell Gwyn, Edward VII and Lillie Langtry; Nell and Lillie were actresses into the bargain. John F. Kennedy was, he might have thought, exercising a benevolent *droit du seigneur*.

But in this case there was only one rendezvous between the attractive, princely president and the reigning movie queen; to follow the Arthurian simile: the mists of Avalon are easily dispersed by shining reality's clear light on to the scene.

It is important to establish definitively the truth of this matter not only for the sake of historical accuracy but also because of a far more damaging rumour that began after Marilyn Monroe's death. The unfounded and scurrilous accounts of a concomitant or subsequent sexual affair with Robert F. Kennedy, the president's younger brother and attorney general, has been even more persistent than that of the presidential liaison. It has also led to the completely groundless assertion of a link between

Robert Kennedy and Marilyn's death – a connection so outrageous as to be hilarious were it not also injurious to the man's reputation.*

The rumours of an affair with Robert Kennedy are based on the simple fact that he met Marilyn Monroe four times, as their schedules during 1961 and 1962 reveal, complementing the testimony of (among others close to Kennedy) Edwin Guthman, Kennedy's closest associate during this time. But Robert Kennedy never shared a bed with Marilyn Monroe.

Guthman, a Pulitzer Prize-winning investigative reporter and journalist, was Special Assistant for Public Information in the Kennedy administration as well as senior press officer for the Justice Department. The travel logs of the attorney general's schedule for 1961–2 (preserved in the John F. Kennedy Library and in the National Archives) support the detailed accounts provided by Guthman. These, collectively, attest to the fact that Robert Kennedy and Marilyn Monroe enjoyed a socially polite relationship – four meetings and several phone calls over a period of less than ten months. But their respective whereabouts during this time made anything else impossible – even had they both been inclined to a dalliance, which is itself far from the truth on both sides.

Marilyn's first meeting with Robert Kennedy occurred several weeks before her introduction to the president. 'On either October 2 or 3, 1961,' said Guthman,

> Kennedy and I were attending a series of meetings with United States attorneys and members of the FBI in Albuquerque, Phoenix, Los Angeles, San Francisco, Portland and Seattle. The attorney general and I attended a dinner party at the Lawfords, and around midnight Marilyn decided to go home. But she had drunk too much champagne, and we were worried for her. Bobby and I would not let her drive her car, and we did so together, delivering her safely to her door.

* The history of this fiction is traced in the Afterword to this book, *The Great Deception*.

The second meeting between the attorney general and
Marilyn occurred on Wednesday 1 February 1962, when he and
his entourage dined at the Lawfords en route from Washington
to the Far East on a month-long diplomatic journey. 'That
evening,' according to Guthman, 'Marilyn was quite sober – a
terrifically nice person, really – fun to talk with, warm and interested in serious issues.'

Pat Newcomb, also present at the dinner, remembered that
Marilyn

> really cared about learning. The day before [the dinner
> party], Marilyn told me, 'I want to be in touch, Pat – I want
> to really know what's going on in the country.' She was espe-
> cially concerned about civil rights – she really cared about
> that. She had a list of questions prepared. When the press re-
> ported that Bobby was talking to her more than anyone else,
> that's what they meant. I saw the questions and I knew what
> they were talking about. She identified with all the people
> who were denied civil rights.

The next day, 2 February, Marilyn wrote two letters. To Isadore Miller, Marilyn sent a two-page letter in which she wrote
to her 'Dear Dad',

> Last night I attended a dinner in honor of the Attorney
> General, Robert Kennedy. He seems rather mature and bril-
> liant for his thirty-six years, but what I liked best about him,
> besides his Civil Rights program, is he's got such a wonderful
> sense of humor.

That same day, she wrote to Arthur Miller's son Bobby:

> I had dinner last night with the Attorney General of the
> United States, Robert Kennedy, and I asked him what his
> department was going to do about Civil Rights and some
> other issues. He is very intelligent and besides all that, he's

got a terrific sense of humor. I think you would like him. I was mostly impressed with how serious he is about Civil Rights. He answered all of my questions and then he said he would write me a letter and put it on paper. So, I'll send you a copy of the letter when I get it because there will be some very interesting things in it because I really asked many questions that I said the youth of America want answers to and want things done about.

The third and fourth meetings were the most casual of all. Peter and Patricia Lawford had invited Marilyn to attend a dinner party for Robert Kennedy on Wednesday 27 June. The Lawfords came for Marilyn early that evening, and with them was the attorney general – at Marilyn's specific invitation, for she had invited them all to see her new home. From there, they proceeded to the Lawfords' house for dinner: later, the attorney general's driver delivered her back to Fifth Helena. 'They all came over to see the house,' according to Eunice. 'She certainly didn't go sneaking around with Mr Kennedy or have a love affair with him!'*

All other accounts simply cannot be proven. Those who claim Robert Kennedy and Marilyn Monroe had a tryst in Los Angeles on 18 November 1961, for example, fail to deal with the fact that on that date, Kennedy was in New York, addressing a convocation at Fordham University; Marilyn, who was preparing for her photographic sessions with Douglas Kirkland,

---

* On Monday and Tuesday, 25 and 26 June, the attorney general was in Detroit, Chicago and Boulder addressing (among other groups) conferences of United States attorneys. On Tuesday afternoon, Kennedy arrived in Los Angeles, where he met FBI and IRS agents to discuss matters of criminal intelligence. On Thursday morning, he left Los Angeles for Oklahoma City, Nashville and Roanoke, whence he returned to Washington on 30 June. On this entire week, the record is unambiguous. The National Archives; FBI Files no. 77-51387-274 and 260 (documenting the attorney general's itinerary); and the Jerry Wald appointment books at the University of Southern California all confirm that the attorney general spent most of Wednesday afternoon, 27 June, with Wald, discussing the possibility of a film based on Kennedy's book *The Enemy Within* (1960).

dined in Los Angeles with the Greensons after a psychiatric session at the doctor's home. Such prevarications are equalled only by those who place the lovers' meetings on 24 February and 14 March 1962: on the first date, Kennedy was in Bonn, Germany, and Marilyn was in Mexico; on the second, he was in Washington addressing the American Business Council while she had just moved into her new home and had in her company Joe DiMaggio. As so it goes.

As long as he knew Robert Kennedy, said Edwin Guthman, he never had the remotest impression of an affair with Marilyn – much less any other woman.

Ethel was the woman in his life, and he seemed uninterested in any other except in the normal, socially acceptable and public way of such things. That summer, Marilyn did indeed call [Kennedy] several times at his Washington office. Bobby was a good listener, and he took an interest in her questions, her life, even her troubles. But the truth is that for me, for Bobby, and for Angie [Novello, Kennedy's secretary], the calls became something of a joke, and certainly nothing secret or whispered. We would say to one another something like, 'Oh, here she is again, with questions about this or that.' But these were always brief conversations. He was not a man to spend a lot of time on small talk with anyone. And to have an affair? Well, frankly it wasn't in his character.

To a person, Hollywood and New York reporters who knew Marilyn Monroe and Robert Kennedy are unanimous in agreement. 'The man [with whom she had the brief affair] was not Bobby Kennedy, but his brother John,' wrote Earl Wilson. 'There was no doubt it was Jack and not Bobby,' according to Marilyn's old friend Henry Rosenfeld. And Richard Goodwin, assistant special counsel to President Kennedy, a director of the subsequent Robert Kennedy campaigns and a leading scholar on the Kennedy family, put the matter simply: 'Anyone who knew Bobby Kennedy knew that it was not in his temperament [to have an affair]. We had many intimate talks over the years, and Marilyn Monroe's name never came up. Given Bobby's relation to his brother, it would have been unthinkable for him to 'take over' the relationship, as some have claimed.'* As for Marilyn, she asked Rupert Allan and Ralph Roberts if they had heard rumours of a romance between her and Robert Kennedy; when they replied that indeed they had, she insisted they were false. (Furthermore, according to Ralph and Rupert, Marilyn did not find the younger Kennedy physically appealing.)†

Four days after the 1 February dinner at the Lawford house, Marilyn was in New York, en route to visit Isadore Miller, then living in Florida, and from there she was going on for a shopping trip to Mexico. Her devotion to Miller in his lonely widowhood, like her affection and generosity to Arthur's children, continued uninterrupted until her death, even after Arthur's marriage to Inge Morath early in 1962. After Marilyn moved into her new home that March she often sent Isadore, Bobby and Jane gifts, made frequent offers of airline tickets for them to visit her in California, and asked what she might do for them as their friend.‡

---

* Sidney Skolsky and all of Peter Lawford's closest friends, including William Asher, Milton Ebbins and Joseph Naar, insist the Monroe–Kennedy friendship was platonic. Skolsky summed up their belief: 'As for Robert Kennedy, she never mentioned him,' (p. 234) and said that Norman Mailer, 'writing about Bobby, put together purple prose to make greenbacks' (quoted in Wilson, p. 60) – an assertion Mailer himself admitted in 1973.

† J. Edgar Hoover, who had kept a detailed dossier on Marilyn since before her marriage to Miller, would very much have appreciated confirmation of rumours about Marilyn and Robert Kennedy, but his files remained empty on the matter. 'It would have been impossible for Hoover not to have known about such goings-on had they occurred,' said Edwin Guthman, 'and he certainly would have used this information during Bobby's later campaigns for office.'

‡ To Isadore Miller on 2 February 1962: 'Do give my invitation some serious thought because remember, you haven't been west of the Rockies yet. But most of all, I would love to have you spend time with me . . . I'll sure enjoy seeing you. I send all my love and I miss you.' To Bobby Miller, same date: 'I would love it if you and Janie [his sister] wanted to come for a few days or a week – you are welcome to stay as long as you want to. I will take care of your plane tickets and meet you at the airport. You and Janie are always welcome. I guess we are all a little sloppy about writing, but I think we all know what we mean to each other, don't

In New York, Marilyn was first happily reunited with the Strasbergs. They attended the Old Vic's production of *Macbeth* at the City Center with her on 6 February. Marilyn then spent three days discussing with Paula the first, incomplete draft of the script for *Something's Got to Give*, and she attended several open and private classes at the Actors Studio. At the same time, she received many messages from California each day – about her new home; about the starting date for the film (she had yet to meet Weinstein); about calls from Joe, who was surprised to locate her in New York when he had made a special journey to visit her in Los Angeles; from Greenson, who called at least once daily. All these messages were meticulously recorded, logged and preserved by Cherie Redmond.

In addition to the calls, there were meetings with representatives of *Life* magazine regarding a forthcoming interview, and a conversation with Alan Levy that formed the basis of a long article in *Redbook* later that year. Like Marilyn's friends, Levy found her thoughtful and articulate.

Eunice, meanwhile, had obtained from Marilyn several hundred dollars' advance on her weekly salary and left Los Angeles on Monday 12 February. She visited her brother-in-law Churchill Murray in Mexico City, checked into a hotel and awaited Marilyn's arrival for their shopping expedition. No matter that Pat Newcomb was entirely prepared to attend Marilyn as friend and companion on the trip: Greenson had arranged that Eunice was to be with them.

'It wasn't hard to understand,' Pat said later. 'Eunice was simply Greenson's spy, sent down to report back everything Marilyn did. Soon even Marilyn began to see this.'

On Saturday the seventeenth, Marilyn arrived in Miami, where she was met by Pat Newcomb and by her new personal Los Angeles hair stylist George Masters (who had the painstaking task of maintaining Marilyn's platinum colour). For three days, Marilyn entertained Isadore, taking him to dinner at

we? At least I know I love you kids and I want to be your friend and stay in touch. I love you and miss you both. Give my love to Janie too.'

the Hotel Fontainebleau's Club Gigi and to a cabaret show at the Minaret. That spectacle was a disappointment, according to Miller, but when he suggested that they leave, Marilyn, who had been recognized, was unwilling to hurt the performers' feelings by rising to depart. The next evening she gave a dinner for several of Isadore's friends, and after she departed on Tuesday, he found $200 in an overcoat pocket. He had spent more than that on her in times past, she replied when he telephoned later to protest. 'You see,' he said later, 'Marilyn wanted me to protect her [like a father], but she also protected me.'

Apart from her hospital treatments, Marilyn had not been much in the public eye for over a year, and so Pat Newcomb and George Masters joined her for the trip to Mexico City: two press conferences had been arranged at the Hilton, to reveal a slim, shimmeringly lovely Marilyn shopping for her new home and speaking enthusiastically (despite her misgivings about the project) of going to work the following month on *Something's Got to Give*. Over eleven days beginning 21 February, Marilyn met the press and then, in the company of Fred Vanderbilt Field and his wife Nieves (to whom she was just then introduced through mutual friends), Marilyn toured Cuernavaca, Toluca, Taxco and Acapulco. They rummaged in local shops, bought ethnic furniture and housewares and ordered Mexican tiles for Marilyn's new kitchen and bathrooms. And as Pat and Eunice both noted, Marilyn took no sleeping pills, no drugs of any sort during this time.

While Pat expertly supervised press relations throughout the trip, George saw that Marilyn was – even on a casual outing – perfect to behold. 'Whenever she was being made up and I was doing her hair that extraordinary platinum,' George recalled,

some incredible change occurred and she became 'Marilyn Monroe.' Her voice changed, her hands and body motions altered and suddenly she was a different woman from the plain girl with faded blue jeans and a worn shirt I'd seen a few moments before. I've never seen anything like this complete change of personality. She was brilliant. She knew how to become what people expected.

He also found Eunice extraordinary, but (like Marilyn's other friends) in a different way. 'She was – how can I put it? – a very weird woman, like a witch. Terrifying, I remember thinking. She was terrifically jealous of Marilyn, separating her from her friends – just a divisive person.'

But such efforts on Eunice's part were unavailing when it came to a new and brief acquaintance Marilyn made that month. A Mexican Monroe fan named José Bolaños located them, claiming to be a writer as well as an admirer. Slim and dark with movie-star good looks, he was Marilyn's occasional escort for social events during the journey. Then, from Los Angeles, came the news of another Golden Globe Award for Marilyn, to be presented in March – whereupon she said to Pat, 'I guess I can go to the dinner with Sidney Skolsky.' Instead, Pat suggested that it would be good publicity for her to invite Bolaños to fly back as her escort for that evening.

At their expense, he was thrilled to do so. On Friday 2 March the little entourage returned to Los Angeles, and the following Monday she again received the Hollywood Foreign Press Association's award as 'the world's favourite female star'. George Masters, who helped prepare Marilyn for the evening, recalled that she ordered a green, floor-length beaded dress and then summoned two seamstresses from Fox; she stood for seven hours while the women recut the dress so that it would be dramatically backless instead of scooped-neck.

The presence of Marilyn with José at the dinner ignited rumours of a new Latin lover. Whatever the extent of the relationship (it does not seem to have been very romantic), José was back in Mexico soon after the award dinner, for another Joe had arrived, as if on cue. Unwilling to contest the presence of the legendary slugger, José retreated to his previous position as Marilyn's ultimate Mexican fan, with what supplementary memories may never be known.

Joe's unexpected arrival was not due to jealousy. He had heard (as who familiar with Hollywood news did not) that Marilyn's deportment at the award dinner that Monday evening was uncharacteristically embarrassing: she was, as her friend Susan Strasberg observed, 'drunk, barely in control, her voice slurred – and she wore a dress so tight she could hardly move.' For once, the silence in the room betokened not admiration or awe but, even in Hollywood, shock.

There were both chemical and emotional causes for her unusual conduct. She had received several injections on Saturday, Sunday and Monday from Hyman Engelberg – 'vitamin shots', as Eunice Murray euphemistically called them, but clearly more potent combinations of drugs. Among them were Nembutal, Seconal and phenobarbital (all dangerous and habit-forming barbiturates) and, for quick sleep, chloral hydrate (the so-called Mickey Finn knockout drops). These drugs, also provided for Marilyn in capsule form by prescription, were not so strictly controlled by the government as they were later.

As the noted pathologist Dr Arnold Abrams observed later, 'It was simply irresponsible to provide this sort of thing in the amounts Marilyn Monroe received them, even in 1962. These were known to be toxic drugs requiring careful monitoring. This was not 1940, when there was far less knowledge about this kind of medication.' To make matters worse, Greenson, too, began to provide heavier doses of sleeping pills; only later did he and Engelberg try to co-ordinate their prescriptions, with completely ineffectual results.

For physicians held in such apparent high regard, they failed egregiously to note the difference between *relaxation* and *relief from stress*. When Marilyn Monroe awoke after an intake of barbiturates, she was just as anxious as before – over professional matters that were quickly exacerbated by drugs. Tranquillizers like Valium and Librium (then being widely introduced) clearly relaxed people, but there was an erroneous assumption that they also relieved stress. Quite the contrary: the patient simply awoke with the same anxieties, which often seemed worse because of the depressing effect of the drugs themselves. Pat Newcomb, Rupert Allan and Ralph Roberts knew that Marilyn's medicine cabinet and bedside table resembled sample drawers at Schwab's: she had a veritable pharmacopoeia at her disposal.*

'During and after *The Misfits*,' as Roberts remembered, 'Greenson took no steps to get Marilyn off drugs: in fact he provided them.' And with an eventual tolerance of 300 milligrams of Nembutal nightly, she was indeed in a precarious situation – of this neither physician could have been unaware. As Pat Newcomb said, 'It is hard to understand negligence such as that.' Maintaining a roster of rich, famous and inadequate clients may provide at least a partial explanation, if not an excuse. 'I never liked Greenson,' said Allan Snyder years later, 'and never thought he was good for Marilyn. He gave her anything she wanted, just fed her with anything. There seemed something strange and phony about his entire relationship with Marilyn. And when he got himself on the Fox payroll, I was certain of it.'

There was also an element of emotional turmoil behind Marilyn's heavy sedation that weekend. On Saturday 3 March she saw Greenson for the first time in a month: cheerful when she arrived, she was tearful and depressed after the session. Indeed, she did not return to José Bolaños (who had checked in with her at the Beverly Hills Hotel that night), but instead remained with the Greensons. The content of her therapeutic session cannot be determined. Separately, it is known that Marilyn was greatly distressed by the news that Nunnally Johnson had ended his work on *Something's Got to Give* and left the project, which now seemed destined for disaster because no one could resolve (much less update) the script's complicated emotional threads, nor could any satisfactory conclusion be found

---

* That same year, as was subsequently documented in her divorce petition, Engelberg's wife was maintained by him on appallingly massive doses of barbiturates and hypnotics – ostensibly to keep her calm during the trauma of the termination of their thirty-year marriage. But the result of this prodigal administration of dangerous drugs was very nearly disastrous.

for the story. 'I don't know whether it will ever be made or not,' Johnson wrote to his old colleague Jean Negulesco. 'They seem to be too scared at Fox.'

For several days, Arnold Shulman (the original scenarist) was recalled, but it seemed to him that

> the studio simply wanted to forget about the picture, which they couldn't do because they had a tableful of signed contracts to pay off. I adored Marilyn, and when I confronted Peter Levathes and a few other good men at Fox that this was my understanding of the whole rotten scheme, it was unmistakable that this was their plan.

Fox, as David Brown recalled, was nearly bankrupt at the time, and among the films and television series then shooting at the studio, *Something's Got to Give* was the most expensive. In addition, the situation was disastrous whether the picture was completed or not. If completed and released as scripted, it would be one of the most pallid, unfunny, emotionally confused 'comedies' ever to come from a major studio – as the eight hours of outtakes and almost sixty minutes of edited, completed footage reveal. The final disposition of things in June leaves the distinct impression of a film no one believed would ever be completed – except Marilyn, who was, according to David Brown,

> an artist who knew exactly what she needed and what was good for her career – and she knew very well that if she were the cause of the picture's collapse, it would have been the very *worst* thing for her career. She knew she would have to do the picture once she had signed for it. She was a thorough professional, whatever her personal problems. She hadn't become Marilyn Monroe without serious ambition, after all, and it didn't desert her in 1962.

Shulman summed up the matter as he saw it: the new team of studio executives in charge at a time of unimaginable financial chaos wanted to force Marilyn's hand – to make her quit the project – enabling them to sue her for breach of contract. 'No matter what anybody writes,' Shulman told Marilyn that weekend, 'they're going to ruin the deal.'

When Marilyn arrived at Greenson's home that weekend, then, she had reason for anxiety: Marilyn – who could hardly be called paranoid about this matter – rightly believed that the new regime at Fox considered her a dispensable commodity.

But Greenson's method for dealing with her put the emphasis on his own needs, not hers. His technique was again an infringement of a cardinal rule of patient care: he invited her into the security of his home, under the pretext that hers would not be ready to move in to until late the following week. As an almost incidental issue, there was José Bolaños, of whom Greenson could not have approved (otherwise the man would not have been summarily dismissed). So there was Marilyn, the Greenson subordinate, again dependent on her therapist instead of on her own resources, attached to him instead of to her own choices and her own friends.

Even attorney Milton Rudin, who 'loved and admired [Greenson] like a brother', recognized that whatever Greenson's conscious motives, 'he involved Marilyn beyond [the point] he should have with the family. He was worried about her all the time – and then he involved me in the situation, too. Well, it was easy to feel sorry for Marilyn.'

By Tuesday 6 March, Marilyn was still at the Greenson house, and it was then that Joe arrived in Los Angeles, traced her to Franklin Street, and went to visit, hoping to help prepare for the move to Fifth Helena, by then firmly scheduled for Thursday and Friday. But when he arrived, a strange and disturbing thing happened, witnessed by a visiting trainee doctor.

On arrival, the young doctor learned that Marilyn Monroe was upstairs, 'in residence' as she had often been during the previous year, and now under sedation for emotional collapse. This arrangement, he then believed (and still did many years later), was

> out of line for a prominent training analyst who was sup-
> posed to be teaching students both the proper frame in which
> to help people and the proper professional identity to keep in
> working with patients.

But things became even more odd:

> Joe DiMaggio came to the house, and Marilyn Monroe was
> upstairs. Learning that Joe had come, she wanted to see him.
> But Greenson forbade them to meet. He asked Joe to remain
> downstairs to talk with him, and after a while Marilyn began
> to make a minor fuss upstairs – like a person confined in a
> hospital against her will who wanted to see her family or her
> visitors. Nevertheless, Greenson insisted on detaining Joe,
> and Marilyn was eventually close to a tantrum.

Then came the strangest moment of all:

> Joe excused himself and insisted that he was going to go up to
> see Marilyn, and Greenson turned to me and said, 'You see,
> this is a good example of the narcissistic character. See how
> demanding she is? She has to have things her way. She's
> nothing but a child, poor thing.'

The student said nothing, but the event disturbed him for years and led to his total loss of respect for his mentor. No professional expertise is required to recognize the classic signs of projection, for it was obviously Ralph Greenson himself who had to exert control and whose narcissistic personality demanded that he have his own way with her. It is also remarkable that Greenson would ignore every accepted protocol of professional ethics by discussing his patient with a third party, regardless of the close relationship.

Henry Weinstein recalled a similar breach of ethics by Greenson, when the psychiatrist said to him one day, 'Henry, don't you pay any attention to these fantasies of hers. She has a lot of them – one that is a typical fantasy of girls, for example, is that they want to go to bed with their fathers. That was her fantasy.' Whether this was indeed Marilyn's expressed dream or fear is impossible to know: by this time, Greenson himself was so deeply overwhelmed by his projection and countertransference that he may well have seen *himself* as the father figure to whom she was sexually attracted. In any case, his conversation about Marilyn with Weinstein was unconscionable. Marilyn's growing distrust of Greenson was indeed not paranoid. 'I think,' Weinstein said years later, 'that Ralph was dependent on her.'

It is astonishing that Greenson conducted himself with a patient in this manner, and that not a single one of his colleagues stood up to correct him. The reason may have been not only his enormous influence in the professional community, but also because he circulated among them the spurious and unsubstantiated report that Marilyn Monroe was 'schizophrenic', and that he himself was being supervised in caring for her by a man well known in Los Angeles for treating schizophrenics: Milton Wexler, who was not a medical doctor but the holder of an academic degree in psychology.

'At that time,' continued Greenson's young colleague,

everyone was experimenting with ways to treat schizophrenics, and Wexler had his own method. Greenson used Wexler as his supervisor, and thus gave his unorthodox treatment of Monroe an apparent legitimacy. One of the techniques was to invite the patient into the home – not only to provide what may have been lacking earlier, but to have a constant connection so the patient would never have undue anxiety on week-ends, or [suffer] any separation trauma.

Marilyn was, then, being further locked into her childhood instead of being freed from it. And Greenson, once upstaged by his sister Juliet, brought Marilyn into his home to domesticate her, to demythicize her, to control her and reduce her celebrity – all of it, of course, in the name of treating her emotional maladies and her insecurity. At home in his private clinic, with his professional supervisor providing a convenient endorsement of his tactics, Greenson became the prototype of the analyst who believed himself free of the conventional boundaries. With his own psyche so overwhelmingly intertwined with Marilyn's, he was no longer able to see the harm of his own actions. Greenson's attempt to keep Marilyn and Joe separate, then, reveals that he sensed a threat to his primacy – just as he had with her dear friend Ralph Roberts, who was 'one Ralph too many'.

Marilyn was the fairest game of all for such manipulation: impressed by learned and paternal men who seemed to offer protection; thrice divorced and uncertain of her own worth, acceptability, talent and capacity for love; about to have her own home for the first time – she mutely accepted what Greenson made of himself for her: the all-providing saviour figure every healthy and unneurotic therapist dreads to become. Everything that happened between Monroe and Greenson from that spring to her death suggests a perilous obsession. 'She was a poor creature I tried to help,' he said later, 'and I ended up hurting her.' These were perhaps the truest words he could have chosen to summarize their association.

As he had at Payne Whitney, however, Joe managed to extricate Marilyn from the situation. They returned to Doheny Drive, whence the movers, on 8 and 9 March, transferred her few pieces of furniture to 12305 Fifth Helena Drive; deliveries from Mexico and New York were awaited in the coming weeks. Joe stayed the weekend with Marilyn, left at the house a pair of pyjamas and a toothbrush, and proceeded on Tuesday the fourteenth for business with Monette.

Ralph Roberts, who had returned to Los Angeles, was as usual a great help to Marilyn as she settled in. Because she had not yet chosen the curtains for her bedroom, her first request of him was to tack up the blackout drapery she had had at Doheny

Drive, a single heavy piece of black serge that extended several feet wider than the window. 'When she went to bed, she could not bear a flicker of light from outside and always slept in a closed, warm, unlocked room.' Better than anyone, Ralph Roberts was in a position to know these habits: he treated Marilyn with a massage several times weekly, and by the time he departed, she had already retired for the night.

The script of *Something's Got to Give*, meanwhile, limped along its dreary way. On 11 March, Walter Bernstein was brought in to see what he could do with the seemingly endless unamusing scenes and turgid dialogue. By this time, as he recalled, the story and script costs alone had topped $300,000 – six times what the production had budgeted. But Fox had lost $22 million the previous year and (thus Bernstein) 'executives were not easily awed by figures'. Eager to please both the studio and star, Bernstein set to his task and went to Marilyn's home for script conferences. 'She was very charming and accommodating,' he recalled.

> She showed me proudly around her new house, and she was really lovely to be with. Things she had to say about the script were right on target. 'Marilyn Monroe wouldn't do this,' she said, and 'Marilyn Monroe wouldn't make this kind of move, they'd come to her,' and so forth. Some of this was typical movie star ego, but she was very shrewd about what would play and what wouldn't. Perhaps most of all, I remember her saying, 'Remember, you've got Marilyn Monroe. You've got to use her.'

She was, Bernstein added, particularly pleased with the Swedish-accented English she had perfected with a voice coach, to be used for one of the picture's few genuinely droll sequences. Weinstein, too, recalled that at their first meeting Marilyn said, 'Henry, I think you ought to use this scene instead of that one . . . and this plot development, because let's face it, if this part of the story is a struggle for a man between me and another woman, there's no contest!' It was at such time, Weinstein re-called, that 'she was very sure of herself, and her points were so well taken that we went ahead with virtually an entire rewrite.'

Charming and alert she may have been, but on 15 March Marilyn was attacked by a virus, suffering chills and a high fever. Besides her duties as publicist, Pat Newcomb became a friend in need, shuttling back and forth with tea and sympathy as well as business papers and ignoring Eunice's clear resent-ment of anyone trespassing on what she regarded as her turf. The housekeeper had plenty to occupy her, as she informed Greenson, who immediately ordered Marilyn to double Eunice's weekly salary to $200 – 'based on the fact that Marilyn's business secretary [Cherie Redmond] was receiving $250', as Eunice said. Likewise, Eunice engaged her son-in-law Norman Jeffries, his brother Keith and two friends for the work to be done in and around the house – without telling Marilyn of the personal relationship. Moreover, according to Cherie's daily account logs for March and April, Eunice asked for Marilyn's signature on blank cheques for Norman and Keith – a request that was rightly denied.

In her remarkably self-serving memoir, Eunice Murray ex-pressed her disdain for Cherie Redmond, a shrewd lady with a keen eye and an honest pen who came highly recommended by Milton Rudin. For her part, Cherie resented Eunice's authori-tarian attitude: 'It's not particularly inspiring,' as she wrote to Hedda Rosten, 'and in some ways terribly time-consuming, to work through Mrs Murray – and from Tinkers to Evers to Chance never facilitates things.' Her analogy to a baseball double-play was apt for a system that did not help at home or work. But with her quiet persistence, Eunice was not only re-porting but now arranging, too.

In the light of her background and life experience (not to mention her presence as Greenson's alter ego), Murray's pro-prietary attitude is easy to understand. Chosen for its resemblance to the home she lost and which was (as she said) the 'bond' between herself, Greenson and Marilyn, the house at

Fifth Helena became a kind of totem for her. Having lost her own family and her husband, the doctor was Eunice's surrogate husband: a paternalistic ministerial figure whose vocation it was to help others, and with whom she had associated herself for fifteen years, continuing her adulation of her sister and brother-in-law.

With complete charge over Marilyn granted by Greenson, Eunice had the opportunity to correct her past by recreating it: for her, Marilyn's house was hers – hence her virtual appropriation of its design, care and refurbishing. Just as she was making 12305 Fifth Helena her home, so was Marilyn her daughter and Greenson her husband returned. In Marilyn Monroe's life, Eunice Murray seemed for a time to regain everything to which she had ever aspired and then lost: the situation enabled her to be at last the unrealized, successful sister and the nurse-caretaker Carolyn had become. One of the major problems in all this was that Eunice was living more and more in a dangerous fantasy life. Perhaps without their full realization, then, Ralph Greenson and Eunice Murray were fulfilling one another's needs: the doctor was creating, as his wife said, a fantasy foster-home, a haven for all those he could save; and the nursemaid was taking Marilyn as her life's mission.

The object of this dangerous tangle of emotions was, however, stronger than most people believed. Determined to accept an invitation to join President Kennedy and other guests for the last weekend of March at Bing Crosby's home in Palm Springs, Marilyn threw off her illness. At the Crosby home, she radiated grace and wit for the guests and spent her one night in the president's bed.* It was at this time that Kennedy invited her to join the Madison Square gala to be held in May; she not only accepted the offer but said she would sing 'Happy Birthday'.

---

* 'Not in her worst nightmare,' according to her confidante Susan Strasberg, 'would Marilyn have wanted to be with JFK on any permanent basis. It was okay for one night to sleep with a charismatic president – and she loved the secrecy and drama of it. But he certainly wasn't the kind of man she wanted for life, and she was very clear to us about this.'

This pleasant weekend may at least partly explain why, the following Monday, Marilyn was (according to Walter Bernstein) 'in good humor and full of energy' at a meeting with her producer, director and writer. While she was there, the studio doctor Lee Seigel took Marilyn into an inner office and administered one of his famous 'vitamin shots', those venerable Hollywood drug concoctions that kept employees energetic or sedated, depending on the company's need and/or the star's wishes. 'Seigel was the Dr Feelgood at Fox,' recalled Ernest Lehman, who wrote and produced some of Hollywood's finest screenplays. 'I remember him giving me an intravenous injection once, as he did to hundreds of people at Fox. It was a dangerous mixture of amphetamines and God only knows what else.' The same sort of treatments were also being supplied to Marilyn every few days by Engelberg.

At the meeting, Marilyn learned that the start of *Something's Got to Give* was now postponed to the end of April; with that – despite an executive order from the studio that she must not risk a relapse of her illness by travelling to New York – Marilyn departed to discuss the film's problems with the Strasbergs. She was especially anxious, she told them, because an ending to the script still seemed beyond anyone's imagination, and in such a quandary Paula's assistance would be more than ever necessary as she groped her way through each day's scenes. This arrangement Lee negotiated at a fee of $5000 a week, half to be paid by Marilyn herself. Once an ardent Socialist, Lee now knew the value of a dollar.

As usual, Marilyn was as prodigal as she was needy of Paula. Around then she wrote a cheque for a thousand dollars, becoming one of the founding members of something called the Hollywood Museum Associates, a group planning a movie and television archive that never materialized; her cheque was never returned. The Miller children continued to receive occasional gifts for no other reason than her affection for them; and Marilyn sent to one of her studio hairdressers, Agnes Flanagan, a duplicate of a garden swing Agnes had admired one day at

Fifth Helena. Such acts of spontaneous generosity were still typical, as Allan Snyder and Evelyn Moriarty recalled, and one had to be very careful shopping with Marilyn. 'If you went to a store with her and pointed out a shirt or something you admired,' according to Snyder, 'you could be sure it would arrive at your home next day!'

This attitude was perhaps all the more remarkable because Marilyn, one of the handful of unfailingly bankable stars whose films, by this time, had earned Fox more than sixty million dollars, was honouring a commitment she could easily have simply torn up – to make *Something's Got to Give* for $100,000. By comparison, Cyd Charisse (in a supporting role) was hired for $50,000; Tom Tryon (in an even less important role) was to be paid $55,000; and Dean Martin and George Cukor were receiving $300,000 each for a film budgeted at $3,254,00. 'The arithmetic,' as another Fox producer said at the time, 'makes Marilyn look like a doll. She could have got a million and a percentage of the gross any day of the week. The studio has got itself a tremendous bargain.' If this is so, it remains unclear why her representatives did not negotiate for a higher salary: as David Brown noted, 'an agent should have come in to write a new contract – it would have been that simple.'

But nothing in the executive offices at Pico Boulevard was ever simple, especially in 1962. The budget on the Burton–Taylor extravaganza *Cleopatra*, which shut down in London and was reshooting everything in Rome, sped towards thirty million dollars, and the studio back lot was sold to pay for it; in addition, the commissary and the talent school were shut down, and the lawns on the property went unwatered. In June 1961, Fox had 29 producers, 41 writers and 2154 employees on its weekly payroll, working on 31 films; there were now 15 producers, 9 writers and 606 staff for only 9 films. The 55 contract players in 1961 cost Fox a weekly total of $26,995; a year later, there were 12 actors under contract at a total of $7480. Peter Levathes, his eye on the bottom line, announced proudly to Spyros Skouras that *Something's Got to Give* would be produced on time and within its budget, requiring only forty-seven working days. This was a well-meant but almost comical proclamation, for when shooting finally began on 23 April the script was still incomplete, Marilyn was ill, and Dean Martin had not yet completed a prior commitment.

Marilyn engaged a limousine and driver from the Carey Cadillac Company that spring, and records provide a chart to the course of her life. According to the detailed invoices charged to her and signed by her daily driver, Rudy Kautzky, her schedule up to the first day of shooting was unvarying, Mondays to Saturdays from 2 April. She began with a facial at Madame Renna's on Sunset Boulevard, usually around noon; this was followed by a session with Greenson in his Beverly Hills office and a reading of script lines with Paula, who was in residence at the Bel-Air Sands Hotel on Sunset. Marilyn then visited either Engelberg, Seigel or specialists who treated other ailments that plagued her; these doctors administered injections, sometimes wrote their own prescriptions and often gave Marilyn what she requested. She was then driven for food shopping at the Brentwood Mart on San Vicente Boulevard or at Jurgensen's in Beverly Hills, and in late afternoon she was driven back for a second session with Greenson at his home:
by now he was sometimes bringing her in for twice-daily counselling.

The routine was broken only for costume and makeup tests at Fox on 10 April and wardrobe fittings at home on 16 April. 'She was so happy to be back at work,' according to Henry Weinstein. 'The tests were marvelous. I never saw anyone so pleased and delighted as Marilyn during those tests.' According to film editor David Bretherton, Allan Snyder (still her preferred makeup artist and close friend) and Marjorie Plecher (costumier for the film and subsequently Mrs Snyder), Marilyn was more beautiful than ever when she arrived for the tests: they all noticed a clarity of expression, a luminous radiance and eagerness to work hard.

Weinstein's recollection that all during mid-April she lay at home in a 'barbiturate coma' and his panicky rush to the studio on 11 April to urge that the picture be cancelled can only be due to his unfamiliarity with a Nembutal hangover. In fact, as the limousine records indicate, she left with her driver at nine-fifteen that morning for a usual day of appointments: Weinstein, youthfully eager but injudicious, had arrived at six.

Thenceforth, except for the final outcome of a hopelessly derailed and cancelled picture, the making of *Something's Got to Give* paralleled the production of any other Monroe picture. Terrified of appearing before the camera, as Weinstein and the entire company recalled, Marilyn delayed, malingered and over-rehearsed; frightened of not sleeping sufficiently, she frequently took too many pills – no one bothered to monitor her intake – and so she was groggy and confused for several early morning hours; but determined to acquit herself well, she was brilliant when she finally arrived. Word-perfect, willing to work and re-work a scene to the director's pleasure, generous with her co-stars and fiercely dedicated to pleasing her audience, she was, as David Brown said, the consummate professional. As everyone became convinced – Snyder, Newcomb, Strasberg, Roberts, even Levathes – the source of the trouble was the conjunction of Greenson and Murray, a team they were powerless to counter. To her further alarm, Pat Newcomb discovered in mid-April that Eunice had moved into the guest room of Marilyn's home.

'Marilyn couldn't walk across a room without advice and counsel and people with vested interest,' Levathes said years later.

Her so-called advisors created the difficulties and caused her a terrible identity crisis. I thought Marilyn was a nice woman – not a shallow person who made no distinctions, but someone who thought about her life, who knew the differences between sham and reality. She had depth; it wasn't all fluff. She was enormously complex during her suffering and her absences from the production, but at her best there was no one like her.

Cukor agreed: the advice she was getting was utter rubbish.

On Sunday, 22 April, after a session with Greenson, Marilyn rode down to Hermosa Beach, south of Los Angeles. There the veteran hair colourist Pearl Porterfield (who had cared for, among others, the wavy white coiffure of Mae West) prepared Marilyn for her first day on the set of *Something's Got to Give*. Eunice was so impressed with the look when Marilyn arrived home that henceforth she had her thin brown hair washed and styled by Pearl Porterfield, too.

Marilyn's first scene was scheduled for Monday morning, 23 April, but when she awoke she had a blinding headache, no voice, and impaired respiration: she was seen by her dentist (the only physician she could reach at five in the morning), who diagnosed acute sinusitis. For the rest of that week, she was ordered to rest at home, visits to Greenson being the sole exception. But such occurrences are hardly rare in movie-making, and there were contingency plans. Her point-of-view shots (what her character sees) were photographed that day, and from Tuesday to Friday scenes with Cyd Charisse and Dean Martin were filmed.

Finally, on Monday 30 April, Marilyn appeared on the set promptly at nine for her first scenes in the picture. With her hair brilliantly white, her skin unblemished, her eyes clear and alert, she wore the required costume for her entrance: a red and white floral-print sheath, a white coat and white shoes. For seven hours – and over forty times, according to a careful count of the outtakes – she repeated the closeups in which, as Ellen Arden, she returns to her home for the first time in five years. Standing at the poolside, she gazes in silent wonder at her little boy and girl, splashing playfully, at first oblivious of her presence and then, when they chat with her, of her identity. The scene is a miracle, and not only because Marilyn in fact had a severe sinus infection and a temperature of 101°: she was forcing herself to work.

Finding her way through all the emotional complications of

the character's scene, she is alternately happy to see her children, frightened of their reaction, concerned for their welfare, proud of their growth and charm. In fully thirty of the forty takes Cukor directed, there is preserved Marilyn Monroe at the peak not only of her beauty but of the depth of her inner resources. With the daily help of Paula Strasberg, Marilyn had reached into her own lost childhood, and perhaps into the sorrow of her own failed pregnancies, and there she had found the mysterious complex of feelings that enabled her to give a simple scene its wistful, fully human regret. As in nothing she had done since *Bus Stop* and *The Prince and the Showgirl*, there is in this incomplete film the relic of an astonishing performance. Her smile is unforced, her brows arch and her eyes just begin to glaze with tears, as if a wash of memories has evoked both penance and longing.

The Marilyn Monroe of this film is wholly unlike that of *All About Eve* or *Niagara*, of *Gentlemen Prefer Blondes* or *The Seven Year Itch*. She is mature, serene, fragile – but graceful and resplendent, too. None of the emotions were manufactured: they were, to the contrary, deeply felt, imagined, *lived* in some way. The laughter with the children moments later is neither cute nor manic, but joyous, wise, confident that somehow all will be well. No one who sees them (or the few moments preserved in the 1990 commercial documentary that bears the film's title) can for a moment see this as anything but the efforts of a responsible and sensitive actress evoking recognizable human feeling and continuing to grow as an artist, just as she wished.

Marilyn worked until four o'clock that afternoon, when she returned home and collapsed into bed. Next day, Engelberg pronounced her ill with a sinus infection and unable to work – a judgement confirmed when Fox sent Seigel, who rang the executive offices to say he would not ask even the film's cocker spaniel to perform in such a condition. Marilyn was ordered to bed for the remainder of the week, and the studio was so informed. There was an ancillary issue at stake, too: with the hugging scenes Marilyn was required to do with them, her closeness was considered risky for the health of the two children.

'She was genuinely ill,' according to Marjorie Plecher, 'as anyone could see. But the studio didn't want to believe her.' Allan Snyder agreed: Marilyn, never strong physically, had been susceptible to colds and respiratory infections over the fifteen years he had known her, and that week she spiked a high fever with her sinus infection: 'But no one wanted to hear about that.' Pat Newcomb also knew this to be true.

On each of the daily production call sheets for 1–4 May, Marilyn's absence was announced as if it were a last-minute development each morning. Evelyn Moriarty said she was always informed a day or two in advance of Marilyn's continuing leave: 'Marilyn did *not* simply not show up!' Alternative shooting could thus be hastily scheduled.

Despite illness, Marilyn worked with Paula for hours at home. But then Fox pulled another tactical error, sending a messenger at ten or eleven each night with revised script pages printed, according to tradition, on a different-colour paper from the previous or original pages of dialogue; these new lines had been composed by this writer or that one, by Cukor, by anyone willing to risk what now seemed impossible. With all this confusion, 'Marilyn was shattered,' according to Nunnally Johnson, who kept in touch with her and the production. She saw her comeback film as a terrible failure, and she was right. 'And then more and more [revisions] arrived, until in the end there were only four pages left from the original script.' When Cukor and Weinstein learned the distress this was causing Marilyn, they tried to mislead her by having the changes inserted into a freshly bound script with all pages on the same colour paper as the original. 'She was much too smart [not to say experienced] to be misled by that trick,' concluded Johnson.

That same week, when she complained to Weinstein and Levathes, Marilyn reminded them that she had permission to attend President Kennedy's birthday gala in New York later in May. Evelyn Moriarty recalled that this absence was posted weeks in advance: indeed, the call sheet circulated on 10 May for 17 May noted that production would shut down that morning at eleven-thirty 'because of Miss Monroe's permission to go to N.Y.' It would have been unimaginable for the studio to refuse the presence of Hollywood's most famous star at a command performance. In addition, performers with other commitments were readily released for this special event, each sent to provide a portion of the evening's entertainment. Marilyn's intended appearance was already known and promulgated in New York, as Hedda mentioned to Cherie in a letter posted in the first week of May.

For the occasion, Marilyn was submitting to hours of fittings with Jean Louis, who had created the notorious gown worn by Marlene Dietrich in 1953 for her nightclub premiere – a skin-tight sheath of sequins, brilliants, rhinestones and chiffon that covered and flattered while giving the illusion of nudity. In Dietrich's case, a foundation garment was also required; Marilyn, however, would wear merely a sheer body stocking embroidered with sequins, so that she would seem to glitter in the spotlight. Literally sewn into it the evening of the party, she would wear, as *Life* magazine stressed later, 'nothing, absolutely nothing, underneath', and would appear enveloped only by reflected, diffused light – a veritable star indeed. Eunice made plain her disapproval of such a daring outfit: 'It might have been more graceful if it were looser,' she said, to which Marilyn gaily replied, 'Be brave, Mrs Murray – be brave!'

Although both Marilyn's and the studio's physicians ordered her to remain home from Tuesday to Friday (1–4 May), Cherie – now working on Marilyn's behalf at Fox – was required to telephone Eunice daily to ascertain the patient's health. Her log for 1 May contains a curious annotation: 'At 4.00, I called [Eunice], who said she would ask Marilyn how she felt and bring me back a message. But she didn't come back on the line. I didn't call her back and left at 6.30.' There are several such omissions on Eunice's part during April and May: she seems to have been afflicted with either a gradually failing memory or an astonishing lack of courtesy. In any case, Eunice seemed to be taking on the characteristics of one or another of Marilyn's doctors.

All that first week of May, Cukor shot around her, filming scenes with Dean Martin and Phil Silvers, Dean Martin and Cyd Charisse, a courtroom sequence on another sound stage, and Marilyn's point-of-view shots. Again, Greenson insisted on seeing Marilyn twice daily, and on these outings her limousine logs include daily stops to the Vicente Pharmacy, the Horton & Converse drugstore or one or another Westwood chemist. Her analyst was still providing abundant medications – not for her sinus condition (that would have been the responsibility of Engelberg or another specialist, whom she also visited), but for her anxiety and depression over *Something's Got to Give*. But the barbiturates and tranquillizers prescribed had exactly the opposite effect to what Greenson supposedly sought. Instead of encouraging Marilyn to work, the pills made her more and more dysfunctional: taken with the antibiotics, they became even more powerful sedatives and hypnotics, gradually rendering her confused, foggy and somnolent. Her condition could have been mistaken, by any passer-by, as that of a confirmed alcoholic. To young Joan Greenson fell again the task of transporting Marilyn, often in a drug haze and with speech impaired, to and from her home when Rudy was off duty.

In such a condition, Marilyn's behaviour toward friends would occasionally be demanding or socially inappropriate. She sometimes treated Pat like a personal servant rather than a professional assistant, ordering a second telephone line to be installed at Pat's home in order to have constant access to her publicist, for any request or complaint, any hour day or night. Yet when Pat's car went down with a terminal complaint, Marilyn presented her with a new one, waving away the cost.

At seven o'clock on the morning of Monday 7 May, Marilyn dutifully arrived for work, but half an hour later, alternately perspiring and shaking with chills, she was sent home. Fearing this, Cukor and his unit manager had arranged an alternative schedule, and the company proceeded south to Balboa Island for other scenes. But by the time they arrived, the weather had turned inclement and remained so the next day. Everyone was back on the set on Thursday, when *Something's Got to Give* completed fourteen days of shooting (only one with Marilyn) and was four and a half days behind schedule – by no means a morbid situation, and one typical of many productions. With the usual Hollywood ingenuities (to cover, for example, accidents, illness, weather, revised scripts or new sets), plans could be rearranged: in fact the 10 May call sheet proposed only one additional day of shooting to compensate for losses thus far incurred.

On Friday 11 May, Marilyn rang the studio and asked Evelyn to bring some items from her dressing room, a task the stand-in was glad to do. Arriving at Fifth Helena and hoping for the chance to visit Marilyn, Evelyn was summarily and curtly dismissed by Eunice: 'I'm sorry, Miss Monroe is in conference.' As Evelyn later learned, Marilyn was simply at the other end of the house, or in the bath and unaware of her friend's arrival. 'But what could I do?' Evelyn asked rhetorically years later. 'Mrs Murray was like a class monitor for Dr Greenson' – or, one might add, like Mrs Danvers, the nightmarish housekeeper who terrorized the second Mrs de Winter after the death of Rebecca.

On Saturday, Paula arrived at the house with her sister Bea Glass, who had prepared home-made soups and delicacies Marilyn liked. Joe had come to stay for the weekend, and so there was briefly a circle of affectionate serenity around Marilyn, who was cheerful despite her lingering illness. Pat summarized the feelings of several confidants when she said that of all Marilyn's entourage, 'Paula was among the most loyal and helpful. She took the rap for Marilyn's lateness, but she gave Marilyn a great deal. And she never tried to own Marilyn, or to cut others out of Marilyn's life.' Ralph Roberts, who also visited, saw a warm and supportive atmosphere around Marilyn: 'Joe was really the only one in her life then, and that gave us hope, for the rest of us knew there was something terribly wrong in Marilyn's relationship with Greenson – even Rudy was aware of it.'

Still, Greenson had established a profound dependency – and then he betrayed it. On 10 May he and his wife left for a five-week trip abroad: he was to deliver a lecture in Israel and they were to proceed to Switzerland for a long overdue visit to her mother, who had suffered a stroke in February. Weinstein implored Greenson not to go: 'Ralph had made himself very central to her functioning,' Weinstein recalled, 'and frankly, I was surprised and annoyed. He left when all of this was going on.' But the trip was one Greenson's wife much anticipated, perhaps as much for the chance to put some distance between her husband and the patient to whom he was inordinately and inextricably attached: by this time, anyone who knew patient and therapist also knew that she had become virtually his career. Greenson himself admitted to a close friend that 'Hildi was afraid to leave me home alone.'

Greenson must have been fearful of leaving his patient, too – fearful for himself, his relationship with her, his control of her. What he did prior to his departure, however, was markedly injudicious.

When I left for a five-week summer vacation, I felt it was indicated to leave her some medication which she might take when she felt depressed and agitated, i.e., rejected and tempted to act out. I prescribed a drug which is a quick-acting anti-depressant in combination with a sedative – Dexamyl. I also hoped she would be benefited by having something from me to depend on. I can condense the situation by saying that, at the time of my vacation, I felt that she would be unable to bear the depressive anxieties of being alone. The administering of the pill was an attempt to give her something of me to swallow, to take in, so that she could overcome the sense of terrible emptiness that would depress and infuriate her.

With this, the countertransference to which he referred – his dependence on Marilyn's dependence on him – is as clear as the monumentally egocentric eroticism which had by this time taken control of him: Ralph Greenson was by now in the grip of an obsession over which, henceforth, he had no control. Hildi was quite right to be 'afraid to leave [him] alone'. As for Dexamyl, it was an acceleration of the drug routine, a combination of Dexedrine and amobarbital – an amphetamine combined with a short-acting barbiturate that was eventually removed from the drug market because of the difficulty of achieving the correctly balanced ratio between the two chemicals.

Before his departure, Greenson recommended that Paula be dismissed from the production of *Something's Got to Give*: still projecting his own feelings on to others, he told Marilyn that Paula was simply taking advantage of her and her money. Marilyn said nothing, and in fact, although Paula soon departed for a brief trip to New York, Marilyn conveyed no such notice of dismissal to her or the studio.

But she was annoyed with Eunice, and within days of Greenson's departure she handed her a cheque and dismissed her. 'By this time,' according to Pat, 'Marilyn was on to Mrs Murray. She resented her and wanted to get her out. Naturally those of us who were close to Marilyn were delighted.' With this single action alone, as Marilyn told her friends, she was making an important step in self-assertion, in establishing her independence from a woman whose meddling interference she resented and whose snooping was offensive. Acting the adult and taking responsibility for her action – this was, she always thought, the goal of her psychotherapy in any case.

The deed must have encouraged and invigorated her, for that day Marilyn sped off to Fox and, for ten hours, submitted with remarkable patience and good humour to over fifty takes of a scene involving the family cocker spaniel. Expert in rehearsals, the dog (named Tippy by Marilyn, after the one she had lost in childhood to a neighbour's rage) refused to follow off-camera commands and cues, leaping around and behind her, panting and drooling over Marilyn for hours. Anyone else might have balked at kneeling so long on the ground waiting for an animal, but Marilyn laughed and joked that she knew how the Method could delay players until they find the right mood, and there was no reason a dog should not be similarly indulged. The hours of outtakes from this scene, often frustrating and uncomfortable for her, remain vastly amusing decades later. 'He's getting good!' she calls to Cukor after something like her twentieth take with the dog, and several times the film clips show Marilyn collapsing with laughter over the recalcitrant animal's antics.

Her energy and good humour continued on Tuesday and Wednesday, 15 and 16 May. But with writers scribbling furiously, Weinstein attempting to wrest from Cukor a sense of how this picture could continue without a firm finale, and several key roles still uncast, the only scenes to be filmed were retakes of Marilyn with the children at poolside.

The following morning she was again on time for work, chatting excitedly about her departure for New York. At the same time, Fox's telephone lines were jammed with a succession of calls to and from New York, aimed at preventing her journey. First, Weinstein learned from Cukor that if she was absent for Thursday afternoon and Friday's shootings, the picture would be six days behind schedule, and the director would now have to account for the delays to the new executives. By this time, as Weinstein recalled, they had all forgotten an additional reason Marilyn would not be at work on the seventeenth: she had had a letter of agreement appended to her contracts since 1956, to the effect that she would not be required at the studio during her menstrual period. 'She had set that day aside before we began production,' Weinstein recalled years later, 'and we had agreed we weren't going to shoot that day.' This turned out to be a convenience for the film – but how could the producer and director say that her absence actually gave them time to work out the final script problems and complete the casting on this chaotic picture?

This was a matter of concern to Cukor and Weinstein only because of the fierce attention such matters were receiving from the financiers in New York and from Levathes, their legate at the studio. 'I had no idea whether it was a good picture or not,' Milton Gould said years later. 'I was not a moviemaker. My job was to solve money problems.' His was an honourable task bravely assumed: but not to care 'whether it was a good picture or not' was also to act with pronounced myopia. Such an attitude in fact signalled the start of a trend that has long endured: creative decisions subsequently made by attorneys and business graduates, perhaps intelligent and benevolent, but ignorant of the fundamentally crazy and unpredictable nature of moviemaking and the impossibility of maintaining religious dedication to production schedules. These new men were concerned only for the so-called bottom line, with no reference to the value of the entertainment product.

The result of this short-sightedness was predictable. Anxious, Weinstein ('whose termination I had already planned', said Gould) called Milton Ebbins, Lawford's man in charge of West Coast preparations for the gala: 'You've got to do something, Milt. You're Peter's friend. You've got to help me. Marilyn is set to go to New York, and this just can't happen.'

'What do you mean, it can't happen?' countered Ebbins.

'Milt, she can't go. We're in the middle of a picture. Can't you do something?'

'Listen, Henry. Number one, I don't represent Marilyn Monroe. And number two, what's this sudden problem? This has been planned for weeks. It's the president's birthday, for God's sake!'

'Well, there's going to be a lot of trouble, Milt. If she goes – I don't know – she may lose the picture.'

'"Lose the picture"? What does that mean?'

'You know – '

There was a moment of silence, as Ebbins recalled, and then he replied: 'Look, Henry, I can't believe she's going to lose anything. Marilyn's not that dumb. And Mickey [Milton Rudin] is not that dumb. Mickey never called me, never said a word!'

As Evelyn Moriarty recalled, there had been no effort to prevent Marilyn's trip to New York until that week – and now every weapon in the corporate arsenal appeared. 'When Peter [Levathes] called to tell me Marilyn was leaving for New York on Thursday,' according to Milton Gould, 'I told him to forbid it. He did, but she went anyway. That's when I told him to fire her.' This final drastic measure took several weeks, however much Gould may have hoped the matter would be adjudicated with all despatch; but at last his bidding would be executed. The reasoning was simple: the studio could save over three million dollars by scrapping a film with only half a dozen sets and twenty actors – a project doomed from the first day of script conferences and in which the director and the star had no confidence. If they could find a persuasive reason – a star's illness, for example – Fox's insurance company might be persuaded to reimburse the monies spent. At least the picture might be temporarily shelved, rewritten, perhaps recast and recommenced later.

Had Fox not rushed to production (as Milton Rudin, for one, wisely counselled against), *Something's Got to Give* would either have been turned into a good film (first on paper, where all good films are made, and at which stage David Brown urged care and caution); or it would never have got beyond a prose treatment, saving money, jobs and the health of many. Of these machinations Marilyn knew nothing as she sped to New York.

'The whole thing was ridiculous,' Henry Weinstein said years later, reassessing the way the event was mismanaged.

At Fox, the men up front were trying to prove they were bosses. Had I been more experienced, I would have gone with her to New York with some press people from Fox. We could have made an advertising event out of it, going around with our own camera crew and signs reading *Something's Got to Give – Marilyn Monroe!* – instead of worrying about the schedule. But these men were concerned only about power, which of course is a Hollywood fixation. And to be concerned about power when you have Marilyn Monroe is stupidity.

At 11.30 on the morning of 17 May, as previously agreed, Marilyn's scenes were concluded – just as Peter Lawford and Milton Ebbins, who were to escort Marilyn and Pat to New York, arrived at Fox by helicopter to whisk them away to Los Angeles International Airport. 'Of course a car would have done just as well,' as Ebbins later said, 'but Peter loved to fly around in that helicopter. I told him I was surprised he didn't use it to go shopping at Sears.'

An hour later, Fox's attorneys filed a breach of contract notice (dated the previous day, 16 May), mailed both to MCA and to Milton Rudin, charging Marilyn with failure to work and a stern warning of dire consequences to follow. Had the studio's legal department collected every sabre from the prop rooms, the sound of rattling could not have been louder; to follow, one might have expected the muted clanking of chains.

Marilyn arrived that evening at her New York apartment, where early next morning Fox's New York office delivered a copy of the breach of contract letter to her door: now she knew clearly that she was in danger of being fired. Her reaction (as Pat Newcomb and Ralph Roberts recalled) was undisguised, justifiable outrage: how could Greenson have blithely left her for Europe? Surely his connection to the production, to Weinstein and to Rudin put him in a unique position to know this action would be taken against her. How could her 'team', as the men at Fox called Weinstein, Greenson and Rudin, not protect her at such a time? Why, indeed, ought she to be receiving this letter at all? Why did she have advocates if they could not be trusted to defend her against such ridiculous charges? Only her friends and her insistence on acquitting herself in the present task enabled her to prepare with a residual equanimity.

On Friday evening, the composer and producer Richard Adler, who was staging the birthday salute for the president, came to Marilyn's apartment to rehearse with her at the white piano. Over and over, for perhaps three hours, she sang 'Happy Birthday to you ...' Adler, recalled Ralph Roberts, 'became more and more perturbed, because he was afraid she was going to sound too sexy. He even called Peter Lawford to ask Marilyn to tone down her manner. But of course she just smiled and went right on preparing it the way she thought it would be best.'

Madison Square Garden, on Saturday evening, 19 May, was packed with more than fifteen thousand people who paid from one hundred to one thousand dollars for a ticket to a vast birthday party that served to pay off the Democratic National Committee's deficit from the 1960 presidential campaign.* Jack Benny, the elegant and witty master of ceremonies, introduced the performers – among them Ella Fitzgerald, Jimmy Durante, Peggy Lee, Henry Fonda, Maria Callas, Harry Belafonte, Mike Nichols and Elaine May – but there had to be a musical interlude when Marilyn's turn came, for she was as usual late. At last she arrived at the Garden, and was ready to go onstage after a last minute touch-up by Mickey Song, who styled the Kennedy brothers' hair. 'We kept working around her lateness,' remembered William Asher, the producer of the event, 'and the comedian Bill Dana suggested that Peter introduce her as "the late Marilyn Monroe."' Which is exactly what Peter did. In one of the most awkward and jarring moments in the history of events recorded by television, Marilyn – barely able to walk in her skin-tight body stocking – inched her way to the podium and Lawford announced, 'Mr President: the late Marilyn Monroe.'

Removing an ermine jacket and revealing herself in what Adlai Stevenson called 'skin and beads', a nervous Marilyn tentatively began to sing 'Happy Birthday'. It was not, as Adler

* Kennedy's birthday was being celebrated ten days early; that year he would turn forty-five.

had feared, tawdry or inappropriate, but breathless, with just a hint of parody – as if she would wink at a cliché. Did not a handsome young president deserve a new rendition, something different from what might be heard at the party of a seven-year-old? When the audience cheered and applauded after her smoky, nightclub rendition of the first verse, she jumped with delight, waving her arms and shouting, 'Everybody – sing!' A second chorus accompanied the arrival of a six-foot cake with forty-five candles, borne aloft by two chefs. Marilyn concluded her stint with a few lines sung to the tune of 'Thanks For the Memory':

Thanks, Mr President,
for everything you've done,
The battles that you've won –
The way you deal with U.S. Steel . . .

Halfway into his twenty-minute address, Kennedy thanked the performers individually, commenting that 'Miss Monroe left a picture to come all the way East, and I can now retire after having had "Happy Birthday" sung to me in such a sweet, wholesome way.' It was but one of many laugh lines in a typical Kennedy speech that combined political rhetoric, wit, good cheer and earnest allusions to important social issues. Backstage afterwards, the actors and performers greeted the president. Marilyn, who had invited Isadore Miller to be her guest that evening, introduced him to Kennedy: 'I'd like you to meet my former father-in-law,' she said proudly.

After the gala, a private reception was held at the East Side home of Arthur Krim and his wife Mathilde, who recalled, 'Marilyn came dressed in a body stocking covered with sequins, which looked as if they were just stuck to her skin because the net was a flesh color.' George Masters added that Marilyn 'reveled in that Jean Louis gown. She was flamboyant but somehow elegant and subtle about her nudity, as if it were the most natural thing in the world not to wear underwear.' Her main concern that evening was to see that Isadore, amid the crushing crowd of guests, had a chair and a plate of food. She never abandoned him to strangers, nor did she wander among the crowd seeking small talk, praise or compliments.

In a way, the evening was unimaginably important to Marilyn Monroe. Not only had the lost child found her momentary place in Camelot – she had made real the recurring dream of her childhood. For there she was, all but nude before her adorers, utterly without shame, somehow as innocent as a jaybird. 'There was a softness to her that was very appealing,' said Mathilde Krim. 'She was – well, just extraordinarily beautiful.'

Chapter Twenty-one

On Sunday 20 May – the day following the great gala – Marilyn rushed back to Los Angeles, where she found Eunice Murray calmly cooking supper for her at Fifth Helena. The housekeeper had, it seems (or so she said), taken the cheque and dismissal as simply signifying time off for a vacation, and here she was, cheerfully back at her post. Marilyn, tired and frankly glad to have someone to awaken her next morning, to prepare the breakfast, make some calls and attend to some household details, tacitly rescinded the discharge, which was never again mentioned.

Next morning she was on the set, working eight hours after a cool reception from her producer, director and crew. They must have known of the threat against her, but the picture still had its own problems. For one thing, the script was unfinished – and they called *her* unprofessional, as Marilyn later told Paula sarcastically. She was, in fact, clear-headed in her suspicions against her team and the entire management at Fox: the latter's incompetence during the last weeks of production and the amateurish inefficiency on and off the set suggest that the plan was indeed simply to justify Gould's order that Marilyn be dismissed and the picture shelved.

Despite all the commotion, all they could ask of Marilyn that Monday, 21 May, was to do more retakes of her scenes with the children, for Dean Martin had gone down with a cold. The production report for Tuesday notes that Martin 'reported for work, but that due to Marilyn Monroe's susceptibility and on the advice of her doctor, she refused to work with him until his recuperation.' But that day, too, she worked all morning with the children, completing medium and close shots for their pool-side conversation. Martin was still down with his cold on Wednesday and Thursday and remained at home until Friday. Marilyn worked those three full days, and one of them, as everyone hoped, made immediate international news.

On Wednesday 23 May, no other actor was required on the set but Marilyn for the scene in which, as the long lost Ellen Arden, she was to take a midnight swim after her return home. As she did so, she was to be seen by her husband from his bed-room upstairs, where he was with his new wife; this was to lead to some silent comic interplay and gesticulating between them to prevent her being discovered. From nine in the morning to four in the afternoon (with only a twenty-minute break for lunch), Marilyn remained in the pool, paddling, swimming, splashing and waving, while closeup, medium and long shots were taken again and yet again. In the script, she was to be swimming naked, with the illusion of nudity easily obtained by the flesh-coloured, two-piece bikini Marilyn wore all day.

There was, however, a problem. When cinematographer William Daniels gazed through his viewfinder at the long shot of Marilyn with her back to the camera, sitting at the edge of the pool towel-drying her hair, he noticed that the back strap of the bikini's top was clearly visible to the Technicolor camera. This he reported to Cukor, who approached Marilyn – who in turn readily tossed aside her bikini top for this simple, quick, rear-view image. In a few moments the shot was easily made.

But then Marilyn had an idea, one entirely natural for the woman who had posed nude for Tom Kelley on red silk in 1949; who had her skirt blown high for Billy Wilder over a subway grating in 1954; and who most recently had appeared at a presi-dential party with the scantiest covering. The shots she suggested were not in the script (and, she knew, would never be approved by the Motion Picture Production Code in 1962). But for publicity – to advertise *Something's Got to Give* all over the world – why not take several shots of her nude as she wrapped round herself the blue terry-cloth robe for the next sequence? She had been so many icons, after all: why not Venus Rising From the Waves? This would cost the picture not a cent, and it might bring in millions: Marilyn Monroe, soon to appear in *Something's Got to Give* – and, it was (wrongly) implied, naked, just the way you see her now in a magazine.

Weinstein and Cukor thought this was inspired, and things happened quickly. Two freelance photographers (William Woodfield and Lawrence Schiller) were hastily summoned to join the Fox studio photographer (James Mitchell). For just under an hour, many stills were made of Marilyn from various angles – but with nothing like total nudity, front or rear.

By the end of the day she was exhausted, but there was a burst of applause from the crew and even an embrace from Cukor. 'Do you think this was in bad taste?' Marilyn asked Agnes Flanagan as she headed for her dressing room. 'I told her,' said Agnes, a dignified Irish grandmother, 'that there was nothing suggestive about it at all.'

On Thursday 24 May, Marilyn was back on the set for solo closeups and over-the-shoulder two-shots with Cyd Charisse – despite an earache from her watery scenes. Martin was in his fourth sick day and there were last-minute rearrangements, but no one seemed much concerned; the picture was only nine days behind schedule, and these could easily be justified (especially with this surprise new publicity campaign). The production required only a conclusion to the messy, tangled script. On Friday 25 May, ignoring a low-grade fever and a slight discharge from her right ear, Marilyn worked without complaint, joining Martin and Charisse for eight complicated shots. In these, she spoke with a brilliantly phoney Swedish accent, Marilyn's character trying to pass herself off as a foreign maid in her own home. The outtakes remain among the indisputable examples of her greatly underestimated talent: she wanted, Marilyn said, to do a sendup of every Garbo mimic in history, and that is just what she gave Cukor. Now he and Weinstein began to worry even more – that despite the rumblings from executive offices here and in New York, something might not have to give at all: they could be getting a film worth saving.

Marilyn spent the weekend mostly alone, but she and Pat shopped for food on Saturday; the atmosphere, they agreed, was far pleasanter without Eunice lurking at weekends. Marilyn had placed a cotton-wool pad in her ear and was taking antibiotics she had left over from her bout of sinusitis, but by Saturday there was a frank infection and her temperature had risen to 102°. A massive injection of penicillin cured her in record time, but she could not report for work on Monday.

On Tuesday 29 May, she and Dean Martin worked six hours on dialogue, doing forty-six takes of five shots and completing one-and-a-quarter pages of script. As the outtakes reveal, Marilyn worked the scene carefully, executing a brief but gradually building anger, her voice always controlled, her eyes slowly blazing with resentment at an accusation of infidelity. Each time Cukor cut in, asking for a retake or giving direction, Marilyn listened patiently, sometimes asking a question, always nodding her agreement and eager to give what was best for the scene.

On Wednesday, Memorial Day, there was no call for anyone to report for work. On Thursday 31 May, Marilyn acted for the first time with her friend Wally Cox, for whom she had lobbied in the role of the shoe clerk roped in to pretend that he was marooned on a desert island with her for five years. Not only was this an astonishing day's work – thirty-eight takes of four setups, resulting in two-and-a-half pages of filmed script – it was also one of the most hilarious scenes Marilyn Monroe ever acted for film. Wearing a cashmere suit with a mink collar and matching mink hat, she whispered, cajoled, begged the milquetoast character to lunch with her – all the while trying on a pair of shoes two sizes too small ('Well, go barefoot for five years!'). Once again, she made an indifferent scene memorable by investing it with just the right, light comic touch – her voice lilting but confident, her gestures properly elegant. Had *Something's Got to Give* ever been released, the public would at least have seen Marilyn Monroe at arguably the loveliest point in her life.

The following day, 1 June 1962, Marilyn turned thirty-six. Evelyn Moriarty had planned a birthday celebration, but Cukor refused to allow any merriment until he had had a full day's work from his cast. In an overlong, actionless scene with Wally Cox and Dean Martin, Marilyn gave one of the subtlest performances of her career; it was also, alas, her final performance in a motion picture. With few words but with mock innocence, she tried to convince Martin that the meek Cox was her island partner. Marilyn had only to smile, to turn slightly to the left, to glance ever so lazily to the right – and there was film acting of a high calibre indeed, the result of fifteen years of hard effort at her craft. Here were gazes and intonations signifying wistfulness and victory, witty ruse and earnest yearning to be reunited with her husband: somehow, despite all the stress and pain of the last two months, she gave a performance of which any actress could be forever proud.

At six o'clock, Evelyn was permitted to wheel out a cake she had purchased that morning at the Farmers Market. Sparklers glittered on it and the traditional song echoed as Allan Snyder and Wally Cox poured champagne for everyone. Eunice angled her way on to the lot, drifting through distractedly as if she were a slightly boozy fairy godmother, and left saying nothing. But birthday or not, people departed quickly – it was Friday evening, someone said. Something was dreadfully wrong; an unusually tense atmosphere prevailed. In half an hour the party was over, and there were only herself, Wally and Evelyn left, sipping Dom Perignon from paper cups. Marilyn and Wally climbed into the limousine; she had with her the wardrobe's cashmere suit and mink hat. There were no plans for the evening – Joe had put through a call from Europe, where he was on business with Monette – and so Marilyn had accepted an invitation to appear at a fund-raising baseball game for charity.

She looked magnificent, posed happily for newsmen, and retired alone at ten o'clock.

However memorable her appearance and significant her work that week, she must have been miserably lonely by Friday night, not to say frightened of losing her job. But most of all, as she told friends in telephone calls that evening, she was enraged at Greenson, on whom she had been conditioned to rely completely. To her, it seemed the ultimate act of betrayal: an axe was about to fall, and she had no defences against it. Indeed, how else could she have felt after being so long a member of his family? Weinstein and Rudin had been right: a film at this time of her life, when she was so deeply (if ill-advisedly) committed to therapy, had been unwise, as even her tendency to a series of real physical maladies indicated. That she acquitted herself so brilliantly was a testament to her essential inner strength, her willingness to work, her desire not to let others down.

'What happened that week-end [after her birthday], I don't know, but to me it was more important than the weekend she died.' Thus spoke Henry Weinstein almost thirty years later.

At the time, he could not have known the bizarre events that were just beginning. Early Saturday morning, 2 June, weeping uncontrollably, Marilyn telephoned Greenson's son and daughter, Dan and Joan, who had been instructed by their father to respond if she called; once again, it is hard to comprehend the appropriateness of involving his children in what Greenson himself called a dangerous case. They entered Marilyn's bedroom, where they found her indescribably lonely and depressed, then giddy and disoriented – the classic signs of Dexamyl overdose. Following their father's instructions, they called Milton Wexler, who sped to the house, found 'a dangerous arsenal . . . a formidable array of sedatives on her bedside table and swept them all into his black bag' (thus Eunice). That night (actually on 3 June, at one in the morning), Dr Milton Uhley was summoned, in the absence of Engelberg, to provide sedation.

On Monday 4 June, Marilyn, sober but livid with rage, felt no obligation to work in a situation from which she felt entirely disconnected. Eunice, unaccustomed to seeing her in such undiluted anger, put through a call to Greenson in Switzerland, but he had not arrived yet from Israel. At the same time, Paula – who had flown back to Los Angeles and was in residence at the Chateau Marmont, prepared to help – telephoned Fox that Marilyn would not report until she had had discussions with her advisers. Prudently, Paula did not add her agreement with Marilyn that she ought not to work on a picture from which she was about to be dismissed. Marilyn, meanwhile, was on the telephone to Lee and to the Rostens, and to Ralph Roberts, Pat Newcomb, Allan Snyder and Agnes Flanagan. She had, it may be presumed, been taught in therapy to assert herself: now she was ensuring that her friends knew how bereft she felt. That day, two pages of the script for *Something's Got to Give* were filmed; there would be no more work, although the picture was not formally shut down for a week. Just before six that afternoon, Phil Feldman, vice-president of business operations at the studio, telephoned Milton Rudin, who could provide no answer as to whether Marilyn would be on the set on Tuesday or Wednesday.

On Tuesday evening, 5 June, Fox warned Rudin that they were prepared to file suit against Marilyn for breach of contract, to which Rudin replied that he understood their position, and all he could say was that at Marilyn's request he had telephoned Greenson in Switzerland, requesting that he return to facilitate a resolution to the situation. Weinstein, frantic, had also called Greenson, who was indeed en route even as they spoke; he arrived in Los Angeles the evening of Wednesday 6 June. 'Fox needed a reason to shut down that picture,' according to Evelyn Moriarty, who, along with the rest of the cast and crew, were piecing together the week's events. Paula, weary, called her and asked, 'Evelyn, do we have any friends?' Well may she have asked.

Greenson went directly from the airport to Fifth Helena on the evening of 6 June, then went home, and early next morning was back at Fifth Helena. And at this point events took a grotesque turn.

The contradictions in Greenson's conduct must be faced in all their complexity. On the one hand, he considered Marilyn's condition so perilous that he left specific instructions for her care with his children, three colleagues and his brother-in-law, her attorney. Having made the decision to depart, he then leaped at once to return, abandoning his wife and doing exactly what a therapist in such a situation is trained to avoid: playing the saviour and making himself central in her life. Marilyn's anger notwithstanding, he could have left her career problems in the hands of Rudin and Fox, where they were rightfully being adjudicated; that, however, would have been to admit peers – for him, competition.

What transpired at their reunion cannot be determined, but his attitude toward Marilyn was clear from a letter he wrote two weeks later to a friend named Lucille Ostrow which reveals the extent of his rage at himself, at Marilyn, and at a situation he had permitted to go beyond control. He had not only missed his vacation, he complained to Ostrow: he also missed a few days in New York planned as an interval – a business meeting with Leo Rosten, a party in Greenson's honour to be given by Dore Schary, and an appointment with his publisher. All these he cancelled, he said, to rescue his patient. Greenson added that he felt like an idiot, for on his return Marilyn recovered quickly and was delighted to be rid of the burden of a terrible picture. Furious for the inconvenience, Greenson ended the letter by saying that he had cancelled his other patients and was now seeing only this schizophrenic one regularly again: she had, in other words, completely taken over his time and his life – but (one might ask) at whose insistence? He was, Greenson told Ostrow, depressed and lonely; very likely without yet admitting it to himself, he bitterly resented what he had allowed Marilyn to do to him and his family. The letter, dated and postmarked 22 June 1962, is a bitter diatribe of therapist against patient.

'Everybody [on *Something's Got to Give*] was aware that Greenson had put Marilyn in a cocoon-like situation,' said Walter Bernstein.

> I always felt that she had become an investment to people like him – an investment not only financially, in caring for her, but even in the fabrication of her illness. It had become a need for him and others that she be considered sick, dependent and needy. There was something sinister about Ralph Greenson. It was well known that he exerted enormous influence over her.

Susan Strasberg agreed: his close involvement with her was an open secret no one really discussed.

But the influence and involvement then led beyond resentment to outrage and anger – indeed, to a rage that far exceeded hers. 'If I behaved in a way which hurt her,' he wrote to Kris on 20 August, 'she acted as though it was the end of the world and could not rest until peace had been re-established, but peace could be reconciliation and death.' This odd comment was followed by his admission that he became 'impatient with her constant complaints' and that he was 'being led by counter-transference feelings.'

But it was Greenson himself who had a lifelong tendency to irrational fits of anger. An actor and writer who sought his help was told that he ought to go elsewhere because the man 'needed a psychiatrist who could love him. You don't understand – psychiatrists must *love* their patients.' The young man replied that he understood perfectly if 'love' meant concern, but that otherwise this advice did not seem right. 'But then Greenson became a violent, screaming hysteric. He completely lost control, and in fact it frightened me. "How dare you challenge me!" he shouted. "*I* am the expert, not you! You are wrong, you are mad – you are a schizophrenic!"' The man found Greenson, after three meetings, a 'profoundly unstable man. And then I learned that most of his patients were bored, tennis-playing

Beverly Hills matrons or movie stars, and he hated them – in fact, he made no secret of it.' Other ex-clients felt uncomfortable at the constant intrusion of sex and questions about intimate sexual matters, whenever possible, into therapeutic discussions.

The anger was evident with peers and friends, too: Ralph Greenson was simply not a man to be challenged. In 1957 he received a letter from his old friend John Frosch, editor of the *Journal of the American Psychoanalytic Association*, reporting that an essay Greenson had submitted was not suitable for publication in its present form. This infuriated Greenson, and he answered in angry disbelief, wondering why Frosch was treating him so badly and why he bore such an obvious vendetta? On 4 February 1957, Frosch replied, shocked at his friend's tone, saying that Greenson was behaving in a completely irrational manner, that he saw this as strictly a professional decision. Greenson should consider revising his article and resubmitting it, Frosch concluded, but that never happened.

There are several primary documents connecting Marilyn's final dismissal from *Something's Got to Give* with Greenson's return from Switzerland and the events of 7 and 8 June: Greenson's letters to Ostrow and Kris; the memoranda of the Fox meetings on 5, 6 and 7 June; Eunice Murray's incomplete 1973 memoir; and the account of an eminent Beverly Hills plastic surgeon named Michael Gurdin.

Dr Gurdin became part of the story on the morning of 7 June, when Greenson brought Marilyn to his office. 'She was disheveled,' Gurdin recalled,

> and there were black and blue marks on both lower lids, poorly covered by makeup. The story Greenson gave me was that she was in her shower, slipped and fell. Now it was obvious to me that Miss Monroe was under the influence of

drugs – her voice was thick and slurred. But her major concern was that she had a picture commitment, and that she was fearful that her nose was broken. She actually talked very little, and the questions I put to her regarding her injury were answered by Dr Greenson. She did not answer. I did not take any X-rays because she did not want them. I examined her carefully, and I could find no evidence of a fracture.

According to Dr Gurdin, Marilyn's injuries could indeed have been the result of a fall, as he was told,

but it is possible that she could have been struck on the face. Either a fall or an assault would give those same signs, for if an injury is sustained to the nose to have any bleeding under the skin, you won't see it on your nose, you'll see it under the eyes – because the tissues under the eyes are very soft and loose, and blood escapes into them. Also, there's a direct connection between the tissue under the nose and eyes.

Once Gurdin had pronounced Marilyn fracture-free, a flurry of telephone calls was made. First, Greenson telephoned Rudin (who was at Lake Tahoe), who asked his partner Martin Gang to call Phil Feldman and report that Greenson, having returned, was now in charge of Marilyn's relationship with the studio. Since she had accused Rudin of being 'with them' (i.e., of siding with Fox rather than with her) and since Greenson was 'the medical member of the team in charge', Greenson would determine Marilyn's ability to return to the picture – which, he said, might occur within the week. Greenson asked to be quoted as follows: 'I am convinced that she can finish the picture in the normal course,' a statement vague enough to come from any politician. Greenson then telephoned Eunice and instructed her to say nothing to the press, nor to anyone who called from the Arthur Jacobs office, from New York or from the studio. He then advised her that the injury to Marilyn's face was no cause for concern and she should forget about it. Nothing was communicated to Weinstein.

In all these calls and announcements, there is clearly a serious problem. Greenson never mentioned Marilyn's accident and their visit to Gurdin, an occurrence that could ironically have helped her. Fox rightly expected a reason to be offered for her absence that week, but they received none. Instead of buying time for another week by simply showing Fox that a woman with bruises was hardly fit for the camera, not a word was spoken by Greenson (the only one besides Gurdin who knew about the accident, if such it was). Just as crucial, his letters to Kris and Ostrow (and Murray's memoir) are noteworthy for their presentation of Marilyn as a gravely ill patient, a schizophrenic and a desperate abuser of dangerous drugs: would not his account of her nearly tragic, drug-induced accident have supported these allegations? She could have sustained career-threatening if not life-threatening injury, after all.

Why, then, did Greenson not mention this accident, telling Fox straightaway that Marilyn had hurt herself? And why did Murray's memoir omit it years later? Why did Greenson not invite a studio doctor to come to Fifth Helena to see for himself that Marilyn was unable to work that day and the next? Why was neither Pat Newcomb nor her boss, Arthur Jacobs, informed of the injury? It was their job to finesse such delicate matters with the press and public should the news somehow leak out.

Would not Greenson have telephoned Engelberg if he found Marilyn injured, or taken her to Engelberg's office? To avoid publicity at all costs, would it not have better suited his purposes to have a doctor come to the house? No, these were not options because Marilyn herself – not hours but moments after the blow – had insisted on seeing the man who had cared for her face years earlier. Had the accident occurred as Greenson told Gurdin, why was it not mentioned by Eunice in her account; why did Greenson not use it to help keep Fox at bay? And why did Marilyn, who no longer trusted her advisers, not insist on

attending the crucial luncheon meeting at Fox next day, the conference that would determine her fate and that of the picture?
Doubtless because she was temporarily disfigured (and very
likely sedated).

There can be only one explanation. Greenson wanted to con-
fide in no one and wished to prevent Marilyn being seen or
questioned about the injury by Gurdin or anyone else for one
reason only: he was the one responsible for it. Exhausted, frustrated, highly strung, confident of his authority to the point of
egomania, he was a man known to become enraged when challenged. Furious at Marilyn for having sabotaged his vacation,
having disobeyed his orders, causing him professional and
personal embarrassment before his family and the studio and
then saying that she was (thus the letter to Ostrow) not very ill
after all and would be glad to be rid of the picture, Greenson
had become violent and struck her. As long before with Joe, she
silently endured the moment of abuse, convinced that she had
been a naughty child and that punishment was due.

The hairstylist Sidney Guilaroff, not a man to be lightly dismissed, came to visit Marilyn that weekend but was brusquely
turned away by Greenson, who came to Fifth Helena for weekend sessions on 9 and 10 June: 'I went to see her,' Guilaroff
recalled, 'but Greenson kept me out. He kept a lot of people
from her.' For over a week she was virtually incarcerated at
home until her bruises healed, and so forced to decline several
social invitations she might otherwise have accepted. Among
these was an invitation from Pat and Peter Lawford, who were
to be guests of honour at the home of Robert and Ethel Kennedy in Virginia. Her telegram of regret, dated 13 June, linked
her struggle with Fox to the famous 'Freedom Riders' fighting
on behalf of civil rights for minorities:

Dear Attorney General and Mrs Kennedy:
    I would have been delighted to have accepted your in-
vitation honoring Pat and Peter Lawford. Unfortunately, I
am involved in a freedom ride protesting the loss of the

minority rights belonging to the few remaining earthbound stars. After all, all we demanded was our right to twinkle.
Marilyn Monroe.

A second visit to Gurdin, on 14 June, confirmed that all would soon be well. During that week, there were visits by Greenson and Engelberg, who later submitted bills (Engelberg's were for injections).

The meetings were held at Fox next day, Friday 8 June, and to them Greenson brought a double burden. He had to convince hostile studio executives that he could deliver Monroe to the set; and he had to prevent knowledge of her injuries – which, if ever known, would ignite a scandal and ruin his career for ever, making Marilyn, in the bargain, a more sympathetic figure before the studio and the public.

Greenson performed brilliantly. He, Rudin, Feldman and Frank Ferguson (an assistant secretary of Fox) met in the executive offices, where Greenson began by stating that his patient had endured two unfortunate incidents: a virus she contracted in New York and (his ego ever uninjured) his absence from her life. He added that Pat Newcomb was 'dispensable' as publicist and Paula Strasberg as coach (doubtless because, like Ralph Roberts, they were friends to Marilyn and disliked him). In addition, he reminded them that he had pulled Marilyn through a crisis once before, during *The Misfits*, and he could do so again.

The discussion continued along these lines, and when Feldman attempted to raise the stakes, asking if Marilyn would accept a new director or cameraman, Greenson was unfazed. He said, according to Feldman's detailed notes, that he would 'be able to get his patient to go along with any reasonable request and *although he did not want us to deem his relationship as a*

Svengali one, he in fact could persuade her to anything reasonable that he wanted.'*

Continuing this pathetic expression of egomania, Greenson astonished everyone by saying that he was ready to assume responsibility for all creative areas of the picture: to select the new director and cameraman, to decide which scenes Marilyn would or would not perform and which takes would finally be printed. 'I pointed out to Dr Greenson,' noted Feldman, 'that although I was sure he knew his business, I agreed with Mickey [Rudin] that he [Greenson] was not necessarily expert in our motion picture business.'

The meeting, which began at 12.30, continued through luncheon. A few minutes before four, when Rudin returned to his office, there was already a message awaiting him from Fox: the studio considered Marilyn Monroe in breach of contract and was prepared to proceed with all available legal remedies. In fact they had so proceeded on Thursday afternoon, and the Friday meeting was an empty formality. Moments before the Los Angeles County Court closed that 7 June, a suit was filed against Marilyn Monroe Productions, Inc., and its employee Marilyn Monroe, in the amount of $500,000. Sheila Graham, who got the news from Henry Weinstein on Thursday, published it in her column in the *Citizen-News* that night; otherwise it was unreported in the press until Friday and Saturday, 8 and 9 June.

When the news broke widely over that weekend, Marilyn was, as Allan Snyder, Marjorie Plecher and others remembered, unutterably depressed, for she could not believe that Fox would go so far as to fire her. She had, after all, made twenty of her twenty-nine films there and longed to believe that at last she was valued and had friends.

The dismissal, said Peter Levathes in an official statement, 'was made necessary because of Miss Monroe's repeated wilful

---

* Italics are the author's. Considering the visit to Gurdin the previous day, Greenson's allusion to Svengali sounds chilling.

breaches of her contract. No justification was given for her failure to report for photography on many occasions. The studio has suffered losses through these absences.' This was a simple case of muscular exertion by Levathes, acting at last on orders from Gould, Loeb and the rest of the board. Then, Levathes seemed to admit that Twentieth Century-Fox was itself a place fit only for madmen: 'We've let the inmates run the asylum,' he added, which meant that actors were lunatics and executives little more than keepers of a madhouse – not an allusion likely to win staff support.

Weinstein, years later, offered his own explanation, and it was at least partly correct. The real reason Marilyn was fired, he said, was that '*Cleopatra* was way behind schedule and costing millions, and here we had this small picture behind schedule. It looked as if Skouras and his appointed head Levathes were losing control of their talent. And so she was a pawn – an interesting pawn, a sad pawn, it's tragic, it's funny – but a pawn. And that's the real Hollywood story.' And, he might have added, it is often enough the story of Hollywood.

'They just didn't understand,' said David Brown, a veteran of problems more difficult even than this,

and they decided to play hardball like businessmen: 'We'll sue you … We'll hold you to every last clause … You'll never work in this town again,' and so forth and so on. These executives were storm troopers delivering messages. It was all so unnecessary.

It was also very soon regretted by the men at Fox, who scrambled to correct a potentially disastrous oversight.

That the company had much earlier begun negotiations for Marilyn's replacement on the picture was obvious on Saturday, when newspapers showed a photo of George Cukor, smiling too broadly with Lee Remick, who was signed on Saturday to replace Marilyn; in fact, Remick landed the role only after Kim Novak and Shirley MacLaine turned it down. And with this single announcement about Remick's engagement, the men at Fox revealed their delirious incompetence, for Dean Martin's contract gave him the right to approve his leading lady. Loyal to Marilyn, Martin at once telephoned his agent Herman Citron and announced he would not proceed with *Something's Got to Give* – news that touched and cheered Marilyn to the point of tears.

The rollercoaster continued its crazy route. Early Monday morning, a meeting-room at Fox was crowded with Levathes, Cukor, Feldman, Martin, Citron and casting director Owen McLean. The purpose was to convince Martin not to force the studio to close down the picture; and Levathes begged him not to reject Lee Remick. But Martin replied that Levathes was not quite accurate: he was not rejecting Remick, he simply would not do the picture without Marilyn, for whose participation he had signed to do this silly movie in the first place. 'Mr Martin,' reported the transcript of the meeting,

> said that he felt the chemistry between himself and Miss Monroe was right and that was why he took the picture and for no other reason, and that Miss Monroe meant a lot more at the box office than Miss Remick and that the point of the end of the story seemed to be that he would leave Miss Charisse for Miss Monroe – and that therefore this was not a role for Miss Remick, and that he wanted to do the picture only with Miss Monroe.

That was that. The studio was caught short by Dean Martin's loyalty, his insistence on his contractual rights and his canny sense of the best casting.

At this point, the vigilant Milton Rudin stepped in. He called Feldman on Monday afternoon to ask why he had not been informed that a lawsuit had been filed, since he assumed conversations were continuing in good faith. He then rightly asked why Fox was giving out derogatory statements to the press about Marilyn, since he fully expected her to return to work very soon. Contrariwise, Rudin added, he had advised Arthur Jacobs and his staff to issue no defensive publicity at all on Marilyn's behalf, nor to provide any reply to the many calls everyone was now receiving. The conversation concluded when Rudin asked Feldman who was to replace Martin if they went forward with Remick. Feldman replied that he did not know, whereupon 'Mr Rudin said maybe we ought to get President Kennedy.'

Bumbling along with their strong-arm tactics, Fox instructed their law firm (Musick, Peeler and Garrett) to continue to turn a skirmish into outright war. That same Monday, an amended lawsuit was filed, raised the ante against Marilyn from half a million to $750,000. This they had to do very hurriedly, before anyone learned that their suit from the previous week contained an error that could have led to an instant dismissal of the case: the first brief claimed that 'since April 16, the defendant failed, refused and neglected to render services' on *Something's Got to Give*. Marilyn had not begun work on the picture until 30 April, after which she willingly and satisfactorily rendered very much service indeed. This clause, omitted from the 7 June suit, was supplement by an inclusion of the 16 May warning.

Nothing, Fox seemed to reason, would succeed like overkill, and so on 19 June they continued in their litigious actions, suing Dean Martin (whose company, Claude Productions, was producing the picture) for $3,339,000 – the entire cost of the shelved production as they then computed it. This, like those against Marilyn, was eventually abandoned by Fox when an entire new platoon of executives strode through the studio gates. The shakeup began before the end of June, when the (forced) retirement of Spyros Skouras was announced.

Meantime, Peter Levathes quickly realized that in abandoning *Something's Got to Give* and losing Monroe and Martin, the company was also losing the fantastic publicity from the photographs of the swimming scene and the peek-a-boo nude shots – glorious colour images that by this time had appeared worldwide. Where and when, it was being asked, would this film be released? And as for the matter of cost, Lee Remick came at no bargain price: her salary was $80,000, and more than fifteen days of footage would have to be scrapped. It would in the long run be easier to find the budget for, essentially, a new picture.

Thus (hooray for Hollywood), discussions for an eventual resumption of *Something's Got to Give* were resumed just a week after Marilyn's dismissal, as negotiations began for a complete script revision by Hal Kanter. At the same time, there were telephone calls and meetings to determine how Marilyn Monroe and Dean Martin could be brought back in October, after he had completed another scheduled picture. 'When [Levathes] made his announcement that he was going to fire Marilyn,' said Nunnally Johnson, 'I phoned him to suggest that if anyone was to be fired it should be the director. It was Marilyn who brought people into the theaters, not this director.' All this was being discussed throughout June and July, despite the objections of Milton Gould, who left the board of Fox on the departure of Skouras.

Meanwhile, Marilyn was far from idle, for there were discussions about other films, too. In addition, the brouhaha with Fox and subsequent news of renewed negotiations led every magazine in America to ask for a photo story and interview. For those she agreed to accommodate, her good friend Allan Snyder was as usual asked to do her makeup. About the same time, Truman Capote (on familiar terms with the messy business of serious drug addiction), was surprised to find that 'she had never looked better . . . and there was a new maturity about her eyes. She wasn't so giggly anymore.' As Marilyn herself said at this time, 'There's a future, and I can't wait to get to it.'

By 23 June, a week after her second visit to Gurdin, her bruises had vanished, and Marilyn met the photographer Bert Stern, on assignment from *Vogue*, for the first of five photo sessions between that day and 12 July; she also spent three days (29 June–1 July) on and around Santa Monica beach with the photographer George Barris for a *Cosmopolitan* photoessay. Believing that she was at her best posing rather than acting and proud of her lithe and youthful figure, she was as ever the most patient and co-operative model, at ease with her lover the still camera, for which she had to remember no dialogue. For these long sessions, Marilyn wore mink for glamour shots, cavorted in bikinis and, draped in diaphanous veils and beneath a white sheet, posed semi-nude.

'She was very natural, without the affectation of a star complex,' according to Stern. 'There was a rare quality that I haven't seen before or since – as if there were no other person in the world while you were there. Marilyn devoted herself single-mindedly to the task and was ornery or impatient only when she was fed up with the glamour shots, the fashion shots *Vogue* wanted. She did not seem depressed or anxious about anything: she sipped her Dom Perignon and was delighted to be doing what she most enjoyed.'

'How's this for thirty-six?' she asked Stern, holding a sheer scarf over her naked breasts. George Masters, who was her hair-stylist for the Stern sittings, recalled that 'she said she never felt better, and she looked utterly fantastic, like something shining and ethereal. This was a lady who talked a lot that week about the future. She had no time for brooding over the past, even the recent past.'

Regarding her age and her prospects, Marilyn was frank and articulate when speaking to a reporter: 'I'm thirty-six years old,' she said,

I don't mind the age. I like the view from here. The future is here for me, and I have to make the most of it – as every woman must. So when you hear all this talk of how tardy I am, of how often it seems that I make people wait, remember – I'm waiting too. I've been waiting all my life.

She continued to speak with quiet sincerity, but her tone changed. For a moment it was as if Cherie had sprung from some lost scene of *Bus Stop* and was alive again in Marilyn:

You don't know what it's like to have all that I have and not be loved and know happiness. All I ever wanted out of life is to be nice to people and have them be nice to me. It's a fair exchange. And I'm a woman. I want to be loved by a man, from his heart, as I would love him from mine. I've tried, but it hasn't happened yet.

The reporter naturally followed up with questions about her marriages, but Marilyn was as always the soul of discretion. Joe was 'Mr DiMaggio', and Arthur 'Mr Miller', and she would not be led to a discussion of her private life. In the fifteen years he knew her, said Allan Snyder, he never heard an unkind or vindictive word about an ex-husband or a former lover – not even about those professionals who treated her unfairly. 'To think of Marilyn Monroe calling a press conference to air her grievances against anyone is laughably out of character. Why, she wouldn't even say a single bad word to a friend or a reporter!' Nor did she extend a problematic relationship with an individual to include that person's family: on 19 July, showing her gratitude for their concern during Greenson's absence, Marilyn invited Dan and Joan (without their parents, it should be noted) to Fifth Helena for a casual supper celebrating Joan's birthday.

Marilyn recognized that something was askew in her relationship with Greenson, for she confided to friends that she felt it was unhealthy for her to depend on someone whose attitude and actions were unpredictable (she provided no details) and with whom she seemed to be making no progress. But in the paradoxical way of many patients in therapy, she continued to consult him daily during July. Greenson had, after all, successfully convinced Marilyn of her need of him. And in this regard, he enlisted Hyman Engelberg as accomplice.

According to invoices later submitted, Engelberg visited Marilyn at home every day but six during July: except for the fourth, sixth to the ninth and the sixteenth, she received injections – liver and vitamin shots, she said. But these transformed her mood and energy with alarming rapidity. 'She asked to postpone our talk,' recalled Richard Meryman, who arrived late one afternoon for the second of a series of interviews for *Life*. 'She was tired out, she said,' after meetings at Fox. But then they were interrupted by the arrival of Engelberg: Marilyn bounded out to the kitchen, received a shot and returned to Meryman – suddenly eager to talk on and on, which she did until midnight and after. That evening (unlike the other meetings) her speech was rapid and disjointed – hardly the effect of 'liver and vitamin shots'.

There were Engelberg's so-called youth shots. When Pat Newcomb learned of them, she told Marilyn to remember she was only thirty-six, 'but she implied that whatever she was receiving was going to keep her young. Of course it was hard to argue with her, because she looked so great – better than I'd ever seen her in films.' But this was cause for alarm, for Engelberg tracked down Marilyn wherever she was to provide the injections: Pat never forgot the day he found the two women at a Brentwood restaurant, where 'he took her back to some private place to give her the shot.' In this way, Engelberg was clearly as proprietary with Marilyn as Greenson; his first wife recalled him almost dancing with schoolboyish glee, showing off to his friends and announcing as he shook a set of keys, 'I have access to Marilyn Monroe's apartment', and then, 'I have the keys to Marilyn's house!' When therapy or the usual dose of Nembutal failed to put Marilyn to sleep, Greenson routinely telephoned Engelberg, who in 1961 dashed down from his house on St Ives Drive to Doheny, and in 1962 made the longer trip to Fifth Helena. Greenson was quite open about the arrangement: as he said, he arranged for a physician to provide the injections 'so that I had nothing to do with the actual handling of medication.'

The issue of her doctors and her work may have been among the items on her agenda when Marilyn placed a total of eight telephone calls that summer to the office of her new friend, Attorney General Robert Kennedy. According to Pat Newcomb and Edwin Guthman, their conversations were simply social, friendly calls, brief and uncomplicated, for they were not encouraged by the busy Mr Kennedy. But he had assured her during their last meeting in June that he was indeed interested in her career and concerned for her health during and after the trials of *Something's Got to Give*. Following their conversations about matters political and social at two previous dinners, Kennedy may not have anticipated that Marilyn, from afar, would depend on his compassion and encouragement in her private life, too. According to Edwin Guthman, however, there was never time in Kennedy's office for him to devote to lengthy social calls, and Marilyn was gently but firmly discouraged from prolonging their conversations.

In support of this, the telephone records document very brief calls. On Monday 25 June Marilyn called Kennedy's office to confirm his presence at the Lawford's on Wednesday evening and to invite him and the Lawfords to visit her home for a drink before dinner; she spoke only to his secretary, Angie Novello, for one minute. On Monday 2 July she placed two calls, again to Novello and for the same length of time. The remainder of the calls were placed during the last two weeks of July, only one of them lasting more than one minute: on the thirtieth, Marilyn called Kennedy to say that she was sorry to have missed his Los Angeles speech the previous weekend; she had gone to Lake Tahoe.* These calls and four meetings comprise the entire relationship between the two.

During July, Marilyn relied on three sources of encouragement: friends like Ralph Roberts and Allan Snyder (and, by phone, Norman Rosten in Brooklyn); the admiration and encouragement of a few journalists and photographers; and the return to her life of Joe DiMaggio.

'We often stopped in at her house in the evening for a drink in June and July,' said Allan Snyder and his wife Marjorie. 'She

---

* All these calls were put through the main switchboard at the Department of Justice (Republic 7–8200) and then transferred to the attorney general's secretary. Marilyn's address book lists only this number; she never had access to Kennedy's private line.

was in very good spirits, showing us her newest addition to the house – some tiles, a carpet, a new chair.'

Since his return from Europe, Marilyn and Joe had frequently exchanged telephone calls, and he visited her once in June (on the twentieth) and twice in July (on the eighth and twenty-first); as all her friends knew, Joe's presence and concern were her great strength, and ever since he rescued her from Payne Whitney they had maintained constant contact. Now, they shared simple suppers on the floor of her living-room, since the shipment of Mexican furniture was delayed; they rented bicycles at the Hans Ohrt Bicycle Shop in Brentwood and free-wheeled along San Vicente Boulevard towards the ocean; and they shopped together.

Joe and Marilyn seemed much like the happy couple of ten years earlier – but they were more serene, both of them respectful of their differences, he less alarmed by her public persona, yet somehow touched by her essential sweetness and simplicity, and perhaps impressed with her courage and core of strength. He agreed with her concern about the ongoing therapy with Greenson, and promised to support whatever decision she made.

A decade had made a difference. Joe sat quietly, nodding appreciatively as she purchased an entire new wardrobe in Beverly Hills, at Saks Fifth Avenue and Jax: cashmere sweaters; blouses; two evening dresses; unfussy, spike-heeled shoes; half a dozen pairs of trousers in various pastel colours. The morning of 21 July he brought her home from Cedars of Lebanon after yet another procedure to alleviate her chronic endometriosis.* As subsequent events revealed, his presence then must have marked a major step forward in the reunion, for the following week he informed Monette that he was resigning his position and would no longer be working for the company after the end of July.

* The notes of her regular surgeon, Leon Krohn MD (chief of the gynaecological service at Cedars) leave no doubt that the later rumours of an abortion are sheer fiction.

As for the interviews, it is no surprise that Marilyn was most articulate, secure and frank in Engelberg's absence. On the fourth, fifth, seventh and ninth of July, for example, she gave what was her last interview, for *Life* magazine, a series of conversations conducted by Richard Meryman at Fifth Helena. Only during the second meeting, after Engelberg's visit and treatment, were her remarks unusable; the final draft was drawn from the other three, during which Marilyn was at her best.

Regarding some unflattering remarks in the gossip columns:

I really resent the way the press has been saying I'm depressed and in a slump, as if I'm finished. Nothing's going to sink me, although it might be kind of a relief to be finished with movie-making. That kind of work is like a hundred-yard dash and then you're at the finish line, and you sigh and say you've made it. But you never have. There's another scene and another film, and you have to start all over again.

Leading Meryman on a tour of her home, she pointed out her plans for a small guest suite:

a place for any friends of mine who are in some kind of trouble. Maybe they'll want to live here where they won't be bothered till things are okay for them.

On fame:

What goes with it can be a burden. Real beauty and femininity are ageless and can't be contrived. Glamour can be manufactured. Fame is certainly only a cause for temporary and partial happiness – not for a daily diet, it's not what fulfills you. It warms you a bit, but the warming is only temporary. When you're famous every weakness is exaggerated. Fame will go by and – so long, fame, I've had you!

I've always known it was fickle. It was something I *experienced*, but it's not where I live.

Replying to Meryman's question as to how she 'cranked herself up' to do a scene:

I don't crank anything – I'm not a Model T. Excuse me, but I think that's kind of disrespectful to refer to it that way. I'm trying to work at an art form, not in a manufacturing establishment.

On her chronic tardiness:

Successful, happy and on time – those are all the glib American cliches. I don't want to be late, but I usually am, much to my regret. Often, I'm late because I'm preparing a scene, maybe preparing too much sometimes. But I've always felt that even in the slightest scene the people ought to get their money's worth. And this is an obligation of mine, to give them the best. When they go to see me and look up at the screen, they don't know I was late. And by that time, the studio has forgotten all about it and is making money. Oh, well.

On her recent troubles at Fox:

Executives can get colds and stay home and phone in – but the actor? How dare you get a cold or a virus! I wish *they* had to act a comedy with a temperature and a virus infection! I'm there to give a performance, not to be disciplined by a studio. This isn't supposed to be a military school, after all.

On being a sex symbol:

A sex symbol becomes a thing, and I just hate to be a thing. You're always running into people's unconscious. It's nice to be included in people's fantasies, but you also like to be accepted for your own sake. I don't look on myself as a commodity, but I'm sure a lot of people have, including one corporation in particular which shall be nameless. If I'm sounding 'picked on,' I think I have been.

On her interest in social and humanitarian causes:

What the world needs now is a greater feeling of kindship. We are all brothers, after all – and that includes movie stars, laborers, Negroes, Jews, Arabs – everyone. That's what I'm working on, working to understand.

On her future:

I want to be an artist and an actress with integrity. As I said once before, I don't care about the money. I just want to be wonderful.

But Marilyn had been burned so often by the press that she seemed not to trust Meryman entirely, and by the conclusion of their sessions she seemed to him cool and withdrawn. When the photographer Allan Grant arrived to take the photos that would accompany the interview, Marilyn was, as Pat and Eunice recalled, in a giddy mood, making funny faces and joking. 'What are you, some kind of a nut?' Meryman asked with remarkable insensitivity. This stopped her cold, for his remark had obviously hurt, and she was wary when he delivered a transcript of their conversation on 9 July.

Marilyn requested only one cut from her taped remarks: 'She asked me to take out a remark she had made about quietly giving money to needy individuals.' Like the best of herself, her charity would remain private, a secret between her and those she longed to help. She walked with him to the driveway, and then, just as he was about to depart, she stepped forward. 'Please,' she said in a whisper, 'please don't make me a joke.'

After completing the month's scheduled photo sessions and interviews, Marilyn and her old friend Sidney Skolsky were reunited – the first meeting in over a year – for a project that had long been important for both of them: he would produce and she would star in a film of Jean Harlow's life. But first they would need the co-opertion of Harlow's mother, 'Mama Jean' Bello, and so on Sunday 15 July they travelled to Indio, a town near Palm Springs. There they found the charmingly eccentric old lady, surrounded by relics, photographs and mementos of her beloved 'Baby Jean'. Her approval was immediately forthcoming, for she took one look at Marilyn and declared that she could swear her baby had come back from the dead.

To those who knew the continuing parallels in the lives of the two platinum blondes, Mama Jean would not have sounded far from the mark. In fact, an outline of Jean Harlow's last months provides an eerie stencil for Marilyn's:

On 30 January 1937 the newly re-elected Franklin Delano Roosevelt invited Jean to his Birthday Ball in Washington; in order to attend, she had to leave the filming of *Personal Property*, which caused a dustup in Hollywood – at least until Louis B. Mayer realized the enormous publicity value of her appearance.

That spring of 1937, Jean spoke with Carolyn Hoyt, an interviewer from *Modern Screen*: 'I have achieved, of late, a degree of peace. I feel now at peace with myself and with my world. I have attained this by forcing myself to realize that all I can do is done in the best way I know – and that, as they say, is that.' The sentiments might have been uttered by Marilyn to Meryman.

Also during the spring of 1937, Jean's recurring illnesses were blithely treated with only sedatives and narcotics by the notorious Dr E. C. Fishbaugh, who prescribed the same, and with the same harmful effects, for Fay Wray's alcoholic husband.

On 7 June 1937 – twenty-five years to the day before Marilyn was fired from *Something's Got to Give* – Jean Harlow died of kidney failure, her last film incomplete. She was twenty-six, a creature of Hollywood, loved by millions, at last recognized for her talents – yet in the end failed by her Hollywood colleagues.

After taking tea with Mrs Bello, her guests returned to Los Angeles. The three agreed to meet again in August, and before that, Marilyn and Sidney decided to meet two weeks later, at four o'clock on the afternoon of Sunday 5 August to work on a treatment for *The Jean Harlow Story.*

Despite her almost daily injections, the difficulties of her sessions with Greenson and the uncertainties of the future, there was a fresh maturity in Marilyn Monroe that summer. And although she was dependent on certain chemicals, they seemed only fitfully to stymie her life – and this itself may be testimony to her fundamental strength, her resolve to overcome obstacles past and present. 'Summarizing this time,' said Pat Newcomb, 'I would say that yes, she was in control of things.'

Ralph Roberts heartily agreed. 'She was really taking control of her life and asserting herself that summer,' he said, sentiments echoed by, among others, Rupert Allan and Susan Strasberg. Roberts recalled that during the last months of her life, Marilyn was more optimistic than she had been in two years. She nurtured a close friendship with Wally Cox and renewed one with Wally's special friend, Marlon Brando. 'And she saw,' Roberts added, 'that Greenson was severing all her close relationships, one by one. He had tried to cut me and the Strasbergs and Joe out of her life – and now Marilyn said he thought it would be better if she dismissed Pat Newcomb, too. By the end of July, Marilyn realized that if she was going to have any friends left, any life of her own at all, she might have to disconnect from Greenson.'

This decision would soon be firm, but first there was the matter of her relationship with Fox. By Wednesday 25 July, Hal Kanter had completed his revision of *Something's Got to Give* and submitted it to Peter Levathes, Weinstein's future being now as uncertain as that of Skouras and company.

Marilyn welcomed Levathes to her home on that same day, 25 July. Before his arrival, she was awake early and, determined to look her best, greeted Agnes Flanagan (who washed and styled her hair) and Allan Snyder (who deftly applied a morning makeup). Cautious about a discussion without an agent or attorney present, Marilyn then asked Pat Newcomb to come over and stand unseen behind a bedroom door, to witness her meeting with Levathes.

In 1992, he provided an account of that morning with Marilyn, and his recollection was later confirmed by Pat:

As so often with Marilyn's history at Fox, we simply decided to reinstate her. I was the one responsible for firing her, so I wanted to be the one to personally rehire her. No one wanted bad blood. She told me she didn't want her name tarnished, nor did she wish to ruin anyone. She did not seem unhappy or depressed at all, she asked if we could review the new script and we did. She read it and was very astute about it, thinking carefully before she made some excellent suggestions. Marilyn saw, for example, great comic potential for a scene she had in mind: 'A woman who has been off on a desert island for years wouldn't eat so delicately with knives and forks.' And she suggested another scene in which her character just forgot about shoes, because she was unused to wearing them. I remember saying, 'Marilyn, these are beautiful ideas!' She was very happy and creative and glad to have a say in the revised script. She was in fine spirits and looking forward to getting back to work.

It seemed to Levathes that all the anguish, all the pain could have been avoided but for 'her so-called advisors, who caused her a terrible identity crisis.' He told her that the lawsuits would be dropped, and that she was to be rehired at a higher salary; to whom, he asked, ought the new contract be sent? Marilyn hesitated, then said she would reply later that week. She seemed to him very pleasant and reasonable, and before he departed she said something that stayed with him over the years:

You know, Peter, in a way I'm a very unfortunate woman. All this nonsense about being a legend, all this glamour and publicity. Somehow I'm always a disappointment to people.

He never saw her again, for very soon his fortunes changed, if not as dramatically as hers.

When I said good-bye, she returned to the task she was engaged in when I arrived. There was an array of photos of her [by Bert Stern and George Barris], contact sheets and prints all over the floor, and she was making decisions about them. This was not, I thought, a shallow person, and I was sorry I never really knew her. She was a woman who made distinctions, who thought about her life, who knew the difference between sham and reality. She had depth. Of course she was enormously complex and I had a sense of some real underlying suffering there. But at her best there was no one like her. The wounds with Fox were healed, and when I last saw her, she was like a young and beautiful starlet, eager to do a picture that now had real possibilities.

Their hopes were unrealized, for soon there was another corporate earthquake at Fox. Darryl F. Zanuck was elected president of Twentieth Century-Fox, Levathes was booted out, and Milton Gould and John Loeb resigned from the board. Every decision made before Zanuck's return was to be reevaluated, but after forty years in the business, even he (who never had a great appreciation of Marilyn's talents) knew something about the box-office. If anything had to give, he said, it would not be Marilyn Monroe. Zanuck personally attended the meetings on the recommencement of *Something's Got to Give*.

For the last weekend of July, Marilyn had been invited to be the Lawfords' guest at the new Cal-Neva Lodge in Lake Tahoe, where Frank Sinatra was going to sing. To this she had readily agreed, and (as Ralph Roberts and Rupert Allan knew), she had telephoned Joe and asked him to meet her there. Although

Robert Kennedy was due to arrive in Los Angeles that weekend and she had originally planned to hear an address he was to give, there were now more important matters on Marilyn's agenda. Except for her appearance at Sinatra's Saturday evening performance, she and Joe kept a low profile during the entire weekend. 'She didn't want to be seen about too much,' recalled Roberts, 'because she was afraid of any discord between Joe and Frank.'

Marilyn did, however, want to meet Dean Martin briefly, who was also at the Lodge that weekend – not only to express thanks for his support during the June crisis but also to discuss briefly a movie project that Arthur Jacobs wanted to produce for her and Dean, a comedy called *I Love Louisa*. Next week, Marilyn said, she was going to watch some of the films of director J. Lee Thompson, whom Arthur had suggested.

For years there were scurrilous and unfounded rumours of Marilyn accidentally overdosing on barbiturates that weekend and requiring emergency revival; and rumours of Marilyn socializing with various figures from the criminal underworld with whom she became sexually involved (among them Johnny Roselli, Bugsy Siegel and Sam Giancana). But the actor Alex D'Arcy, who knew Marilyn (since appearing with her in *How To Marry a Millionaire*) and was also a close friend of Roselli – a key mob figure in Los Angeles – hotly denied both insinuations: 'There was absolutely never any affair between Marilyn and any of these men,' he said. 'In fact there was no connection between Marilyn and the mob at all! She was in Lake Tahoe to be with Joe!' Betsy Duncan Hammes, who also knew Roselli and Sinatra well, agreed: 'I was in Lake Tahoe that weekend and I saw Marilyn eating dinner. Giancana and his crowd weren't there, and I would have known if they were.'

On Sunday evening, Marilyn returned to Los Angeles with the Lawfords, and Joe headed for San Francisco, to appear in an exhibition game and to tell his family what he and Marilyn had decided that weekend. As Valmore Monette confirmed, 'Joe told me that he had decided to remarry her. He thought things would be different than they had been before and that everything would work out well for them now. I knew that was why he left us and was going back out there in 1962.'

Marilyn and Joe planned a wedding date of Wednesday 8 August in Los Angeles, and a radiant Marilyn returned home with Joe's pyjamas. 'She was fighting to take responsibility for her own life,' said Susan Strasberg, 'and so she was getting out of relationships that were not good for her and back into one that was. She knew she needed some sort of emotional and spiritual anchor.' The same need could be said of Joe, who had become a kind of commercial Flying Dutchman, respected but lonely.

On Monday 30 July, Marilyn saw excerpts from Thompson's films in Arthur Jacobs's screening room and, on the spot, agreed to accept him as director for *I Love Louisa* early in 1963.* Jacobs added that Jule Styne, who had given Marilyn 'Diamonds Are a Girl's Best Friend' for *Gentlemen Prefer Blondes*, had agreed to write new songs for her. The same day, Marilyn tried to reach Milton Rudin, for she wished to make a new will; attentive and supportive as he had been, however, Rudin felt that he could not sign a will and certify that she was of sound and disposing mind, for he believed her to have serious problems with both pills and paranoia. In a way, Rudin was correct, for Marilyn's problems were far from solved, and she knew she had to face her dependence on drugs and on Greenson just as she had to continue a maturation that in many ways was just now beginning. But that she was of unsound mind is quite another assertion.†

*

* The film, starring Dean Martin, Robert Mitchum and (in the role designed for Marilyn) Shirley MacLaine, with songs by Jule Styne, was released in 1964 as *What A Way to Go!*

† As for her will, the 1961 draft stood. At the time of her death, Marilyn left only the house, assessed at a value of $60,000; furniture, furnishings and personal effects valued at $3,200; $2,200 in bank accounts; and $405 cash on hand. The value of her Estate over the years grew as a result of the subsequent commercial marketing of her name and image.

Ever since her teens, Marilyn had believed she had nothing to offer but what Grace Goddard, photographers and studios claimed: the mass appeal of her beauty and her body. She also believed that 'Marilyn Monroe', although at least partly a false pretender, represented a part of her true self. She had indeed encouraged an image of sexual allure and availability, and the endorsement and acceptance of her in those terms were important.

But there was another aspect of her personality – or more accurately, a real identity behind the persona. Marilyn had often tried to repress and disguise the image with black wigs and dark glasses, without makeup. She tried to separate herself from that 'Marilyn Monroe' by reducing 'her' to another, a third person – 'her' – 'Would you like to see me be her?' Unlike other screen stars, Marilyn never fused the two. Marlene Dietrich, for example, eventually believed the illusion created for her, and the fall that injured her body at the age of seventy-five also wounded something within. Believing her youth and illusory self were all she had, Dietrich had to withdraw from public view when the youth and glamour faded, and for the last sixteen years of her life she was virtually a recluse.

Marilyn, on the other hand, always reaching for an *integration* of her personality, knew in some way that her emotional health depended on a *separation* between the public Marilyn and the private self. Sorrow, confusion and neuroses prevented her rising above the image she deplored, to become the woman she yearned to be. Her film roles continually forced her to rely on what she wanted to put behind her; no wonder, then, that most of all she longed to sleep. When she awoke, she was restrained, forced to assume 'Marilyn Monroe' again, the conundrum of the sexually available, ever popular teenage waif who somehow retained her innocence. That her popularity was caused by an image she hated – and now, for the first time in 1962, she was openly admitting – showed how clearly she realized the split in herself. This can hardly, however, be called schizophrenic; in fact it reveals a remarkable clarity of self-perception.

Had she not been a woman who (as Levathes said) 'made distinctions, who thought about her life, who knew the difference between sham and reality', there would have been no need for a struggle, no need for her to admit that she needed to grow, no anguished cries to get on with her life: 'There's a future and I can't wait to get to it.'

When Marilyn left Fox in 1954, she had taken a bold step in abandoning the identification of herself with its false image; new friends, new work, studies – all these would, she hoped, enable her to transcend her own limitations. Only a courageous woman would so act.

But part of the problem was, then as in 1962, that part of her still depended on outer approval, still considered herself a child – only a body without a soul worth probing, and in this regard we are very close to sounding the reasons for her mass appeal decades later. She still believed the Gladys/Grace tales of family madness, and her retreat into an adopted false self was something she could not entirely abandon. Something in Marilyn still feared that she might for ever slip back to being the patronzied child-bride, the girl who would do best to forget her unknown lineage and assume the identity of America's ultimate pin-up darling after World War II.

In a profound sense she was still telling the culture about the Kinsey Report a decade later, for she was still the worrisome union of national needs: sex with innocence; worshipping gaze with the fear of experience; adolescent longing and adult responsibility; desire and, in its aftermath, too often disappointment when too much is demanded. What was endemic to a culture – from just after the war, when she entered movies (1947) to the beginning of a social revolution (1962) – was almost inextricable from Marilyn Monroe.

Kinsey spoke of sex, wrote about it, enquired into its most intimate details, and Hollywood was more and more parading the new sexual frankness. The boys he interviewed had been to the war and were entitled to be considered men. But the men seen on television and in the movies in the 1950s were mostly boys:

Cary Grant in *Monkey Business* is nothing so much as a handsome preppie; the 'romantic lead' of *Gentlemen Prefer Blondes* turns out to be a rich child; even in *River of No Return*, where the wild man to be tamed is no less than Robert Mitchum, a boy is necessary to link the couple.

Amid all this confusion, Marilyn Monroe and her aspirations had to be mocked by the culture. The thought of so independent a woman was anathema: the country wanted a child-woman – a busty, sexy gal, not too bright, whom distance made somewhat unreal, the stuff of dreams, someone who would not (and whom we could not allow to) grow up.

Just as harmful as the studios that reflected the culture and in ways more tragic, she had become unwittingly trapped in the pop-Freudian circle that urged her continually to consider her childhood – the worst possible agenda for the star's unending absorption with self. But her parent surrogates (Strasberg, Miller, Kris, Greenson) suggested it, demanded it. And so to please them she underwent Freudian therapy. Instead of freeing her, it froze her. In the end, it was wondrous that she did not break down sooner, for each time she tried to go forward there were those whose advantage it was to keep her ever the subordinate child.

On the morning of Tuesday 31 July Marilyn telephoned Jean Louis's assistant, Elizabeth Courtney, who was to come over as soon as possible for the final fittings of a new gown Jean had designed for her. 'She was so happy,' recalled Courtney – and with good reason, for this was to be her wedding dress. That afternoon, after a ninety-minute session with Greenson, Marilyn returned home and spent several hours on the telephone, placing calls to (among others) a florist, her local wine shop and a caterer.

'I want to be loved by a man, from his heart, as I would love him from mine,' she had said in an interview that June. 'I've tried, but it hasn't happened yet.' Now at last, the fulfilment of that longing seemed very close indeed.

Chapter Twenty-two

On Wednesday 1 August, Nunnally Johnson told Marilyn's old friend Jean Negulesco that he was going to be invited to direct *Something's Got to Give* 'because Marilyn has asked for you'. Negulesco, who had directed her in *How To Marry a Millionaire*, said he would be delighted to replace Cukor, for he considered Marilyn 'a hurricane of glamour [who] had such a right sense of knowing the character she was playing – the way to enter a scene, to hold singular attention as the scene developed [and] the way to end a scene.'* With Negulesco's acceptance, everything was in place for the picture to recommence at the end of October. Marilyn was signed at a salary of $250,000, two-and-a-half times the amount of her original contract.

Evelyn Moriarty heard the news about Negulesco and telephoned Marilyn, who was, according to Evelyn, 'in great spirits – she was so happy to be going back to work. We talked about the script and the new director – all sorts of things. She was really in tip-top condition, and we all looked forward to starting the picture.' Marilyn also told Evelyn that Arthur Jacobs was going to produce *I Love Louisa* for Fox later that year, so there was even *more* to anticipate. With these projects and *The Jean Harlow Story* being developed, Marilyn's career had never seemed brighter.

As for her immediate plans, Marilyn was preoccupied with

---

* In a desperate move to save the picture, Fox had decided to replace Cukor.

preparations for a small reception to follow her wedding, and was drawing up a list of friends to be invited at the last moment. She also confirmed that the wine, sandwiches and salads would be delivered the following week from Briggs, the local emporium she frequented on nearby San Vicente Boulevard. Joe was due in los Angeles Sunday night or Monday morning; they would be married on Wednesday and then proceed for a honeymoon in New York, where they both had close friends. Then perhaps they would spend a week on Long Island or Cape Cod.

Marilyn's telephone records for 1 August also list a call to Leon Krohn's office at Cedars of Lebanon Hospital. Krohn, whom she trusted without reservation and to whom she often went for advice on other than medical matters, had by this time attended her for a decade. From the 1952 appendectomy through the anxieties and heartbreak of *Some Like It Hot* and her subsequent third miscarriage right up to her recent minor surgery, 'Red' Krohn was the gentlest of men and her most perceptive physician. He had been a good friend to her and Joe during their divorce proceedings, too, and so it was natural for her to call him with brighter news. She asked Krohn to dine with her that evening, saying she had something important to tell him; he replied that he would ring back after his hospital rounds. Then she telephoned again, late in the afternoon, and said she would call him in a few days.

The reason for this postponement is not entirely clear, but before the day was over Marilyn had gone to Greenson for a two-hour session and Engelberg had come to Fifth Helena thereafter, in the early evening. The sudden change of dinner plans may have been the result of an injection, or just simple exhaustion; it may also, however, have been related to the tensions of Marilyn's relationship with Eunice, whom she could at last dismiss permanently – and she now had the perfect opportunity to do so, on the eve of her renewed life with Joe.

Besides Eunice's proprietary attitude, her attempt to control Marilyn's life and her alliance with Greenson, there were three final moments that pushed Marilyn's patience too far and sealed the housekeeper's fate. First, as Cherie Redmond wrote from the studio to Marilyn at the end of July, Marilyn's mail from Fox and from her private post office box were now 'being held by Mrs Murray', whose liberties were becoming more and more presumptuous. Informed of this, Marilyn was rightly angry, since she felt once again like a child in her own home under the supervision of her own employee.

Second, at Marilyn's invitation, Ralph Roberts had come that Wednesday morning to give her a massage. Eunice 'made her presence known,' as he recalled, 'and she looked at me with such hatred and venom, as if she were saying, "I thought we'd gotten rid of you." It was chilling how intimidating this little woman could be, how manipulative of Marilyn and divisive with Marilyn's friends. Mrs Murray was Greenson's minion, that's all, his on-the-spot representative.' Eunice's attitude to Ralph did not escape Marilyn, who was further annoyed.

The third incident fixed Marilyn's determination. Eunice had planned to accompany her sister and brother-in-law on a European vacation beginning Monday 6 August. But she had chosen not to tell Marilyn of this in advance and had not even made travel reservations: apparently she was unsure about leaving Marilyn at all. Cherie Redmond remarked on this indecision when she wrote to Hedda, 'It seems to me that Mrs Murray's devotion to MM is so intense – that may not be the right word, but you know what I mean – that she wouldn't want to go away.'

Whatever the rationale, several things were clear: on Wednesday 1 August, Eunice at last told Marilyn she would like to take a vacation on the following Monday. Marilyn, who must have been delighted with the news but perhaps did not show it, wrote her a cheque for a month's wages and told Eunice not to return in September. Thus Marilyn, who always avoided confrontations, could fire the housekeeper with the excuse that she herself would be travelling for an indeterminate time and that her own future plans were as uncertain as Eunice's sudden announcement. Although she made no mention of it in her memoir,

Eunice probably also learned from Marilyn that afternoon about the marriage plans, for Marilyn knew that Eunice disliked DiMaggio as much as she did Roberts. In addition, Marilyn put through several calls to her New York maid, Hattie Stevenson, apparently to ask if she might be available on a short-term basis in Los Angeles that autumn.

Eunice's reaction could only have been shock, hurt and possibly even anger. Here she was, finally in the ideal situation she longed for, in the replica of her dream house she had chosen, working with the wise father-figure Ralph Greenson, determining more and more the life of her 'daughter' Marilyn, nursing her as her sister Carolyn nursed children. At last she seemed to have fulfilled her lifelong dream of living up to the standard set by her sister; at last she had been able to correct the situation of her unhappy marriage and, through Marilyn, regain her lost home and head a kind of family.

Marilyn ... Marilyn's busy life ... Marilyn's house ... Marilyn's insecurities ... Marilyn's dependence on Greenson – all these had become the emotional accoutrements of Eunice Murray's identity, had provided her with a purpose. Without the house on Fifth Helena and its famous resident, without Greenson to serve and Marilyn to 'nurse', there would be no life for Eunice at all. Like Rupert Allan (who had returned to Los Angeles from Monaco for six weeks), Ralph Roberts and Pat Newcomb recalled that the imminent departure of Eunice Murray was in fact one of the important things Marilyn did in her own best interest. 'I knew her attitude toward Greenson had changed,' Roberts recalled, 'and concerning Mrs Murray – well, Marilyn simply said how much the woman annoyed her, bored her to distraction.' The end of the employment, especially after the temporary separation in May, was not unexpected. 'Marilyn just couldn't stand her living there any more,' said Pat. 'The truth is that Marilyn at last felt in control of things, and so she fired Mrs Murray. It was over. And with Marilyn, when it was over, it was over. Eunice was out.' Her last day of work would be Saturday 4 August; until then, there was a good deal of work to occupy them both. This was only the beginning of Marilyn's healthy self-assertion, but the real challenge still lay ahead – confronting Greenson with her new autonomy.

Marilyn spent that afternoon at Fox, conferring about the resumption of *Something's Got to Give*; this was so cordial and creative a meeting that an outsider might have thought there had been only a brief hiatus for some minor reason, with no troubled history at all.

On Thursday morning, 2 August, Marilyn went to Greenson for a session and, as his subsequent invoices to her Estate testified, he drove to her house for a second meeting later that day. Clearly, there was a crisis. It is unimaginable that she would not have told him about the dismissal of Eunice and her forthcoming marriage, and to these news items he could not have reacted with any pleasure or approval. It would also have been logical for her to have discussed her temporary interruption of therapy in the light of her travel plans, and with that, Greenson may have thought he, too, was about to be dismissed.

'Greenson's connection to the studio she perceived as the ultimate betrayal,' said Ralph Roberts.

She deeply resented what she saw as his use of her. And she saw at last what was fundamentally true: that Hollywood was not her life, and that dependence on him was not her life. Her resentment of Greenson had reached the breaking point – so much was clear to all of us. He had tried to get rid of almost everyone in her life, and she didn't have that many people to begin with. But when he tried it with Joe – I think that's when she began to reconsider the whole thing. As for Engelberg and the pills and the shots, well it was obvious, wasn't it? If you can't control Marilyn one way, there were always drugs.

Emboldened by her action with Eunice, Marilyn was about to

take the step that she believed would free her as much as her re-marriage to Joe. 'She realized she had to get rid of Greenson,' according to Roberts, 'and she seemed ready to do so. After all, she had support from a lot of us for that!'

Marilyn had been, as Pat Newcomb knew first-hand, furious with her analyst over three things in three months: first, Greenson was in Switzerland when she returned from New York to find trouble brewing at Fox. 'Marilyn was very angry about his not being there for her,' according to Pat – just as Marilyn had subsequently experienced physically *his* anger, which was a second cause of her resentment and whose perfidy she needed several days or weeks to realize. Third, she never forgot the way Greenson had tried to separate her from Joe.

'Several times, she threatened to fire Greenson – to leave him,' Pat recalled, 'but I never took her threats seriously.' Now at last Marilyn was about to turn a warning into a promise ful-filled. Eunice was to be booted out and Marilyn was about to marry, effectively abandoning Greenson and his therapy for a husband and a honeymoon. She may not have been explicit about a firm termination of their relationship, as she had been with Eunice, but it was certain that she was moving on.

In his essay on 'Special Problems in Psychotherapy with the Rich and Famous', Greenson neatly described the end of his re-lationship with this special client in a passage immediately following a lightly veiled disquisition on Marilyn, her back-ground and her problems. The glittering generalizations show how emotional an issue this was for him, for all scholarly dis-cretion is crushed beneath the weight of his unhappy memories:

> Rich and famous people believe that prolonged psychoth-erapy is a rip-off. They want their therapist as a close friend, they even want his wife and his children to become part of the therapist's family . . . These patients are seductive.

Anyone in the audience who knew of his most famous client must have thought of Marilyn as he continued his projection of feelings on to her, and the implicit admission of his own history and dejection:

> Rich and famous people need the therapist twenty-four hours a day and they are insatiable. They are also able to give you up completely in the sense they are doing to you what was done to them by their parents or their servants. You are their servant and can be dismissed without notice.

For Greenson, Marilyn had indeed become the rival Juliet, one to be controlled through the appearance of the most benevolent counsel. Talented, adored, applauded, beautiful, the actress in a way had taken the place of his sister in his complex feelings.

For her part, and to his satisfaction, Marilyn had come to a point where she had worked only with Greenson's approval; she arranged her social life according to his lights; she accepted or rejected roles only with his approbation (Huston's film about Freud, for example, was out of the question, no matter how much she longed to be in it). Muffling by proxy the applause for Juliet that he so resented, he had kept Marilyn in his home. Putting forth the notion of her schizophrenia and receiving the blessing of his colleague Milton Wexler for such unorthodox treatment (but apparently not for the prodigal administration of a drug regime), Greenson had brilliantly orchestrated everything under the pretext of reordering her life. 'Come inside with me,' he seemed to say. 'Renounce your fame, and therefore affirm my supremacy,' his actions said. With Marilyn Monroe, Ralph Greenson finally became not only a musician but orchestrator and conductor.

But he was indeed, as he himself had feared anyone thinking, the incarnation of the musician Svengali to this new Trilby, the performer of the world. Just as Eunice had done, Greenson was, with Marilyn, reversing the resented past pattern: he was subjugating the other. Eunice Murray had become a crippled version of the increasingly healthy Marilyn: now Ralph Greenson was himself retreating into a psychoneurotic fear of abandonment and rejection, precisely the mental attitudes Marilyn was learning to put behind her.

Apparently, no firm decision was taken that Thursday about a termination to her therapy: this was to be something discussed by them over the next several days, or perhaps when Joe arrived and they announced their future plans; in any case, it would not have been an easy task for Marilyn to confront Greenson with this dramatic news.

Whatever the substance of their sessions, Marilyn asked Eunice to drive her on several errands in Beverly Hills and West Hollywood. Their last stop was The Mart, an antique collector's paradise on Santa Monica Boulevard, where Marilyn went in search of a bedside table. 'I have a Spanish house in Brentwood,' she told the store's owner, Bill Alexander, 'and I'm so happy, because I'm going to be married to someone I was married to once before.' They chatted about furnishings, and Marilyn selected a table to be delivered on Saturday. She would have lingered to browse and talk further, but, said Alexander, 'her housekeeper and companion seemed anxious and nervous and said, "Marilyn, we should be leaving. I will wait for you in the car."' Around six o'clock, Marilyn invited Allan Snyder and Marjorie Plecher to the house for champagne and caviar. They recalled how happy and optimistic she was, radiating charm and wit and good health.

On Friday 3 August 1962 – as reported by the Associated Press wire service that evening and by the *Los Angeles Times* next morning – Robert and Ethel Kennedy and four of their children arrived by air in San Francisco, where they were met by their good friends John Bates and his family. The Kennedys were guests at the Bates ranch outside Gilroy – 80 miles south of San Francisco, 350 miles north of Los Angeles and high in the Santa Cruz Mountains – for that entire weekend preceding the attorney general's opening address at a convention of the American Bar Association on Monday 6 August.

This social note would have no relevance at all to the life and death of Marilyn Monroe were it not for the fact that from 1962 the most outrageous assertions were made – not only about a tryst between Robert Kennedy and Marilyn Monroe that weekend, but also about Kennedy's direct involvement in her death. The origin and accumulation of these claims – and the absurd alternative theories of a murder cover-up variously involving organized crime, the FBI and the CIA – are despatched in the Afterword to this book. But a brief outline of the attorney general's weekend, and of the several witnesses who attest to his considerable distance from Los Angeles, should be herewith provided.

The Kennedys and the Bates were already friends, and in a way the Bates family was reciprocating a previous weekend they had enjoyed at Hickory Hill, Robert Kennedy's Virginia compound. John Bates, then forty-four, had graduated from Stanford University in 1940 and had served for three years in the Navy. Through a college fraternity brother named Paul B. Fay, a close friend of John F. Kennedy, Bates met and also became a friend of Robert Kennedy. After the war, Bates took his law degree at Berkeley in 1947 and joined the San Francisco firm of Pillsbury, Madison & Sutro, where he worked with such distinction that he eventually became a senior management partner.

By the time John Kennedy became president, John Bates was one of California's most prestigious and respected attorneys, holding, among other positions, the chair of the judiciary committee of the Bar Association of San Francisco. It was no surprise, then, that the new administration invited him to head the anti-trust division of the Department of Justice. Bates, however, preferred to remain with his law firm and to retain his California residence, where he and his wife were raising their three children.

'It was a difficult decision,' said Bates years later, 'but I gratefully declined. When I learned that the attorney general was to address the Bar Convention, I wanted to show my appreciation for the offer to join the Kennedy administration, and so my wife and I invited Bob to join us for the weekend.' Kennedy's presence at the remote Bates ranch in Gilroy that weekend is beyond dispute: in fact it was documented not only by the Bates family and household employees in detail, but also by *The Gilroy Dispatch* the following Monday. 'The attorney general and his family were with us every minute from Friday afternoon to Monday,' said John Bates, 'and there is simply no physical way that he could have gone to Southern California and returned.' Accounts to the contrary by the media and so-called eyewitnesses Bates always considered 'outrageous, ridiculous and disgraceful.'

Bates is quite correct, for the airstrip nearest to his ranch is at San Jose, an hour's journey by car. Because of the deep canyons, steep mountains and high power lines, helicopter flights have been always dangerous in and out of Mount Madonna, the site of the Bates ranch. The only practicable means of transport from Gilroy to Los Angeles in 1962 was by car, a journey of no less than five hours each way.

The Kennedy schedule for that weekend has been well-preserved in the Bates family guest books and documented in their photograph albums. On Saturday morning, 4 August, both families rose early and ate large breakfasts before Robert and Ethel Kennedy joined John and Nancy Bates for a ride.

The foreman of the Bates ranch, Roland Snyder, was another witness to the weekend. 'I saddled the horses for Mr and Mrs Bates and for Mr and Mrs Kennedy, then they lined up and I took their picture and they took off for Mount Madonna. They were here all weekend, that's certain. By God, he wasn't anywhere near L.A. – he was here with us.'

The morning ride was followed by swimming and a barbecue lunch back at the compound. 'I was fourteen at the time,' recalled John Bates Jr, 'and was about to go off to boarding school. I remember Bob [Kennedy] teasing me about it, saying, "Oh, John, you'll hate it!"'

During Saturday afternoon, the attorney general – in a typical Kennedy-style challenge – suggested that everyone race a mile to an open field for a game of touch football. 'The best flat meadow for field games,' according to John Bates,

> was at the top of the ranch. So off we went, and all eleven of us played. We then went back to the compound for a swim and some games, and then the children showered and dressed for dinner. I remember Bobby sitting with the children as they ate and telling them stories. He truly loved his children.

After the children were put to bed, the four adults sat down to dinner: Nancy Bates remembered their discussion of Kennedy's forthcoming speech, which was reviewed and edited by Ethel (and on which the attorney general worked intermittently during the weekend). 'Dinner lasted until about ten-thirty,' said John Bates, 'and we were in our bedrooms not long after that.'

Sunday morning, 5 August, the Bates and Kennedy families were up early for the trip to Mass in Gilroy, their presence documented by the local press next day. After luncheon back at the Bates ranch, John drove the Kennedys to San Francisco, where they were to stay at the home of Paul Fay during the convention. That afternoon and evening the Kennedys spent in San Francisco with John and Nancy Bates and other friends of both the Bates and Kennedy families (among them Mr and Mrs Edward Callan and Mr and Mrs Joseph Tydings). It is significant that over a span of more than thirty years not one of the dozen people who were with Marilyn on 3 and 4 August – at her home and at Peter Lawford's – ever mentioned the presence of Robert Kennedy. In fact, when the stories began to be taken for truth, everyone took pains to deny these allegations. Finally, the FBI records confirm without any doubt precisely this schedule kept by the attorney general and his family that weekend.*

Friday 3 August was a warm and unusually humid summer day,

---

* See FBI file no. 77-51387-293 dated 6 August 1962 and registered 21 August 1962.

full of activity for Marilyn. She awoke early and refreshed, perhaps because she had not taken sleeping pills the night before. Then she spent ninety minutes with Greenson at Franklin Street and stopped at Briggs to add some items to her party list for the following week. Back at her home, Hyman Engelberg was waiting, apparently at Greenson's request. He injected her and gave her a prescription for twenty-five Nembutal capsules. These were added to a store of chloral hydrate, the instant 'knockout pills' – actually a liquid enclosed in a gelatine capsule – that had been prescribed by Greenson to wean Monroe off barbiturates, as he later detailed. Lee Seigel had also written for her a prescription for an unknown quantity of Nembutal on 25 July and repeated it on 3 August. The precise numbers of pills available to Marilyn Monroe during the last months of her life was lost in the confusion of the days after her death and the conflicting accounts of several medical and legal sources, but clearly she had no trouble obtaining drugs in quantity.

The easy availability of a profusion of drugs was partly due to a failure of communication between Greenson and Engelberg. This was made more difficult by Engelberg's protracted and painful divorce from his wife of twenty-nine years, and he was often difficult to locate in late July and early August. Engelberg said later that he was careful to limit Monroe's supply of Nembutal to one a day, and Greenson claimed that a primary object of his therapy was to break his patient's drug dependency – but if their statements accurately expressed their protocols, both doctors were failing spectacularly.

That Engelberg's injections were something more than vitamins is evident from the 32-minute call documented by her General Telephone records. Norman Rosten recalled that during their conversation she was 'cheerful, excited . . . high, bubbly, breathless. She seemed high . . . She raced from one subject to another [with] barely a pause.' But although her tone seemed manic, Marilyn had a lot of news and was clear about her plans: she said she was feeling better than ever, that she would soon be back at work, that her house was nearing completion, that she was getting several film offers. It was, Marilyn said, time for them all to put the past behind them and begin to live before they were too old.

Other telephone calls kept Marilyn busy throughout Friday afternoon, as her records document. She spoke with the handyman Ray Tolman at his home in Fullerton, to arrange for him to work at the house early the following week: there was heavy cleaning to do, as well as some important repairs necessary. She then telephoned Elizabeth Courtney and Jean Louis to ask if they could deliver her new dress for a final fitting the next day: but suddenly remembering that would be Saturday, she corrected herself, said she did not want to interrupt their weekend and added that she could wait until Monday.

In mid-afternoon, Jule Styne, who was looking forward to composing her songs for *I Love Louisa*, telephoned from New York with another idea. He proposed to Marilyn a film musical version of Betty Smith's novel *A Tree Grows in Brooklyn*, which had been a successful Fox film in 1945. To this idea she responded enthusiastically and added that since she was coming to New York the following week, they could meet in his office. Thus an appointment was fixed for the following Thursday, 9 August, at 2.30: 'She was very excited about the idea,' recalled Jule Styne, 'and she would have been wonderful in it. We spoke of [Frank] Sinatra for the other leading role.' Marilyn also agreed to give a long interview for a photoessay accompanying her appearance on the cover of *Esquire*, and there were various social engagements as well. 'My husband and I were expecting her to arrive that week,' according to Paula Strasberg, who had begun to book theatre tickets for her visit.

Arthur Jacobs called to say that their meeting with J. Lee Thompson was scheduled for Monday at five o'clock to discuss *I Love Louisa*. Marilyn was delighted at the rapid progress of this project, too. Her diary was filling up fast, and as even Eunice had to admit later, there was nothing sombre about her attitude: 'There was too much to look forward to.' The phone calls were interrupted when Marilyn decided she should dash over to Frank's Nursery, where she ordered several citrus trees, flowering plants and succulents; delivery was arranged for the following day. Very likely she planned her wedding to be held outdoors, and the garden and pool area needed plantings and colour; no doubt Eunice Murray and Ralph Greenson were in her mind even as she spoke.

Yet Marilyn Monroe was functioning soberly and creatively even after a second meeting with Greenson that Friday afternoon. She called Pat Newcomb, whom she invited to dine out with her. Pat, however, was suffering a bout of bronchitis – to which Marilyn replied, 'Why don't you come out here and stay for the night? You'll have all the privacy you want, you can sun in the back yard and have all the rest you want.' As Pat said later, 'I accepted her invitation. She was in a very good mood, a very happy mood.'

And so the two women dined quietly that Friday evening at a local restaurant, and then returned to Fifth Helena. Eunice Murray had gone to her home for the night, and Marilyn and Pat retired early. Pat slept soundly in the small second bedroom diagonally opposite Marilyn's, but Marilyn endured another night of only intermittent sleep.

A few minutes after eight on the morning of Saturday 4 August, Eunice Murray arrived at Fifth Helena for her last day at work, which was to include supervision of the garden plantings. Marilyn wandered into the kitchen at about nine, wrapped in her white terry-cloth robe, and poured herself a glass of grapefruit juice. An hour later, Lawrence Schiller drove up: he had been one of the trio photographing the swimming scene on the set of *Something's Got to Give*, and he had come to discuss a magazine feature exploiting the pictures; as ever, Marilyn had retained the right to approve or reject photos for American magazines. That morning, according to Schiller, Marilyn was fresh and alert, 'seemingly without a care', and tending a flowerbed in front of the house when he arrived. She gave him a tour of her remodelled guest cottage and then marked the photographs with a grease pencil, indicating her selection and rejection.

The morning was hardly a dramatic one. Marilyn signed for several deliveries (the bedside table from The Mart, the trees from Frank's Nursery) and spoke with friends on the telephone. Ralph Roberts called, and they arranged to have a barbecue at Fifth Helena the following evening, after she returned from her second visit to Mama Jean Bello with Sidney Skolsky. It seemed, that sunny summer morning, that the recent crisis with Fox had somehow propelled her to a stage of freedom and a strength of purpose that had been her goal since 1955, when she deserted Hollywood for New York. Never before had her professional prospects been so various or so potentially rewarding, both financially and artistically.

Just before noon, Pat Newcomb got up, only to find her client and friend surly and sarcastic. 'Marilyn seemed angry that I had been able to sleep and she hadn't – but something else was behind it all.' Nevertheless while Marilyn telephoned friends, Eunice prepared lunch for Pat, who remained throughout the afternoon. She lay quietly, sitting under a heat lamp for her bronchitis and sunbathing beside the pool while Marilyn attended to her own business.

Shortly after one o'clock, Ralph Greenson arrived. Except for an interval between three and four-thirty, he remained with Marilyn until after seven that evening: 'He spent most of the day with her,' as Milton Rudin said, based on his later conversations with Greenson. While Marilyn and Greenson retreated to her bedroom for a therapy session, Eunice as usual answered the telephone: there was apparently only one caller – a collect call from Joe DiMaggio Jr, then on duty with the Marines in nearby Orange County. Then twenty, he had maintained close ties with Marilyn, as had the Miller children, and scarcely a month passed without their exchanging several phone calls. But because Marilyn was closeted with her doctor, Eunice told Joe that Marilyn was not home. This occurred, as he told the police, at about two o'clock.

At about three, according to Pat Newcomb, Greenson 'came out and told me to leave, that he wanted to deal with Marilyn alone. She was upset, and he told Mrs Murray to take her out for a walk on the beach, in the car. And that's the last I saw of her.'

With that, Greenson returned home, while Eunice drove Marilyn to Peter Lawford's home; the housekeeper then went shopping for groceries as Marilyn instructed (so Eunice documented in her memoir) and then returned for Marilyn within an hour.

William Asher, who had directed the presidential gala, was a director in Lawford's production company and was also a regular at Lawford's social events, recalled Marilyn's visit to the beach that afternoon between three and four. 'I was there along with a few other people who had dropped by, when Marilyn arrived and took a walk on the beach.' Asher knew Marilyn through his frequent visits to the Lawfords, and through negotiations for yet another prospective new film project then being discussed – a comedy about a train heist to star Marilyn, Lawford, Sinatra, Dean Martin and Sammy Davis Jr. Harry Brown (who had written *Ocean's Eleven* for the same quartet of men) had completed a treatment for the new project, and Milton Rudin was already negotiating contracts.

But there was a drastic change in the sober manner and clear speech Eunice and Pat had observed in Marilyn that morning. After Greenson's visit and by the time she arrived at the beach she was drugged, according to Asher – 'not staggering, but clearly under the influence, and she wasn't too steady in the sand.' Whether at Greenson's suggestion or by her own choice, Marilyn during or after their session had taken sufficient sedation to make her speech now slurred and her gait wobbly: as her autopsy later revealed, there was a high concentration of sodium pentobarbital (Nembutal) in her liver, for which several hours of accumulation would be required.

There were several reasons for Marilyn to be given or to resort on her own to her habit of taking tranquillizers that day, and they were the same causes of her scratchy humour Pat had seen that morning. Eunice's final hours in her employment must have made the atmosphere at Fifth Helena awkward, as would the imminent interruption of her therapy necessitated by her marriage and trip to New York. Marilyn was also restless because of her insomnia the previous night; she was eager for Joe's arrival; and however enthusiastic she was about her many projects, she was as usual nervous and insecure about her participation in any professional activities. Asher remembered that Marilyn watched part of a volleyball game on the beach and then departed at about four o'clock.

At 4.30, Joe DiMaggio Jr, put through a second collect call to Marilyn, and Eunice Murray again told him she was not at home – but this cannot have been true, for by this time Eunice and Marilyn had returned from the beach together. The fact is that, as Greenson mentioned in his letter of 20 August to Marianne Kris, he returned to Marilyn's house at exactly that time to continue what was becoming virtually a day-long therapy session, during which Eunice again answered the telephone. Greenson also wrote to Kris words that reveal most pointedly the extent of his emotional upset and the likelihood that they had at least discussed terminating her therapy: 'I was aware that she was somewhat annoyed with me. She often became annoyed when I did not absolutely and wholeheartedly agree [with her] . . . She was angry with me. I told her we would talk more, that she should call me on Sunday morning . . .'

At about five, however, Marilyn did take a call from Peter Lawford, who was trying to assemble a few friends for the usual Saturday night casual Mexican supper, and he hoped Marilyn would return to the beach to join them – George Durgom, a personal manager of (among others) Lawford and of Jackie Gleason; Lawford's closest friend, the agent Joe Naar and his wife Dolores, and Milton Ebbins and his wife (Patricia Lawford was in Hyannis Port visiting her ailing father). This invitation she declined, but Peter persisted: 'Oh, Marilyn, come on down. You can go back early.' He then said he would call again, hoping she would reconsider.*

* The Naars and the Ebbinses eventually withdrew, too, after Lawford told them Marilyn, Marlon Brando and Wally Cox – the original trio invited – had all begged off.

But there were two other telephone calls that Marilyn was not able to intercept. The first came from Isadore Miller, to whom Eunice said that Marilyn was dressing and would call him back; Isadore never received a return call. The second call was from Ralph Roberts, at about 5.40 or 5.45, just before he drove to Jurgensen's in Beverly Hills to purchase the food for their barbecue next evening. 'But it was Greenson who picked up the phone,' according to Roberts. 'When I asked for Marilyn, he said abruptly, "Not here," and immediately hung up on me without asking if I wanted to leave a message. Nothing else, just a blunt "Not here," and he put down the receiver.'

His manner may not have sprung from simple rudeness, however clear was the resentment of Ralph the analyst towards Ralph the friend. At precisely this time, Greenson was expecting a call from Hyman Engelberg, whom he had been trying to reach, and whom he wanted to come and provide Marilyn with medication – most likely an injection to help her sleep, as the physician so often did. Earlier that same day, amid the awkwardness of separating from his wife, he had received a message through his answering service from Greenson, asking him (as his first wife clearly recalled) to come to Fifth Helena. Engelberg had refused. Now, just after six, Greenson traced him to his home on St Ives Drive. To Greenson's dismay, Engelberg again declined, leaving the psychiatrist to cope alone.

At seven o'clock or seven-fifteen, Greenson claimed, he departed, leaving Marilyn alone with Eunice Murray. And shortly thereafter begins the series of inconsistencies, misrepresentations and outright lies masking the truth of the tragic and unnecessary death of Marilyn Monroe.

First, there is a conflict between Ralph Greenson's account of Eunice's remaining with Marilyn, and Eunice's tale. In *The Last Months*, Eunice's co-author and sister-in-law Rose Shade wrote that 'before he left, [Greenson] asked [Eunice] if she planned to stay over that night, and she said she did. That was all.' Two weeks after Marilyn's death, however, Greenson expressly noted in a letter to Marianne Kris, 'I asked the housekeeper to stay over night, *which she did not ordinarily do on Saturday nights.*'* In 1973, Greenson said he made this request because he 'didn't want Marilyn to be alone', which was curious considering that by then everyone knew this was to be Eunice's last day of employment under Marilyn. Things become more ominous still in the light of what Eunice told the district attorney in 1982: that 'this was the *first time Dr Greenson had asked Murray* to spend the night at Monroe's residence', and that she had no knowledge of Marilyn's ordinary sleeping habits or attire.†

Greenson and Murray were less than forthcoming and much less than consistent in subsequent accounts over the years. But two telephone calls provide important clues to a final resolution of the mystery surrounding Marilyn's last night.

The first call came from Joe DiMaggio Jr, who persisted in his day-long efforts to get through to Marilyn. He finally succeeded between seven and seven-fifteen, when she picked up the telephone and the two had a pleasant conversation during which he informed her that he had decided to break his engagement to a young woman Marilyn did not like.‡ As Joe Jr told police, he found her alert, happy and in good spirits – especially when he shared this news. Their chat lasted about ten minutes. Even Eunice Murray confirmed that during this conversation Marilyn was 'happy, gay, alert – anything but depressed.' Greenson repeated a similar impression: he said Marilyn called him after hearing from Joe Jr, and that she sounded 'quite pleasant and more cheerful.'

The second call came from Peter Lawford, still hoping to persuade Marilyn to attend his little supper party. Lawford spoke

* Italics are the author's.
† Italics are the author's.
‡ Joe DiMaggio Jr was able to fix the time of his conversation. In his subsequent police interview, he said that Marilyn picked up the phone while he was watching on television the seventh innings of a baseball game: the Baltimore Orioles against the Anaheim Angels, being played in Baltimore that Saturday evening. The game began just after seven-thirty Eastern Daylight Time, which would have put the seventh innings at about ten o'clock (or seven o'clock Pacific Daylight Time).

with Marilyn soon after Joe Jr had – at 7.40 or 7.45 – and heard a woman in a very different condition.

Lawford heard Marilyn muttering in thickened speech, her voice slurred and almost inaudible. Distressed and disoriented, she frightened Peter, himself no stranger to the effects of barbiturates, alcohol and drugs, and familiar with Marilyn's own habits in this regard. Attempting to rouse her to consciousness, he shouted her name several times over the telephone, asking what was wrong. Finally, with a great effort, she seemed to inhale, and then Marilyn Monroe said, 'Say goodbye to Pat, say goodbye to the president, and say goodbye to yourself, because you're a nice guy.' At that point, Lawford said later, 'I really started to get angry and frightened.' Oddly, Marilyn whispered, 'I'll see, I'll see,' and then she was silent.

Thinking Marilyn had hung up the telephone, Lawford immediately tried to call her back, but he heard only an engaged signal that blocked the line for the next half-hour. When he asked an operator to interrupt the conversation, he was told that the phone was off the hook or out of order. Frantic, he telephoned Milton Ebbins, who had also been invited to and declined the now defunct supper party. 'Peter was obviously deeply concerned,' Ebbins recalled – and he would remain concerned throughout the evening, despite repeated assurances from several people that Marilyn was well and there was no cause for alarm.

There was, of course, very much cause for just that.

In less than half an hour, something terrible happened to Marilyn Monroe, as the coroner later noted:

Monroe was laughing and chatting on the telephone with Joe DiMaggio's son . . . and not thirty minutes after this happy conversation, Marilyn Monroe was dying . . . This was one of the strangest facts of the case.

Peter Lawford understood her few words as indicating that she was dangerously drugged or even dying. Something was so wrong and different that he was convinced this was not what some people later claimed – a cry of 'Wolf!' With panic in his voice, he then tried to obtain help for her from whomever among his friends he could enlist. And in this effort he persisted so fiercely that even an eventual call from no less than Milton Rudin was not enough to allay his fears.

First, there was Ebbins:

Peter said, 'Let's go over there [to Marilyn's house]. I want to go over there right away – I think something terrible is happening to Marilyn.' But I said, 'Peter, don't do it! You're the president's brother-in-law! If you go over there, it she's drunk or drugged or something, you'll see headlines all over the place and you'll get yourself involved. I'll tell you – let me call Mickey Rudin, and if he says so, then you can go, because otherwise, if you go, you're really opening a can of worms.'

Ebbins then called Rudin – a logical choice, since he was Marilyn's attorney – reaching his office at 8.25. He learned that Rudin was attending a party at the home of Mildred Allenberg, the widow of Sinatra's agent, and Ebbins called Rudin there. 'Rudin asked me to let him check it out – to see if there was any trouble,' Ebbins recalled. 'So he telephoned Mrs Murray.' With this account Rudin concurred: 'I did not call [Greenson]. He had had enough, quite frankly. He had spent the day with her. But I did call the housekeeper.'

Rudin reached Eunice at about 8.30 or a few moments later, in the room at the guest cottage. After asking her to check on Marilyn, he waited 'for about four minutes, and then she came back to me and said, "She's fine." But I had a feeling she never went out to take a look.' Rudin's intuition served him well, as Eunice's account of his call suggested: 'If only [Rudin] had told [me] that he had received a worried call from someone,' she lamented in her book. 'If only . . .' then *what*? She would have actually taken the trouble to ascertain Marilyn's condition? But in her memoir, Eunice wrote nothing about Marilyn's non-response: she did not say that she went to the door, that she knocked, called out to her – nothing.

Rudin then called Ebbins and reported his conversation with Eunice; Ebbins in turn reported to Lawford. Still, Lawford was neither satisfied nor convinced: becoming more and more drunk as the evening progressed (and Ebbins knew from subsequent calls), he persisted in his anguished concern for Marilyn, calling other friends to enlist help.* Among these was Joe Naar, who lived on Moreno Avenue, half a mile from Fifth Helena. Lawford called him at about eleven, asking him to drive over to determine Marilyn's welfare 'because she sounded as if she might have overdosed', as Naar said later. As he was dressing to do just that, Naar received another call – this time from Ebbins, countermanding Lawford's request and saying that everything was fine: Rudin had just contacted him to the effect that 'Marilyn's doctor has given her a sedative [thus Naar, quoting Ebbins] and she was resting. The doctor was Greenson.'

While Ebbins continued to keep people away from Fifth Helena, Lawford repeatedly sounded the alarm, calling Asher as late as one o'clock Sunday morning, imploring him to make the trip to Marilyn's house. Only at one-thirty did Lawford desist in his efforts – because by then he had learned the truth in a telephone call from Ebbins, who had heard the news from Rudin. According to Lawford, Rudin had telephoned Ebbins at exactly that time from Fifth Helena, where Rudin and Greenson 'had found Marilyn dead at midnight'. Lawford's confidence as to the time was based on his simultaneous glance at a bedside clock.

In fact, according to Milton Rudin, Marilyn was dead before midnight. He recalled, in his first full discussion of this night for the record, that he returned home early from the Allenberg dinner party and before he prepared to retire, he received a call

* However, he heeded the advice to stay away. As both his maid Erma Lee Riley and his friend George Durgom insisted, Lawford never left his home that night.

from his brother-in-law Ralph Greenson: 'I got a call from Romey. He was over there. Marilyn was dead.' Rudin said he drove at once to the scene.

The brief timespan during which Marilyn's death must have occurred becomes narrower still in the light of another telephone call, this one received by Arthur Jacobs at the Hollywood Bowl, where he was attending a concert with the producer Mervyn LeRoy and his wife, and with the actress Natalie Trundy – later to be Mrs Arthur Jacobs – on the eve of her birthday. 'At about ten or ten-thirty,' according to Natalie Jacobs,

> someone came to our box and said, 'Come with us right now, please, Mr Jacobs. Marilyn Monroe is dead.' That I will never forget. Arthur asked the LeRoys to take me home. I don't know why, but I had the distinct impression it was Mickey Rudin who called Arthur at the Bowl, and that he [Rudin] had been called by Greenson from Marilyn's house.

Well before midnight, then, several people close to Marilyn were aware of a terrible disaster and were moving to control it.

According to Natalie Jacobs, Arthur arrived at Fifth Helena, conferred with those already present and then departed. The burden of the worldwide public relations tangle that was soon to begin would be handled by Marilyn's friend, Pat Newcomb. Pat was not at home that evening and could not be reached until several hours later. She was finally informed of Marilyn's death about five o'clock Sunday morning by Rudin. 'I remember his exact words,' according to Pat. 'He said, "There's been an accident. Marilyn has taken an overdose of pills." I asked, "Is she okay?" and he said, "No, she's dead. You'd better get over here." That I remember.

These first-hand reports fully contradict the entire official report of Marilyn Monroe's death, which depends on Ralph Greenson's and Eunice Murray's versions of the events.

To be accepted, the accounts of Greenson and Murray relied

on the consensus that no one thought there was anything amiss until around three o'clock Sunday morning, 5 August – fully ninety minutes after Lawford's telephone call from Ebbins and almost five hours after the news was reported to Jacobs.

At three, Eunice said, she awoke, 'for reasons I still don't understand' (as she said with her typical blend of feigned innocence, coy vagueness and a *soupçon* of bogus mysticism). She then noticed a light under the door to Marilyn's room, tried to open the door, found it locked, and then, her concerns aroused, telephoned Greenson. He instructed her to take a poker, then to go outside the house and part the curtains through the open grille-covered front casement windows, to see if Marilyn was asleep and apparently well. Eunice did as she was told and saw Marilyn lying nude and motionless on the bed. This she reported back to Greenson on the telephone. He rushed over and, using the same fireiron, broke a second, unbarred window (at the side of the house) which he unlatched, thereby climbing into Marilyn's bedroom. A moment later he unlocked the bedroom door from within to admit Eunice, saying quietly to her, 'We've lost her.' At 3.50, Greenson telephoned Engelberg, who pronounced Marilyn dead. At 4.25, the two doctors then called the police, who arrived at the house ten minutes later.

The first flaw in the story was the idea that light shone under the door: new, deep-pile white carpeting had recently been laid in Marilyn's bedroom, so thick that for two weeks it had prevented the door from being fully closed, which it could not be until a slightly pressed arc was worn into the carpet. No light could be seen beneath the door. Confronted with this later, Eunice quickly amended her account to say that she became alarmed when she noticed the telephone cord leading under the doorway.

But there were even more serious problems.

For one thing, there was never an operating lock on Monroe's door, a fact Murray conceded years later in written correspondence. On 9 February 1987, the archivist and genealogist Roy Turner wrote to Eunice (whom he had befriended), asking,

'Was Marilyn's door locked when you found her?' She replied in one handwritten word following his question: 'No.' This would have been entirely true, for Marilyn never locked her bedroom door; leaving the door unlocked had been a lifelong habit, especially reinforced since the Payne Whitney experience. 'She didn't lock doors,' Pat said years later. 'I never thought about that, but it's true.' Ralph Roberts and Rupert Allan concurred.*

Moreover, the idea that Eunice parted the curtains of Marilyn's bedroom window with a poker and found the actress, sprawled dead across her bed, is impossible to accept. The window coverings were not draperies but the heavy blackout fabric from Doheny Drive, nailed across the casement and beyond both sides of the window by Ralph Roberts soon after Marilyn moved in. Disturbed by the slightest light when trying to sleep, Monroe had them installed in one piece: there was no overlap in the middle for Eunice to push aside even if the windows had been open.

The question of timing also proved troublesome for Eunice. When she was interviewed by Sergeant Jack Clemmons, the first police officer arriving on the scene at 4.35 on the morning of 5 August, Eunice said she had called Greenson to the house at about midnight. But soon she must have realized the problems this would cause, for Greenson had not called the police until four and a half hours later. And so, by the time a detective interviewed her later that Sunday morning, she had changed the time of her call to Greenson to three o'clock. The summons at about midnight would, however, have been consistent with the news reported to Lawford by Ebbins, that Rudin and Greenson were at the house before one-thirty, and that Marilyn was already dead.

* Between 15 March and 30 June, according to their invoice no. 7451, the A-1 Lock & Safe Company of 3114 Wilshire Boulevard, Santa Monica, installed only two locks in the house: a cabinet lock for Cherie Redmond's files, and a replacement lock for the front door of the house. Additionl locks were not installed until 15 and 21 August, after Marilyn's death (A-1 invoice no. 7452).

Greenson told the police the same story as Murray, but his version never changed because he agreed to be interviewed but rarely, never wrote a memoir and was never challenged. The failure in both versions to mention the presence of Milton Rudin further damages the credibility of Greenson's account.

The weakness of this official version effected many results, not least among them a series of fantastic conspiracy theories, the inventions of nefarious plots and counterplots, government-inspired murder and so on. The problem is obvious for any theory involving the FBI, the CIA, organized or disorganized crime, the Kennedys or Kennedy cronies: there is simply no concrete evidence to support any such claim.*

The psychiatrist and the housekeeper always neatly escaped scrutiny themselves – he because of his accomplishments, prestigious position and canny retreat behind the curtain of professional confidence, and she by virtue of a brilliantly calculated public image, reinforced via print and television interviews, as a dear little old lady.

But as their individual histories and their actions that final evening revealed, and as the medical record would soon confirm, it was these two alone who had something to hide.

---

* For a detailed treatment of the alternatives proposed for the death of Marilyn Monroe, see the Afterword.

Chapter Twenty-three

5 AUGUST 1962

In the early morning hours of 5 August, Sergeant Jack Clemmons was serving as acting watch commander, replacing an off-duty lieutenant normally in charge at the West Los Angeles station of the Los Angeles Police Department. At 4.25 his desk telephone rang and a caller said simply, 'Marilyn Monroe is dead, she committed suicide.' Because this was a quiet night at the station, Clemmons decided to investigate the matter personally.

Arriving at 12305 Fifth Helena Drive about ten minutes later, Clemmons was led into Marilyn's bedroom, where he found her lying nude, prone and lifeless, with a sheet pulled over her body. In the room were Greenson and Engelberg; by this time, Milton Rudin had departed. Clemmons then observed (and later wondered about the fact) that Eunice was busy operating the washing machine at the time of his arrival.

According to the sergeant, Eunice then offered him a sketchy account of the night's events, including the fact that she had discovered Marilyn's body 'at midnight'. Clemmons asked immediately why it had taken so long for police to be notified, and at once Greenson replied that the doctors 'had to get permission from the publicity department at the studio before we could notify anyone' – an absurdity as stated, but at the same time a possible allusion to the earlier presence of Arthur Jacobs.

By this time, word of the catastrophe was quickly circulating as newspapers and wire services monitored police radio frequencies; within minutes, more policemen began to arrive on the scene – among them were Officer Marvin Iannone (later chief of police in Beverly Hills) and Detective Sergeant Robert E. Byron, who assumed control of the case and who proceeded to question Greenson, Engelberg and Murray. At this point, Eunice changed the time of her discovery of Marilyn's body to about three o'clock.

Like Clemmons before him, Byron was unimpressed with the statements he was able to elicit, especially those of Eunice: 'It is officer's opinion that Mrs Murray was vague and possibly evasive in answering questions pertaining to the activities of Miss Monroe during this time,' he noted in his official report.

Another officer who responded to the scene before dawn that Sunday morning was Don Marshall, a plain-clothes officer also in the West Los Angeles division. Marshall arrived to find Clemmons still in charge of the scene, and he was assigned to 'take a look around and see if Monroe had left a suicide note.' Marshall spent the next several hours carefully examining any and all papers he could find in the house.

Near the bed was an English-language telegram from Paris, offering Marilyn an opportunity to appear in a one-woman show, but otherwise Marshall's thorough search satisfied him there was indeed no suicide note. He remained on duty at Fifth Helena throughout the day, during which he questioned Marilyn's neighbours, Mr and Mrs Abe Landau, who lived at 316 South Carmelina, only a few yards away at the corner of Fifth Helena Drive. The Landaus, reported Marshall, assured him they had heard no disturbance the night before, and that in fact Miss Monroe had been 'a very good neighbor'.

At this point, the level of activity increased, as Pat Newcomb had joined the gathering crowd that now included Greenson, Engelberg, several police officers and Milton Rudin, who by now had returned to the scene. Pat remained at the house for about two hours before returning home to cope with a stream of calls from the press worldwide. Then, shortly after five-thirty, Marilyn Monroe's remains were covered with a pink woollen blanket, strapped on to a steel gurney, trundled out the driveway and loaded into a battered Ford panel truck for an interim stop at the Westwood Village Mortuary – exactly why is unclear, for the circumstances of death required an autopsy, which could only be done downtown, at the office of the coroner. Most likely, this hiatus occurred so that Rudin, as Marilyn's attorney, had the opportunity to contact Inez Melson, her business manager and the conservator of Gladys's affairs, and Joe DiMaggio, whom Rudin rightly foresaw would best manage the funeral details.

Just after eight o'clock that Sunday morning, 5 August, the remains were at the City Morgue. At 10.30, deputy coroner Dr Thomas Noguchi, on weekend duty, completed the autopsy.

Back at Fifth Helena, the police remained in charge. Later there were ridiculous reports that Fox executives had ordered the 'burning a pile of documents in the huge Mexican fireplace'. There were also rumours that 'the locks on Monroe's metal filing cabinet had been smashed with a crowbar and the drawers rifled' in order to remove documents compromising the security of the United States Government. This is all utter nonsense, according to Officer Don Marshall, who was present all day: 'Nobody was destroying anything.'*

There was, however, some repair in progress. Eunice telephoned her son-in-law Norman Jeffries, asking him to replace the small pane of glass Ralph Greenson had supposedly shattered with the fireplace poker; this would prevent any disturbance to the interior of the house once the property was legally sealed off by police late Sunday night. With that and her laundry done, Eunice finally left Fifth Helena Drive – one day beyond her scheduled date. She had left Marilyn Monroe's home in very tidy condition indeed.

Miles away, another kind of care was being taken by Thomas Noguchi as he performed the autopsy on Marilyn Monroe.

---

* A small cache of Marilyn's personal letters and papers was removed next day by Inez Melson, after whose death in 1986 they passed first to a collector, thence to DS.

With him was a brilliant observer who would also be crucial toward an understanding of Marilyn's death.

In 1962, John Miner was deputy district attorney of Los Angeles County and chief of its Medical Legal Section; as such, he was also liaison officer to the chief medical examiner-coroner's office. Miner also taught forensic psychiatry at the University of Southern California and was particularly respected for his legal and medical expertise in assessing suicides and deaths judged possible suicides. During his tenure as liaison officer to the coroner, Miner attended the post mortem examination for every death reported as unnatural, more than 5000 autopsies. That year the medical examiner-coroner of Los Angeles County was Dr Theodore Curphey, who appointed Dr Thomas Noguchi, deputy medical examiner, to perform the autopsy on Marilyn Monroe.

The preliminary report from the Office of the County Coroner, dated and signed by Noguchi at 10.30 on Sunday morning, it contained in File Number 81128 in the Los Angeles County Coroner's Mortuary, Hall of Justice, City of Los Angeles. The first supplement, a report of chemical analysis of the blood and liver, was dated and signed by R. J. Abernethy, Head Toxicologist, at eight o'clock on the morning of 13 August (File Number 81128-I). Subsequently, on 10 August, Curphey's preliminary judgement was that death occurred because of a 'possible overdose of barbiturates'. On 17 August this was amended to 'probable suicide', and on 27 August, Curphey made his final statement still more forcefully, as 'acute barbiturate poisoning – ingestion of overdose'.

This decision was based on the major chemical findings of toxological analyses, which seemed clear and unambiguous.

First, there were no external signs of violence. Second, there was in the blood a count of 8 milligrams of chloral hydrate and 4.5 milligrams of Nembutal – but in the liver there was a count of 13 milligrams, a much higher concentration of Nembutal. These figures are crucial toward a comprehension of how she died.

5 August 1962

On her bedside table, police had found full and partly full bottles of several drugs, among them antihistamines and medications for her sinusitis. There were also an empty bottle that had contained twenty-five 100-milligram Nembutal capsules, a prescription dated 3 August 1962 on the authorization of Dr Hyman Engelberg; and ten capsules remaining from an original bottle of fifty 500-milligram chloral hydrate capsules, a prescription dated 25 July and repeated on 31 July on the authorization of Dr Ralph Greenson.

This was important information for the Suicide Prevention Team, convened at the coroner's request to come up with a psychological profile of the deceased at the time of death and the likelihood of suicide. 'It was obvious to us, after speaking with Dr Greenson about Marilyn's psychiatric history,' said Dr Robert Litman, a member of the team, 'that the only conclusion we could reach was suicide, or at least a gamble with death.' But Litman and his colleagues did not believe that Marilyn took her life deliberately: 'Since our studies from 1960, we have found that no authenticated case where barbiturates were involved that a person was so drugged he didn't know what he was doing.'

And yet Litman and his colleagues submitted a verdict of suicide because that had been Curphey's initial judgement, because they had consulted only their colleague Greenson and because, as the Suicide Prevention Team, they pursued and rightly dismissed other options. She was neither psychotic nor, as Dr Norman Farberow, another member of the team, added significantly, 'an addict among addicts, and she had no physical dependency on drugs. Her intake could be considered light to medium. And she was certainly not mentally unbalanced so far as I could determine.' Besides, as Litman said, 'We wanted to get this over with, to come to a decision, close the case, issue a death certificate and move on. But of course, that turned out to be a misplaced hope. Nobody ever moved on.'

Thomas Noguchi, John Miner and at least three other highly

645

respected forensic pathologists reached a quite different conclusion from that of Curphey and the Suicide Prevention Team.*

'I did not think she committed suicide,' said John Miner thirty years later. 'And after interviewing Dr Greenson I was even more convinced that Miss Monroe did not commit suicide. In fact, he did not believe it himself.'

Miner's medical reasons for disbelieving the suicide verdict were supported by his interview with Greenson, from whom he learned that Marilyn was not only making plans for the future but that 'she felt that she had put everything bad behind her and could now go forward with her life.'

A systematic review of post mortem chemical analyses provides the final crucial step from John Miner's informed intuition to positive conclusions about Marilyn Monroe's death. Whatever drugs caused it could only have been introduced into the body in one of three ways: by mouth, by injection, or by enema.

Marilyn could not have died by oral ingestion of capsules for several reasons.

First, the ratio of Nembutal found in the blood compared to that in the liver suggested to any competent forensic pathologist that Marilyn lived for many hours after ingestion of that drug. There was also 'not a large reservoir left in the stomach or gastrointestinal tract to be drawing from'; in fact, as Noguchi's report stated, there was no trace of drugs in the stomach or in the duodenum, where absorption occurs. This means that while Marilyn was alive and mobile, throughout the day, the process

---

* For what follows, the author is grateful for corroborative reports filed with John Miner by two internationally renowned pathologists: Dr Milton Halpern, former chief medical examiner of the City of New York; and Dr Leopold Breitenecker, medical examiner for the City of Vienna, professor at the University of Vienna and one of the great European forensic pathologists. In 1982, Dr Boyd G. Stephens, chief medical examiner-coroner of the City and County of San Francisco, provided the City of Los Angeles with an independent review of the autopsy evidence. In 1992, DS further consulted Dr Arnold Abrams, Medical Director of Pathology at St John's Hospital, Santa Monica.

of metabolizing the Nembutal she had taken had already reached the stage where much of the toxic material had reached the liver and was beginning the process of excretion. 'The barbiturates were absorbed over a period not of minutes but hours,' according to John Miner, 'precisely as is indicated by the high concentration in the liver.' This report is consistent with what is known of Marilyn's activities earlier that day, and what Greenson himself called her 'somewhat drugged' condition.

Second, suicide by deliberate Nembutal overdose would have been an action entirely inconsistent with everything in Marilyn Monroe's life at the time – especially after the call from Joe DiMaggio Jr, as reported by him and by both Murray and Greenson.

Third, had she for some unknown reason suddenly decided to commit suicide, she would have taken a large dose at one time (not many capsules throughout the day, which she well knew how to ingest intermittently and at which dosages). The barbiturate would have reached a toxic level rapidly, and she would have died. But in that case, there would almost certainly be a residue of pills in the stomach: 'Forty or fifty pills simply are not going to dissolve so quickly in the stomach,' as Dr Arnold Abrams reported. 'The odds that she took pills and died from them are astronomically unlikely.'

The possibility of barbiturate injection must also be rejected. A dose large enough to be lethal, injected intramuscularly or intravenously, would have resulted in an instantaneous death and a much higher level of barbiturate in the blood. As the District Attorney observed in his 1982 review of the case and specifically of these blood levels, 'This leads to a reasonable conclusion that Miss Monroe had not suffered a "hot shot" or needle injection of a lethal dose.' Such a massive injection would also have left a swelling and bruise, the gradual disappearance of which would have ceased with death. But 'every inch of her body was inspected with magnifying glasses,' according to Miner (thus, too, Noguchi), 'and there was simply no needle mark.'

The only possible route of administration of a fatal dose of drugs is confirmed by the discovery, during autopsy, of a bizarre condition Miner said was unique in his review of more than ten thousand autopsies: a major area of Marilyn's colon bore 'marked congestion and purplish discoloration', a condition consistent with a rectal administration of barbiturates or chloral hydrate. 'This abnormal, anomalous discoloration of the colon has to be accounted for,' said Miner in 1992. 'Noguchi and I were convinced that an enema was absolutely the route of administering the fatal drug dose.'

Abrams agreed:

I have never seen anything like this in an autopsy. There was something crazy going on in this woman's colon. And as for suicide, I simply can't imagine a patient self-administering a fatal dose of barbiturates or even a sedative dose by taking the trouble to prepare and administer the solution! You don't know what the necessary fatal dose will be, and you have no guarantee that it's going to be absorbed before it's expelled. Look: if you're going to kill yourself with barbiturates, you do it with pills and glasses of water.

As for Nembutal suppositories (sometimes fancifully suggested as the cause of death), these would only have reached about ten centimetres into the rectum: but in Marilyn's case, the entire sigmoid colon, a section very much higher, was grossly discoloured. Administration by enema was indeed the route by which the fatal dose was administered.

In this regard, it must be recalled that Marilyn had a history of taking enemas 'for hygienic and for dietetic purposes', as Miner said (and as her designers, like William Travilla and Jean Louis, had known for a long time). 'This was also much the fad among actresses in that era.'

But this conclusion does not solve the problem of what was administered in this enema and by whom. An explanation is still required of precisely what happened in Marilyn Monroe's bedroom between the end of her conversation with Joe DiMaggio Jr at 7.15 or 7.25, and her almost incoherent replies to Peter Lawford at 7.40 or 7.45. Perhaps the most poignant fact is that Marilyn seems to have been aware, as she answered Lawford's call, that she was slipping over the edge from the kind of normal drug-induced sleep or sedation she knew so well, towards death – and she knew there was nothing she could do to reverse the situation. Quite contrary to those who say that Marilyn was crying 'wolf' is the plain, tragic fact that she knew she was dying and could neither rouse herself nor summon help: 'Say goodbye . . .'

The exact circumstances of Marilyn Monroe's sad and unnecessary death can, in the light of all this evidence, at last be established.

First, it is important to remember that Ralph Greenson had ceased prescribing Nembutal for Marilyn Monroe. He was, as he said, 'cutting down her dependence on Nembutal [which he no longer prescribed] by switching her to chloral hydrate [which he did] as a sleep-inducer.' In fact, he said he had asked Hyman Engelberg not to prescribe Nembutal without his permission: they were to monitor the drugs each was providing. But the previous day Engelberg wrote Marilyn a prescription for Nembutal without Greenson's knowledge.

'On Friday night,' Greenson wrote to Marianne Kris two weeks after Marilyn's death, 'she had told the internist that I had said it was all right for her to take some Nembutal, and he had given it to her without checking with me, because he had been upset for his own personal reasons. He had just left his wife.' During Saturday, however, Greenson observed that Marilyn was 'somewhat drugged', as he told Kris; he was too sophisticated and familiar with Marilyn not to recognize on what medication she was 'somewhat drugged'.

While the precise amount of Nembutal was unknown to him, the ineffectiveness of it was clear – she was awake, angry and difficult to manage. Greenson's solution to this was revealed in the toxicological analysis: chloral hydrate, his drug of choice for her, was present in the blood and not the liver. And because the level of chloral hydrate was twice that of the Nembutal (which had accumulated in the liver, having been ingested gradually over many hours), it is clear that the chloral hydrate was administered after the Nembutal had been taken.

In his haste that evening, Greenson perhaps overlooked one crucial factor, the adverse interaction of the two drugs. Chloral hydrate interferes with the body's production of enzymes that metabolize Nembutal. It was the chloral hydrate that pushed Marilyn over the edge. Some of the Nembutal was being processed by the liver, but much (4.5 milligrams, more than a lethal dose) had not been metabolized. As Milton Rudin recalled Greenson saying on the night of Marilyn's death: 'God damn it! Hy [Engelberg] gave her a prescription I didn't know about!' John Miner recalled a similar, incomplete statement: 'If only I'd known about that other prescription . . .'

'If only', then what? Would Greenson indeed have foregone that last heavy dose of chloral hydrate?

Two weeks later, he described his departure that night to Marianne Kris in the most pacific tone: 'I told Marilyn,' Greenson wrote to Kris, 'that she should call me on Sunday morning when she awakened, and I left.' But in the event, Greenson felt irritated, resentful and rejected; unable to accept that his romantic self-image of saviour had been terminated and aware that he could no longer continue in the mode of control he had so carefully constructed, he chose the easier route. 'He'd had enough, he was exhausted, he'd spent the day with her,' Milton Rudin said of him. And so, before departing, Greenson arranged for Marilyn to take a sedative enema, since she was physiologically resisting the effects of oral medication. Chloral hydrate would enable her to sleep. Short of the usual Engelberg injection, which Greenson tried but failed to obtain, the most powerful route of administration, as he knew, was an enema – something on which Marilyn often relied for other purposes. But she did not know that a chloral hydrate enema could be dangerous, even fatal, as a sequel to Nembutal.

'She probably regarded this as an ordinary enema being given to her,' said Miner. 'It would have been inserted slowly, not unpleasantly, not causing any immediate urgency for evacuation. After several minutes' – during which time she took Lawford's call – 'she then would have lapsed into unconsciousness. The absorption continued, and though still alive, she was dying.'

But who, at last, gave the chloral hydrate enema?

The only person who could have done it was Eunice Murray, and this was indeed her last act as Marilyn Monroe's employee and Ralph Greenson's watchdog. 'I always felt the key was Mrs Murray,' said John Miner thirty years after the fact, speaking fully for the first time.

But Eunice was acting under orders from Greenson, the man she had looked to for fifteen years as her protector and employment provider. As her son-in-law Philip LaClair insisted years later, 'Eunice did only what Ralph Greenson told her to do. She always followed his orders closely, because she had no formal training as a nurse. There's a lot I could say about Greenson, but I won't.'

Accustomed to delegate the administration of medicine to others, it was logical for Greenson to ask Eunice to do this particular deed. Moreover, giving an enema is not within the range of a psychiatrist's duties, especially not a male psychiatrist with a female patient: no matter how obsessive his attachment, Greenson's ego would not permit so intimate a physical act. But asking an untrained woman with no nursing credentials to give a drug in such a way that its method of administration is potentially lethal – no matter how careful the instructions might have been – is professionally imprudent and in fact downright reckless.

On the other hand, it is possible that Ralph Greenson never actually left Fifth Helena Drive that night – he may not have had to return at all. For years he claimed he went out to dinner with friends, but even when he was questioned, the 'friends' were never named, they never stepped forward of their own accord, and the Greenson family, interviewed frequently after his death, never identified them. Milton Rudin, for one, believed that Greenson was at home all evening. Even had he remained at Fifth Helena, Greenson would likely have absented himself (however proximately) during Eunice's nursing task; either way, responsibility for that task was his.

This scene of the drama closes with another important detail previously remarked upon but never taken into account: Eunice's inexplicable washing of garments and linens, as Clemmons attested and as Miner later learned. 'Why, under these circumstances,' as Miner asked rhetorically, 'would a housekeeper be doing the laundry at such an hour – unless the bedclothing had become soiled as a result of the administration of these drugs?' Abrams concurred: 'Eventually, of course, when she slipped into her terminal coma, the enema had to be expelled. Thus the washing of the sheets,' which, as Miner added, 'was an especially hard thing to understand unless Mrs Murray was destroying evidence.'

To the horror of everyone involved, what may have been intended as Marilyn's long, deep sleep became her death.

There were numerous details to be arranged that night, along with the sanitizing of what was, to say the least, an ugly situation. 'Arthur said it was horrendous,' Natalie Jacobs recalled him saying after that night. 'He never gave me any details, and I never asked him. He said only that it was too dreadful to discuss.'

This appalling situation explains the long delays between the arrival of Greenson at Fifth Helena and the summons to police five hours later. If indeed he left at all, Greenson returned immediately after Rudin's call to Eunice had sent her to Marilyn's room – where everything had gone wrong. Marilyn was unresponsive; she had expelled the enema; and there were other aspects of the 'horrendous' scene occurring in the case of someone comatose, moribund or even, by this time, dead.

Certainly, as the telephone calls indicated and as Rudin conceded, Greenson arrived before the small hours, locating

Engelberg only later at his temporary residence in West Los Angeles, where he was living because of his marital separation. Presumably there was an attempt to revive Marilyn, to reverse the effects of the drug. (Henry Weinstein recalled that at least once before, Greenson summoned Engelberg to pump out Marilyn's stomach when she had apparently taken too many Nembutal in her Doheny Drive apartment.) Also, according to both Eunice and a note in the District Attorney's 1982 report, an ambulance was summoned around midnight and then dismissed on arrival – because she was dead, and because California law prohibits the transport of a corpse in an ambulance. Greenson and Murray must have felt an almost paralysing panic as the enormity of the disaster became clear to them. How does one announce one's involvement in, or explain one's discovery of, the death of Marilyn Monroe, so much adored by all the world?

Once it was clear that Marilyn was beyond resuscitation, there were details to be staged. A window had to be broken, so that it would appear as if a forced entry had been necessary. There was the blackout fabric to be removed (which it was, and neatly folded by the time police arrived), to substantiate the story concocted about Eunice pushing back the curtains with a poker. Most of all, there was an account Greenson and Murray had to fabricate and which they had to rehearse. And there was soiled linen to be cleaned.

Had Ralph Greenson himself administered the fatal enema, Eunice Murray would have said so – if not during his lifetime, then after his death, when she had a great deal to gain financially and the public's lingering suspicion of which to unburden herself. After Marilyn, Eunice worked neither for Greenson nor anyone else as nurse or housekeeper. One imaginative suggestion has been that Greenson provided her with hush-money, making a financial settlement to cover his own calamitous indiscretion. But a payoff does not accord with the poverty in which Eunice subsequently lived, moving from one small Santa Monica apartment to another until her daughters took her in frail old age.

Very soon, then, there was a dark and dreadful collusion firmly in place.

Ralph Greenson could never reveal what he knew about Eunice Murray because this would have effectively ended his career. He had hired a non-professional – and a troubled woman, at that – and asked her to perform a medical task because he could not locate Engelberg. This was a rank and reckless lack of professionalism, perhaps subconsciously justified by him because of his anger at his beloved but unresponsive patient. This was, after all, the most famous movie star in the world: he could not tell the truth of the matter. In fact, Greenson could be rather smug about the success of the coverup, for when the photographer William Woodfield later asked him about the large prescriptions of chloral hydrate he had allowed Marilyn, Greenson replied casually, 'Well, I've made a number of mistakes in my time.'

For her part, Eunice Murray could not point the finger at anyone else because she had done the actual deed. All she and Greenson could do was weakly to state that they did not believe Marilyn Monroe took her own life deliberately. 'Nobody then or later,' as John Miner said, 'undertook to realize that Mrs Murray was concealing information. She simply wasn't telling the whole truth and never did thereafter.' Miner was correct, for apart from the insufficiency of her stories about the light and/or telephone cord beneath Marilyn's bedroom door, Eunice did not lie so much as deny. Rightly, she denied the presence of Robert Kennedy: 'I don't recall him being there at all' in July or August, she said – because, indeed, he was not. Rightly, she denied the presence that night of Peter Lawford and of unknown assailants. Asked about her published memoir as a basis for solving the mystery, Eunice's last statement on the record about the death of Marilyn Monroe sounds very like the beginning of a confession: of her book *The Last Months*, she said in 1987, 'I wouldn't swear to my version at all.'

As for Engelberg, his distribution of dangerous and habit-forming drugs, not to say his continued reliance on

Greenson, put him in no position to expose anyone's deeds – which he very likely considered at worst an unfortunate accident.

But it was much more than that, and herein lies the unspeakable sadness of Marilyn Monroe's fate.

She had been under the supervision of a man who can at best be termed obsessive, and this she realized to the extent that she knew their relationship had to end. This he realized, too, admitting to colleagues that he had reached a classic state of countertransference; his work with her could no longer be justified.

'Dr Greenson took her death very personally,' said John Miner,

> for he was involved with this lady to a strong degree. He was deeply shaken, even devastated by it. Even though a psychiatrist is supposed to maintain a defense mechanism, he could not restrain himself. In his own way, he loved this girl in the sense that she was a wonderful person to him. He had become very emotionally attached to her.

And more than attached, for Greenson deeply resented her increasing independence – thus his systematic attempt to separate her from good friends. His patient's death indicates the awful possibilities when an analyst does not keep to his boundaries and yet continues, knowing full well that his own emotions are intimately intertwined with his patient. In the end, he no longer regarded either his own responsibilities nor her needs. When he said he had 'tried to help but ended up hurting her,' Greenson spoke perhaps the truest self-assessment of his life.

Out of patience, fearing the loss of his best beloved, enraged at himself and at what he considered her ill-advised dismissal of Eunice and of himself (which was imminent if not actual), Ralph Greenson ordered Marilyn Monroe sedated – as he had for so long, with Engelberg's assistance – so that the rupture of their relationship might not occur: 'Call me on Sunday morning.'

But it was finally just as the other Ralph, the loving Ralph Roberts, had said, 'If you can't control Marilyn one way, there are always drugs.' John Huston may have known more than he let on when, told of her death, he said angrily, 'Marilyn wasn't killed by Hollywood. It was the goddam doctors who killed her. If she was a pill addict, they made her so.'

As for Eunice Murray, she had experienced the fullness of her life with Marilyn, in the replica of her own house, with a surrogate daughter and working with a surrogate ministering husband. But the situation had failed her, and so in a way as she administered the sleeping drug she was putting this entire part of her life to rest, however ignorantly and unaware of the final effect. She was the stooge of Ralph Greenson – an unpretty term but in this case an accurate one for an emotionally crippled and dependent woman, and so she must have felt when she cried out at the age of eighty-five, twenty-five years later, 'Oh, why – at my age – do I have to keep covering up for this thing?'

The monumental self-absorption and ego-neuroses of her two caregivers enabled them to observe Marilyn at the happiest time of her life, at a stage of growth so full of promise – yet strive to keep her dependent on them and on them only.

At the last, the custodians could not sustain what they perceived as her rejection of their tyranny. 'We've lost her,' Greenson said ironically to Murray, announcing her death. On his utterance of this statement they both agreed: in a way they had already lost her, when she made her decision to dismiss them.

Ralph Greenson may have helped patients to whom he did not become obsessively attached. But in a serious way he was a personal and professional failure: an egocentric, slick entertainer; a storyteller jealous of the limelight; a possessive and tyrannical man who could pass for a brilliant therapist only in Hollywood, where even social performance is applauded and admired. He treated Marilyn Monroe not as a growing, maturing woman, one who was becoming healthier and stronger. On the contrary, he wished to keep her frail, collared to dependence on him forever. Weary of interrupting his personal life to deal with the struggles of his primary patient – an involvement he had himself worked hard to create – he was at the end resentful that Marilyn was withdrawing from his orbit, was moving out of his control, towards Joe and therefore away from him. Having spun for himself the mantle of guardian and protector, father and caregiver, he found it was an intricate web. He had worked tirelessly to limit Marilyn's outside contacts, to make his devotion her only love and his care her only support. In any relationship, this is a dangerous programme; in a therapeutic situation, it is catastrophic.

Her imminent departure was intolerable to him, the ultimate rejection by his ultimate patient. He considered her, therefore, as one who failed to be his, and in the end he treated her just as such a man would – capriciously, placing her in a perilous situation. In some dark corner of his mind, he may have known or feared or even wished that his temerity would lead to disaster.

And herein lies the tragedy of Marilyn Monroe's death. Something brave, new and mature was emerging in her those last months, as every deed, interview, human interaction and performance witnesses. She was finally taking control of her life, as those closest to her testified; she was in some way banishing the crippling ghosts that had so long surrounded her. Never contemptuous of those who had hurt or misguided her, she was now kinder still, more concerned than ever for those her life had touched. Only in this spirit can her finest qualities be appreciated – her refusal to malign husbands or lovers for the sake of a good interview; her rejection of self-pity; her devotion to Isadore Miller, to Arthur's children, to the young DiMaggio. There were remarkable, almost miraculous acts of hope in her own future: her return to Joe, her new projects, her willingness to cast out the unhelpful people, the old and the jaded parts of her life.

This buoyant spirit had been activated before, when she first turned her back on Hollywood in 1955, feeling that her life was stymied. That spirit returned to her now, too, and it must have had something to do with Joe DiMaggio – although not everything, for theirs was hardly a passionate love in its first full bloom, and they were both too wise not to know there were shoals yet to be negotiated. 'But there's a future, and I can't wait to get to it,' she had recently told one reporter. Enthusiasm and humility, a green hope coupled with the longing to go on, to transcend what had been – rarely has so graceful a spirit been so cruelly silenced.

Silenced indeed. Marilyn Monroe died at the mercy of those who believed their mission was to save her – not for her sake, but for themselves. They wanted to own her. Marilyn Monroe's death gives new meaning to the phrase California Gothic.

Late Saturday afternoon, Marilyn had begun to write to Joe, whom she so anxiously awaited; it would be pleasant to think that she was writing it after he telephoned. But something interrupted her, and the note was found, folded in her address book. When the house was searched for a suicide letter before her body was removed next morning, the address book was left untouched, or perhaps the note was discreetly left in place by the searcher. Like her life, it was something good, in process:

Dear Joe,

If I can only succeed in making you happy, I will have succeeded in the biggest and most difficult thing there is – that is, to make *one person completely happy*. Your happiness means my happiness, and

Chapter Twenty-four

6-8 AUGUST 1962

The body desired by millions belonged to no one: on Monday morning, 6 August, Marilyn Monroe's remains still lay unclaimed at the Los Angeles County morgue. And so, to no one's surprise, Joe DiMaggio stepped in to adjudicate the last details. Late that afternoon, she was brought back to the Westwood Village Mortuary on Glendon Avenue, a few steps from busy Wilshire Boulevard.

Ten years earlier, at the start of her great dash to stardom, Marilyn had asked her friend Allan Snyder to come to a hospital just before she was to be discharged: she wanted to look her best for the public and the cameras. For fifteen years, no one understood her fears and her features better than he, no one was more patient and loyal in devoting his craft to her benefit.

Promise me something, Whitey,' she had said, using his familiar nickname while he brushed and lined, highlighting here and toning there.

'Anything, Marilyn.'

'Promise me that if something happens to me – please, nobody must touch my face but you. Promise you'll do my makeup, so I'll look my best when I leave.'

'Sure,' he said, teasing. 'Bring the body back while it's still warm and I'll do it!'

A few weeks later, Allan received a gift box from Tiffany's. Wrapped in a light blue pouch was a gold money clip with an engraving:

Marilyn Monroe

Whitey Dear
While I'm still warm
Marilyn

Now it was time to call in the promise. On Tuesday 7 August
the telephone rang at Snyder's Malibu home.

'Whitey?' Joe was calling from his hotel room in Santa
Monica. 'Whitey, you promised – will you do it, please – for
her?'

No explanation was necessary. They both remembered.

'I'll be there, Joe.'

And so Allan drove to the mortuary, Swiftly, deftly, rever-
ently, he took up his bases and brushes, his liquids and rouges,
and worked there in the cool room. He had done this job so
many times, had worked on her while she laughed and chatted
or simply slept; he had prepared Marilyn for so many public
appearances before she emerged from dressing rooms, airplanes
and clinics. Now, as Allan completed his task, Joe entered.

On Wednesday morning, 8 August, Allan returned early,
knowing that the makeup would surely need retouching.

Joe was still there. He had spent the night with his beloved,
his fingers clasped tightly, his gaze fixed on Marilyn's features:
it was the solitary vigil of an adoring knight, worshipping from
twilight to dawn on the eve of a great battle. Now Joe sat
motionless, leaning forward as if by sheer force of love and
longing he could urge her back to life for their wedding. To
strangers, reporters and writers, he never uttered her name
again, nor did he ever remarry.

Joe made a hard decision during those three days. There
would be no Hollywood stars or directors at the funeral, no
producers or studio executives, no newsmen, reporters or
photographers: they had only hurt Marilyn, he said. Instead,
only thirty relatives and friends were to be admitted, among
them Berniece, who had come from Florida out of respect for
the half-sister she scarcely knew but had come to admire from
afar; Enid Knebelkamp, Grace's sister; the Snyders; Lee and

Paula Strasberg; May Reis; Ralph Roberts; and the Greenson family, with Eunice Murray. Jim Dougherty, remarried, was on duty with the Los Angeles Police Department, and Arthur Miller, also remarried, likewise declined to attend.

Gladys, still at Rockhaven, never knew of her daughter's death. She was released from the sanitarium several years later and, after living for a time with Berniece, entered a Florida nursing home where she died of congestive heart failure on 11 March 1984, at eighty-two. When questioned, Gladys seemed not quite certain who Norma Jeane was or who she had become.

The service began in the mortuary chapel at one o'clock, when an organist offered a selection from Tchaikovsky's sixth symphony and one of Marilyn's favourite melodies, 'Over the Rainbow', from *The Wizard of Oz*. A local minister preached, taking his text from the Book of Amos: 'How wonderfully she was made by her Creator.' Then, as Joe had requested, Lee Strasberg spoke briefly: 'We knew her,' he said, his voice shaking and his eyes glazed with tears, 'as a warm human being, impulsive, shy and lonely, sensitive and in fear of rejection, yet ever avid for life and reaching out for fulfilment. The dream of her talent was not a mirage.'

Before the casket was closed, Joe bent over, weeping openly as he kissed Marilyn. 'I love you, my darling – I love you,' he said, placing a nosegay of pink roses in her hands. Henceforward for twenty years, flowers would be delivered weekly from Joe to her burial place – just as he had promised Marilyn when she told him of William Powell's pledge to the dying Jean Harlow. Joe then led the group from the chapel to the crypt, a hundred yards away. They passed the grave markers of Ana Lower, buried here in 1948, and of her niece Grace McKee Goddard, who had followed five years later.

That day they were gathered at the centre of the neighbourhood where Marilyn had spent almost all her life. It was the same small arena where she had grown and gone out to work in such a brief but brilliant radiance, this local girl who now belonged to the world. There were Hawthorne and the old Bolender house to the south; the Los Angeles Orphans Home eastward in Hollywood, near the place where Gladys and Grace worked at film-cutting benches and took the girl to the movies; and very close, Nebraska Avenue, where she lived with Aunt Ana, and Emerson Junior High School, where Norma Jeane was 'the Mmmmm Girl', dating the wisecracking Chuck Moran. Near them, too, were University High; the house where she married Jim; the sound stages of Twentieth Century-Fox; and Fifth Helena Drive.

They stood silently while the coffin was placed in a marble wall-crypt to which a bronze plaque was attached:

Marilyn Monroe
1926-1962

After the mourners had departed, reporters, newsreel photographers and the public were at last permitted to approach. In the cemetery garden, cameras clicked and movie film whirred all afternoon and through the quiet evening.

Afterword

THE GREAT DECEPTION

After the publication of his book *The Life and Curious Death of Marilyn Monroe* in 1974 (see note in Chapter 11), Robert Slatzer continued to trumpet his alleged relationship with Marilyn Monroe, developing without proof information about himself and about her affair with Robert Kennedy into a cottage industry. Quoted in magazine articles, cited in books and featured on sensational television shows, Slatzer became the ultimate torchbearer and self-proclaimed authority. Marching as a heroic pursuer of justice, he played point-man in a long-running, grotesque literary charade that matches any other for brazen audacity.

Others contributed to the legend. They include Lionel Grandison, a former coroner's aide who said that the police falsified Marilyn's autopsy; Jack Clemmons, the sergeant who first arrived at Marilyn's home on the morning of 5 August 1962; Milo Speriglio, a private detective who published his own fantastic allegations based on Slatzer's questionable testimony; and Jeanne Carmen, who has described herself as one of the star's closest friends but who, like Slatzer himself, was completely unknown to anyone who knew or worked with Marilyn (see Chapter 19). Slatzer and company regularly trot on to television talk shows, where they cheerfully corroborate one another's outlandish assertions.

In part, the success of Slatzer's enterprise witnesses the permanent fascination the world has with Marilyn Monroe, the first public icon to suffer an untimely death during the 1960s.

The subsequent allegation that her murder was politically motivated elevated her to the pantheon of that era's tortuous history, and the supposed involvement of the Kennedys tapped into the realm of conspiracy and fable pre-eminently attached to that family.

But how did such a colourful tale originate?

The first plank of it was put into place by New York gossip columnist Dorothy Kilgallen even before Marilyn died. On Friday 3 August 1962, she published the news that Marilyn was 'vastly alluring to a handsome gentleman who is a bigger name than Joe DiMaggio'.* She was then rivalled by columnist Walter Winchell (who, like Kilgallen, had been hostile to Marilyn since 1955): he pointed to 'one of the President's appointees . . . who ran like a Husband [*sic*] – back to his wife.' Winchell was following a lead from the right-wing fanatic Frank A. Capell, a man who – like Winchell himself – deeply hated the Kennedy clan, believing them soft on communism. Since 1938, as confidential investigator and then chief of the Subversive Activities Department for the Sheriff of Westchester County, New York, Capell had seen Communists lurking everywhere. But he was no ideal American: moving to the compliance division of the War Production Board, he was indicted and pleaded guilty in 1945 to three counts of conspiring with a colleague to solicit bribes from government contractors. Forced into civilian life, he began publishing a Communist-baiting newsletter, *The Herald of Freedom*.

One of Capell's buddies was Jack Clemmons, the first policeman on the scene after Marilyn's death. Clemmons was also connected to the Police and Fire Research Organization (more familiarly, 'Fi-Po'), a team dedicated to exposing 'subversive activities which threaten our American way of life'. In this capacity, Clemmons met Capell just six weeks after Marilyn's death to investigate supposed Communist affiliations in Hollywood.

---

* Kilgallen did not name her source for this curious titbit: Howard Perry Rothberg, a New York interior designer with no connection at all to Marilyn or her circle.

Clemmons then introduced Capell to Maurice Ries, president of the Motion Picture Alliance for the Preservation of American Ideals, an anti-Communist forum that made headlines in the 1950s when it charged the Screen Writers Guild with fostering a Communist invasion of the movie world. At a meeting attended by all three men, Ries held forth on the hundreds of files he had compiled on celebrities, turning at last to the case of Marilyn Monroe.

'I'll tell you a story,' Ries said. 'Marilyn had been having an affair with Bobby Kennedy, and Bobby promised to marry her, and then he changed his mind and wanted to get rid of her. And she was threatening to go public with the story, and the Kennedy's had her murdered to shut her up.'

'It sounds very interesting,' Clemmons said, adding later, 'Capell said we should look into this. He said, "Jack, will you help me?" and I said, "Yeah, Frank, I'll help you." '

His assistance took the form of a call to the coroner's office, where Clemmons learned that no residue of pills had been found in Marilyn's stomach during autopsy. 'For a long time that was really the only hard physical evidence we had,' Clemmons recalled. But it was enough to convince him and Capell that Ries was right in his theory, and at once Capell (said Clemmons) 'kept feeding information to Walter Winchell, and over a period of time Walter Winchell printed the whole theory in his column.'

Capell's own version of the story was published in 1964 as *The Strange Death of Marilyn Monroe* by his own Herald of Freedom imprint. In this seventy-page pamphlet, he offered an odd combination of autopsy, police and court reports with a haphazard and somewhat hysterical review of alleged Communist affiliations of almost every principal in Marilyn's life, from Arthur Miller to Ralph Greenson to Hyman Engelberg. Capell used the snippets published by Winchell (which was virtually a case of Capell citing himself) and grandly announced his verdict. After a lengthy conjecture about Marilyn's romance with Robert Kennedy, Capell claimed that, 'because of the closeness of their friendship, she was led to believe his intentions were serious.' He then states that, since Kennedy was a Communist sympathizer, he 'wanted her out of the way' because of his 'mad ambition', and so he covered up her murder by 'deploying his personal Gestapo'. Such a paranoid imagination is perhaps unknown since the days of Senator Joseph McCarthy.

At this point, into the picture stepped J. Edgar Hoover, who learned of the imminent publication of Capell's book through Winchell, Hoover's close friend and regular conduit for celebrity news. The FBI director at once gleefully wrote to Robert Kennedy: '[Capell's] book will make reference to your alleged friendship with the late Miss Monroe. Mr Capell stated that he will indicate in his book that you and Miss Monroe were intimate, and that you were in Miss Monroe's home at the time of her death.' Appropriately, Kennedy made no reply.

In 1964 and 1965, Capell and Clemmons collaborated still further, joining a radical right-wing ideologue named John Fergus in yet another defamatory political attack – this one aimed at Senator Thomas H. Kuchel of California, a Republican who incurred the wrath of racist groups by supporting the landmark Civil Rights Act of 1964.

Capell, Clemmons and Fergus were indicted in February 1965 by a California grand jury for conspiracy to libel by obtaining and distributing a false affidavit asserting that Senator Kuchel had once been arrested on a morals charge – specifically, that he had a homosexual encounter in the back of a car. The affidavit was based on an actual case from 1950, but one involving entirely different people and in no way connected to Kuchel. After the indictment, Capell and Clemmons issued the unintentionally hilarious statement that the press had demonstrated 'disregard for our accepted standards of fair play'. After a two-month trial, it was determined that the conspirators engaged in 'arm-twisting' to obtain a false affidavit, and 'with smirking satisfaction began to apply it to their own purposes'. The judge accepted guilty pleas from Capell and Fergus; charges against

Clemmons were dropped on condition he resign from the Los Angeles Police Department.

With the framers of the 'Kennedy-killed-Monroe' fiction thus disgraced by 1965, the matter should have died. But the vein of malicious gossip it tapped was too appealing, the Kennedy–Monroe story too inflammatory to forget. Nothing more came into print before Robert Kennedy's death in 1968, although the rumour mill continued to grind out pernicious morsels. Stories were matched and swapped, embellished and improvised. But after Kennedy's assassination, the whispers became shouts.

The biggest noise was caused by the publication of Norman Mailer's *Marilyn*, published in 1973. Mailer admitted that he depended heavily on Fred Lawrence Guiles's *Norma Jean* [*sic*], written and serialized before Robert Kennedy died and published (without substantiating notes or sources) the following year. Guiles, taking his lead from Winchell, wrote of her affair with 'a married man not in the [movie] industry . . . an Easterner with few ties on the coast'. The man was 'a lawyer and public servant with an important political career . . . an attorney [who stayed] at his host's beach house' where he and Marilyn met for their rendezvous. No one had any doubt of the man's identity, and as Guiles wrote later, 'the [RFK] liaison with Marilyn, which my book doubtless exposed despite my precautions [!], has been written about over and over again.'

Despite his telling observation that 'Guiles's version . . . may be no more than a compendium of the lies he was told,' Mailer then proceeded to compound the fiction by fantasizing that Robert Kennedy *might* have had a hand in Marilyn's death or even that government intelligence agents *might* have killed her in an attempt to frame the attorney general. By simply being the first to name Robert Kennedy, Mailer had his best-seller.

Excoriated by critics for his foggy ruminations, he was interviewed by Mike Wallace on the CBS news programme *60 Minutes* (on 13 July 1973), where Mailer had to concede, 'I'd say it was ten to one that [Marilyn's death] was an accidental suicide.' Why, then, did he trash Robert Kennedy? Mailer was nothing if not candid: 'I needed money very badly.' He got it, but the public was hooked on a monumental deception.

Meanwhile, Robert Slatzer pressed ahead, fruitlessly demanding an official Los Angeles County investigation into Marilyn's death and enlisting the services of a private detective, Milo Speriglio. Their grandstanding was not much heeded until the appearance of an article – 'Who Killed Marilyn Monroe?' – in the October 1975 issue of *Oui*, a monthly 'adult' publication best described as a soft porn magazine. The writer, Anthony Scaduto (whose only sources were Slatzer and Speriglio), ran further with the Kennedy angle than anyone thus far; he also introduced two ingenious new elements into the tale.

The first was the supposed existence of a red leather diary kept by Marilyn – a notebook, Slatzer said, in which she had carefully recorded government secrets told to her by the attorney general. In this book there were, it was claimed, the details of (among other items) a plot to assassinate Fidel Castro, a secret Slatzer said Marilyn threatened to reveal to the world along with her Kennedy affairs when the attorney general ended their romance.

The second 'revelation' was the supposed existence of tape recordings, made by Marilyn herself, of her conversations with both John and Robert Kennedy – tapes, like the diary, that somehow no one actually *possessed* (or even heard) but whose 'existence' made good copy. As Speriglio, who could never be accused of understatement, blithely told Scaduto, 'Marilyn knew more about what the president was doing, thinking, planning, than the public, the press, the Congress, the Senate, the Cabinet and even the Attorney General.'

With this article, Scaduto took a permanent seat on the band wagon. In 1976, writing under the pseudonym Tony Sciacca, he expanded his article into a book, *Who Killed Marilyn?* The missing tape recordings, he now claimed, were said to have been made not by Marilyn herself but by a wiretap specialist named

Bernard Spindel, whose clients included James Hoffa, chief of the teamsters' union. Otherwise, the same dreary, totally unsupported allegations continued.

As with Capell, this lunacy was generally disregarded. But it also generated an internal investigation within the Los Angeles Police Department. Eventually, the department's Organized Crime Investigation Division prepared a point-by-point refutation of Scaduto's story, based on meticulous documentation and new interviews with Peter Lawford and Medical Examiner Thomas Noguchi. In an uncharacteristic literary smirk, the report turned a line from Scaduto against him: 'The evidence is as thin as Depression-food-line soup.'

But then an avalanche fell on to the shelves: slapdash memoirs – among them books by Marilyn's early photographers David Conover and André de Dienes, who (taking cues from Slatzer) added details of sexual intimacy and claims of a close confidence that lasted until Marilyn's death; and accounts by Ted Jordan, James Bacon and Hans Lembourn, who made assertions concerning passionate affairs with her.

Milo Speriglio also scampered on to the field with a book, offering a few new sensations, among them the incriminating gist of a secret interview with Robert Kennedy (another item no one could actually locate). Speriglio also brought forth the coroner's aide, Lionel Grandison, who claimed he saw extensive bruising on Marilyn's body that was not noted in the autopsy report. Grandison added that he saw the red diary about which Slatzer told Scaduto, but that it had somehow disappeared after the night she died. With the righteousness worthy of those declaring a holy war, Speriglio and Slatzer then demanded a new investigation into the circumstances of Marilyn's death. Appeals were made to the County Board of Supervisors, and this time official Los Angeles was persuaded. In August 1982, District Attorney John Van de Kamp ordered a so-called threshold investigation to determine whether reasonable cause existed to open a full-scale murder inquiry. The results of this investigation, submitted later that year, were important not for what they revealed about Marilyn's death, but for the light they shed on Slatzer, his cronies and their ravings. Grandison, for example, turned out to be a less than credible source, for he was dismissed from the Coroner's office for gruesome crimes 'involving the theft of property from dead bodies'.

The District Attorney also paid close attention to the allegations of a wiretap, and he found that Bernard Spindel was indeed 'a rather notorious illegal wiretapper' who had been retained by Hoffa 'in an effort to secure embarrassing information on Robert Kennedy'. Spindel had stated in late December 1966 that he had conducted electronic surveillance of Marilyn's home and obtained material 'surrounding the causes of the death of Marilyn Monroe, which material strongly suggests that the officially reported circumstances of her demise are erroneous.'

But the timing of this claim was more than suspect. Spindel's home had been raided by the Manhattan District Attorney's office earlier in December 1966 during an investigation of illegal wiretapping that resulted in the indictment of twenty-eight practitioners of that craft. Days later – his evidence 'stolen' – Spindel uttered his provocative announcement (after four years of mysterious silence). There the matter of the tapes lay until Slatzer and Speriglio recognized the value of a new story prop.

By 1982, Spindel was dead and District Attorneys in Los Angeles and New York, who could have made quite a coup had they succeeded in finding support for the existence of the 'Marilyn tapes', concluded that the whole thing was a fraud. 'Spindel's asserted desire to have the tapes made public,' wrote Assistant District Attorney Ronald Carroll in his final report, 'appears to have been a ploy . . . The [Spindel] tapes were in fact heard by staff investigators and none of the tapes contained anything relating to Marilyn Monroe.' William Graf, later chief investigator for the United States Environmental Protection Agency, added that Spindel was 'a known boaster'.

It is frankly unimaginable, if the tapes (like the diary) had ever existed, that *someone, somewhere* – over the course of so many years – would not have been able to come up with *something tangible*. In addition, Spindel's claim raises a logical question: if compromising tapes were made available to Hoffa, why did he never use them to derail the prosecution launched against him by Robert Kennedy – procedures that eventually whisked Hoffa off to prison? And why, despite enormous cash rewards offered since 1966, has no one ever produced either the telltale tapes or the diary? The answer is obvious: like the sexual affair between Marilyn Monroe and Robert Kennedy and his involvement in her death, these materials simply never existed.

Los Angeles District Attorney John Van de Kamp announced the reults of his inquiry in December 1982 with the simple statement, 'The facts, as we have found them, do not support a finding of foul play . . . Permit me to express a faint hope that Marilyn Monroe be allowed to rest in peace.'

It was not to be. Belief in a 'Kennedy murder coverup' persisted, and it was to report on the District Attorney's 1982 conclusions (see notes to Chapter 22) that Anthony Summers came on the scene. A British investigative reporter whose 1980 book *Conspiracy* had spread new seed on the fertile field of John Kennedy assassination theories, Summers found that, despite the repeated claims of Slatzer and his friends, no one had dealt once and for all with the rumours of a Kennedy connection to Marilyn's death. With that, Summers set to work in 1983. *Goddess: The Secret Lives of Marilyn Monroe* was published in 1985.

Attracted by the fantastic tale that Robert Kennedy had a hand in Marilyn's death (and before that, two feet in her bed), Summers hailed Slatzer as a legitimate source, an intimate of Marilyn who afforded important insights into her motivations and affairs. Jeanne Carmen was given equal stature, as was a New York fan named James Haspiel – a man who, like Slatzer, parlayed a few photographs of himself with Marilyn into a career (and, eventually, wrote an insufferable book that had the temerity to offer a nightmarish fantasy of Robert Kennedy suffocating Marilyn to death with a pillow). Summers admitted that 'Capell's role as an investigator, given his right-wing zealotry, was hopelessly flawed,' but he failed to add that

Capell's work was the basis for the claims of Slatzer, Winchell and others whom Summers himself endorsed.

In uncritically accepting stories from all quarters, Summers found himself in the impossible situation of juggling several conspiracy theories, most of them mutually exclusive. Thus Los Angeles Police Chief William Parker is reported leading the official coverup in an effort to become J. Edgar Hoover's replacement at the FBI. Contrariwise, Summers wrote that Hoover himself intervened and supervised the coverup, on orders from Robert Kennedy. Summers credits as 'the most cogent account' that of Joe and Dolores Naar, who said they spent the evening of 4 August at Lawford's home and that Kennedy was absent. A few pages later, it is reported that Kennedy was indeed with Lawford that evening.

Worse, Summers ignored and/or frequently misrepresented those he claims to have interviewed. On the matter of Marilyn's supposed despondency over the end of her affair with Robert Kennedy, for example, he quotes her publicist's widow, Natalie Trundy Jacobs: 'Arthur and I would stay at her house till five or six in the morning talking to her, trying to stop her drinking or taking pills.' But Natalie Jacobs has consistently denied ever making such a statement to Summers: on the contrary, her account has never varied: she met Marilyn once only, at Arthur's home for dinner and a film screening. Similarly, Ralph Roberts and Rupert Allan (to name only two more) were outraged at Summers's manipulation and misuse of their comments to him.

Despite these and a number of factual bloopers,* television documentaries based on *Goddess* were prepared in England and America. But a segment on the ABC News programme *20/20* was rightly cancelled by network executive Roone Arledge, who dismissed the entire Slatzer–Summers epic as nonsensical gossip – a wise professional decision for which he was unjustly

---

* Summers maintains, for example, that Marilyn inherited Marlene Dietrich's dressing room at Fox. This is nonsense, for Dietrich never worked at that Hollywood studio.

reprimanded by colleagues who knew nothing about the life and death of Marilyn and instead raised cries of journalistic censorship. Arledge, alas, was unfairly termed an interfering Kennedy loyalist.*

The political smear launched by Frank Capell and Jack Clemmons finally reached critical mass. Despite the assassination of Robert Kennedy in 1968 and the eventual passing of the Redbaiters, the rumours endured. The attorney general was unjustly transformed in the public's mind from a compassionate champion of civil rights to a darkly amoral character willing to kill for his reputation, and *Goddess* became the popularly accepted and unworthy source book.†

In its latter stages, the unfolding story of the Capell-Clemmons-Slatzer treachery reached the level of black comedy. Slatzer and Speriglio both returned to the well, each publishing a second book rehashing their old charges for what they hoped would be a new and larger audience. Slatzer even managed to sell his ridiculous story to ABC-TV, which in 1991 produced a movie of the week called *Marilyn and Me*.

Double Cross, ghost-written by an anonymous author for the godson and brother of Chicago mobster Sam Giancana, postulated that a pair of men colourfully named Needles and Mugsy travelled to Los Angeles on orders from Giancana. Needles and Mugsy waited patiently while Robert Kennedy had a final lovers' quarrel with Marilyn, and then slipped into her home to administer a fatal barbiturate suppository. The goal was to embroil Kennedy in a politically devastating scandal. Logic seems not to have been the authors' strong suit, for had this

---

* Even the best can be persuaded. ABC News commentator Hugh Downs, for one, surprisingly and loftily claimed that Marilyn's affairs with both Kennedy brothers were 'not in dispute' and 'known to everyone'. Cf. Downs, on the documentary 'The Class of the 20th Century', Merrill W. Mazuer, prod. for CEL Communcations, Inc./A & E Network (US cable television), 1991.

† Summers's unfounded allegations about Monroe and the Kennedys continued right through his next book, on J. Edgar Hoover, published in 1993.

been the mobsters' goal, Marilyn would certainly have been more valuable to them alive.

But the most astonishing compendium of error was *Marilyn: The Last Take*, by the entertainment writer Peter Harry Brown and the Beverly Hills society columnist Patte Barham, for this book quoted people and sources inaccurately, embellished incidents and, under the guise of offering the last word, offered only the time-worn Kennedy/Marilyn scenario.

From page one, *The Last Take* was a disastrously misleading book. At the outset, the authors imagined a melodramatic episode in which long-forgotten reels of *Something's Got to Give* were stealthily removed from the vaults of Twentieth Century Fox and spirited to the Los Angeles home of Greg Schreiner, president of Marilyn Remembered. There (thus Brown-Barham) the film was unspooled for a select group of Monroe admirers and then surreptitiously returned to the studio. These details might work in an espionage novel, but they bear no resemblance to the truth, which was at once simpler and more honourable: a New York collector had obtained outtakes of the unfinished film and sent them to Sabin Grey, who screened them at his home during a regular monthly meeting of Marilyn Remembered. Peter Brown, who ultimately assisted the expert Fox News producer Henry Schipper in the creation of a documentary on Marilyn's last film, should have known better. But he and Barham were never deterred from a good story by mere facts.

The long list of errors was astonishing – among them:

• Marilyn never travelled on Air Force One, as the authors claimed.

• The respected surgeon Michael Gurdin MD, was unconscionably misquoted. In 1992, Dr Gurdin took an hour to refute Brown and Barham's misrepresentation of their brief telephone conversation with him about his care of Marilyn. 'I don't know why they got wrong everything I told them,' the doctor said.

• Eunice Murray was not 'a veteran psychiatric nurse'; indeed, she never graduated from high school.

- *Something's Got to Give* was not the only film in production at Fox during the spring of 1962: among others was *The Stripper* (then titled *Celebration*), with Joanne Woodward.
- From 1951 to 1955, Marilyn was represented by agent and producer Charles K. Feldman, not by the William Morris Agency.
- Marilyn's limousine and driver were engaged by her, not by Fox, and the car had no studio logo engraved on the door.
- George Cukor was never an 'openly gay' Hollywood director: in fact he had to be extremely private about his sexual orientation, like everyone else so inclined during the so-called Golden Age of Hollywood.
- Marilyn's poodle Maf was a gift from Patricia Newcomb, not Frank Sinatra. And Newcomb never 'worked for the Kennedys on a variety of special projects'.

A quick survey of Brown and Barham's notes to their key chapter, on Marilyn's 'tangled, disastrous affairs with President John F. Kennedy and Attorney General Robert Kennedy' is alarming. Heading two pages of sources supposedly confirming these affairs are the names of Marilyn's masseur Ralph Roberts, Deputy District Attorney Ronald Carroll, Anthony Summers, Rupert Allan, Natalie Jacobs, Patricia Newcomb, former Kennedy press aide Edwin Guthman and the ubiquitous Robert Slatzer. Of this group, Roberts, Allan, Newcomb and Guthman have always insisted that no romance ever existed between Robert Kennedy and Marilyn Monroe (nor did they ever say otherwise to these two authors); and Carroll, Jacobs and Guthman have consistently denied any such knowledge. This leaves only Slatzer, Summers and those in their tradition.

Furthermore, Brown and Barham's notes amusingly elevate tabloid television talk shows to the level of academic scholarship: '*Geraldo, Sally Jessy Raphael, Donahue* and *Hard Copy* have all produced segments on the [RFK] affair and provided further evidence of what is now a historically accepted fact – that Monroe had tempestuous affairs with both [Kennedy] brothers.' The same notes go so far as to include, of all things, a book review of *Goddess* as further 'evidence'. The lure of such storytelling is obvious, and it was enunciated by Norman Mailer quite early in the history of this remarkably persistent legend. It has to do with money.

But the price runs higher than cash paid for shameful books. The cost includes the erosion of ideals, a loss of faith in good men and women, a cavalier disregard for the reputations of decent people and a profound indifference to the truth.

Against this grim cyclorama of deceit and sensation, *Marilyn Monroe: The Biography* was begun.

Notes

Materials from the Milton Green Papers are from two separate collections, designated **MG** and **MG2**, and have been in each group classified according to folder, file and page numbers. Thus, MG X, 3, p.24, references File number 10, folder 3, page 24 from the first group. Where there are unpaginated sheets, a page number is not provided. **RT** refers to the genealogical and ancestral papers of the family of MM and materials related to her first sixteen years. These were collected over almost a decade by the archivist Roy Turner, and the number following the designation **RT** refers to an assigned folder number for these papers.

RT refers to the genealogical and ancestral papers of the family of MM and materials related to her first sixteen years. These were collected over almost a decade by the archivist Roy Turner, and the number following the designation **RT** refers to an assigned folder number for these papers.

Magazine editor Jane Wilkie conducted important interviews with both James Dougherty and Natasha Lytess. There remain two versions of the Dougherty interview: **JWP** I refers to the unedited, complete notes of Wilkie's interviews with Dougherty in 1952; **JWP** II refers to the final version, ghost-written by Wilkie and published as: James Dougherty, 'Marilyn Monroe Was My Wife', *Photoplay*, March 1953, pp.47–85.

On several occasions from 1958 to 1960, Wilkie also interviewed MM's drama coach Natasha Lytess, from which an important cache of papers emerged. This material also exists in two forms: extensive transcribed, unedited notes and a completed, polished memoir. Both remain unpublished and were subsequently acquired by DS from Wilkie. In the Notes, **JWP/NL** I refers to the unedited transcript, **JWP/NL** II to the edited version.

BH refers to the notes and manuscripts prepared by Ben Hecht as the original ghost writer suggested by MM's confidant, the columnist Sidney Skolsky, to write MM's autobiography, which was eventually reworked by Milton Greene for publication as *My Story* (New York: Stein & Day, 1974). Hecht's notations are preserved in his Collection at The Newberry Library, Chicago, and are so identified.

IMP refers to the Inez Melson Papers, a box of MM's personal documents and letters kept by Inez Melson, her business manager from 1952 to 1962. Melson died in 1986, and the collection was acquired by DS in 1991.

For interviews which occurred on only one occasion, the author has, for reasons of space economy, generally mentioned the details of his interview only on their first citation; subsequent citations from the same source refer to the same interview unless otherwise noted.

Notes

CHAPTER 1

page

3.   neat as a pin: MG X,3.
5.   to pray for: Quoted by Gladys Monroe in a letter to MM: MG III, 2; cf. also RT 16.
6.   failure to provide: Divorce petition of Della Monroe Graves vs. Lyle Arthur Graves, Superior Court of Los Angeles County, Petition #B-8426.
9.   extreme cruelty: Divorce petition, Baker vs. Baker, Superior Court of Los Angeles County, Petition #D-10379.
12.   She was a birdlike: Olin G. Stanley to RT, 12 Oct. 1982.
13.   For the Martin Mortensen–Gladys Baker marriage, see California State Board of Health, Bureau of Vital Statistics, register no. 13794.
13.   wilfully and without: Divorce claim of Mortensen vs. Baker, File #053720, in and for the County of Los Angeles in the Superior Court of the State of California.
13.   I sure would like: Olin G. Stanley to RT, no date.
14.   shamelessly boasted: Gifford vs. Gifford, Divorce Petition #D-24788, Superior Court of the State of California.

CHAPTER 2

18.   I was probably: Quoted in MG IV, 8, p.12; cf. also Guus Luijters, *In Her Own Words: Marilyn Monroe* (London: Omnibus, 1991), p.28.
20.   for no reason: Ida Bolender, in the David L. Wolper Productions Inc. film documentary, *The Legend of Marilyn Monroe* (1964). Hereinafter indicated as 'Wolper, *Legend*'.
20.   Medical files of Della M. Monroe: Norwalk State Hospital, Norwalk, California: Record #5093; Death Certificate #4081, Registry No. 132.
20.   contributory manic depressive: *Ibid.*
21.   Despite all the: James E. Dougherty, *The Secret Happiness of Marilyn Monroe* (Chicago: Playboy Press, 1976), p.9; also Dougherty to DS, 20 June 1992.
21.   Her mother paid: Quoted in Ezra Goodman, *The Fifty-Year Decline and Fall of Hollywood* (New York: Simon & Schuster, 1961), p.225.
22.   One morning: MM, quoted in Wolper, *Legend*. Also to MG, in II, 6, p.4.
22.   She discussed her father: Rupert Allan to DS, 17 Aug. 1992.
22.   She didn't come: Georges Belmont, interview with MM originally conducted for the French magazine *Marie Claire*, published in 1960 and reprinted in *Marilyn and the Camera* (Boston: Bulfinch/Little, Brown, 1989), p.14. Hereinafter cited as 'Belmont'.
22.   To go to: 'Hollywood's Topic A-Plus' *Life*, vol.32, no.14 (7 April 1952), 104.
22.   no one ever: Quoted in *People*, vol.18, no.6 (9 Aug. 1982), 44. This statement recurs frequently in MM's notes in MG I and II.
23.   We took her: Ida Bolender, in Wolper, *Legend*.
23.   Every night: Robert L. Heilbroner, 'Marilyn Monroe', *Cosmopolitan*, vol.153, no.5 (May 1953), 40.
23.   I always felt: Maurice Zolotow, *Marilyn Monroe* (reprint of the 1960 original, New York: Harper/Perennial, 1990), p.21. Hereinafter cited as 'Zolotow'.
24.   They were terribly: Belmont, p.14.
25.   It was hard: Quoted by MM in MG II, 6, p.5.

Notes

26.   I dreamed: Often attributed to MM – e.g., 'To Aristophanes & Back', *Time*, vol.lxvii, no.20 (14 May 1956), 74.
26.   You could have: Quoted by MM in MG, II, 6, p.6.
27.   We all had: Robert Cahn, 'The 1951 Model Blonde', *Collier's*, 8 Sept. 1951, p.50.
27.   I loved playing: Margaret Parton, 'A revealing last interview with Marilyn Monroe', first published in *Look*, 19 Feb. 1979, p.26.
29.   a people well: Christopher Rand, *Los Angeles: The Ultimate City* (New York: Oxford University Press, 1967), p.135.
31.   Life became: Belmont, p.14.
31.   Aunt Ida: Belmont, p.14. Cf. also *Time*, loc. cit., 76.
33.   There's a movie star: Quoted by MM in MG, II, 5, p.7.
33.   Jean Harlow: MM in MG, III, 3, p.2. See also Belmont, pp.14, 17.
33.   There I'd sit: MM in *Life*, vol.53, no.5 (3 Aug. 1962), 33; also numerous similar observations *passim* in MG.
34.   For an account of Tilford Marion Hogan's death, see the *Laclede* (Missouri) *Blade*, 2 June 1933; cf. also File #17075, Missouri State Board of Health, for the death certificate.
36.   The doctor who prescribed: Eleanor Goddard to DS, 21 Feb. 1992.
36.   reality: Gladys Monroe, medical report from Los Angeles General Hospital dated October 1934: 'Mrs Monroe [*sic*] visited her family four days, returning of her own will in an agitated state. Referred by Dr Fellowes to Dr ...' This is the only decipherable portion of the record, torn and yellowed, and was preserved by MM in MG, VIII, 4, p.1.
37.   Grace loved: Zolotow, p.18.
38.   Grace Goddard was nice: James Dougherty to Roy Turner, in RT 47.
39.   It was just: Charlotte Engleburg to Roy Turner, n.d.

CHAPTER 3

41.   there wasn't anyone: Quoted in Eve Golden, *Platinum Girl: The Life and Legends of Jean Harlow* (New York: Abbeville Press, 1991), p.230. O'Sullivan repeated identical remarks on the 1992 Turner Network Television mini-series *When the Lion Roars*, a history of MGM. MGM film editor Margaret Booth was among several who enthusiastically agreed.
41.   There's no reason: Quoted by MM in MG XII, 2, p.24.
43.   My mother: MG III, 3, p.3.
43.   Her illnesses: File of Gladys Monroe Baker from Los Angeles General Hospital, 1935; put on deposit by MM in MG VI, 2, p.18.
44.   I was sorry: 'To Aristophanes & Back', *Time*, loc. cit., 76.
44.   You can imagine: MG III, 3.
46.   Norma Jeane was: Jody Lawrance, quoted in Ezra Goodman, op. cit., p.227.
48.   Doc had a: James Dougherty to DS, 20 June 1992.
48.   slept in: Belmont, p.15.
48.   MM's many dramatic accounts of the orphanage persisted to days before her death: cf. *Life*, vol.53, no.5 (3 Aug. 1962), 38.
48.   normal, healthy: Portion of a record of the Los Angeles Orphans Society retained by MM, filed in MG IV, 3 (undated, unpaginated).
49.   the man: Many times from 1949 to 1962, e.g., to her publicist Rupert Allan, among others.
49.   fix things: MG XI, 2, p.8.
49.   trying to fit: MM, in Wolper, *Legend*.
50.   made their appearance: *New York Times*, 8 June 1937, pp.1, 30.
50.   Time after time: MM to BH, folder 12.

51. Grace's expense records were preserved by MM and were later discovered by RT, from whom DS received them.
51. she was able: Arthur Miller, *Timebends* (New York: Grove Press, 1987), p.9.
51. anxious and withdrawn: Los Angeles Orphans Home Society, report dated 20 February in the file of Norma Jeane Baker, retained in MGIV,2. The signature is illegible.
51. I was never used: *Life*, loc. cit., 38.
51. I sometimes told: MM in MG, IX, 22, p.4
53. I suddenly stopped: *Ibid.*, III, 6.
53. You have: *Ibid.* MM recited this anecdote with variations: in some citations (Belmont, p.15 *et alibi*) the cosmetic job that day was Mrs Dewey's idea.
53. This girl: *New York Times*, loc. cit., 30.
53. She added little: *Ibid.*
54. between grief: MM in MG III, 5, p.37.
54. The incident of Doc's molestation was recounted to DS by Dougherty, 22 April 1992.
54. I can't trust: *Ibid.*, p.39.
54. At first: MG II, 3, p.17.

CHAPTER 4

56. destitute and in need: Olive Brunings Monroe, Petition No. 434981 submitted to the State of California in accordance with Sections 1570–1573 of the State Welfare and Institutions Code.
56. I remember: Ida Mae Monroe Masciello to RT, 1984.
57. The world: MG II, 4, p.34.
58. Later I thought: MG XI, 4.
60. sexually assaulted: Sam Shaw and Norman Rosten, *Marilyn among friends* (London: Bloomsbury, 1987), p.95. Rosten wrongly states her age in 1937.
61. She was very: Eleanor Goddard to DS, 21 Feb. 1992.
62. She changed: Quoted in Zolotow, p.34.
62. Talk about marriage: MG VI, 2, p.40.
65. but nothing did: MG VIII, 3, p.46.
65. Los Angeles was: Gladys Phillips Wilson to DS, 14 Feb. 1992.
66. She was very much: Mabel Ella Campbell, in Wolper, *Legend*.
67. I was very: MG VI, 3, p.3.
67. She was neat: Ron Underwood to RT, 2 Dec. 1986.
67. She always seemed: Marian Losman Zaich to RT, 16 Dec. 1986.
67. You used to have: MM to BH, 3.
68. Suddenly, everything: *Life*, loc. cit., 33.
72. We danced: MG XII, 4, p.37.
72. the smiling and beaming: *The Emersonian*, vol.5, no.15 (20 June 1941), n.p.
75. After tabulating: 'What Is Your Favorite Type of Girl?' in *The Emersonian*, loc. cit.
75. and I'd say: Often – e.g., Belmont, p.15.
75. A for Ambitious: *The Emrsonian*, loc. cit.
76. You couldn't support: Dougherty, p.18.
77. dreamboat: MG XII, 61.
77. She was: Quoted in Robert L. Heilbroner, 'Marilyn Monroe', *Cosmopolitan*, vol.134, no.5 (May 1953), 42.
77. What a daddy: Quoted by Eleanor Goddard to DS; similarly in MG XII, 61.
77. I noticed: JWP, pp.1–2.
77. expertly maneuvering: Dougherty, op. cit., pp.19-20.
77. extra close: *Ibid.*, p.22; also JWP, p.11.

78. She very neatly: Dougherty, op. cit., p.24.
79. her respect: Dougherty to DS, 20 June 1992.
79. she was loud: Tom Ishii to RT, 1985.
80. The thought: JWP, p.2; cf. also Wolper, *Legend*.
80. so that she wouldn't: Elia Kazan, *A Life* (New York: Knopf, 1988), p.404.
81. Grace McKee arranged: Belmont, p.16.
81. but not have: JWP, p.2.
82. liked the winding: *Ibid.*, p.9.
83. never let go: Dougherty, *Secret Happiness*, p.30.

CHAPTER 5

84. I'm the captain: James Dougherty, JWP II.
84. there were never any problems: Dougherty, *Secret Happiness*, p.37; see also Dennis Rowe, 'Shattered: The Myth of Frigid Marilyn', in the *Sunday Mirror* (London), 30 May 1976.
85. I wouldn't: Rowe, loc. cit.
85. My marriage didn't: MG XII, 4, p.12.
85. I really didn't: MG IX, 3, p.34.
85. She was so sensitive: James Dougherty, in the JWP I, p.5.
86. She called me: *Ibid.*, p.13.
86. She loved them all: Eleanor Goddard to DS, 20 Feb. 1992.
86. she couldn't cook: JWP I, p.4.
87. You ought to: *Ibid.*, p.5.
87. Our life was: *The Listener* (London), 30 Aug. 1979, p.272; see also *People*, vol.5, no.21 (31 May 1976), 38.
87. Pull off the road: Dougherty, *Secret Happiness*, p.46.
88. Of course I: MG XII, 10, p.22.
88. used to stay: JWP I, p.5.
88. Her mentality: *Ibid.*, p.8.
88. an enchanting idea: in Wolper, *Legend*.
89. terrified: MG XII, 10, p.23.
89. I insisted: James Dougherty to DS, 20 June 1992.
89. Your old lady: Earl Wilson, *The Show Business Nobody Knows* (Chicago: Cowles Book Co., 1971), p.281.
89. very shy and sweet: Robert Mitchum in Feldman/Winters documentary *Marilyn: Beyond the Legend*.
90. She was just: Elyda Nelson, 'The True Life Story of Marilyn Monroe', *Modern Screen*, Dec. 1952, p.62.
90. because she wore: Rowe, loc. cit.
90. She was a perfectionist: JWP I, p.4.
90. Just her presence: Dougherty, *Secret Happiness*, p.53.
92. We got along: JWP I, p.1.
92. There was a scarcity: Quoted in the *Sunday Express* (London), 9 Aug. 1987.
93. I'll admit: *Ibid.* Same source for the ensuing dialogue between the Doughertys.
94. She begged me: James Dougherty to DS, 20 June 1992.
96. she had developed: Eleanor Goddard to DS, 21 Feb. 1992.
98. In her rational: Dougherty, *Secret Happiness*, p.80.
100. There was a luminous: David Conover, *Finding Marilyn* (New York: Grosset & Dunlap, 1981), p.12.
100. What happened: *Ibid.*
101. Mom froze: JWP I, p.6.

101.   a white bathing: Robert Stack, with Mark Evans, *Straight Shooting* (New York: Macmillan, 1980), p.84.
101.   all this business: Quoted by Dougherty in JWP I, p.7.
102.   As far as: MG XII, 3, p.25
103.   too curly: Emmeline Snively in the Los Angeles *Daily News*, 4 Feb. 1954, p.14.
103.   perfect teeth: from the Blue Book application card filled in by an unknown staff member for 'Norma Jean [*sic*] Dougherty', dated 2 August 1945.
103.   dance a little: *Ibid*.
103–4.   I don't think: Quoted in Ted Thackrey in the Los Angeles *Herald-Examiner*, 7 Aug. 1962; Snively also spoke on camera for Wolper.
104.   The problem: MG III, 2, p.20.
104.   When you stop: MG III, 2, p.22.
105.   very serious: Lydia Bodrero Reed to DS, 19 June 1992.

CHAPTER 6

107.   She was: JWP II, p.7.
108.   she still seemed: Quoted in Thackrey, loc. cit.
108.   naive but disturbing: André de Dienes, *Marilyn Mon Amour* (New York: St Martin's Press, 1985), p.27.
109.   So far: JWP I, pp.7–8.
109.   The truth is: MG VII, 4.
109.   I longed to: de Dienes, p.51.
109.   The plain truth is: Alex D'Arcy to DS, 18 June 1992.
109.   She needed: de Dienes, p.71.
109.   Come to me: *Ibid*., p.67.
111.   In my dreams: de Dienes, p.70.
112.   Isn't this better: Golden, op. cit., p.178.
113.   nearly went berserk: JWP, p.8.
113.   the lost look: William Burnside, 'My life with young Marilyn', *Observer Magazine*, 11 May 1975; see also Kate Wharton, 'Photos that echo a sad story of love', *Today* (UK), 23 April 1986.
114.   Her lyric was reprinted in *The Observer* magazine of 6 May 1984, p.23; a copy is also in MG III, 3.
114.   She liked: Earl Moran, in 'A Marilyn for All Seasons', *Life*, vol. 6, no.7 (July 1983), 15.
114.   a shy girl: Joseph Jasgur to DS, 7 Feb. 1992.
115.   When she saw: Laszlo Willinger in Feldman/Winters documentary, *Marilyn: Beyond the Legend*.
115.   where a female: Ken DuMain to DS, 26 Aug. 1992.
116.   She wandered: Eleanor Goddard to DS, 21 Feb. 1992.
117.   calculating: Dougherty, *Secret Happiness*, p.105.
117.   a woman without: JWP, p.11
117.   Regarding MM's financial support of her mother: 'Marilyn neverf shirked a responsibility she legally did not have,' according to Inez Melson, her business manager in later years. 'No matter how little she made, she contributed to her mother's care, and her will ensured that the care continued after Marilyn's death.' See Inez Melson, quoted in *The Listener* (London), 30 Aug. 1979.
118.   First she thought: *Ibid*., p.8.
118–20. The dialogue between the Doughertys was told by Dougherty to Jane Wilkie: JWP II, pp.1–11.
119.   She thought we: Dougherty to DS, 20 June 1992.

119.   extreme mental cruelty: Complaint, 'Norma Jeane Dougherty, Plaintiff, Vs. James Edward Dougherty, Defendant', Case no. 31146 in the Eighth Judicial District Court of the State of Nevada, Clark County, filed 5 July 1946.

120.   I married and: Philip K. Scheuer, 'Wolves Howl for "Niece" Just Like Marilyn Monroe', *Los Angeles Times*, 29 Aug. 1950.

121.   She'd been: Allan Snyder to DS, 2 May 1992. Snyder also provided the subsequent quotation from Shamroy.

122.   When I first: Leon Shamroy, quoted in Robert Cahn, 'The 1951 Model Blonde', *Collier's*, 8 Sept. 1951, p.51. See also Zolotow, pp.60–61.

125.   I told her: Ben Lyon to Earl Wilson, quoted in the Los Angeles *Daily News*, 13 June 1953, p.10.

125–6.   The dialogue is cited by MM in MG X, 8, pp.22–3.

CHAPTER 7

127ff.   For a succinct history of 20th Century-Fox, see Joel W. Finler, *The Hollywood Story* (London: Octopus and New York: Crown, 1988), pp.88–113. A fair treatment of Darryl F. Zanuck may be found in Marlys J. Harris, *The Zanucks of Hollywood* (New York: Crown, 1989).

129.   an energetic and: Philip Dunne, 'Darryl from A to Z', *American Film*, vol.ix, no.9 (July–Aug. 1984), 50.

129.   She was very: Lipton in Wolper, *Legend*.

130.   Desperate to absorb: Allan Snyder to DS, 2 May 1992.

133.   When I told: Lipton in Wolper, *Legend*.

133.   It was my: MG XVI, 4, p.12.

135.   crazy, destroyed: MG XVI, 4, p.17.

136.   She asked us: *Ibid*.

136.   All I could think of: MG XVI, 4, p.19.

137.   she did all: Phoebe Brand, quoted in Zolotow, p.72.

137.   Movie stars were paid: MG XII, 3.

138.   the look of: Lucille Ryman Carroll to DS, 20 Feb. 1992.

139.   Marilyn was: Lee Strasberg, quoted in Cindy Adams, *Lee Strasberg: The Imperfect Genius of the Actors Studio* (New York: Doubleday, 1980), p.153.

141–2.   MM's comments on *Glamour Preferred* are recorded in MG II, 5, p.26.

144.   I was invited: MG VIII, 4; cf. also Meryman, 33; and the later expanded version of Meryman in *Life*, vol.15, no.8 (August 1992), 75.

145.   If four or five: quoted in Neal Gabler, *An Empire of Their Own: How the Jews Invented Hollywood* (New York: Crown, 1988), p.113.

146.   Marilyn spoke: Amy Greene to DS, 5 May 1992.

CHAPTER 8

150.   Not very much: MG XIV, 3, p.2.

150.   She was like: Jane Wilkie to DS, 20 Oct. 1992.

150.   Marilyn was inhibited: JWP/NL I, p.5.

150.   There were days: MG II, 8, p.12.

151.   I took her: JWP/NL I, p.5 and II, p.9.

151.   She was in love: MG II, 8, p.2.

152.   the one human: *Ibid.*, p.3.

153.   I began to feed: JWP/NL II, pp.8–9.

153.   I felt like: MG XIV, 3, p.24.

154.   Please don't do: JWP/NL II, p.5.

155.   but first of all: Milton Berle to DS, 9 April 1992.
155.   She told me very tearfully: Adele Jergens to DS, 9 April 1992.
155.   the only security: JWP/NL I, p.10.
156.   Under Marilyn's: Goodman, op. cit., p.234.
157.   He said that: MG III, 7, p.24.
159.   Marilyn was beginning: JWP/NL II, p.10.
160.   I'm not going: *Ibid.*, p.11; see also MG III, 4, p.15; and similar remarks cited to DS by Rupert Allan, Lucille Ryman Carroll and Amy Greene.
161.   Johnny Hyde knew: Peter Leonardi to Earl Wilson, quoted in Wilson's *Show Business Laid Bare* (New York: Putnam's, 1974), p.67.
161.   She never had: The late Leon Krohn MD spoke to producer Ted Landreth in 1984 for his BBC-TV documentary *Marilyn: Say Goodbye to the President.*
161.   He was willing: MM, quoted in Jane Corwin, 'Orphan in Ermine', *Photoplay*, vol.45, no.3 (March 1954), 109.
161.   I knew nobody: JWP/NL I, p.4.
162.   chump: Kazan, p.403.
162.   tramps and pushovers: *Ibid.*, p.406.
163.   It's amazing: Quoted in Roger G. Tyalor, *Marilyn In Art* (Salem, New Hampshire: Salem House, 1984), n.p.
164.   I began to see hope: JWP/NL II, p.8.
164.   Natasha was jealous: MG VIII, 2, p.1.
166.   I think I: Tom Kelley, quoted in 'Marilyn: The Naked Truth!' *Los Angeles Magazine*, vol.36, no.6 (June 1991), 90.
166ff. Whenever the topic of the calendars arose, Marilyn claimed she was 'broke and behind in the rent', or 'hungry and behind in my rent'. See, e.g., Belmont, p.18 *et alibi.*
167.   I'm only comfortable: Earl Wilson, *Show Business Laid Bare* (New York: Putnam's, 1974), p.67.

CHAPTER 9

169.   I bought: MG VI, 3, p.25.
170.   Her shrewdness: JWP/NL I, p.9.
171.   It was the: MG VI, 3, p.29.
171.   She had the: de Dienes, p.91.
171.   so they just: Earl Wilson's syndicated column (e.g., in the Los Angeles *Daily News*) for 30 July 1949.
171-2. a pretty dull: Earl Wilson, *The Show Business Nobody Knows* (Chicago: Cowles, 1971), p.288.
173.   You know: Quoted in Sidney Skolsky's column in the Los Angeles *Citizen-News*, 30 Sept. 1952.
173.   They showed me: 'The Men Who Interest Me . . . By Mrs Joe DiMaggio', *Pageant*, vol.9, no.10 (April 1954), 53.
173-4. Why, you're: This little dialogue has been attributed to their meeting in 1953, which Milton and Marilyn put forth as their first encounter and which most people accepted – including Amy Greene (who married Milton that year). But Rupert Allan heard it in his home in 1949.
174.   painting with the: Often in MG: e.g., I, 4, p.31; see also Al Morch, 'The photographer who captured Marilyn Monroe', *San Francisco Examiner*, 13 July 1981, p.D5.
174.   Telegram to MG from MM preserved in MG I, 1.
175.   sad to see Milton: Rupert Allan to DS, 17 June 1991.
175.   voluptuously made: Quoted in Lawrence Grobel, *The Hustons* (New York: Avon, 1989), p.334.

175. When she finished: John Huston, *An Open Book* (New York: Knopf, 1980), pp.286–7. With minor variations, this is the account reported also by Grobel; by Axel Madsen; and by Gerald Pratley (see Bibliography).
176. But she was: Quoted in the London *Daily Mirror*, 1 April 1980.
176. For the better: JWP/NL II, p.9.
176. She impressed me: John Huston in Wolper, *Legend*.
177. It was the first: JWP/NL II, p.10.
178. I don't know: *Ibid.*, p.9.
178. Body control: Quoted by George Masters to DS.
179. For the reminiscences of Agnes Flanagan, see Crivello, p.250.
182. eager young hustler: Nunnally Johnson, quoted in Carl E. Rollyson Jr, *Marilyn Monroe: A Life of the Actress* (Ann Arbor: UMI Research Press, 1986), p.33.
182. Almost everybody thought: MG XII, 3, p.14.
183. Joe sponsored: David Brown to DS, 11 Nov. 1992.
185. had done a good: Joseph L. Mankiewicz, *More About All About Eve* (New York: Random House, 1972), pp.76–7.
185. Every now and then: *Ibid.*, p.78.
185. very inquiring: George Sanders, *Memoirs of a Professional Cad* (New York: Putnam's, 1960), pp.70–71.
186. but somehow she: Mankiewicz, op. cit., p.79.
186. soft-spoken: Fredda Dudley Balling to Constance McCormick, quoted in the Constance McCormick Collection in the Film Archives of the University of Southern California.
187. because I wanted: MG IV, 3, p.22.
187. She fed Josefa: JWP/NL I, p.11.
188. was a channel: JWP/NL II, p.10.
188. I signalled: *Ibid.*, p.11.
189. He had a tendency: Steffi Sidney Splaver to DS, 5 June 1992. There is also an amusing account of Skolsky's place in Hollywood history in Goodman, pp.46–9 and 392–5.
191. Do you think: Quoted by Skolsky in Goodman, p.394.
191. From then on: Sidney Skolsky, *Don't Get me Wrong – I Love Hollywood* (New York: Putnam's, 1975), p.214.
191. He had confidence: *Pageant*, loc. cit.
191. I don't know: MG VIII, p.5.
193. I saw: JWP/NL I, p.13.
194. Joe Schenck was: Sam Shaw to DS, 8 March 1992.
194. Natasha often accused: MG III, 3, p.9.
194. just by standing: *Life*, vol.30, no.1 (1 Jan. 1951), 37.

CHAPTER 10

196. It wasn't until: JWP/NL II, p.16.
198. she was frightened: Quoted in 'MM Remembered', *Playboy*, vol.11, no.1 (Jan. 1964), 191.
198. She can't stop: Quoted in Kazan, p.404.
198. She hadn't even: *Ibid.*, p.403.
199. technique of seduction: *Ibid.*, p.404.
199. a simple, decent-hearted: *Ibid.*, pp.404–5.
199. Marilyn simply wasn't: *Ibid.*, p.415.
201. I'm not interested: Many times in her life: e.g., the incident here, cited in Pete Martin, 'The New Marilyn Monroe', *The Saturday Evening Post*, 5 May 1956, p.150.

202.   the shock of: Miller, p.303.
202.   When Miller withdrew his script rather than alter its premise, he received a telegram from Harry Cohn complaining that 'THE MINUTE WE TRY TO MAKE THE SCRIPT PRO-AMERICAN YOU PULL OUT' (see Miller, p.308). The wheels were set in motion for the absurd charges of anti-Americanism against Arthur Miller.
204.   the air around: Miller, p.306.
204.   was something like: *Ibid.*, pp.307, 327.
204.   She fell in love: JWP/NL I, p.9.
205.   if I had stayed: Arthur Miller, quoted in James Kaplan, 'Miller's Crossing', *Vanity Fair*, vol.54, no.11 (Nov. 1991), 241.
205.   Most people: MM to AM, 9 March 1951: she kept a working copy (MG III, 3).
205.   If you want: AM to MM, 13 March 1951, cited in Fred Lawrence Guiles, *Legend: The Life and Death of Marilyn Monroe* (New York: Stein and Day, 1984), p.173.
205.   It scared hell: Kazan, op.cit.
205–6. you could hear: Sidney Skolsky, 'Hollywood Is My Beat', Hollywood *Citizen-News*, 2 May 1951.
206.   hardly enough room: Quoted in Robert Cahn, 'The 1951 Model Blonde', *Collier's*, 8 Sept. 1951, p.50.
206.   the whole crew: June Haver in 'MM remembered', *Playboy*, loc. cit.
206.   she grabbed: Jack Paar, on the television programme *Donahue*, 5 May 1983.
206.   one of the brightest: Ezra Goodman in the Los Angeles *Daily News*, 6 June 1951.
206.   Marilyn Monroe is superb: New York *Times*, 3 Aug. 1951, p.10.
207.   Our bodies: Quoted by MM in MG VI, 4, p.31. They were both in fact citing the epigraph to the first chapter of his book; cf. Michael Chekhov, *To the Actor: On the Technique of Acting* (New York: Harper & Row, 1953), p.1.
208.   I am going: MG XII, 4, p.13. MM recalled this exercise exactly as Chekhov had recited it; cf. also his book, p.6.
208.   Merely discussing: Chekhov, *ibid.*
208.   artists of such magnitude: Chekhov, pp.163-6.
210.   She is particularly concerned: Cahn, loc. cit.
210.   She's the biggest: Quoted in Goodman, p.234.
211.   How much of the story: Skolsky, p.220.
211.   The studio: Richard Meryman, 'A Last Long Talk With A Lonely Girl', *Life*, vol.53, no.7 (17 Aug. 1962), 33.
211.   Like a famous predecessor: Cahn, loc cit.
212.   terribly late: Rupert Allan to DS, 17 Aug. 1991.
212.   the brightest star: Rupert Allan, 'Marilyn Monroe . . . a serious blonde who can act', *Look*, vol.15 (23 Oct. 1951), 40.
213.   Nothing happened: Robert Wagner, in *Remembering Marilyn*, 1988 TV documentary, narrated by Lee Remick; dir. Andrew Solt. Vestron Video/Image Entertainment LaserDisc.
213.   indifferent, amusing: e.g., Wanda Hale, in the New York *Daily News*, 7 Nov. 1951.
214.   Hold a good thought: e.g., Skolsky, p.216; also Susan Strasberg to DS, 29 Aug. 1992.
214.   Every element had to be: Marjorie Pelcher Snyder to DS, 2 May 1992.
214.   scared as hell: Quoted in Peter Bogdanovich, *Fritz Lang in America* (New York: Praeger, 1967), p.81.
214.   She fought: JWP/NL I, p.20.
214.   She wasn't disciplined: Quoted in Ella Smith, *Starring Miss Barbara Stanwyck* (New York: Crown, 1985), p.233.
215.   We don't want: Bogdanovich, op. cit., p.82.

215. a forceful actress: Alton Cook, *World-Telegram & Sun*, 20 June 1952.
216. Natasha, I'm terrified: JWP/NL I, p.15.
218. surefire money attraction: *Variety*, 13 Aug. 1952.
218. We had a hell: Quoted in *Hollywood Studio Magazine*, vol.20, no.8 (August 1987), 35.
218. I'm trying to: Aline Mosby, 'Actress has memory of heartbreak', Los Angeles *Daily News*, 7 Jan. 1952.
219. dazzled by the richness: Miller to the editors of *Current Biography*, 1973, p.297.
220. Dear Mr Chekhov: Copy preserved in MG III, 4, p.2.
220. For Nunnally Johnson's recollections of MM, cf. Tom Stempel, *Screenwriter: The Life and Times of Nunnally Johnson* (San Diego, A.S. Barnes, 1980), pp. 168–74.
220. The more important: Howard Hawks, quoted in Pamela Trescott, *Cary Grant – His Movies and His Life* (Washington: Acropolis Books, 1987), p.144.
221. We're not married: MM to Mort Jelline, Los Angeles *Daily News*, 26 Feb. 1952.

CHAPTER 11

224. I didn't let: Quoted in Roger Kahn, *Joe & Marilyn* (New York: William Morrow, 1986), p.18.
225. everybody who calls: *Ibid.*, p.44.
226. almost a mental: *Ibid.*, p.238
226. one of the most: Quoted in *Current Biography*, 1951, p.163.
226. very slow: *Ibid.*, p.32; cited from an interview by Clay Felker with former player Andy High.
226. loner: *Ibid.*, p.164; see also Maury Allen, *Where Have You Gone, Joe DiMaggio?* (New York: Dutton, 1975), 171ff.
227. I was surprised: MG VIII, 3, p.14.
227. Joe is looking: Sidney Skolsky's syndicated column for 17 March 1952; ironically, that evening Joe took Marilyn to her first baseball game – at Gilmore Stadium, where the Hollywood Stars (a minor league professional team) were playing the Major League All Stars for a Kiwanis Club benefit. Joe played centre field.
228. It's like a: Quoted in Maurice Zolotow, 'Joe & Marilyn: The Ultimate L.A. Love Story', *Los Angeles* magazine, Feb. 1979, p.240.
229. She got really: Quoted in Luitjers, p.111.
229. I first met: JWP/NL II, p.20.
232. although I really: MG II, 3, p.56.
233. MM's comments were repeated by her in MG II, 3, p.34; see also her virtually identical words in Mosby's article in the Los Angeles *Herald Express*, 13 March 1952, pp.1, 10.
234. I've been on: MM quoted in 'Four For Posterity', *Look*, vol.16, (18 Jan. 1962), p.83. She was not pleased, however, when the calendar photo turned up on drinking glasses, ashtrays and cocktail napkins later that year. Lawyers for MM and Fox tried, without much success, to stop the flow of artefacts bearing her nude form.
234. the biggest news: Joe Hyams to DS, 19 Sept. 1991.
234. the way she: Halsman, quoted in Wagenknecht, p.?.
235. the successor to Harlow: see, e.g., Jim Henaghan, 'So Far to Go Alone!', *Redbook*, June 1952, p.43.
235. If anything was 'wrong': David Brown to DS, 11 Nov. 1992.

237.   Gladys's letter to MM was preserved and included in IMP.

237.   I knew there was nothing: A note appended by MM to the foregoing letter in IMP.

238.   n: Grace Goddard's letter to MM, dated 28 Oct. 1952, was preserved in IMP.

238.   Unbeknown to me: Erskine Johnson, 'Marilyn Monroe confesses mother alive, living here', Los Angeles *Daily News*, 3 May 1952.

240–1.   The notes taped by MM to her body were well publicized and copies kept in IMP.

242.   She never had: Quoted in John Kobal, *People Will Talk* (New York: Knopf, 1985), pp.615, 613.

243.   If you wanted: Joseph Cotten, *Vanity Will Get You Somewhere* (London: Columbus Books, 1987), p.110.

243.   Am I making: *Ibid.*, p.111.

244.   the best natural: Quoted in Sidney Skolsky's column for 16 July 1952.

244.   marvelous to work with: Quoted in Kobal, p.615.

245.   A lot of guys: Maury Allen, p.177.

245.   It's the seventh: Sidney Skolsky's syndicated column (e.g., the Hollywood *Citizen-News*) for 24 July 1952.

245.   That's why: Quoted in Kobal, p.616.

246.   I think I'll: Jay Breen, 'She just lets the conversation drift toward her', Los Angeles *Daily News*, 9 Sept. 1952.

246.   I didn't want: MG IV, 4, p.23.

246.   nothing, but nothing: Earl Wilson's syndicated column (e.g., Los Angeles *Daily News*), 27 Aug. 1952.

247.   but La Monroe: Quoted in Dick Williams's column, Los Angeles *Mirror*, 18 Sept. 1952.

247.   She did the same: George Hurrell, quoted in Kobal, p.266.

247.   This picture might give: Los Angeles *Daily News*, 2 Sept. 1952, p.26.

248.   I am very: *Ibid.*

248.   People were staring: *Newsweek*, 15 Sept. 1952, p.50.

248.   That dress was: UPI wire service item, 5 Sept. 1952.

248.   Photographers stood: Sidney Skolsky's column for 5 Sept. 1952.

250.   some estangement: See e.g., Los Angeles *Times*, 5 Nov. 1952.

253.   when she put: Ron Nyman to DS, 24 July 1992.

254.   She was damned: Lionel Newman, in remarks dated 26 Oct. 1972, for sleeve notes to a collection of MM songs recorded on 20th Century Records (T-901), 1972.

254.   I feel as though: Barbara Berch Jamison, 'Body and Soul: A Portrait of Marilyn Monroe Showing Why Gentlemen Prefer That Blonde', *New York Times*, 12 July 1953, sec.II, p.5.

254.   There wasn't: Joseph McBride, *Hawks on Hawks* (Berkeley: University of California Press, 1982), p.124.

254.   She loved to: Hal Schaefer to DS, 24 April 1992.

254.   My great ambition: *New York Times*, 18 Feb. 1953.

255.   I had to get out: MG I, 4, p.14.

255.   She wants to: Sidney Skolsky's column (e.g., the Hollywood *Citizen-News*), 17 Dec. 1952.

255.   I want to: MM to Irene Crosby, her stand-in on *Gentlemen Prefer Blondes*, quoted in Skolsky for 17 Dec. 1952.

255.   She was terrified: Jane Russell to DS, 18 March 1985; likewise on *The Sally Jessy Raphael Show*, 15 April 1992 and see also David Galligan, ' "Sex Symbol" Jane Russell', *Drama-Logue*, vol.17, no.7 (13–19 Feb. 1986), 7.

255.   Neither of us: Jamison, loc. cit.

256.   far more intelligent: Jane Russell, *Jane Russell: My Paths and My Detours* (New York: Franklin Watts, 1985), p.137.

256.   no makeup: *Ibid.*

256.	that she was just a: Jack Cole, quoted in Kobal, p.605.
256.	the most frightened: Hawks, in McBride, op. cit.
257.	I'm really eager: MM to Dick Williams, in the Los Angeles *Daily Mirror*, 10 March 1953.
257–8.	On the auction of the Reinhardt materials, see the Los Angeles *Times* for 5 and 6 December 1952.
258.	Surely you will: Gottfried Reinhardt, *The Genius* (New York: Knopf, 1979) p.396.

CHAPTER 12

259.	Marilyn, this man: JWP/NL I, p.19.
259.	She had to be: 'Billy, Please Dress Me Forever', *News of the World* (5 May 1991), 5.
260.	that looked as if: 'Florabel Muir Reporting', Los Angeles *Mirror*, 10 Feb. 1953.
260.	burlesque show: Joan Crawford, in Bob Thomas's Associated Press syndicated column (e.g., Hollywood *Citizen-News*), 2 March 1953.
261.	One thing that makes: Joan Crawford, quoted in the Hollywood *Citizen-News*), 10 June 1953.
261.	Marilyn's the biggest: Quoted in Aline Mosby, ' "They're just jealous of Miss Monroe, says Betty Grable",' Los Angeles *Daily News*, 16 March 1953.
262.	a love affair: Jean Negulesco, *Things I Did . . . and Things I Think I Did* (New York: Linden Press/Simon & Schuster, 1984), p.219.
262.	under the spell of: Dorris Johnson and Ellen Leventhal, eds., *The Letters of Nunnally Johnson* (New York: Knopf, 1981), p.203.
262.	By this time: Alex D'Arcy to DS, 18 June 1992.
262–3.	On the Lytess–Monroe attachment delaying production, see Los Angeles *Times*, 14 April 1953.
263.	Monroe cannot do: Charles K. Feldman, inter-office memo to staff at Famous Artists Agency dated 20 Feb. 1953. In the Charles Feldman Papers at the American Film Institute, Los Angeles.
264.	no meannesss in her: Lauren Bacall, *By Myself* (New York: Knopf, 1979), p.208.
264.	Honey, I've had mine: Doug Warren, *Betty Grable: the Reluctant Movie Queen* (New York: St Martin's Press, 1981), p.000
265.	I don't want: The incident is recalled in Anne Edwards, *Judy Garland* (New York: Simon & Schuster, 1975), p.202.
267.	trying to direct: Charles K. Feldman to MM, 10 Aug. 1953; from the Feldman Collection at the American Film Institute.
267.	I pleaded with: Otto Preminger, *Preminger: An Autobiography* (New York: Doubleday, 1977), p.128.
268.	Marilyn, you don't: JWP/NL I, p.2.
268.	Marilyn thought there: Robert Mitchum in the Gene Feldman/Suzette Winters television film documentary *Marilyn: Beyond the Legend*.
268.	We put her through: Paul Wurtzel to DS, 19 Feb. 1992.
268.	n: see Luitjers, pp.57-8.
269.	Here are the: Allan Snyder to DS, 2 May 1992.
270.	She thought they: Quoted in Bart Milles, *Marilyn on Location* (London: Pan/Sidgwick & Jackson, 1989), p.150.
273.	Regarding news accounts of the Kinsey reports, see *Time* magazine, 31 Aug. 1953.

Notes

275. She was superb: Jack and Joan Benny, *Sunday Nights at Seven* (New York: Warner, 1990), p.243.

275. Success has helped: Sidney Skolsky's syndicated column, 'Hollywood Is My Beat', Hollywood *Citizen-News*, 25 Nov. 1953, p.15.

276. For the circumstances of Grace Goddard's suicide, see California State File number 53–087308. As for Grace's husband, he never saw Marilyn Monroe after 1945. Ervin 'Doc' Goddard married twice more – first to Anna Alice Long and then to Annie Rundle, who died with him in a car crash in Ventura on 4 Dec. 1972.

278. She had proved: Negulesco, p.223; on the pre-theatre party, see Johnson, *Letters*, pp.205-6.

278. since Gloria Swanson: Mike Connolly, in *The Hollywood Reporter*, 6 Nov. 1953.

278. This is just: Quoted in Luitjers, p.56.

278. For Marilyn's observations and agent Hugh French's reaction, see a letter from him to Charles K. Feldman dated 9 Oct. 1953 and preserved in the Feldman Collection at the American Film Institute, Los Angeles.

279. convinced Marilyn: Ray Stark to Charles K. Feldman, memorandum dated 1 Dec. 1953, preserved in the Feldman Collection.

280. she cooperated to: Hugh French to Charles K. Feldman, cable dated 19 Dec. 1953, preserved in the Feldman Collection.

CHAPTER 13

282. pill-pals: Sidney Skolsky's syndicated column for 6 June 1954 (see, e.g., the Hollywood *Citizen-News*). Additional information on Skolsky supplying MM with pills was confirmed by Steffi Sidney Splaver to DS, 5 June 1992.

283. not fighting over: Loyd Wright Jr, quoted in the Los Angeles *Times*, 6 Jan. 1954.

284. I was put into: Quoted in Marie Torre, 'Marilyn Monroe', New York *Herald-Tribune* TV and Radio Magazine (section 9), 14–20 Aug. 1955, p.6. A nearly identical statement is in MG XII, 4, p.35.

284. I read the script: Quoted in Sidney Skolsky's column in the Hollywood *Citizen-News*, 1 Feb. 1954.

284. I couldn't believe: Zanuck, quoted in Dick Williams's column in the Los Angeles *Mirror*, 15 Jan. 1954.

285. Marilyn herself: *Time*, vol.lxiii, no.4 (25 Jan. 1954), 108.

285. the inheritor: *Life*, vol.36, no.4 (25 Jan. 1954) 32.

286. I'd like to have: Widely quoted in the international press: see, e.g., Allen, p.180; Kahn, p.254; Los Angeles *Examiner*, 15 Jan. 1954. On the motel room, see Allen, p.180.

286. It usually rents for: Quoted in Hedda Hopper, 'DiMaggio and Monroe Hide for Honeymoon', Los Angeles *Times*, 17 Jan. 1954.

286. radiant: San Francisco *Examiner*, 17 Jan. 1954.

287. I just bumped: 'Marilyn and DiMaggio on Their Way to Japan', Los Angeles *Times*, 30 Jan. 1954. The broken thumb was picked up by the Associated Press and widely reported.

287. my Slugger: Often throughout 1954, and reported, e.g., in Roger Manvell, *Love Goddesses of the Movies* (New York: Crescent, 1979), p.116.

288. Airport officials: United Press International wire item dated 30 Jan. 1955; see, e.g., the Los Angeles *Times* for 31 Jan. 1954, part I, p.26 ('Hair-Tugging Mob Greets Marilyn, Joe').

288. went virtually unnoticed: *Time*, 15 Feb. 1954, p.32.

288. like I was: Kahn, p.255.

Notes

288. For O'Doul's recollections, see Kahn, *ibid.*
289. The press conference was widely reported by wire services; see, e.g., *Time*, loc. cit.
289. the marriage seemed: Quoted in Allen, p.183; see also Gay Talese, 'The Silent Season of a Hero', in *Esquire* (vol.LXVI, no.1 (July 1966), 43.
289. For accounts of MM's tour of Korea, see C. Robert Jennings, 'The Strange Case of Marilyn Monroe vs. the U.S. Army', *Los Angeles* magazine, Aug. 1966, pp.31-63; Allen, pp.181-4; Kahn, pp.255-6.
290. There were seventeen: From the original draft of Hecht's version of MM's autobiography, BH, Box HE, pages 133-6.
291. She was Marilyn Monroe: Quoted in Los Angeles *Times*, 20 Feb. 1954.
291. She gave us: Ted Cieszynski to DS, 10 Feb. 1992.
291. This is my first: Jennings, loc. cit., p.60.
292. When I went to Korea: Skolsky, p.212.
292. It was so wonderful: Cited frequently – e.g., Talese, p.43; Kahn, p.256.
293. Joe hates: Sidney Skolsky's syndicated column (Hollywood *Citizen-News*) for 10 March 1954.
294. For the dialogue between MM and Skolsky, see Skolsky, p.213.
294. Marilyn wept: Ben Hecht to Jacques Chambrun, 14 April 1954.
295. Sit down and: Quoted by MM to Arthur Miller, *Timebends* (New York: Grove Press, 1987), p.370.
296. But you're married: Quoted by Lucille Ryman Carroll to DS, 20 Feb. 1992.
299. At night: JWP/NL II, p.22.
299. called me at two or three: JWP/NL I, p.7.
300. tired of having: Jack Gordean and Hugh French, memo to Charles K. Feldman reporting a meeting with Marilyn on or about 26 June 1954.
301. It's ridiculous: Hal Schaefer, quoted in Los Angeles *Examiner*, 6 Oct. 1954 and in *Confidential*, vol.3, no.4 (Sept. 1955), 56. The latter magazine, thought at the time to be a mere gossip tabloid, was in fact an impeccably researched and carefully written monthly, however sensational were the aspects of celebrities' lives it chose to present. *Confidential* was, for example, the first magazine to challenge the Hollywood hypocrisy that there were no homosexuals in the film industry. Employing investigative reporters, attorneys, fact-checkers and established journalists, *Confidential* also delivered some of the most revealing stories of its time on executive mismanagement and studio fraud.
302. It's okay, baby: *Confidential*, p.58. This event was confirmed to DS by producer Milton Ebbins, in an interview on 22 Sept. 1992.
302. very unhappy when: Louella O. Parsons, 'Joe Jealousy [sic] of Marilyn Told in Rift: Cites Visits to Voice Coach in Hospital', Los Angeles *Examiner*, 6 Oct 1954, p.1.
302. She had very little: Hal Schaefer to DS, 24 April 1992.
303. stupid part: MG IV, 3, p.25.
303. Breathe from your stomach: Quoted in Robert Cahn, 'Marilyn Monroe Hits a New High', *Collier's*, 9 Sept. 1954, pp.99-101.
304. Miss Monroe's wriggling: Bosley Crowther, in the New York *Times*, 16 December 1954.
304. For Irving Berlin's comment, see Manvell, p.117.
304. I had a code: JWP/NL I, p.6.
304. If Marilyn wasn't: Rita Moreno, on 'The Class of The 20th Century', Merrill W. Mazuer, prod. for CEL Communications, Inc./The A & E Network (US cable television), 1991.
305. I've heard: Susan Strasberg, *Bittersweet* (New York: Putnam's, 1980) pp.55-6.
305. I kept: MM, quoted on MG Dictabelt #4, dated 11 April 1957.
306. What the hell: Quoted in Graham McCann, *Marilyn Monroe* (New Brunswick: Rutgers University Press, 1988), p.46.

693

Notes

307.   He has the: MM, quoted in *Pageant*, vol.9, no.10 (April 1954), 55.
307.   He wouldn't speak: Quoted in Maurice Zolotow, 'The Mystery of Marilyn Monroe', *The American Weekly*, 23 Oct 1955, p.30.
307.   When I married: Norman Rosten, *Marilyn: An Untold Story* (New York: Signet/NAL, 1973), p.104.
307.   I have too many: Quoted in Gloria Steinem, 'Growing Up with Marilyn', *Ms*, vol.1, no.2 (August 1972), 38.
310.   But although she was: George Axelrod to DS, 6 Nov. 1991.
311.   She was shaking: Tom Ewell, quoted in the Los Angeles *Daily News*, 5 Oct. 1954, p.51.
311.   The location work: Sam Shaw to DS, 7 March 1992.
311.   Wilder and Wurtzel confirmed the production schedule to DS in interviews on (respectively) 19 Nov. 1991 and 19 Feb. 1992.
312.   It would make her nervous: The entire dialogue was published by Winchell in his syndicated column just days after MM died: see, e.g., the Los Angeles *Herald-Examiner*, 8 Aug 1962.
312.   look of death: Billy Wilder to DS, 19 Nov. 1991.
313.   The violence between Marilyn and Joe was widely reported by witnesses: see McCann, p.46.

CHAPTER 14

314.   On MM's illness, see *The Hollywood Reporter*, 30 Sept. 1954.
314.   I hope you: quoted in Los Angeles *Daily News*, 5 Oct. 1954, p.51.
314.   I knew she: Tom Ewell, quoted in *Hollywood Studio Magazine*, vol.20, no.8 (Aug. 1987), 33.
315.   Others could give: Darryl F. Zanuck to Billy Wilder, letter dated 20 Sept. 1954, preserved in the Charles K. Feldman Collection at the American Film Institute, Los Angeles.
315.   I have to sleep: Sam Shaw to DS, 7 March 1992; see also Shaw and Rosten, *Marilyn among friends*, p.16.
315.   When you got her: Billy Wilder to DS, 19 Nov. 1991.
316.   I wanted so much: MG V, 3.
316.   letter perfect: George Axelrod to DS, 22 April 1992.
317.   For the neighbours' recollections of Marilyn's night-time walks, see the Los Angeles *Herald-Examiner*, 6 Oct. 1954.
318.   because of incompatability: for the news release and subsequent statements to the press, see, e.g., Los Angeles *Times*, 6 Oct. 1954; *Time*, vol.lxiv, no.16 (18 Oct. 1954), 47; and news wire services, 4–7 Oct. 1954.
318.   grievous mental suffering: Los Angeles *Times*, 6 Oct. 1954.
318.   n: common as political: *Ibid.*
319.   It is my home: Los Angeles *Mirror*, 6 Oct. 1954; see also Beverly Hills *Newslife*, 7 Oct. 1954.
320.   Miss Monroe will: Quoted in Beverly Hills *Newslife*, 7 Oct., p.1; also on news film worldwide, and on both the United Press International and Associate Press news wire services.
320.   The marriage was: Ray Parker and Roby Heard, 'What Made Marilyn and Joe Bust Up?' Los Angeles *Mirror*, 5 Oct. 1954, p.4.
320.   The marriage was: *Ibid.*, 7 Oct. 1954, part 1, p.6.
320.   Joe is a sweet guy: Quoted by Aline Mosby in, 'Marilyn, Joe Rift Widens', Hollywood *Citizen-News*, 7 Oct. 1954.
321.   bored: Susan Strasberg to DS, 2 June 1992.
321.   He didn't like: MG III, 4.
321.   I feel alive: quoted in the Los Angeles *Times*, 8 Oct. 1954.

Notes

321.   I can't understand: Joe DiMaggio, quoted in the Newark *Evening News*, 18 Oct. 1954.

321.   But Marilyn's determination: Skolsky, p.224–5.

323.   Mr DiMaggio: Inez Melson, quoted in the Newark *Evening News*, loc. cit.

325.   She has been: Charles K. Feldman to Darryl F. Zanuck, letter dated 21 October 1954, preserved in the Feldman Collection.

325.   I feel like: 'Life Goes to A Select Supper for Marilyn', *Life*, vol.37, no.22 (22 Nov. 1954), 162; this was picked up from Skolsky's column of 9 Nov.

325.   that the so-called elite: Sidney Skolsky's column, 'Hollywood Is My Beat', Hollywood *Citizen-News*, 9 Nov. 1954.

326.   I have come: Quoted in Shaw and Rosten, p.78.

326.   I've always admired: MM told the exchange to Skolsky, who included it in his column dated 9 Nov.

326.   It's because of: *Ibid*.

326.   for correction of: Hollywood *Citizen-News*, 8 Nov. 1954; Los Angeles *Daily News*, 9 Nov. 1954.

326.   There's no chance: MM to Aline Mosby, quoted in the Hollywood *Citizen-News*, 8 Nov. 1954.

327.   She wanted me: Ella Fitzgerald, quoted in Gloria Steinem, *Marilyn* (New York: Henry Holt, 1986), pp.90–91.

328–9.   He, too, wanted: Michael Korda to DS, 30 June 1992.

329ff.   Background material on the formation of MMP is found in MG (all files and folders) and was also provided by Jay Kanter (MM's MCA agent in New York from :955) to DS, 15 April 1992.

329.   For a brief outline of Lew Wasserman's extraordinarily powerful career, see 'Lew!', *California*, vol.10, no.3 (March 1985), 95–144.

330.   never had a chance: MG I, 2, p.3.

332.   With us she had: Amy Greene to DS, 5 May 1992.

332.   Marilyn seemed to me: Jay Kanter to DS, 15 April 1992.

333.   because of their: ILS, 2 Feb. 1955: MG III.

333.   We will go: New York *Times*, 8 Jan. 1955; New York *Daily News*, 8 Jan. 1955.

333.   The night at the Copacabana was recalled by Amy Greene to DS, 5 May 1992.

335.   It is the damndest: ILS to Aubrey Schenck, 13 Jan. 1955: MG II.

335.   You're looking good: Quoted in Sidney Skolsky's syndicated column (e.g., Hollywood *Citizen-News*) for 12 Jan. 1955.

336.   It might be fatal: Irving L. Stein, corporate memorandum dated 27 Jan. 1955, in MG I. Hereinafter, Stein's corporate memoranda, letters, etc., are designated ILS.

336.   Get Joe DiMaggio: ILS, 31 Jan. 1955.

336.   only while DiMaggio: ILS, 2 Feb. 1955: MG IV.

336.   Is this a: Earl Wilson, 'Marilyn, Joe Tryst Hints Reconciliation', syndicated column (e.g., Boston *Mirror-News*), 25 Jan. 1955.

338.   Regarding MM's ease in wandering the streets of New York if she did not make herself up: she discussed this on Edward R. Murrow's CBS television show *Person to Person* on 8 April 1955.

338.   n: Regarding *Variety*'s promotion for her recordings, see the issue dated 16 Feb. 1955, p.43.

338.   For accounts and histories of Lee Strasberg and the Actors Studio, see Evangeline Morphos, ed., *Lee Strasberg: A Dream of Passion* (Boston: Little, Brown, 1987); Cindy Adams, *Lee Strasberg: The Imperfect Genius of the Actors Studio* (Garden City: Doubleday, 1980); and Steve Vineberg, *Method Actors* (New York: Schirmer, 1991). Much important information also came to DS in several important interviews with Susan Strasberg during 1989, 1990 and the spring and summer of 1992.

339.   We were like: Eli Wallach, quoted in Joanne Kaufman, 'Studio System', *Vanity Fair*, vol.55, no.11 (November 1992), 238.
339.   We were all dedicated: Shelley Winters, *ibid.*, 272.
340.   He sometimes got: Anne Jackson, *ibid.*
340.   Lee was enshrined: Kazan, p.539.
341.   It made me: Marlon Brando, quoted in the New York *Times*'s obituary of Lee Strasberg, 18 Feb. 1982, p.D20.
341.   Lee-you-should-excuse: Quoted in Adams, p.3.
341.   Crying, after all: Quoted in Viner, p.109.
342.   All this talk about The Method: Laurence Olivier, quoted by Basil Langton to DS, 11 May 1990; see also Maurice Zolotow, 'The Olivier Method', New York *Times*, 7 Feb. 1960, sec.2, p.1.
343.   My father wanted: Susan Strasberg to DS, 3 and 10 June 1992: see also Susan Strasberg, *Marilyn and Me: Sisters, Rivals, Friends*, p.31.
344.   Milton did more than: Amy Greene to DS, 5 May 1992.

CHAPTER 15

345.   I had teachers: MG VI, 4.
346.   It seemed to me: ILS, 28 Feb. 1955.
347.   My problem is: Her remarks have three sources: Belmont, p.19; MG III, 3, p.17, in notes taken at a meeting with Stein on 10 March 1955; and MM to Susan Strasberg, quoted to DS, 3 June 1992.
349.   The incidents and dialogue with the Rostens are recounted in Norman Rosten, *Marilyn: An Untold Story* (New York: Signet/NAL, 1973), pp.11–12, 27–8.
349.   When she came: Norman Rosten, quoted in Kahn, p.67.
351.   and the resulting: Miller, p.354.
351.   It was wonderful: James Kaplan, loc. cit., p.242.
353.   It meant a lot: MM on Edward R. Murrow's CBS-TV show *Person to Person*, 8 April 1955.
353.   The circumstances of the Murrow television broadcast is Amy Greene's account to DS, 5 May 1992.
354.   Imagine what you: Eve Arnold, on the BBC-TV documentary *Eve and Marilyn* (1987).
355–6.   For Susan Strasberg's contributions, see *Marilyn and Me*, pp.143, 145: also, Strasberg to DS, 3 June 1992.
355.   She wore: Stanley Kauffman, 'Album of Marilyn Monroe', *The American Scholar*, vol.60, no.4 (autumn 1991), 568.
355.   Sam Shaw's memories of MM to DS, 7 March 1992.
356.   Looking at her: Truman Capote, 'An Abbess in High-heeled Shoes', *People*, 27 Oct. 1980, p.56.
356.   I just felt: The incident is recorded in Adams, p.256.
357–9.   The notes by MM are recorded in MG III, VI, VII, IX, as are the poems on pages 362–3.
359.   My father was: Susan Strasberg to DS, 3 June 1992.
360.   Don't you ever: quoted in Adams, p.263.
361.   Our household revolved: Strasberg, *Marilyn and Me*, p.19.
361.   it was hard: John Strasberg, quoted in *ibid.*, p.44.
362.   When I have problems: quoted in Adams, p.258.
362.   Oh, no: MM quoted by Gloria Steinem in *Ms*, vol.1, no.2 (Agust 1972), 36.
362.   Hi, it's me: Quoted by Susan Strasberg to DS; also in *Bittersweet*, p.56.
363.   anybody who had: Kim Stanley to John Kobal, p.699.

363.   endeavour to develop: Frank Corsaro, on the 1991 American Masters documentary on The Actors Studio, prod. Chloe Aaron, dir. Dennis Powers for PBS.

363.   I know they say: For MM on Kafka, see Tom Hutchinson, *Marilyn Monroe* (New York: Exeter Books, 1982), p.69.

363.   That's all they're: Shaw and Rosten, p.95.

364.   We're just good friends: *New York Journal-American*, 2 June 1955, p.1; *New York World-Telegram and Sun*, same day; and also the New York *Daily News*, p.4.

364.   Marilyn was afraid: Lois Weber Smith, quoted in Allen, pp.199–200.

365.   Marilyn told me: Rupert Allan to DS, 3 Aug. 1991.

365.   The supplanting of Milton by Lee was suggested in Dorothy Kilgallen's column in the *New York Journal-American* on 28 June 1955.

365.   How do we: ILS, 30 June 1955, MG IX.

365–6.   For details of MM's time with the Strasbergs on Manhattan and on Fire Island, and for the night-time dialogue between MM and their daughter on p.371, I am grateful for several interviews with Susan Strasberg during May, June and July 1992.

366.   One day she: Amy Greene to DS, 5 May 1992.

367.   had a great sense: *Eve and Marilyn*, BBC-TV (1987).

368.   She was pleased: John Springer to DS, 5 March 1992.

368.   This is the girl: Quoted in Wagenknecht, p.47.

369.   The dialogue with Gilels is reported by Rosten (pp.24–5), who was present.

370ff.   Regarding the FBI file on Marilyn Monroe, there are eighty pages declassified, beginning at document number 105–40018–1. Documents dated 19 Aug. 1955 and 27 April 1956 concern MM and her request for a visa and the history of her last two years. They are documents numbered 105–40018. The document containing the FBI's recording of the item from the London *Daily Worker* is numbered 100–351585–A, dated 15 Aug. 1955.

370.   I expect our divorce: Joe DiMaggio , on the INS news wire service dated 21 Aug. 1955; see e.g., *Los Angeles Herald-Examiner* this date.

370.   I never should: MM to Amy Greene, quoted to DS, 5 May 1992.

371.   You all start: George Axelrod, *Will Success Spoil Rock Hunter?* (New York: Samuel French, 1955), p.7.

372.   I saw: Quoted by George Axelrod to DS, 22 April 1992.

374.   I'm beginning to: MM, quoted in Pete Martin, 'The New Marilyn Monroe', *Saturday Evening Post*, 12 May 1956, p.110.

CHAPTER 16

375.   There is persuasive: *Time*, 30 Jan. 1956, p.62.

375.   But then she had us: Laurence Olivier, *Confessions of an Actor* (New York: Simon & Schuster, 1982), pp.205–6.

376.   The questions and answers at the press conference were widely reported: see, e.g., *Time*, vol.lxvii, no.8 (20 Feb. 1956) 94 and *The Manchester Guardian*, 10 Feb. 1956 ('Miss Monroe Meets Her Idol: Alliance of Pulchritude and Art').

377.   Shall I take: Josephine DiLorenzo and Theo Wilson, 'Marilyn Can Act Too, Sez Olivier', *New York Daily News*, vol.37, no.197 (10 Feb. 1956), 3.

377.   The strap breaking: John Moore to DS, 23 Aug. 1992.

377.   Before we went: Eve Arnold on the BBC-TV documentary, *Eve and Marilyn* (1987).

377.   artless: Quoted in Hugo Vickers, *Cecil Beaton* (Boston: Little, Brown, 1985), p.393.

Notes

377.   Brooklyn became Nirvana: Sam Shaw to DS, 7 March 1992.
377.   heavenly: often, e.g. in Hedda Hopper's syndicated column for 24 Jan. 1956.
378.   There are all: ILS, 6 Jan. 1956: MG IV.
378.   Teenage boys: Vincent X. Flaherty, 'Will Marilyn Become an Intellectual?' *Los Angeles Examiner*, 6 July 1956, section 1, p.2.
378.   America's best known: Walter Winchell's radio broadcast of 12 Feb. 1956, recorded as FBI document number 62–31615–966.
378.   For an account of Miller's troubles with the FBI, see Natalie Robins, *Alien Ink* (New York: Morrow, 1992), pp.310ff.
379.   the next stop: Walter Winchell's broadcast of 10 June 1956, recorded as FBI document number 62–31615–983.
379.   Miss Monroe, after completing: Memo from SAC, Los Angeles, to Director, FBI dated 1 June 1956, FBI document number 23–100–422103.
380.   Regarding the final disposition of MMP shares and control, information is detailed in ILS memoranda throughout October and December 1955, culminating in the memorandum of 11 February 1956.
380.   Be conservative: the Wasserman memorandum to Stein was dated 14 Feb. 1956; subsequent calls and correspondence on this matter occur to 21 Feb.
381.   Marilyn Monroe, Blonde: Quoted in 'The New Marilyn', *Look*, vol.20 (29 May 1956), 73.
381.   This was really: Maureen Stapleton to DS, 22 April 1992.
383.   I couldn't see: Quoted in *Redbook*, Feb. 1958, p.96.
383.   very deep: Anna Sten to John Kobal, p.140.
383.   often brilliant: Robert Schneiderman, 'Drama teacher remembers Marilyn Monroe', *Spotlight Chicago*, week of 4 Aug. 1992, p.6.
384.   The press reception at the airport was documented on film and has been included in virtually every documentary on MM: see, e.g., Feldman and Winters, *Marilyn: Beyond the Legend*, and Wolper, *Legend*.
384.   For the court appearance of MM, see these newspapers, all dated 1 March: Hollywood *Citizen-News*; *Los Angeles Mirror*; *Los Angelese Time*; *Los Angeles Examiner*.
385.   She seemed content: Allan Snyder to DS, 2 May 1992.
385.   Irving Stein's statement is from ILS, memorandum dated 3 March 1956: MG VII.
386.   In Marilyn's powerful: JWP/NL II, p.25.
388.   But Marilyn can't act: Joshua Logan, *Movie Stars, Real People and Me*, (New York, Delacorte, 1978), p.35.
388.   I have worked: *Ibid.*
390.   she wants to: Milton Greene to ILS, 17 March 1956: MG IV.
390.   Like a child: Guy Trebay, 'Don Murray', *Interview*, October 1973, p.21.
391.   Milton seemed to want: William Woodfield to DS, 20 Sept. 1991.
391.   surrounded with intrigue: Ezra Goodman, *The Fifty-Year Decline and Fall of Hollywood* (New York: Simon & Schuster, 1961), p.239.
392.   I can't do it: Miller, p.379-80.
393.   expressly for her: Logan, p.39.
394.   Hold on to your chairs: *New York Times* review by Bosley Crowther, 1 Sept. 1956, p.19.
395.   effectively dispels: Arthur Knight, in the *Saturday Review of Literature*, 8 Sept. 1956.
395.   one of the great: Logan, pp.36, 48; speaking in the documentary *Marilyn: Beyond the Legend*, dir. Gene Feldman/Wombat Productions, 1987; see also the *Los Angeles Daily Mirror*, 10 Oct. 1956.
395.   For the meeting with Sukarno, see *New York Times*, 2 June 1956, p.13; for MM's remarks on the encounter, see Rosten, p.73.
396.   Al Delgado's letter to Jay Kanter, dated 15 June 1956, is included in MG III.
398.   a live witness: Robins, p.313.
398.   Marilyn Monroe's new romance: *Ibid.*

Notes

398ff. Miller's appearance in Washington and his statements before the HUAC were documented in, among many other journals and magazines, the *New York Times* on 22 June 1956, pp.1, 9; *New York Daily News*, 22 June 1956, pp.3, 6; *Chicago Tribune*, 25 June 1956, pp.1, 9.

399.   No question: *New York Sunday News*, 1 July 1956.

399.   provided Marilyn agreed: Miller, p.406.

399.   I will marry: *New York Mirror*, 21 June 1956 *et alibi*. See also the important history in Éric Bentley, ed., *Thirty Years of Treason: Excerpts from Hearings before the House Committee on Un-American Activities, 1938–1968* (New York: Viking, 1971), p.819.

399.   Have you heard: Rosten, p.34.

399.   It was awfully: Amy Greene to DS, 5 May 1992; Rupert Allan to DS, 21 July 1991.

400.   Arthur was learning: Susan Strasberg to DS, 3 June 1992; see also *Marilyn and Me*, p.105.

401.   [Jean] was always: Maureen O'Sullivan, quoted in Golden, p.158.

403.   stand by in case: Milton Greene's telephone call to Irving Stein is recorded in ILS dated 29 June 1956: MG XI.

403.   The account of Marilyn's hesitation at her marriage was provided to DS by Amy Greene, 5 May 1992.

403.   Well, I hope: George Axelrod to DS, 22 April 1992; Axelrod's statement was included in an essay on Miller by Kenneth Tynan, in *Profiles* (London: Nick Hern/Walker Books, 1989), p.119.

405.   ILS memorandum dated 2 July 1956: MG IV.

406.   result in capital gain: ILS to MG, 16 October 1956: MG XI, 4.

407.   ILS memorandum dated 14 July 1956: MG IV.

407.   he ought to stay out: Kay Brown, quoted in ILS memorandum dated 12 Sept. 1956: MG V, 3.

407.   Yes, but: *Daily Telegraph*, 16 July 1956.

408.   Unlike many other: Jack Cardiff to DS, 26 May 1992.

408.   to take her: Quoted in *Los Angeles Herald-Examiner*, 5 Aug. 1982; similar remarks are recorded in MG VIII, 4, 3.

409.   He tried to be: W. J. Weatherby, *Conversations with Marilyn* (New York: Mason/Charter, 1976), p.84.

409.   All you have: The remark is widely quoted by witnesses, among them Susan Strasberg to DS, 23 April 1990; by Amy Greene; by actress Maxine Audley, *et al.* Olivier never denied he said this.

409.   suspicious, sullen: Rosten, p.43.

409.   It was something: Quoted in Bart Mills, *Marilyn on Location* (London: Pan/Sidgwick & Jackson, 1989), p.108.

410.   I think Arthur: Quoted by Rupert Allan to DS, 15 July 1991.

410.   Miller looked on: Sidney Skolsky's syndicated column for 25 Nov. 1961.

410.   The Strasberg interference: the phrase, almost a motto at the time, was used in conversations with DS by Allan Snyder, Rupert Allan, Amy Greene and Jack Cardiff; its equivalent is much cited by Arthur Miller.

410.   My mother had once: Susan Strasberg to DS, 3 June 1992; see also *Bittersweet*, p.84.

411.   poisonous and vacuous: Kaplan, loc. cit., p.242.

411.   nearly religious: Miller, p.423.

411.   Miller's comments on Paula were spoken to Fred Lawrence Guiles, *Legend*, p.316.

411.   Greene thought: Guiles, p.309.

411.   it was important for Milton: Jay Kanter to DS, 15 April 1992.

411.   getting involved: Albert Maysles to DS, 30 March 1992.

412.   were wrecking her: Allan Snyder to DS, 2 May 1992.

412.   two months supply: MG to ILS, 27 Sept. 1956: MG VII.

413. Too many people: Quoted in Hutchinson, p.78.
413. had been wrong to form: Margaret Hohenberg to ILS, reported to MG in telephone call on 27 Dec. 1956 and so dated in ILS: MG IV.
414. she had some: letter from MG to Joe Carr and Irving Stein, dated 27 Sept. 1956: MG IV.
414ff. ILS memoranda dated 1–3 September 1956: MG IV and VI.
415. thoroughly ill-mannered: *Daily Express*, 22 May 1980.
415. It was a: Henry Brandon, 'Sex, Society and the Theatre', *Sunday Times* (London), 20 March 1960, p.15.
415. She's quite remarkable: Quoted in *Time*, 6 Aug. 1956, p.31. That the citation from Hopkins was a favourite line of Marilyn was reported to DS by Ralph Roberts (to whom she often quoted it), 1 May 1992.
415. You did well: quoted in Sidney Skolsky's column for 14 June 1957; and in Taylor, *Marilyn in Art*, n.p.; see also Miller, p.426.
417. No one had: Laurence Olivier, *On Acting* (New York: Touchstone/Simon & Schuster, 1986), p.316; and the same author's *Confessions of an Actor* (New York: Simon & Schuster, 1982), p.213.

CHAPTER 17

422. I was off: Miller, p.460.
422. I felt an urgency: Miller, pp.458–9.
422. a mere child: Miller, p.448.
422. a rose-tinted: Kazan, p.540.
422. For Norman Rosten's recollections of Marilyn's never-ending struggle for the perfect home design, see *Marilyn: An Untold Story*, p.67.
423. I love them: MM to Richard Meryman in a taped interview for *Life* magazine in July 1962.
423. You must excuse me: the anecdote about the neighbour and the new coat is documented in Wagenknecht, p.xvii.
423. Michael Korda to DS, 30 June 1992.
424. But there was another: Amy Greene to DS, 5 May 1992.
424. adopted daughter: Michael Molnar, *The Diary of Sigmund Freud* (New York: Robert Stewart/Charles Scribners Sons, 1992), p.174.
425. some of the most: Edward A. Gargan, 'Tribute to Marianne Kris', *New York Times*, 8 Dec. 1980. See also Henry Nunberg, 'In Memoriam Marianne Kris', *The Psychoanalytic Study of the Child*, vol.38 (New Haven: Yale University Press, 1983), 1–7 (Kris, as it happened, was Nunberg's aunt); and the obituary in *New York Times* on 25 Nov. 1980, p.D23.
426. as if I were: MM, quoted by Rupert Allan to DS, 10 June 1991.
427. too stand-offish: Comments by Miller's brother, sister and in-laws are cited in Robert J. Levin, loc. cit., p.95.
428. For Kazan's estimation of the Monroe–Strasberg connection, see Kazan, p.540.
428. Lee makes me think: Rosten, p.49.
428. Whether it was: Strasberg, *Marilyn and Me*, p.103.
428–9. It is not: MM drafted the letter in early April but kept it for reflection and revision; it was cabled to Jack Warner on 22 April 1957; see the production files for *The Prince and the Showgirl* in the Warner Bros archives at the University of Southern California.
430f. MM's statement through Miller's attorney was issued on 11 April and was noted in the next day's edition of *The New York Times*, p.22.
430. absolutely irrational: Robert H. Montgomery Jr, to John Wharton, memorandum preserved in MG IX, memoranda for April 1957.

430.   For the news accounts of the reorganization of MMP, see: *New York Times*, 17 April 1957, p.36; *Los Angeles Times* and the *Los Angeles Examiner*, 17 April 1957; *Time*, vol.lxix, no.17 (29 April 1957), 94.

430.   It seems: *Los Angeles Times*, 12 April 1957, part III, p.8.

431.   He knows perfectly: *Ibid.*

431.   The truth is: Jay Kanter to DS, 15 April 1992.

431.   Arthur was taking: MM to Amy Greene, quoted to DS, 5 May 1992.

432.   shitty friends: Arthur P. Jacobs to Irving Stein: MG VI, memorandum for 20 April 1957.

432.   She was ultrasensitive: MG XIII, 4; see also *Los Angeles Herald-Examiner*, 5 Aug. 1982.

433.   She had no desire: Olie and Joe Rauh, as told to Harriet Lyons, 'The time Marilyn Monroe Hid Out at Our House', *Ms* magazine, August 1983, p.16.

434.   She loved children: Allan Snyder to DS, 2 May 1992.

435.   a new kind: Miller, p.457.

436.   She knows how: Strasberg, *Bittersweet*, p.122.

436.   Arthur was writing: Olie Rauh, loc. cit., p.16.

437.   If I shouldn't: Susan Strasberg to DS, 3 June 1992; similarly, see *Marilyn and Me*, p.170.

437.   a façade of marital: Rosten, p.79.

437.   hiding: *Ibid.*, p.61.

437.   The accident was reported by the Associated Press, dateline 25 March 1958.

437.   floating off in: Rosten, p.55.

438.   The maid's not: quoted by John Moore to DS, 23 August 1992.

438.   She shouldn't wear: Associated Press story dated 29 April 1958.

438.   But I've never: quoted by John Moore to DS, 23 August 1992.

439.   For I.A.L. Diamond's memoir of *Some Like It Hot*, see his article, 'The Day Marilyn Needed 47 Takes To Remember to Say, "Where's the Bourbon?"' *California*, vol.10, no.12 (Dec. 1985), 132–6.

440.   because she gives me: MM, to Hedda Hopper in New York, April 1958. Heavily edited, the comments appeared as part of Hopper's article 'Just Call Her Mrs Miller!' in the *Chicago Sunday Tribune Magazine*, 22 June 1958, p.14.

441.   because May: Vanessa Reis to DS, 16 Feb. 1992.

441ff.   The comments of Billy Wilder throughout this chapter were made to DS, 19 Nov. 1991.

442.   She picked: Allan Snyder to DS, 2 May 1992.

442.   Marilyn time: Rosten, p.24.

442.   I never heard: Quoted in *The Listener*, 30 Aug. 1979.

443.   Well, I think: MM to Richard Meryman, July 1962.

443.   organically: MM, quoted in *Los Angeles Times*, 9 July 1958.

443.   relaxing a little: MM, quoted in Luitjers, p.63.

444.   It seemed to me: In notes prepared by Leon Krohn MD for Ted Landreth, during preparation for the BBC-TV documentary *Say Goodbye to the President* in 1984.

444.   I have a feeling: MM to Norman Rosten, quoted in Rosten, pp.76–7.

445.   very easy to work: Avedon, in Wagenknecht, p.59.

445.   the spontaneous joy: Arthur Miller, 'My Wife Marilyn', *Life*, vol.45, no.25 (22 Dec. 1958), 146.

445.   Arthur Miller's letter to MM was typed Friday evening, 12 Sept. 1958 and sent via air mail that night. It arrived on Monday at the suite of 'Mrs Marilyn Miller' at the Bel-Air Hotel. MM obviously thought the letter so important that she kept it until her death. IMP.

447.   more and more living with her: Rosten, p.79.

447.   For Olie Rauh's opinion of Arthur's arrival in California, see Rauh, loc cit., p.16.

Notes

447. going through some: Jack Lemmon, quoted in McCann, p.105.
449. I have discussed: Billy Wilder to DS; see also Tom Wood, *The Bright Side of Billy Wilder* (New York: Doubleday, 1960) p.158, and Maurice Zolotow, *Billy Wilder in Hollywood* (New York: Putnam's, 1977), p.265.
449. MM's telephone call to Audrey Wilder was relayed by Billy Wilder to DS; see also Diamond, loc. cit., p.136; with slight variations, the anecdote is also recounted in Zolotow, *Billy Wilder in Hollywood*, p.271, and in Wood, p.162.
449. Anyone can remember lines: Quoted in Mills, p.122.
450. Could I have: Rosten, p.72.
450. Incomplete records of Dr Kris's prescriptions for MM are attached to her bills and to pharmacy invoices through 1957 (and are so preserved in MG III, IV and VI, since they were items for her accountant's perusal); for 1959, see IMP.
451. Susan Strasberg's comments on 1959 were shared with DS in June 1992; see also *Marilyn and Me*, pp.187–9.
451. warm and plain: 'Tribute to Marilyn Monroe from a friend . . . Carl Sandburg', *Look*, vol.26 (11 Sept. 1962), 90–94.
452. uncomfortable: Mervin Block to DS, 6 Oct. 1992. Other details of the press junket were provided by John Moore to DS.
452. For Miller's creative stasis during this time, see Allan Seager, 'The Creative Agony of Arthur Miller', *Esquire*, vol.lii, no.4 (Oct. 1959), 123–6.
453. I guess: quoted in Gloria Steinem, 'Growing Up with Marilyn', *Ms* vol.1, no.2 (August 1972), 38.
454. He told me: Tynan, p.146.
455. I'm sure he accepted: Arthur Miller, quoted in Hervé Hamon and Patrick Rotman, *Yves Montand: Tu vois, je n'ai pas oublié* (Paris: Seuil/Fayard, 1990), p.499.
455. He looked at me: Rosten, p.21.
455–6. She was always: Frankie Vaughan, quoted in Hutchinson, p.74.
456. *un titre prémonitoire:* Signoret's description, cut from the final published edition of her memoirs, is cited in Hamon and Rotman, p.503.

CHAPTER 18

457. Marilyn was a: Sidney Skolsky in the *Hollywood Citizen-News*, 20 Jan 1960.
457. Next to my husband: Widely quoted – e.g., in 'Marilyn meets Montand', *Look*, vol.24, (5 July 1960), 96.
457. Everything she do: *Ibid.*, 93.
458. There was no script: Quoted in Goode, p.202.
458. a sacrifice of great blocks: Miller, p.466.
459. came running: Hamon and Rotman, p.512; trans. DS. See also Zolotow, p.347.
459. Arthur Miller, the big liberal: Skolsky, p.227–8.
459. was a terrible ordeal: quoted in Kobal, p.606.
459. There was something: Vanessa Ries to DS, 16 Feb. 1992.
460. no real communication: Gavin Lambert, *On Cukor* (New York: Putnam's, 1972), pp.174–5.
460. The incident with Frankie Vaughan and his son was documented by Vaughan in Paul Donovan, 'The day Marilyn cried on Frankie's shoulder', *Today* (London), 2 June 1986.
461. I saw Marilyn: Quoted in Kirk Crivello, *Fallen Angels* (Secaucus, N.J.: Citadel, 1988), p.261.

Notes

461ff. For the shared fears that drew MM and Montand together, see Hamon and Rotman, pp.519ff.

461. a whole succession: Simone Signoret, *Nostalgia Isn't What It Used to Be* (London: Grafton, 1979), pp.322–3.

462. Comments by Jack Cole and Jerry Wald may be found in *Life*, vol.49, no.7 (15 Aug. 1960), 68; and in Kobal, pp.605–7.

462. Is there anything: Frank Radcliffe, quoted in Del Burnett, 'Marilyn: A Personal Reminiscence', *American Classic Screen*, March 1981, p.14.

462. What am I afraid of: MM's notes, scribbled on a pad, were found by a journalist who published them in *The American Weekly* on 1 May 1960.

464. I'll miss you: Hamon and Rotman, p.531.

464. I bent over: *Ibid.*, pp.531–2ff.

466. I liked her: George Cukor, quoted in *Los Angeles Herald-Examiner*, 5 Aug. 1982, p.A8.

466. She gave me: quoted in Kobal, pp.606–7.

466. there was a childishness: Inez Melson, in the television special *That's Hollywood*, narrated by Tom Bosley; written and produced by Philip Savenick.

466. On Ralph Greenson's background and childhood, see his incomplete and unpublished memoir, 'My Father the Doctor', in Box 12 of the Ralph R. Greenson Collection in the Department of Special Collections at the University of California at Los Angeles; henceforth extracts from this collection are designated RRG.

468ff. The materials relevant to *Captain Newman, M.D.* are contained in RRG Box 15 and in the June 1962 supplement to his biography at the UCLA Medical School.

470. a charismatic speaker: RRG, Box 1.

471. He wanted to amuse: Benson Schaeffer MD, to DS, 28 Dec. 1992.

471. Only later was it: A highly respected California psychoanalyst requested DS to preserve his anonymity.

472. a hard-living man: Elisabeth Young-Bruehl, *Anna Frued* (New York: Summit, 1988), p.371.

472. 'Special Problems In Psychotherapy With the Rich and Famous', dated 18 August 1978: RRG, Box 2, Folder 19.

472. 'Drugs in the Psychotherapeutic Situation': RRG, Box 2, Folder 4. Other lectures cited on 657 and 658 are located in the same Box.

474. I was going to be: the quotations attributed to Ralph Greenson are derived from a letter he wrote to Marianne Kris on 20 Aug. 1962. From the Ralph Greenson Papers, Special Collections, UCLA.

475. I'm thirty-four: quoted in Eve Arnold, p.85.

475. You're both narcissists: quoted by Esther Maltz (formerly Mrs Hyman Engelberg) to DS, 28 July and 23 Oct. 1992.

475. prescribe medication for her: Ralph Greenson to Marianne Kris, 20 Aug. 1962: Greenson Papers, Special Collections, UCLA.

476. I have lived: Alfred Hitchcock to DS, 18 July 1975.

477. Westerns and the West: Miller, p.462.

478. This is an attempt: James Goode, *The Story of The Misfits* (Indianapolis: Bobbs-Merrill, 1961), p.17.

478ff. On the making of *The Misfits*, see (in addition to Goode), *Time*, vol. lxxvi, no.6 (8 Aug. 1960), 57; Arlene Croce, 'The Misfits', *Sight and Sound*, summer 1961, pp. 142–4; Alice T. McIntyre, 'Making *The Misfits*', *Esquire*, vol.lv, no.3 (March 1961), 74–81; Rosten, pp.82–9.

479. Each of the players: Goode, p.17.

480. What makes you so sad?: Miller, *Timebends*, p.369.

480. desperately unhappy: Rupert Allan to DS, 17 Aug. 1991.

481. But the character: Sam Shaw to DS, 7 March 1992.

481. Miller's was the: Shaw and Rosten, p.186.

482.   I have not: Quoted in 'Mosaic for Marilyn', *Coronet*, February 1961.
482.   I never really: Jon Whitcomb, 'Marilyn Monroe – The Sex Symbol Versus The Good Wife', *Cosmopolitan*, vol.149, no.6 (Dec. 1960), 54–5.
482.   But I promised: McIntyre, loc. cit., p.79.
482.   Harlow was always: Quoted in *Coronet*, February 1961.
482.   by throwing a fit: Luitjers, pp.67–8.
483.   I had to: Most of these remarks were edited out of the 1962 *Life* magazine interview by Meryman; the few remaining comments were much altered. As offered here, they are drawn from the original taped conversations.
483.   She had considerable: Goode, p.43.
483.   I'm Mitzi Gaynor: Goode, p.117.
484.   Cut!: Goode, p.182.
484.   a mean streak: Anjelica Huston to Barbara Walters on ABC-TV, 6 Nov. 1991.
484f.   For the account of the perils of making *Moby Dick* in 1955, see Michael Freedland, *Gregory Peck* (New York: Morrow, 1980), pp.137–8, and Axel Madsen, *John Huston* (New York: Doubleday, 1978), pp.149–50.
484.   I want you: Madsen, p.149.
485.   I'm doing this one: For the account of Gable's stunts in *China Seas*, see Jay Robert Nash and Stanley Ralph Ross, *The Motion Picture Guide* (Chicago: Cinebooks, 1985), vol.II, p.417.
485.   For an account of Gable's stunts in *The Misfits*, and for Dunlevie's remark, see Jack Scagnetti, *The Life and Loves of Gable* (Middle Village, N.Y.: Jonathan David, 1976), p.152.
486.   You can all: Gable's remark and the incident are recounted in Goode, pp.208–9.
486.   They don't care: Gable, quoted in Lawrence Grobel, *The Hustons* (New York: Avon, 1989), p.494.
486.   had begun staying: Miller, p.474.
487.   But I like: Huston, quoted in Gerald Pratley, *The Cinema of John Huston* (Cranbury, N.J.: A. S. Barnes, 1977), p.130.
487.   Well, I ran: quoted in *Newsweek*, 12 Sept. 1960, p.102; *ibid.* for Huston's gambling schedule.
487.   I spent a lot: John Huston, *An Open Book* (New York: Knopf, 1980), p.287.
487.   The telltale sign: Grobel, p.496.
487.   losing steadily: Goode, p.48; see also pp.31, 35, 61, 73, 82, 159. Huston's gambling habits are also detailed in William F. Nolan, *John Huston: King Rebel* (Los Angeles: Sherbourne Press, 1965), pp.184–5.
487.   What should I ask: The dialogue is recorded in Goode, p.246 and repeated by Grobel, p.496.
488.   For details of Paula Strasberg's illness, I am grateful to Susan Strasberg, who discussed the matter in several interviews during June and October 1992.
488.   I think we're doing: Goode, p.126.
488.   I was almost: Miller, p.477.
488.   n: MM's doctor-administered injections of Amytal were gruesomely recounted by Miller, p.481: these were, he wrote, enough to sedate her for a major operation. See also Miller, pp.528–9.
488.   It took so long: Allan Snyder to DS, 2 May 1992.
489.   On Huston's loss of $16,000 on 16 August, see Goode, p.108.
489.   the one great lesson: often quoted – e.g., in Lyn Tornabene, *Long Live the King* (New York: Putnam's, 1976), p.361–2.
490.   I think she: Hedda Hopper's column for 1 Sept. 1960; prepared the previous day at her office by wire service.
490f.   The relevant daily production history of *The Misfits* can be determined from Goode, pp.115–24, from call sheets preserved by members of the cast and crew, and from the reminiscences of Evelyn Moriarty, Allan Snyder, Rupert Allan and Ralph Roberts.

491.   Huston's account was unvarying: 'Drugs ravaged her, and she broke down. I had to send her to a hospital for a week' (in Wolper, *Legend*).
492.   n: Goode, p.124.
492.   And with that: Evelyn Moriarty to DS, 17 Feb. and 9 Aug. 1992.
492.   When the press: Ralph Roberts to DS, 2 March 1992.
493.   My guess is: Hyman Engelberg, quoted in the *New York Times*, 30 Aug. 1960, p.24.
493.   looking wonderfully: Miller, p.485.
494.   When she was told: Goode, pp.257–8.
494.   I know Arthur's: Quoted in Charles Hamblett, *Who Killed Marilyn Monroe?* (London: Leslie Frewin, 1966), p.128.
494.   All my life: Henry Hathaway, quoted in Kobal, p.613.
496.   serious, accurate: Paul V. Beckley, in the *New York Herald Tribune*, 3 Feb. 1961.
497.   I can't do it: Grobel, p.498.
497f.   Detailed information on Greenson's increasingly bizarre relationship with MM, and his family's relationship with her, came collectively from Rupert Allan, Ralph Roberts, Susan Strasberg, Pat Newcomb, and from three sources close to the Greenson family who requested that DS preserve their anonymity.
498.   I was her therapist: Ralph Greenson to Marianne Kris, 20 Aug. 1962.
499.   the sad fact: quoted in *Time*, vol.lxxvi, no.21 (21 Nov. 1960), 61.
499.   I kept him waiting: Skolsky, p.230. He locates this conversation in Los Angeles after Gable's death, but that is impossible: it must have occurred between the first heart attack and the second, fatal one, for when Gable died MM was in New York.

CHAPTER 19

502.   I really am: Alan Levy, 'Marilyn Monroe: "A Good Long Look at Myself"', *Redbook*, Aug. 1962, p.77.
502.   splendid: W. Somerset Maugham, in a letter to MM dated 31 Jan. 1961.
504.   because the press: Pat Newcomb to DS, 3 Aug. 1992. Henceforth, all quotations attributed to Pat Newcomb are taken from this interview unless otherwise noted.
504.   incompatibility of character: Divorce proceeding reported in the *New York Times*, 22 Jan. 1961, p.86; see also *ibid.*, 25 Jan. 1961, p.35; and the UPI wire service despatches dated 21, 23 and 25 Jan. 1961.
504.   I am upset: UPI wire service story dated 21 Jan. 1961; see, e.g., the *Hollywood Citizen-News*, that date.
504.   It would be: *Ibid.*
504.   Mr Miller is: MM to Hedda Hopper in July 1961, released in her syndicated column on Sunday 16 July.
505ff. The details of MM's stay at the Payne Whitney Clinic of New York Hospital were provided in interviews with Norman Rosten, Ralph Roberts, Susan Strasberg and Pat Newcomb. For the medical evaluation of her as 'extremely disturbed and potentially self-destructive', see a report obtained by the *New York World Telegram* and published on 10 Feb. 1961, p.1.
506f.   MM's letter to the Strasbergs was first printed in the London *Daily Mirror*, 5 Aug. 1981; in abbreviated form, it is also in Guiles, *Legend*, p.402.
507.   On DiMaggio's life from 1955 to 1961, see Bob Dean, 'Marilyn to Wed Again?' *Photoplay*, May 1961; also Allen, p.194ff.
507.   He carried a torch: quoted in Allen, p.186.
508.   He loved her: *Ibid.*, p.197.

508.   take the hospital: Quoted by many of MM's friends – e.g., in Rosten, p.93.
508.   Kris's remarks to Roberts were relayed to DS and are also found in Susan Strasberg, *Marilyn and Me*, p.228.
514.   I feel wonderful: UPI wire service story for 6 March 1961; see, e.g., *Los Angeles Examiner*, 'Marilyn Whisked From Hospital', that date.
514.   as radiantly: *Ibid.*
515.   She had just been discharged: Wagenknecht, p.49.
515.   Joe DiMaggio deeply loved: Allen, p.189.
515.   The attraction to Joe: *Ibid.*, p.199.
516.   I'm very happy: Jonah Rudd, 'Now that I am 35', the London *Daily Mail*, 5 June 1961.
516.   There's no doubt: Milton Ebbins's recollections about Sinatra and MM, and about MM up to the night of her death, were provided in his interviews with DS in Beverly Hills on 6 Aug. and 22 Sept. 1992.
518.   It was scary: A composite statement of the same sentiments, expressed by MM to Rupert Allan and Susan Strasberg.
519.   I told [Arthur]: Rosten, p.91.
520f.   Details of the Greenson–Monroe relationship derive from previously dated interviews with Ralph Roberts, Susan Strasberg, Allan Snyder, Pat Newcomb, Rupert Allan; from a conversation with Greenson's then brother-in-law and attorney, Milton Rudin; and from interviews with three lay people who knew Greenson personally and two of his Los Angeles psychiatric colleagues, whose five separate requests for anonymity DS has honoured.
521.   He overstepped: Robert Litman MD, to DS 23 April 1992.
522.   Help Help: Norman Rosten, 'About Marilyn', *McCall's*, Aug. 1972, p.132. These words were not new from MM but apparently recaptured by her: they are found as early as 1956, shortly after she arrived in London and found Arthur's notebook entry (MG IV, 5, p.5).
522.   Henceforth in the text, all the remarks attributed to Ralph Roberts derive from the interview with DS on 2 March 1992, and from subsequent, supplementary telephone conversations in May, June, August and September of that year. See also Susan Strasberg, *Marilyn and Me*, p.230.
523.   She began to get rid: Ralph Greenson to Marianne Kris, 20 Aug. 1962: Greenson Papers, UCLA Special Collections.
524.   I never heard: Betsy Duncan Hammes to DS, 22 July 1992.
525.   You must have: David Brown to DS, 11 Nov. 1992.
525.   in a shambles: Milton Gould to DS, 10 Nov. 1992.
525.   a tall, dark: Negulesco, p.224.
526.   There was nothing: Arnold Shulman to DS, 28 July 1992.
527.   Have you been trapped: Johnson and Leventhal, p.206.
527.   quick, she was gay: *Ibid.*, p.207.
528ff.   The production history of *Something's Got To Give* described herein and in the following chapter derives from an interview with the original producer, David Brown (with DS, 11 Nov. 1992), and from Brown's book, *Let Me Entertain You* (New York: Morrow, 1990), pp.53–6; from Patricia Newcomb; from the Fox production files; and (as detailed below) from interviews with those involved in the production, especially Evelyn Moriarty, Henry Weinstein, Allan Snyder and Marjorie Plecher Snyder.
527.   The change: Peter G. Levathes to Spyros P. Skouras, cable dated 10 Jan. 1962, in Box 45 of the Skouras Collection, Stanford University.
527.   how much: Peter G. Levathes to DS, 8 Oct. 1992.
528.   essentially a different: Douglas Kirkland to DS, 24 July 1992.
529.   If I am: Many times, e.g., to Richard Meryman, July 1962, as in *Life*, loc. cit.
530.   I encouraged her: Greenson, in a deposition to the Estate of Marilyn Monroe, preserved in RRG/UCLA.

530. The doctor thought: Eunice Murray, in Wolper, *Legend*; see, similarly, Eunice Murray, with Rose Shade, *Marilyn: The Last Months* (New York: Pyramid, 1975), p.43; hereinafter referred to as Murray.

530. there was nobody else: Ralph Greenson to Marianne Kris, 20 Aug. 1962: Greenson Papers, Special Collections, UCLA.

530f. Details on the background and biography of Eunice Joerndt Murray Blackmer were ascertained from the Advancement Office of Urbana University, in Urbana, Ohio; from the Annual Catalogue of the Urbana University School Academy and Junior College for 1917–18; from the Library and Archives of the Swedenborg School of Religion in Newton, Mass.; from Eunice's son-in-law, Philip LaClair (interview 22 July 1992); from County records in Albuquerque, N.M. and Bath, Me.; from Frank Higgins, *Urbana College* (Urbana, Ohio: Urbana College, 1977); from the obituary of John Murray in the *Albuquerque Tribune*, 24 Nov. 1958.

531. mere shadow: Eunice Murray Blackmer to Audrey Stevens, 13 May 1983.

531. constantly to engage: Higgins, pp.6–7.

532. controversial, alienating: *Ibid.*, p.108.

533. a house they had planned: Murray, p.6.

533. It was strictly: Philip LaClair, 22 July 1992.

534. in any kind: Murray, p.7.

535. very strange lady: Allan Snyder to DS, 2 May 1991.

CHAPTER 20

NB: Citations from the daily production reports and call sheets for *Something's Got to Give* cited in the text are drawn from those files: Picture No. A-855, Twentieth Century-Fox Film Corporation, 1962.

536. Regarding the cost and mortage of 12305 Fifth Helena, see the *Los Angeles Times*, 11 Aug. 1962 and the relevant Los Angeles County tax records for 1962.

536. I felt badly: Quoted in Murray, p.49.

536. she was talked: Evelyn Moriarty to DS, 17 Feb. 1992.

538. but there isn't: Cherie Redmond to Hedda Rosten, MM daily secretarial and business report from Los Angelese to New York, dated Sunday, 25 Feb. 1962.

538ff. For accounts of the brief encounters between MM and President Kennedy (hardly constituting a romance), DS relied on interviews with Allan Snyder, Rupert Allan, Susan Strasberg, Pat Newcomb, Milton Ebbins and Joseph Naar; see also Skolsky, pp.233–4; and Wilson, *Show Business Laid Bare*, pp.56ff.

541ff. On Robert Kennedy's friendship (it can be called nothing else) with MM, DS relied on interviews with Edwin Guthman (29 Oct. 1992) and those listed in the note above; see also Skolsky, p.234; Wilson, pp.60, 84. In his appearance on the television programme *60 Minutes* in 1973, Norman Mailer admitted that, contrary to the allegations in his then recently published book on Monroe, he did not believe that she was romantically involved with Robert Kennedy, but that his publisher had offered him a lot of money when he 'needed quick cash', and that this element made a good story. Granted.

544. They all came over: Eunice Murray, quoted in the *Chicago Tribune*, 11 Sept. 1973, sec.2, p.1.

545. The man: Wilson, p.56.

545. There was no doubt: *Ibid.*, p.84.

546. (n) writing about Bobby: quoted in *ibid.*, p.60.

547.   MM's telephone message logs, kept in longhand and then typed by Cherie Redmond, are in IMP.

547.   According to Redmond's message logs (for 5 February, 8 March, 9 May, 12, 22, 29 June and 6 July), Eunice's repeated requests for cash advances continued throughout that year – a habit MM found annoying.

548.   For Isadore Miller's brief recollections of the Florida visit, see Wagenknecht, pp.52-4.

548.   On MM's freedom from drug dependence during her Mexican trip, see Murray, pp.59ff.; also Pat Newcomb to DS, 3 Aug. 1993.

549.   Whenever she was: George Masters to DS, 8 Aug. 1992. See also George Masters and Norma Lee Browning, *The Masters Way to Beauty* (New York: NAL/Signet, 1978), pp.68–83.

549.   Regarding MM's dress at the Golden Globe ceremony: George Masters to DS, 8 Aug. 1992.

550.   drunk, barely: Susan Strasberg to DS, 3 June 1992; see also *Marilyn and Me*, p.239.

550.   vitamin shots: Murray, p.78.

550.   It was irresponsible: Arnold Abrams MD to DS, 2 Nov. 1992.

551.   The details of MM's visit to Greenson on 3 March 1962 were provided by two sources who requested anonymity – one a medical colleague of Greenson, the other a person close to him.

551.   It is hard: Pat Newcomb to SA, 3 Aug. 1992; see also Guiles, *Legend*, p.441.

552.   I don't know: Nunnally Johnson to Jean Negulesco, quoted in Negulesco, p.223.

552.   the studio simply: Arnold Shulman to DS, 7 July 1992; see also Shulman's comments in Strasberg, *Marilyn and Me*, pp.240–2.

553.   he involved her: Milton Rudin to DS, 31 Oct. 1992.

554.   The doctor present in the Greenson house was under supervision by Greenson for psychotherapeutic training that year, and he was an eyewitness to the DiMaggio event. Still in practice in Los Angeles, he has requested that his name not be used as a source for this event. In fact, there was a second witness, also a physician still in practice in Beverly Hills.

555.   Henry, don't you pay any attention: quoted by Weinstein to DS, 10 Dec. 1992.

556.   She was a poor creature: quoted in McCann, p.176.

557.   executives were not: Walter Bernstein to DS, 5 March 1992; see also his reminiscences in 'Marilyn Monroe's Last Picture Show', *Esquire*, vol.lxxx, no.1 (July 1973) 104–78; published in the UK in the *Observer Review*, 9 Sept. 1973.

557.   She was very charming: Bernstein to DS, 5 March, 1992.

558.   based on the fact: Murray, p.71

558.   Regarding Eunice's management of Marilyn's home and life, and her choice of workmen, see her book, pp.72ff.

558.   It's not particularly: Cherie Redmond to Hedda Rosten, 27 April 1962.

560.   n: Susan Strasberg to DS, 5 Nov. 1992.

560.   For the injection by Seigel, see Bernstein, loc. cit.

560.   Seigel was: Ernest Lehman to DS, 29 Aug. 1992.

560.   every few days: Murray, p.78.

561.   Regarding the gift to Agnes Flanagan: see Crivello, p.250.

561.   The arithmetic: *Close-Up*, vol.5, no.21 (14 June 1962) 5. The producer is unnamed.

561.   Receipts detailing each hour of Marilyn's appointments April–June were preserved by Carey Cadillac. They were signed and dated by the driver, Rudy Kautzky, and bear invoice numbers 21703–22005.

561.   For Cukor's opinions, DS interviewed (on 20 April 1992) Richard Stanley, the director's assistant during the last seven years of Cukor's life.

563.   She was so happy: Henry Weinstein to DS, 10 Dec. 1992.
566.   Seigel's reports are preserved in the production files for the film, in reports for 30 April–4 May, and in the documentary *Marilyn: Something's Got to Give* (Fox Entertainment News, 1990), ex.prod. William K. Knoedelseder Jr, prod., wr., narr. Henry Schipper. Fox Video #1955.
566.   Marilyn did not: Evelyn Moriarty to DS, 17 Feb. 1992.
566.   Marilyn was shattered: Johnson and Leventhal, p.208.
567.   The president's birthday gala in May had of course been planned for months: MM told Rupert Allan, among others, that the invitation to Marilyn was issued personally by JFK in March, and as filming approached, she also made it clear to Fox that she would have to be released for two days in New York that May. The studio would not, of course, object to a star appearing at so prestigious an event.
567.   nothing, absolutely: *Life*, June 1987, p.70.
567–8.   It might have been: Murray, p.101.
568.   At 4.00: Daily log for 1 May kept by Cherie V. Redmond, in IMP.
569.   Evelyn Moriarty's meeting with Eunice Murray was told to DS by Evelyn on 17 Feb. 1992.
570.   Ralph had made himself: Henry Weinstein to DS, 10 Dec. 1992.
570.   Hildi was afraid: Ralph Greenson to Marianne Kris, 20 Aug. 1992: Greenson Papers, Special Collections, UCLA.
570.   When I left: Ralph Greenson, Folder 4, Box 2: Greenson Papers, Special Collections, UCLA. This material was the rough draft form of what became a portion of chapter twelve of his book *Drugs in the Psychotherapeutic Situation*, pp.204–5. MM is not specifically mentioned as the patient, but the only five-week summer vacation he took from 1959 to his death in 1979 was in 1962. With no other woman patient was he so involved, and the language of this passage is virtually a copy of his descriptions of MM in his letter to Marianne Kris dated 20 Aug. Even if the patient were *not* MM, the words and tone of this passage are frighteningly self-referential, not to say frankly sexual. One need not be trained in the fine points of Freudian language to be astonished at Greenson's lack of discretion.
573.   She had set that day: Henry Weinstein to DS, 10 Dec. 1992.
573.   I had no idea: Milton Gould to DS, 10 Nov. 1992.
573.   The Weinstein–Ebbins dialogue was reconstructed for DS by Milton Ebbins, 6 Aug. 1992.
574.   Peter Levathes firmly denied (to DS, 8 Oct. 1992) the absurd allegation set down by some writers to the effect that he received a telephone call from Robert Kennedy, ordering the release of MM from work so she could come to New York on 17 May.
575.   The whole thing: Henry Weinstein to DS, 10 Dec. 1992.
577.   We kept working: William Asher to DS, 25 Sept. 1992.
577.   skin and beads: Quoted in Arthur M. Schlesinger Jr, *Robert Kennedy and His Times* (Boston: Houghton Mifflin, 1978), p.590.
578.   I'd like you: Quoted in Wagenknecht, p.54.
578.   Marilyn came: Mathilde Krim, on 'The Class of the Twentieth Century', A & E Cable Television Network, 1992. Narrated by Richard Dreyfus.
578.   reveled in that: George Masters to DS, 8 Aug. 1992.
578.   Regarding the presidential gala: for years there has circulated the rumour that, after the reception, MM joined Kennedy for a tryst in his bedroom at the Carlyle Hotel. 'This is absolutely impossible,' recalled Ralph Roberts. After Milton Ebbins and two other guests left the Krim residence on East Sixty-ninth Street with Marilyn, they delivered her to her apartment at about two o'clock, and there Roberts awaited to give her her pre-arranged massage. 'When I departed, it was almost four and she was asleep' (RR to DS, 2 March 1992).

CHAPTER 21

581.   MM was attended at home for her ear infection and resulting insomnia by Dr Milton Uhley, then on call for Engelberg. He billed her for three visits to her home: the evening of 27 May, after midnight on 28–9 May, and from one to four the morning of 3 June.

584.   What happened: Henry Weinstein, in the Schipper documentary *Marilyn: Something's Got to Give*, 1990.

584.   a dangerous arsenal: Murray, p.107.

585.   Henceforth, all details of MM's telephone calls are derived from the complete records of General Telephone and Electronics for the two numbers installed at her residence, 476–1890 and 472–4830. These were provided to DS through the mediation of producer-director Ted Landreth, who obtained them from Neil Spaatz, Senior Detective with the Los Angeles Police Department and later head of security for Playboy Enterprises.

585f.   Details of the telephone calls and meetings involving Weinstein, Feldman, Levathes, Rudin, Greenson and Gang were all set down in a nine-page studio memorandum by Phil Feldman titled 'Marilyn Monroe Situation' and dated 6–11 June 1962. DS obtained them in early 1992 from a private source. Henceforth these documents are designated 'Feldman'.

587.   Everybody was aware: Walter Bernstein to DS, 5 March 1992.

587f.   The accounts of Greenson's conduct with the actor-writer and another patient were provided by those who for obvious reasons have requested anonymity.

588.   Correspondence between Greenson and John Frosch of the *Journal of the American Psychoanalytic Association* in 1957 is located in Box 14, Folder titled '1957 Correspondence', Greenson Papers, Special Collections, UCLA.

588.   She was disheveled: the citations from Michael Gurdin MD, are derived from the DS interview with him, 21 Sept. 1992.

589.   with them: Feldman, 6 June 1962.

589.   the medical member: *Ibid*, 7 June 1962.

589.   I am convinced: *Ibid*.

591.   I went to see: quoted in the *Los Angeles Times*, 11 Aug. 1962.

592.   Feldman, 8 June 1962, pp.1–3.

593.   was made necessary: quoted in the *Citizen-News*, 9 June 1962, p.2.

594.   We've let the inmates: quoted in the *Los Angeles Herald-Examiner*, 12 June, 1962, p.2.

594.   *Cleopatra* was way: Henry Weinstein, in Schipper's documentary *Marilyn: Something's Got to Give*, 1990.

595.   Feldman, 11 June 1962.

596.   Mr. Rudin said: *Ibid.*, p.3.

596.   since April 16: Complaint no. 797856, Twentieth Century-Fox Film Corporation, Plaintiff, vs. Marilyn Monroe, Marilyn Monroe Productions, Inc., Defendants.

597.   When [Levathes]: Johnson and Leventhal, p.209.

597.   she had never: quoted in Gerald Clarke, *Capote: A Biography* (New York: Simon & Schuster, 1988), p.269.

597.   There's a future: quoted in McCann, p.173.

598.   She was very natural: Bert Stern to DS, 10 May 1992.

598.   she said: George Masters to DS, 8 Aug. 1992.

598.   I'm thirty-six: in *Photoplay*, September 1962, p.87.

599.   To think of: Allan Snyder to DS, 2 May 1992.

599.   Regarding the so-called 'liver and vitamin injections', the first Mrs Hyman Engelberg told DS that she never heard of them: 'Dr Greenson used Hy to sedate [Marilyn].' Esther Maltz to DS, 23 Oct. 1992.

600.   She asked to postpone: Richard Meryman, 'A Last Long Talk With A Lonely Girl', *Life*, vol.53, no.7 (17 Aug. 1962), 33.

600.   I have access: Esther Maltz (formerly Mrs. Hyman Engelberg) to DS, 28 July 1992.

600.   so that I had nothing: Ralph Greenson to Marianne Kris, 20 Aug. 1962: RG Papers, Special Collections, UCLA.

600.   The calls placed by MM to the Department of Justice are recorded on her GTE bill (documented above under the note on page 807). Edwin Guthman, previously cited in this matter, provided for DS an account of how the calls were or were not put through to the attorney general, and how Angie Novello fielded them.

601.   That Angie Novello talked with MM more often than RFK did, see Schlesinger, p.591.

602.   Regarding DiMaggio's visits to MM, see 'Joe's Plan to Be Near Marilyn', *San Francisco Chronicle*, 14 Aug. 1962.

602.   For the history of MM's gynaecological problems and procedures, see above, on Leon Krohn's notes.

602.   Regarding DiMaggio's termination with Monette, see Maury Allen, p.197, and the *Los Angeles Herald-Examiner*, 14 Aug. 1962.

602ff.   MM's remarks are excerpted from Meryman, loc. cit. This was available the week before, on 27 July; according to Eunice Murray (p.116), MM read and liked it.

605.   What are you: quoted by Murray, p.115.

606.   On plans for *The Jean Harlow Story*, see Skolsky, pp.235–6.

608.   As so often: Peter G. Levathes to DS, 21 Feb. 1992.

610.   There was absolutely: Alex D'Arcy to DS, 1 July 1992.

610.   I was in Lake Tahoe: Betsy Duncan Hammes to DS, 22 July 1992.

610–1.   Joe told me: quoted in Maury Allen, p.197. Rupert Allan's interview with DS, 19 July 1991. Privy to the secret wedding plans were, among others, Valmore Monette, Rupert Allan and (documented in Chapter 22 below) Bill Alexander. But MM and DiMaggio intended to keep the wedding secret until after the ceremony, to avoid the kind of publicity that had surrounded them in 1954.

611.   She was fighting: Susan Strasberg to DS, 4 June 1992.

611.   Regarding MM's new will: Milton Rudin to DS, 31 Oct. 1992.

614.   Regarding Elizabeth Courtney's report on the Jean Louis gown for MM, see *Los Angeles Times*, 12 Aug. 1962.

614.   I want to be loved: See note on p.603.

CHAPTER 22

615.   because Marilyn has asked: Negulesco, p.226.

615.   a hurricane of glamour: *Ibid.*, p.227.

615.   in great spirits: Evelyn Moriarty to DS, 26 Feb. 1992.

616.   Notes on interviews with Leon Krohn were shared with DS by producer Ted Landreth, who interviewed Krohn for a BBC-TV documentary. MM's telephone records confirm her call to Krohn (Los Angeles telephone number 662–9111) at Cedars of Lebanon Hospital that day.

617.   being held by: Cheri V. Redmond to MM, 30 July 1962.

618.   The dismissal of Eunice Murray was well known to Newcomb, Roberts, Allan and perhaps to Joe as well. See also Guiles, *Legend*, p.433.

620.   'Special problems In Psychotherapy With the Rich and Famous', Box 2, Folder 19 (dated 18 Aug. 1978): RG Papers, Special Collections, UCLA.

622.   I have a Spanish: Bill Alexander to DS, 27 Aug. 1992.

623.   It was a difficult: John Bates to DS, 20 Nov. 1992. Also contributing to the accounts of that weekend were Nancy (Mrs John) Bates and John Bates Jr. A

separate interview was conducted on the same date with Roland Snyder, the retired foreman of the Bates ranch, who was also with the Kennedys at the ranch that entire weekend.

624.   I saddled: Roland Snyder to DS, 20 Nov. 1992.
624.   I was fourteen: John Bates Jr, to DS, 20 Nov. 1992.
625.   Regarding RFK's presence at Mass, see *The Gilroy Dispatch*, 6 Aug. 1962.
626ff. Greenson and Engelberg submitted bills for 3 August. Norman Rosten summarized his conversation with MM in Rosten, pp.120–1, Allen, p.203 and Shaw and Rosten, pp.189–190. The telephone calls to Ray Tolman and to Rosten appear on MM's GTE telephone bill for that date. The calls to Courtney and Louis were noted by Murray, p.122. Jule Styne discussed his telephone call to MM with DS on 25 Nov. 1992. Other material from Pat Newcomb to DS, 3 Aug. 1992, and it is also documented in Wilson, *The Show Business Nobody Knows*, p.299.
626.   Engelberg told the District Attorney of this prescription in the December 1982 report, the official title of which is: Report to the District Attorney on The Death of Marilyn Monroe by Ronald H. Carroll, Assistant District Attorney; Alan B. Tomich, Investigator. This final report was preceded by a series of investigative interviews conducted on 16 and 20 August, 3, 7 and 27 September, 1, 12 and 18 October, and compiled as the Los Angeles County District Attorney Bureau of Investigation, Investigator's Report, File $ 82–G–2236. The interviews were conducted by Carroll and/or by investigator Alan B. Tomich. Henceforth, the full report is designated as 'DA 1982', and the interviews as 'InvRep'. The citation here is from DA 1982, p.25.
626.   The Engelberg divorce is Los Angeles County civil case #D–617021; additional information was provided by the former Esther Engelberg (later Mrs Albert Maltz) to DS, 23 Oct. 1992.
626.   Regarding the prescriptions by Greenson et al.: see Ralph Greenson to Maurice Zolotow, reported in the *Chicago Tribune*, 14 Sept. 1973, sec.2, p.4; the *Citizen-News*, 7 Aug. 1962; and the District Attorney Report of 1982, p.25.
626.   Regarding the two physicians' prescriptions for MM, Engelberg made a formal statement to investigators from the District Attorney's office on 27 Sept. 1982, in which he stated that he approved ony one Nembutal a day for her, and Greenson claimed to the Suicide Prevention Team on 17 Aug. 1962 that a primary goal of his therapy with MM was to break her drug dependency.
627.   She was very excited: Jule Styne to DS, 14 Dec. 1992.
627.   Regarding MM's deal with *Esquire*, see the *Los Angeles Herald-Examiner*, 14 Aug. 1962.
627.   My husband and I: Paula Strasberg, quoted in the *New York Daily News*, 6 Aug. 1962.
627.   There was too much: Murray, p.122.
628.   Why don't you come: Newcomb to DS, 3 Aug. 1992; also Newcomb quoted in the New York *Journal-American*, 15 Aug. 1962.
628.   seemingly without: quoted in Murray, p.125.
629.   Greenson billed MM's Estate for a visit to Fifth Helena on 4 August.
629.   He spent most: Milton Rudin to DS, 31 Oct. 1992.
629.   Regarding the telephone calls to MM from Joe DiMaggio Jr, he described these to the police on 9 Aug., who included them in their 1962 report on MM's death: 'Interview With Persons Known to Marilyn Monroe, Police Follow-Up Report', 10 Aug. 1962; interviews conducted by Detective Sergeant Robert E. Byron.
630.   Regarding Eunice's shopping, see Murray, p.128.
630.   I was there: William Asher to DS, 25 Sept. 1992. Milton Ebbins confirmed to DS that Asher was at Lawford's that afternoon and had related MM's presence to Ebbins shortly thereafter.

631. Although Greenson admitted in his letter to Kris that he arrived at four-thirty, he wrote that this was at MM's request and gives no indication of the preceding events of the day, much less of his earlier visit.

631. Regarding Greenson's visit to MM, see his statement to the police, 5 Aug. 1962; Zolotow, *Chicago Tribune*, loc. cit., and Murray, p.129.

631. In 1975 and 1982, Peter Lawford told police investigators that he placed his first call to MM at five o'clock that afternoon.

632. The call from Isadore Miller and Murray's response are reported in the London *Daily Express*, 8 Aug. 1962.

632. Regarding Greenson's calls to Engelberg: Esther Maltz (formerly Mrs Hyman Engelberg) to DS, 23 Oct. 1992.

633. I asked the housekeeper: Greenson to Marianne Kris. 20 Aug. 1962.

633. this was the first: Eunice Murray to Investigator Al Tomich, 27 Sept. 1982: DA 1982; Murray, p.2.

633. Regarding the younger Joe DiMaggio's last call to MM, see note to page 635 above. See also his statement to the *Los Angeles Times*, 8 Aug 1962, that MM was alert and in good spirits.

633. happy, gay, alert: Murray, p.130.

634. quite pleasant: Greenson to Kris, 20 Aug. 1962; Greenson to Zolotow, loc. cit.

634. The time of Lawford's call can be precisely fixed because Milton Ebbins recalled that Lawford called him at excactly 7.40 PM – a time Lawford later confirmed with William Asher and Joe Naar, among others. Ebbins, Asher and Naar interviews with DS dated, respectively, 6 Aug. 1992; 25 Sept. 1992; 22 July 1992.

634. Lawford's account as herein related was his consistent account as told in a police interview in 1975, and as reported in the *Los Angeles Times* on 29 Sept. 1985. Lawford was also interviewed by District Attorney investigators in 1982, but at that time he changed his story, saying simply that he could not get through to MM's line at eight o'clock. However, Milton Ebbins reported to DS that Lawford told him on the night of MM's death of his last conversation with the actress at 7.40. Lawford told the same story, in somewhat less detail, to Bill Asher and Joe Naar. It would have been natural for him to alter the account somewhat in 1982, by which time the unjustly believed rumours of the Kennedy involvement in MM's death would have led Lawford to remove himself as far as possible from direct contact with her that night. Lawford later reported that he ended his string of fearful phone calls at 1.30 in the morning, after yet another call from Ebbins. Lawford told investigators from the district attorney's office in 1982 that, 'Ebbins advised that he had just received a telephone call from Rudin, who stated that he and Dr Greenson had found Monroe dead in her residence at midnight.' Lawford added that he was sure of the time of the call because he remembered looking at his bedside clock.

   Again, Ebbins denied making the 1.30 call. By his account, following his (roughly) nine o'clock conversation with Rudin, he did not speak with the attorney again until four in the morning, at which time Rudin informed him of the death. 'I said, "Mickey, what are you doing up at this hour?" He said, "I got problems." I asked, "How's Marilyn?" and he said, "Not good." He said, "Her doctors and I just broke into the bedroom. They've been working on her, and they just pronounced her dead." ' This account (Ebbins to DS, 6 Aug. 1992) seems unlikely, for it contradicts the collective witness of Asher, Naar and Rudin and supports the false claim of Greenson and Eunice Murray themselves – namely, that the doctor had to break into MM's bedroom to gain access to it.

634. Regarding Lawford's second telephone call: see Harrison Carroll, 'Lawford Tells of Phoning Marilyn', *Los Angeles Herald-Examiner*, 6 Aug. 1962:

'Lawford may have been the last person to talk to the blonde star before she was found dead in her bed . . . Eunice Murray earlier reported that Marilyn received such a call.'

634.   Say goodbye: Lawford to Los Angeles Police Department, 16 Oct. 1975; also Lawford to Earl Wilson, *Show Business Laid Bare*, p.88.

634.   Peter was obviously: Milton Ebbins to DS, 6 Aug. 1992.

634.   Monroe was laughing: Thomas T. Noguchi with Joseph DiMona, *Coroner* (New York: Simon & Schuster, 1983), p.65.

635.   That Ebbins reached Rudin's office at 8.25 PM is confirmed by Rudin's report to the police, based on his office records for that evening. Attorneys' offices (especially in Hollywood) routinely have round-the-clock answering services for emergencies.

635.   I did not call: Milton Rudin to DS, 31 Oct. 1992.

635.   Rudin's account is from this same interview with DS. Also, see Rudin's account in the police interview dated 10 Aug. 1962.

636.   If only: Murray, p.132.

636.   Joseph Naar's account: to DS, 22 July 1992. George Durgom, who died in 1992, suffered from Alzheimer's disease the last several years of his life while this book was being researched and could not be interviewed.

636.   had found Marilyn dead at midnight: The entire episode was recounted by Lawford in InvRep (Lawford), p.2.

636.   Ebbins denied (to DS, 22 July and 6 Oct. 1992) calling Naar that evening. 'He must be mistaken,' he said of Naar, who was and remains a friend of Ebbins. Naar, however, was emphatic (to DS, 22 July 1992): 'I could swear it was Ebbins who called.' The information Naar received in that call is consistent with what Ebbins affirmed he later learned.

637.   At about ten or ten-thirty: Natalie Trundy Jacobs to DS, 28 Feb. 1992.

638.   for reasons I still: Murray, p.ooo.

638f.   Murray's and Greenson's reports are here represented as given to the Los Angeles police in 1962: report #62–509 463.

638.   We've lost her: quoted in Robert Welkos and Ted Rohrlich, 'Marilyn Monroe Mystery Persists', the *Los Angeles Times*, 29 Sept. 1985, part 2 p.1.

638.   Murray's altered account from a 'light beneath the door' to a 'telephone cord' was made in Wolper, *Legend*.

639.   Murray's written answer to Roy Turner's typewritten letter dated 9 Feb. 12987; Pat Newcomb to DS, 3 Aug. 1992; Ralph Roberts to DS, 2 March 1992; Rupert Allan to DS, 19 June 1992.

CHAPTER 23

641.   Clemmons's account is derived from an extended lecture and presentation he gave in Los Angeles on 22 March 1991, before an audience of those devoted to MM called 'Marilyn Remembered'. His report is also contained in DA 1982, pp.7–8, 26–8.

642.   It is officer's opinion: Los Angeles Police Department Report: Re-Interview of Persons Known to MM, dated 10 Aug. 1962.

642.   take a look: Don Marshall (Los Angeles Police Department, Retired) to DS, 2 Sept. 1992.

642.   a very good: quoted by Marshall.

643.   burning a pile: Peter Brown and Patti Barham, *The Last Take* (New York: Dutton, 1992), p.322.

643.   Nobody was destroying: Don Marshall to DS, 14 Sept. 1992.

645.   It was obvious: Robert Litman MD to DS, 23 April 1992.

645.   Since our studies: Robert Litman MD, quoted in Howard Hertel and Frank

Notes

Laro, 'Marilyn Monroe's Death Listed by Coroner as Probably Suicide', *Los Angeles Times*, 18 Aug. 1962.

646.   I did not think: John Miner to DS, 11 June 1992. All further citations of Miner are derived from this interview.

646.   not a large: DA 1982, p.4.

646.   (n) Citations from Arnold Abrams to DS: 2 Nov. 1992.

647.   On the impossibility of an injection, see also DA 1982, p.4.

647.   This leads: *Ibid.*

648.   marked congestion: Coroner's Report, File #81128: autospy performed on 5 Aug. 1962, signed by T. Noguchi MD, Deputy Medical Examiner. See also Noguchi, p.78.

649.   cutting down: To Zolotow, in the *Chicago Tribune*, 14 Sept. 1973, sec.2, p.4.

651.   Eunice did only: Philip LaClair to DS, 22 July 1992.

653.   Weinstein's recollections concerning Engelberg's gastric lavage (stomach-pumping) of MM at Doheny Drive were reported in an interview to DS, 10 Dec. 1992.

653.   Regarding Eunice's statement about the ambulance, so she said in a taped telephone conversation with Roy Turner, 9 Feb. 1987.

654.   Well, I've made: Quoted by William Woodfield to DS, 20 Sept. 1991.

654.   I don't recall: Eunice Murray to Roy Turner, taped telephone conversation, 9 Feb. 1987.

654.   I wouldn't swear: *Ibid.*

655.   tried to help: quoted in McCann, p.176.

656.   Marilyn wasn't killed: John Huston to Reuters News Service, 22 Aug. 1962.

656.   Oh, why do I: Murrary, during the filming of the BBC-TV documentary, *Marilyn: Say Goodbye to the President*, as heard by the producer, Ted Landreth and reported to DS.

658.   Dear Joe: IMP.

CHAPTER 24

659.   The dialogue between MM and Allan Snyder was recalled for DS by Snyder on 2 May, 1992.

661.   I love you: *Los Angeles Herald-Examiner*, 8 Aug. 1962, p.1.

NOTES TO AFTERWORD

666.   vastly alluring: Lee Israel, *Kilgallen* (New York: Delacorte, 1979), pp.338–40.

666.   one of the President's appointees: 'The Midnight World of Walter Winchell', *Photoplay*, December 1962, p.91.

666ff.   On Frank A. Capell, see the profile in the *New York Times*, 18 Feb. 1965.

666.   subversive activities which threaten: William Turner, *Power on the Right* (Berkeley: Ramparts Press, 1971), p.224.

667.   I'll tell you a story: This dialogue and the account of the meeting was reported by Clemmons himself in an address in Los Angeles on 22 March 1991, to the group known as Marilyn Remembered.

668.   the closeness of their friendship: Frank A. Capell, *The Strange Death of Marilyn Monroe* (Zarephath, New Jersey: The Herold of Freedom, 1964), pp.62, 69–70.

668ff.   On Winchell and Hoover, see Natalie Robins, *Alien Ink* (New York: Morrow, 1992).

668.   [Capell's] book: FBI File #77–51387.
668.   On Capell, Clemmons, Fergus and the Kuchel case, see, e.g., *The Los Angeles Times*, 20 June 1965.
669.   a married man: Fred Lawrence Guiles, *Norma Jean: The Life of Marilyn Monroe* (New York: McGraw-Hill, 1969), p.315.
669.   the [RFK] liaison: Guildes, *Legend*, p.16; like *Norma Jean*, this book also lacks documentation.
669.   Guiles's version: Norman Mailer, *Marilyn* (New York: Grosset & Dunlap, 1973), p.237.
670.   See Anthony Scaduto, 'Who Killed Marilyn Monroe?' *Oui*, Oct. 1975, pp.35ff.
671.   The evidence is as thin: Report of the Los Angeles Police Department Organized Crime Investigation Division, dated 22 Oct. 1975.
671ff.   On the results of the District Attorney's threshold investigation, see the Los Angeles County District Attorney Bureau of Investigation, Investigator's Report, File #82–G–2236: this report is treated extensively in the notes to Chapter 22.
672.   a known boaster: *Ibid*.
673.   Capell's role as: Anthony Summers, *Goddess: The Secret Lives of Marilyn Monroe*, 2nd ed. (New York: Signet/Onyx, 1986), p.453.
674.   On Parker and Hoover: *Ibid*., p.374.
674.   On Kennedy's order to Hoover: *Ibid*., p.405.
674.   the most cogent account: *Ibid*., p.390.
676.   I don't know why: Michael Gurdin MD to DS, 21 Sept. 1992.
677.   tangled, disastrous affairs: Brown and Barham, p.386.
677.   Geraldo, Sally Jessy: *Ibid*., p.386.
677.   evidence: *Ibid*., p.387.

Bibliography

In addition to the essays, articles and reviews cited in the text, the following books were consulted.

Adams, Cindy. *Lee Strasberg: The Imperfect Genius of the Actors Studio*. Garden City: Doubleday, 1980.

Allen, Maury. *Where Have You Gone, Joe DiMaggio?* New York: Dutton, 1975.

Anderson, Janice. *Marilyn Monroe*. London: Hamlyn, 1983.

Arnold, Eve. *Marilyn Monroe – An Appreciation*. New York: Knopf, 1987.

Axelrod, George. *Will Success Spoil Rock Hunter?* New York: Samuel French, 1955.

Bacall, Lauren. *By Myself*. New York: Knopf, 1979.

Baker, Roger. *Marilyn Monroe: Photographs from UPI/Bettmann*. New York: Portland/Crescent, 1990.

Belmont, Georges (interviewer). *Marilyn Monroe and the Camera Eye*. Boston: Bullfinch/Little, Brown, 1989.

Benny Jack, with Joan Benny. *Sunday Nights at Seven*. New York: Warner, 1990.

Bentley, Eric, ed. *Thirty Years of Treason: Excerpts from Hearings before the House Committee on Un-American Activities, 1938–1968*. New York: Viking 1971.

Bogdanovich, Peter. *Fritz Lang in America*. New York: Praeger, 1967.

Brown, David. *Let Me Entertain You*. New York: William Morrow, 1990.

717

Bibliography

Carpozi, George, Jr. *Marilyn Monroe: Her Own Story*. Belmont Books, 1961.

Chekhov, Michael. *To the Actor: On the Technique of Acting*. New York: Harper & Row, 1953.

Conover, David. *Finding Marilyn*. New York: Grosset & Dunlap, 1981.

Cotten, Joseph. *Vanity Will Get You Somewhere*. London: Columbus Books, 1987.

Crivello, Kirk. *Fallen Angels*. Secaucus, N.J.: Citadel Press, 1988.

Crown, Lawrence. *Marilyn at Twentieth Century Fox*. London: Comet/Planet, 1987.

de Dienes, André. *Marilyn Mon Amour*. New York: St Martin's, 1985.

Doll, Susan. *Marilyn: Her Life and Legend*. New York: Beekman House, 1990.

Dougherty, James E. *The Secret Happiness of Marilyn Monroe*. Chicago: Playboy Press, 1976.

Edwards, Anne. *Judy Garland*. New York: Simon & Schuster, 1975.

Eells, George. *Robert Mitchum*. New York: Franklin Watts, 1984.

Eisner, Lotte H. *Fritz Lang*. London: Secker & Warburg, 1976.

Finler, Joel W. *The Hollywood Story*. London: Octopus, and New York: Crown, 1988.

Fowler, Will. *Reporters: Memoirs of a Young Newspaperman*. Santa Monica: Roundtable Publications, 1991.

Franklin, Joe, and Laurie Palmer. *The Marilyn Monroe Story*. New York: Rudolph Field, 1953.

Freedland, Michael. *Gregory Peck*. New York: Morrow, 1980.

Golden, Eve. *Platinum Girl: The Life and Legends of Jean Harlow*. New York: Abbeville Press, 1991.

Goode, James. *The Story of The Misfits*. Indianapolis: Bobbs-Merrill, 1961.

Goodman, Ezra. *The Fifty-Year Decline and Fall of Hollywood*. New York: Simon & Schuster, 1961.

Bibliography

Grobel, Lawrence. *The Hustons.* New York: Avon, 1989.

Guiles, Fred Lawrence. *Legend: The Life and Death of Marilyn Monroe.* New York: Stein and Day, 1984.

——. *Norma Jean: The Life of Marilyn Monroe.* New York: McGraw-Hill, 1969.

Hamblett, Charles. *Who Killed Marilyn Monroe?* London: Leslie Frewin, 1966.

Hamon, Hervé, and Patrick Rotman. *Yves Montand: Tu vois, je n'ai pas oublié.* Paris: Seuil/Fayard, 1990.

Harris, Marlys J. *The Zanucks of Hollywood.* New York: Crown, 1989.

Haspiel, James. *Marilyn: The Ultimate Look at the Legend.* New York: Henry Holt, 1991.

Hoyt, Edwin P. *Marilyn: The Tragic Venus.* Philadelphia: Chilton, 1965.

Hudson, James A. *The Mysterious Death of Marilyn Monroe.* New York: Volitant, 1968.

Huston, John. *An Open Book.* New York: Knopf, 1980.

Hutchinson, Tom. *Marilyn Monroe.* New York: Exeter Books, 1982.

Johnson, Dorris, and Ellen Leventhal, eds. *The Letters of Nunnally Johnson.* New York: Knopf, 1981.

Kahn, Roger. *Joe & Marilyn: A Memory of Love.* New York: William Morrow, 1986.

Kaminsky, Stuart. *John Huston: Maker of Magic.* Boston: Houghton Mifflin, 1978.

Kazan, Elia. *A Life.* New York: Alfred A. Kopf, 1988.

Kobal, John, ed. *Marilyn Monroe: A Life on Film.* London: Hamlyn, 1974.

——. *People Will Talk.* New York: Knopf, 1985.

Lambert, Gavin. *On Cukor.* New York: Putnam's, 1972.

Logan, Joshua. *Movie Stars, Real People and Me.* New York: Delacorte, 1978.

Luijters, Guus. *Marilyn Monroe, in her own words.* London: Omnibus, 1991.

McBride, Joseph. *Hawks on Hawks.* Berkeley: University of California Press, 1982.

Bibliography

McCann, Graham. *Marilyn Monroe*. New Brunswick: Rutgers University Press, 1988.

Madsen, Axel. *John Huston*. New York: Doubleday, 1978.

Mailer, Norman. *Marilyn*. New York: Grosset & Dunlap, 1973; New York: Galahad, 1988.

——. with photographs by Milton H. Greene. *Of Women and Their Elegance*. New York: Simon and Schuster, 1980.

Mankiewicz, Joseph L. *More About All About Eve*. New York: Random House, 1972.

Masters, George, and Norma Lee Browning, *The Masters Way to Beauty*. New York: NAL/Signet, 1978.

Meaker, M. J. *Sudden Endings*. Garden City: Doubleday, 1964.

Mellen, Joan. *Marilyn Monroe*. New York: Pyramid, 1973.

Miller, Arthur. *Timebends*. New York: Grove Press, 1987.

Molnar, Michael. *The Diary of Sigmund Freud*. New York: Robert Stewart/Charles Scribners Sons, 1992.

Monroe, Marilyn. *My Story*. New York: Stein and Day, 1974.

Moore, Robin, and Gene Schoor. *Marilyn & Joe DiMaggio*. Manor Books, 1977.

Morphos, Evangeline, ed. *Lee Strasberg: A Dream of Passion*. Boston: Little, Brown, 1987.

Murray, Eunice. *Marilyn: The Last Months*. New York: Pyramid, 1975.

Negulesco, Jean. *Things I Did . . . and Things I Think I Did*. New York: Linden Press/Simon & Schuster, 1984.

Nolan, William F. *John Huston: King Rebel*. Los Angeles: Sherbourne Press, 1965.

Olivier, Laurence. *Confessions of an Actor*. New York: Simon & Schuster, 1982.

——. *On Acting*. New York: Touchstone/Simon & Schuster, 1986.

Overholt, Alma. *The Catalina Story*. Avalon and Los Angeles: no publisher listed, 1962.

Palmer, Edwin O. *History of Hollywood*. New York: Garland Publishing, 1978.

Parsons, Louella O. *Tell It To Louella*. New York: Putnam's, 1961.

Bibliography

Pepitone, Lena, and William Stadiem. *Marilyn Monroe Confidential*. New York: Simon and Schuster, 1979.

Pratley, Gerald. *The Cinema of John Huston*. Cranbury, N.J.: A. S. Barnes and Co., 1977.

Preminger, Otto. *Preminger: An Autobiography*. New York: Doubleday, 1977.

Rand, Christopher. *Los Angeles: The Ultimate City*. New York: Oxford University Press, 1967.

Ricci, Mark, and Michael Conway. *The Complete Films of Marilyn Monroe*. Secaucus: Citadel, 1964.

Riese, Randall, and Neal Hitchens. *The Unabridged Marilyn: Her Life from A to Z*. New York: Congdon & Weed, 1987.

Robins, Natalie. *Alien Ink*. New York: Morrow, 1992.

Rollyson, Carl E., Jr. *Marilyn Monroe: A Life of the Actress*. Ann Arbor: UMI Research Press, 1986.

Rosten, Norman. *Marilyn: An Untold Story*. New York: Nal/Signet, 1973.

Russell, Jane. *Jane Russell: My Paths and My Detours*. New York: Franklin Watts, 1985.

Scagnetti, Jack. *The Life and Loves of Gable*. Middle Village, N.Y.: Jonathan David, 1976.

Schlesinger, Arthur M., Jr. *Robert Kennedy And His Times*. Boston: Houghton Mifflin, 1978.

Shaw, Sam, and Norman Rosten. *Marilyn among friends*. London: Bloomsbury, 1987.

Signoret, Simone. *Nostalgia Isn't What It Used to Be*. London: Grafton, 1979.

Shevey, Sandra. *The Marilyn Scandal*. New York: William Morrow, 1988; Berkley/Jove, 1990.

Skolsky, Sidney. *Don't Get Me Wrong – I Love Hollywood*. New York: Putnam's, 1975.

——. *Marilyn*. New York: Dell, 1954.

Slatzer, Robert. *The Life and Curious Death of Marilyn Monroe*. New York: Pinnacle, 1974.

Smith, Ella. *Starring Miss Barbara Stanwyck*. New York: Crown, 1985.

Spada, James, and George Zeno. *Monroe: Her Life in Pictures*. New York: Doubleday, 1982.

Speriglio, Milo. *The Marilyn Conspiracy*. New York: Pocket Books, 1986.

Spoto, Donald. *Laurence Olivier: A Bibliography*. New York: HarperCollins, 1992.

Stack, Robert, with Mark Evans, *Straight Shooting*. New York: Macmillan, 1980.

Steinem, Gloria, with photographs by George Barris. *Marilyn*. New York: Henry Holt and Company, 1986.

Stempel, Tom. *Screenwriter: The Life and Times of Nunnally Johnson*. San Diego: A. S. Barnes, 1980.

Strasberg, Susan. *Bittersweet*. New York: Putnam's, 1980.

— —. *Marilyn and Me: Sisters, Rivals, Friends*. New York: Warner Books, 1992.

Summers, Anthony. *Goddess: The Secret Lives of Marilyn Monroe*. New York: Macmillan, 1985; Signet, 1986.

Taylor, Roger G. *Marilyn in Art*. Salem: Salem House, 1984.

— —. *Marilyn Monroe: In Her Own Words*. New York: Delilah/Putnam, 1983. (UK: *Marilyn on Marilyn*. London: Zachary Kwintner, 1983).

Tornabene, Lyn. *Long Live the King*. New York: Putnam's, 1976.

Trescott, Pamela. *Cary Grant – His Movies and His Life*. Washington: Acropolis Books, 1987.

Tynan, Kenneth. *Profiles*. London: Nick Hern/Walker Books, 1989.

Vineberg, Steve. *Method Actors*. New York: Schirmer, 1991.

WPA. *Los Angeles: A Guide To the City And Its Environs*. New York: Hastings House, 1941.

Wagenknecht, Edward. *Marilyn Monroe: A Composite View*. Philadelphia: Chilton, 1969.

Warren, Doug. *Betty Grable: The Reluctant Movie Queen*. New York: St Martin's Press, 1981.

Weatherby, W. J. *Conversations with Marilyn*. New York: Mason/Charter, 1976.

Bibliography

Wilson, Earl. *Show Business Laid Bare*. New York: Putnam's, 1974.

——. *The Show Business Nobody Knows*. Chicago: Cowles Book Co., 1971.

Wood, Tom. *The Bright Side of Billy Wilder, Primarily*. New York: Doubleday, 1970.

Young-Bruehl, Elisabeth. *Anna Freud*. New York: Summit, 1988.

Zolotow, Maurice. *Billy Wilder in Hollywood*. New York: Putnam's, 1977.

——. *Marilyn Monroe*. New York: Harcourt Brace, 1960.

The Films of Marilyn Monroe

The following abbreviations are used for the credits of Marilyn Monroe's twenty-nine completed and released motion pictures:
P: Producer
D: Director
Sc: Author of screenplay
b/o: based on
C: Cinematographer
b/w: black and white (all others in Technicolor or DeLuxe)
Rel: Release date

Scudda-Hoo! Scudda-Hay!
P: Walter Morosco for Fox. Sc/D: F. Hugh Herbert, b/o a novel by George Chamberlain. C: Ernest Palmer. Rel: Apr. 1948. **MM** as Peggy; with June Haver, Lon McCallister, Walter Brennan, Ann Revere, Natalie Wood, Henry Hull, Tom Tully.

Dangerous Years
P: Sol Wurtzel for Fox. D: Arthur Pierson. Sc: Arnold Belgard. C: Benjamin Kline, b/w. Rel: Dec. 1947: filmed after *Scudda-Hoo! Scudda-Hay!* but released first. **MM** as Eve; with William Halop, Ann E. Todd, Darryl Hickman, Jerome Cowan.

Ladies of the Chorus
P: Harry A. Romm for Columbia. D: Phil Karlson. Sc: Harry Sauber and Joseph Carol. C: Frank Redman, b/w. Rel: Oct. 1948. **MM** as Peggy Martin; with Adele Jergens, Rand Brooks, Nana Bryant.

Love Happy
P: Lester Cowan for United Artists (Mary Pickford). D: David Miller. Sc: Frank Tashlin and Mac Benoff, b/o a story by Harpo Marx. C: William C. Mellor, b/w. Rel: Apr. 1950. **MM** as an unnamed client of Groucho Marx (as a private detective); with Harpo Marx, Chico Marx, Ilona Massey, Eric Blore, Vera-Ellen, Raymond Burr.

A Ticket to Tomahawk
P: Robert Bassler for Fox. D: Richard Sale. Sc: Sale and Mary Loos. C: Harry Jackson. Rel: May 1950. **MM** as Clara; with Dan Dailey, Anne Baxter, Rory Calhoun, Walter Brennan, Marion Marshall.

The Asphalt Jungle
P: Arthur Hornblow Jr, for MGM. D: John Huston. Sc: Huston and Ben Maddow, b/o a novel by W. R. Burnett. C: Harold Rosson, b/w. Rel: May 1950. **MM** as Angela Phinlay; with Sterling Hayden, Louis Calhern, Jean Hagen, Sam Jaffe, James Whitmore.

All About Eve
P: Darryl F. Zanuck for Fox. Sc/D: Joseph L. Mankiewicz. C: Milton Krasner, b/w. Rel: Oct. 1950. **MM** as Miss Caswell; with Bette Davis, Anne Baxter, George Sanders, Celeste Holm, Gary Merrill, Hugh Marlowe, Thelma Ritter, Gregory Ratoff.

The Fireball
P: Bert Friedlob for Fox. D: Tay Garnett. Sc: Garnett and Horace McCoy. C: Lester White, b/w. Rel. Nov. 1950. **MM** as Polly; with Mickey Rooney, Pat O'Brien, Beverly Tyler.

Right Cross
P: Armand Deutsch for MGM. D: John Sturges. Sc: Charles Schnee. C: Norbert Brodine, b/w. Rel: Nov. 1950. **MM** as Dusky Le Doux; with Dick Powell, June Allyson, Ricardo Montalban, Lionel Barrymore.

Home Town Story (not, as usually listed, *Hometown Story*)
P, D, Sc: Arthur Pierson for MGM. C: Lucien Andriot, b/w.
Rel: May 1951. **MM** as Iris Martin; with Donald Crisp, Jeffrey
Lynn, Marjorie Reynolds, Alan Hale Jr.

As Young As You Feel
P: Lamar Trotti for Fox. D: Harmon Jones. Sc: Trotti, b/o a
story by Paddy Chayefsky. C: Joe MacDonald, b/w. Rel: Aug.
1951. **MM** as Harriet; with Monty Woolley, Jean Peters, Thelma
Ritter, Constance Bennett, Albert Dekker.

Love Nest
P: Jules Buck for Fox. D: Joseph Newman. Sc: I. A. L.
Diamond, b/o a novel by Scott Corbett. C: Lloyd Ahern, b/w.
Rel: Oct. 1951. **MM** as Roberta Stevens; with June Haver,
William Lundigan, Leatrice Joy, Jack Paar, Frank Fay.

Let's Make It Legal
P: Robert Bassler for Fox. D: Richard Sale. Sc: F. Hugh Her-
bert and I. A. L. Diamond, b/o a story by Mortimer Braus. C:
Lucien Ballard, b/w. Rel: Nov. 1951. **MM** as Joyce; with Clau-
dette Colbert, Macdonald Carey, Robert Wagner, Zachary
Scott, Barbara Bates.

Clash by Night
P: Harriet Parsons for Jerry Wald and Norman Krasna, RKO.
D: Fritz Lang. Sc: Alfred Hayes, b/o the play by Clifford
Odets. C: Nicholas Musuraca, b/w. Rel: June 1952. **MM** as
Peggy; with Barbara Stanwyck, Robert Ryan, Paul Douglas,
Keith Andes.

We're Not Married
P/Sc: Nunnally Johnson for Fox. D: Edmund Goulding. C:
Leo Tover, b/w. Rel: July 1952. **MM** as Annabel Norris; with
David Wayne and (in other segments of this anthology film)
Ginger Rogers, Fred Allen, Louis Calhern, Zsa Zsa Gabor.

Don't Bother to Knock

P: Julian Blaustein for Fox. D: Roy Baker. Sc: Daniel Taradash, b/o a novel by Charlotte Armstrong. C: Lucien Ballard, b/w. Rel: July 1952. **MM** as Nell Forbes; with Richard Widmark, Anne Bancroft, Donna Corcoran, Jim Backus and Lurene Tuttle.

Monkey Business

P: Sol Siegel for Fox. D: Howard Hawks. Sc: Ben Hecht, Charles Lederer and I. A. L. Diamond, b/o a story by Harry Segall. C: Milton Krasner, b/w. Rel: Sept. 1952. **MM** as Lois Laurel; with Cary Grant, Ginger Rogers, Charles Coburn and Hugh Marlowe.

O. Henry's Full House

P: Andre Hakin for Fox. D: Henry Koster. Sc: Lamar Trotti, b/o stories by O. Henry. C: Lloyd Ahern, b/w. Rel: Oct. 1952. **MM** as a streetwalker, in a segment of this five-part anthology film; with Charles Laughton and David Wayne.

Niagara

P: Charles Brackett for Fox. D: Henry Hathaway. Sc: Brackett, Walter Reisch and Richard Breen. C: Joe MacDonald. Rel: Jan. 1953. **MM** as Rose Loomis; with Joseph Cotten, Jean Peters, Casey Adams, Richard Allan, Denis O'Dea, Don Wilson, Lurene Tuttle.

Gentlemen Prefer Blondes

P: Sol Siegel for Fox. D: Howard Hawks. Sc: Charles Lederer, b/o works by Anita Loos and Joseph Fields. C: Harry J. Wild. Rel: July 1953. **MM** as Lorelei Lee; with Jane Russell, Tommy Noonan, Charles Coburn, Elliot Reid, George Winslow, Norma Varden.

How To Marry a Millionaire
P: Nunnally Johnson for Fox. D: Jean Negulesco. Sc: Johnson, b/o plays by Zoe Akins and Dale Eunson and a book by Doris Lilly. C: Joe MacDonald. Rel: Nov. 1953. **MM** as Pola Debevoise; with Betty Grable, Lauren Bacall, William Powell, David Wayne, Rory Calhoun, Alex D'Arcy, Cameron Mitchell, Fred Clark.

River of No Return
P: Stanley Rubin for Fox. D: Otto Preminger. Sc: Frank Fenton, b/o a story by Louis Lantz. C: Joseph LaShelle. Rel: April 1954. **MM** as Kay Weston; with Robert Mitchum, Tommy Rettig, Rory Calhoun.

There's No Business Like Show Business
P: Sol Siegel for Fox. D: Walter Lang. Sc: Phoebe and Henry Ephron, b/o a story by Lamar Trotti. C: Leon Shamroy. **MM** as Vicky; with Ethel Merman, Dan Dailey, Donald O'Connor, Mitzi Gaynor, Johnny Ray.

The Seven Year Itch
P: Charles K. Feldman and Billy Wilder for Fox. D: Billy Wilder. Sc: Wilder and George Axelrod, b/o Axelrod's play. C: Milton Krasner. Rel: June 1955. **MM** as The Girl; with Tom Ewell, Evelyn Keyes, Victor Moore, Robert Strauss.

Bus Stop
P: Buddy Adler for Fox. D: Joshua Logan. Sc: George Axelrod, b/o the play by William Inge. C: Milton Krasner. Rel: Aug. 1956. **MM** as Cherie; with Don Murray, Arthur O'Connell, Eileen Heckart, Betty Field, Hope Lange.

The Prince and the Showgirl
P: Milton H. Greene and Laurence Olivier for Warner Bros. D: Laurence Olivier. Sc: Terence Rattigan, b/o his play. C: Jack Cardiff. Rel: June 1957. **MM** as Elsie Marina; with Laurence Olivier, Sybil Thorndike, Jeremy Spenser, Richard Wattis, Esmond Knight, Maxine Audley.

728

Some Like It Hot
P, D: Billy Wilder for Walter Mirisch/United Artists. Sc: Wilder and I. A. L. Diamond, b/o a story by R. Thoeren and M. Logan. C: Charles Lang Jr, b/w. Rel: March 1959. **MM** as Sugar Kane; with Jack Lemmon, Tony Curtis, George Raft, Pat O'Brien, Joe E. Brown, Joan Shawlee.

Let's Make Love
P: Jerry Wald for Fox. D: George Cukor. Sc: Norman Krasner, Hal Kanter. C: Daniel L. Fapp. Rel: Sept. 1960. **MM** as Amanda Dell; with Yves Montand, Wilfrid Hyde White, Tony Randall, Frankie Vaughan, Madge Kennedy.

The Misfits
P: Frank E. Taylor for UA/Seven Arts. D: John Huston. Sc: Arthur Miller. C: Russell Metty, b/w. Rel: Feb. 1961. **MM** as Roslyn Tabor; with Clark Gable, Montgomery Clift, Eli Wallach, Thelma Ritter, Kevin McCarthy, Estelle Winwood, Ralph Roberts.

Incomplete: *Something's Got to Give*
P: Henry Weinstein. D: George Cukor. Sc: Nunnally Johnson, Walter Bernstein, Hal Kanter et al., b/o the 1940 film *My Favorite Wife*. C: Franz Planer, Leo Tover, William Daniels. **MM**'s thirtieth film was cancelled during production; extant footage shot from April to June 1962. **MM** as Ellen Arden; with Dean Martin, Cyd Charisse, Phil Silvers, Wally Cox. The production was formally shut down on 12 June 1962. *Marilyn Monroe* died on 4 August 1962. The film was rewritten, recast, reproduced and released in 1963 as *Move Over Darling*, with Doris Day and James Garner.

Index

Index

Index

Index

Index

Sukarno 395; marries Miller 401–5;
in England for filming of *The Prince
and the Showgirl* 407–20; has
miscarriage 414–15; meets Edith
Sitwell again 415; meets the Queen
417; returns to New York and
housewifery 421–3; begins sessions
with Dr Marianne Kris (*q.v.*) 424–8;
and breakdown of MMP and
relationship with Greene 423, 424,
429–32; with Miller 434–9;
alternating moods 434, 437, 438;
ectopic pregnancy 435; co-stars in
Some Like It Hot 439–40, 441–2,
448, 449; miscarriage and depression
450, 451; marriage in decline 451,
452; meets McCullers and Sandburg
451; on promotional tour of *Some
Like It Hot* 451; fondness for
Isadore Miller (*q.v.*) 452; receives
David di Donatello 453; new
project shelved by illness and
operation 453–4; in *Let's Make
Love* 454, 458, 460–2, 464–5, 466;
meets Khrushchev 455; friendship
established with Ralph Roberts
(*q.v.*) 456; with Miller and the
Montands 457–8; loses confidence
in Miller 458–9; quarrels with Miller
459–60; friendship with Evelyn
Moriarty 460; celebrates 34th
birthday 464; affair with Montand
464–5; consults Ralph Greenson
(*q.v.*) 467, 473–5; in *Misfits* 475–95
passim, 496–7; breaks with Miller
499; upset by Gable's death 499;
reunited with Pat Newcomb (*q.v.*)
500; divorces Miller 500, 504–5;
Strasberg aborts TV appearance
502–3; Kris places in psychiatric
hospital 505–7; rescued by
DiMaggio 508; at Columbia-
Presbyterian Hospital 508–9, 514;
letter to Greenson 509–14; attends
Augusta Miller's funeral 515; with
DiMaggio in Florida 515; affair with
Sinatra 516–17; gall bladder
operation 518; return to Los
Angeles with Roberts 519–20;
absorbed into Greenson's life

520–3; recalled by Fox 524; trapped
into *Something's Got to Give* 526–8;
Kirkland photographs 528–9;
Greenson encourages to buy house
529–30, 535, 536–8; forced to hire
Eunice Murray (*q.v.*) 530, 533;
'affairs' with President Kennedy
538–41, 560; and Robert Kennedy
541–6; in New York with Strasbergs
547; trip to Mexico 547–8, 549;
embarrassing behaviour at award
dinner due to drugs 549, 550–1;
distressed over *Something's Got to
Give* 552–3; in Greenson house
553–6; rescued by DiMaggio 556–7;
continues on *Something's Got to
Give* 557, 558, 561, 562–75 *passim*;
and Greenson's trip abroad 570–1;
dismisses Eunice Murray 571; Fox
files breach of contract notice 575;
and Kennedy's birthday gala 560,
567, 573, 574, 576–8; back on set
579–83; celebrates 36th birthday
583; Greenson and her dismissal
from *Something's Got to Give*
584–97; photographic sessions
597–8; *Life* magazine interviews
600, 603–5; has 'youth shots' from
Engelberg (*q.v.*) 599–600, 603;
telephones Robert Kennedy 600–1;
reunited with DiMaggio 601–2;
visits Jean Harlow's mother with
Skolsky 606–7; Fox reinstates
608–10; weekend with Lawfords
609–10; plans marriage to DiMaggio
611, 615–16, 657, 658; last days
615–22, 626–34; death 634–8;
mortuary preparation 659–60;
funeral 660–2; official report on
death 638–40; police investigations
639–43; postmortem and
preliminary report 630, 643–5;
suicide verdict 644, 645–6; cause of
death established 646–57
personality traits etc.: alcohol
consumption 437; childhood
pretend games 27–8, 57; love of
children 90, 170, 203, 434, 460, 500;
concern for the poor and weak
133–4, 164–5, 203; love of dogs 28,

Index

Index

748